EC Consumer Law Compendium

EC Consumer Law Compendium

The Consumer Acquis and its transposition in the Member State

Edited by

Hans Schulte-Nölke

Christian Twigg-Flesner

Martin Ebers

sellier.
european law
publishers

The EU Consumer Law Compendium has been prepared under a contract with the European Commission by the University of Bielefeld (Germany) for DG Health & Consumer Protection (http://ec.europa.eu/consumers/cons_int/safe_shop/acquis/index_en.htm).

It represents the views of the contractor or authors. These views set out in this book have not been adopted or in any way endorsed by the Commission and should not be relied upon as a statement of the views of the Commission. In particular, the views expressed by the authors on the adequacy of national transpositions measures are without prejudice to the opinions of the Commission. The Commission does not guarantee the accuracy of the data included in this Compendium, nor does it accept responsibility for any use made thereof.

ISBN 978-3-86653-063-8

The Deutsche Nationalbibliothek lists this publication in the Deutsche Nationalbibliografie; detailed bibliographic data are available in the Internet at http://dnb.d-nb.de.

Design: Sandra Sellier, Munich. Production: Karina Hack, Munich. Printing and binding: Friedrich Pustet KG, Regensburg. Printed on acid-free, non-ageing paper. Printed in Germany.

General Overview

Part 2:
Transposition of the individual Directives

Part 3:
Common structures in the Directives

Part 4:

Annex A:

Annex B:

Annex C:

Contents

Introduction

1. The Project. The EC Consumer Law Compendium presents the results of a wide-ranging study prepared for the European Commission by an international research group. It is part of the research the Commission has undertaken in the process of preparing the review of the consumer acquis. For the first time, the transposition of 8 important consumer directives into the national laws of 25 Member States is analysed. The findings of this study reveal the substantial differences between the various national implementing measures as a result of utilising minimum harmonisation clauses and regulatory options. The purpose of this introduction is to sketch some of the key aspects of this study and its methodology. A more detailed description can be found in the call for tenders which led to the contract for the production of the Compendium, concluded between the European Commission and the University of Bielefeld,[1] as well as in various Commission documents.[2]

2. Scope of the Study. The study covers eight Directives, namely:

- The Doorstep Selling Directive (85/577/EEC);
- The Package Travel Directive (90/314/EEC);
- The Unfair Terms in Consumer Contracts Directive (93/13/EEC);
- The Timeshare Directive (94/47/EC);
- The Distance Selling Directive (97/7/EC);
- The Price Indication Directive (98/6/EC);
- The Injunctions Directive (98/27/EC); and
- The Consumer Sales Directive (1999/44/EC).

The choice of these Directives may seem somewhat arbitrary. In particular, on the one hand, Directives 98/6/EC (Price Indication) and 98/27/EC (Injunctions) might seem out of place, because all the other directives share a common feature in that they regulate contract law aspects of EC consumer law. On the other hand, the abovementioned list does not contain several directives which one would expect to be included in a list of core measures of EC consumer contract law, such as the Consumer Credit Directive (87/102/EEC) or the Distance Selling of Financial Services Directive (2002/65/EC). But the choice of which directives to include in this study was had been made by the responsible Commission section when issuing the call for tenders and was, therefore, not questioned by the contractors. There is obviously a political motive for this choice: with regard to the Consumer Credit Directive 87/102, it is worth noting that it had been undergoing a thorough review during the time when the Consumer law Compendium was elaborated. As to the Distance Selling of Financial Services Directive 2002/65, which is – other than the previous directives – a full har-

---

1 N° of the call for tenders: 2003/S 153-138854; published in different places on the website of the European Commission, e.g. under ted.europa.eu (document n° 2003-138854); Service Contract No. 17.020100/04/389299: "Annotated Compendium including a comparative analysis of the Community consumer acquis".

2 COM (2004) 651 final, pp. 3-4.

monisation measure, the period since it was enacted might have been considered as too short for a profound assessment of its impact on the laws of the member states.

3. Outputs of the Study. The study has led to two main outputs: firstly, a legal Database has been created linking the eight directives, relevant ECJ jurisprudence, national transposition measures as well as national case-law. This Database is available online and will kept up-to-date for the coming three-year period.[3] Secondly, the study has produced this Compendium which is, as the Commission has put it, a "comparative analysis of the different national regulations, including possible barriers to trade or distortions of competition resulting from them". Both parts of the study, the Compendium presented in this volume and the Database, complement each other. For example, in order to avoid cluttering the text with thousands of footnotes (i.e., more than the several thousand already present), we, as the authors of the Compendium, often refrained from giving a full reference of particular transposition measures in individual member states. The relevant information can easily be found in the Database. It also goes without saying that we are aware of much of the legal literature and studies existing in the field of this study, as far as these materials are written in the languages accessible to us. However, we decided to include only limited references where necessary. More bibliographical information can also be obtained from the Database.

4. Time Schedule. It was a great challenge to undertake a comprehensive transposition review for eight directives in 25 member states. This has never been attempted before to such an extent and density. In the course of this endeavour, it turned out that the task needed much more effort and time than originally expected. Work began in October 2004 and was initially envisaged to be concluded in April 2006 for the (then) 25 Member States. When it became clear then that the study could not be finalised at this point of time, the Commission granted an extension until December 2006. This is the reason why the Compendium and the Database were first presented in December 2006. Although work is underway to extend the analysis to include also the two new Member States which acceeded to the Union in 2007, this first print edition of the Compendium only contains the findings regarding the 25 Member States. Information on the transposition of the eight directives in Bulgaria and Romania will be included in a possible second edition of this Compendium, but can already be retrieved from the database in the meantime.

5. Methodology. The preparatory research in the 25 member states was conducted by colleagues from the individual countries. A list of participants and contributors is appended to this introduction. The initial step, in order to build up the Database and to draft this Compendium, was to develop questionnaires which were to structure the national reports in a way that would enable the editors of the study to identify the relevant issues for each member state. Already at this stage, several of the national contributors participated in the drafting of questionnaires. This has proven to be extremely useful. Thus, we were able to ensure as far as possible that the questions were understood in the same way by lawyers from so many different legal backgrounds – an aspect frequently given less attention than necessary when undertaking comparative research involving the transposition of European directives: the interaction between the European and national level is possibly one of the most fascinating fields of enquiry in a study such as this, but one can easily come to the wrong conclu-

---

3 Directly accessible via http://www.eu-consumer-law.org; or – via the homepage of the European Commission: http://ec.europa.eu/consumers/rights/cons_acquis_en.htm.

sions if the questionnaires used to gather relevant information are open to wide and differing national interpretation. This is something which, we hope, we were able to avoid.

Guided by these questionnaires, individual researchers or teams from each of the 25 member states drafted reports on the respective national transposition measures for each directive. As an added value, these reports also revealed how national laws were influenced by EU legislation and whether there have been difficulties or shortcomings of transposition.

On the basis of the national reports, the authors of this Compendium drafted, on the one hand, a very short characterisation of the general "transposition culture" of each member state (Part 1) and on the other hand, a detailed report on each directive, which intends to draft an EC-wide legal map after the transposition of the eight directives (Part 2). These reports are intended to chart the transposition across the 25 member states, and individual authors have determined how much depth was required in order to present a meaningful analysis of this process. A balance had to be struck between lengthy papers giving an exhaustive account on the transposition of each provision of every directive in all 25 member states, and a sketch providing only a very broad brush overview. The intention has been to draw out those aspects where the national transposition measures differ, rather than to list every provision that has been accurately transposed. The level of depth may therefore vary for each individual section, hopefully thereby having ensured that the Compendium provides a valuable picture of the state-of-play across the European Union, without obscuring the broader picture with too much detail.

These core parts of the Compendium are complemented by key conclusions with regard to common structures in the directives (Part 3) and particular recommendations to solve some of the problems highlighted in this study (Part 4). Of course, these conclusions and recommendations express just the personal views of the individual authors, although we do not shy away from encouraging deep reforms to these directives in the course of the ongoing review of the consumer acquis.

6. Editors and Authors. The research project was conducted in close co-operation of numerous contributors. It was co-ordinated by Hans Schulte-Nölke. This part of the study, the Compendium, was edited by him together with Christian Twigg-Flesner and Martin Ebers. The editors also served as the authors of individual parts of the study, partially together with other co-authors as indicated in the relevant parts.

7. Cut-off date. We originally intended that the Consumer Law Compendium should reflect the law in force on 1 October 2005. Thanks to the extended timetable referred to earlier, we were able to include some later developments. Therefore, we have also been able to incorporate many important changes in the law or other developments which took place up to mid-2006, in some cases even until mid 2007. It goes without saying that since then, the development of national consumer laws has continued. Thus, some information contained in this Compendium might soon be overtaken by new national developments (if this has not occurred already!). In particular the consolidated text of the Spanish Consumer Law (Real Decreto Legislativo 1/2007), which entered into force on 1 December 2007 could not be taken into account before the manuscript went to print. The overall picture of the enormous differences between the national laws in the fields regulated by the consumer directives is not very much changed by the amendments in individual member states. It is nevertheless envisaged to publish a second edition of this Compendium after some time, which then will reflect such amendments. In the meantime, the Database mentioned above will provide information on changes since the publication of the Compendium. It is envisaged that the Database will be updated quarterly, beginning from July 2008.

8. Caveat and Invitation for Comments. Overall, the Compendium contains about 6000 individual references to national laws. Almost all of these have been double-checked by at least one national consumer law expert, in many cases also by other interested experts, e.g. from consumer organisations or national ministries. We have taken all reasonable care to process the enormous bulk of material in more than 20 languages, but despite all diligence, the complexity of the exercise most certainly will also have led to some inaccuracies which are not just due to subsequent amendments of the national laws. The editors would like to point out that they have to take the academic responsibility for such shortcomings, not the national correspondents or proof-readers. We apologise for any of the inaccuracies readers may find. The editors and all contributors hope that the study will be acknowledged as a very serious attempt to draw a map of European consumer law in the field of the eight directives. We would gratefully welcome any, in particular critical, comment, which helps to improve it.

9. Acknowledgments. Finally, we would like to thank the many many people who contributed and supported the project. First of all, we need to mention the national correspondents who invested an enormous amount of time into this project and who patiently answered dozens of questionnaires and questions without complaining. We especially have to thank those who took the responsibility to evaluate the Database the Compendium. The Database team and many other interested people from enterprises, national authorities and consumer law organisations gave invaluable comments and recommendations. We are also very grateful to many members of the Acquis Group who, even though not formally involved in the project, gave advice and support. It has proven impossible to name everyone who supported this exercise, but the list of contributors and supporters enclosed may give an impression.

We are grateful for a lot of comments made on earlier versions of the study by many Commission officials who helped us to avoid some inaccuracies. Last, but certainly not least we also thank the responsible Commission officials, in particular and pars pro toto Giuseppe Abbamonte and Mikolaj Zaleski, who, despite of all time constraints caused by our delay, constantly supported us to an extent much beyond one could have expected.
We wish to reiterate that comments and suggestions are most welcome: schulte-noelke@uni-osnabrueck.de.

Bielefeld, Hull and Barcelona, January 2008

Hans Schulte-Nölke,
Christian Twigg-Flesner,
Martin Ebers

Contributors to the Project

1. General Co-ordinator of the Consumer Law Compendium Project

Prof. Dr. Hans Schulte-Nölke, Director of the Centre for European Legal Practice at the University of Bielefeld (from April 2008 Professor at the University of Osnabrück).

2. Editors of the Comparative Analysis

Name	Institute/Function
Prof. Hans Schulte-Nölke	Director of the Centre for European Legal Practice at the University of Bielefeld
Dr. Christian Twigg-Flesner	Senior Lecturer in Private Law Law School University of Hull
Dr. Martin Ebers	At present University of Barcelona

3. Co-Authors

Name	Institute/Function
Andreas Börger	PhD Researcher Centre for European Legal Practice at the University of Bielefeld
Sandra Fischer	PhD Researcher Centre for European Legal Practice at the University of Bielefeld
Leonie Meyer-Schwickerath	PhD Researcher Centre for European Legal Practice at the University of Bielefeld
Dr. Christoph M. Scheuren-Brandes	Senior Researcher Centre for European Legal Practice at the University of Bielefeld (attorney-at-law in Hamburg)

4. Language and Editing Work

Name	Institute/Function
Zahour Akhtar	PhD Researcher Centre for European Legal Practice at the University of Bielefeld
Lucy Goodhew	Research Assistant Centre for European Legal Practice at the University of Bielefeld
David Kraft	Research Assistant Centre for European Private Law at the University of Münster
Christian Rodorff	PhD Researcher Centre for European Private Law at the University of Münster
Filip Wejman, LL.M. (Harvard)	Senior Researcher Centre for European Legal Practice at the University of Bielefeld (at present located at the University of Krakow)

5. Database Team

Name	Institute/Function
Dr. Thomas Simons	Database editor in chief Legal and editorial aspects of the Database IPR Verlag GmbH, Munich
Michael Nagel	EDP quality Manager IPR Verlag GmbH, Munich
Raimund Beck	Database editor Web design IPR Verlag GmbH, Munich
Alexander Hentschel	Database editor Database development IPR Verlag GmbH, Munich
Sibylle Calabresi-Scholz	Legal and editorial aspects of the Database IPR Verlag GmbH, Munich

6. National correspondents contributing to the project

Country	Name	Institute/Function
Austria	Prof. Peter Bydlinski	Institute for Civil Law Karl-Franzens-Universität Graz
	Dr. Martin Stefula	Judge
	Thomas Schoditsch	Institute for Civil Law Karl-Franzens-Universität Graz
Belgium	Prof. Gert Straetmans	University of Antwerpen
	Dr. Stefan Rutten	Assistant Universität of Antwerpen
Cyprus	Christiana Markou LL.M.	Practising Lawyer and PhD Researcher
Czech Republic	Prof. Luboš Tichý	Faculty of Law Charles University Praha
Denmark	Prof. Peter Møgelvang-Hansen	Law Department Copenhagen Business School
	Søren Sandfeld Jakobsen, PhD	Associate Professor Law Department Copenhagen Business School
Estonia	Dr. Margus Kingisepp	Associate Professor on Civil Law University of Tartu Institute of Law Tallinn
Finland	Dr. Tuomas Majuri LL.M.	Ministry of Finance Financial Markets Department
France	Dr. Elise Poillot	Maître de Conférences à l'Université Jean Moulin-Lyon 3 et Directrice adjointe de l'Institut de Droit Comparé Edouard Lambert
	Dr. Michel Cannarsa	Chargé d'enseignements à l'Université Jean Moulin Lyon 3
Germany	Dr. Martin Ebers	At present Universitat de Barcelona
Greece	Prof. Ioannis Karakostas	Faculty of Law University Athens
	Dr. Paraskevi Paparseniou	Lecturer Faculty of Law University Athens
	Theodor Katsas	Faculty of Law University Athens
Hungary	Prof. Judit Fazekas	Faculty of Law, University of Miskolc
	Dr. Edit Ujvari	Faculty of Law, University of Miskolc
	Barbara Zubriczky	Hungarian Competition Authority and PhD Researcher, Faculty of Law, University of Bielefeld

Country	Name	Institute/Function
Ireland	Fidelma White	Senior Lecturer Law Department, University College, Cork
	Prof. Henry Ellis	Law Department, University College, Cork
Italy	Prof. Gianmaria Ajani (supervision)	Sistemi giuridici comparati Dipartimento di Scienze Giuridiche, Università di Torino
	Dr. Piercarlo Rossi	Sistemi giuridici comparati Dipartimento di Scienze Giuridiche, Università di Torino
	Dr. Cristina Poncibò	Sistemi giuridici comparati Dipartimento di Scienze Giuridiche, Università di Torino
Latvia	Baiba Broka	Lecturer of Department of Private Law University of Latvia, Riga
Lithuania	Gediminas Pranevicius, LL.M.	Lecturer Intellectual Property Law Riga Graduate School of Law and Practising Solicitor
Luxembourg	Marc Thewes	Avocat à la Cour Thewes & Reuter, Luxembourg
Malta	Dr. Paul Edgar Micallef	Consumer Affairs Council, Malta
	David Gonzi	Legal Researcher, Malta
Netherlands	Prof. Carla Sieburgh	Radboud Universiteit Nijmegen Faculteit der Rechtsgeleerdheid Nijmegen
	Hanneke Spath	Radboud Universiteit Nijmegen Faculteit der Rechtsgeleerdheid Nijmegen
Poland	Dr. Magdalena Sengayen	Centre for Socio-Legal Studies Oxford University
Portugal	Prof. Dr Miguel Gorjão-Henriques	Assistant Professor Faculty of Law, University of Coimbra; Specialist Lawyer in European Law and Competition – Vieira de Almeida & Associados
	Ana Raquel Moniz LL.M.	Faculty of Law University of Coimbra
Slovakia	Mgr. Lenka Nosalova	Lecturer Department of Marketing, Trade and World Forestry, Technical University Zvolen Slovakia
	Dr. Julius Koval	Slovak Association of Consumers
Slovenia	Prof. Peter Grilc	Faculty of Law University of Ljubljana

Country	Name	Institute/Function
	Doc.dr. Špelca Mežnar	Assistant Professor at the Civil Chair at the Faculty of Law, University of Ljubljana
	Doc.dr. Damjan Možina	Assistant Professor at the Civil Chair at the Faculty of Law, University of Ljubljana
	Asist. Ana Vlahek, univ.dipl.iur.	Assistant at the Civil Chair at the Faculty of Law, University of Ljubljana
	Asist. Jerca Kramberger, LL.M.	Assistant at the Civil Chair at the Faculty of Law, University of Ljubljana
Spain	Prof. Sergio Cámara Lapuente	Profesor Titular de Derecho Civil Departamento de Derecho Universidad de La Rioja La Rioja
Sweden	Prof. Lars Gorton	Department of Law University of Lund
	Dr. Eva Lindell-Frantz	Assistant Professor Department of Law University of Lund
	Lennart Johansson	Department of Law University of Lund
United Kingdom	Dr. Christian Twigg-Flesner	Senior Lecturer in Private Law Law School University of Hull

7. Independent Evaluator appointed by the Commission

Centre for European Economic Law / Study Centre for Consumer Law,
Prof. Dr. Jules Stuyck, University of Leuven

8. Acquis Group

Many members of the Acquis Group (http://www.acquis-group.org) have contributed with all sorts of invaluable advice and other support, namely Prof. Dr. Gianmaria Ajani, University of Turin; Prof. Dr. Reiner Schulze, University of Münster, and Prof. Dr. Fryderyk Zoll, University of Krakow.

Part I: Overview of the Member States' Legislative Techniques

A. Austria – Legislative techniques

Directive	Transposed in (Translation)	Date of Transposition (due date)	ECJ decisions in relation to Austria
Directive 85/577	Art. 3, 4 of the Consumer Protection Act	1 October 1979 (31 December 1987)	
Directive 90/314	Art. 31b-31f of the Consumer Protection Act	1 January 1994 (1 January 1993)	**1.** ECJ 14 May 1998 C-364/96 – *Verein für Konsumenteninformation v. Österreichische Kreditversicherungs AG*, [1998] ECR I-01949 **2.** ECJ 15 June 1999 C-140/97 – *Rechberger, Greindel, Hofmeister etc. v. Republik Österreich* [1999] ECR I-03499 **3.** ECJ 12 March 2002 C-168/00 – *Simone Leitner v. TUI Deutschland GmbH & Co KG*, [2002] ECR I-02631
Directive 93/13	Art. 6 of the Consumer Protection Act	1 October 1979 (31 December 1994)	**1.** ECJ 1 October 2002 C-167/00 *Verein für Konsumenteninformation v. Henkel*, [2002] ECR I-08111
Directive 94/47	Timeshare Act	1 April 1997 (29 April 1997)	
Directive 97/7	Distance Selling Act	1 June 2000 (4 June 2000)	**1.** ECJ 11 July 2002 C-96/00 *Rudolf Gabriel*, [2002] ECR I-06367
Directive 98/6	Price Indication Act	1 June 1992, the Act was amended in 2000 (18 March 2000)	
Directive 98/27	Art. 28-30 of the Consumer Protection Act	1 October 1979, amended in 1999 (1 January 2001)	
Directive 99/44	CC Art. 922-933b; Art. 8-9b of the Consumer Protection Act	1 January 2002 (1 January 2002)	

I. State of consumer protection in the field of the Directives before transposition

By 1979 AUSTRIA had already adopted its Consumer Protection Act which contained provisions for Doorstep Selling (including a right of withdrawal), Unfair Contract Terms and actions for injunction. However, before the transposition of the European Directives, Austrian law contained no effective regulations concerning Package Travel, Timesharing or Distance Selling.

II. Legislative techniques of transposition

AUSTRIA transposed most of the European Directives at issue by making amendments and additions to the existing Consumer Protection Act instead of enacting single transposition laws or amending the ABGB (Austrian Civil Code). This was the case with the transposition of the Directives 85/577, 90/314, 93/13 and 98/27. For Timeshare and Distance Selling, however, the legislator adopted separate Acts. In the course of the transposition of the Consumer Sales Directive Austria considerably modified both the Austrian Civil Code and the Consumer Protection Act.

III. Timeliness of transposition

AUSTRIA transposed all Directives in time except for Directive 90/314 which (as in many other member states) was transposed with a delay of one year.

IV. Use of minimum harmonisation

When transposing the European Directives AUSTRIA made use of minimum clauses on various occasions. The provisions to implement Directive 85/577 are considerably more extensive than the Directive itself, as the core scope of application of the right of withdrawal in Art. 3(1), sent. 1 of the Consumer Protection Act is basically defined in the negative: the provisions apply if the consumer has *not* concluded the contract at the supplier's business premises and *not* at a trade fair or market stand (see OGH 28 July 2004, 7 Ob 78/04b as well as OGH 11 February 2002, 7 Ob 315/01a). Even where the consumer has concluded the contract at the supplier's business premises, Art. 3(2) nevertheless affords him a right of withdrawal, if he has been enticed there by the business or his representative, in the course of a promotion or through individual contact on the street. For timeshare contracts the Timeshare Act provides a period of withdrawal of 14 days whereas the Directive requires only 10 days.

V. Other extensions

Generally the definition of the term "consumer contract" is broader than in the EC Directives. The AUSTRIAN notion in the Consumer Protection Act comprises all types of bilateral contracts and also unilateral legal transactions such as public offers for reward, offers for the conclusion of a contract or withdrawal. According to the Consumer Protection Act even legal entities may be protected as consumers. These extensions concern the transposition of Directives 85/577, 90/314, 93/13, 97/7 and also 94/47 (since the Timeshare Act refers to the notion of consumer as defined in the Consumer Protection Act).

A significant deviation from Directive 85/577 consists in the fact that contracts for real property or for the supply of foodstuffs or beverages are not excluded from the scope of application of the Consumer Protection Act. Furthermore, in contrast to the Directive (Art. 3(1) 3rd indent), the scope of application of the distance selling regulations in Austrian law extends to distance contracts, which are concluded with telecommunication operators through the use of public payphones.

The national provisions on Unfair Contract Terms cover both standard terms and individually negotiated terms, which are excluded from control according to Article 3(1) of the Directive. Also in contrast to Directive 93/13 (Art. 4(2)), Austrian law does not exclude control of the main subject matter of the contract or of the adequacy of the price and remuneration.

The Austrian provisions on Package Travel also go beyond Article 1 of the corresponding Directive since they are applicable even to travel services of less than 24 hours duration without overnight accommodation. Finally, the provisions to implement Directive 99/44 also extend their scope beyond those of the Directive, since in Austrian law the exceptions envisaged in Art. 1(2) (b) of the Directive were not adopted; in addition to the above, in principle, real property is also encompassed.

VI. Possible infringements of EC Law

The AUSTRIAN legislator has in the past accommodated the case law of the ECJ, and repeatedly approximated consumer law to European imperatives. To suffice the guidelines laid down in *Simone Leitner*, in 2003 the provisions on package travel in Art. 31e(3) of the Consumer Protection Act were amended to provide a right to appropriate compensation in respect of loss of holiday enjoyment where the travel organiser deliberately or negligently fails to perform a considerable part of its obligations. The *Heininger* decision (concerning the German Doorstep Selling Act) also led to changes in Austrian law: The Consumer Protection Act prescribed in 2003, states that the right of withdrawal ceases to exist, at the latest, one month after complete performance by both contractual parties. This also applied where the consumer was not informed of his right of withdrawal. According to present-day law, the consumer's right of withdrawal, in contrast, does not expire if the consumer has not been informed of his right of withdrawal. The problem nevertheless remains, that according to Austrian law, the notification of the right of withdrawal does not have to be dated. This is correctly regarded as a breach of Art. 4 of Directive 85/577.

Furthermore, it is argued that CC Art. 864(2), on the sending of unsolicited goods, breaches Art. 9 of Directive 97/7. According to the preparatory works of the Act (explanation of the Government's reference, 311 of the addenda to the stenographic protocol of the national council, XX. Legislative period) CC Art. 864(2) is to be understood as meaning that the recipient of unsolicited goods is not obliged to keep the goods or return them, but rather that he is entitled to dispose of them, however, if he uses the goods for himself then he can be liable for restitution.

Finally, it is also being discussed as to whether and to what extent the redress rule of CC Art. 933b suffices Art. 4 of Directive 99/44. Extremely diverging opinions are proffered as to the substance of the directive's provision. In contrast to the Directive, the implementing provision of CC Art. 933b does limit the redress to the expenditure of the business in question. Moreover, the claim for redress expires two months after performance of the warranty-related duties incumbent on the entitled party.

More detailed information is provided in the individual reports on the transposition of the Directives (cf. in particular, the executive summaries of the reports on Package Travel in Part 2.B. and on Unfair Contract Terms in Part 2.C.).

B. Belgium – Legislative techniques

Directive	Transposed in	Date of Transposition (due date)	ECJ decisions in relation to Belgium
Directive 85/577	Articles 86-92 of the Act of 14 July 1991 on trade practices and consumer information and protection, TPA	29 February 1992 (31 December 1987)	
Directive 90/314	Act of 16 February 1994 regulating package travel contracts and travel intermediation contracts, TOA	4 October 1994 (1 January 1993)	
Directive 93/13	Act of 14 July 1991 on trade practices and consumer information and protection, TPA	29 February 1992 (31 December 1994)	
Directive 94/47	Act of 11 April 1999 on the purchase of the right to use immovable properties on a timeshare basis	1 July 1999 (29 April 1997)	**1.** ECJ 25 February 1999, C-319/98, *Commission v. Belgium*, [1999] ECR I-01201
Directive 97/7	Articles 76-83 of the Act of 14 July 1991 on trade practices and consumer information and protection, TPA *Note*: The existing section in the TPA on distance contracts was completely revised by the Act of 25/5/1999 in order to transpose the Directive	1 October 1999 (4 June 2000)	
Directive 98/6	Royal Decree of 30 June 1996 concerning the indication of the price of products and services and the order form	18 March 2000 (18 March 2000)	
Directive 98/27	Act of 26 May 2002 concerning intra-Community injunctions in view of protecting consumers	20 July 2002 (1 January 2001)	
Directive 99/44	Act of 1 September 2004 on the protection of consumers in respect of the sale of consumer goods	1 February 2005 (1 January 2002)	

Directive	Transposed in	Date of Transposition (due date)	ECJ decisions in relation to Belgium
	Note: From 1 January 2005, the articles 1649bis-1649octies are embedded in the Belgian Civil Code, as a constitutive part of the section relating to the sale of goods		

I. State of consumer protection in the field of the Directives before transposition

Before the transposition of the European Directives, there had already been a tradition of regulation of certain areas of consumer protection law in BELGIUM. The former *loi sur les pratiques du commerce* (Trade Practices Act, TPA) of 1971 contained a provision on itinerant trade which was defined as each sale, offer or promotion aimed at selling products (movable property) to a consumer (defined as an exclusively non-professional person) by a merchant or an intermediary outside his central place of business, his branch(es) mentioned in the Register of Commerce or the premises normally used for trade fairs. The subsequent Trade Practices Act of 14 July 1991 transposed Directive 85/577 and largely anticipated the implementation of Directive 93/13. Furthermore, the Act provided protection in certain fields related to travel contracts and distance selling. However, in Belgian law there was no specific regulation on timesharing contracts concluded by consumers. The Royal Decree of 30 June 1996 (RD 1996) imposed the obligation on sellers to indicate unit prices on products sold in bulk or pre-packaged products with a variable quantity. As to injunctions, only those (national) consumer organisations recognised by the Minister of Economic Affairs or represented in the "*Raad van Verbruik*" (Consumers' Council), were entitled to commence an action for injunction.

II. Legislative techniques of transposition

All of the Directives at issue have been transposed by the national legislator and, except for the Royal Decree of 30 June 1999 on price indication (statutory instrument), all transposition laws have been enacted by an Act of Parliament.

The legislative techniques applied are diverse. For package travel contracts, timesharing contracts and intra-Community injunctions the BELGIAN Parliament, in each case, enacted a special, separate Act. In contrast, Directives 93/13, 85/577 and 97/7 have been implemented via amendments and insertions to the existing Trade Practices Act (TPA) of 14 July 1991. Moreover particular forms of marketing are limited by trade rules, for example, the Law of 25 June 1993 on the continuation of itinerant activities and the organisation of public markets (*Belgisch Staatsblad*, 30 September 1993, 21526, 'the Law on itinerant activities'): According to this act, the itinerant sale of subscriptions to periodicals without prior authorisation constitutes an offence. Finally, for consumer sales the Parliament adopted a special legislative Act which was inserted into the Belgian CC as a constitutive part of the section relating to the sale of goods.

III. Timeliness of transposition

BELGIUM has transposed Directives 93/13, 97/7, 98/6 in due time. In the case of the provisions on Unfair Contract Terms, after the Commission had pointed out a number of shortcomings in transposition, the Belgian Parliament amended the Trade Practices Act twice in order to secure conformity with the Directive. The other Directives have been implemented with a delay of between 19 months (Directive 98/27) and 50 months (Directive 85/577). For its failure to implement Directive 94/47 in time the Commission has successfully brought an action against Belgium before the ECJ.[4]

IV. Use of minimum harmonisation

When transposing the European Directives BELGIUM made extensive use of the minimum clauses: Unlike Directive 90/314, the Travel Act requires the information supplied, pursuant to TPA, Article 7 (Art. 4(1) of the Directive), to be *in writing*.

As to unfair contract terms, the TPA as well as the Liberal Professions Act (LPA) contain a "blacklist" of clauses that are always considered unfair (per se unfair), whereas the Directive uses a list of clauses that *may* be considered unfair. If the consumer demonstrates that a contract term comes within the clauses listed in TPA, Article 32, no further judicial assessment is required. For timesharing contracts under Belgian law the withdrawal period is extended to 15 working days (Art. 5(1) of Directive 94/47: 10 days). The Timesharing Act also obliges the vendor to provide more information in the prospectus and the contract than required by the Directive.

V. Other extensions

Article 1(7) of the TPA defines consumers as all natural or legal persons who are exclusively acting (buying products or services) for purposes outside their business or trade. Consequently a person who acquires a product or service for a combined private and professional purpose will cease to qualify as a 'consumer' for the purposes of the TPA. In contrast to the Directives, under the TPA and LPA, legal persons may qualify as consumers, but in the light of recent case law of the Court of Cassation (*Cour de Cassation, Hof van Cassatie)* it is difficult to see how legal persons may be regarded as consumers since the TPA requires consumers to act exclusively for purposes outside business and trade.

As to doorstep selling, the TPA does not provide for a similar exemption as in Article 1(2) of Directive 85/577 and consequently applies to products or services even when the consumer knew or should have known that they form part of the seller's commercial and professional activities. The definition of travel intermediary contracts is broader than the definition in the Directive: the Travel Act (TA) also covers contracts where a seller takes up the obligation to perform just *one* action which enables the consumer to travel or stay somewhere (TA, Art. 1, 2°). As to unfair contract terms, the TPA applies not only to pre-formulated standard contracts but also, without any reservation, to individually negotiated terms in consumer

4 ECJ judgment of 25 February 1999, C-319/98 – *Commission v. Belgium*, [1999] ECR I-01201.

contracts. The scope of application of the provisions on distance selling is broader since many of the exemptions in Art. 3 of the Directive (concerning automatic vending machines, public payphones, auctions, supply of foodstuffs) have not been adopted.

VI. Possible infringements of EC law

The ECJ decided in C-20/03 – *Burmanjer, Van Der Linden, De Jong*[5] (based on a reference for a preliminary ruling from the *Rechtbank van eerste aanleg te Brugge*, Belgium), that "Art. 28 EC does not preclude national rules under which a Member State [Belgium] makes an offence of the itinerant sale of subscriptions to periodicals within its territory, without prior authorisation, where such rules apply, and without distinction based on the origin of the products in question, to all the economic operators concerned carrying on their activity within that State, provided that such rules affect in the same manner, in law and in fact, the marketing of products originating in that State and that of products from other Member States." Now, however, it is for the aforementioned *Rechtbank Brugge* to determine, taking into consideration the facts of the main proceedings, whether the application of Belgium law is such as to ensure these requirements.

As to the rules on standard terms the wording of some of the clauses listed in the Belgian list of unfair terms in Article 32 of the TPA was criticised for demonstrating a certain a lack of coherence: some of the clauses of the black list may overlap, some of the rules of the TPA need further clarification e.g. the exclusion of key-clauses. There is also controversy regarding the real nature of the sanction of nullity and the competence of the Commission and unfair contract terms that are not well-defined. Since the Annex of the Directive displays merely an indicative grey list, it is arguable that the aforesaid does not constitute an infringement of EC law.

As to timesharing, the rule that advance payments cannot be demanded before the end of the withdrawal period is subject to certain limitations in Art. 9(1), 1° of the Timesharing Act. The prohibition applies to the regular withdrawal period but not to the prolonged withdrawal period in case of lack of information. One could argue that this constitutes an infringement of Art. 6 of Directive 94/47.[6]

The provisions on distance selling refer to the general scope of application of the TPA which is limited to 'moveable property'. According to well-established case law the TPA is also applicable to service contracts relating to immovable property, provided those services qualify as commercial acts. In case of rental of immovable property this may possibly lead to a scope which diverges from that of Directive 97/7.

---

5 ECJ judgment of 26 May 2005, C-20/03 – *Burmanjer, Van Der Linden, De Jong* [2005] ECR I-4133.

6 Cf. Part 2 D.III.4.

C. Cyprus – Legislative techniques

Directive	Transposed in	Date of Transposition	ECJ decisions in relation to Cyprus
Directive 85/577	The Law for Consumer Contracts Concluded Away from Business Premises of 2000, L.13(I)/2000	28 January 2000	
Directive 90/314	The Package Travel, Holidays and Tours Law of 1998, L.51(I)/98	1 March 1999	
Directive 93/13	The Unfair Terms in Consumer Contracts Law of 1996, N.93(I)/96	1 July 1997	
Directive 94/47	The Timeshare Contract Law of 2001, L.113(I)/2001	27 July 2001	
Directive 97/7	The Law for the Conclusion of Consumer Distance Contracts of 2000, L.14(I)/2000, as amended by L. 237(I)/04	28 March 2000	
Directive 98/6	The Selling and Unit Price Indication Law of 2000, L.112(I)/2000	24 March 2001	
Directive 98/27	In all legislative measures transposing consumer protection Directives. Examples include: • Misleading Advertising Law • The Law for the Conclusion of Consumer Distance Contracts of 2000, L.14(I)/ 2000, as amended by L. 237(I)/04. • The Timeshare Contract Law of 2001, L.113(I)/2001 as amended by the Timeshare Contracts (Amendment) Law of 2004, L. 127(I)/2004.	 28 March 2000 27 July 2001	
Directive 99/44	The Certain Aspects of the Sale of Consumer Goods and Associated Guarantees Law of 2000. (L. 7(I)/2000)	28 January 2000	

I. State of consumer protection in the field of the Directives before transposition

Before the transposition of the Directives CYPRUS had already established a high level of consumer protection in some areas of law. Some fields of consumer protection, for instance, price indication, injunctions, package travel and timesharing, were already subject to some special regulations and so the consumers were provided with a significant amount of protection. In contrast to that, doorstep and distance selling contracts were not subject to any special regulations and therefore the state of protection could only be granted by provisions of law that applied and still apply to contracts in general and to contracts for the sale of goods. Furthermore, consumers enjoyed the rights being conferred to them by the English Common Law which is applicable in Cyprus by virtue of Article 29 of the Courts Law of 1960, L 14(I)/60.

II. Legislative techniques of transposition

In CYPRUS the obligation of implementation was mostly met by making special legislative Acts that implemented the particular Directive into national law. Directive 94/47, for instance, was transposed by the Timeshare Lease Law of 2001 (Law 113 (I) of 2001). The Law for the Consumer Contracts Concluded Away from Business Premises of 2000 (Law 13 (I) of 2000), for example, serves as transposition for Directive 85/577. Articles 2 and 3 of Directive 98/27 have been transposed by implementing corresponding provisions in each legislative Act that was introduced to transpose other consumer protection directives.

III. Timeliness of transposition

CYPRUS became a member state of the EC on 1 May 2004, when all the deadlines of transpostion had already expired. Thus, Cyprus was required to ensure that the Directives were transposed – as part of the aquis communaitaire – in accordance with its Treaty of Accession. Except for Directive 93/13 and Directive 90/314 which were transposed in 1997 and 1999, all the Directives were implemented in 2000 and 2001. Concerning Directive 97/7 and Directive 99/44, Cyprus was even able to transpose these Directives within the given time frame.

IV. Use of minimum harmonisation

CYPRIOT legislation has made use of minimum harmonisation on various occassions. As an example, concerning Directive 94/47, Cypriot transposition law states that the withdrawal period shall be 15 calendar-days instead of 10 calendar-days provided by the Directive. The withdrawal period of 7 working-days prescribed in Directive 85/577 and Directive 97/7 is longer as well, namely 14 calendar-days, in Cypriot transposition law. Regarding Directive 97/7, the Cypriot legislation goes furthermore beyond the Directive's provisions. What regards the effects of withdrawal, the seller has to reimburse all sums paid by the consumer immediately, instead of within 30 days as provided by the Directive. In the case of unavailability of the goods or services ordered by the consumer, the seller must offer a refund as soon as possible, at the latest within 14 days, which is sooner than the period of 30 days in Art.7(2) of the Directive. Furthermore, the Cypriot transposition law of Directive 97/7 saddles the supplier with the additional obligation to provide the consumer with a standard form of the notice of renunciation of the contract, which the consumer must complete, in case he decides to exercise the aforesaid right. This also applies to Directive 94/47 and Directive 85/577. Here the supplier has to perform the contract within 14 days after the conclusion of the contract, an element which is not required by the community text.

Concerning Directive 98/6, on the one hand, the law implementing the Directive has not been extended to situations outside the scope of the Directive. On the other hand, however, the law is wider than the Directive. The Directive does not specify the place where prices must be indicated, but the transposition law requires them to be indicated on the products themselves, on their packaging or on the shelves where the products are displayed to prevent any confusion to the consumer.

Cyprus has also made use of the minimum clause in Article 7 of Directive 98/27. Qualified authorities are given more extensive rights to bring an action at national level. They are entitled to seek a larger variety of orders, which include ordering the infringing trader to take measures correcting the violation or ordering any other act or measure that may be necessary or reasonable under the circumstances of a particular case. Most importantly, they can bring an action not only for infringements against collective consumer interests but also against the interests of one or more specific individual consumer.

V. Other extensions

Often CYPRIOT law provides more definitions than the European provisions: For timeshare contracts these are "Authorised Officer", "Court", "Credit Contract", "Informative Document", "Minister" and "Ordered Service". Regarding unfair contract terms the definitions of "Business", "Court" and "Director" are added. In the implementation of Directive 99/44 "Authorised Service", "Contract of Sale", "Court", "Minister" and "Permanent Means of Communication" are defined and the wording "the quality of the goods" is specified (which means the safety of the goods, the reasonable durability in time and use, the appearance and finishing, and the non-existence of defects).

Furthermore, the Doorstep Selling transposition law also covers contracts concluded as a result of an unsolicited visit to the consumer, regardless of where the aforesaid visit takes place.

VI. Possible infringements of EC law

More detailed information is provided in the individual reports on the transposition of the Directives (cf. in particular, the executive summaries of the reports on Package Travel in Part. 2.B., on Unfair Terms in Part 2.C., on Distance Selling in Part 2.E. and on Injunctions in Part 2.G.).

D. Czech Republic – Legislative techniques

Directive	Transposed in	Date of Transposition	ECJ decisions in relation to the Czech Republic
Directive 85/577	Civil Code (Act No. 40/1964)	1 January 2001	
Directive 90/314	Civil Code (Act No. 40/1964) Act No. 159/1999 on conditions of business operation in the tourism industry	1 January 2001 1 October 2000	
Directive 93/13	Civil Code (Act No. 40/1964)	1 January 2001	
Directive 94/47	Civil Code (Act No. 40/1964)	1 January 2001	

Directive	Transposed in	Date of Transposition	ECJ decisions in relation to the Czech Republic
Directive 97/7	Civil Code (Act No. 40/1964) Consumer Protection Act No. 634/1992 Act on cross-border payments No. 124/2002 Act on technical specification of products No. 22/1997, as amended by Act No. 226/2003	1 January 2001 31 December 1992 1 January 2003 1 September 1997	
Directive 98/6	Act on Prices No. 526/1990 as amended by an Act 276/2002 and 124/2003 Consumer Protection Act No. 634/1992	1 January 1991 31 December 1992	
Directive 98/27	Consumer Protection Act No. 634/1992 Civil Code (Act No. 40/1964)	31 December 1992 1 January 2001	
Directive 99/44	Act on technical specification of products No. 22/1997 Civil Code (Act No. 40/1964) Act on general security of products No. 102/2001	1 September1997 1 January 2001 1 July 2001	

I. State of consumer protection in the field of the Directives before transposition

Before 1989 there was no particular legislation concerning consumer protection in the CZECH REPUBLIC, as the Communist Civil Code of 1964 did not recognise such a category. The Act 367/2000 by which several Directives were transposed amended the Civil Code.

II. Legislative techniques of transposition

The CZECH REPUBLIC has a Consumer Protection Act (No. 634/1992) which came into force on 31 December 1992 and was amended a few times. It contains the rights and duties of the trader, the rights of the consumer and functions of the public administration in the field of consumer protection. In addition, the Czech Republic enacted different kinds of laws dealing with the regulations of the Directives, for example, the Act on Prices (No. 526/1990), the Act on technical specification of products (No. 22/1997) and the Act on cross-border payments (No. 124/2002).

III. Timeliness of transposition

The CZECH REPUBLIC became member of the European Union on 1 May 2004. So the timeliness of the transposition of the Directives in the Czech Republic cannot be judged by comparing the dates when their laws came into force with the given deadlines. Transposing the Directives into Czech law was part of the necessary preparations for membership according to the Treaty of Accession.

IV. Use of minimum harmonisation

The CZECH legislator has made use of minimum harmonisation in the transposition of Directive 97/7, Directive 94/47 and Directive 99/44. Regarding Directive 97/7 Czech law grants a period of withdrawal of 14 days to the consumer. In the case of Timeshare contracts the period of withdrawal is 15 days. Concerning the Consumer Sales Directive, the CYPRIOT legislator has not transposed the exeptions stated in Art. 2(4) and 3(6).

V. Other extensions

According to the CC also a legal person who is not acting within his commercial activity is considered as consumer.

VI. Possible infringements of EC law

More detailed information is provided in the individual reports on the transposition of the Directives (cf. in particular, the executive summaries of the reports on Doorstep Selling in Part 2.A., Package Travel in Part 2.B., Unfair Terms in Part 2.C., Timesharing in Part 2.D., Distance Selling in Part 2.E., Injunctions in Part 2.G. and on Consumer Sales in Part 2.H.).

E. Denmark – Legislative techniques

Directive	Transposed in[7]	Date of Transposition (due date)[8]	ECJ decisions in relation to Denmark
Directive 85/577	Act No. 451 of 9 June 2004 on certain consumer contracts	23 December 1987 (31 December 1987)	
Directive 90/314	Regulation No. 503/2004 on registration and security etc. in the Travel Guarantee Fund Regulation No. 776/1993 on Package Travels Act No. 315/1997 on the Travel Guarantee Fund Act No. 472/1993 on Package Travels	1 July 1993 (31 December 1993) 1 October 1993 (31 December 1993) 1 July 1993 (Act no 454/1993) (31 December 1993) 1 October 1993 (31 December 1993)	
Directive 93/13	Consolidated Act No. 699/2000 on Marketing Practices	1 May 1975 (Act No. 297/1974) (31 December 1994)	

7 The acts, consolidated acts and regulations listed under this heading are the present acts and regulations containing the transposed rules. They are not necessarily the same as the original instruments of transposition.

8 The dates mentioned (without brackets) refer to the original instrument of transposition.

Directive	Transposed in[7]	Date of Transposition (due date)[8]	ECJ decisions in relation to Denmark
	Consolidated Act No. 781/1996 on Formation of Contract	1 January 1995 (Act No. 1098/1994) (31 December 1994)	
Directive 94/47	Act No. 234 of 2 April 1997 on consumer contracts relating to the purchase of the right of use to real estate on time-share basis	2 April 1997 (30 April 1997)	
Directive 97/7	Consolidated Act on Means of Payment Act No. 451 of 9 June 2004 on certain consumer contracts Consolidated Act No. 699/2000 on Marketing Practices	31 May 2000 (1 January 2002)	
Directive 98/6	Executive Order No. 866 of 18 September 2000 on information on sales price and price per unit for consumer goods The price indication rules were transferred to the Marketing Practices Act in July 2006.	18 September 2000 (18 September 2000)	
Directive 98/27	Act No. 1257/2000 on the protection of the consumers' interests	1 December 2000 (11 December 2000)	
Directive 99/44	Consolidated Act No. 237/2003 on Sales of Goods Consolidated Act No. 699/2000 on Marketing Practices	1 December 2002 (Act No. 213/2002) (1 January 2002) 1 July 1999 (Act No. 342/1999). (1 January 2002)	

I. State of consumer protection in the field of the Directives before transposition

DANISH national law had already provided a great amount of consumer protection before the Directives in the field of consumer protection came into force. For example, concerning package travel, "The Travel Guarantee Fund" was established by an Act of Parliament in 1979 in order to secure a refund of money, accommodation and, when necessary, repatriation. With regard to unfair contract terms, a general clause, which was added to Art. 36 in the Formation of Contracts Act in 1975, gives the consumer the possibility to completely or partly disregard an agreement if it would be "unreasonable or contrary to principles of fair conduct". As another instrument of consumer protection "good marketing practices" were implemented as rules on preventive control of unfair contract terms in Art. 1 of the first Marketing Practices Act in 1975. By transposing the Directives, consumer protection was expanded and some of the rules that were already in force were clarified.

II. Legislative techniques of transposition

DENMARK met the obligation of transposition by amending the existing national laws and by making special legislative acts. For instance, Directive 97/7 was transposed into national law by amending different statutes, in particular the Act on Certain Consumer Contracts, and the Marketing Practices Act. Act No. 1257/2000 on the protection of the consumers' interests serves as an implementation of Directive 98/27.

III. Timeliness of transposition

For the most part, DENMARK transposed the Directives into national law within the timeframe.

IV. Use of minimum harmonisation

Except for the transposition of Directive 98/27, DENMARK has always made use of the minimum clause. As an example, in the case of distance selling contracts, the period of withdrawal is 14 days instead of the seven days provided in the Directive. Regarding Directive 99/44, for instance, the consumer also has the right to rescind the contract even when the lack of performance is minor in cases where the seller has not fulfilled an offer (or a demand) to repair/replace the product. Concerning Directive 90/314 and Directive 94/47 the minimum clause has been used while implementing the European provisions into national law. In contrast, regarding Directive 99/44 and Directive 85/577, for instance, existing rules which provided the consumer with wider protection than the Directive have simply been upheld.

V. Other extensions

In order to provide the consumer with greater protection, DENMARK has often extended the definitions which were given in the Directives. For instance, by transposing Directive 99/44, Directive 97/7 and Directive 94/47 Denmark has extended the term of consumer in a way that it does not only cover natural persons, but also legal persons, provided that they act outside their profession. The transposition of Directive 94/47 extended the Directive in various ways. Not only the definition of the term of consumer, but also the term of vendor and the definition of the contract are wider than in the Directive. Regarding the latter, the Act is not limited to contracts where the right of use of the immovable property is set to a maximum length of one week per year and, in addition, the Act also applies to contracts where there has been no agreement on a payment of "a certain global price". The provisions implementing the Doorstep Selling Directive into Danish law do not only cover contracts concluded at an excursion organised by the trader, but all contracts concluded outside the trader's business, for example in streets, squares, restaurants or railway stations. The consumer's right of withdrawal also applies if the consumer has expressly requested a visit from the trader and also if the trader contacts the consumer by telephone. The price indication rules were transferred to the Marketing Practices Act in July 2006 and now also apply to services.

VI. Possible infringements of EC law

There seem to be no infringements of EC law.

F. Estonia – Legislative techniques

Directive	Transposed in	Date of Transposition	ECJ decisions in relation to Estonia
Directive 85/577	Regulation No. 66/2004 Consumer Protection Act Law of Obligations Act	15 April 2004 15 April 2004 1 July 2002	
Directive 90/314	Tourism Act Law of Obligations Act	1 March 2001 1 July 2002	
Directive 93/13	Trading Act Regulation No. 130 of 10 May 2004 Consumer Protection Act Law of Obligations Act	15 April 2004 10 May 2004 15 April 2004 1 July 2002	
Directive 94/47	Trading Act Regulation No. 130 of 10 May 2004 General Part of the Civil Code Act Law of Obligations Act	15 April 2004 10 May 2004 1 July 2002 1 July 2002	
Directive 97/7	Electronic Communication Act Regulation No. 130 of 10 May 2004 Private International Law Act Consumer Protection Act Law of Obligations Act	1 January 2005 10 May 2004 1 July 2002 15 April 2004 1 July 2002	
Directive 98/6	Regulation No. 76 of 14 April 2004 Consumer Protection Act	26 April 2004 15 April 2004	
Directive 98/27	Regulation No. 130 of 10 May 2004 Private International Law Act Consumer Protection Act	10 May 2004 1 July 2002 15 April 2004	
Directive 99/44	Trading Act Regulation No. 130 of 10 May 2004 Private International Law Act Consumer Protection Act Product Safety Act Law of Obligations Act	15 April 2004 10 May 2004 1 July 2002 15 April 2004 1 May 2004 1 July 2002	

I. State of consumer protection in the field of the Directives before transposition

In ESTONIA, consumer law used to be regulated by the Civil Code of the former Estonian Soviet Socialist Republic of 12 June 1964, in force since 1 January 1965. There were no special rules on doorstep selling, package travel, unfair contract terms and the other fields of the Directives in consideration; only general contract law applied. With the Law of Obligations Act (LOA), which came into force on 1 July 2002, the largest part of Civil Code of

Estonian Soviet Socialist Republic (part III „Obligation Law“) was declared null and void. The LOA served as transposition of several Directives, for example Directive 97/7. On 15 December 1993 the Parliament passed the Consumer Protection Act (CPA) which came into force on 1 January 1994. The CPA contained general provisions concerning responsibilities and restrictions of the seller (Art. 7 and 8), but no special rules comparable to the Directives. Therefore, on 11 February 2004, a new Consumer Protection Code came into force in order to completely harmonise Estonian law with the acquis communautaire.

II. Legislative techniques of transposition

The Law of Obligations Act (LOA), made by the national legislator, was inserted into the existing civil law codification. Furthermore, some Directives, for instance Directive 85/577, Directive 98/6 and Directive 98/27, were additionally implemented by statutory instruments set up by the Minister of Economy and Communication. These statutory instruments were implemented by amending the existing statutory laws.

III. Timeliness of transposition

ESTONIA became a Member State of the European Union on 1 May 2004. On that date the transposition deadlines for all the Directives in consideration had already expired. Estonia was required to ensure that the Directives were transposed – as part of the aquis communaitaire – in accordance with its Treaty of Accession.

IV. Use of minimum harmonisation

Concerning the transposition of the Directives on consumer protection ESTONIA has made use of the minimum clauses given in the Directives. In the area of doorstep selling and distance selling, Estonian law grants a withdrawal period of 14 days. Concerning Directive 98/27, an action can also be taken by an individual consumer.

V. Other extensions

Extensions can, for instance, be found in the transposition of Directive 85/577, Directive 90/314 and Directive 93/13. Concerning Directive 90/314 and Directive 93/13 the scope of application is not restricted to consumers. Consumers, non-commercial and commercial legal persons are covered by the law transposing the Directives. Furthermore, the contracts of package travel service that fall into the scope of application of the package travel regulations do not necessarily have to cover a period of more than 24 hours as prescribed in the Directive., as long as the service includes accommodation. Regarding Directive 85/577, the regulation in Art. 3(2) of the Directive, which stipulates that some kinds of contracts are banned from the scope of application, has not been implemented into ESTONIAN law.

VI. Possible infringements of EC law

More detailed information is provided in the individual reports on the transposition of the Directives (cf. in particular, the executive summaries of the reports on Package Travel in Part 2.B., Unfair Terms in Part 2.C. and on Injunctions in Part 2.G.).

G. Finland – Legislative techniques

Directive	Transposed in	Date of Transposition (due date)	ECJ decisions in relation to Finland
Directive 85/577	The Consumer Protection Act 20.01.1978/38	1 September 1978 (23 December 1987)	
Directive 90/314	Act of Package Travel Undertakings 28.11.1994/1080 Package Travel Regulation 28.11.1994/1085 Package Travel Act 28.11.1994/1079	1 July 1995 (31 December 1992) 1 July 1995 (31 December 1992) 1 July 1995 (31 December 1992)	1. ECJ 11 February 1999 C-237/97 – *AFS Intercultural Programs Finland ry* [1999] ECR I-00825
Directive 93/13	The Consumer Protection Act 20.01.1978/38	1 September 1978 (31 December 1994)	
Directive 94/47	The Consumer Protection Act 20.01.1978/38	1 September 1978 (29 April 1997)	
Directive 97/7	The Consumer Protection Act 20.01.1978/38 The Personal Data Act, 1.06.1999/523 Com data protection Act, 1.09.2004/516	1 September 1978 (4 June 2000)	
Directive 98/6	Regulation on Price Indications in Marketing of Consumer Goods, 30.12.1999/1359 The Consumer Protection Act 20.01.1978/38	1 April 2000 (18 March 2000) 1 September 1978	
Directive 98/27	Act on Cross Border Injunction Procedure 21.12.2000/1189	1 January 2001 (1 January 2001)	
Directive 99/44	The Consumer Protection Act 20.01.1978/38	1 September 1978 (1 January 2002)	

I. State of the consumer protection in the field of the Directives before transposition

Before the transposition of the European Directives at issue FINLAND had already established a high level of consumer protection which is heavily based on a single act. The Consumer Protection Act of 1978 applying only to goods, even so, covered a great number of both selling and marketing situations such as Doorstep Selling, Unfair Contract Terms and Consumer Sales and included a right of withdrawal. Consequently, the concept of consumer is in relation to EC-law relatively uniform. In case of a lack of specific provisions, for one concerning Package Travel, general rules and principals were applicable.

II. Legislative techniques of transposition

As FINLAND set up an effective consumer protection a long time before any European initiatives, nearly all Directives were implemented in a technical way and transposed by amendments and additions to the existing law, namely the Consumer Protection Act. However, Directive 90/314 and Directive 98/27, covering situations for which specific provisions did not exist in Finland before, are each codified in a special act where the principal of *lex specialis derogat lex generalis* applies.

A special feature of the Finnish system is the capital role of public authorities having considerable discretion. According to 3:4 Consumer Protection Act, The Consumer Ombudsman, who is Chief of the Consumer Agency, supervises the consumer protection. He can also apply interim measures such as injunctions (3:3.2 Consumer Protection Act) in case of application of unfair contract terms as well as enacting non-binding guidelines (such as for the marketing of Package travels) which are nevertheless, authoritative sources for the traders referring to relevant acts and recent case law. Besides, he may assist a consumer in an individual case (Act on Consumer Agency, Article 9), especially in case the trader does not comply with the decision of the Consumer Complaint Board.

The consumer authorities can react relatively fast to the changing marketing practices and trading activities. This allows flexibility and wider applications of general clauses, a fundamental element of Nordic consumer protection. As a result, when transposing the European Directives, the Finnish legislator does not favour the implementation of black lists (for example, one contained in Directive 93/13) or other similar legal instruments.

All in all, the Directives have not changed Finnish consumer law very much and it can be argued that the impact on businesses, consumers and lawyers has been low. The Directives have not lowered the level of consumer protection for they are harmonised to a minimum, with the exception of Directive 98/27. Some slight amendments might have improved the level of protection.

III. Timeliness of transposition

On the whole, FINLAND transposed the European Directives within the time limit. Only Directive 90/314 was implemented with a remarkable delay of more than two years.

IV. Use of minimum harmonisation

FINLAND is likely to use the minimum clauses in order to maintain the high level of consumer protection which often goes beyond the directives (this is expressed in the travaux preparatoires (HE 2001/89 vp) at 2.7.), for instance, in the Consumer Protection Act, by granting a longer period for right of withdrawal (14 days compared with 7 days of the European provision) or ignoring the time limit of two years of Art. 5(2) of Directive 99/44. To quote an example concerning package travel the passenger has already a right to withdraw from the contract when he has sufficient reasons not to participate in a trip to a dangerous region even if the organiser does not plan to cancel it (Art. 15(1) of the Package Travel Act). Besides, contrary to the Directive, the duty to provide a travel brochure is mandatory (Art. 6 of the Package Travel Act) and the assistance duty applies also in cases where the traveller himself has caused difficulties (Art. 16 of the Package Travel Act). The provisions relating to force majeure situations are more specific (Art. 12 of the Package Travel Act).

Another special derogation concerns Directive 99/44. It is important to notice that the Directive does not impose obligations to the consumer (tilaaja), whereas Chapter 8 of the Consumer Protection Act imposes obligations and liabilities on the consumer in the case of breach of contract.

V. Other extensions

Generally, the FINNISH provisions contain a wider scope of application than the European Directives. An exception is Directive 98/27 which is harmonised without extension of the scope or providing higher protection.

VI. Possible infringements of EC law

More detailed information is provided in the individual reports on the transposition of the Directives (cf. in particular, the executive summaries of the reports on Package Travel in Part 2.B. and on Timeshare in Part 2.D.).

H. France – Legislative techniques

Directive	Transposed in	Date of Transposition (due date)	ECJ decisions in relation to France
Directive 85/577	L. Art. 121-21 et seqq. C.Cons.	29 June 1989 (31 December 1987)	**1.** ECJ 14 March 1991 C-361/89 – *Patrice di Pinto* [1991] ECR I-01189
Directive 90/314	Loi no. 92-645 du 13 juillet 1992 fixant les conditions d'exercice des activités relatives à l'organisation et à la vente de voyages ou de séjours. Now implemented into the Art. L 211-8 et seqq. Code du tourisme	14 July 1992 (1 January 1993)	**1.** as to Art. 7 ECJ 1 December 1998 C-410/96 – *André Ambry* [1998] ECR I-07875
Directive 93/13	L. 132-1 C. Cons.	28 February 1995 (31 December 1994)	**1.** ECJ 21 November 2001 C-473/00 – *Cofidis SA c. Jean-Louis Fredout* [2002] ECR I-10875

Directive	Transposed in	Date of Transposition (due date)	ECJ decisions in relation to France
Directive 94/47	L 121-60 et seqq. C.Cons.	9 August 1998 (29 April 1997)	
Directive 97/7	L. 121-16 et seqq. C. Cons.	25 August 2001 (4 June 2000)	
Directive 98/6	Arrȩté du 16 novembre 1999 relatif à la publicité, à l'égard du consommateur, des prix de vente ŕ l'unité de mesure de certains produits préemballés	24 November 1999 (18 March 2000)	
Directive 98/27	L. 421-6 C. Cons.	25 August 2001 (1 January 2002)	
Directive 99/44	Art. L. 211-1 et seq. C. Cons.	17 February 2005 (1 January 2002)	

I. State of consumer protection in the field of the Directives before transposition

Before the transposition of the European Directives in the field of consumer law FRANCE had already integrated a profound consumer protection in its national legislation. With regard to door-to-door sale, for instance, the law No. 72-1137 of 1972 established rules comparable to the ones of Directive 85/577 of 20 December 1985. With the law No. 78-23 of 1978 a special code of consumer law had been enacted and in chapter IV an administrative controlling system of unfair terms was regulated. In 1992 the existing laws related to consumer protection were combined in the French Consumer Code by the law No. 93-949 of 26 July 1992. The contents of the prior laws remained unmodified except for editorial changes.

II. Legislative techniques of transposition

In the course of the transposition of the Directives FRANCE chose to integrate most of the European provisions in the existing Consumer Code instead of enacting single transposition laws or amending the Civil Code. As an example, the transposing law No. 89-421 of Directive 85/577 was codified in Art. L. 121-16. et seq. C. Cons.; the law No. 95-96 and the regulatory act no. 2001-741 implementing Directive 93/13 modified Art. L. 132-1 C. Cons.; in Art. L. 121-60 et seq. C. Cons. the regulations transposing Directive 94/47 were embodied. Most recently, on 24 February 2005, the French legislator created a Tourism Code including herein the transposition legislation of Directive 90/314 (law no. 92-645, decree no. 94-490).

III. Timeliness of transposition

In general, FRANCE exhausted the given time to transpose the Directives. The transposition acts have been enacted just in time or slightly after the deadline, the implementation of Directive 93/13 being two months later than the date determined in the Directive. Only Directive 99/44 was not transposed at all in the time frame granted by the European legislator (up until 1 January 2002). On 14 July 2003 the European Commission initiated an infringement procedure because of the lack of transposition. Directive 99/44 is now codified in Art. L. 211-1 et seq. C. Cons. (regulatory act no. 2005-136 from 17 February 2005).

IV. Use of minimum harmonisation

Whereas the FRENCH legislation sometimes goes beyond the European provisions, other regulations almost literally adopt the Directive texts (such as the provisions transposing Directive 97/7 and Directive 98/6).

V. Other extensions

As an example of the FRENCH extension of consumer protection, the regulations implementing Directive 93/13 can be considered. In France, no express definition of the consumer can be found. Nevertheless, the jurisdiction has a wider understanding of the notion of consumer. As the Cour de Cassation ruled on 5 March 2002 tradesmen acting without direct connection to their profession can also be regarded as consumers.

VI. Possible infringements of EC law

The French manner of transposition has given reason for complaints from the European Court of Justice. In C-410/96 - *Ambry* the implementation of Art. 7 Directive 90/314 was objected. The French provisions stipulated that insurance could only be effected with a company registered in France. The court ruled that this violated the European regulations of free market barriers. Also the withdrawal period of 7 "jour francs" for distance contracts is a breach of EC law.

More detailed information is provided in the individual reports on the transposition of the Directives (cf. in particular, the executive summaries of the reports on Distance Selling in Part 2.E. and on Injunctions in Part 2.G.).

I. Germany – Legislative techniques

Directive	Transposed in (Translation)	Date of Transposition (due date)	ECJ decisions in relation to Germany
Directive 85/577	Doorstep Selling Cancellation Act Since 1 January 2002: CC Art. 13, 14, 312, 312a, 312f, 355-359 BGB and Art.14 Regulation on duties to supply information in civil law	1 May 1986 (31 December 1987)	**1.** ECJ 17 March 1998 C-45/96 *Bayrische Hypotheken- und Wechselbank AG v. Edgar Dietzinger* [1998] ECR I-01119 **2.** ECJ 13 December 2001, C-481/99,

Directive	Transposed in (Translation)	Date of Transposition (due date)	ECJ decisions in relation to Germany
			Heininger v. Bayrische Hypo- und Vereinsbank AG [2001] ECR I-09945 **3.** ECJ 25 October 2005 C-350/03 *Elisabeth und Wolfgang Schulte v. Deutsche Bausparkasse Badenia* [2005] ECR I-9215 **4.** *ECJ 25 November 2005* Case C-229/04 *Crailsheimer Volksbank eG v. Klaus Conrads, Frank Schulzke und Petra Schulzke-Lösche und Joachim Nitschke* [2005] ECR I-9273
Directive 90/314	CC Art. 651a-651m, Regulation on information duties of travel organisers Since 1 January 2002: Art. 4-11, 15 Regulation on duties to supply information in civil law	1 November 1994 (1 January 1993)	**1.** ECJ 8 October 1996, joined cases C-178/ 94, C-179/94, C-188/94, C-189/94 and C-190/94, *Dillenkofer v. Bundesrepublik Deutschland* [1996] ECR I-04845
Directive 93/13	Act Concerning the Regulation of the Law of Standard Business Terms Since 1 January 2002: CC Art.13, 14, 305-310	25 July 1996 [last part Art. 12, 24a AGBG] (31 December 1994)	**1.** ECJ 1 April 2004, Case C-237/02 *Freiburger Kommunalbauten GmbH Baugesellschaft & Co KG ./. Ludger Hofstetter und Ulrike Hofstetter,* [2004] ECR I-02403
Directive 94/47	Timeshare Act Since 1 January 2002: CC Art. 13, 14, 481-487 and Art. 2, 14 Regulation on duties to supply information in civil law	1 January 1997 (29 April 1997)	
Directive 97/7	Distance Selling Act Since 1 January 2002: CC Art. 13, 14, 241a, 312b-312d, 312f, 355-359, 676h and Art. 1, 14 Regulation on duties to supply information in civil law	30 June 2000 (4 June 2000)	
Directive 98/6	Price Indication Regulation	1 September 2000 (18 March 2000)	
Directive 98/27	Art. 22, 22a Act Concerning the Regulation of the Law of Standard Business Terms Since 1 January 2002: Injunctions Act	30 June 2000 (1 January 2001)	
Directive 99/44	CC Art. 13, 14, 275, 323, 326, 346-354, 433-480, 651	1 January 2002 (1 January 2002)	

I. State of consumer protection in the field of the Directives before transposition

Before the transposition of the European Directives at issue there had not been special rules on consumer protection law in GERMANY. From 1976 onwards, the Unfair Contract Terms Act protected all natural and legal persons (including businesspersons) confronted with standard contract terms drafted in advance by another party. The Doorstep Selling Cancellation Act was adopted almost simultaneously with Directive 85/577. Although generally based on the protection concept of the Directive, the Doorstep Selling Cancellation Act did not explicitly mention the term "consumer", instead the Act referred only to "*Kunde*" which can be translated as customer. The notion "consumer" was used for the first time in German private law in 1987 in the Consumer Credit Act which served the transposition of Directive 87/102.

The level of consumer protection of the German provisions so formulated lagged considerably behind the requirements of Community law prior to transposition of the Directives. Neither did there exist a general right of withdrawal in doorstep sales, distance sales and time sharing contracts, nor were any detailed information requirements in the area of these Directives prescribed in German law. In terms of monitoring unfair terms no clauses could be controlled before transposition of the Directive which were created for single use or incorporated into the contract on the initiative of a third party. Sales law guarantees were subject to a six month limitation period before implementation of the directive; moreover guarantees could in principle be excluded or restricted.

II. Legislative techniques of transposition

Regarding the legislative techniques of transposition in GERMANY three different phases can be identified: In the first phase Germany transposed the European Directives by making marginal modifications to already existing pieces of law. This applies to the provisions on doorstep selling (transposed in the Doorstep Selling Cancellation Act, which was enacted shortly before the Directive was adopted), package travel (transposed via modifications to the already existing rules on travel contracts) and to the provisions on unfair terms (transposed by amendments to the already existing Unfair Contract Terms Act).

In the second phase, the German legislator adopted separate special Acts following the European guidelines; the legislative method applied came close to a word for word transposition. This was the case with the Timeshare Act and the Distance Selling Act. By the time of transposition of Directive 97/7 the German legislator opted for a two-pronged approach: On the one hand the Community law provisions were regulated in accordance with the then employed legislative technique, i.e. in a separate consumer act outside of the CC. On the other hand, for the first time, the central structural elements of consumer law in the CC were standardised and rules established that apply to all consumer contracts. These include the unitary definitions of consumer (CC Art. 13) and business (CC Art. 14) as well as the rules on withdrawal and returns (CC Art. 361a, 361b old version, now: CC Art. 355, 356).

This strategy was pursued further in the third phase with the Act to modernise the law of obligations in relation to transposition of Directive 99/44. The formerly separate consumer protection Acts (on doorstep selling, distance selling, unfair contract terms, timesharing and consumer credit contracts) were integrated into the CC. At the same time the withdrawal provisions of the CC were unified to a greater extent than before. Likewise in relation to sales contracts the legislator opted for a so-called "big solution". The rules of Directive 99/44 were implemented not only for consumer sales, but for all sales contracts. Many of the rules of Directive 99/44 are now applicable to all kinds of sales contracts irrespective of whether or not a consumer is involved; solely in CC Art. 474-479 special rules exist which apply exclusively to contracts between consumers and businesses concerning moveable goods (*Verbrauchsgüterkauf* – sale of consumer goods). Certain principles of Directive 99/44 (for example the concept of rescission) are even to be found in the general part of the law of obligations and are thus applicable to all contracts *in personam* (e.g. in the case of rules on rescission, to all "synallagmatic contracts").

III. Timeliness of transposition

GERMANY transposed most of the Directives either in time or with a relatively slight delay of a couple of months (Directive 97/7 and Directive 98/6). Solely Directive 90/314 (as in many other member states) was transposed with a notable delay of nearly two years (on this point, see the decision of the ECJ in the case of *Dillenkofer*, op. cit.).

IV. Use of minimum harmonisation

When transposing the European Directives GERMANY made use of minimum clauses on various occasions. The time limit for withdrawal for doorstep selling, distance selling and timesharing contracts has been extended to 14 calendar days, whereas the Directives only require seven (Directive 85/577 and 97/7) and ten days (Directive 94/47). If at no time the consumer is informed of his right of withdrawal in accordance with the statutory provisions, then according to German law, an unlimited right of withdrawal exists not only for doorstep selling, but also for distance selling and timesharing contracts, as the legislator implemented the requirements of the *Heininger* decision for all rights of withdrawal. According to Directive 97/7 by contrast, the right of withdrawal, even in the event of non-notification thereof, expires after six months (Art. 6(1), sent. 4 of Directive 97/7) and for timesharing contracts, after three months and ten days (Art. 5(1) of Directive 94/47).

Moreover, the German rules on Doorstep selling protect the customer even if only the negotiations, but not the conclusion of the contract, take place in a doorstep situation. The national rules apply also to cases where the customer is approached in public or on public transport. Furthermore the revocation period has been extended to 14 days (the Directive requires only seven days).

For distance contracts and timesharing contracts the information duties are in part more comprehensive than as laid down in the Directives. In contrast to Directive 90/314 the corresponding provisions of the CC also encompass occasional travel organisers; furthermore neither a minimum length of 24 hours nor an overnight stay are required. Also the possible remedies for the travellers for non-performance are more comprehensive in German law.

Certain rules of Directive 99/44 also exist in relation to consumer guarantees, as under German law, a seller who has issued a guarantee may be liable irrespective of any fault or negligence.

V. Other extensions

Generally, the definition of the term "consumer" is broader than in the EC Directives, as in contrast to Community law the notion of consumer in CC Art. 13 also encompasses the employee acting in the course of a business. As mentioned above, both the provisions on unfair terms and the rules for guarantees in sales contracts basically apply to all kinds of contracts irrespective of whether or not a consumer is involved.

Certain rules of Directive 99/44 (such as e.g. the norms on rescission, *ante*) have general application for all bilateral contracts. Concerning Price Indication the German provisions are also applicable to contracts for services. The German provisions on injunctions are not limited to infringements listed in the Annex of the Directive, instead, applications for injunctions can be filed for violations of all consumer protection laws.

VI. Possible infringements of EC law

More detailed information is provided in the individual reports on the transposition of the Directives (cf. in particular, the executive summaries of the reports on Doorstep Selling in Part 2.A., Package Travel in Part 2.B., Distance Selling in Part 2.E. and on Consumer Sales in Part 2.H.).

J. Greece – Legislative techniques

Directive	Transposed in	Date of Transposition (due date)	ECJ decisions in relation to Greece
Directive 85/577	Article 3 Consumer Protection Act 2251/1994	16 November 1994 (31 December 1987)	
Directive 90/314	Presidential Regulation No. 339/96 on package travel, to implement Directive 90/314/EEC of the Council of 13 June 1990 on package travel including package holidays and package tours (Official Journal 225/11.9.1996)	11 September 1996 (1 January 1993)	
Directive 93/13	Art. 2 Consumer Protection Act 2251/1994 (Official Journal 191 A`/ 16 November 1994)	16 November 1994 (31 December 1994)	
Directive 94/47	Presidential regulation 182/13.8.1999 for the approximation of Greek legislation to the provisions of Directive 94/47/EC (Official Journal 171/ 25.8.1999)	6 January 1999 (29 April 1997)	**1.** ECJ 14.9.1999 Case C-401/98 *Commission v. Hellenic Republic* [1999] ECR I-05543

Directive	Transposed in	Date of Transposition (due date)	ECJ decisions in relation to Greece
Directive 97/7	Amendment of Article 14 of the Consumer Protection Act 2251/1994 via ministerial resolution Z1-496/2000 (Official Journal 1545/18.12.2000)	(4 June 2000)	
Directive 98/6	Resolution n Z1– 404/28.6.2001 (ΦΕΚ Β΄ 827/28.6.2001) of the minister for the economy and development	28 June 2001 (18 March 2000)	
Directive 98/27	Presidential regulation No. 301/2002 to approximate Greek legislation to the rules of Directive 98/27	(1 January 2001)	
Directive 99/44	Act 3043/2002 to amend Arts. 534 et seq. of the Civil Code (Liability of the seller for defective products) and Art. 5 of the Consumer Protection Act	(1 January 2002)	

I. State of consumer protection in the field of the Directives before transposition

Although there were no comprehensive provisions on consumer protection prior to transposition of the directives in GREECE, certain sub-areas were, however, already subject to regulation. According to the Greek Civil Code, it was only possible to intervene in party autonomy in exceptional circumstances, e.g. if the conduct of the other contractual party was contrary to good morals, good faith or the social or economic purpose of the law (CC Art. 174, 178-179, 281, 288).

Article 9(1) subpara. c(γ) of Act 393/1976 laid down certain information duties for travel agencies which offered package tours, however, the travel contract was not regulated as an independent type of contract, but treated as a contract for services. The legislator addressed the issue of time sharing relatively early on. Pursuant to Art. 1(2) of Act 1652/1986 time sharing contracts are concluded through a notary, whilst the ministerial resolution A 9953/DIONOSE/1789/1987 prescribes a comprehensive list of obligatory contractual requirements, whose content by and large corresponds to the minimum requirements of the Annex to the Directive 94/47. Art. 31 of Act 1961/1991 on consumer protection lays down the mandatory requirement that contracts concluded away from business premises must be done so in writing and confers a right upon the consumer to withdraw from the contract within ten days of receipt of his copy of the contract. The contract of sale and thus also the liability of the seller for defective products was subject to general regulation, independent of the nature of the parties, in CC Art. 534 to 561, whilst the Greek legislator regulated the case of sale of new, durable goods (long-life consumer goods) in Art. 5 of Act 2251/1994 on consumer protection, which obliged the supplier to provide a written guarantee to the consumer-buyer.

II. Legislative techniques of transposition

Various concepts were chosen to transpose the consumer protection directives in GREECE: Directives 85/577, 93/13, 97/7 and most parts of Directive 98/27 were transposed via respective amendments in the Consumer Protection Act 2251/1994. Directive 99/44 was transposed by amending the provisions of non-conformity with the contract of the CC (Art. 534 et seq.) and also Art. 5 of the Consumer Protection Act. With Directives 85/577, 93/13, 99/44 this occurred through respective Parliamentary Acts, whereas Directive 97/7 was transposed via ministerial regulation on the basis of statutory authority and Directive 98/27 via presidential regulation. Directives 90/314 and 94/47 by contrast, were transposed by the President of the Republic by separate legal acts via presidential regulation, copying the wording of the Directives almost verbatim. The Greek provisions on unit prices were approximated via resolution of the minister for economy and development.

III. Timeliness of transposition

The transposition of the directives in GREECE did not always happen in a timely fashion, in some respects the European guidelines went unheeded for many years. Following an action by the Commission, the ECJ declared Greece to be in breach of its Treaty obligations in respect of the Timeshare Directive (C-401/98 – *Commission v. Hellenic Republic*).

IV. Use of minimum harmonisation

In many respects the GREEK legislator secures a level of protection beyond that of the Directives: By means of example the provisions on Doorstep Selling require not only a written explanation of the right of withdrawal, but also prescribe that the whole contract is to be in written form and specify certain minimum particulars to be contained therein. Also the time limit for withdrawal is ten days (as oppose to seven calendar days in Directive 85/577). The provisions on package travel contain, alongside additional information duties, an operating licence of the tourist accommodation, an extension of the requirement to hold insurance, to the extent that the consumer has a direct insurance claim against the insurance provider in respect of all claims arising out of imperfect performance or non-performance of the travel contract; this even applies in the absence of insolvency or bankruptcy of the organiser/agent.

In consumer sales the rights of redress of the consumer stand alongside each other, i.e. there is no hierarchy of remedies. The new Art. 540 of the CC allows the purchaser to require a reduction in price or to rescind the contract, even where non-conformity could be remedied by repairing the good or by replacement thereof without disproportionate expenditure on the part of the seller. Furthermore, CC Art. 536, sent. 1, in contrast to Art. 2(5), sent. 1 of Directive 99/44, does not require that the non-conformity be attributable to incorrect installation; therefore the seller is also liable in cases where non-conformity with the contract exists independently of assembly of the product.

V. Other extensions

The notion of consumer in Art. 1(4)(a) of the Consumer Protection Act 2251/1994 encompasses natural or legal persons, for whom the products/services on the market are intended, so long as they are their final addressee. In contrast to the European law concept it is not necessary that the final addressee uses the good or service solely for his own private needs, also the addressee who uses the good/service for business purposes is protected. The provisions on contracts of sale (CC Art. 534 et seq.) also apply to all contracts and not only those which fall within the objective or subjective scope of the directive. The Greek legislator regarded the rules of Directive 99/44 to be of general application and consequently, in amending the corresponding provisions of the CC, opted to regulate all contracts for sale of moveable and immovable goods between all parties (B2B, B2C, C2C) in a uniform fashion, to avoid legislative inconsistencies in the regulation of similar problems.

For distance contracts the legislator has extended the scope of the national provisions to also apply to construction contracts and the contracts for the purchase of immovable property (and concerning rights thereover) as well as to contracts concluded in the course of auctions.

VI. Possible infringements of EC law

The Greek legislator, in transposing Art. 1(2) of Directive 85/577 into Greek law through Art. 3(2) of the Act 2251/1994, neglected to include the supply of other, non-requested services by the supplier in the context of visits by a sales representative on the basis of an express invitation by the consumer. Likewise, subject to criticism is the transposition of Art. 7(1) of Directive 97/7, according to which the supplier is required, unless the parties have agreed otherwise, to execute the order within a maximum of 30 days from the day following that on which the consumer forwarded this order to the supplier. According to Greek law, namely Art. 4(8) of the Act 2251/1994, the time limit first begins after the supplier has received the order.

More detailed information is provided in the individual reports on the transposition of the Directives (cf. in particular, the executive summaries of the reports on Distance Selling in Part 2.D. and on Consumer Sales in Part 2.H.).

K. Hungary – Legislative techniques

Directive	Transposed in	Date of Transposition	ECJ decisions in relation to Hungary
Directive 85/577	Government Decree No. 370/2004 (XII.26.) on Doorstep Selling Hungarian Civil Code	26 December 2004 1 May 1960	
Directive 90/314	Government Decree No. 214/1996. (XII.23.) on Travel Contract and Mediation of Travel Government Decree No. 213/1996. (XII.23.) on Travel Organisation and Agency Activities	1 January 1997 1 January 1997	
Directive 93/13	Hungarian Civil Code Government Decree No. 18/1999. (II.5.) on Unfair Contract Terms Law-Decree No. 13 of 1979 on the International Private Law	1 May 1960 1 March 1999 1 July 1979	1. ECJ judgment of 10 January 2006, C-302/04 – *Ynos Kft v. János Varga* [2006] ECR I-00371

Directive	Transposed in	Date of Transposition	ECJ decisions in relation to Hungary
	Unfair Contract Terms Decree No. 2/1978 Act CXII of 1996 on Credit Institutions and Financial Enterprises	1 March 1978 1 January 1997	
Directive 94/47	Government Decree 20/1999. (II. 5.) on contracts for the purchase of the right to use immovable property on a timeshare basis Act CXLI of 1997 on Real Estate Registration Hungarian Civil Code	1 January 2000 1 May 1960	
Directive 97/7	Government Decree No. 17/1999. (II.5.) on Distance Contracting Act CXLI of 1997 on Real Estate Registration Hungarian Civil Code Unfair Contract Terms Decree No. 2/1978	1 January 2000 1 May 1960 1 March 1978	
Directive 98/6	GM Decree No. 7/2001. (III.29.) on the indication of the prices of products and services offered to consumers Act CLV of 1997 on Consumer Protection	23 December 1997	
Directive 98/27	Act CLV of 1997 on Consumer Protection Government Decree No. 89/1998. (V.8.) on Consumer Supervisory Authorithy Law-Decree No. 13 of 1979 on the International Private Law Ministry of Justice Decree No 13/2004 (IV.16) IM listing the acts of legislation corresponding to the directives listed in the Annex to Directive 98/27/EC on injunctions for the protection of consumers' interests	23 December 1997 1 July 1979	
Directive 99/44	Hungarian Civil Code Act CLV of 1997 on Consumer Protection Government Decree No. 249/2004. (VIII. 27.) Government Decree No.181/2003. (XI. 5.) Government Decree. No. 151/2003. (IX.22.) on guarantees of consumer durables GKM Decree. No. 49/2003. (VII.30.) Unfair Contract Terms Decree No. 2/1978 Law-Decree No. 13 of 1979 on the International Private Law	1 May 1960 23 December 1997 1 March 1978 1 July 1979	

I. State of consumer protection in the field of the Directives before transposition

With regard to Doorstep Selling HUNGARY had already enacted some decrees dealing with consumer protection before the transposition of Directive 85/577 which corresponded to the Directive in general. Only the scope of application was wider than the one prescribed by the Directive and elements of the right of withdrawal differed from the regulations of Directive 85/577.

Before the transposition of Directive 98/6 regulations on the indication of the unit price had not existed in Hungary, meaning that only selling prices were apparent on the goods or on price lists hung beside the goods. More general provisions have been included in the Hungarian Consumer Protection Act (Act No CLV of 1997 on Consumer Protection). As before the transposition of Directive 94/47 there was no particular piece of legislation regulating specifically the area of timeshare in Hungary, the Consumer Protection Act and the Competition Act have been applied in this context. The public administrative body, responsible for the enforcement on deceptive practices, namely the Hungarian Competition Authority, has been dealing with several complaints regarding this area of law, where case handlers have been applying the relevant section of the Competition Act (Act LVII of 1996 on the Prohibition of Unfair and Restrictive Market Practices). According to Article 8(1) thereof "It shall be prohibited to deceive consumers in economic competition." Before the transposition of Directive 90/314 in 1996 the activities of travel agencies were regulated in two government decrees (VO 2/1992. (I. 13.), VO 11/1978 (III. 1.). Regarding Directives 98/27, 99/44, 93/13 legal techniques were established even before the transposition, for example, the possibility of actio popularis which was guaranteed by the Consumer Protection Act and the Civil Code and legal instruments to protect the consumers. One of the main instruments of this system was the CC which developed a wide field of guarantees. The provisions of the CC were applicable to all contractual relations, which means that these provisions were applicable for contracts between suppliers and consumers and also non-consumers. Consequently the guarantees were also applicable to all kinds of contract and not only to consumer contracts.

II. Legislative techniques of transposition

The different Directives were all transposed into HUNGARIAN law by the enactment of Government Decrees and amendments of the CC. As an example Directive 97/7 was transposed into Hungarian law by the Government Decree No. 17/1999 (II.5.) on Distance Contracting and will be implemented into the CC.

III. Timeliness of transposition

HUNGARY became a Member State of the European Union on 1 May 2004, when the transposition deadlines for all the Directives had already expired. Hungary had to transpose the Directives in accordance with its Treaty of Accession.

IV. Use of minimum harmonisation

Regarding Directive 97/7 HUNGARY has made use of the minimum clause. The supplier has to inform the consumer about the right of withdrawal in good time prior to the conclusion of the contract. The period of withdrawal is 8 days instead of 7 days, as in the Directive. The burden of proof concerning the existence of prior information is placed on the supplier. Doorstep Selling is more restricted than prescribed in Directive 85/577 since it is only allowed to sell products door-to-door, where the purpose of selling is generally known, and where these products are industrially packed and not dissected. Furthermore it is forbidden to visit the consumer at home between 7 o'clock p.m. and 9 o'clock a.m., if the consumer has not agreed to the visit in advance. The period of withdrawal in the case of timeshare contracts is 15 days instead of the 10 days stipulated in Directive 94/47.

The Hungarian legislator has made extensive use of the minimum harmonization clause regarding Directive 99/44. The consumer can hold back a proportionate portion of the price until the repair or replacement of the sold goods is completed. If the goods are replaced or if the consumer rescinds from the contract, he is not obliged to pay any compensation for the loss in value caused by proper use of the good. Furthermore, in the case that the non-conformity of the good could not be detected by the consumer, for example due to the nature of the good or the character of the fault, within the given timeframe, the consumer can enforce his or her guarantee rights within one year and in the case of goods designated for long-term use, within three years of delivery. In addition, any clause in a consumer contract which differs from the statutory guarantee rights, where the consumer is at a disadvantage, is void. In the area of unfair contract terms Hungarian legislation goes beyond the provisions of Directive 93/13, as it is possible for the consumer to contest any unfair contract clause, even if the clause has been negotiated.

V. Other extensions

As already mentioned above, HUNGARIAN Law is wider than the regulations of the Directives. The definition of Package Travel is, for example, wider than prescribed by Directive 90/314, because the definition also includes, in contrast to the Directive, trips with a duration of less than 24 hours. The term "organizer" is wider than prescribed by the Directive. The scope of application covers outgoing and incoming tourism Business. Concerning Directive 97/7 there are several acts which stipulate exceptions of the scope, for instance, government decree 175/2003. (X. 28.) concerning the public safety of endangering materials or Law XXXV of 2000 on pesticides. Whereas the term of consumer of Directive 99/44 covers every natural person, the guarantee rules of the CC can be applied to any person who is a party of a contract, concluded for reasons different from economic or professional activities. "Any person" can be a natural person but also a legal person or other organizations. The rules of guarantees and warranties are applicable on consumer contracts and non-consumer contracts as well. Hungarian rules concern all the types of contracts when the parties are bound to owe mutual service to one another. Consumer protection is also warranted for contracts concerning less than 60 Euros. Contracts of catalogue commerce are also covered by the Hungarian legislation. The consumer can arraign the contract because of unfair contract terms even if they were negotiated between him and the supplier before the conclusion of the contract. The regulations on doorstep selling are also applicable if the price is below 60 Euros.

VI. Possible infringements of EC law

The principle of transparency prescribed in Art. 5, sent. 1 of Directive 93/13 has not explicitly transposed in Hungary. Therefore it is doubtful whether the requirements of the Directive have been sufficiently adhered to; see Part 2 C.V.1.b.

More detailed information is provided in the individual reports on the transposition of the Directives (cf. in particular, the executive summaries of the reports on Unfair Contract Terms in Part 2.C. and on Injunctions in Part 2.G.).

L. Ireland – Legislative techniques

Directive	Transposed in	Date of Transposition (due date)	ECJ decisions in relation to Ireland
Directive 85/577	European Communities (Cancellation of Contracts Negotiated away from Business Premises) Regulations, 1989	1 November 1989 (31 December 1987)	
Directive 90/314	Package Holidays and Travel Trade Act 1995	1 October 1995 (1 January 1993)	
Directive 93/13	European Communities (Unfair Terms in Consumer Contracts) Regulations, 1995 as amended by SI No. 307 of 2000	1 January 1995 (31 December 1994)	
Directive 94/47	European Communities (Contracts For Time Sharing Of Immovable Property – Protection of Purchasers) Regulations, 1997 as amended by SI No. 144/2000	19 May 1997, the amendment came into force on 25 May 2000 (29 April 1997)	
Directive 97/7	European Communities (Protection of Consumer in respect of Contracts made by means of Distance Communication) Regulations, 2001 (SI No. 207/2001 as amended by SI No. 71 of 2005	15 May 2001 (4 June 2000)	
Directive 98/6	European Communities (Requirement to Indicate Product Prices) Regulations, 2001 (SI No. 422/2001, has been replaced by European Communities (Requirement to Indicate Product Prices) Regulations, 2002 (SI No. 639/2002	1 October 2001, the amendment came into force on 1 March 2002 (18 March 2000)	
Directive 98/27	European Communities (Protection of Consumers' Collective Interests) Regulations, 2001	3 October 2001 (1 January 2001)	
Directive 99/44	European Communities (Certain Aspects of the Sale of Consumer Goods and Associated Guarantees) Regulations, 2003	22 January 2003 (1 January 2002)	

I. State of consumer protection in the field of the Directives before transposition

Before the transposition of the EC consumer Directives under consideration, there was no consumer protection comparable to that in most of the Directives established in Ireland (e.g. in the area of the Timeshare Directive, Price Indication Directive and the Injunctions Directive). In other areas of law the general rules of contract law were applied. For instance, contracts negotiated away from business premises were governed under general contract law and other specific statutory instruments, such as the Sale of Goods Act 1893, the Sale of Goods and Supply of Services Act 1980, and the EC (Misleading Advertising) Regulations 1988. The Act of 1980 allowed the Minister responsible to rule by order for contracts negotiated away from business premises for a specific period within which the consumer may withdraw from the contract. In fact, this option has never been used. Also for packages, the general contract law was applicable. Tour operators were regulated under the Transport (Tour Operators and Travel Agents) Act 1982. In the area of distance selling there was no pre-existing legislation, again general contract law was applicable. Protection only existed for inertia selling of goods. For consumer sales, there already existed a comparable protection of consumers by the provision of the Sale of Goods Acts 1893 and 1980. These acts already gave the consumer rights which were similar to those provided by the Directive adopted later. The consumer had the right to reject the goods, terminate the contract and sue for damages. The provisions determining whether a good conforms to the contract were comparable as well. Nevertheless, these acts granted a greater freedom to exclude the liability of the seller and difficulties regarding the burden of proof.

II. Legislative techniques of transposition

Ireland has transposed all Directives in single acts. The Directives have been implemented into Irish law by statutory instruments. Only the Package Travel Directive has been transposed by an Act of Parliament.[9] Ireland often uses the copy and paste technique.

III. Timeliness of transposition

Ireland only transposed the Unfair Contract Terms Directive on time. The Timeshare Directive was implemented slightly late. The other directives were transposed with a delay ranging from nine months for the Injunctions Directive to 33 months for the Package Travel Directive.

IV. Use of minimum harmonisation

IRELAND has not intensively made use of the minimum harmonisation clauses provided in the Directives. Directives 85/577, 94/47, 98/6 and 97/7 have been transposed faithfully without implementing a higher consumer protection level than given in the Directives. Only

---

9 Package Holidays and Travel Trade Act 1995.

when transposing Directive 90/314, Ireland extended the catalogue of information obligations for the brochures. In addition to the Directive, the consumer has to be informed in relation to any tax or compulsory charge, an agent with an address within the State in case the organiser has no office in the consumer's state and the arrangements for security for money paid over and (where applicable) for the repatriation of the consumer in the event of insolvency of the organiser.[10] The regulations transposing Directive 99/44 expressly do not substitute, but complete other existing enactments relating to the sale of goods or the terms of contracts concluded with consumers. The consumer can choose the enactment which is more favourable to him.

V. Other extensions

Generally, the implemented legislation is restricted to the scope given to it by the corresponding Directives.

VI. Possible infringements of EC law

More detailed information is provided in the individual reports on the transposition of the Directives (cf. in particular, the executive summaries of the reports on Injunctions in Part 2.G.).

M. Italy – Legislative techniques

Directive	Transposed in	Date of Transposition (due date)	ECJ decisions in relation to Italy
Directive 85/577	Legislative decree of 15 January 1992 No. 50 "Implementation of the Directive 85/577/EEC to protect the consumer in respect of contracts negotiated away from business premises" Legislative decree of 6 September 2005 No. 206 "Consumer code" (Art. 45-47, 62-67)	6 March 1992 (31 December 1987) 23 October 2005	**1.** ECJ judgment of 14 July 1994, C-91/92 – *Paola Faccini Dori v. Recreb Srl*; ECR 1994, I-3325
Directive 90/314	Legislative decree of 17 March 1995 No. 111 "Implementation of the Directive 90/314/ECC on package travel, package holidays and package tours" Legislative decree of 6 September 2005 No. 206 "Consumer code" Art. 82-100	15 October 1995 (1 January 1993) 23 October 2005	
Directive 93/13	Legislative decree of 6 September 2005 No. 206 "Consumer code" (Art. 33-37) Statute of 6 February 1996 No. 52, Art. 25 (amended by Statute of	23 October 2005 (31 December 2004) 6 March 1992	**1.** ECJ 22 November 2001 C-541/99 and 542/99 – *Cape Snc v Idealservice*

[10] Section 10(1) of the Package Holidays and Travel Trade Act 1995.

Directive	Transposed in	Date of Transposition (due date)	ECJ decisions in relation to Italy
	21 December 1999 No. 526, Art. 25) "Implementation of the Directive 93/13/EEC relating to unfair terms in contracts concluded between a seller or supplier and a consumer"		*Srl; Idealservice MN RE Sas v.* OMAI *Srl* ECR [2001] I-09049 2. ECJ 24 January 2002 C-372-99 – *Commission of the European Communities v. Italian Republic* ECR [2002] I-00819
Directive 94/47	Legislative decree of 6 September 2005 No. 206 "Consumer code" (Art. 69-81) Legislative decree of 9 November 1998 No. 427 "Implementation of the Directive 94/47/EC on the protection of purchasers in respect of certain aspects of contracts relating to the purchase of the right to use one or more immovable properties on a timeshare basis"	23 October 2005 15 February 1999 (1 April 1997)	
Directive 97/7	Legislative decree of 6 September 2005 No. 206 "Consumer code" (Art. 50-58, 62-67)	23 October 2005 (4 June 2000)	
Directive 98/6	Legislative decree of 6 September 2005 No. 206 "Consumer code" (Art. 13-17) Legislative Decree of 25 February 2000 No. 84 "Implementation of Directive 98/6/EC on consumer protection in the indication of the prices of products offered to consumers"	23 October 2005 12 May 2000 (18 March 2000)	
Directive 98/27	Legislative decree of 6 September 2005 No. 206 "Consumer code" (Art. 137, 139, 140)	23 October 2005 (1 January 2001)	
Directive 99/44	Legislative decree of 6 September 2005 No. 206 "Consumer code" (Art. 128-139) Legislative decree of 2 February 2002 No. 24 "Implementation of Directive 99/44/EC on certain aspects of the sale of consumer goods and associated guarantees"	23 October 2005 in force since 18 February 2002 (1 January 2002)	

I. State of consumer protection in the field of the Directives before transposition

Before the transposition of the Directives into ITALIAN law the issue of Consumer Protection was regulated by the general provisions on contract law in the Italian Civil Code.

II. Legislative techniques of transposition

The ITALIAN legislator enacted a few legislative decrees and statutes to transpose the regulations of the different Directives. The new Consumer Code came into force on 23 October 2005. While implementing the regulations of the Directives Italy regularly made use of the copy and paste instrument.

III. Timeliness of transposition

ITALY did not transpose all the Directives on time. The delay concerning Directive 98/6 was quite short, namely two months. Directive 94/47 was transposed 2½ years after the transposition period expired and Directive 90/314 almost three years. The transposition of Directive 98/27 was delayed 4 years. Directive 85/577 and Directive 97/7 were transposed 4½ years after the transposition timeframe ended.

IV. Use of minimum harmonisation

When transposing the European Directives the ITALIAN legislator has made use of minimum harmonisation, but not in a very extensive way. As an example, the Italian provisions concerning the right of withdrawal, in the case of distance selling and timeshare contracts give a longer period of withdrawal, namely 10 working-days. Then, the minimum clause in Directive 94/47 was additionally used to stipulate the voidness of the contract if it is not in written form, to forbid the use of the notion "multiproprieta" in Timeshare contracts and to oblige the vendor to provide a bank or insurance guarantee. Concerning Directive 85/577, it is stipulated that a clause that derogates the place of jurisdiction away from the domicile of the consumer is void. The regulations implementing Directive 97/7 contain, compared with the Directive, some further specifications of information duties.

V. Other extensions

In ITALY, the scope of application is sometimes extended. In the regulation implementing Directive 99/44, other contracts such as those mentioned by the community text are included, more particular "permuta" (contracts of exchange of goods), "somministrazione" (the delivery of goods is distributed during the time), "appalto" and "opera" (the professional agrees to do all the work necessary to produce or build a consumer good). In regard to Distance Selling, the Italian law has a larger scope than the Directive, including contracts concluded by mail, on the basis of a trader's catalogue and in any public space. On the contrary, in the case of Timeshare the scope is not extended, but it is considered that the use of minimum clauses described above leads to better information and protection of the consumer.

VI. Possible infringements of EC law

More detailed information is provided in the individual reports on the transposition of the Directives (cf. in particular, the executive summaries of the reports on Doorstep Selling in Part 2.A and on Package Travel in Part 2.B).

N. Latvia – Legislative techniques

Directive	Transposed in	Date of Transposition	ECJ decisions in relation to Latvia
Directive 85/577	Republic of Latvia Cabinet Regulation No. 327 "Regulations Regarding Contracts Entered Into Outside the Permanent Location of Sale or Provision of Services of an Undertaking (Company) Consumer Rights Protection Law	25 September 1999 1 April 1999	
Directive 90/314	Cabinet Regulation No. 163 "Regulations regarding Package Tourism Services Consumer Rights Protection Law Tourism Law	1 October 2000 1 April 1999 1 January 1999	
Directive 93/13	Consumer Rights Protection Law – Chapter 2 "Contracts"	1 April 1999	
Directive 94/47	Cabinet Regulation No. 325 "Regulations regarding Contracts on Obtaining the Right to Temporary Use of a Residential Building or a Part Thereof" Consumer Rights Protection Law	1 October 1999 1 April 1999	
Directive 97/7	Cabinet Regulation No. 1037/2004 Cabinet Regulation No. 207 "Regulations Regarding Distance Contracts Regulation of 18 June 1994 Consumer Rights Protection Law	30 December 2004 31 May 1999 18 June 1994 1 April 1999	
Directive 98/6	Cabinet Regulation No 178 "Procedures for Diplaying Prices of Products and Services" Consumer Rights Protection Law	1 January 2000 1 April 1999	
Directive 98/27	Cabinet Regulation No. 154/2004 Consumer Rights Protection Law	2004 1 April 1999	
Directive 99/44	Consumer Rights Protection Law	1 April 1999	

I. State of consumer protection in the field of the Directives before transposition

In LATVIA, the first regulations concerning Consumer Protection were established by the Law on Consumer Right Protection 1992 after the collapse of the Soviet Union. The law contained basic rights for consumers, for example, the right to receive goods and services in an appropriate quality, and few criteria regarding the voidness of contractual terms. Between 1992 and 1999 consumer rights protection developed intensively. The Latvian legislator revised the existing law on the basis of the experiences of the western countries and the different Directives of the European Community.

II. Legislative techniques of transposition

In the course of the transposition of the Directives the LATVIAN legislator chose to transpose most of the European provisions into the Consumer Law Protection Act. This act is supplemented by individual cabinet regulations for the different Directives, for example, Cabinet Regulation No 178 "Procedures for Displaying Prices of Products and Services" for Directive 98/6 or Cabinet Regulation No. 325 "Regulations regarding Contracts on Obtaining the Right to Temporary Use of a Residential Building or a Part Thereof" for Directive 94/47. As there were no regulations concerning Timeshare before, Directive 94/47 was completely transposed by using the copy and paste technique. For the same reasons the Latvian legislator has used the technique of copy and paste for the transposition of Directives 93/13 and 97/7.

III. Timeliness of transposition

LATVIA became a Member of the European Union on 1 May 2004. As a new member state joining after the transposition deadlines for all the Directives had expired, Latvia was required to ensure transposition of the directives in accordance with its Treaty of Accession. The Consumer Right Protection Act came into force on 1 January 1999. In this law the Directives 99/44, 93/13, 94/47, 85/577 were transposed. Directives 97/7 and 98/6 were partly transposed. The missing provisions were transposed in Cabinet Regulations (No. 207, adopted on 28 May 2002 for Distance Selling and No. 178 adopted on 8 May 1999 for Unit Prices). Directive 90/314 was transposed in the Tourism law from 17 September 1998 and was amended on 7 October 1999, 24 January 2002 and 27 February 2003. Directive 98/27 was partly transposed in 2001.

IV. Use of minimum harmonisation

The LATVIAN legislator has made no use of minimum harmonisation in the transposition of Directives 98/6, 98/27 and Directive 99/44. On the contrary minimum harmonisation has been used in the transposition of Directives 97/7, 85/577 and 94/47 granting the consumer a period of withdrawal of 14 days instead of seven days as provided in these Directives.

V. Other extensions

The LATVIAN legislator formerly used a wider notion of consumer in Art. 1(1) sec. 3 of the Latvian Consumer Rights Protection Law. Legal persons could also be consumers if they "wish to purchase, purchase or might purchase goods or utilise a service for a purpose which is not directly related to his or her professional activity". Now, since 11 November 2005, legal persons are excluded from the scope of "consumer" in the Consumer Rights Protection Law.

VI. Possible infringements of EC law

In Latvia there is a lack of transposition concerning Directive 97/7. The Latvian regulations do not transpose Art. 8 of Directive 97/7, which provides consumers' rights in case of fraudulent use of their payment cards. In addition, Art. 9, 2nd indent of Directive 97/7 is not transposed in Latvian law either. Another shortcoming can be found in the transposition of Directive 93/13. According to Art. 6(1) of this Directive unfair terms shall not be binding. This regulation is transposed by Art. 6(8) of the Latvian Consumer Rights Protection Law, but there is a technical nuance that, practically, makes an important difference with the idea of the Directive. Latvian Law states that only after a consumer's request, the particular contractual term could be declared as unfair and therefore not binding. Until the consumer makes a claim, all contractual terms are valid and legal. Regarding Directive 90/314 the Latvian law only regulates packages sold or offered in Latvian territory, not in the territory of the Community as prescribed in Art. 1 of the Directive.

More detailed information is provided in the individual reports on the transposition of the Directives (cf. in particular, the executive summaries of the reports on Doorstep Selling in Part 2.A., Unfair Terms in Part 2.C., Timeshare in Part 2.D. and on Consumer Sales in Part 2.H.).

O. Lithuania – Legislative techniques

Directive	Transposed in	Date of Transposition	ECJ decisions in relation to Lithuania
Directive 85/577	Civil Code of the Republic of Lithuania Order of the Minister of Economy of the Republic of Lithuania on the Approval of the Rules of Sale of Goods and Provision of Services in Premises not Designated for this Activity Law on consumer protection	1 July 2001 8 February 2001 30 April 2004	
Directive 90/314	Civil Code of the Republic of Lithuania Law on Tourism of the Republic of Lithuania Law on consumer protection	1 July 2001 1 April 2003 30 April 2004	
Directive 93/13	Civil Code of the Republic of Lithuania Law on consumer protection	1 July 2001 30 April 2004	
Directive 94/47	Civil Code of the Republic of Lithuania Law on consumer protection Order of the Minister of Environment on the Approval of the Minimum List of the Mandatory Data to be Indicated in the Description of the Provided Residential Premises and Agreement when Buying the Right to Use the Residential Premises from Time to Time	1 July 2001 30 April 2004 3 June 2001	
Directive 97/7	Civil Code of the Republic of Lithuania Law on consumer protection	1 July 2001 30 April 2004	

Directive	Transposed in	Date of Transposition	ECJ decisions in relation to Lithuania
Directive 98/6	Civil Code of the Republic of Lithuania Order of the Minister of Economy of the Republic of Lithuania on the Rules of Labeling of Items (Goods) Sold in the Republic of Lithuania and Indication of Prices Law on consumer protection	1 July 2001 20 June 2004 30 April 2004	
Directive 98/27	Law on consumer protection	30 April 2004	
Directive 99/44	Civil Code of the Republic of Lithuania Law on consumer protection	1 July 2001 30 April 2004	

I. State of consumer protection in the field of the Directives before transposition

Before adopting Law No. I-657 of the Republic of Lithuania "On Consumer Protection" of 10 November 1994, LITHUANIAN Consumer law was regulated by the Soviet Civil Code (dating from 7 July 1964). In the Soviet Civil Code, there were no regulations on Consumer Protection comparable to those in the Directives. According to the European Agreement Establishing an Association between the European Communities and their Member States and the Republic of Lithuania, which came into force on 1 February 1998, the Lithuanian legislation had to be harmonised with the acquis communautaire. In this process of integration the Directives were transferred into Lithuanian law.

II. Legislative techniques of transposition

In LITHUANIA there is a Law of Consumer Protection which contains regulations regarding each Directive. For example, the Lithuanian legislator uses a unitary definition of consumer[11] which is applicable for all Directives. The definition of seller[12] is, as well, unitary and applicable to all Directives. Some provisions of the Directives were transposed by amending the Lithuanian Civil Code. Concerning Directives 85/577, 94/47, 98/6 Orders of the Ministry of Economy supplement the regulations of the laws.

III. Timeliness of transposition

LITHUANIA became a Member of the European Union on 1 May 2004. The Law on consumer protection, by which all the Directives are (partly) transposed, came into force on 30 April 2004. As a new member state joining after the transposition deadlines for all the Directives had expired, LITHUANIA was required to ensure transposition of the Directives in accordance with its Treaty of Accession.

---

11 Article 2(1) of the Law on consumer protection.

12 Article 2(2) Law on consumer protection.

IV. Use of minimum harmonisation

The LITHUANIAN legislator has made no use of minimum harmonisation. Consumers are not given greater protection than envisaged in the Directives and the legislation. The Lithuanian legislator has made no use of options either.

V. Other extensions

LITHUANIAN law does not extend to situations outside the scope of the Directives.

VI. Possible infringements of EC law

More detailed information is provided in the individual reports on the transposition of the Directives (cf. in particular, the executive summaries of the reports on Doorstep Selling in Part 2.A., Unfair Terms in Part 2.C., Timeshare in Part 2.D., Distance Selling in Part 2.E., Injunctions in Part 2.G. and on Consumer Sales in Part 2.H.).

P. Luxembourg – Legislative techniques

Directive	Transposed in	Date of Transposition (due date)	ECJ decisions in relation to Luxembourg
Directive 85/577	Act of 26 March 1997 transposing Directive 93/13/EEC and Directive 85/577/EEC	29 April 1997 (23 December 1987)	
Directive 90/314	Package Travel Act of 14 June 1994	6 July 1994 (31 December 1992)	
	Decree of 4 November 1997 on the amount, conditions and use of the financial guarantees provided in article 6 of the law of 14 June 1994	28 November 1997	
	Decree of 4 November 1997 on pre-contractual information and contract conditions of package travel contracts	28 November 1997	
	Decree of 26 novembre 2001 amending Decree of 4 November 1997	20 December 2001 (31 December 1992)	
Directive 93/13	Act of 26 March 1997 transposing Directive 93/13/EEC and Directive 85/577/EEC	29 April 1997 (31 December 1994)	
Directive 94/47	Timeshare Act of 18 December 1998	26 January 1999 (29 April 1997)	
Directive 97/7	Distance Contracts Act of 16 April 2003	8 May 2003 (4 June 2000)	
Directive 98/6	Decree of 7 September 2001 on price indication (as amended by the decree of 29 July 2004)	3 October 2001 (18 March 2000)	

Directive	Transposed in	Date of Transposition (due date)	ECJ decisions in relation to Luxembourg
Directive 98/27	Act on injunctions of 19 December 2003	31 December 2003 (1 December 2001)	
Directive 99/44	Consumer Sales Act of 21 April 2004	29 April 2004 (1 January 2002)	

I. State of consumer protection in the field of the Directives before transposition

Legislation in the grand duchy shows that a considerable effort had been made to promote consumer rights before any European initiatives. The main fields of LUXEMBOURG'S pre-existing consumer legislation cover prices, packaging, labelling, advertising, selling methods and unfair competition, the quality and safety of consumer products and services and consumer credit. The main gaps are liability for products and services, access to justice, control over unfair terms and consumer education.

In Luxembourg law consumer interests are not always easy to distinguish from general interests or the interests of competition. Consumer protection is actually considered as a kind of reflex to competition law. However, legislative measures in the field of competition law have a long tradition. The core of unfair competition law is contained in the Act of 27 November 1986 regulating certain trade practices and sanctioning unfair competition (Loi du 27 novembre 1986 réglementant certaines pratiques commerciales et sanctionnant la concurrence déloyale).

One of the most important legal acts is the one of 25 August 1983 on the legal protection of the consumer (Loi du 25 août 1983 relative à la protection juridique du consommateur), modified by the Act of 26 March 1997 on the basis of Directive 93/13 concerning unfair contract terms. This law deals with consumer protection mainly on the contractual level. Another provision of great relevance is the Act of 16 July 1987 on hawking, peddling, display of goods and solicitation of orders (Loi du 16 juillet 1987 concernant le colportage, la vente ambulante, l'étalage de marchandises et la sollicitation de commandes). In addition, a law of 11 August 1982 on the protection of privacy, prohibits persons molesting others by repeated and unannounced telephone calls or in written form and other messages (Loi du 11 août 1982 concernant la protection de la vie privée).

II. Legislative techniques of transposition

As to the transposition of European Directives the LUXEMBOURG legislator uses both the copy and paste technique and the technique of implementation through amendment of pre-existing domestic law. Partly the copy and paste technique prevails – e.g. with regard to the transposition of Directives 94/47, 97/7, 98/6 and 99/44 – and, partly the amendment technique – e.g. regarding Directives 85/577 and 93/13. In order to implement the latter Directives, the Luxembourg legislator revised two Acts of great relevance: the Act of 25 August 1983 on the legal protection of the consumer and the Act of 16 July 1987 on hawking, peddling, display of goods and solicitation of orders.

III. Timeliness of transposition

LUXEMBOURG has not managed to implement the above-mentioned Directives by their deadline. Indeed, the transposition into national law was carried out with a couple of years' delay (on average two to three years). In the case of Directive 85/577, the European Commission launched a legal action against Luxembourg for non-transposition.

IV. Use of minimum harmonisation / Other extensions

LUXEMBOURG has practically made no use of the minimum harmonisation clauses. Options in the Directives in favour of higher consumer protection are rarely used. Generally, the implementing legislation is restricted to the scope given to it by the corresponding Directives. On occasion, there are slightly more generous definitions, which has the effect of broadening the scope of application. One example might be Art. 1(3) of the Act of 16 April 2003 on the protection of the consumer concerning distance selling contracts, which provides a broader definition of the "supplier" in comparison to Art. 2(3) of Directive 97/7.

V. Possible infringements of EC law

More detailed information is provided in the individual reports on the transposition of the Directives (cf. in particular, the executive summaries of the reports on Unfair Terms in Part 2.C.).

Q. Malta – Legislative techniques

Directive	Transposed in	Date of Transposition	ECJ decisions in relation to Malta
Directive 85/577	Doorstep Contracts Act	15 March 1987 full implementation of Directive – 1 January 2001	
Directive 90/314	Malta Travel and Tourism Services Act Package Travel, Package Holidays and Package Tours Regulations, 2000	25 August 2000 25 August 2000 1 November 2001 (date of coming into force)	
Directive 93/13	Consumer Affairs Act	15 October 2002	
Directive 94/47	Protection of Buyers in Contracts for Time Sharing of Immovable Property Regulations, 2000	15 September 2001	
Directive 97/7	Distance Selling Regulations, 2001	4 September 2001	
Directive 98/6	Consumer Affairs Act (Price Indication) Regulations	1 October 2002 (date of coming into force)	
Directive 98/27	Consumer Affairs Act	15 October 2002 (fully in force)	
Directive 99/44	Consumer Affairs Act	1 July 2002	

I. State of consumer protection in the field of the Directives before transposition

In general, the amount of protection in MALTA before the transpositions was not comparable to the one laid down in the Directives. In a lot of cases, there were no special legal rules that dealt with the area of consumer protection, so the general provisions of the Civil Code were applied. However, before the implementation of Directive 85/577 and Directive 98/6, consumers were already granted a great amount of protection. By enacting the Door-to-Door Salesmen Act[13] (Cap. 317 of the Laws of Malta) in February 1987, the Maltese legislator took the European Directive as a model. The consumer was not only granted the right of withdrawal, but also other measures of protection that in some points, for example, the burden of proof, even went beyond the minimum measures stated in the Directive. The Control of the Sale of Commodities Regulations, 1972, which dealt with the display of prices, obliged the traders to "exhibit conspicuously" a sample of every type of product they had in stock. Each of those samples had to be indicated with a white label showing the selling price which had to fulfil very strict requirements concerning the way the single figures were to be printed.

II. Legislative techniques of transposition

The eight Directives were transposed into MALTESE law either by Acts of Parliament which were enacted by amending existing statutory law or else by regulations promulgated by the responsible Minister under the legislative powers granted to him by Parliament under the applicable law. Whereas, for instance, the Door-to-Door Salesmen Act was amended by Act No. XXVI of 2000 in order to bring the legislation in line with the EC Directive, the Directives 93/13, 98/27 and 99/44 were each transposed into Maltese law by amendments to the Consumer Affairs Act (Cap. 378 of the Laws of Malta). These amendments were enacted by Parliament. The Directives 97/7 and 98/6 were transposed by the Minister responsible for consumer affairs after consultation with the Consumer Affairs Council by virtue of his powers to make regulations under Article 7 of the Consumer Affairs Act, whereas Directive 90/314 and Directive 94/47 were transposed by the Minister responsible for tourism after consultation with the Malta Tourism Authority by virtue of his powers under Article 47 of the Malta Travel and Tourism Services Act.

III. Timeliness of transposition

MALTA became a member of the European Union on 1 May 2004. As a new member state, joining after the transposition deadlines for all the Directives had expired, Malta was required to ensure transposition of the Directives in accordance with its Treaty of Accession.

---

13 The Door-to-Door Salesmen Act was later renamed to Doorstep Contracts Act.

IV. Use of minimum harmonisation

Except for Directives 90/314 and 98/6 the MALTESE legislator has always made use of minimum harmonisation clauses in the Directives. Concerning the Directive 85/577 and 97/7 the period for the consumer to exercise his right of withdrawal has been extended to 15 days as opposed to 7 days as in the Directives. Furthermore, regarding Directive 94/47, separate regulations have been enacted in order to stop the harassment of timeshare salespersons by prospective buyers. These regulations state that the salespersons have to be licensed, that they have to carry personal identification with them while working and that they must not take part in any conduct which is misleading or deceptive. Concerning Directive 93/13, a black list of terms has been included.

Concerning Directive 99/44, Maltese law contains rules dealing with the requirements of commercial or voluntary guarantees which go beyond the Directive's provisions. Extensions have also been made in the context of the implementation of Directive 90/314 with regard to the information duties of the travel organiser. In the brochure, the organiser must give information on all taxes and additional charges. Furthermore, these brochures must include information on arrangements for security for the refund of monies paid and for the repatriation of the consumer in the event of the insolvency of the organiser.

V. Other extensions

In general the scope of application is not extended to such a great extent that one can state that consumers overall have much more protection at law than the minimum required under EC legislation, though there are significant variations as stated above notably with regard to unfair terms and timeshare. Regarding Directives 93/13, 99/44, 97/7 and 98/6 the term "consumer" covers natural persons. However, in relation to the laws transposing these Directives, the Minister responsible for consumer affairs after consulting the Consumer Affairs Council has the power to designate any other class or category of persons including legal persons as consumers. In the case of Directive 98/6 'consumer' also includes the final purchaser. Concerning Directive 93/13, Maltese law extends the protection to all contractual terms without making any distinction as to whether the term was individually negotiated or not.

VI. Possible infringements of EC law

More detailed information is provided in the individual reports on the transposition of the Directives (cf. in particular, the executive summaries of the reports on Doorstep Selling in Part 2.A., Unfair Terms in Part 2.C., Injunctions in Part 2.G. and on Consumer Sales in Part 2.H.).

R. Netherlands – Legislative techniques

Directive	Transposed in	Date of Transposition (due date)	ECJ decisions in relation to the Netherlands
Directive 85/577	Dutch Civil Code Law of 31 December 1989 containing changes to the Doorstep Selling Law	1 January 1992 (26 July 1989)	
Directive 90/314	Dutch Civil Code Decree of 15 January 1993, containing rules concerning data that organisers of organised trips must state on behalf of travellers	1 January 1992 (27 January 1993)	
Directive 93/13	Dutch Civil Code Law of 28 October 1999 to the adaptation of Book 6 of the Civil Code to the Directive unfair terms in consumer contracts	1 January 1992 (17 November 1999)	**1.** ECJ 10 May 2001 C-144/99 – *Commission of the European Communities v Kingdom of the Netherlands* ECR [2001] *I-03541*
Directive 94/47	Dutch Civil Code Decree of 25 June 1997 containing rules concerning data that sellers of the right of part-time use of real estate should mention in the contract on behalf of the buyer	1 January 1992 (29 April 1997)	
Directive 97/7	Dutch Civil Code Dutch General act on terms Media Law Telecommunication Law Personal Data Protection Act Law of 21 December 2000 to the adaptation of Book 7 of the Civil Code to Directive number 97/7/EC of the European Parliament and the Council of Europe of 20 May 1997 regarding the protection of consumers by distance selling	1 January 1992 1 April 1965 25 May 2005 1 January 2001 (4 June 2000)	
Directive 98/6	Decree of 21 May 2003 containing rules in regard to the indication of prices as replacement for the Decree price-indication on goods 1980	11 June 2003 (18 March 2000)	
Directive 98/27	Dutch Civil Code Law of 25 April 2000 on the adaptation of Book 3 and 6 of the CC to the Directive 98/27/EC on injunctions for the protection of consumers' interests	1 January 1992 (1 January 2001)	
Directive 99/44	Dutch Civil Code	1 January 1992 (1 January 2002)	

I. State of consumer protection in the field of the Directives before transposition

Before the transposition of the European Directives in the field of consumer law the NETHERLANDS had already integrated some general provisions concerning consumer protection in the CC (Burgerlijk Wetboek). CC Title 7.1 mentions specific provisions for consumer contracts, for example, the principle of conformity (CC 7:17). This principle means that any good delivered should conform to the contract, which means that the good should have all qualities that a buyer could reasonably expect given its nature and the information given by the seller. With regard to Directive 85/577 the Doorstep Selling Law of 7 September 1973 established rules comparable to those of Directive 85/577. Especially in the field of Unfair contract terms the Dutch Civil Code did not contain specific provisions before 1 January 1992.

II. Legislative techniques of transposition

Most of the provisions established by the different Directives were transposed in the DUTCH CC except the regulations of Directive 98/6. In terms of the transposition of Directive 98/6 the Dutch law established the decree of 21 May 2003 which contains rules in regard to the indication of prices as a replacement for the Decree price-indication on goods 1980. In addition to the amendments of the Dutch Civil Code single transposition laws were enacted, for example, the Decree of the 25 of June 1997, containing rules concerning information that sellers of timeshare rights should mention in the interest of the buyer (Directive 94/47), or the Law of the 28 of October 1999 to the adaptation of CC Book 6 to the Directive of unfair terms in consumer contracts.

III. Timeliness of transposition

With regard to Directive 85/577 the Doorstep Selling Law of 7 September 1973 established rules comparable to those of Directive 85/577. This Act was amended by the Law of the 31 December 1989. Additionally with regard to all Directives except Directive 98/6 the Dutch Civil Code was changed on the 1 November 2004. The Decree of the 15 of January 1993 transposed Directive 90/314 with one month delay. Directive 93/13 was transposed on the 17 November 1999 by the Law of the 28 of October 1999 to the adaptation of CC Book 6 with a delay of 5 years.

IV. Use of minimum harmonisation

In several cases DUTCH law is broader than the scope of the Directive. As an example, Directive 93/13 contains an indicative and non-exhaustive list of terms which *may* be regarded as unfair. Dutch law contains a list of terms that *must* be regarded as unfair. Also several of the limitations allowed in Article 3 of the Directive are not implemented. Various articles and paragraphs of CC Section 7.1 on contracts of sales, including articles and paragraphs similar to those in Directive 99/44, also apply to buyers who are not consumers. Examples are CC

Article 7:17 and CC Article 7:21(1), (2) and (3) and CC Article 7:23(2). In the field of Directive 97/7 the legislator has not made any use of the possibility to offer the consumer more comprehensive protection than the minimum protection prescribed by the Directive. Moreover, Dutch legislation has not been extended to situations outside the scope of the Directive. According to the legislator CC Article 7:17(4) gives greater protection than Article 2(2) lit. (a) of the Directive because the burden of proof of the function of the sample or model is on the seller. The reasoning is that, if a sample or model is shown, it does not necessarily mean that the seller and buyer have entered into a contract of sale of goods, where the goods should conform exactly with the sample. CC Article 7:17(2) gives greater protection than Article 2(2) lit. (b) of the Directive because the goods should conform with the particular purpose, not only as far the seller has accepted this purpose, but also with that which has been determined in the contract, which may be broader.[14] CC Article 7:21(1)(a) grants the right to the delivery of missing goods, which is not granted by Article 3(2) of the Directive. If the seller has not repaired the good within a reasonable time, CC Article 7:21(6) allows the consumer to have a third party repair the goods and hold the seller liable for the costs. CC Article 7:23(2) offers more protection than Article 5(1) of the Directive. The Article is more favourable to the consumer, because (a) the lack of conformity does not have to become apparent within two years after delivery; and (b) with regard to the limitation period, the moment of notification, and not the moment of delivery is taken as the starting point.[15]

V. Other extensions

In some cases DUTCH law offers a greater consumer protection than prescribed by the European Directives. In the case of Doorstep Selling Dutch law also covers contracts where the total payment to be made is less than € 34 and situations in which there is a standing relationship between parties concerning the selling of food. The original broader scope of the law is maintained in a sense that the field of work is broader than Article 1(1) of the Directive indicates and that several of the limitations allowed in Art. 3 of the Directive are not implemented.

The scope of the Doorstep Selling Law contains a broader field of work than is prescribed by Article 1(1) of Directive 85/577.

Regarding the transposition of Directive 94/47 the application of CC chapter 7.1.10A is not limited to contracts for the transfer of property, but is extended to include inter alia contracts of rent or lease. The explanatory note explicitly states that, like Art. 2 first indents of the Directive, CC Art. 48a aims to encompass all the different forms of rights to part time use of immovable property (Kamerstukken II 1995/96, nr. 3, 5). The definition of CC Art. 48a also includes contracts that create indirect rights to part time use of unmovable property (for instance trough membership of a club). This provision allows an extension of the period if the deed does not contain all of the required information. In contrast to Art. 5, 2nd indent of the Directive no distinction is made as to the type of information that has been omitted.

The consumer protection with regard to contract of sales is also applicable to contracts of barter (CC Article 7:50). The consumer protection does not only include tangible moveable

---

14 *Kamerstukken* II 2000/2001, 27 809, nr. 3, p. 5.

15 *Kamerstukken* II 2000/2001, 27 809, nr. 3, p. 9-10.

goods, but also intangible goods such as claims (CC Article 7:47). Various articles and paragraphs of CC Section 7.1 on contracts of sales, including articles and paragraphs similar to those in the Directive, also apply to buyers that are not a consumer.

VI. Possible infringements of EC law

The DUTCH government thought that Dutch law was in compliance with Directive 93/13. Therefore, initially the law was not changed. However, the ECJ ruled that several provisions were not in compliance with Directive 93/13 (Jur. 2001, I-2541). For that reason, a clarification was introduced in the Dutch code, making sure that the assessment of the unfair nature of the terms shall not relate to the definition of the main subject matter of the contract, provided that these terms are in plain intelligible language. Futhermore, an extra provision was introduced to the code which had to make sure that where there is doubt about the meaning of a term, the interpretation most favourable to the consumer shall prevail. In general, the Dutch law on unfair contract terms was already in compliance with the Directive. Directive 99/44 has not been implemented in time. Otherwise no major difficulties have been encountered as a result of incompatibilities of the Directive with the Dutch legal system, or as a result of ambiguities, inconsistencies or other weaknesses in the Directive, or as a result of lack of coherence with other Directives.

More detailed information is provided in the individual reports on the transposition of the Directives (cf. in particular, the executive summaries of the reports on Package Travel in Part 2.B., Unfair Terms in Part 2.C. and on Consumer Sales in Part 2.H.).

S. Poland – Legislative techniques

Directive	Transposed in	Date of Transposition	ECJ decisions in relation to Poland
Directive 85/577	Act of 2 March 2000 on the protection of certain consumer rights and liability for an unsafe product	1 July 2000	
Directive 90/314	The Act on Tourist Services of 29 August 1997	1 July 1998	
Directive 93/13	Act of 2 March 2000 on the protection of some consumer rights and liability for an unsafe product	1 July 2000	
Directive 94/47	The Act of 13 July 2000 on the protection of purchasers in respect of the right to use buildings or dwellings during certain time each year	8 December 2000	
Directive 97/7	Act of 2 March 2000 on the protection of some consumer rights and on liability for unsafe products	1 July 2000	
Directive 98/6	The Act on prices of 5 July 2001	11 December 2001	
Directive 98/27	The Act of 15 December 2000 on the protection of consumers and competition.	1 April 2001	

Directive	Transposed in	Date of Transposition	ECJ decisions in relation to Poland
Directive 99/44	Act of 27 July 2002 on the certain conditions of consumer sale and on the amendment of the Civil Code	1 January 2003	

I. State of consumer protection in the field of the Directives before transposition

Before the implementation of the Directives, in most cases there existed no specific provisions, concepts and definitions dealing with terms of the different Directives in POLISH law. For example the definition of 'consumer' did not exist in Polish law until the Act of 2 March 2000 and there was no right of withdrawal given to the consumers and no specific information duties imposed upon traders. Only general provisions concerning contracts and contractual liability of the Civil Code were applied. But the available remedies did not, however, correspond to the remedies prescribed by the Directives.

Also no specific provisions covering timeshare existed in POLISH law. Timesharing was only known by the Polish legal literature, legal practice and case law. The general provisions of the CC on contractual relations and contractual liability were applied. But there were no obligations of the trader to provide specific information to the consumer, not even the trader's address or other details concerning him. No specific rules concerning the functionality of travel agencies as well as the package travel existed in the POLISH legal system until the 1990s. There was no regulation concerning the qualifications required for persons dealing with tourism. Traders who dealt with such type of business activity had to respect the provisions concerning any business activity (the Act *on economic activity* of 23 December 1988) and relations between the consumers and the travel agents or organisers of tourist events were regulated by the law of contracts (CC).
Since 1990 certain mechanisms aimed to protect consumer interests had been established, but they were still unsatisfactory in comparison with the standards required by the Directives. The idea of unfair contractual clauses had always been based upon the concept of 'standard forms' – '*wzorce*' – as it was perceived that such clauses derived from standard form contracts (adhesion contracts). 'Standard forms' were defined as any contractual clauses (either in the form of ready lists of clauses, standard contractual forms, or sets of rules) unilaterally drafted before the conclusion of the contract justified by the aim of protecting consumer interests. One such Regulation of the Council of Ministers was indeed adopted on 30 April 1995 (*on the conclusion and execution of contracts of sale of movable goods with consumers*). Article 384 of this regulation was repealed as unconstitutional by the Act implementing Directive 93/13.

II. Legislative techniques of transposition

In the course of the transposition of the Directives POLAND enacted single transposition laws for example the Act of 2 March 2000 on the protection of certain consumer rights and liability for an unsafe product or the Act on Tourist Services of 29 August 1997. In terms of the transposition of the Consumer Sales Directive the Polish legislation amended the Polish Civil Code.

III. Timeliness of transposition

Poland, as a new member state joining the European Union after the transposition deadlines for all the Directives had expired, was required to ensure transposition of the Directives in accordance with its Treaty of Accession.

IV. Use of minimum harmonisation

The POLISH legislation makes use of minimum harmonisation in many areas. Regarding the Doorstep Selling Directive, the period for withdrawal is 10 days long and not 7 days as it is prescribed by the Directive. This extension, however, does not constitute a significant advantage to the consumer in comparison with the regime of the Directive, because time periods in Poland are calculated using all calendar days, not working days. If Poland had followed the Directive and introduced a 7-day period it could have been taken as decreasing the level of protection provided by the Directive. Furthermore, the trader is not only obliged to inform the consumer before the conclusion of the contract about his right of withdrawal, but also has to provide him with a standard form for withdrawal.

In the case of Directive 97/7 the consumer does not have to bear the costs for returning the goods and in case of deposit payments by the consumer, statutory interest should be paid to him (calculated from the date of payment). With regards to restrictions of the use of certain means of distance communication, the Polish legislator uses the opt in system whereas the Directive uses the opt out system. Consequently, for the use of telephone, videophone, fax, electronic mail, automated calling system and any other means of distance communication, if their use is for the purpose of making an offer, the consent of the consumer is required.
In the case of Directive 94/47 the Polish Act on the protection of purchasers in respect of the right to use buildings or dwellings during a certain time each year restricts the possibility of amending the contents of the prospectus prepared by the trader only to situations which are beyond the trader's control (in contrast with Article 3.2 of the Directive which also allows amendment if both parties agree to it). The Act also makes express references to the prohibited contractual terms, and even mentions particular examples of a term which may be treated as prohibited. The buyer has the right to withdraw from the contract within a period of 10 days which starts running on the day when the written copy of the contract was supplied to the buyer.

The POLISH Act transposing Directive 98/6 reaches further than the Directive – regarding the obligations for traders. The price must not only be indicated on products, but also on services.

Also in terms of Directive 99/44 the POLISH Act covers a wider range of situations than the scope of the Directive. It requires the sellers to confirm in writing all the crucial clauses of the contract of sale in sales by instalments, sales to order, sales based on a sample or trial period and sales exceeding 2000 PLN. In other sales contracts, the seller must confirm in writing the conclusion of the contract (specifying the seller and his address, date, the goods – their quantity and price) if the buyer so requires. Any seller operating within the territory of POLAND has to impart clear and comprehensible information in Polish language, allowing the use of the consumption goods in a proper manner. In particular, the name of the goods, the producer or importer and the country of origin, any safety and compliance marks, information on licenses to be marketed in Poland, determined by further provisions, efficiency and other information, must be specified. This information must be placed on the product or be joined with it (if the goods are sold individually or in a set), or placed on the premises where the goods are sold (in the latter case – only the name of the goods, the producer, importer and country of origin and the main function must be specified). Furthermore, every seller has to ensure that the appropriate conditions are present at the sales premises to enable the buyer to choose the goods and examine their quality and functioning. The sellers must attach to the goods all the instructions and other information required by other provisions (written in Polish language).

The Act *on tourist services* which implemented Directive 90/314 into the POLISH legal system regulates more than just the provision of package travel - it also regulates the activities of tour agents, tour guides or hotels, for instance, the procedure for licensing such activities.

V. Other extensions

The POLISH transposition laws often have a wider objective or personal scope of application than the Directives. The Act transposing Directive 98/27 applies to 'traders'. The definition of trader covers all physical or legal persons providing public services which are not an economic activity as such, or professions. The Act implementing Directive 90/314 also covers ordinary 'tourist services' which do not involve a package, for example. The POLISH Act implementing Directive 93/13 also applies to financial services such as banking services or insurance. Concerning Directive 98/6 the only type of relations to which the Act does not apply are those between two „physical persons who are not traders", so it is also applicable in case of commercial sales. All types of contracts can be subject to the protection provided by the Act implementing Directive 85/577, and indeed the scope of the Act is wider than the scope of the application of the Directive. For instance, the protection also applies if the consumer requested the visit of the trader (including a visit in the consumer's place of work), or if the contract was concluded on the business premises, provided the offers were collected outside these premises. In fact, Article 1.1 of the Act extends protection to all situations where a trader has invited the consumer to conclude a contract outside business premises.

VI. Possible infringements of EC law

More detailed information is provided in the individual reports on the transposition of the Directives (cf. in particular, the executive summaries of the reports on Package Travel in Part 2.B.).

T. Portugal – Legislative techniques

Directive	Transposed in	Date of Transposition (due date)	ECJ decisions in relation to Portugal
Directive 85/577	Decree Law No. 272/87 of 3 July 1987, repealed by Decree-Law No. 143/2001, of 26 April 2001	1 October 1987 (31 December 1987)	.
Directive 90/314	Decree Law No. 198/93 of 27 May 1993	27 May 1993 (1 January 1993)	**1.** ECJ 30.04.2002 Case C-400/00 *Club-Tour, Viagens e Turismo SA v. Alberto Carlos Lobo Gonçalves Garrido* [2002] ECR I-04051.
Directive 93/13	Decree Law No. 220/95 of 31 August 1995	15 September 1995 (31 December 1994)	
Directive 94/47	Decree Law No. 180/99 of 22 May 1999	23 May 1999 (29 April 1997)	
Directive 97/7	Decree Law No. 143/2001 of 26 April 2001	27 May 2001 (4 June 2000)	
Directive 98/6	Decree Law No. 162/99 of 13 May 1999	14 May 1999 (18 March 2000)	
Directive 98/27	Law No. 25/2004 of 8 July 2004	6 October 2004 (1 January 2001)	
Directive 99/44	Decree Law No. 67/2003 of 8 April 2003	9 April 2003 (1 January 2002)	

I. State of consumer protection in the field of the Directives before transposition

Although the aim of consumer protection has been mentioned in the PORTUGUESE constitution since 1976 (see Art. 110 Portuguese constitution [old version]; since 1989: Art. 60), the Portuguese legislator had regulated only certain parts of consumer protection law prior to the implementation of the European Directives. The Consumer Protection Act, Law 29/81 of 22 August 1981; now: Law No. 24/96 of 31 July 1996, enacted by the Parliament, established a general obligation to protect consumers and introduced the principles of «equality» and «loyalty». The Act was particularly directed against aggressive sales methods impairing the customer's freedom of decision. From 1985 onwards the Decree law 446/85 of 25 October 1985, formed after the German Act on Unfair Contract Terms provided quite comprehensive protection regarding standard contract terms. Its scope of application was not limited to consumers. The general Decree-Law 264/86 of 3 September 1986 contained provisions dealing with organised travels taking place entirely in Portugal.

Certain types of contracts for Timesharing were regulated by Decree-Law 130/89 of 18 April 1989 and Decree-Law 275/93 of 5 August 1993. As to Distance Selling, Decree law 272/87 of 3 July 1987 as amended by Decree law 243/95 of 13 September 1995 prescribed written form for contracts, imposed a number of information duties on the seller and granted right of withdrawal to the purchaser.

There was no special separate Act on consumer sales, but Articles 913-922 of the PORTUGUESE Civil Code generally provided for warranties/guarantees for defective goods and Decree law 24/96 of 31 July 1996 (Consumer protection Act) contained special regulations concerning the quality of goods sold to consumers.

II. Legislative techniques of transposition

Since 1997 the PORTUGUESE Constitution has prescribed that all Directives have to be implemented through a legislative act by the national legislator i.e. either by Parliament or by the Government. In most cases, the Government has chosen to enact a special legislative act separate from the Civil Code and the Consumer Protection Act. Directive 93/13, Directive 94/47 and Directive 98/6 have been transposed via making amendments to already existing pieces of law.

III. Timeliness of transposition

PORTUGAL has transposed Directive 85/577 and Directive 98/6 in due time. The other Directives have been implemented with a delay. The average delay amounts to nearly 20 months.

IV. Use of minimum harmonisation

When transposing the European Directives PORTUGAL made use of the minimum clauses on various occasions. The domestic legislation concerning package travel grant the customer a general right of cancellation, compensation for "ruined holiday" and transfer/assignment of the package. Additionally, organiser and retailer are jointly liable and there is a special Travel Guarantee Fund. As to timesharing contracts there is a prohibition in Art. 6 of the Directive against any advance payments. Under Portuguese law this prohibition may also comprise mortgages, as the law states that it includes any form of advance payment "with any other goal directly or indirectly related to the contract to be concluded". Furthermore the withdrawal period for timesharing contracts is extended to 10 working days as opposed to 10 calendar days under Art. 5(1), indent 1 of the Directive. According to Decree Law 25/2004 qualified entities may bring actions for injunctions for infringements of rights and interests other than those granted in the course of implementation of EC directives. In contrast to Art. 1(2)(b) of Directive 99/44, the corresponding Portuguese provisions are not restricted to movable items, therefore contracts for the sale of immovable goods are also covered.

V. Other extensions

The definition used in the Consumer Protection Act (Law 24/96, of 31 July), upholds a uniform concept of the notion "consumer" in all PORTUGUESE statutes regulating contract law matters. According to Art. 2 CPA, a consumer is a person for whom another person conducting a business as a professional delivers goods, provides services or transfers rights as long as the goods, services or rights are not ordered for professional purposes. Nevertheless, the specific provisions also refer to the "client" (package travel) or "purchaser" (timesharing). Irrespective of the different wording the definitions of consumer and trader/supplier do not seem to deviate significantly from those prescribed by the Directives.

VI. Possible infringements of EC law

It has been criticised that the Unfair Contract Terms Act (Decree law 446/85 of 25 October 1985, amended as described above), unlike Art. 4(1) of the Directive does not explicitly mention that for the assessment of unfairness of a term, all circumstances have to be taken into account. Thus it remains unclear whether individual, concrete particulars of a contract, such as the experience of the party accepting the terms or the situation in which the contract has been concluded, can be regarded.

More detailed information is provided in the individual reports on the transposition of the Directives (cf. in particular, the executive summaries of the reports on Consumer Sales in Part 2.H.)

U. Slovakia – Legislative techniques

Directive	Transposed in	Date of Transposition (due date)[16]	ECJ decisions in relation to Slovakia
Directive 87/577	Act No. 108/2000 on Consumer Protection in Doorstep Selling and in Distance Selling Act No. 634/1992 on Consumer Protection as amended	1 April 2000 16 December 1992	
Directive 90/314	Act No. 281/2001 on Package Travel Civil Code Act No. 634/1992 on Consumer Protection as amended	1 October 2001 1 April 1964 16 December 1992	
Directive 93/13	Civil Code Constitution of Slovak Republic as amended Commercial Code as amended Bond Papers Act Act No. 634/1992 on Consumer Protection as amended Code of international Law Act No. 258/2001 on Consumer Credit Act No. 99/1963 Code of Civil Procedure as amended	1 April 1964 1 October 1992 1 January 1992 16 December 1992 1 April 1964 1 April 1964	
Directive 94/47	Civil Code Act No. 634/1992 on Consumer Protection as amended Code of international Law	1 April 1964 16 December 1992 1 April 1964	

16 Slovakia was required to ensure transposition of the Directives in accordance with its Treaty of Accession.

Directive	Transposed in	Date of Transposition (due date)[16]	ECJ decisions in relation to Slovakia
Directive 97/7	Act No. 108/2000 on Consumer Protection in Doorstep Selling and in Distance Selling Non-Smoker-Protection-Act Civil Code Constitution of Slovak Republic as amended Systems on payments Act Act No. 634/1992 on Consumer Protection as amended Code of international Law Act No. 99/1963 Code of Civil Procedure as amended	1 April 2000 1 July 2004 1 April 1964 1 October 1992 1 January 2003 16 December 1992 1 April 1964 1 April 1964	
Directive 98/6	Price Indication Decree Act No. 634/1992 on Consumer Protection as amended	1 November 2002 16 December 1992	
Directive 98/27	Act No. 634/1992 on Consumer Protection as amended Code of international Law Act No. 99/1963 Code of Civil Procedure as amended	16 December 1992 1 April 1964 1 April 1964	
Directive 99/44	Civil Code Act No. 634/1992 on Consumer Protection as amended Code of international Law Act No. 99/1963 Code of Civil Procedure as amended	1 April 1964 16 December 1992 1 April 1964 1 April 1964	

I. State of consumer protection in the field of the Directives before transposition

Before the transposition of the Directives, SLOVAKIA provided the consumer with protection by applying the CC as well as the Consumer Protection Act to most of the different contracts negotiated between a consumer and a trader. Concerning package travel contracts, for instance, the right of withdrawal and the general responsibilities of the provider are regulated in the CC and the conditions for fair trade of products and services are laid down in the Consumer Protection Act. Regarding injunction matters, the Slovakian law did not conform at all to the content of the Directive, as an injunction only existed in competition law. Besides that, a great amount of consumer protection is to be found in the Slovakian law before the implementation of the Directive.

II. Legislative techniques of transposition

Most of the Directives were transposed by amending existing law codifications or statutory law. For instance, Directive 98/27 was implemented into SLOVAKIAN law by Amendment No. 616/2004 of the Consumer Protection Act and Directive 93/13 was transposed by Amendment No. 150/2004 of the CC. As opposed to that, Directive 85/577 and Directive 97/7 were enacted by a special legislative act, the Act No. 108/2000 on Doorstep Selling and Distance Selling. Directive 98/6 was implemented by a Decree of the Ministry of Economy of the Slovakian Republic which executed the Act No. 18/1996 on Prices which provided consumer protection before the transposition of Directive 98/6.

III. Timeliness of transposition

SLOVAKIA became a Member of the European Union on 1 May 2004. As a new member state, joining after the transposition deadlines for all Directives had expired, Slovakia was required to ensure transposition of the Directives in accordance with its Treaty of Accession.

IV. Use of minimum harmonisation

The SLOVAKIAN legislator has sometimes made use of the minimum harmonisation clauses. Regarding Directive 85/577 and Directive 97/7, Act. No. 377/2004 on Non-smoker Protection provides non-smokers with a greater amount of protection by prohibiting such contracts on tobacco products. Concerning the Distance Selling, Act No. 22/2004 on Electronic Communications states, that in the case of contracts being concluded by use of electronic communication, the provisions of the Act on Consumer Protection in Doorstep Selling and Distance Selling must be applied. As another example, with regard to Directive 90/314, the brochure provided by the travel organiser must contain more information than prescribed in the Directive, namely information concerning contractual penalties for the traveller.

V. Other extensions

In most cases, SLOVAKIA has extended the amount of consumer protection by implementing a broader definition of the term consumer than required by the Directives. In the Act on Consumer Protection, in general, non-commercial and commercial legal persons are regarded as consumers, provided they act outside their area of trade, business or profession and buy products or use services for direct personal use. However, it is noteworthy that, concerning Directive 85/577 and Directive 97/7, these persons are excluded from the scope of application of the Act on Consumer Protection in the case of Doorstep Selling and Distance Selling. Although the transposition of Directive 93/13 and Directive 98/27 does not adopt the wider consumer definition either, a broader definition than the one required by the Directive is laid down.

VI. Possible Infringements

More detailed information is provided in the individual reports on the transposition of the Directives (cf. in particular, the executive summaries of the reports on Timeshare in Part 2.D. and on Consumer Sales in Part 2.H.).

V. Slovenia – Legislative techniques

Directive	Transposed in	Date of Transposition	ECJ decisions in relation to Slovenia
Directive 85/577	Consumer Protection Act (Art. 46-47)	28 March 1998	
Directive 90/314	Code of Obligations (Articles 883-903) Promotion of Tourism Development Act (Articles 33, 34, 36)	1 January 2002 30 January 2004	
Directive 93/13	Consumer Protection Act (Art. 22-24)	28 March 1998	
Directive 94/47	Consumer Protection Act	28 March 1998	
Directive 97/7	Consumer Protection Act (Articles 43-45.a)	28 March 1998	
Directive 98/6	Rules on Price Indication for Goods and Services (issued by the Minister for the Economy)	21 August 1999	
Directive 98/27	Consumer Protection Act (Arts. 70-75)	28 March 1998	
Directive 99/44	Consumer Protection Act (Art. 1, 16, 18, 37) Code of Obligations (Art. 460)	28 March 1998	

I. State of consumer protection in the field of the Directives before transposition

In SLOVENIA much of the legislation on consumer protection was contained in the Consumer Protection Act 1998, with some rules also found in the Code of Obligations. Prior to implementing the various Directives, there was already legislation in place dealing with matters, such as rules on doorstep selling, package travel, limited rules on timeshares ("tourist property"), distance selling and consumer sales. Matters on which there was no specific pre-existing legislation were unfair terms, price indications and injunctions. To the extent that there was earlier legislation, some of the aspects addressed in the corresponding Directives were covered, but in many ways existing law was not up-to-date and in need of some improvements.

II. Legislative techniques of transposition

SLOVENIA has a Consumer Protection Act which contains the vast majority of the rules relevant to the protection of consumers. To the extent that this Act did not already contain adequate provisions to comply with the various Directives, amendments were made to the existing legislation to slot the additional requirements into the Consumer Protection Act. The only measure in respect of which this has not been followed is the Administrative Order implementing Directive 98/6 on price indications, which is a completely separate measure.

III. Timeliness of transposition

SLOVENIA, as a new member state joining after the transposition deadlines for all the Directives had expired, was required to ensure transposition of the Directives in accordance with its Treaty of Accession.

IV. Use of minimum harmonisation

The minimum harmonisation clauses have been used extensively by the SLOVENIAN legislator. In some instances, this was done to preserve existing rules which were already more favourable to consumers, but in others, there appears to have been a deliberate decision to give consumers more protection. For example, the cancellation period in Slovenia is 15 days, rather than the 7 days envisaged under Directive 85/577 and Directive 97/7. Also, "individually negotiated terms" are subject to assessment under the Slovenian rules on unfair contract terms. It is noteworthy that the rules on package travel provide better protection in a number of different aspects.

V. Other extensions

In some instances, the rules which are now considered as implementing an EC Directive extend beyond the immediate scope envisaged in the Directive. For example, the rules on the sale of consumer goods also apply to consumer services, and are also not restricted to consumer goods as defined in Art 1(2)(b) of Directive 99/44.

VI. Possible infringements of EC law

There appear to be a number of instances where the SLOVENIAN transposition deviates from the requirements of a particular Directive. In some instances, this may have the effect of *improving* consumer protection, and as such is probably justifiable on the basis of the minimum harmonisation clause (e.g., in respect of Art. 2(4) of 99/44 – no transposition in Slovenia). There are instances where Slovenian law is more restrictive – for example, Slovenian law excludes the same contracts from the doorstepselling rules as it excludes from the distance selling rules – but only the latter are permitted under Directive 97/7. In respect of some measures (Package Travel, Timeshare, Consumer Sales), it is possible to identify a number of departures from the Directive which could be classed as infringements of EC law, although some may be the result of ambiguities within the Directives themselves.

More detailed information is provided in the individual reports on the transposition of the Directives (cf. in particular, the executive summaries of the reports on Doorstep Selling in Part 2.A., Package Travel in Part 2.B. and on Consumer Sales in Part 2.H.)

W. Spain – Legislative techniques

Directive	Transposed in (Translation)	Date of Transposition (due date)	ECJ decisions in relation to Spain
Directive 85/577	Law 26/1991 of November 21, on consumers' protection in case of contracts executed out of the commercial premises	17 December 1991 (31 December 1987)	**1.** ECJ, 22 April 1999 Case C-423/97 – *Travel Vac SL v. Manuel José Antelm Sanchi* [1999] ECR I-02195
Directive 90/314	Law 21/1995 of July 6, which regulates the package travels	7 October 1995 (1 January 1993)	
Directive 93/13	Law 7/1998 of April 13, on Standard Terms in Contracts; Article 10 of the General Law 26/1984 of July 19 on Consumer Protection	5 May 1998 (31 December 1994)	**1.** ECJ, 27 June 2000 Joined cases C-240/98 to C-244/98 – *Océano Grupo Editorial v. Marciano Quinter* [2000] ECR I-04941. **2.** ECJ, 9 September 2004 C-70/03 – *Commission v. Spain* [2004] ECR I-07999. **3.** ECJ, 26 October 2006 C-168/05 – *Elisa María Mostaza Claro v. Centro Móvil Milenium SL* [2006] ECR I-10421
Directive 94/47	Law 42/1998 of December 15, on time-sharing rights on immovable goods for tourist use and taxation norms	6 January 1999 (29 April 1997)	**1.** ECJ, 22 April 1999 Case C-423/97 – *Travel Vac SL v. Manuel José Antelm Sanchi* [1999] ECR I-02195.
Directive 97/7	Law 47/2002, of December 19, on the reform of the Law 7/1996 on retail trade, for the transposition into the Spanish legal system of Directive 97/7/CE on distance selling, and for the adaptation to other Community Directives	1 January 2003 (4 June 2000)	**1.** 28 November 2002 C-414/01 – *Commission v. Spain,* [2002] ECR I-11121
Directive 98/6	Royal Decree 3423/2000 of December 15 on the regulation of the indication of prices of the products offered to consumers and users	29 December 2000 (18 March 2000)	
Directive 98/27	Law 39/2002 of October 28 for the transposition into the Spanish legal system of some Community Directives on protection of the interests of consumers and users	19 November 2002 (1 January 2001)	
Directive 99/44	Law 23/2003, on consumer sales	11 September 2003 (1 January 2002)	

I. State of consumer protection in the field of the Directives before transposition

SPANISH legislative activity in the field of consumer protection first began in the 1980s under the new regime established after the Spanish Constitution. According to Art. 51 of the Spanish Constitution of 27 December 1978, the public authorities shall guarantee the protection of consumers and users and shall, by means of effective measures, guarantee their safety, health and legitimate economic interests.

Before the transposition of the European Directives at issue, most areas were only governed by the general rules of the SPANISH CC. Alongside these, there existed only very few special rules for the protection of the structurally weaker party to the contract. In relation to the monitoring of Standard Contract Terms for example, although there was no separate Law on unfair contract terms, there did exist a concise regulation on the topic with a protection to some extent comparable to that of the Directive. In 1980 the Law 50/1980 of October 8 on the insurance contract was enacted, whose Art. 3 dealt with (and deals with, since it is still in force) standard terms and unfair terms in contracts of insurance.

With a more general approach, the Law 23/2003 on Consumer Protection embraced a full regime on unfair contract terms in contracts concluded by consumers. Moreover, the Law 26/1984 contains some general definitions and rules, which have been complemented by special statutes and regulations on the various matters of consumer protection. The Law 26/1984 of July 19 on Consumer Protection includes a general definition of "Consumer" (consumidor) and "User" (usuario) (Art. 1(2) and (3)), provisions on information duties (Art. 13-17), rights to representation, consultation and participation (Art. 20-22) and rules on strict liability enabling consumers and users to obtain compensation for damage caused by the use of a thing, product or service (Art. 25-31; however, these provisions do not apply to civil liability for damage caused by defective products; see on this ECJ, case C-183/00 – *María Victoria González Sánchez v. Medicina Asturiana SA*).

II. Legislative techniques of transposition

First of all it is worth mentioning that every Autonomous Community ("*Comunidad Autónoma*" such as Basque Country, Catalonia, Asturias, Madrid, etc.) still has its own rules on consumer protection, normally in its Law on Internal Trade, but some of them have enacted specific Decrees on it. The exclusive competence of these Autonomous Communities, however, is limited to the public law provisions relating to consumer protection, as for example, the regulations governing that the relationships between individuals shall be under exclusive competence of the State (with a few exceptions in only a few regions). Therefore, the regulations at regional level actually contain administrative provisions (licences, authorisations, concessions, etc.).

The national legislator transposed the European Directives applying various legislative techniques. For Directives 85/577, 94/47 and 99/44 the SPANISH Parliament passed individual implementing acts. Directive 98/6 was integrated into domestic law through a Decree Law. Directive 97/7 and Directive 98/27 have been implemented solely via amendments to existing statutory laws.

In the course of the transposition of Directive 93/13 and Directive 90/314 the legislator adopted a set of different measures consisting of national separate transposition laws, amendments to existing statutory laws on national and regional level, codes of conduct (business associations agreed upon 2 different models for standard terms on package travels) and administrative sanctions.

III. Timeliness of transposition

SPAIN has transposed none of the European Directives at issue in time. The delay differs from 9 months (Directive 98/6) to a considerable 40 months (Directive 93/13); on average 26 months. The failure to implement Directive 97/7 has given rise to complaints from the Commission to the ECJ (Case C-414/01, *Commission v. Spain*, [2002] ECR I-11121).

IV. Use of minimum harmonisation

When transposing the European Directives SPAIN made use of minimum clauses on various occasions. The use of the right of withdrawal requires no special formality. For brochures on package travels Art. 3(1)(h)-(j), (d) and (f) of the Law 21/1995 prescribe more comprehensive information duties than Art. 3 of Directive 90/314. It is also compulsory for the organiser or retailer to make a brochure containing this information available to the consumer. Moreover, the duty of the consumer to communicate any failure in performance in Art. 5(4) of the Directive has not been transposed into SPANISH Law. Finally, the Spanish law provides a right of withdrawal for the consumer whose existence does not depend on an alteration of terms or any other non-performances. This cancellation right (that is not in Directive 90/314) is only accompanied by a requirement to make a small compensation to the seller (Art. 9(4) of the Law 21/1995). Law 42/1998 on timesharing contains more comprehensive information duties than Art. 3(1) and Annex of the Directive 94/47. Additionally, the consumer benefits from the fact that Art. 7(2) of Law 42/1998 requires the owner of the building to conclude an insurance contract covering the liability for torts caused by the titleholder of the timeshare rights.

In case of non performance of information duties, the SPANISH provisions on distance selling state that the consumer shall not bear the costs of returning the goods (Art. 44(5) *in fine* Law 7/1996). In inertia selling, Art. 43 *in fine* Law 7/1996 prescribes rules even more protective of the consumer, since he has no duty to return the goods and can keep them free of charge, and in case of depreciation in value, the consumer has no duty to compensate for damages or deterioration. If the dispatch of the goods was based upon an evident mistake, the burden of proof of that fact is for the seller and the addressee has a right of compensation.

Pursuant to Art. 10 of the Law 23/2003 on consumer sales the consumer has an action not only against the seller (the rule in the Directive), but also directly against the producer if the consumer cannot claim against the seller or that claim is too burdensome. In Directive 99/44 the subsidiary remedies (reduction of price or rescission) are only available when both the repair and the replacement are impossible or disproportionate in relation to the value of the goods, whereas in the SPANISH rule it is sufficient that just one of the primary remedies is impossible or disproportionate (Art. 6 and 7 of the Law 23/2003). The limitation period (prescription) for the action of the consumer is three years (Art. 9(3) of Law 23/2003) in Spain, thereby increasing the minimum two years of the Directive.

V. Other extensions

The definition of the term consumer in the SPANISH legal system is not coherent. However, the transposition laws for most Directives (exceptions: Directive 90/314 and Directive 98/27) contain a reference (e.g. Art. 1(3) of the Law 23/2003 on consumer sales) to the general definition of consumer in Art. 1(2) of the Law 26/1984 of July 19 on Consumer Protection. This general definition of "consumer" is wider than the one mentioned in the EC Directives since it also covers atypical transactions of a business which are not related to a further transfer. Moreover, the definition of "consumer" also encompasses legal persons; cf. for more details Part 3 A.III.1 and 3 of this study.

The Spanish provisions on doorstep selling (Law 26/1991) do not explicitly include contracts concluded during an excursion organised by the trader (Art. 1(1) of the Directive) but uses a broader wording: contracts concluded away from the commercial premises. It also adds in Art. 1 (c): "contracts concluded in public transport". The Spanish provisions on distance-selling have a wider scope of application since they include contracts concluded at auctions by electronic means (Art. 38(3)(a) of the Law 7/1996).

VI. Possible infringements of EC law

Most possible infringements of EC law are caused by "dual transpositions" in different Acts, lack of coordination, inconsistencies within the SPANISH legal system and poor legal transposition techniques in general:

- The requirements articulated by the ECJ in C-70/03 (ECJ judgment of 9 September 2004, C-70/03 – *Commission v. Kingdom of Spain* [2004] ECR I-0799 concerning the transposition of Art. 5 and Art. 6 of Directive 93/13) have thus far not been implemented in Spanish law, but there is currently a draft being discussed in the Spanish parliament, modifying not only the wrong transposition, but also some other questions on unfair terms (e.g. round-off clauses against the consumer, unfair practices in service contracts, unfair clauses on requisites for termination).
- SPAIN has not transposed the rule of Art. 4(2) of Directive 93/13 on the exclusion of price and subject matter of the contract from the assessment of unfairness. This "silence" has produced problems of interpretation on the application of the rule into Spanish Law; academia and case law use different approaches to solve the problem with contradictory solutions.
- Art. 6(g) of the Law 23/2003 on consumer sales excludes the right of replacement in case of second hand goods and fungibles. The SPANISH academic community considers this contrast with the Directive to be excessive (the Directive does not restrict the right in respect of such goods) and even regards it as a defective transposition.

It has been criticised that SPANISH law does not provide an exact definition of the term "means of distance communication" (Art. 2(4), Annex Directive 97/7). Furthermore the division of the norms on distance contracts into "sales" (Arts. 38-48 LOCM) and "services" (First Additional Disposition of the LOCM) lead to several inaccuracies in transposition.

More detailed information is provided in the individual reports on the transposition of the Directives (cf. in particular, the executive summaries of the reports on Doorstep Selling in Part 2.A., Package Travel in Part 2.B., Distance Selling in Part 2.E. and on Consumer Sales in Part 2.H.).

X. Sweden – Legislative techniques

Directive	Transposed in (Translation)	Date of Transposition (due date)	ECJ decisions in relation to Sweden
Directive 85/577	Doorstep Selling Act SFS 1992:1111, later replaced Law on Consumer Protection on Distance Contracts and Doorstep Selling Contracts 2000:274), which was finally replaced in 2005 by a new Distance and Doorstep Selling Act SFS 2005:59	1 January 1993 (31 December 1987)	.
Directive 90/314	Package Tours Act 1992:1672	1 January 1993 (1 January 1993)	
Directive 93/13	Act on terms and conditions in consumer relations 1994:1512	1 January 1995 (31 December 1994)	**1.** ECJ 5 July 2002 – *Commission v. Kingdom of Sweden*, C-478/99, ECR 2002 I-041047
Directive 94/47	Timeshare Contracts Consumer Protection Act 1997:218	1 July 1997 (29 April 1997)	
Directive 97/7	Law on Consumer Protection on Distance Contracts and Doorstep Selling Contracts 2000:274, replaced in 2005 by a new Distance and Doorstep Selling Act (SFS 2005:59)	1 June 2000 (4 June 2000)	
Directive 98/6	Price Information Act 1991:601	18 March 2000 (18 March 2000)	
Directive 98/27	Act (2000:1175) on access to justice for certain foreign consumer authorities and consumer organisations	1 January 2001 (1 January 2001)	
Directive 99/44	Consumer purchase Act 1990:932	1 July 2003 (1 January 2002)	

I. State of consumer protection in the field of the Directives before transposition

SWEDEN can be considered a precursor in the development of consumer protection law. In the 1970s consumer law had already evolved as a separate part of the law alongside the general law. The Swedish approach combined methods of private law such as widespread general clauses like section 36 of the Swedish Contract Act (SFS 1915:218 as amended by SFS 1976:185) in civil law and different administrative methods to improve consumer protection.

Measures were taken to fend off the use of unfair marketing practices such as contract clauses which are regarded as unfair by the Consumer Contract Terms Act (SFS 1971:112, later substituted by Act SFS 1994:1512). Such cases are dealt with separately via the Consumer Ombudsman, a key feature of Nordic legal systems, or via the Swedish Consumer Agency. Judicial protection is provided by the Market Court, a special court dealing exclusively with consumer protection law. It constitutes the only and final instance since Market Courts' judgments cannot be appealed.

Additionally there is a Complaints Board (*Allmänna reklamationsnämnden*) which has been established in order to achieve a more speedy and efficient resolution of disputes involving consumers. The Complaints Board is divided into different departments and handles consumer purchases, package tour disputes, consumer services, etc. Although some of its decisions can be appealed to the courts, there are certain restrictions. Often third parties, for example, trade organisations follow the Complaints Board's decisions and they are also taken into account by the courts in deciding subsequent cases.

In addition to the General Purchase Act, a special consumer purchase Act had been in effect since 1973, marking another step in the development of consumer law as a separate domain of law. In 1981 the legislator adopted the Doorstep Selling Act (SFS 1981:1361) which placed certain information duties upon the seller and granted a right of withdrawal to the customer. The Act also applied to contracts concluded via telephone, thus representing an early stage of distance selling legislation. In the following years the legislation on doorstep selling, distance selling, unfair terms and consumer sales was updated several times. There was no legislation on package travel, but the Swedish Consumer Agency together with the major Swedish organisations of travel professionals negotiated general agreements on package travel which in practice lead to contracts whose fairness was not substantially less than that envisaged in the Directive. In 1990 the Swedish Parliament adopted a special Price Information Act.

II. Legislative techniques of transposition

The legislative techniques applied are more or less unitary as all Directives have been transposed by the national legislator via Acts of Parliament (*Riksdagen*). Since SWEDEN had a long tradition of consumer protection law long before its accession to the EU most Directives could be transposed by making minor amendments to existing pieces of law. However there were no specific provisions on package travel and timesharing. Thus these Directives have been transposed by introducing new, separate Acts. Furthermore, it is worth noting that doorstep selling and distance selling are regulated in a common Act (Distance and Doorstep Selling Act SFS 2005:59).

III. Timeliness of transposition

In this respect it has to be noted that SWEDEN acceded to the EU with effect from 1 January 1995. In contrast to many other member states the Swedish legislator paid close attention to the time limits set for implementation of the Directives at issue. In fact, nearly all Directives were transposed in good time, some even before accession. Only Directives 94/47 and 99/44 were transposed with a slight delay of 2 and 6 months respectively.

IV. Use of minimum harmonisation

When transposing the European Directives SWEDEN made use of minimum clauses at different occasions. The Distance and Doorstep Selling Act SFS 2005:59 provides an extended withdrawal period of 14 days instead of 7 days as prescribed by the corresponding Directives (Art. 5(1) of Directive 85/577, Art. 6(1) of Directive 97/7).

V. Other extensions

The consumer concept in SWEDISH law is not unitary. The Distance and Doorstep Selling Act defines consumers as natural persons that act for mainly private purposes. As regards the administrative law method, according to section 1 in the Consumer Contract Terms Act (1994:1512) a consumer is a natural person who is acting for purposes which are mainly outside his or her business. The reason for this difference in the wording is to avoid any deviation from EC law, this goal seems to have been achieved.

In respect of package travel, the Swedish provisions use the term "package tour" which has an established legal meaning, so it can be argued that the scope of application may be broader than that of the Directive. Section 1 of the Consumer Contract Terms Act 1994:1512 is applicable to all unfair contract terms, even if they have been individually negotiated.

Unlike Directive 98/6, the domestic Price Information Act (Art. 10) applies to all kinds of services and products including financial services, electricity, phone subscriptions, arts and antiques (with the exception of sales at auctions). However, the law does not cover real estate or marketing of job vacancies. In the course of transposition of Directive 99/44 the legislator adopted separate acts on consumer services and consumer insurance.

VI. Possible infringements of EC law

More detailed information is provided in the individual reports on the transposition of the Directives (cf. in particular, the executive summaries of the reports on Package Travel in Part 2.B.).

Y. United Kingdom – Legislative techniques

Directive	Transposed in	Date of Transposition (due date)	ECJ decisions in relation to the United Kingdom
Directive 85/577	Consumer Protection (Cancellation of Contracts concluded away from business premises) Regulations 1987, SI 1987/2117	1 July 1988 (31 December 1987)	
Directive 90/314	Package Travel, Package Holidays and Package Tour Regulations 1992 SI 1992/3288	23 December 1992 (31 December 1992)	
Directive 93/13	Unfair Terms in Consumer Contracts Regulations 1999; SI 1999/2083.	(first implementation: 1 January 1994) 1 October 1999 (31 December 1994)	
Directive 94/47	Timeshare Act 1992	(29 April 1997)	
Directive 97/7	Consumer Protection (Distance Selling) Regulations 2000 SI 2000/2334 Privacy and Electronic Communications (EC Directive) Regulations 2003 SI 2003/2426	31 October 2000 (4 June 2000) 11 December 2003	
Directive 98/6	The Price Marking Order 2004 (SI 2004/102)	22 July 2004 (replacing earlier order)	
Directive 98/27	Enterprise Act 2002, Part 8 and Schedule 13	20 June 2003 (replacing earlier rules)	
Directive 99/44	Sale and Supply of Goods to Consumers Regulations 2002 (SI 2002/3045), amending Sale of Goods Act 1979, Supply of Goods and Services Act 1982 and Supply of Goods (Implied Terms) Act 1973; Unfair Contract Terms Act 1977	31 March 2003 (31 December 2001)	

I. State of consumer protection in the field of the Directives before transposition

Consumer protection had been the subject of legislative action in the UNITED KINGDOM a long time before any European iniatives. In respect of half of the Directives, there was pre-existing legislation which dealt with similar aspects to the Directives. Thus, Part III of the Fair Trading Act 1973 enabled the Director-General of Fair Trading to take action to prevent traders from engaging in unlawful conduct, although no such powers were available to consumer organisations. The Unfair Contract Terms Act 1977 regulated some types of contract terms, but provided both more and less protection (more in that it applied to negotiated clauses, but less because it did not apply to all contract terms). The Sale of Goods Act 1979 had been reformed with consumer interests in mind in 1994, although there was no statutory right to repair or replacement. And the Timeshare Act 1992 contained a number of requirements regarding such contracts, but, again, did not cover quite the same ground as the corresponding Directive. In other areas, there was no pre-existing legislation at all, e.g., Doorstep and Distance Selling (with minor exceptions, e.g., inertia selling) and Package Travel.

II. Legislative techniques of transposition

The UNITED KINGDOM may have a reputation for the "copy and paste" approach to implementing European directives, but that does not portray the approach it has adopted accurately. There is, in fact, a degree of variation in how the various Directives have been transposed. Thus, there are separate pieces of legislation for the Directives on Doorstep Selling, package travel, unfair terms, distance selling and unit prices. Directive 94/47 was implemented through amendments of the Timeshare Act 1992. Similarly, Directive 99/44 was implemented by amendments to the relevant legislation on the sale and supply of goods. Directive 98/27 was first transposed through the "Stop-Now" Regulations, but soon replaced with the new integrated enforcement regime in Part 8 of the Enterprise Act. It is therefore a fair observation that the United Kingdom does attempt to integrate the relevant Directive into pre-existing domestic law (and note that a proposal has been tabled to combine the Unfair Contract Terms Act 1977 and the Unfair Terms in Consumer Contracts Regulations 1999).

III. Timeliness of transposition

The UNITED KINGDOM has not managed to transpose all the Directives by their deadline; indeed, it is usually slightly late. In the case of Directive 99/44, the transposition occurred only days before the Commission launched legal action against the United Kingdom for non-transposition (subsequently withdrawn).

IV. Use of minimum harmonisation

The UNITED KINGDOM has rarely made use of the minimum harmonisation clauses (although it often exercises options in the Directives in favour of higher consumer protection), and usually only in a very restricted manner. The one notable exception is Directive 99/44, where the clause forms the basis for retaining much of the pre-existing law overlapping with the Directive. On the whole, the United Kingdom takes a restrictive approach to what is referred to as "gold-plating", i.e., exceeding the minimum standard set by a Directive.

V. Other extensions

Generally, the implementing legislation is restricted to the scope given to it by the corresponding Directives. On occasion, there are slightly more generous definitions of "consumer", which has the effect of (marginally) broadening the scope of application. In particular, the new remedies in consumer sales may be available to a professional buyer (including a company) if the goods in question are ordinarily supplied for private use or consumption.

VI. Possible infringements of EC law

In respect of most of the 8 Directives under consideration, there seem to be no obvious problems regarding their compatibility with EC law. One may note that the Timeshare Act is very difficult to follow, and that the plethora of criminal penalties in the Package Travel Regulations also makes this rather cumbersome to read. The one area where there do seem to be significant difficulties is the implementation of Directive 99/44, in respect of which it is possible to identify many problems. More detailed information is provided in the individual reports on the transposition of the Directives (cf. in particular, the executive summaries of the reports on Consumer Sales in Part 2.H.).

Part 2: Transposition of the individual Directives

A. Doorstep Selling Directive (85/577)

Drafted by Hans Schulte-Nölke and Christoph M. Scheuren-Brandes

Executive summary

1. Transposition deficiencies

Besides various deviations in terms of wording, some transposition deficiencies can be identified in national jurisdictions. Potentially significant examples may be:
- Exclusion of all contracts concluded before a notary public from protection under the national transposition law (e.g. GERMANY, LITHUANIA, MALTA, SPAIN);
- Start of the withdrawal period even where the trader has failed to provide (sufficient) information (e.g. CZECH REPUBLIC, ITALY, LITHUANIA, SLOVENIA);
- Exclusion of contracts concluded during an excursion (e.g. LATVIA).

2. Enhancement of protection

a. Extension of scope

Some member states have extended the scope of their national doorstep selling laws, thereby broadening the protection afforded by the Directive to cover other persons or situations:
- Extension of the notion of "consumer" to, for example, certain legal persons (e.g. AUSTRIA, BELGIUM, GREECE, SPAIN);
- Inclusion of situations other than those covered by Art. 3 of Directive 85/577 or prohibiting doorstep selling of specific goods in general (e.g. AUSTRIA, BELGIUM, ESTONIA, FRANCE, GERMANY, GREECE, HUNGARY, ITALY, LATVIA, POLAND). Such additional situations include, for instance:
  - contracts concluded on the trader's premises if the consumer has been enticed there;
  - contracts concluded in public places; and
  - contracts concluded at fairs and exhibitions.
- Not making use of restrictions/exemptions provided for by Directive 85/577 *[for more detail see b.]*

b. Use of options and exemptions

With regard to the use made by the national legislator of the options available under Directive 85/577, the following observations can be made:

- The option granted in Art. 3 para. 1 (option to exclude contracts under 60 ECU) has been exercised by 16 member states;
- Art. 3 para. 2 lit. a (exemption of contracts concerning immovable property) has been exercised by at least 15 member states;
- Art. 3. para. 2 lit. b (exemption of contracts on goods for current consumption provided by regular roundsmen) has been exercised by at least 14 member states;
- Art. 3 para. 2 lit. c (exemption of contracts concluded on the basis of a trader's catalogue) has been exercised by at least 8 member states;
- Art. 3 para. 2 lit. d (exemption of insurance contracts) has been exercised by at least 14 member states;
- Art. 3 para. 2 lit. e (exemption of contracts for securities) has been exercised by at least 13 member states;
- The option granted in Art. 3 para. 3 (option to exclude contracts concluded during a visit requested by the consumer) has been exercised by at least 10 member states.

The following table provides a brief overview of the use of options and exemptions in the member states:

Key:
❶ = Art. 3 para. 1;
❷ = Art. 3 para. 2 lit. a;
❸ = Art. 3 para. 2 lit. b;
❹ = Art. 3 para. 2 lit. c;
❺ = Art. 3 para. 2 lit. d;
❻ = Art. 3 para. 2 lit. e;
❼ = Art. 3 para. 3

Member state	Options exercised	Member state	Options exercised	Member state	Options exercised	Member state	Options exercised
AT	❶ ❹ ❼	FR	❼	LT	❶❸❺❻	SL	❶❷❸❺❻❼
BE	❶[17] ❷ ❸ ❺ ❻ ❼	DE	❶ ❷ ❹ ❺ ❻ ❼	LU	– – –	ES	❶❷[18] ❹❻
CY	❷❸❹❺❻❼	EL	❷❸❹❺❻❼	MT	❶❷❸❺❼	SE	❶❷❸❼
CZ	❷❸❹❺❻	HU	❼	NL	❶	UK	❶ ❷ ❸ ❹ ❺ ❻
DK	❷ ❸ ❺ ❻	IE	❶❷❸❹❺❻	PL	❶❷❸		

17 There is, however, no general exclusion of sales below 60 euro. Art. 87 lit. (f) of the Trade Practices Act solely excludes sales with a non-commercial, exclusively charitable aim and not exceeding 50 euro.

18 SPAIN has only partially transposed Art. 3 para 2 lit. a. Though the first subparagraph is almost literally transposed, the second one has not been implemented at all ("contracts for the supply of goods and for their incorporation in immovable property or contracts for repairing immovable property shall fall within the scope of this Directive").There is widespread criticism that this second subparagraph has not been transposed.

Member state	Options exercised	Member state	Options exercised	Member state	Options exercised	Member state	Options exercised
EE	❶ [19]	IT	❶ ❷ ❸ ❺ ❻	PT	❶❷❸❺❻❼		
FI	❶	LV	---	SK	❺		

c. Use of minimum clause

All member states have made use of the minimum clause. Some examples of major importance are:

- Art. 4:
  - Additional information requirements imposed on the trader (e.g. trader's phone number);
  - Standard format for information on the right of withdrawal; and
  - Formal requirements governing the contract as a whole.
- Art. 5 para. 1:
- Extension of the withdrawal period
- Art. 7:
  - Time limit favouring the consumer for settlement of the transaction; (reimbursement of purchase price and reshipment of goods); and
  - Lien on the goods supplied in order to secure the consumer's reimbursement claim.

d. Additional consumer protection instruments not provided for by the Directive

Some member states have introduced or maintained consumer protection instruments, which are not contained in Directive 85/577. Potentially significant examples are:

- General ban on doorstep selling (in particular with regard to certain products);
- Licensing requirement for doorstep selling; and
- Time restrictions on doorstep selling late in the evening or early in the morning.

3. Inconsistencies or ambiguities

Examples of inconsistencies or ambiguities in Directive 85/577 are:

- It is unclear whether a natural person in a "mixed purpose" case (i.e. where the consumer might also be acting in a professional capacity) is protected by Directive 85/577 as a "consumer".
- It is unclear whether a not-for-profit organisation can also be regarded as a "trader".
- Directive 85/577 does not contain any rules on the calculation of time periods and, furthermore, does not state whether the withdrawal period also ends when the last day is a Sunday, Saturday or a public holiday.
- Directive 85/577 may be applicable in conjunction with other consumer protection directives (e.g. Consumer Credit, Timeshare). It is unclear whether different informa-

19 The exclusion is limited to sales below 15 euro, where the sum is paid immediately.

tion requirements and different particulars pertaining to the right of withdrawal might impinge on the application of Directive 85/577.

4. Gaps in the Directive

The review did not reveal many gaps in the Directive. Potentially significant examples may be:

- Contracts negotiated in a doorstep selling situation, but concluded afterwards by means of remote communication, in particular on the phone (such contracts are covered neither by the Doorstep Selling Directive nor by the Distance Selling Directive);
- The absence of a provision on the burden of proof regarding the facts and circumstances that would lead to the application of the national transposition law.

5. Potential barriers to (cross-border) trade

Although business models built on cross-border doorstep selling do not seem to be very common and, therefore, not very relevant for the functioning of the internal market, different national provisions on doorstep selling may affect the internal market.[20] As such, some potentially significant barriers to trade might be:

- Additional information requirements;
- Formal requirements imposed on the consumer should he/she wish to exercise the right of withdrawal (because this leads to an additional information requirement);
- Obligatory standard forms for the presentation of information required;
- Strict formal requirements governing the contract as a whole;
- No standard period for the consumer to exercise the right of withdrawal;
- No standard procedure after the right of withdrawal has been exercised, with regard to
  - Reshipment costs for goods and time limits for reshipment and reimbursement of the purchase price;
  - Compensation for any depreciation in value.

6. Conclusions and recommendations

In the course of the review, the following issues could be considered:

- Definition of "consumer" (in particular with regard to "mixed purpose" cases);
- Definition of "trader" (in particular with regard to not-for-profit organisations);
- Inclusion of contracts concluded in public places, outside business premises;
- Inclusion of contracts initially negotiated in doorstep selling situations, but ultimately concluded in a shop or via remote communication;
- Introduction of a provision on the burden of proof;
- Provisions on the formal requirements for exercising the right of withdrawal;
- Set form for uniform information on the right of withdrawal;
- Harmonisation of the withdrawal period and procedure where the right of withdrawal is exercised, including the beginning of that period and the calculation of its duration.

---

20 See for example the recent ECJ case *A-Punkt-Schmuckhandel* – C-441/04.

I. Legislation in the member states before transposition of the Doorstep Selling Directive

The member states had no coherent legislation concerning consumer protection in the case of door-to-door sales before Directive 85/577 entered into force. The level of protection varied tremendously from very robust in some countries (e.g. DENMARK and SWEDEN) to practically non-existent in others (e.g. CZECH REPUBLIC, POLAND, HUNGARY). Door-to-door sales had already been subject to regulations in some member states before the European Commission announced its intention to regulate door-to-door sales at the European level. For instance, door-to-door sales were generally prohibited (except for legally regulated or permitted activities) in LUXEMBOURG by the "Act on Peddling and Itinerant Trade" (1970) and in BELGIUM by the "Trade Practices Act" (1971) and the Royal Decree 82 of 28 November 1939 on Itinerant Trade Activities. The SWEDISH "Law on Door-to-Door Sales" (1971) as well as the FRENCH "Law no. 72-1137 on Canvassing and Door-to-Door Sales"[21] (1972) and the DUTCH "Peddling Act" (1973) all provided for a right of withdrawal.[22] Moreover, the NETHERLANDS introduced a registration requirement for itinerant salesmen in order to tackle improper conduct. The time frame for exercising the right of withdrawal varied from 7 to 8 days and started either with the registration of the contract (e.g. NETHERLANDS) or upon notice being given to the consumer (e.g. SWEDEN). Thereafter, DENMARK (1978), FINLAND (1978) and AUSTRIA (1979) also introduced regulations on door-to-door sales.

After Directive 85/577 came into force, DENMARK implemented it by simply amending its existing laws in 1987, whereas GERMANY (1986), PORTUGAL (1987), the UNITED KINGDOM (1987), IRELAND (1989), GREECE (1991) and SPAIN (1991) enacted new laws. The new member states, in particular, did not, for the most part, have any comparable regulation before preparing to join the EU. Thus, as in the case of CYPRUS and POLAND, only the general provisions concerning contracts and contractual liability applied. The CZECH REPUBLIC primarily adopted comparable consumer protection regulations by amending its Civil Code with Act 367/2000. The first regulatory act in the consumer protection field in LATVIA came into force in October 1992 with the "Law on the Protection of Consumer Rights". LITHUANIA enacted the "Law on Consumer Protection" in September 2000 with a chapter on the "Sale of goods or provision of services away from business premises". In SLOVAKIA, Act 108/2000 on Consumer Protection in Doorstep Selling and Distance Selling was enacted in 2000. As the only exception, MALTA enacted the "Door-to-Door Salesmen Act" already in February 1987.

II. Scope

In its first three articles, Directive 85/577 regulates the conditions under which its provisions shall apply, i.e. 'to protect the consumer in respect of contracts negotiated away from business premises'. Whereas Art. 1 describes the general scope of the Directive, Art. 2 determines the persons to whom it shall apply. Art. 3 contains exemptions from the Directive's scope.

---

21 The French law 72-1137 influenced the drawing up of Directive 85/577.

22 Different wording: "Right of regret" in Sweden.

I. Persons covered under the Directive

The Directive applies to "contracts under which a trader supplies goods or services to a consumer" (Art. 1 para. 1).

a. Consumer

In Art. 2 of Directive 85/577, a "consumer" is defined as "a natural person who (...) is acting for purposes which can be regarded as outside his trade or profession". The member states have chosen different legislative techniques to transpose this definition. In particular, many member states have introduced a common definition of "consumer" applicable to several or all of their transposition laws for the individual consumer protection directives (for a general overview, see Part 3.A.II.). One significant variation in the field of doorstep selling is the inclusion of legal persons under the definition of "consumer", as in BELGIUM.[23] In SLOVAKIA, legal persons in general can be considered as "consumers" under the Slovakian Act on Consumer Protection, but they are explicitly excluded from its scope of protection with regard to Doorstep Selling.[24] In LATVIA,[25] a 2005 reform excluded legal persons from the scope. In the CZECH REPUBLIC, there is a general definition of "consumer" for all consumer contracts.[26] Legal persons who meet the criteria can be considered as consumers, too.

The POLISH[27] Civil Code uses a wider definition of "consumer", requiring that the legal act carried out by a natural person must not be directly related to his business or professional activity. On the contrary, the BELGIAN legislator requires that the person must act exclusively for purposes outside his business or trade in order to be considered as a "consumer". According to FRENCH case law, under specific conditions, associations of natural persons can also be considered as "consumers". Under SPANISH law, a "consumer" can be a natural or legal person and has to be the final recipient of the goods or services.[28] The law defines which persons are not final recipients, i.e. those persons aiming "to integrate them (i.e. goods or services) into production, processing or marketing processes". For instance, even trade unions can be considered as "consumers" in Spain.[29] In GREECE, a natural or legal person is always a "consumer" if he is the last link in the supply chain, regardless of whether the goods and services are meant for professional or business use. Similarly, a natural person who is the final recipient of the goods and services (*consommateur final privé*) is considered to be a "consumer" in LUXEMBOURG. In GERMANY, what are termed dual-use cases - where a private person uses the goods and services for private as well as business purposes - have been the subject of discussion, illustrating the fact that an exact determination and definition of

23 Article 1(7) of the Act of 14 July 1991 on trade practices and consumer information and protection. Conversely, the Belgian Trade Practices Act defines consumers as persons acting exclusively for purposes outside their business or professional activity.

24 Article 1 of Act No. 108/2000 on Consumer Protection in Doorstep Selling and Distance Selling.

25 Amendment of Art. 1(1) of the Consumer Rights Protection Law, in force since 11 Nov 2005.

26 CC sec. 52.

27 CC Art. 22.

28 Article 1(2) of Law 26/1984 of July 19 on Consumer Protection.

29 Audiencia Provincial Teruel, judgment of 31 Oct 2002, 171/2002 "C.S.I.-C.S.I.F" v "G.T.A.P., S.L.".

the notion of a "consumer" is not possible in every single case. German courts would probably focus on the question of which purpose, private or business, is predominant.[30] In ITALY, as well, the prevalent use is decisive. The court should determine this by considering the circumstances of the case, e.g. the nature of the goods and/or services indicated in the contract and the nature of the agreement.[31]

AUSTRIAN jurisdiction has dealt with the question of whether transactions to establish a company (*Gründungsgeschäfte*) fall within the Directive's scope. The Austrian Supreme Court, OGH,[32] held that the fact that an individual subsequently loses his consumer status does not mean he forfeits the protection afforded to him as a consumer. In contrast, ITALIAN jurisdiction[33] held that a person concluding contracts in order to start a business cannot be considered as a consumer.

b. Trader

Directive 85/577 considers a "trader" to be a natural or legal person who, "for the transaction in question, acts in his commercial or professional capacity, and anyone acting in the name or on behalf of a trader". Some member states, DENMARK, IRELAND and LATVIA, strictly follow the Directive's definition. Nevertheless, variations exist in the majority of member states:

AT[34]	Cumulative conditions: the trader has to possess (and not own) a business (e.g. "leaseholder"); and the legal transaction has to form part of the professional activity[35]; the person concerned is the party to the legal transaction disregarding third persons who might be involved without being party; public legal persons are always seen as traders because of a special legislative order; not-for-profit organisations can also be considered as traders.
BE[36]	The definition includes "all traders or craftsmen", "not-for-profit organisations which pursue an economic activity within the framework of their statutes", "governmental institutions that pursue a commercial, financial or industrial activity", "legal persons in which the government holds the majority of shares and which pursue an industrial, commercial or financial activity" and "persons acting in the name or on behalf of a third party, legal persons or other, and who pursue an industrial, financial or commercial activity".
CY[37]	Only a slight variation.
CZ[38]	Use of term "supplier"; otherwise only slight variation.
EE	Person who "sells, offers or markets in any other manner".
FI	Private and public legal person; no mention of representative; purpose of trader's activity must be economic.

30 OLG Naumburg, judgment of 11 Dec 1997, NJW-RR 1998, 1351 (concerning consumer credit).

31 Tribunale Bari, judgment of 31 Aug 2001, Lavopa v. Soc. Inditel S.p.A.

32 OGH judgment of 20 Oct 2004, 2 Ob 178/05y.

33 Cass., judgment of 14 April 2000, 4843 Ambrogio Ciocca v. Soc. Galassia.

34 Consumer Protection Act, Art. 1(1).

35 According to an OGH judgment of 14 July 2005, 6 Ob 135/05d, a legal transaction concluded between suppliers falls outside the scope even if one contract party subsequently stops trading.

36 Article 1(6) of the Act of 14 July 1991 on trade practices and consumer information and protection.

37 Article 2 of the Law for Consumer Contracts Concluded Away from Business Premises of 2000, L.13(I)/2000.

38 CC § 52(3).

EL[39]	Natural or legal persons, which also includes public or local authority undertakings and not-for-profit private organisations.
ES[40]	Different wording in the transposition law: "businessman" instead of "trader" and the terms "which/who supplies goods or services" are omitted; no direct transposition of the definition, but indirectly both interpretations of the notion of "trader" – sensu strictu and a third person acting on behalf or in the name of the trader – apply.
LT	Definitions in different regulations[41]; definition in Law on Consumer Protection includes the definitions of trader and service provider; no mention of other persons like agents or intermediaries, not-for-profit legal persons or consumers starting up a business; definition in Consumer Credit also concerns agents.
MT	Definition includes commercial partnership; persons acting on behalf of the trader or under his direction are included; also includes a 'door-to-door salesman'[42]; furthermore, the Minister responsible for consumer affairs may, after consulting the Consumer Affairs Council, declare any other category or class of persons to be a "trader"; the trader must be licensed in order to operate a doorstep selling business.
NL[43]	Use of term "canvasser"; the seller's objective is also referred to in the definition "who tries to induce a private individual to enter into a contract [...] in connection with any recommendation"; also includes not-for-profit legal persons.
PL[44]	Translation of the Polish notion of business would be wider than "trader", meaning a person carrying out an economic activity related to some undertaking.
PT	Use of term "supplier", i.e. a natural or legal person acting in his/her professional capacity; other persons acting on behalf of the contracting party are not explicitly included in the definition, but the provisions would apply to them as a general rule.
SE	As in other Swedish consumer protection legislation.
SK	Slightly different wording[45]; licensing requirement; other persons acting for the trader are included.[46]
SL[47]	Other persons acting on behalf of the contracting party are not explicitly included in the definition, but the provisions would apply to them too.
UK[48]	Different wording: a person acting for the purposes of his business, including anyone acting in the name or on behalf of such a person.

39 Article 4 lit. (d) and Art. 3 of Law 2251/1994 on Consumer Protection.

40 Article 1(1)(a) and (b) of Law 26/1991 of November 21 on consumer protection in the case of contracts performed away from commercial premises.

41 CC, Art. 6.350(1), sent. (1); Law of Consumer Protection, Art 2 para. (2) and (3).

42 Defined as a person who offers the provision or supply of any type of goods or services by means of a doorstep contract, whether the offer is unsolicited by the person to whom it is made, or is solicited by the latter person in response to any advertisement. It, does not include vendors of foodstuffs and drinks who sell their goods from door to door.

43 Doorstep Selling Law, Art. 1 para (1)(c) and para. (2).

44 CC, Art. 43.

45 § 2(1)(b), § 2(3) of Act 634/1992 on Consumer Protection; § 2 of Act 108/2000 on Consumer Protection in Doorstep Selling and Distance Selling.

46 According to Amendment 118/2006 Z.z. (entry into force on 1 April 2006). This act amended § 2 of Act 108/2000 on Consumer Protection in Doorstep Selling and Distance Selling.

47 Consumer Protection Act, Art. 3(1).

48 Article 2(1) of the Consumer Protection Regulations 1987 (cancellation of contracts concluded away from business premises).

2. Situations falling within the scope of the Directive

The Directive's provisions apply to "contracts under which a trader supplies goods or services to a consumer and which are concluded:

- during an excursion organised by the trader away from his business premises, or
- during a visit by a trader
  (i) to the consumer's home or to that of another consumer;
  (ii) to the consumer's place of work; where the visit does not take place at the express request of the consumer" (Art. 1 para. 1).

a. General application

Generally speaking, most member states have implemented the same type of contracts and situations falling within the scope of Directive 85/577, though occasionally different wording has been used. Contrary to the provisions of Directive 85/577, contracts under LATVIAN law concluded during an excursion are not protected by the transposition law.

It is worthless that the ECJ has clarified some details with regard to the situations covered by the Directive. Member states' national courts have to take into account this case law when applying their domestic doorstep selling laws. In its judgment *Travel VAC*, C-423/97, the ECJ held that where a contract is concluded after a trader has invited a consumer to go in person to a specified place at a certain distance from the place where the consumer lives (other than the premises where the trader usually carries out his business and not clearly identifiable as premises for sales to the public), in order to present to him the products and services he is offering, this contract must be considered to have been concluded during an excursion organised by the trader away from his business premises within the meaning of the Directive. In the same judgment, the ECJ clarified that the consumer does not need to prove that he was influenced or manipulated by the trader. It is sufficient that the contract is concluded in circumstances such as those described in the Directive.

Moreover, in its judgment *Crailsheimer Volksbank*, C-229/04, the ECJ held that, when a third party intervenes in the name or on behalf of a trader to negotiate or conclude a contract, the application of the Directive cannot be made subject to the condition that the trader was, or should have been, aware that the contract was concluded in a doorstep selling situation. As a result, the GERMAN courts, which had ruled differently prior to this decision, now comply with ECJ case law.

Many member states have extended the scope of their doorstep selling laws. The following types of extensions can be observed:

aa. Expanding the list of doorstep situations

Several member states have expanded the list of situations in which consumers are protected, e.g. GERMANY, where contracts concluded following a surprise or sudden approach by the trader on public transport or in an open public space are covered. Moreover, German law does not stipulate that an 'excursion' is necessarily organised by the trader away from his business premises. Rather, a 'recreational event' organised by the businessperson or by a third party operating at least in the interest of the businessperson[49] is sufficient. With regard to the possibility that the trader does not organise the excursion himself, the BELGIAN legislator has also clarified that the excursion can be organised either by the trader directly or on his behalf.[50] The FRENCH and PORTUGUESE[51] doorstep selling laws also apply in cases where the consumer has been invited by the trader to somewhere other than the trader's business premises. In ITALY, the transposition law is applicable to contracts concluded in "transitional situations", e.g. temporary work, study, medical treatment or in public places – provided that any possible order form is signed. Furthermore, the transposition law also applies to contracts concluded via television or audiovisual media.[52] In LITHUANIA, contracts concluded during a visit to an educational institution (e.g. school, university, etc.) or any other such venue fall within the scope of the national legislation enacted to transpose Directive 85/577.[53] Moreover, in DANISH legislation, all contracts concluded outside the trader's business premises are protected by the national transposition law, e.g. contracts concluded in the streets, on squares, in restaurants, at railway stations or in other public places, and on the telephone.[54] In ESTONIA, MALTA and SPAIN, contracts negotiated away from the trader's premises also fall within the scope of protection. In the CZECH REPUBLIC, contracts concluded with a trader outside his business premises, as well as contracts concluded with a trader without any permanent business premises, are covered.

Specific rules for contracts concluded at fairs are contained in BELGIAN[55] and SLOVENIAN[56] law. In CYPRUS,[57] the scope has been extended to visits by the trader to "any other location". GREEK[58] law refers to "the location outside his business premises chosen by the trader". Therefore, the scope is broader as a multitude of possible locations is included. More important is the criterion that the contract must "stem from the trader's initiative". On the one hand, it is restrictive, as it excludes contracts in situations initiated by the consumer. On the other hand, the question of whether a contract is concluded outside business premises is secondary to the question of whether it stemmed from the trader's initiative. As a consequence, contracts concluded on the trader's business premises can also fall within the scope

---

49 According to a BGH judgment (of 28 Oct 2003, X ZR 178/02), at such a recreational event, the recreational aspect and offers of sale must intermingle in such a way that the consumer, on account of the advertising and running of the event, is made to feel at ease and relaxed and would have difficulty withdrawing from any offer aimed at concluding a contract.

50 Article 86(1)(2) of the Act of 14 July 1991 on trade practices and consumer information and protection.

51 The situation dealt with by the ECJ in Travel Vac. is explicitly covered in Portuguese legislation.

52 Article 45(1) of Legislative Decree 6/09/2005, n. 206 "Consumer Code".

53 Article 14(1) of the Law on consumer protection, CC, Art. 6.357.

54 Article 3(1) of Act 451 of 9 June 2004 on certain consumer contracts.

55 Article 86(1)(3) of the Act of 14 July 1991 on trade practices and consumer information and protection.

56 Consumer Protection Act, Art. 46(3).

57 Article 3(1)(b) (iii) of the Law for Consumer Contracts Concluded Away from Business Premises of 2000, L.13(I)/2000.

58 Article 3(1) of Law 2251/94 on consumer protection.

if there is evidence of the trader's initiative, e.g. if the consumer has been enticed onto the business premises with gifts or recreational events.

In AUSTRIA, as the scope is defined negatively,[59] contracts concluded on excursions can also fall within its ambit. According to an OHG judgment,[60] the situation must typically indicate that the consumer is in danger of being caught unaware. This is not the case if, within the context of a holiday offered at an appropriate price, there is, alongside different sightseeing trips, an organised visit to a workshop where goods manufactured there are on sale.

It may be worth considering, within the framework of the planned review, whether the limited list of situations in which the consumer is protected (Art. 1 para. 1) may be expanded following such examples as DENMARK, ESTONIA, MALTA or GERMANY. Such an expansion might amount to a general clause covering all contracts concluded away from business premises, which are not distance contracts. A more concrete expansion could be to include particular contracts concluded in public places.

bb. Goods and services

The Directive is quite unclear with regard to the kind of contracts or other transactions that are covered. In the English version, Art. 1 para 1 refers to "contracts under which a trader supplies goods or services". The ECJ case *Bayerische Hypotheken- und Wechselbank*, C-45/96, which dealt with a guarantee, revealed a linguistic difference between two groups of language versions. For instance, the French and German versions read: « contrats conclus entre un commerçant fournissant des biens ou des services » and „Verträge, die zwischen einem Gewerbetreibenden, der Waren liefert oder Dienstleistungen erbringt, (...) geschlossen werden". These versions seem to be broader, because they only require the trader to supply goods and services in general, whereas the English version seemingly demands that the specific contract concluded in the doorstep situation relates to the supply of goods or services. A guarantee put up by a consumer for the benefit of a bank readily falls under the German and the French version (because the bank – in general – provides services), while doubt is cast over this in the English version (because the guarantee put up by a consumer can hardly be considered as a service provided by the bank). The ECJ in *Bayerische Hypothekenbank* states that, in principle, a guarantee falls under Art. 1 of the Directive.[61] The problem in this case was that the guarantor was assuring repayment of a debt contracted by another person who, for his part, was acting within his commercial or professional capacity. The ECJ held that such a guarantee for a business loan does not come within the scope of the Directive.[62] Thus, only a guarantee for a private loan can fall under the Directive. It might be considered whether this may constitute a gap in consumer protection that should be remedied in a possible review of the Directive.

---

59 Consumer Protection Act, Art. 3 para. 2 "conclusion of the contract not on the supplier's business premises and equally not at a market stall or stand at a fair".

60 OGH, judgment of 10 Nov 1993, 7 Ob 599/93.

61 Cf. Para. 20 of the judgment.

62 Cf. Para. 23 of the judgment.

As regards guarantees, the GERMAN courts followed the abovementioned ECJ decision. In 1998, the German Supreme Court, BGH,[63] ruled that a guarantee does not fall under the definition of Directive 85/577 if it secures a financial liability entered into by the principal debtor acting within his official business capacity. In contrast, in AUSTRIA, the OGH,[64] held in a 2005 ruling that, at the time the guarantee is concluded, the creditor must be a supplier and the guarantor a consumer, even if the guarantee secures a debt of a principal debtor acting in his business capacity.

Most member states refer in their transposition laws to goods and services without much further explanation.[65] However, the DUTCH legislator has clarified that not only movables are included, but also other economic rights.[66] In France, the Supreme Court (Cass. Civ.[67]) ruled that a contract containing provisions to the effect that the consumer shall rent out a place in his immovable property, so that the "supplier" may install a relay station there, falls within the scope of French doorstep selling provisions. The provisions are held to be applicable, although the supplier does not, strictly speaking, provide the consumer with goods or services. In PORTUGAL, the object of the specific contract must be goods or services.

From a consumer protection perspective, the term "goods and services" may be considered as too narrow, because, for instance, donations or subscriptions to (charitable and other) associations are not covered. However, it is perhaps doubtful whether such protection should be stipulated at the EC level.

cc. Offers and/or unilateral legal acts

Art. 1 para. 3 and para. 4 of the Directive attempt to clarify that the consumer must also be able to withdraw from an offer made in a doorstep situation, irrespective of whether the offer is binding (as it usually is, e.g. under GERMAN law) or not binding (as it usually is, e.g. under ENGLISH law). These provisions are somewhat incomplete, because it goes without saying that unilateral legal acts that are binding on the consumer must also be covered. Some member states have explicitly clarified that at least offers made in a doorstep situation fall under their doorstep selling rules (e.g. IRELAND, UNITED KINGDOM). Others must rely on their courts with regard to this issue. AUSTRIA has explicitly stipulated that its doorstep selling laws cover all legal transactions between a consumer and a trader and thereby do not only include all forms of bilateral contracts (except "work only" contracts), but also unilateral acts such as rescissions, withdrawals, contractual stipulations or membership of clubs.[68] Those member states which also apply their doorstep selling laws to contracts concluded not

---

63 BGH, judgment of 14 May 1998, IX ZR 56-95.

64 OGH, judgment of 20 Oct 2005, 2 Ob 178/05y.

65 In the United Kingdom, in the context of UTCCR 1999 (Transposition of Directive 93/13), the Court of Appeal has suggested that "goods or services" in the UTCCR should be read very widely indeed to include tenancy agreements. It is not clear if this will be followed in the context of Doorstep Selling.

66 Doorstep Selling Law, Art. 1 para. (1) (c) and para. (3) and (4).

67 Cass. Civ., judgment of 30 March 2005, Case no.04-11.831 Fouque/SFR.

68 Consumer Protection Act, Art. 1(1)(1).

during, but after the doorstep situation (see next paragraph) automatically cover offers as well.

dd. Contracts negotiated in a doorstep situation, but concluded subsequently

Some member states also cover contracts concluded on business premises when the consumer has previously been influenced in a doorstep situation. This is, for instance, the case in AUSTRIA, where the transposition law also covers contracts concluded on the trader's business premises if the consumer has been enticed there. In POLAND, the scope of protection has been extended to cover contracts concluded on business premises, provided that the contractual offers were made outside these premises.[69] GERMAN law protects the consumer when he has been induced in a doorstep situation to conclude a contract. In France, if a contract is concluded on business premises, but the consumer has first been invited by telephone to go there, the provisions on doorstep selling apply.[70]

ee. Visits requested by the Consumer

With regard to the specific provisions of the Directive dealing with visits requested by the consumer, varying transposition laws can be found. For instance, some member states have not implemented the provision that contracts concluded during a visit at the express request of the consumer can be excluded from the protection. In DENMARK, FRANCE, ITALY, LATVIA and POLAND, the protective provisions also apply to visits taking place at the express request of the consumer, whereas in BELGIUM,[71] the CZECH REPUBLIC[72] and SLOVENIA, the provisions only apply to unsolicited visits. However, in BELGIUM, the acceptance of a telephone offer from the seller to visit the consumer at home does not constitute a prior request made by the consumer.[73] A consumer who shows interest in a product or a service on offer in an advertising brochure is not the same as a consumer who requests a seller to visit him at home with a view to negotiating the purchase of that product or service.[74] In the UNITED KINGDOM,[75] unsolicited visits as well as visits which were arranged by previous unsolicited visits or

---

69 Article 1(3) of Act of 2 March 2000 on the protection of certain consumer rights and liability for an unsafe product.

70 Cour de cassation, Chambre criminelle, 10 January 1996, Receuil Dalloz, 1996, Informations Rapides, 120.

71 The protective provisions are not applicable if, and only if, the consumer explicitly solicited the visit and did so prior to the visit with the purpose of negotiating the purchase of the products or services. The burden of proof for the request rests with the seller. (CA Ghent, judgment of 3 Feb 2004, 2003/AR/960 Mini-Flat n.v. / Chris Vandelannoote).

72 CC § 57(1), last sent.

73 Trade Practices Act, Art. 87(a).

74 CA Brussels, judgment of 25 Feb 2005, 1999/AR/202 s.a. Euroconstruction/Mr. and Mrs. Danielswiez-Claes.

75 On 7 September 2006, the UK government announced two proposals to amend the legislation on doorstep selling in the UK: firstly, the right of withdrawal will also be made available in circumstances where the visit by the trader to the consumer was solicited, i.e., agreed in advance; secondly, contracts are to provide cancellation notices more prominently and clearly indicate the circum-

by telephone fall within the scope.[76] In CYPRUS, the protective provisions apply to unsolicited visits and if the trader has been invited to discuss an item other than the one he is actually offering. According to AUSTRIAN[77] law, the consumer has no right of withdrawal if the business relationship was initiated by the consumer.[78] According to Austrian jurisdiction, "initiating" means that the consumer is instigating contact and demonstrating a willingness to conclude a specific consumer transaction.

In LITHUANIA,[79] solicited visits also fall within the scope where the consumer is provided with goods and services other than those that are requested. A similar regulation can be found in GREECE. However, where the trader offers products other than those which he has been invited to discuss, the protective provisions do not apply if the consumer knows or should know that the products offered are part of the trader's standard product range or that the products offered are linked to the products which the trader has been invited to discuss. According to PORTUGUESE law, visits requested by the consumer or the trader fall within the scope of protection if the consumer is not aware that the trader also sells the specific kind of goods or services. In MALTA, contracts concluded exclusively on the consumer's initiative are excluded from the scope of protection except for cases where the consumer only orders a catalogue, samples or similar items. Where the consumer requests the trader to visit, demonstrate a product/service or participate in an event, this is not considered to be on the consumer's initiative.[80] SPANISH[81] law contains some specifications relating to what is meant by the consumer's initiative. According to Spanish jurisdiction, the visit request must be specific and unambiguous.[82]

---

stances when the right of withdrawal may be lost. The first amendment will require primary legislation, because this exceeds the scope of the Directive, and there is no power to adopt secondary legislation under the European Communities Act 1972 to make this change.

Details of the proposals can be found at http://www.dti.gov.uk/files/file33819.pdf (accessed 7 September 2006).

76 Article 3(3)(a) and (b) of the Consumer Protection Regulations 1987 (Cancellation of Contracts concluded away from business premises).

77 Consumer Protection Act, Art. 3(3), 1st indent.

78 OGH, judgment of 8 Nov 1995, 7 Ob 594/94. According to the OGH judgment of 13 Feb 2002, 2 Ob 11/02k, this can also be the case if the consumer, after a telephone call by the trader couched in general terms, shows interest in concluding a very specific transaction. The burden of proof rests with the trader.

According to the OGH judgment of 9 Oct 1984, 4 Ob 521/84, a consumer who is not just requesting general information at a fair, but rather makes explicit his desire to enter into preliminary negotiations with the aim of concluding a specific transaction, is initiating a business contact with the supplier.

In its judgment of 14 July 1998, 4 Ob 183/98k, the OGH held that the consumer has initiated the transaction, if he takes a closer look at coats on display in a hotel foyer out of curiosity and on his own initiative. This applies even if the supplier then made the initial verbal contact and began the sales discussion.

79 Law on Consumer Protection, Art. 14(3) 2nd indent.

80 Doorstep Contracts Act, Art. 3 lit. (a).

81 Article 1(1)(b) of Law 26/1991 of November 21 on consumer protection in the case of contracts performed outside commercial premises.

82 A demand for free personal information is not considered to be such a request from the consumer because it only aims to gather information. The burden of proof for the request lies with the

b. Exemptions provided for in the Doorstep Selling Directive

aa. Art. 3 para. 1 (Contracts under 60 ECU)

Art. 3(1) of Directive 85/577 provides for the option for member states to exclude contracts that do not exceed the sum of 60 ECU from the scope of their national transposition law. Member states who have not exercised this option are, for instance, CYPRUS, the CZECH REPUBLIC, DENMARK, FRANCE, GREECE, HUNGARY, LATVIA, LUXEMBOURG and SLOVAKIA. Although many member states have indeed exercised this option, they have fixed different limits varying from EUR 10 (POLAND) up to EUR 50 (BELGIUM), as set out in the chart below. In BELGIUM, additionally, the sale must be made for non-commercial and exclusively charitable purposes. In ESTONIA,[83] there is a limit of EUR 15 which only applies where the consumer pays the sum at the moment the contract is concluded. PORTUGUESE law is applicable to contracts under EUR 60, although some provisions (regarding contract form, content and terms and conditions) are only applicable to contracts exceeding this amount.[84]

	Member States
Not transposed	CY, CZ, DK, FR, EL, HU, LU, LV, SK *(9)*
Exclusions	AT (EUR 15 /EUR 45), BE[85] (EUR 50), DE (EUR 40), EE[86] (EUR 15), ES (EUR 48.08), FI (EUR 15), IE (£ 40 = EUR 50.79), IT (EUR 26), LT (LTL 200) MT (20 Maltese liri = EUR 46.68), NL (EUR 34), PL (EUR 10), PT (EUR 60, cf. text above) SE (300 SEK = EUR 32.57), SL (3000 Slovenian Tolars = EUR 12.52), UK (£ 35 = EUR 50.82) ***(16)***

bb. Art. 3 para 2

Equally, the member states have not consistently exercised the options to limit the scope as provided for in Art. 3 para. 2 of Directive 85/577. The general picture on the use of these options has already been set out in the Executive Summary of this chapter. It may be noted that, for instance, in GREECE, ITALY, IRELAND (exclusion of insurance and assurance contracts), PORTUGAL, POLAND and the UNITED KINGDOM,[87] the same situations are basically exempt from protection as provided for under Directive 85/577. In contrast, LATVIAN law does not contain any restrictions in the general definition of the contract.

---

trader. Audiencia Provincial Burgos, judgment of 26 Oct 2001, 528/2001 "Entidad técnica de distribución X. S.L." v María Cruz S. R. y Raúl A.S.

83 Consumer Protection Act, Art. 46(2).

84 Article 16(4) of Decree-Law 143/2001 of April 26.

85 The exclusion is limited to sales which do not exceed the sum of EUR 50 and are made for non-commercial and exclusively charitable purposes.

86 The exclusion is limited to sales where the sum is paid immediately.

87 Article 3(4)(a) of the Consumer Protection Regulations 1987 (Cancellation of Contracts concluded away from business premises); (variation: instead of referring to contracts of "securities", the UK excluded "any agreement the making or performance of which by either party constitutes a regulated activity", e.g. dealing in and arranging deals in investments, managing, safeguarding and administering investments, establishing a collective investment scheme; no application to consumer credit contracts).

It is worth highlighting the following features with regard to the individual transposition laws. GERMANY, LITHUANIA, MALTA and SPAIN exclude contracts concluded before a notary public. This exclusion is broader than what is provided for in Art. 3 para. 2 lit. a (contracts related to immovable property) and may therefore infringe the Directive. In particular, the Maltese[88] legislator, in implementing the exemptions laid down in Art. 3 of the Directive, goes beyond the Directive's scope by excluding contracts negotiated solely in writing, contracts concluded before a court, notary or another person who is bound to inform the parties of their rights and obligations even if they are concluded in a doorstep situation (which is – for some of these cases – hard to imagine).[89] Moreover, the Maltese Minster is empowered by law to make other contracts exempt from the national Doorstep Contracts Act. In Spain, Art. 3(2)(a), sent. 1 has been transposed almost literally, only excluding contracts related to immovable property, whereas the second sentence (contracts for the supply of goods for incorporation in immovable property and contracts for the repair of the latter) has not been transposed at all.

In the NETHERLANDS, contracts in the case of an ongoing relationship between the parties concerning the sale of food are exempt.[90] The LITHUANIAN derogation for the supply of foodstuffs, beverages or other goods intended for current consumption in the household does not require that the goods were supplied by "regular roundsmen".[91] In SPAIN, the doorstep selling of foodstuffs and beverages is prohibited,[92] but not their delivery at the consumer's request.

The exemption of contracts concluded on the basis of a trader's catalogue (as per Art. 3 para. 2 lit. c of Directive 85/577) has not been transposed in BELGIUM, ITALY, LITHUANIA and HUNGARY. Hungarian[93] law explicitly states that the provisions on distance selling are applicable. CYPRUS has exercised this option with some variations regarding the conditions the contract has to meet in order to be excluded from the protective rules (e.g. the time limit for cancellation or return of goods – extended to at least fourteen days – and the information which must be provided in the catalogue and the contract).[94] The GREEK legislator has made a further exemption: the protective provisions do not apply to itinerant traders with small businesses.[95]

---

88 Doorstep Contracts Act, Art. 3.

89 The Maltese legislator has presumed that these contracts would not generally stem from a doorstep situation. This exemption may be considered to be necessary because the definition of "doorstep contract" includes contracts that have been negotiated at any other place or premises other than the door-to-door salesman's business premises .

90 Doorstep Selling Law, Art. 1(3).

91 Article 3(3.1) of the Order of the Minister of Economy of the Republic of Lithuania on the Approval of the Rules on the Sale of Goods and Provision of Services on Premises not Designated for this Activity, Art. 14(3) 1st indent of the Law on consumer protection, CC, Art. 6.357(3) 1st indent.

92 Article 5(2)(d) of Law 26/1984 of July 19 on Consumer Protection, Art. 2(1) 1st sent., no. 6 of Law 26/1991 of November 21.

93 § 1(6) of Government Decree 370/2004 (XII.26.) on Doorstep Selling.

94 Article 4(c) of the Law for Consumer Contracts Concluded Away from Business Premises of 2000, L.13(I)/2000.

95 Article 3(7) of Law 2251/94 on consumer protection.

c. Burden of proof

The burden of proof with regard to the circumstances that would give rise to protection under the national transposition laws is not subject to the Directive's provisions. Nonetheless, this element can either increase the level of consumer protection or at least complicate the enforcement of the consumer's rights. Where the burden of proof regarding the facts necessary to trigger application of the protection law rests with the trader, consumer protection is enhanced. Where the burden of proof rests with the consumer, enforcement is more complicated. Both solutions can be found in the member states' laws. For instance, AUSTRIA, GERMANY, GREECE, POLAND AND SWEDEN place the burden of proof on the consumer, whereas, in DENMARK, MALTA and SPAIN, for example, the trader carries the burden of proof. The BELGIAN courts also tend to place the burden of proof on the trader.[96] There is no specific rule in PORTUGAL. In LATVIA, no particular rule on doorstep contracts can be found either, though it is considered that the Consumer Protection Act's purpose is to place the burden of proof on the trader. In the UNITED KINGDOM, a general rule applies: the claimant has to prove he is entitled to the legal right.

III. Consumer protection instruments

1. Information requirements

The member states mostly transposed the requirement to provide written notice established in Art. 4 of Directive 85/577. In some member states, the protective measures have been beefed up. In BELGIUM, GREECE, MALTA, the NETHERLANDS, PORTUGAL and SPAIN, the whole contract has to be in writing. In other member states, only the information on the right of withdrawal has to be in writing, e.g. AUSTRIA, the CZECH REPUBLIC,[97] DENMARK, FINLAND, FRANCE, HUNGARY, IRELAND, LUXEMBOURG, LITHUANIA, POLAND, SLOVENIA SLOVAKIA[98] and SWEDEN. ESTONIAN and GERMAN[99] law require the information to be either

---

96 In a judgment of 23 March 2005 the Ghent Court of Appeal ruled that, taking into account the precise circumstances in which the contract was negotiated, the contract term stipulating the prior and express request of the consumer to negotiate the contract was sufficient proof. In the same vein, the CA Brussels ruled on 9 May 2005 that a contract negotiated away from business premises was to be considered null and void (in the absence of a withdrawal clause) if the trader could not prove that the consumer had previously requested a visit. On 14 September 2005, the CA Ghent explicitly stated that the burden of proof as to the prior and express request of the consumer rests with the trader. However, the term in the contract indicating the consumer's express request was not considered sufficient proof of such a prior and express request, as it was drafted in exceptionally small print which was difficult to decipher. Furthermore, the Court crucially added that such a clause did not, in any case, prove that the consumer's request was particularly aimed at negotiating a sales contract. This stance was confirmed by the Ghent CA in its judgment of 12 October 2005.

97 Including the name and contact details of the person against whom that right may be exercised.

98 § 7(2)(d) of Act 108/2000 on Consumer Protection in Doorstep Selling and Distance Selling; notice must at the latest be given at the time the contract is concluded.

99 In Germany, according to a judgment of the BGH (judgment of 4 July 2002, I ZR 55/00), notice pertaining to a right of withdrawal may not, in principle, contain any information other than what

in writing or otherwise available in a durable format accessible to the consumer. When a contract is entered into in SPAIN, an information note in the format approved by the Minister of Economic Affairs and Communications must be given to the consumer. Finnish law sets a general duty to provide a doorstep selling document in accordance with the model approved by the Ministry of Trade and Industry. Similar to the Finnish regulation, French legislation requires, alongside a version of the contract, delivery of a detachable withdrawal document containing the information on the right of cancellation. In addition, the contract must contain certain information.[100] In CYPRUS, the trader must inform the consumer about the right of withdrawal in a separate written notice and attach a standard cancellation form, which the consumer can use to exercise his right of withdrawal. In LATVIA, upon entering into a contract, the seller or service provider shall issue the consumer with a written withdrawal form identifying the specific contract involved. The consumer, in order to acknowledge the receipt of the withdrawal form, must make a note on a copy of that form.

Furthermore, in IRELAND and the UNITED KINGDOM, two written forms of information documents exist: a "cancellation notice" comprising the data set by the Directive and a "cancellation form", which is prescribed in an annex to the doorstep regulations. ITALIAN regulations state that the notice of the right of withdrawal shall be enclosed with the order form to be signed separately from any other contractual provisions and in print of the same size or larger than in the other parts of the form. A copy of the order form, containing details of the date and place of signature, has to be sent to the consumer. MALTESE law requires a clause accompanying the contract set in clear, bold and highlighted letters, in which the right of withdrawal has to be communicated in writing. Herein, in addition to the Directive's requirements, the licence number of the door-to-door salesman has to be stated. A similar requirement to provide the licence (certificate) exists in SLOVAKIA. POLISH law is different in requiring that the consumer be informed before the contract is concluded; *inter alia*, the consumer has to be provided with a standard withdrawal form, including the name and address[101] of the trader. In LITHUANIA,[102] the trader is obliged to provide the consumer with a document specifying the identity and address of the trader and the identity (name, surname) of the person to whom the consumer may address his withdrawal.

As to the sanctions imposed on the trader where he has failed to provide sufficient information, these range from contracts being declared partially null and void in GREECE and in SPAIN[103] to their being declared invalid in their totality (FRANCE, HUNGARY and the NETH-

is prescribed by law. Only in exceptional circumstances may it contain supplementary information clarifying, though not differing from, the content of the notice.

100 Code de la Consommation, Art. L. 121-23 states that a contract must be established and that it shall contain the following information: 1. the name of the provider and trader, 2. address of the provider, 3. address of the place where the contract has been concluded, 4. precise description of the goods and services, 5. conditions regarding performance of the contract, 6. total price, 7. right of withdrawal.

101 Before the transposition of Directive 85/577, Polish law did not require the provision of the address, but only the trader's office.

102 Law on Consumer Protection, Art. 14(4) 4th and 5th indents; CC Art. 6.357(4) 4th and 5th indents.

103 According to the judgment of the Audiencia Provincial Cantabria of 8 Mar 2004, 118/2004 "Finanzia Banco de Crédito, S. A." v Iván, the trader must inform the consumer not only of their

ERLANDS). BELGIAN law declares a contract null and void and imposes fines between EUR 250 and EUR 10,000[104] in addition to a cease and desist order. Damages can only be obtained through separate proceedings based on the Belgian Civil Code.

Fines or more severe sanctions in the case of infringements of protective provisions (e.g. the information requirement) under national transposition law are provided for in BELGIUM, ESTONIA, FINLAND, FRANCE, GREECE,[105] HUNGARY, ITALY, IRELAND, LUXEMBOURG, LATVIA, PORTUGAL, POLAND, SLOVENIA and SLOVAKIA.

In MALTA, the contract is rendered null and void and therefore unenforceable against the consumer. Furthermore, the licence, which any door-to-door salesman needs, can be withdrawn or suspended by the Director, who also issues them. A person who then operates as a door-to-door salesman without a licence is guilty of an offence and, on conviction, liable to a fine and/or imprisonment.[106]

With regard to the sanctions for an infringement of the obligation to inform the consumer of his right of withdrawal, the ECJ stated, in the cases *Schulte* and *Crailsheimer Volksbank*, that, where the consumer would have been able to avoid exposure to the risks inherent in the contract, Article 4 of the Directive requires the member states to ensure that their legislation protects consumers who have been unable to avoid exposure to such risks by adopting suitable measures to allow them to avoid bearing any potential consequences should those risks materialise. It will have to be seen how the member states intend to comply with this requirement. The GERMAN courts which referred the issue to the ECJ now consider whether to grant the consumer a claim for damages (based on the breach of a pre-contractual obligation) in such cases.[107]

2. Right of withdrawal

a. Length of withdrawal period

As illustrated in the chart, the time limit for exercising the withdrawal right ranges from 7 calendar days to 15 calendar days in the different member states, with some opting to express that period as a number of working days.

---

right to withdraw from the contract, but also that the contractual formalities, to be performed by the trader are mandatory and that failure to comply with them results in the contract's being declared null and void.
The legislative text uses the term "null and void"; prevalent academic interpretation and also the Audiencia Provincial Cantabria in its judgment of 26 Feb 2003, 88/2003 "BSCH., S.A." v Ángel Juan C. M., consider that this means only partially null and void.

104 An indexed fine between EUR 1,375 and EUR 55,000.

105 Article 14(3) of Law 2251/1994.

106 Doorstep Contracts Act, Art. 4 and Art. 5.

107 See, for example, BGH judgment of 16 May 2006, XI ZR 6/04.

Withdrawal Period	Member State
7 calendar days	CZ, ES, FR, IE *(4)*
7 working days	BE,[108] LT, LU, SK, UK *(5)*
8 calendar days	NL *(1)*
8 working days	HU *(1)*
One week	AT *(1)*
10 calendar days	PL *(1)*
10 working days	EL, IT[109] *(2)*
14 calendar days	CY, DE[110], DK, EE, FI, LV, PT, SE *(8)*
15 calendar days	MT, SL *(2)*

The longest withdrawal period (15 calendar days) can be found in MALTESE and SLOVENIAN law. In BELGIUM, LITHUANIA, LUXEMBOURG, SLOVAKIA, and the UNITED KINGDOM, the withdrawal period is 7 working days. The period is 7 calendar days in the CZECH REPUBLIC, FRANCE, IRELAND and SPAIN[111] and 8 calendar days in the NETHERLANDS. In HUNGARY, the consumer has 8 working days to withdraw from the contract. In AUSTRIA, the period is one week. According to POLISH law, the period is 10 calendar days, whereas according to GREEK and ITALIAN law, the consumer can withdraw from a contract within 10 working days.

In the CZECH REPUBLIC, where goods are not delivered, the consumer can withdraw from the contract within one month. In ITALY, if the trader does not inform the consumer about his right of withdrawal or supplies incorrect information, the period is extended to 60 days.[112] This approach to transposition has been criticised, because the consumer might not be sufficiently protected if he does not receive information about his right of withdrawal or if he receives no written notice, but only oral information. Consequently, the consumer might not be aware of the possibility to withdraw from the contract within 60 days. In LITHUANIA, POLAND and SLOVENIA, the withdrawal period is extended to three months where there is a failure to provide (sufficient) information. In the CZECH REPUBLIC, the period is extended to one year after the conclusion of the contract. Under the ECJ's ruling in the C-481/99 – *Heininger* case, any limitation of the withdrawal period where no notice about the right of withdrawal is given is in breach of Art. 4 of Directive 85/577. Therefore, the transposition provisions in the CZECH REPUBLIC, LITHUANIA, POLAND, SLOVENIA and ITALY infringe that article.

In CYPRUS, DENMARK, ESTONIA, FINLAND, LATVIA, PORTUGAL and SWEDEN, the withdrawal period is up to 14 calendar days. In GERMANY, the withdrawal period is generally up to two weeks, provided that information on the right of withdrawal is given to the consumer before or at the time the contract is concluded. If information on the right of withdrawal is given to the consumer after the conclusion of the contract, the consumer has one month to withdraw from the contract. If no (correct) notice of the right of withdrawal is given to the consumer,

---

108 Article 1(9) of the Trade Practices Act contains the following definition of working days: "all days other than Sundays and public holidays. If a period expressed in working days ends on a Saturday, the period is extended till the next working day".

109 After entry into force of the Consumer Code; previously 7 days.

110 Two weeks.

111 The law on doorstep selling refers to "7 days". According to CC, Art. 5(2), the period is deemed to be in calendar days unless it is specified otherwise in the law.

112 CC, Art. 65(3).

the withdrawal period does not start (i.e. there is no limitation on the right to withdraw from the contract). In the UNITED KINGDOM, if correct information is not given at the time the contract is concluded, the contract remains unenforceable against the consumer forever. This is, however, presumably subject to the doctrine of waiver/affirmation, although no case law is available.

b. Start of the withdrawal period

Art. 5 of Directive 85/577 states that the consumer shall have the right to renounce the effects of his undertaking by sending notice within not less than seven days from receipt of the information about the right to withdraw. The member states have laid down rather different provisions for the beginning of the period. For instance, in AUSTRIA, GERMANY and LITHUANIA, the withdrawal period starts upon receipt of the notice regarding the right of withdrawal. In IRELAND,[113] LATVIA and the CZECH REPUBLIC,[114] the period starts with the conclusion of the contract. In ESTONIAN and POLISH law, the withdrawal period begins with the conclusion of the contract if the consumer receives due notice before entering into the contract; if not, the withdrawal period begins upon receipt of the notice regarding the right of withdrawal. In CYPRUS, the period starts on the day following the date of conlusion of the contract or on the day the trader performs the contract, whichever comes last. In SLOVAKIA,[115] the period starts upon receipt of the goods or upon conclusion of the contract. SPANISH law provides for a period that is "seven days from receipt", which is rather unclear, because it could mean after receipt of the information or after receipt of the goods sold under the contract. Legal literature has criticised this gap, as have some courts, which have already ruled that the period begins upon receipt of the goods.[116] In other member states, only the date on which the contract is concluded is decisive, e.g. in BELGIUM,[117] FRANCE,[118] MALTA[119] and the UNITED KINGDOM (given that the information has been provided beforehand or simultaneously). DANISH law distinguishes between contracts under which the trader supplies goods and contracts under which services are provided. In the case of contracts for services, the withdrawal period begins upon conclusion of the contract. If the trader supplies goods, the withdrawal period starts upon their delivery. The same distinction is made in HUNGARY. However, where the goods are delivered after the contract is con-

---

113 Article 5(1) – and the Schedule containing a cancellation form – European Communities Regulations, 1989 (Cancellation of Contracts Negotiated away from Business Premises).

114 CC § 57(1), sent. 1.

115 § 7(1)(d) of Act 108/2000 on Consumer Protection in Doorstep Selling and Distance Selling.

116 SAP Madrid, 26 March 2002 Oscar M. O. v "Servicios Integrales de F., S. L:", and the Spanish Constitutional Court judgment of 30 September 1993, *obiter dicta* (5th legal reason). Most scholars agree (VÉRGEZ, 4038; BOTANA, *Contratos*, 252; GARCÍA VICENTE, 188-189, disagrees, supporting the day of receipt of the information).

117 The withdrawal period starts the day after the contract is signed (Trade Practices Act, Art. 88).

118 Consumer Code, Art. L. 121-25. According to case law, the withdrawal period starts on the day after the contract is concluded (Cour de cassation, Chambre criminelle, 5 October 1987, Recueil Dalloz, 1987, Informations Rapides, 236).

119 The CA explicitly ruled that the period begins from the date the contract is signed and not from when the goods are delivered to the consumer; judgment of 14 Jan 2002, 615/99SM Commonwealth Educational Society Limited vs Saviour and Bernardette Saliba.

cluded, it is from this delivery that the withdrawal period starts. Similar provisions can be found in SLOVENIA and SWEDEN. According to GREEK law, the consumer can exercise his right of withdrawal within 10 days from receipt of the written contract or, as the case may be, upon subsequent receipt of the goods. It is disputed whether the later event is always decisive, especially if the delivery of goods takes place more than ten days after receipt of the contract.[120]

Under ITALIAN law, the withdrawal period starts with the signing of an order form containing the information on the right of withdrawal. If no order form is used, the withdrawal period starts upon receipt of the information itself. Additionally, in the case of contracts for the supply of goods, the withdrawal period starts upon delivery of the goods where the contract has been concluded in the trader's absence, or where the product presented or demonstrated is different from the one in the contract. In FINLAND, the withdrawal period starts when the door-to-door selling document (set form) is supplied. There is a special provision concerning the sale of tangible goods according to which the withdrawal period begins with the delivery of the goods if this delivery is later than the receipt of the document.[121] Under GREEK law, the withdrawal period starts with the conclusion of the contract or, if goods are handed over at a later date, with the delivery of the goods to the consumer. An equivalent rule can be found in PORTUGAL. In the NETHERLANDS, the trader is obliged to register the contract at the *Kamer van Koophandel* (Chamber of Commerce). Therefore, the withdrawal period starts on the day of registration.

c. Postal Rule / Dispatching Rule

Contrary to the Distance Selling Directive, Directive 85/577 contains a provision specifying how the consumer can exercise the right of withdrawal within the time limit. Member States like AUSTRIA,[122] BELGIUM,[123] DENMARK, ESTONIA, GERMANY,[124] GREECE,[125] HUNGARY,[126] ITALY, LITHUANIA,[127] POLAND, PORTUGAL, SLOVAKIA,[128] SLOVENIA, SPAIN[129] and SWEDEN have included a dispatching rule. The FRENCH provisions do not contain a dispatching rule,

---

[120] In Greek literature, it is considered that, if the goods are delivered within ten days from receipt of the contract, the period of withdrawal will be extended by ten days. Where delivery of the goods takes place after the period of 10 days has expired (counting from receipt of the contract), it is disputed whether or not the consumer is given a new 10-day period counting from the delivery of goods.

[121] Consumer Protection Act, Art. 6(9).

[122] Consumer Protection Act, § 3(4).

[123] Trade Practices Act, Art. 88 and Art. 89(2).

[124] CC, § 355(1), sent. 2.

[125] It is recognised in academic literature that the period is guaranteed if the notice is dispatched before the end of the period (*Karakostas*, Dikaio Prostasias tou katanaloti, margin no. 206).

[126] Only in the case of written notice, § 4(3) of Government Decree 370/2004 (XII.26.) on Doorstep Selling.

[127] CC Art. 1.122(2).

[128] § 7(2) of Act 108/2000 on Consumer Protection in Doorstep Selling and Distance Selling.

[129] Article 5(1) 2nd indent of Law 26/1991.

but as the withdrawal notice must be sent by recorded delivery, the letter can be regarded as being served at the time of posting.

In the DUTCH[130] regulations on doorstep selling – and running counter to the general rule – the message is assumed to have reached the addressee when the letter is first given to him. In LATVIA, a postal rule is provided for under civil law. In IRELAND, there is a form of postal rule stipulating that the cancellation shall have effect from the date of delivery of the cancellation form by hand or the date on which it is posted. In CYPRUS[131] and the UNITED KINGDOM,[132] the transposition law contains a postal rule stating that the withdrawal notice sent by post shall be deemed to have been served at the time of posting, whether it has been received or not. A similar provision exists in FINLAND[133]: if the withdrawal notice is sent appropriately, it can be invoked even if it is delayed, altered or lost. This point could be clarified when reviewing the Directive, also with regard to the question of whether such a rule purely ensures the timeliness of the withdrawal (as in GERMANY) or whether it even makes a withdrawal valid should the declaration never reach the supplier (e.g. because the letter got lost after being dispatched), as in Cyprus, Finland and the United Kingdom.

In CZECH law, there is no postal or dispatching rule. In MALTA there is no dispatching rule either. The withdrawal can be exercised without any formal requirements. It is only necessary that the intention of the consumer is substantially conveyed to the trader. On the one hand, the term 'delivery' may be interpreted to mean that the notice only needs to be dispatched and not received. On the other hand, the requirement that the intention be conveyed to the consumer seems to imply that the door-to-door salesman must have actually received the notice.

d. Formal requirements

The formal requirements the consumer must fulfil when he exercises his right of withdrawal are not consistent in the member states' transposition laws. The following chart shows some of the differences.

Right of Withdrawal – Formal Requirements	Member State
None	DK,[134] EE,[135] FI, HU,[136] NL, MT, PT, ES, SE[137] *(9)*
Written	AT, CY, CZ[138], IE, LT, LV, PL[139], SK[140], SL, UK *(9)*

130 Doorstep Selling Law, Art. 25(4).

131 Article 8 of the Law for Consumer Contracts Concluded Away from Business Premises of 2000, L.13(I)/2000.

132 Regulation 4(7) of the Consumer Protection Regulations 1987 (Cancellation of Contracts concluded away from business premises).

133 Consumer Protection Act, Ch. 12 sec. (1)(c).

134 Article 19 of Act 451 of 9 June 2004 on certain consumer contracts.

135 Law of Obligations Act, Art. 49, 188.

136 Other forms are also possible, but the dispatching rule only applies in the case of use of a written notice, § 4(3) of Government Decree 370/2004 (XII.26.) on Doorstep Selling.

137 Article 4(5) of Regulation 2005:59.

138 CC § 57(1), sent 1.

Right of Withdrawal – Formal Requirements	Member State
Text form	DE *(1)*
Return of goods	DE, ES, FI (3)
Letter sent by recorded delivery	BE, FR, EL,[141] IT, LU *(5)*

In several member states, the right of withdrawal can be exercised without any formal requirements, e.g. in ESTONIA, FINLAND, HUNGARY, the NETHERLANDS, MALTA,[142] PORTUGAL, SPAIN[143] and SWEDEN. In BELGIUM, FRANCE, ITALY and LUXEMBOURG, the consumer has to inform the trader via a letter sent by recorded delivery. GREEK law also requires recorded delivery, but Greek literature and case law accepts a withdrawal without formal requirements as well. This is similar in PORTUGAL. Portuguese law presumes that the notice is always considered effective if it is sent by recorded delivery, but it is considered that case law would accept another notice mechanism if it could be proven that notice has been given. In other member states, a written notice has to be sent to the trader, e.g. in CYPRUS, the CZECH REPUBLIC, IRELAND, LATVIA,[144] LITHUANIA, POLAND, SLOVENIA and the UNITED KINGDOM. In LATVIA, the consumer additionally has to make a note on the withdrawal form in order to confirm receipt of the form. Besides a written notice, SLOVAKIAN law provides for the possibility to mutually agree other formal requirements for exercising the right of withdrawal in the contract. According to AUSTRIAN law, the consumer can withdraw from the contract by giving written notice. He may also send the contract to the trader with a withdrawal notice. Furthermore, a verbal withdrawal notice is possible if the trader agrees to this form of withdrawal.[145] In POLAND, the consumer is provided with a standard withdrawal form by the trader. Therefore, it can be assumed that the consumer should make use of this form, but it

139 As Article 3(1) of the Act requires the trader to provide the consumer with a standard form for the withdrawal notice, it appears that the consumer should make use of this standard form.

140 Other party agreements possible.

141 Greek literature and case law accept a withdrawal without formal requirements as well.

142 As a result of the amendments under Act XXVI of 2000, a consumer who wishes to cancel a doorstep contract – in contrast to the previous legal requirements – is obliged to substantially convey his intention of cancelling the contract within the 15-day period. This cancellation notice can be communicated either verbally or by telephone or fax, or be delivered by hand or ordinary or registered mail. There is no obligation on the consumer to use the cancellation form provided by the trader. For the purposes of the law as amended, it is enough if it is clear from the communication that the consumer is cancelling the contract. According to the judgment of the CA of 10 Mar 2004, 3/2003 Saviour u Patricia Muscat vs Commonwealth Educational Society Limited, the burden of proof lies with the trader. Only as far as the withdrawal from a contract in relation to the law before the 2000 amendments is concerned, can the consumer withdraw in accordance with the procedure established by that law, i.e. by using the cancellation form provided to him by the door-to-door salesman, and by delivering that form either personally or by registered mail to the trader. Qorti tal-Magistrati, judgment of 12 June 2003, 47/1999/1 Commonwealth Educational Society vs Victor Debono.

143 According to an Audiencia Provincial Asturias judgment of 15 Sept 2003, 369/2003 Laura v "Cambridge Institute 1908, S. L.", the withdrawal is also valid if it is exercised verbally within the period of seven days, particularly when the trader has failed to comply with his/her legal duty to provide a withdrawal form or document.

144 Consumer Rights Protection Law, Art. 12(4).

145 OGH judgment of 13 Feb 2002, 2 Ob 11/02k.

remains unclear whether he can also withdraw by other means. In GERMANY, the withdrawal notice has to be sent to the trader in text form. Moreover, in Germany, FINLAND (in the case of tangible goods[146]) and SPAIN, it is possible to withdraw from a contract by returning the goods to the trader. DANISH law equally does not require the consumer to send a cancellation notice, but to return the goods received before the cancellation period expires.

e. Effects of withdrawal

As the Directive only requires that, by exercising the right of withdrawal, the consumer is released from any obligations under the cancelled undertaking (Art. 5 para. 2), the member states have been given leeway to shape and specify their provisions. Art. 7 states explicitly that the effects of withdrawal shall be governed by national laws, particularly regarding the reimbursement of payments for goods or services provided and the return of goods received.

As the ECJ stated in its judgment *Schulte* and *Crailsheimer Volksbank*, it is up to the member states to regulate the effects of withdrawal – the transposition laws have to consider the aims of the Directive, essentially its *effet utile*.[147] More specific guidance has only been given by the ECJ in these judgments for the very specific case of credit contracts concluded for the financing of houses. The ECJ clarified that the Doorstep Selling Directive does not preclude:

- a requirement that a consumer who has exercised his right to cancel under the Directive must pay back the loan proceeds to the lender, even though, according to the scheme drawn up for the investment, the loan serves solely to finance the purchase of the immovable property and is paid directly to the vendor thereof;
- a requirement that the amount of the loan must be paid back immediately;
- national legislation requiring that, in the event of cancellation of a secured credit agreement, the consumer not only repay the amounts received under the agreement but also pay the lender interest at the market rate.

Thus, the differences between the member states are significant. For instance, AUSTRIA, the CZECH REPUBLIC, GERMANY, GREECE, LUXEMBOURG and SLOVENIA apply their general principles of the right to withdraw from a contract. The effects are – especially in AUSTRIA, the CZECH REPUBLIC,[148] GERMANY and GREECE – the mutual return of any contractual agreements performed by the parties, as well as the reimbursement of profits or payment of compensation where the products/services have been rendered obsolete. In Greece, the trader may not receive any payments as long as the period of withdrawal has not expired. Where a contract governs the provision of a service that has already been performed by the trader, Greek academic literature diverges on the question of whether the consumer must pay a market-linked refund in accordance with the costs he has saved, or whether the right of withdrawal can no longer be exercised.

---

146 Consumer Protection Act, Ch. 6 sec.(9).

147 ECJ, C-350/03 – *Schulte*, no. 69.

148 In addition, the contract is null and void from the beginning (CC sec. 48(2)) on the grounds of unjustified enrichment (CC sec. 457).

In BELGIUM, doorstep selling contracts are not regarded as having been concluded as long as the withdrawal period has not expired. In FRANCE,[149] no payments may be made, no goods delivered, nor services provided before the 7-day withdrawal period has expired. According to LITHUANIAN[150] law, the consumer is released from the contract and the trader obliged to take back the goods delivered and to reimburse the sums paid by the consumer. In DENMARK, MALTA, PORTUGAL, POLAND and SLOVAKIA,[151] the consumer is equally released from the contract in the case of withdrawal. The consumer has to return any goods received and the payments have to be reimbursed. In SLOVAKIA, the goods must be returned within 7 days. The trader must then take back the goods and refund the sums paid within 15 days. In POLAND, the goods should be returned as soon as possible, but not later than 14 days. The goods have to be returned unaltered unless an alteration or change was necessary. The trader has to pay statutory interest on the consumer's payments that are to be reimbursed. In PORTUGAL, the return period is 30 calendar days, starting with the delivery of the goods. It is worth noting that, in DENMARK, the consumer is obliged to return the goods to the trader *before* the cancellation period expires in order to benefit from the right of withdrawal. In order to fulfil this requirement, it is sufficient that the consumer has delivered the goods to a courier who transports them back to the trader.[152] Under Danish law, the consumer is liable for reshipment costs. ITALIAN law releases the consumer from the contract. However, the consumer has to return the goods within 7 days (at his own cost), while the trader has to reimburse the purchase price within 30 days. Consequently, only the trader may exercise the *exceptio inadimpleti* (CC, Art. 1460), while, after exercising the right of withdrawal, the consumer bears any risk of deterioration until the purchase price is reimbursed (CC, Art. 1177).[153] According to ESTONIAN law, the trader shall reimburse the purchase price to the consumer immediately after the withdrawal, but never more than thirty days thereafter. This is in contrast to SWEDEN, where the trader is obliged to collect the goods from where they have been delivered and the consumer is entitled to the reimbursement of his money within a period of 30 days. In FINLAND, the consumer is released from any contractual obligations and the trader has to reimburse the purchase price. The consumer has to make the goods or other returnable services provided available for the trader at the place to which they have been delivered. If the trader does not collect the goods, the consumer's duty to keep the goods on behalf of the trader expires two months after withdrawal. Nevertheless, the trader and the consumer may stipulate in the contract terms that goods delivered by mail have to be returned by the consumer. In LATVIA, the consumer must return the goods to the seller at the location where the goods were received. The consumer may also return the goods to another location specified by him, provided that this does not cause any inconvenience to the trader. The trader has to reimburse all the payments made by the consumer.

Under GERMAN law, the consumer has to compensate for any depreciation in value if he is not able to return the goods or services supplied to him or if the condition of the goods has

---

149 CC Art. L.121-26.

150 Law on Consumer Protection, Art. 15(4); CC, Art 6.357(9).

151 The contract is null and void from the beginning.

152 Article 19(2) of Act 451 of 9 June 2004 on certain consumer contracts.

153 A. *Stoppa*, Le vendite negoziate fuori di locali commerciali, in: C.M. *Bianca*, La vendita e la permuta, 181; M. *Cartella*, La disciplina di contratti negoziati fuori di locali commerciali, in: Giur. Comm, 1992, I, 740.

deteriorated.[154] The consumer has to compensate for depreciations in value even if the deterioration has only been caused by the contractual use of the goods, provided that the consumer has been advised about this duty by the trader.[155] The consumer can be made liable for reshipment costs under the terms of the contract if the value of the goods does not exceed EUR 40. Under LITHUANIAN law, the consumer may exercise his right of withdrawal only if the goods received from the trader have not been damaged or their appearance has not been substantially altered. This provision might inhibit the consumer in exercising his right of withdrawal. HUNGARIAN law states that, after withdrawal, the parties have to return any goods received or other contractual agreements performed. The consumer has to compensate for any depreciation in value only where he has defaulted on the contract. If the consumer is not able to return any goods received in full or if services have already been performed in full, it is not possible to withdraw from the contract. In contrast to these rather restrictive provisions, the consumer is entitled to keep the goods received in CYPRUS and SWEDEN even if he has exercised his right of withdrawal. This is subject to the trader's not requesting the goods within a period of 21 days (Cyprus) and three months (Sweden). In Cyprus, the consumer can treat the goods as an unconditional gift after another period of 21 days has expired. The consumer is entitled to keep the goods and deal with them as he likes if the trader has not requested their return within a total of 42 days from the day the right of withdrawal is exercised. Under SPANISH law, the consumer does not have to compensate for any depreciation in value if the goods have only been used in accordance with the terms of the contract.[156]

In IRELAND, the contract is rendered null and void on cancellation, so that any sum paid by the consumer to the trader is subject to provisions governing unjustified enrichment. The trader is obliged to collect the goods at a reasonable time and place, as specified by the consumer. In the NETHERLANDS, the consumer is released from all obligations. As a result, any contractual agreements performed have to be returned. In the UNITED KINGDOM and IRELAND, the reimbursement of the purchase price is secured by a lien, which the consumer has on the goods that have been supplied under the contract. The consumer is obliged to make the goods available for collection from his home and to take reasonable care of those goods. In Ireland,[157] if the trader has not returned all monies due, ownership rights for the goods pass to the consumer three months after the date on which the consumer has delivered or posted the cancellation notice.

It should be noted that such differences in national provisions in terms of the length and the beginning of the withdrawal period and the effects of withdrawal may cause a barrier to trade, because the trader, who has to inform the consumer of his withdrawal right, may have to adapt this information to comply with respective national laws. It is therefore impossible to draft a notice for cross-border use.

---

154 CC § 346(2).

155 CC § 357(3) sent. 1.

156 Article 2(1)(7)(c) of the Law 26/1991 of November 21 on consumer protection in the case of contracts performed outside commercial premises.

157 Article 6(4) European Communities Regulations, 1989 (Cancellation of Contracts negotiated away from business premises).

3. Other consumer protection instruments in the field of doorstep selling

As the right of withdrawal is the only consumer protection instrument Directive 85/577 provides for, many, if not all, member states have enacted other protection instruments applicable in the field of doorstep selling. A few examples may illustrate this. SLOVAKIA, for instance, has introduced a time limit for doorstep selling activities (working days: from 8 A.M. to 7 P.M.; non-working days: from 10 A.M. to 3 P.M.),[158] and additionally requires the trader to be licensed. In MALTA, a licence is necessary, too. Operating as a door-to-door salesman without a licence is an offence and, on conviction, the salesman is liable to a fine and/or imprisonment. Furthermore, a person who calls at a consumer's home or place of work to negotiate a doorstep contract and refuses to leave when so requested is guilty of an offence and, on conviction, liable to a fine. In FRENCH law, a ban on doorstep selling applies to contracts related to legal consultation, the drafting of legal documents, as well as to distance learning. HUNGARIAN law prohibits the sale of the following goods in doorstep selling situations: products subject to excise duties, seeds, drugs and medication, pesticides, flammable products, hazardous waste, precious metals and stones (also jewellery), food (except for fruit and vegetables), and goods prohibited by other legislative acts.[159] The ECJ has frequently ruled in the course of its *Keck* case law that such provisions concerning pure selling arrangements do not infringe Art. 28 EC Treaty, as long as the provisions do not affect products from other member states more than they affect domestic products.[160] However, the recent example of the ECJ case, C-441/04 – *A-Punkt-Schmuckhandel*, shows that such provisions may, in practical terms, hinder cross-border business. In this case, a trader sold jewellery in a private home in Austria and thereby infringed an Austrian provision prohibiting the sale of silver jewellery in a doorstep situation. The seller, a company with headquarters in Germany, sold jewellery itinerantly in different EU countries and relied on the fact that the sale of silver jewellery in private homes was legal in, for example, GERMANY, ITALY or the UNITED KINGDOM. The upshot of this situation is that a trader cannot expand his business model throughout Europe.

In BELGIUM, alongside section 11 (Doorstep Selling) of the Trade Practices Act, there are two other Acts[161] containing consumer protection measures in the field of doorstep selling. The scope is mainly (but not exclusively) focused on market fairs and fairground activities. The trader and his representatives must be licensed.[162] Furthermore, the itinerant sale of certain goods is prohibited (medicines, medical and orthopaedic devices, products normally sold by an optician, precious metals and stones (also jewellery), weapons and ammunition)[163] and there is a time limit on doorstep selling activities, which must be conducted between 8 a.m. and 8 p.m.[164]

---

158 Article 5(1) of Act 108/2000 on Consumer Protection in Doorstep Selling and Distance Selling.

159 Article 1(1) of Government Decree 370/2004 (XII.26.) on Doorstep Selling.

160 See, as a recent example, the ECJ case C-441/04 – *A-Punkt-Schmuckhandel*.

161 Act of 25 June 1993 on the Practice and the Organisation of Itinerant and Fairground Activities (Itinerant Trade Act) and the Royal Decree of 24 September 2006 on the Exercise and the Organisation of Itinerant Activities.

162 Itinerant Trade Act, Art. 3 and Royal Decree on Itinerant Activities, Art. 20-22.

163 Royal Decree on Itinerant Activities, Art. 5.

164 Royal Decree on Itinerant Activities, Art. 19.

Further consumer protection instruments may become applicable as a result of other EC measures. Contracts concluded in doorstep situations may also fall under other consumer protection directives containing information requirements (e.g. Consumer Credit) or a right of withdrawal (e.g. Timeshare). In its judgment C-423/97 – *Travel* VAC, No. 23, the ECJ ruled that, in general, such directives are applicable in parallel, unless there is a provision which rules out the application of other directives. An example of such a provision can be found in Art. 13 of the Distance Selling Directive. Like most of the other directives, Directive 85/577 does not contain any such provision. It is therefore unclear to what extent the different information requirements provided for under the relevant directives, and different particulars pertaining to the right of withdrawal (if any), might impinge on the application of Directive 85/577.

Bibliography

Discussion Paper on the Review of Directive 85/577/EEC to protect the consumer in respect of contracts negotiated away from business premises, **http://ec.europa.eu/consumers/ cons_int/safe_shop/door_sell/doorstepselling_discussionpaper.pdf**; Study on Door to Door Selling – Pyramid Selling – Multi Level Marketing, **http://ec.europa.eu/consumers/ cons_int/ safe_shop/door_sell/sur10_01.pdf**; Report of the Hearing on 15-16 March 2000 on Door to Door selling – Pyramid selling – Multi level marketing, **http: //ec.europa.eu/consumers/ cons_int/safe_shop/door_sell/door02_en.pdf**;
Ajani, Gianmaria/Rossi, Piercarlo, Codice del consumatori, 2005, **Badenas Carpio, Juan Manuel/Boldó Roda, Carmen,** Régimen jurídico de la llamada "venta directa" Las ventas domiciliarias y a distancia, Valencia 2003, **Benda, Vladimír,** Ochrana spotrebiteľa pri predaji v obchode, podomovom obchode a pri zmluvách uzatváraných mimo miesta podnikania, Thesis – Department of Civil law,Faculty of Law of Comenius University in Bratislava, Bratislava 2000, **Georgiades, Olga**, Sale of Goods in Cyprus Following Harmonisation with the Acquis Communautaire and Consumer Protection, Nicosia 2005, **Holberg, Benedikte/ Kristensen, Lene Pagter/Møgelvang-Hansen, Peter/Nielsen, Tina Morell/Øe, Henrik,** Forbrugeraftaleloven, Copenhagen 2006, **Howells, Geraint/Weatherill, Stephen,** Consumer Protection Law, Aldershot 2005, **Hulva, Tomáš**, Ochrana spotřebitele, Praha 2005, **Łętowska, Ewa**, Prawo umów konsumenckich, Warszawa 2002, **Macrì, Carmine**, Contratti negoziati fuori dai locali commerciali, Torino 1998, **Micklitz, Hans-W.**, Europäisches Verbraucherrecht, Baden-Baden 2003, **Micklitz, Hans-W.**, Richtlinie 85/577/EWG des Rates betreffend den Verbraucherschutz im Fall von außerhalb von Geschäftsräumen abgeschlossenen Verträgen (Haustürwiderrufsrichtlinie), in: Grabitz/Hilf, Das Recht der Europäischen Union, Loseblatt, Band III, A 2, München 1999, **Rott, Peter**, Die Umsetzung der Haustürwiderrufsrechtlinie in den Mitgliedstaaten, Baden-Baden 2000, **Skorini, Paparigopoulou X.**, I prostasia tou katanaloti sti simbasi ektos emporikou katastimatos,1999, **Sporne, Ilva**, Par atteikuma tiesībām patērētāju līgumos, Jurista Vārds 2001, **Vargová, Zuzana**, Implementácia Smernice 85/577/EHS na ochranu spotrebiteľa v súvislosti so zmluvami uzatvorenými mimo miesta podnikania do slovenského a rakúskeho právneho poriadku, Thesis – Department of International a European law,Faculty of Law of Comenius University in Bratislava, Bratislava 2003, **Wiedmann, Thomas,** Haustürgeschäfte (§§ 312, 312a, 355 ff. BGB), in: Gebauer/ Wiedmann, Zivilrecht unter europäischem Einfluss, Kap. 6, Stuttgart 2005.

B. Package Travel Directive (90/314)

Drafted by Hans Schulte-Nölke and Leonie Meyer-Schwickerath

Executive Summary

1. Transposition deficiencies

Although the Directive has been transposed in all member states, the analysis has revealed many transposition deficiencies with regard to some of the details. The following examples could constitute potentially significant transposition deficiencies:

- No duty to include in the brochure the deadline for informing the consumer in the event of cancellation where the minimum number of participants is not reached in SWEDEN (Art. 3(2)(g)).
- Duty to provide information about passport and visa requirements only for own citizens (CZECH REPUBLIC), citizens or residents (CYPRUS), citizens of the member state where the package is offered (AUSTRIA, GERMANY). This is contrary to Art. 4(1)(a) of the Directive, which requires this information with regard to all nationals of the member state(s) concerned.
- No formal requirement regarding the information to be given before the start of the journey (Art. 4(1)(b)) in ESTONIA and Germany.
- No requirement for details to be provided about the place to be occupied by the traveller (Art. 4(1)(b) no. (i)) in Czech and ITALIAN law.
- Delaying the point at which the necessary elements of the contract must be communicated in Austrian and German law (instead of "before conclusion of the contract" as stated in Art. 4(2)(b), the confirmation document including certain elements must be handed over to the traveller "at or immediately after conclusion of the contract").
- Several member states still have limitations on the insurance sum to be paid despite the ECJ ruling in the *Rechberger* case.

2. Enhancement of protection

a. Extension of scope

Some national laws provide for a wider scope in the field of package travel, for example by broadening the:

- Notion of 'organiser' (Art. 2(2)); e.g. inclusion of persons operating occasionally.
- Notion of 'package' (Art. 2(1)); e.g. extension to travel contracts containing only one service, extension to combined trips of a duration of less than 24 hours or without overnight accommodation.

b. Use of minimum clause

Most member states made use of the minimum clause. Key examples are listed below:

- Art. 3(2): additional requirements concerning the brochure (e.g. manifold additional information to be included, compulsory provision of a brochure).
- Art. 4(1)(a): additional information requirements before conclusion of the contract (e.g. optional insurance, price of the package, security for money paid in the event of insolvency).
- Art. 4(1)(b): increase in information requirements before the start of the journey.
  - Additional information requirements (e.g. details of the package).
  - Setting a time limit for provision of this information (e.g. at the latest 7 calendar days before departure).
- Art. 4(2): additional elements to be included in the contract (e.g. conditions for cancellation by the traveller or organiser and/or retailer, maximum amounts for possible claims by the agency); stricter formal requirements for the contract (e.g. only "in writing" instead of also "such other form as is comprehensible and accessible to the consumer").
- Art. 5: liability (e.g. extension of compulsory cover for the organiser/retailer, direct insurance claim for the consumer against the insurer in cases of improper performance or non-performance of the contract, even where the organiser/retailer is not insolvent).
- Art. 5(4): no transposition of the provision requiring that the consumer communicate any failure in the performance.
- Art. 7: additional refund (e.g. other needs resulting from non-performance).

3. Use of options

The majority of member states made use of the options provided for in the Directive:

- Art. 5(2) sent. 4 (scope for limiting compensation in accordance with international conventions) has been transposed by the vast majority of member states *(21)*.
- Art. 5(2) sent. 4 (scope for limiting compensation under the terms of the contract for damages other than personal injury) has also been transposed by the majority of member states *(18)*, but with great variations in detail.

4. Inconsistencies or ambiguities

Some potentially significant inconsistencies or ambiguities in the Directive are:

- The use of the term 'pre-arranged' in the definition of 'package' (Art. 2(1)) is misleading because the ECJ (C-400/00 – *Club-Tour*) has clarified that combinations of tourist services tailored by a travel agency to the specific requests of the consumer are also covered.
- The notion of 'organiser' (Art. 2(2)) does not tally with the commonly used definition of "acting professionally in the course of his business" and also includes private persons and not-for-profit organisations; the exact meaning of acting "occasionally" is unclear.
- The notion of 'consumer' (Art. 2(4)) deviates substantively from the definition in the other consumer protection directives.
- By using the wording 'organiser and/or retailer', the Directive did not clearly decide whether the organiser, the retailer or both carry obligations vis-á-vis the consumer. This decision is left to the member states' discretion. They have to ensure that at least one of

the two is liable in any case. The member states' transposition laws do not only show great differences, but have also created many uncertainties. Especially in those member states that provided for a different and separate liability for the organiser and the retailer (with each of them being liable for problems occurring in their respective spheres), it may be rather unclear who is liable for what.

- Unclear formal requirements for the information due under Art. 4(1)(a) and (b) ("in writing or any other appropriate form").
- Unclear formal requirements for the contract in Art. 4(2) ("in writing or such other form as is comprehensible and accessible to the consumer"; "copy of these terms").
- It is unclear whether exemptions from information requirements in the case of last-minute contracts are applicable only with regard to Art 4(2)(b), or also with regard to other information duties (in particular Art. 4(1)).
- The wording in Art. 4(3) ("having given the organiser 'or' the retailer reasonable notice") does not clarify whether the member states or the consumer may choose the addressee. Moreover, it is unclear whether "reasonable notice" just refers to a reasonable period of time, and indeed how long such a period should be.
- It is unclear whether Art. 4(4) ("upward 'or' downward revision") requires transposition to deal with both possibilities (and not only with the possibility to increase [and not to decrease] the price).
- The use of the term "withdrawal" in Art. 4(5) and (6) may be confused with the 'cooling-off periods' provided for in other Directives, which are commonly described as a "right of withdrawal".
- In Art. 4(7), it is unclear whether the duty to compensate the consumer "where appropriate" constitutes an independent specific liability rule or just refers to the general rule in Art. 5(2) of the Directive.
- Art. 5 does not explicitly state that – according to the ruling of the ECJ in the *Simone Leitner* case – the consumer must also have a right to compensation for non-material damage and, in particular, that such compensation can arise from the loss of enjoyment the consumer has suffered because of the improper performance of the travel contract.

5. Gaps in the Directive

The analysis of the way in which the Directive has been transposed in the member states did not reveal substantial gaps. Although some member states broadened the scope of their travel laws in different respects, these findings do not lead to the conclusion that there is an urgent need to extend the scope of the Directive. However, some contributors suggested some extensions to the scope (e.g. one-day trips, conferences, flights) or new protection instruments (e.g. the insertion of general rules on cancellation fees if the consumer cancels without a justified reason).

6. Potential barriers to (cross-border) trade

The following examples are quite likely to cause barriers to trade in the European market:

- Additional elements to be included in the brochure (Art. 3(2)) or the contract (Art. 4(2)) diverging across different member states.

- Additional information to be provided before the contract is concluded (Art. 4(1)(a)) and before the start of the journey (Art. 4(1)(b)).
- Stricter formal requirements in member states with regard to the information due under Art. 4(1) (e.g. information must solely be "in writing").
- Stricter formal requirements in member states with regard to the contract pursuant to Art. 4(2)(b) (e.g. contract must solely be set out "in writing").
- Substantial differences in member states' laws concerning the possibility to limit compensation in the case of damages resulting from non-performance or improper performance of services included in the package. These differences leave organisers and retailers who want to market package tours in several member states practically no choice other than to refrain from agreeing any compensation limits.
- Substantial differences in the obligations for retailers in member states. These mean, on the one hand, that, in some member states, all the organiser's duties are imposed upon retailers who sell packages for foreign organisers and, on the other hand, that a consumer who purchases a package organised by a foreign organiser in his home country might only have the right to claim against the foreign organiser (although, under Art. 5 of the Rome Convention, this is generally governed by the law of the country in which the consumer has his habitual residence).

7. Conclusions and recommendations

In order to remove ambiguities, inconsistencies or barriers to trade, the following issues could be considered:

- Definition of 'package': inclusion of tailor-made packages offered by travel agencies according to the ECJ ruling in *Club-Tour*. This would mean deleting the misleading term "pre-arranged"; should there be a political decision to extend the scope, this could, in particular, include packages with a duration of less than 24 hours or without overnight accommodation.
- Definition of 'consumer': bringing the definition into line with other definitions in EC consumer law.
- Definition of 'organiser': bringing the definition into line with other definitions of "professional" or "supplier" in EC contract law, thereby also deleting the phrase "other than occasionally".
- Clarification that the organiser is obliged and liable in all cases and that it is left to member states to determine whether the retailer is jointly liable.
- Definition of the terms "in writing" or "any other appropriate form" in Art. 4(1)(a) and (b), as well as of "in writing or such other form as is comprehensible and accessible to the consumer" and "copy of these terms" in Art. 4(2), thereby possibly making use of the definition of "another durable medium" as per Art. 2(f) of Directive 2002/65. This would also adapt the Directive to the requirements of e-commerce.
- Clarification of whether, in the case of last-minute contracts, exemptions from information requirements may also be permissible with regard to Art. 3(2) (brochure) and Art. 4(1)(a) (information to be provided before conclusion of contract).
- Clarification that the wording in Art. 4(3) ("having given the organiser 'or' the retailer reasonable notice") leaves the choice of addressee to the consumer (and not to the member states); moreover, clarification of whether "reasonable notice" just refers to a reasonable period for giving notice, and of how long such a period should be; finally,

clarification that member states do not have to introduce a formal requirement (e.g. in writing) for the notice.
- Clarification that the transposition of Art. 4(4) ("upward 'or' downward revision") must deal with both possibilities (replacement of 'or' by 'and').
- Clarification of whether in Art. 4(7) the duty to compensate the consumer "where appropriate" constitutes an independent specific liability rule or just refers to the general rule in Art. 5(2) of the Directive.
- Clarification that Art. 5 also grants a right to compensation for non-material damage, in particular, that such compensation can arise from the loss of enjoyment (*Simone Leitner*).
- Regulation of the possibility to contractually limit compensation in the case of damages resulting from non-performance or improper performance of services included in the package in Art. 5(2).
- Insertion of a general provision obliging member states to ensure that adequate and effective means exist to ensure compliance with the Directive in the interests of consumers.

In order to ensure that the member states can no longer introduce or maintain additional protection instruments and thereby create barriers to trade, it might be worth considering full harmonisation in the most sensitive areas like pre-contractual information duties, brochures and formal requirements for information duties. This might also cover contractual exclusion clauses.

I. Member state legislation prior to the adoption of the Package Travel Directive

Prior to the adoption of Directive 90/314, only a few European countries had directly legislated in the field of travel contracts. Of course, general rules and principles of contract law (e.g. with regard to the quality of the goods or services provided, information duties, doctrine of misrepresentation) were applicable to package travel agreements, *inter alia*, in AUSTRIA, DENMARK, FINLAND, IRELAND, LATVIA,[165] MALTA,[166] the NETHERLANDS, POLAND, SLOVAKIA and the UNITED KINGDOM.

Some member states had individual acts regulating travel contracts. However, national rules in this area differed substantially, both in terms of coverage and detail. In 1973 and 1977, ITALY ratified the International Convention on Travel Contracts (CCV). This convention provided comparable consumer protection to that afforded under the Directive with regard to the travel organiser's liability.[167] In BELGIUM, travel contracts were also regulated by the

[165] Until the adoption of the Tourism Law on 17 September 1998, no special regulation existed regarding tourism and package travel contracts. Thus, the Civil Law "Law of Obligations" applied as general legal rules for the particular contractual relationships.

[166] Prior to the Package Travel Regulations enacted in 2000 in order to transpose Directive 90/314, no specific rules existed and the primary rules of contract law in the Maltese CC were applicable.

[167] Directive 90/314 was initially implemented by Decree 111 of 17 March 1995 concerning "all-inclusive" travel packages, holidays and excursions. The field of package travel is now regulated in Art. 82 et seq. of the Consumer Code.

CCV and, in certain respects, by the Trade Practices Act.[168] The latter banned misleading information and listed in detail the information the consumer had to be provided with. In FRANCE, there were some regulations comparable to those in Directive 90/314 concerning information duties, pricing, reimbursement requirements, organiser's liability and the travel guarantee fund.

Before the Directive was transposed, SLOVENIAN law had, in general, similar provisions to those currently in force. The current Code of Obligations is based on the former Law of Obligations and only minor insertions were needed in order to achieve compliance with the Directive. Whereas GREEK legislation obliged travel agencies to provide the consumer with a minimum level of information, which had to be signed by both contractual parties, HUNGARIAN law only regulated the financial aspects of package travel in two decrees. These included provisions for cover in the event of the organiser's insolvency to be provided via insurance payments or cash deposits.

PORTUGUESE law had already had for some time specific rules dealing with travel organised within its borders, although these did not give any definition of a 'consumer', but used the term client instead.[169] In SPAIN, before the introduction of the Directive, administrative regulations governing package travel contracts were in place, but no private law existed in this field. Nevertheless, the administrative regulations had some impact in private law, since they were included in travel contracts concluded under the general rules governing contracts for accommodation, transport or service hire.

In 1979, GERMANY introduced a sub-chapter on package travel contracts in §§ 651a-k of the Civil Code. However, these provisions did not afford the same standard of consumer protection as the Directive because, for instance, they did not lay down many information requirements, nor any effective security provisions should the tour organiser become insolvent.

Non-binding guidelines in the field of package travel existed in AUSTRIA, DENMARK, FINLAND and SWEDEN. The Austrian "general travel conditions", partially regulating the Directive's content (e.g. information duties, conditions for a price revision), received the status of "soft law" and could be voluntarily respected by travel agencies and organisers. Moreover, a legal duty to indicate the acceptance of all or some of the conditions was imposed on the organiser. In Denmark, guidelines on travel advertisements were issued by a Consumer Ombudsman under the Marketing Practices Act, while problems could be brought before the Travel Arbitration Court, a private complaints board. The Finnish Consumer Agency produced non-binding guidelines concerning the marketing of package travel, which included especially detailed provisions on information brochures and pre-contractual information. Despite its non-binding character, any marketing material contravening the guidelines could be deemed an unfair commercial practice as defined in Chapter 2 of the Consumer Protection Act.[170] Moreover, the Consumer Protection Act was also applicable to travel packages, thus meaning that the general marketing provisions also applied to the regulation and amendment of contract terms. In Austria, a "Travel Guarantee Fund" was created in 1986 and could be joined on a voluntary basis. In Denmark, a comparable fund was estab-

---

168 Trade Practices Act of 14 July 1991.

169 Rules amended by the time of accession by Decree-Law 264/86.

170 Consumer Protection Act 20.1.1978/38.

lished by an Act of Parliament in 1979, and in Finland, under the Travel Agency Regulation, travel agencies were obliged to pledge collateral in order to refund customers in the event of insolvency. Sweden indirectly protected consumers via general agreements on package travel negotiated by the Swedish Consumer Agency with the major Swedish travel organisations. Any violation of these agreements by a professional was deemed unfair, meaning that the provisions on unfair consumer contracts were applicable.

II. Scope of application

1. Consumer

The definition of a 'consumer' in Directive 90/314 deviates substantively from the definition commonly used in other consumer protection directives.[171] The consumer is usually characterised as a "natural person acting for purposes outside his/her professional activity". The definition of 'consumer' used in Art. 2(4) of the Directive is, however, divided into three parts: any "person who takes or agrees to take the package ('the principal contractor') (...) any person on whose behalf the principal contractor agrees to purchase the package ('the other beneficiaries') or any person to whom the principal contractor or any of the other beneficiaries transfers the package ('the transferee')".

Unusually, the notion of 'consumer' is not explicitly limited to "natural" persons, but includes any person taking the package. Thus, the Directive's notion of a 'consumer' seems to encompass legal persons as well as tradesmen concluding a contract for business purposes.

a. Transposition in general

In transposing the Directive, the vast majority of member states integrated the definition into a special Act. Only some countries included the definition in existing legislation, namely GERMANY and the NETHERLANDS in their Civil Codes and ITALY in its Consumer Code. The majority of member states adopted the structure of the Directive's definition. However, about a quarter of member states have not used any definition, but refer only to the main contracting party.

Table: Use of the definition's elements

Tripartite definition	AT, CY, CZ,[172] DK, EL, ES, FI, IE, IT, MT, NL, PL, SE, SK, UK *(15)*
Bipartite definition (main contract partner and other beneficiaries)	BE, LV *(2)*
Single definition (main contract partner)	HU, LT *(2)*
No legal definition at all	EE, FR, DE, LU, PT, SL *(6)*

171 For more detail, see Part 3.A.

172 Seemingly, some changes have been made in the regulation of package travel. This may lead to some amendments with regard to the information about the CZECH REPUBLIC.

The term 'consumer' has only been used in some member states (e.g. CYPRUS, GREECE, IRELAND, MALTA, SPAIN and the UNITED KINGDOM[173]). Two thirds of member states have used a different term in implementing the Directive. The terms used in lieu of 'consumer' vary from 'traveller' (e.g. AUSTRIA, ESTONIA, GERMANY, the NETHERLANDS, SWEDEN), 'purchaser' (FRANCE, LUXEMBOURG, SLOVAKIA), and 'customer' (the CZECH REPUBLIC, DENMARK, POLAND[174]), to 'client' (LATVIA, PORTUGAL) and 'tourist' (LITHUANIA).

It is evident that many member states have tried to avoid the term 'consumer' in the field of Package Travel in order not to contradict the commonly used notion of consumer. EC law apparently uses the notion of 'consumer' inconsistently and leaves it up to member states to find a solution for transposing the different content of the term. Sometimes, national legislation therefore also uses the 'consumer' definition inconsistently. As such, it is not easy to identify a general scheme or principle throughout the EU determining who is actually protected in the field of Package Travel.

Table: Use of terms

Consumer	CY, EL, ES, IE, IT, MT, UK *(7)*
Traveller	AT, BE, DE, EE, FI, HU, NL, SE, SL *(9)*
Purchaser	FR, LU, SK *(3)*
Customer	CZ, DK, PL *(3)*
Client	LV, PT *(2)*
Tourist	LT *(1)*

b. Transposition in particular

Despite variations in the wording, the majority of national laws seem to mirror largely the content of the Directive's definition and, especially, seem to include its second and third parts. About one third of member states have not legally defined the notion of 'consumer', but rather refer only to the contracting party ('traveller', 'purchaser' or 'passenger') without further clarification (e.g. GERMANY, FRANCE, LUXEMBOURG, SLOVENIA).

173 Regulation 2(2) of the Package Travel, Package Holidays and Package Tour Regulations 1992 modifies the meaning of 'consumer' (i.e. different for the definition of 'contract') and is also used as shorthand ("as the context requires").

174 In the latest version of the Act on Tourist Services of 29 August 1997 in force since 1 January 2006, there is still no definition of 'consumer'. Instead, the Act uses three notions: 'tourist', 'visitor' and 'customer', the latter being defined as a person who enters into a contract that is not part of his economic activity (Art. 3(11): a person who, acting outside the scope of his business, is willing to conclude, or has concluded, a contract for tourist services in his own name or on behalf of another person; a person for whom such a contract has been concluded or a person to whom the rights to use the tourist services under the contract concluded previously have been transferred).

Table: Transposition method

	The principal contractor	The other beneficiaries	The transferee
Substantively equivalent to the Directive	AT,[175] BE, CY, CZ, DK, EL, ES, FI,[176] HU, IE, IT, LV, MT, NL, SE, SK, UK *(17)*	AT, BE, CY, CZ, DK, EL, FI, IE, IT, MT, NL, SK, SE, UK *(14)*	AT, BE, CY, CZ, DK, EL, FI, IE, IT, MT, NL, SK, UK *(13)*
Variations	LT, PL *(2)*	ES, PL *(2)*	ES, PL *(2)*
Not explicitly transposed		HU, LT, LV *(3)*	HU, LT, LV, SE *(4)*
No legal definition at all	DE, EE, FR, LU, PT,[177] SL[178] *(6)*		

aa. The principal contractor

In contrast to the Directive, POLAND excludes professionals from the definition, thus possibly contradicting the Directive's definition. GERMAN law[179] only mentions the 'traveller' as one of the contracting parties, i.e. a person concluding a travel contract in his/her own name, even though he/she does not make use of the travel service his/herself. This is essentially the same in the CZECH REPUBLIC and the NETHERLANDS[180], where the 'traveller' is simply the other party to the contract. In FRANCE[181] and LUXEMBOURG[182], the law only mentions the notion of 'purchaser', whereas HUNGARIAN[183] and ESTONIAN[184] law opt for the term 'traveller'. In SLOVAKIA, the 'purchaser' is a person who concludes a contract with the travel bureau. LITHUANIA introduces a new definition, which deviates significantly from the 'consumer' definition in the Directive. Lithuanian law[185] uses the term 'tourist', defined as "a natural person who, for family, professional, business, ethnic, cultural, recreational, health, religious or special reasons, travels within a country or other countries and remains for at least one night, but no longer than one year, outside his permanent place of residence if this is not for the purposes of study or paid work".

---

175 Consumer Protection Act, § 31b(2)(3). Furthermore, § 2 no. 4 and no. 5 of the Regulation on travel agencies implementing Art. 7 of the Directive 90/314 explicitly limits the notion of traveller to persons who make the booking.

176 According to the explanatory memorandum of the law, the definition of 'traveller' covers all three parts of the definition.

177 Portuguese law uses exclusively the term 'client'.

178 In Slovenian law, no explicit definition of a 'consumer' is given; it only mentions the rights and obligations of the 'passenger/traveller' without further explanation. It is accepted, that, under the Code of Obligations, the traveller might be any person (therefore the traveller-organiser relationship is not limited to the consumer-professional relationship).

179 CC § 651a(1).

180 CC Book 7 Art. 500(1)(a).

181 Tourism Code, Art. L 211-11.

182 Package Travel Act, Art. 8.

183 In Hungarian legislation, the principal contractor is referred to as the 'traveller'.

184 Law of Obligations Act, Art. 866(1).

185 Law on Tourism, Art. 2(14).

Table: National transposition

Substantively equivalent to the Directive	AT, BE,[186] CY, CZ, DK, EL, ES,[187] FI, HU, IE, IT, LV, MT, NL, SE, SK, UK *(17)*
Variations: exclusion of professionals	PL *(1)*
Variations: concept of tourist	LT *(1)*
No legal definition at all	DE, EE, FR, LU, PT, SL[188] *(6)*

bb. The other beneficiaries

About half of member states have introduced a similar notion of 'the other beneficiaries' into their concept of consumer. Again, POLISH law explicitly excludes professionals, whereas SPANISH law deliberately omitted legal persons from the definition. LATVIAN law uses a different expression from the one in the Directive: anyone who purchases a package tourism service on behalf of a third person is protected instead of "on whose behalf the principal contractor agrees to purchase the package" as per the Directive's definition.[189] In a number of member states (ESTONIA, FRANCE, GERMANY, LUXEMBOURG, PORTUGAL, SLOVENIA), there is no legal transposition of this part of the definition. In Germany, only persons with their own claim are explicitly mentioned. Nevertheless, because the concept of a contract for the benefit of a third party is applied, even those without their own rights (such as travelling relatives), are protected. SWEDISH law[190] defines "anyone who purchases a package tour, either directly or through a third party" as a 'traveller'. Thus, persons on whose behalf the traveller purchases a package tour are also indirectly included in the definition. In SLOVAKIA, a person for whose benefit the tour contract is concluded is also included in the definition.

Table: National transposition

Substantively equivalent to the Directive	AT, BE, CY, CZ, DK, EL, FI, IE, IT, MT, NL, SE, SK, UK *(14)*
Variations: exclusion of legal persons	ES *(1)*
Variations: exclusion of professionals	PL *(1)*
Not explicitly transposed	HU, LT, LV *(3)*
No legal definition at all	DE, EE, FR, LU, PT, SL *(6)*

cc. The transferee

The notion of the 'transferee' has been introduced into national legislation by the vast majority of member states, though with different methods. In those member states that have not explicitly transposed this notion, it is possible that the transferee is indirectly covered

186 In Belgian law, there is no explicit reference to "agrees to take the package" as per the Directive.

187 The legal text explicitly mentions natural and legal persons.

188 Only the term 'traveller' is mentioned in Slovenian law (indirectly defining it as the person to whom the organiser is obliged to supply a package) whereas principal contractor, transferee and beneficiaries are not mentioned.

189 It is unclear whether this definition also covers the beneficiary of a travel package purchased by a third person.

190 § 3(3) Package Tours Act 1992:1672.

under general rules of contract law. For instance, under GERMAN and SLOVAKIAN law, the rules governing assignment or transfer of a contract ultimately mean that the transferee is considered as the traveller and therefore protected as such. BELGIAN law indirectly covers the transferee by including "everyone who benefits from the contract (...) whether or not he concluded the contract himself".[191] FINNISH law[192] also indirectly includes this third part of the Directive's definition by characterising the 'traveller' as a person "who has the right to participate in a holiday on the basis of a contract that some other person or corporate body has concluded". Again, the SPANISH legislator opted to omit legal persons from the definition. The SLOVAKIAN definition of 'purchaser' includes the person to whom the tour is transferred according to the terms of the CC. In CZECH law, the 'transferee' is a person who takes the package instead of the primary customer – he becomes the 'customer' himself from the date on which the travel agency receives notification of the transfer.[193]

Table: National transposition

Substantively equivalent to the Directive	AT, BE, CY, CZ, DK, EL, FI, IE, IT, MT, NL, SK, UK *(13)*
Variations: exclusion of legal persons	ES *(1)*
Variations: exclusion of professionals	PL *(1)*
Not explicitly transposed	HU, LT, LV,[194] SE[195] *(4)*
No legal definition at all	DE, EE, FR, LU, PT, SL *(6)*

2. Organiser

According to Art. 2(2) of the Package Travel Directive, an 'organiser' is a "person who, other than occasionally, organises packages and sells or offers them for sale, whether directly or through a retailer".

It should be noted that this definition refers to the definition of 'package' and that the ECJ, in its ruling in C-400/00 – *Club-Tour*, held that, with regard to this definition, the term must be interpreted so as to include holidays organised by travel agents at the request of, and in accordance with, the specifications of a consumer. This ruling explicitly includes combinations of tourist services put together at the moment the contract is concluded between the travel agency and the consumer. As such, the term 'organiser' does not only cover the typical tour operators selling pre-arranged packages via travel agencies and other retailers. Travel agencies or internet platforms which, at the specific request of the consumer, spontaneously combine several tourist services, such as flights and hotel accommodation, offered by different service providers and thereby fulfil the definition of 'package', are covered by the notion of 'organiser'.

---

[191] Article 1, sent. 1(5) of the Act of 16 February 1994 regulating package travel contracts and travel intermediation contracts.

[192] § 3(2) Package Travel Regulation 28.11.1994/1079.

[193] CC sec. 852f(1).

[194] It is unclear whether the definition of 'client' also covers the transferee of a travel package purchased by a third person.

[195] It is unclear whether the definition of 'traveller' also covers the transferee of a package tour purchased by a third person.

Unlike other consumer protection directives where the term 'trader' (or similar) is used – defined as the person acting within his/her professional activity – the definition of 'organiser' in the Package Travel Directive comprises all persons not acting 'occasionally'. Thus, on the one hand, its scope covers both natural and legal persons. On the other hand, not only tradesmen, but also individuals or non-commercial organisations not acting occasionally meet the requirements of the definition. This interpretation has been confirmed by the ECJ in the C-237/97 – *Afs intercultural* case, in which a non-commercial entity, the 'AFS Intercultural Programs Finland ry', was regarded as an 'organiser' pursuant to Directive 90/314. The Directive itself does not offer any explanation as to the content of the term 'occasionally' and could thus be considered imprecise. In the course of a review of the consumer directives, it may also be worth considering whether the term 'organiser' should be harmonised with the definitions of 'trader' (etc.) in the other consumer directives.

a. Transposition in general

The majority of member states transposed the term 'organiser' with slight variations in wording, such as 'travel/tour organiser'. ESTONIA and LATVIA introduced the notion of 'tour/ tourism operator'. Moreover, Latvian law uses the generic term of 'undertaking (company)' in its two transposition laws[196] when mentioning the consumer's counterparty. According to the Regulations on Package Tourism Services[197], the "services are prepared by the tourism operator or the package tourism undertaking". The Latvian Tourism Law defines the 'package tourism undertaking' as "an undertaking (company) that carries out the functions of both a tourism operator and a tourism agency"[198], whereas the 'tourism agency' acts as an intermediary[199]. Thus, in using the different terms and defining a 'tourism agency' as an intermediary and yet part of the definition of 'organiser', the legislative texts are clearly inconsistent and are likely to cause confusion. POLISH law contains three main categories of trader: the 'tourism organiser', the 'tourism intermediary'[200] and the 'tourism agent'[201]. The term 'tourism organiser', defined as a trader organising tourist events, is in line with the Directive's definition.[202] Although it is not explicitly stated in Polish law that the organiser sells package tours, it seems logical that, in interpreting the rule according to Community law, this is also part of the organiser's activities.

IRELAND uses the Directive's definition of 'organiser'[203], but also the term 'package provider' as a catch-all for the organiser, or both the organiser and retailer if the retailer is also party to

---

196 Cabinet Regulation No. 163 "Regulations regarding Package Tourism Services".

197 Cabinet Regulation 163, Art. 2.

198 Tourism Law, § 1(1)(6).

199 Tourism Law, § 1(1)(19).

200 A trader who, at the request of a customer, conducts any legal or material acts concerning the conclusion of contracts for tourist services.

201 The closest definition to the one of 'retailer' in the Directive. 'Tourism agent' is a trader who permanently acts as an intermediary in concluding contracts for tourist services in the name of tourism organisers.

202 Article 3(5) of the Act on Tourist Services.

203 S. 2(1) 11th indent, sent. 3 of the Package Holidays and Travel Trade Act, 1995.

the contract[204]. FRENCH[205] and LUXEMBOURG[206] law do not stipulate the nature of the consumer's counterparty, but only mention a "natural or legal person".

Terms related to the business of travel agencies are used in the CZECH REPUBLIC, PORTUGAL and SLOVAKIA. Portuguese law uses the notion of 'travel or tourism agency' (agência de viagens e de turismo[207]), defined as a company exercising activities listed in the transposition law which are typically associated with travel agencies[208]. Czech law generally refers to a 'travel agency operator' who must be a licensed trader. Slovakian law "applies to services provided by travel bureau operators (...)".[209] The travel bureau is considered to be a qualified trader, licensed to conclude package travel contracts (in contrast to the 'travel agency' (retailer)). However, it remains somewhat unclear whether – besides the term 'travel bureau' – the term 'travel agency' may also define the organiser.

Thus, many national transposition laws do not distinguish as clearly as the Directive between 'organiser' and 'retailer'. This seems to be due to the fact that travel agencies/bureaus may carry out different roles, i.e. that of an organiser and that of a retailer (cf. also ECJ C-400/00 – *Club-Tour*). The Directive's definition shows that the acting party's function takes precedence, and not any general classification as a 'travel agency'. A travel agency may either act as an 'organiser', combining different elements of a trip, or as an agent (hence a 'retailer'), selling packages combined by other organisers. The Directive itself could make clearer who is bound by the duties imposed by the Directive and state unequivocally that a travel agency has to be considered as an 'organiser' if it meets the relevant criteria. The ECJ has given some guidance for making this distinction in the cases C-400/00 – *Club-Tour*, and C-237/97 – *AFS Intercultural*.

Table: Use of terms

Organiser	AT, BE, CY, DE, DK, EL, ES, FI, IE, IT, LT, MT, NL, PL, SE, UK *(16)*
Operator	EE, LV* *(2)* (* *more than one term)*
Undertaking	LV* *(1)*
Package provider	IE *(1)*
Travel organiser	SL *(1)*
Travel agency	CZ, PT *(2)*
Travel bureau	SK *(1)*
Travel company	HU[210] *(1)*
No mention of any term	FR,[211] LU *(2)*

204 S. 2(1) 13th indent of the Package Holidays and Travel Trade Act, 1995.

205 Tourism Code, Art. L 211-1 and Art. L 211-2.

206 Package Travel Act, Art. 1.

207 Article 1(1) of the Decree-Law 209/97.

208 Arts. 1(2), 2 (1) of the Decree-Law 209/97. According to Portuguese legislation, the concept of company/undertaking includes, *inter alia*, limited liability one-person establishments (e.g. European Economic Interest Groupings), cooperatives or commercial corporations – c.f. Art. 1(2) of Decree-Law 209/97. Before the amending Decree-Law 12/99, individuals with unlimited liability could also be considered as a company/undertaking.

209 § 1 of the Package Travel Act 281/2001.

210 Government Decree 213/1996 uses the term 'travel company', which covers 'organisers' and 'retailers' according to the other relevant decree to which it refers in the definition.

211 Article L 211-1 of the Tourism Code states, however, that it applies to "any natural or legal person involved in the organisation or selling of travel".

b. Transposition in particular

aa. Overview

About one third of member states have transposed the content of the Directive's definition of 'organiser'. The vast majority of EU countries have, however, introduced variations in the definition (for more details, see point bb. below). GERMAN law does not offer an explicit definition of who should be considered an organiser. The relevant provisions simply use the term 'organiser' when addressing the person obliged to provide the package to the traveller. It is commonly recognised, that, in principle, any individual or legal entity who/which is responsible for organising and offering a trip can be an organiser.[212]

Table: National transposition

No substantive deviation	AT, DK, IE,[213] MT, SE, UK *(6)*
Variations	BE, CY, CZ, EE, EL, ES,[214] FI, HU, IT, LT, LV, NL, PL, PT, SK, SL[215] *(16)*
No legal definition	DE *(1)*
Not transposed	FR, LU *(2)*

bb. Variations

Variations exist in several aspects of the definition. About two thirds of member states have omitted the requirement that the person act "other than occasionally". Thus, one could draw the conclusion that a person acting occasionally as a travel organiser also has to comply with the provisions of the relevant national law on package travel. However, many of these member states restrict the definition to persons acting professionally (which should also exclude most occasional activities), though CYPRIOT and ITALIAN law seem to include organisers operating occasionally in the definition. GERMAN legislation applies neither the provisions requiring security funds in the event of insolvency nor the regulations concerning information duties to occasional organisers.[216]

There is, on the whole, no further explanation in national laws as to what is meant by 'occasionally'. IRELAND, however, provides interpretation guidelines by classifying groups whose members may be regarded as acting 'occasionally' (e.g. schools and educational institutions, religious groups).[217] Moreover, the GERMAN legislator, in the relevant explanatory memoran-

---

212 E.g. BGH (German Supreme Court) judgment of 24 November 1999, I ZR 171/97.

213 However, it is down to legal interpretation as to when a person is not acting "occasionally".

214 A slight variation in the wording exists as "natural and legal person" are explicitly mentioned in Law 21/1995 regulating package travel. Cf. No. 2 of the Additional Provision of the same law, which stipulates that the organiser must be a 'travel agent' according to administrative legislation.

215 It should be noted that the Code of Obligations does not define the notion of 'organiser', but only explains that the seller of package travel arranged by an organiser headquartered in another state is deemed to be an organiser as well. A definition of organiser/tourism agent is contained in the Promotion of Tourism Development Act: i.e. a sole trader or a legal person.

216 § 11 of the Regulation on duties to supply information in civil law, CC § 651k(6)(1).

217 S. 3(2) of the Package Holidays and Travel Trade Act, 1995.

dum, stated that a person not organising trips more than twice shall be regarded as acting occasionally.[218]

According to CZECH law, the definition of 'travel agency' is restricted to the nature of the business it carries out (i.e. providing travel agency services).[219] In SPAIN, the organiser must be a 'travel agent' in accordance with the corresponding administrative legislation.[220] In HUNGARIAN law, the scope of the transposing Decree (No. 213/1996) only covers economic operators established in Hungary normally undertaking activities as domestic and international tour operators and agencies, and to Hungarian branch offices of companies registered abroad.[221] Furthermore, the Hungarian Decree explicitly excludes from its scope travel arrangements made by educational institutions for students in the form of a scholarship (including accompanying guides). It equally does not apply to travel arrangements made by non-commercial associations and not-for-profit organisations and provided to members at cost price, without generating any profit.

The LITHUANIAN Law on Tourism states that an 'organiser' only means "a legal person who is regularly engaged in the business of tourism ...".[222] However, the Lithuanian Civil Code does not limit the definition of organiser only to legal persons, but refers purely to a 'person' and does not include the requirement of 'regularly' or 'other than occasionally' providing the services.[223]

Table: Variations

No (explicit) requirement of acting other than occasionally	BE, CY, CZ, DE, EE, EL, FI, HU, IT, NL, PL, PT,[224] SK, SL[225] *(14)*
Classification guidelines on the term 'occasionally'	DE, IE *(2)*
Restriction to commercial persons	BE,[226] CZ, EE, EL, ES, FI,[227] FR,[228] HU, LT, NL, PL, PT,[229] SK, SL *(14)*

---

218 In the explanatory memorandum setting out the legal rationale, the German legislator stipulated that 1 or 2 events per year do not exceed occasional actions, Bundestag Publication 12/5354, p. 13.

219 CC, sec. 852a(1).

220 No. 2 of the Additional Provision of Law 21/1995 regulating package travel.

221 § 1(2) lit. (a), lit. (c), lit. (d), lit. (g) of the Government Decree No. 213/1996.

222 Article 2(5) of the Law on Tourism.

223 CC Art. 6.747(3).

224 Some specific provisions exist for natural or legal persons who run tours occasionally and on a not-for-profit basis.

225 The Code of Obligations does not define who an organiser is. However, the Promotion of Tourism Development Act defines who may be an organiser/seller of tourism: a sole trader or a legal person.

226 According to Belgian law, commercial persons are defined as persons engaged in an economic activity which constitutes an act of commerce as per Art. 2 and 3 of the Commercial Code (Art. 1(2) of the Trade Practices Act).

227 § 1 of the Package Travel Act states that the scope shall encompass packages which are offered for consideration "by a trader who organises or procures tourist services other than occasionally".

228 Article L 212-1 of the Tourism Code specifies that the activities referred to in Art. L 211-1 of the same Code can only be exercised by natural or legal persons who are 'traders' possessing a 'travel

Explicit mention of natural and legal persons	EL, ES, FR, LU *(4)*
Qualified exclusion of not-for-profit organisations	HU[230] *(1)*
Transposition not entirely clear	LU *(1)*

cc. Trade licence requirement

In addition to the requirements laid down in Directive 90/314, some member states stipulate that the organiser must have a licence or authorisation for his activity. For instance, the CZECH regulations[231] require that the travel agency hold a concessionary trade licence, for which a security fund is mandatory. In the recently adopted ITALIAN Consumer Code, the licensing requirement is not stipulated in the definition of organiser, but is listed in Art. 86(1)(b) according to which, *inter alia*, the terms and conditions as well as the licence of the organiser (or retailer) signing the contract become mandatory elements of the contract. The main competences for the licence and authorisation procedure, however, have been transferred to the Italian regions.[232] In HUNGARY, travel companies have to be registered in the statutory public register maintained by the Hungarian Trade Licensing Office. [233] Individual traders may pursue their activities as one-person companies. According to ESTONIAN law, an 'undertaking' has to be listed in the commercial register. Further examples of licensing requirements can be found in FRANCE, PORTUGAL and SLOVAKIA. In the UNITED KINGDOM, a licensing system exists in the field of packages involving flights, requiring persons (not acting as a 'retailer') to hold an Air Travel Organiser's Licence (ATOL) issued by the Civil Aviation Authority (CAA).[234] In POLISH law, organisers are required to enrol in the register for tourism organisers and tourism intermediaries.[235] Whilst the MALTESE Package Travel Regulations do not explicitly require a licence from organisers or retailers, the Malta Travel and Tourism Services Act states that a 'travel agent' needs to be licensed by the Malta Tourism Authority.[236] Accordingly, 'organisers' are also required to be licensed as 'travel agents' under the aforementioned Act. In SLOVENIA, organisers and sellers of tourism have to obtain a licence issued by the Chamber of Commerce.[237]

---

agent licence'. According to Art. 212-3 of the Tourism Code, the holder of such a 'travel agent licence' established in France may not exercise other activities.

229 Some provisions exist with respect to social solidarity institutions or public administrative institutions.

230 Article 1(4) of the Government Decree No. 213/1996.

231 Under sec. 2(1) of the Act No. 159/1999 on conditions of business operation in the tourism industry, the travel agency must have a licence as a prerequisite for trading in package travel (excursions). The conditions for such a licence are listed in sec. 5 of the same Act.

232 Article 11(6) of the Law of 29 March 2001 No. 135 on the reform of national tourist law.

233 Article 2-6 of the Government Decree No. 213/1996.

234 The Civil Aviation Regulations 1995.

235 Article 4(1) of the Act on Tourist Services.

236 Article 27 of the Malta Travel and Tourism Services Act. Under Art. 2 of this Act, a 'travel agent' means any person who advises or undertakes to provide travel arrangements including accommodation for outgoing travel.

237 Article 35 of the Promotion of Tourism Development Act.

SPANISH law stipulates that the organiser (and retailer) must be qualified 'travel agents' according to the corresponding administrative legislation.[238] According to LITHUANIAN legislation, the organiser must be engaged in the business of tourism in accordance with the procedure and terms laid down in law.

3. Retailer

Article 2(3) of Directive 90/314 defines a 'retailer' as "the person who sells or offers for sale the package put together by the organiser". It should be noted that the Directive nearly always uses the term 'retailer' in a formula like "the organiser and/or retailer". This legislative technique gives discretion to member states to determine whether the organiser or the retailer (or both) is obliged to fulfil the duties imposed by the Directive. Thus, if a member state decides that only the organiser shall bear the obligations towards the consumer, this member state does not really need the definition. It should also be borne in mind that, because of the broad definitions of 'organiser' and 'package' given by the ECJ in the C-400/00 – *Club-Tour* judgement, travel agents that organise holidays at the request of a consumer, and in accordance with his specifications (thereby combining tourist services as per the definition of 'package'), will often be considered as 'organisers' and not just as 'retailers'.

a. Overview

Most member states have transposed the definition of 'retailer' in their special act on package travel. Some – like HUNGARY and SLOVENIA – have further definitions in other laws or decrees. By contrast, FINLAND, FRANCE, GERMANY, LUXEMBOURG and PORTUGAL do not provide any definition of 'retailer' in their laws.

Table: Definition of Retailer – Transposition Method

Special act on package travel	BE,[239] CY,[240] DK,[241] EL,[242] ES, HU, IE, LT, LV, MT, PL,[243] SE, SK, UK *(14)*	
General regulation	Civil Code	LT, NL *(2)*
	Consumer Code	IT *(1)*
	Law of Obligations	EE, SL *(2)*
Government decree	AT,[244] HU[245] *(2)*	

238 Second Additional Provision of the Law 21/1995 regulating package travel.

239 Article 1(4) of the Act of 16 February 1994 regulating package travel contracts and travel intermediation contracts.

240 Article 2 of the Package Travel, Holidays and Tours Law of 1998.

241 § 3(2) of the Act No. 472/1993 on Package Travel; § 3(2) of Act No. 315/1997 on the Travel Guarantee Fund.

242 Article 2(1)(3) of the Decree No. 339/96 on package travel.

243 Article 3(7) of the Act on Tourist Services.

244 § 2(3) of the Regulation on travel agencies implementing Art. 7 of the Package Travel Directive.

245 Article 1(2)(b) of the Government Decree No. 213/1996.

Not transposed	DE, FI, FR,[246] LU,[247] PT *(5)*
Transposition not entirely clear	CZ *(1)*

Whereas most member states with a definition use the term 'retailer', some also use terms like 'agent' (DENMARK), 'travel agent' (LITHUANIA, POLAND and SLOVENIA) or 'travel arranger' (BELGIUM). As the definitions are close to the Directive, such variations do not seem to be problematic.

Table: Use of terms

Retailer	AT,[248] CY, DE, EE, EL, ES, HU, IE, IT, LV, MT, UK *(12)*
Agent	DK *(1)*
Travel agent	LT, SL *(2)*
Travel agency	CZ, SK *(2)*
Tourism agent	PL *(1)*
Travel arranger	BE *(1)*
Intermediary	NL *(1)*
No use of a specific term	FI, FR, LU, PT[249] *(4)*
Transposition not entirely clear	SE *(1)*

b. Transposition in particular

The Directive's definition can also be found in CYPRUS, ESTONIA, GREECE, IRELAND, LATVIA, MALTA, SPAIN and the UNITED KINGDOM. DENMARK[250] and POLAND[251] use a seemingly similar definition by not requiring a package "put together by the organiser" but a sale "on behalf of the organiser".

In LITHUANIA, the definition is slightly different: a travel agent acts as an intermediary in selling organised tourist trips and/or various tourist services.[252]

In AUSTRIA[253] and BELGIUM[254], only persons who act commercially[255] can be retailers. Similarly, in SPANISH law, the retailer must be a qualified 'travel agent' according to the corresponding administrative regulation.[256]

246 Even though there is no specific definition of the term 'retailer', the distinction between the latter and the organiser exists: e.g. Art. L 211-11 of the Tourism Code mentions the 'organiser' and the 'vendor'; with respect to liability, Art. L 211-17 of the same Code prescribes joint liability for all persons participating in the organisation or selling of package travel.

247 In Art. 1 of the Package Travel Act, the obligations of an organiser are extended to retailers.

248 Only the two implementing Decrees (Regulation on travel agencies, Regulation on travel agencies implementing Art. 7 of the Package Travel Directive) use the term "retailer"; it is not mentioned in the Consumer Protection Act.

249 The law sometimes uses the term 'travel agent' without specific clarification. Portuguese law seems to have merged the concepts of 'organiser' and 'retailer' to some extent.

250 § 3(2) of Act No. 472/1993 on Package Travel; § 3(2) Act No. 315/1997 on the Travel Guarantee Fund.

251 Article 3(7) of the Act on Tourist Services.

252 Article 2(7) of the Law on Tourism.

253 § 2(3) of the Regulation on travel agencies implementing Art. 7 of the Package Travel Directive.

Under HUNGARIAN[257] law, only retailers acting on behalf of a Hungarian tour organiser fall within the scope of the transposition law. This restriction results from an amendment on 13 May 2005. Because of a possible infringement of Art. 49 EC Treaty, persons acting as commission agents for foreign tour organisers are no longer considered as 'retailers'. DUTCH law, however, contains no definition, but a provision stating that a retailer (known as an 'intermediary') acting on behalf of a foreign organiser is to be considered as the organiser. Member states like FINLAND, GERMANY and PORTUGAL do not provide a definition at all. Nonetheless, the term is mentioned in German law with respect to the regulations concerning the refund of money in the case of insolvency.[258] The implementing provisions of the German Civil Code generally focus on the contractual relationship between the organiser and the traveller. The relationship between the traveller and the retailer is not explicitly regulated. According to the rules of general contract law, this relationship is usually covered by an agency agreement. Thus, the traveller can make the retailer liable only in exceptional cases (e.g. wrongful advice).

The transposition laws in FRANCE[259] and LUXEMBOURG[260] do not, as already mentioned above, use a specific term for retailers, but lay down uniform regulations for organisers and persons which Art. 2(3) of the Directive defines as retailers.

Several member states have supplemented their provisions on retailers with administrative requirements. For instance, the SLOVAKIAN[261] transposition laws require certain qualifications from the retailer (e.g. special training or foreign language skills). It should also be noted that some member states require package tour retailers to hold a trade licence.[262]

Table: National transposition

No substantive deviation	CY, EE, EL, IE, IT, LT, LV, MT, UK *(9)*
No legal definition	DE, FI, NL, PT *(4)*
Restriction to commercial persons	AT, BE, ES, SK *(4)*
Agent of domestic tour organiser	HU *(1)*
Offer or sale of a package tour on behalf of an operator	DK, PL *(2)*
Uniform rules for organisers and retailers	FR, LU *(2)*

254 Article 1(4) of the Act of 16 February 1994 regulating package travel contracts and travel intermediation contracts.

255 In BELGIUM, commercial persons are characterised as being engaged in an economic activity which constitutes an act of commerce as per CommC Art. 2 and 3 (Art. 1(2) of the Trade Practices Act).

256 No. 2 of the Additional Provision of the Law 21/1995 regulating package travel.

257 Article 1(2)(b) of the Government Decree No. 213/1996.

258 CC § 651k (3), sent. 4, (4).

259 In Art. L 211-1 of the Tourism Code, the obligations of an organiser are extended to retailers.

260 In Art. 1 of the Package Travel Act of 14 June 1994, the obligations of an organiser are extended to retailers.

261 § 4(1), § 3(2)(a)-(e) of the Act No. 281/2001 on Package Travel.

262 This has not been systematically scrutinised; one of several examples would be Italy: Art. 83(1)(b) of the Consumer Code.

Qualified to provide services	SL,[263] SK *(2)*
Transposition not entirely clear	CZ, SE *(2)*

4. Package

According to Article 2(1) of Directive 90/314, a "'package' means the pre-arranged combination of no fewer than two of the following when sold or offered for sale at an inclusive price and when the service covers a period of more than twenty-four hours or includes overnight accommodation:

(a) transport;
(b) accommodation;
(c) other tourist services not ancillary to transport or accommodation and accounting for a significant proportion of the package

The separate billing of various components of the same package shall not absolve the organiser or retailer from the obligations under this Directive".

With regard to the notion of package, the ECJ held in its ruling C-400/00 – *Club-Tour*, that the term must be interpreted so as to include holidays organised by travel agents, at the request of, and in accordance with the specifications of, a consumer. According to the same ruling, the requirement that the package be 'pre-arranged' also includes combinations of tourist services put together when the contract is concluded between the travel agency and the consumer.

a. Transposition in general

Some member states have created a special law on package travel in which the definition of package can be found. Others have included the definition of package into an existing, more general law, for example the Civil Code (the NETHERLANDS and LITHUANIA), a Consumer Protection Act or Consumer Code (AUSTRIA, ITALY) or a Tourism Act (ESTONIA, FRANCE, LATVIA, LITHUANIA). The GERMAN legislator has kept an existing definition of travel contract, which can be found in the Civil Code. In POLAND, there is no specific legislative transposition of the definition of package. In Austria, the Directive's definition is transposed in three different legislative acts, each with varying content. Similarly, in SLOVENIA, different expressions are used in the Code of Obligations and the Promotion of Tourism Development Act.

263 Article 37 of the Promotion of Tourism Development Act regulates conditions for travel agents to obtain a licence. Travel agents must e.g. provide documentary proof that their activity is recorded in the relevant register, of their opening hours, of the existence of their own office (which must not be in an apartment and must be accessible to customers during clearly displayed opening hours), that the person in charge of the activity has not been found guilty of a criminal trading offence and that this person has carried out legal transactions and is not prohibited from exercising travel agent activities, that the person in charge of the activity has at least a post-school education (i.e. in Slovenia two years after high school) and three years of work experience in the field.

Table: Transposition Method

In a special act on package travel	BE, CY, CZ,[264] DK, EL, ES, FI, HU,[265] IE, LU, MT,[266] PT, SE, SK, UK *(15)*	
In a general regulation	Civil Code	DE,[267] HU,[268] LT, NL *(4)*
	Consumer Protection Act / Consumer Code	AT, IT *(2)*
	Tourism Act	EE, FR, LT, LV *(4)*
	Other	AT,[269] EE,[270] SL[271] *(3)*
No specific legislative transposition	PL *(1)*	

The majority of member states seem to use the term 'package' (some with slight amendments, e.g. package travel) as proposed in the Directive. FRENCH law, for example, uses the term 'tourist package'.[272] GERMAN and DUTCH law, on the other hand, simply refer to 'travel contracts'. The BELGIAN legislator opts for the term 'travel organisation contract' and the LITHUANIAN legislator uses the term 'contract for the provision of tourist services'. In the POLISH regulation, the term 'tourist event' is used. The AUSTRIAN legislator used the term 'package' in the Consumer Protection Code, whereas the term 'travel event' is used in the Decree on travel insurance.[273]

Table: Use of terms

Package	AT, CY, DK, EE, EL, ES, FI, FR, HU*, IE, IT, LT, LU, LV, MT, PT, SE, SL,[274] UK *(19)*
Travel event	AT *(1)*
Tourist event	PL *(1)*

264 Definition of package; further regulations on package travel can be found in the CC.

265 § 2 sec. (1) and sec. (2) of the Government Decree No. 214/1996, § 1(2)(f) of the Government Decree No. 213/1996.

266 Article 2 of the Travel and Tourism Services Act.

267 There are two slightly different definitions used in the German CC. The wording is identical, but the scope is different: CC, § 651a(1) (concerning the rights of the traveller) is also applicable to trips with a duration of less than 24 hours or without overnight accommodation, whereas, in § 651k(6) (concerning security in the event of insolvency), only services with a duration of at least 24 hours or with an overnight stay are included.

268 CC § 415.

269 § 2(1) of the Regulation on travel agencies implementing Art. 7 of the Package Travel Directive, § 2(1) of the Regulation on travel agencies.

270 § 866 sec. (2) and sec. (3) of the Law of Obligations.

271 Article 33 of the Promotion of Tourism Development Act, Art. 883(1) of the Code of Obligations.

272 Article L 211-2 of the Tourism Code.

273 Regulation on travel agencies implementing Art. 7 of the Package Travel Directive.

274 The Promotion of Tourism Development Act uses the term 'tourism arrangement', whereas the Code of Obligations uses a descriptive term 'package of services comprising transport, accommodation and other connected services'.

Travel contract	BE, DE, NL, HU,[275]* LT *(5)*
Excursion	CZ, SK *(2)*

* *more than once*

b. Transposition in particular

About half of the member states have transposed the definition of 'package' as stated in the Directive, whereas the other member states' definitions deviate from the Directive. Deviations in transposition mainly concern the need for overnight accommodation and duration of at least 24 hours on the one hand and the significant proportion of other travel services on the other. In AUSTRIA, the definitions of 'package' vary across the different legislative acts. In the two legislative decrees[276], the original text of the Directive is used. On the contrary, in the Consumer Protection Act, the definition is wider, not stipulating the need for a duration of at least 24 hours or overnight accommodation. Moreover, the other services do not need to be a significant proportion of the package. The GERMAN legislator has not specifically transposed the definition, but decided to keep the existing definition of a 'travel contract' in the Civil Code, as it was believed that it should be cast wider than the Directive. The definition does not refer to a combination of certain elements. However, it is considered that the form of words used ('entirety of travel services') means the combination of at least two services. Concerning the duration of at least 24 hours and overnight accommodation, different provisions exist. § 651a(1) CC (concerning the rights of the traveller) is also applicable to trips with a duration of less than 24 hours or without overnight accommodation, whereas, in § 651k(6) CC (concerning security in the event of insolvency), only services with a duration of at least 24 hours or with an overnight stay are included. On the whole, the same level of consumer protection as laid down in the Directive must be afforded.

In PORTUGAL, the definition was transposed as per the Directive. Additionally, there are examples given for 'other services'. These are "in particular those connected with sporting, religious or cultural events, as long as they represent a significant part of the trip". SLOVAKIAN law makes use of the term 'excursion'. This is also a previously arranged stay including accommodation only; the duration must be at least three nights and the accommodation must be in a single establishment including tents, caravans or private lodgings.[277] According to the new amendment, in order for a combination of services to be viewed as 'previously' arranged, it is sufficient that they are arranged at the moment the contract is concluded.[278] Furthermore, the notion also includes a combination of services based on individual requirements. On the other hand, insurance for package travellers is explicitly excluded from being a service in that sense.

275 Government Decree No. 214/1996 uses the term 'travel contract' when transposing the definition of 'package', in contrast to the definition in Decree No. 213/1996.

276 Regulation on travel agencies implementing Art. 7 of the Package Travel Directive, Regulation on travel agencies.

277 Article 2(2) of the Act No. 281/2001 on Package Travel. Art. 2(3) of Act No. 281/2001 after entry into force of Amending Act No. 186/2006 on 1 January 2007.

278 § 2(2) of the Act 281/2001 amended by Act 186/2006 (entry into force on 1 January 2007).

In the UNITED KINGDOM, the scope is wider than what is laid down in the Directive as the UK regulation explicitly states that the fact that a combination is arranged at the request of the consumer and in accordance with his specific instructions (whether modified or not) shall not of itself cause it to be treated as other than pre-arranged. On the other hand, e.g. in the CZECH REPUBLIC and GERMANY, a combination arranged at the request of the consumer has not historically been regarded as a package. This might change in the wake of the ECJ ruling in C-400/00 – *Club-Tour*. According to the HUNGARIAN definition, a package requires a combination of transport, accommodation or other services. Examples of other services (meals, guided tours, cultural programmes) are given in the CC, as well in the Government Decree. The other services do not need to be a significant proportion of the package.[279] In the Czech Republic, the definition is very similar to the one in the Directive. Only with regard to the proportion of the other tourist services is it stated that they need to constitute a significant part of the package or that their price must be at least 20% of the overall package price. In the following paragraph, certain contracts are explicitly excluded from being a package, such as those governing combinations arranged on individual request.[280] The POLISH Law on Tourism refers to tourist services, defined as services like tour guiding, accommodation and all other services offered to tourists or visitors. Tourist events[281] are characterised as a combination of at least two tourist services to create one programme and covered by an inclusive price, where these services include sleeping arrangements or have a duration of at least 24 hours or if the programme contains a change of place. Thus, this deviates from the Directive insofar as a duration of at least 24 hours or an overnight stay are not necessary if the package includes a change of place.

Table: Content of the definition

Substantively equivalent to the Directive	AT,[282] BE,[283] CY, DK, EE,[284] EL, ES, FR, IE, LT, LU, MT, NL, UK *(14)*
No explicit transposition of which tourist services need to be combined	DE, LV *(2)*
No need to cover a period of more than 24 hours or to include overnight accommodation	AT,[285] FI, DE, PL[286] *(4)*
'Other tourist services' do not need to be a significant proportion of the package	DE, HU, LV, PL *(4)*
No definition except of 'package of travel services'	DE[287] *(1)*

279 Examples of other services contained in Government Decree 214/1996.

280 § 1(2) of the Act 159/1999 on conditions of business operation in the tourism industry.

281 Article 3(2) of the Act on Tourist Services.

282 Only in § 2(1) of the Regulation on travel agencies implementing Art. 7 of the Package Travel Directive and in the Regulation on travel agencies; not in § 31b(2) of the Consumer Protection Act.

283 Article 1(1), sent. 1(c) of the Act of 16 February 1994 regulating package travel contracts and travel intermediation contracts.

284 The only deviation is the use of 'passenger service' instead of 'transport' in Art. 7 sec. (1) and sec. (2) of the Tourism Act.

285 Only in § 31b(2) of the Consumer Protection Act; not in § 2(1) Regulation on travel agencies implementing Art. 7 of the Package Travel Directive or in the Regulation on travel agencies.

286 It is sufficient that the package contains one change of place; Art 3(2) of the Act on Tourist Services.

287 CC § 651a(1), sent. 1.

Additional examples of other services	HU, IT, PT,[288] SK, SL[289] *(5)*
Further regulations	CZ,[290] SK, SL, UK[291] *(4)*
Transposition not entirely clear	SE *(1)*

Table: Separate billing

No transposition of regulation on separate billing	AT,[292] DE, EE, FI, FR, IE, LV, NL, PL *(9)*
Regulation on separate billing explicitly transposed	AT,[293] BE,[294] CY, CZ, DK, EL, ES, HU,[295] IT, LT, LU, MT, PT, SE, SK, SL, UK *(17)*

5. Contract

According to Art. 2(5) of Directive 90/314, a "'contract' means the agreement linking the consumer to the organiser and/or the retailer".

a. Transposition in general

10 member states have transposed the definition of contract in a special act on package travel, whereas, in six member states, the definition can be found in an existing more general act. In the SLOVAKIAN transposition law, reference is made to the definition of a travel contract in the Consumer Code.[296] GERMANY continues to use an already existing definition of travel contract. 8 member states have not specifically transposed the definition of contract. This seems to be due to the fact that the general definition of contract in many national laws is considered to be sufficient.

---

288 Article 17(2) of the Decree-Law No. 198/93.

289 Article 33(2) of the Promotion of Tourism Development Act states that a trip which includes a pre-arranged combination of two or more services (transfer and other tourist services) when sold or offered for sale at an inclusive price – and to which all provisions of this act apply – is deemed to be a travel arrangement.

290 § 1(1) of the Act No. 159/1999 on conditions of business operation in the tourism industry.

291 Regulation 2(1) of the Package Travel, Package Holidays and Package Tour Regulations 1992.

292 Not mentioned only in § 2(1) of the Regulation on travel agencies implementing Art. 7 of the Package Travel Directive, though it is mentioned in § 31b(2) of the Consumer Protection Act.

293 Only in § 31b(2) of the Consumer Protection Act; not mentioned in § 2(1) of the Regulation on travel agencies implementing Art. 7 of the Package Travel Directive.

294 Article 1(1), sent. 2 of the Act of 16 February 1994 regulating package travel contracts and travel intermediation contracts.

295 § 1(5) of the Government Decree No. 213/1996.

296 Article 6 of the Act No. 281/2001 on Package Travel.

Table: Transposition method

In a special act on package travel	BE, CY, EL,[297] ES,[298] HU, IE,[299] LT,[300] LV,[301] LU, MT, SE, UK[302] *(12)*	
In a general regulation	Civil Code	CZ, DE, LT, NL, SK[303] *(5)*
	Code of Obligations	SL *(1)*
Only general definition of 'contract' with no specific reference to travel contracts	EE,[304] FR,[305] PT *(3)*	
No specific legislative transposition	AT, DK, FI, IT, PL *(5)*	

Several member states (e.g. BELGIUM, HUNGARY, LITHUANIA, the NETHERLANDS) have combined the definition of 'contract' with that of 'package' by defining a contract in the transposition law with reference to the definition of a 'package'. Alternatively, others, such as LUXEMBOURG, SLOVENIA and SWEDEN, refer to the term 'package' as the content of the contract under consideration.

Table: Contract/Package

Single Definition for 'contract'	CY, CZ,[306] DE, EL, ES, IE, LV, MT, SK,[307] UK *(10)*
Combined definition of 'contract' and 'package'	BE, HU,[308] LT, NL *(4)*
'Package' used in definition of contract	LU,[309] SE,[310] SL *(3)*
No specific legislative transposition	AT, DK, EE, FI, FR, IT, PL, PT *(8)*

b. Transposition in particular

The CZECH and MALTESE legislators have made an adjustment to the definition, encompassing the notion that it "depends on the circumstances". These adjustments seem to have no major impact on the content of the definitions.

297 Article 2(1)(5) of the Decree No. 339/96 on package travel.

298 Article 2 of the Law No. 21/1995 regulating package travel.

299 Article 2(1) of the Package Holidays and Travel Trade Act, 1995.

300 Article 2(17) of the Law on Tourism.

301 Article 1(1) of the Cabinet Regulation No. 163.

302 Regulation 2(1) of the Package Travel, Package Holidays and Package Tour Regulations 1992.

303 The Package Travel Act 281/2001 cross-refers to the CC §§52-60 (consumer contracts), 741a-741k (package travel contract).

304 Article 8(1) of the Law of Obligations.

305 CC Art. 1101.

306 CC Art. 852a-852k regulate the travel contract. The CC refers to the definition of package in Act 159/1999 on conditions of business operation in the tourism industry.

307 Use of the notion of 'package travel contract'.

308 § 415-416 of the CC contains general rules with respect to travel contracts; Government Decrees No. 213/1996 and 214/1996 establish special rules.

309 Article 8 of the Package Travel Act.

310 § 3(4) of the Package Tours Act 1992:1672.

Table: National transposition

Substantively equivalent to the Directive	CZ, DE, EL, ES, HU, IE, LU, LV, SE, SK, UK *(11)*
"Except where circumstances otherwise require" or similar adjustment	CY,[311] IE,[312] MT[313] *(3)*
Combination with definition of 'package'	BE, LT, NL, SL *(4)*
No special legislative transposition	AT, DK, EE, FR, IT, PL, PT *(7)*

In GERMANY, LITHUANIA, LUXEMBOURG, the NETHERLANDS, SLOVAKIA[314] and SLOVENIA, the definition only refers to the 'organiser' as the liable contract party and omits the 'retailer'. This is not an infringement of EC law as the wording of the Directive is 'organiser and/or retailer'. In Germany, the decision is due to the fact that the definition of a 'travel contract' in the German Civil Code already existed before the Directive was transposed. The question of which party the rights may be exercised against is sometimes solved by general contract law (e.g. in Germany) or by regulations detailing the persons who may be liable (see chapter on the definition of the 'organiser/retailer'). In HUNGARY, the consumer's counterparty is termed the 'travel company' and LATVIAN law also refers to the 'undertaking' (company). Under CZECH law, the 'travel agency' is the liable party.

Table: Liable parties

Organiser and Retailer	BE,[315] CY (or both), EL, ES, IE, MT (or both), SE, UK *(8)*
Organiser	DE, LT, NL,[316] SK, SL *(5)*
Travel agency	CZ *(1)*
'Companies' (or similar)	HU, LV *(2)*
No special legislative transposition	AT, DK, EE, FR, IT, PL, PT *(7)*
Transposition not entirely clear	LU *(1)*

III. Consumer protection instruments

1. Information Duties

a. Travel Brochure

Art. 3(2) sent. 1 of Directive 90/314 regulates the content of an information brochure when it is made available to the consumer. The brochure must indicate in a legible, comprehensible and accurate manner both the price and adequate information concerning details of the destination and transport, accommodation, the meal plan, the itinerary as well as general

311 Article 2 of the Package Travel, Holidays and Tours Law of 1998.

312 Article 2(1) of the Package Holidays and Travel Trade Act, 1995.

313 Article 2(1) of the Package Travel, Package Holidays and Package Tours Regulations, 2000.

314 CC § 741a uses 'organiser (travel bureau)'.

315 There is a separate definition of travel intermediation contracts in Art. 1(2) of the Act of 16 February 1994 regulating package travel contracts and the travel intermediation contracts.

316 An 'organiser' is also a 'retailer' of an 'organiser' outside the territory of the Netherlands, cf. CC Art. 500(2).

information on passport and visa requirements, payment aspects and the deadline for informing the consumer should the minimum number of participants not be reached.

aa. Transposition in general

Some countries seem to have considered a detailed list of information as unsuitable for transposition in a legislative act. As a result, the laws in several countries, including AUSTRIA, GERMANY and DENMARK, refer to a list of information duties which can be found in a government decree.

Table: Transposition law of information list

Special act on package travel	BE,[317] CY (annex[318]), CZ,[319] EL,[320] ES,[321] IE,[322] LT, MT,[323] PL,[324] SE,[325] SK,[326] UK (schedule) *(12)*	
General regulation	Civil Code	CZ, LT *(2)*
	Consumer Code	IT[327] *(1)*
	Law of Obligations	EE,[328] SL *(2)*
Government decree	AT,[329] DE,[330] DK (annex[331]), FI, HU,[332] LU,[333] LV,[334] NL,[335] PT[336] *(9)*	
No specific legislative transposition	FR[337] (no list) *(1)*	
Transposition not entirely clear	LV, SE *(2)*	

317 Article 5 of the Act of 16 February 1994 regulating package travel contracts and the travel intermediation contracts.

318 Article 5(1)-(2) of the Package Travel, Holidays and Tours Law of 1998.

319 The travel contract is part of the CC, while other aspects are regulated in Act No. 159/1999 on conditions of business operation in the tourism industry.

320 Article 3(2) of the Decree No. 339/96 on package travel.

321 Law 21/1995 regulating package travel.

322 Article 10(1) and (2) of the Package Holidays and Travel Trade Act, 1995.

323 Article 5(1) of the Package Travel, Package Holidays and Package Tours Regulations, 2000.

324 Article 12(1) 1st-10th indent of the Act on Tourist Services.

325 Article 5 of the Package Tours Act 1992:1672.

326 § 8(1) lit. (a) - lit. (j) of the Act No. 281/2001 on Package Travel.

327 Article 85(1) of the Consumer Code.

328 § 867 sec. (1) - sec. (3) of the Law of Obligations.

329 § 2 of the Regulation on Travel Agencies.

330 § 4 of the Regulation on duties to supply information in civil law.

331 Annex to Regulation No. 776/1993 on Package Travel.

332 Government Decree No. 214/1996.

333 Article 2 of the Decree of 4 November 1997 on pre-contractual information and contract conditions of package travel contracts.

334 Article 3 of the Cabinet Regulation No. 163.

335 Decree of 15 January 1993 containing rules concerning information that organisers of package travel must notify in the interest of travellers.

336 Article 20 sec. (1) – sec. (2), Art. 22 of the Decree-Law No. 198/93.

337 Article L 211-9 of the Tourism Code.

In SLOVENIAN law, the content of a brochure (travel programme, travel itinerary) is not further defined. It is only stated that, before the travel confirmation is issued, the traveller shall be given a travel programme containing all the requisite information for the travel confirmation, which itself may refer only to the programme.[338]

Table: Use of terms

Brochure	BE, DE, DK, EL, FI, IE, IT, MT, PL, UK *(10)*
Brochure or other written form	CZ,[339] ES,[340] HU, LT,[341] NL, PL, SE, SK *(8)*
Package description	EE *(1)*
Programme of services	LV *(1)*
Advertising material	AT, CY[342] *(2)*
Pre-contractual information	LU, PT *(2)*
Travel programme	SL *(1)*
Written information	FR *(1)*
Transposition not entirely clear	SE *(1)*

bb. Transposition in particular

(1) Transposition of the Directive's information requirements

In AUSTRIA, DENMARK, ESTONIA, GERMANY, GREECE, LATVIA, LUXEMBOURG and SWEDEN, the national legislators have adopted the list of information as laid down in the Directive.

In SWEDEN, the information duties do not go beyond the requirements stipulated in the Directive and are specified in less detail than in the Directive. For example, instead of 'passport and visa requirements' and 'health formalities', the Swedish legislator uses the term 'immigration'. As member states are obliged to interpret legislative acts in accordance with EC Directives, it can be assumed that this term covers the elements listed in the text of the Directive. Deviating from the Directive, the Swedish regulation obliges the organiser to mention only the minimum number of participants required for the package to take place, but not the deadline for informing the consumer in the event of cancellation.

The LATVIAN legislator has transposed the list of information as laid down in the Directive. Furthermore, a general clause is added, stipulating that the organiser has to provide other information if necessary. Sometimes, the information duties are rendered in a more abridged

338 Article 884(3) of the Code of Obligations.

339 Article 10 of the Act No. 159/1999 on conditions of business operation in the tourism industry used the wording 'brochure or some other demonstrable form'.

340 Article 3(1) of the Law 21/1995 regulating package travel refers to a "programme or information brochure which contains in writing ...".

341 Lithuanian law refers to "descriptive material concerning the services offered and advertised by the tour organiser (travel brochures or other official information)", CC Art. 6.748(1); "travel brochures, catalogues or other descriptive material concerning the tourist's trip", Art. 6(2) of the Law on Tourism.

342 In some cases, the term 'informative material' is used, e.g. Art. 4(1) of the Package Travel, Holidays and Tours Law of 1998.

form than in the Directive. For example, Latvian law refers to payment procedures where the wording of the Directive explicitly mentions the sum of money or the percentage of the price to be paid on account.

FRENCH law[343] refers to "written information" which must describe the transport and accommodation services, the price and payment conditions, cancellation options and visa information. Nevertheless, it must be given only to the interested parties ("les intéressés"), which implies that it is not obligatory in every situation.

In FINLAND, it is not compulsory to provide a brochure. If it is provided, it must contain the general conditions applying to the package travel contract and essential information in relation to the contract.[344]

Table: Transposition of the Directive's information requirements

Substantially equivalent to the Directive	AT, DE, DK, EE, EL, LU *(6)*
Information going beyond the Directive's content	BE, CY, ES, FI, HU, IE,[345] IT, LT, MT, NL, PL, PT, SK, UK *(14)*
Deviations from the Directive's requirements	FR, SE *(2)*
Transposition not entirely clear	CZ, LV, SL *(3)*

Some member states have made it compulsory for the organiser/retailer to provide a brochure, thus making use of the minimum clause in the Directive. These member states are SPAIN[346] and, partially, GREECE[347].

(2) Additional information duties

The transposition laws of other member states stipulate additional information to be included in the brochure.

Sometimes, there are additional information duties above and beyond those listed in the Directive. In CYPRUS, for example, going beyond the requisite information on meals, an estimate is required of how many meals not included in the price may be necessary. Another difference is that the total price may be given in an attached price list accompanying the brochure.

343 Article L 211-9 of the Tourism Code.

344 § 6 of the Package Travel Act of 28 November 1994/1079.

345 Article 10(1) lit. (h)-(j) of the Package Holidays and Travel Trade Act, 1995.

346 Article 3(1) of Law 21/1995 regulating package travel.

347 It is not compulsory for the organiser/retailer to provide a travel brochure. However, it is compulsory for travel agencies responsible for general and national tourism as per Law 393/1976, as well as for their intermediaries. Previously, these intermediaries have already had to give a detailed program of the trip or excursion, which now has to contain the details in Art. 3(2) of Decree 339/96 (e.g. general information concerning passport and visa requirements, health formalities important for the trip and the stay).

For the most part, the list of required information is expanded by adding further information duties. The organiser is obliged to give his name and address in FINLAND, HUNGARY, the NETHERLANDS, PORTUGAL and SPAIN. In the Netherlands, the telephone number and, in Portugal, the licence number must also be given. In Hungary, the organiser is also obliged to give information on his domicile, registration number and telephone number.

Information on the representative in the destination country is obligatory in IRELAND, MALTA, SPAIN (name, address) and in HUNGARY (name, address, telephone hotline). In Hungary, if the organiser has no representative in the destination country, he has to give the number of a Hungarian-language telephone hotline via which the traveller can get help and contact the travel organiser.

Most member states that have added information duties also require the organiser to inform the traveller about security/guarantee provision in the brochure. In BELGIUM, HUNGARY, MALTA, the NETHERLANDS and the UNITED KINGDOM, the organiser must give information concerning security in the event of insolvency, as well as information concerning the security for sums paid over. In Hungary, information on the credit institution must also cover the possibility to obtain information on protection in the event of insolvency directly from the security provider. Additionally, the organiser must provide information about how to contact the insurance company or institution should the organiser fail to provide the return trip or to fulfil his duty to reimburse any relevant fees (including those paid in advance). IRISH law has one information category relating to the security arrangements for money paid over and, where applicable, for the repatriation of the consumer in the event of the organiser's insolvency.[348] Moreover, in Belgium, the organiser must give information concerning cancellation and travel insurance.

In PORTUGAL and SLOVAKIA, the national regulations also lay down special information duties in connection with the liability of the organiser. In Slovakia, the brochure must contain information about instances in which the traveller would be liable for contractual penalties, as well as about the amount of these penalties. In Portugal, it must contain the identity of the bodies which underwrite the organising agency's liability. Furthermore, the organiser must inform the traveller about the maximum amounts of liability for the agency and the complaints procedure in the event of a failure of performance.

In some member states, the brochure must contain information on the legal basis of the contract. In SPAIN, the brochure has to give information on clauses with respect to possible liability, cancellations and other terms of the package. In POLAND, there must be information concerning the legal basis for the travel agreement and the legal consequences arising from it. In HUNGARY, the organiser has to display his general terms and conditions. He does not, however, need to inform the traveller about the general contract conditions used by the retailer. In LITHUANIA, the procedure and terms governing performance of the tour contract have to be stated in the brochure, catalogues or other descriptive material.

Another large field of information concerns the programme and the services comprised in the package, as against those services which are not included in the package and which must be paid for additionally. In 6 member states (BELGIUM, HUNGARY, the NETHERLANDS, PO-

---

348 Article 10(1)(j) of the Package Holidays and Travel Trade Act, 1995.

LAND, PORTUGAL and SLOVAKIA), the brochure must contain information on the programme and/or other services. In Poland, information on the sight-seeing programme and tourist attractions is required and, in Slovakia, the organiser must provide information concerning the programme in situ and concerning the scope and nature of all other elements which are part of the package. In Portugal, visits, excursions or other services included in the price must be mentioned. In Hungary, the organiser is obliged to give information on the conditions for participation in optional programmes. According to the BELGIAN regulation, the brochure must contain information on the nature of the trip and its target group. This information is likely to comprise information on the trip programme. In the NETHERLANDS, there is a more general rule. According to the Dutch transposition law, the organiser is obliged to give information on other services which are a significant part of the trip.

Another area of information concerns taxes and additional charges. In IRELAND, MALTA and PORTUGAL, the organiser is obliged to provide information about these. HUNGARIAN law requires information on visits, excursions and other services which are not included in the package price but need to be paid for additionally. According to LITHUANIAN law, the terms and conditions for the currency exchange have to be stated.

In some member states, legislative acts contain clauses stipulating that the organiser must provide other relevant information in the brochure. Such a general clause can also be found in SPAIN (concerning the nature of the package offered) and in LATVIA. Spanish law also provides for information on the "estimated price of the optional excursions" and "the financing conditions if offered".

Finally, there are further special information duties in some member states. A peculiarity in HUNGARY is the need to give information on the weather conditions and local traditions and rules in the destination countries, where these are different from Hungarian traditions and rules and are important for the trip. Moreover, the brochure must also contain information on health formalities and visa requirements.[349] In SLOVAKIA, the organiser has to inform the traveller about the conditions governing a replacement traveller and the deadline by which the traveller must communicate to the organiser that a substitute will replace him in the package. In ITALY, one further information duty is added to the list in the Directive. The organiser is obliged to provide information about deadlines, procedures and parties in relation to which the right of withdrawal may be exercised, where the contract was concluded away from business premises and at a distance (negotiation). In the NETHERLANDS, the brochure must contain the deadline by which the traveller must inform the organiser that the trip does not meet his expectations. In the UNITED KINGDOM, the brochure must contain information on the arrangements (if any) that apply if the travellers are delayed at the outward or homeward points of departure. In PORTUGAL, the organiser must inform the traveller about the periods in which changes to the price are legally admissible.

It is self-evident that such additional requirements with regard to the content of the brochure may be useful for the consumer in many cases. However, such additional requirements may also cause a barrier to trade because they force organisers to adapt their brochures to the respective national laws of the member states where they want to market their packages. The huge variety of national variations makes it rather difficult, if not impossible, to draft bro-

349 Cf. Part.2.B.III.1.b.bb.(4).(a). Information requirements in the Directive.

chures which can be used throughout the EU. In any case, such an endeavour would be rather costly and could therefore deter organisers from making use of the internal market.

Table: Additional information duties

Name, address	ES, FI, HU, NL, PT *(5)*
Representative	ES, HU, IE, MT *(4)*
Security in the event of insolvency	BE, HU, IE, MT, NL, PT, SK, UK *(8)*
Security for sums paid	HU, IE,[350] MT, NL, UK *(5)*
Liability	PT, SK *(2)*
Cancellation and travel insurance	BE *(1)*
Legal basis of the contract	ES, HU, LT, PL *(4)*
Programme and services	BE, HU, NL, PL, PT, SK *(6)*
Taxes and additional charges	FI, HU, IE, MT, PT *(5)*
Terms and procedures of currency exchange	LT *(1)*
"General clause"; other relevant information	ES, LV *(2)*
Other (special) information	CY, ES, FI, HU, IT, NL, PT, SK, UK *(9)*
No farther-reaching information duties	AT, DE, DK, EE, EL, FR, LU, LV, SE *(9)*
Transposition not entirely clear	CZ, SL *(2)*

b. Pre-contractual information duties

Article 4(1)(a) of Directive 90/314 determines some general pre-contractual information duties with regard to health formalities and to passport and visa requirements applicable to nationals of the member state(s) concerned and, in particular, on the periods for obtaining them.

aa. Transposition in general

Almost all member states have transposed these pre-contractual information duties, though with some variations. SPAIN is the only country not to have implemented the Directive provision as such. Art. 4(2) of the Law 21/1995[351] contains a reference to the fact that the consumer must be informed before conclusion of the contract via receipt of a copy of the contractual terms. However, the required contractual terms do not mirror the content of the pre-contractual information duties, but rather transpose the minimum elements to be contained in the contract, as listed in the Directive's Annex.[352] Information duties on passport and visa requirements or health documents are only mentioned as part of the mandatory brochure in Art. 3(1)(e) of the same law, which transposes Art. 3(2) of Directive 90/314. The Spanish legislator probably felt that, as it is mandatory to supply the brochure, this Directive rule on pre-contractual information duties had been entirely complied with.

---

350 Part of the information category with respect to the insolvency of the organiser.

351 Law 21/1995 of July 6 regulating package travel.

352 Cf. Transposition of Art. 4(2)(a) in Part 2.B.III.1.d. of the analysis.

bb. Transposition in particular

(1) The obligated party

At Community level, these duties are imposed on the organiser and/or retailer. In transposing this Directive provision, many member states have chosen to impose the pre-contractual obligation on both the organiser and the retailer, although they are individually mentioned. By contrast, some member states opted for the organiser as the (only) obligated party. CYPRUS and the UNITED KINGDOM used general terminology ('the other party to the contract'), which leaves it to the content of the contract to determine whether the organiser, the retailer or both carry obligations. This also seems to be the case in AUSTRIAN, FRENCH and LATVIAN law, which use the terms 'professional', 'seller' and 'undertaking' (which can be either the organiser or the retailer according to the circumstances). In SWEDEN, there is no reference to a specific party bound to fulfil the pre-contractual information duties; it is only stated that "the traveller shall be informed". This implies that the contractual party, the organiser or the retailer depending on the individual contract, will have to inform the traveller. LUXEMBOURG, PORTUGAL and SLOVAKIA use the term 'travel agency'[353] when determining the person responsible for performing the information duties. LITHUANIAN legislation has adopted two different legal texts regulating information duties before conclusion of the contract for the organiser[354] and the retailer[355].

There is an interesting feature in FRANCE and LUXEMBOURG. The applicable law requires that the information be provided only if the counterpart is an interested party. Regarding this wording, the logical conclusion to draw is that, in order to be viewed as an interested party, the consumer would have to demonstrate his involvement somehow. Such a requirement is not explicitly laid down in the Directive. However, it can be assumed that Art. 4(1) of Directive 90/314 only stipulates that a consumer must be informed if he has expressed an interest in a certain package.

Table: Obligated party

Organiser and/or retailer	AT, BE, CY, EL, FI, FR,[356] HU, IE, IT, LT, LU, LV, MT, PL, PT, SE, SK, UK *(18)*
Organiser	DE, DK, EE, NL, SL *(5)*
Travel agency	CZ *(1)*
Not transposed	ES *(1)*

353 Luxembourg: travel agent, Portugal: travel agency, Slovakia: travel bureau.

354 Duties for the organiser are transposed in the CC (Art. 6.748(2)) and the Law on Tourism (Art. 6(4)).

355 Duties for the retailer are transposed only in the Law on Tourism (Art. 6(4)).

356 Article L 211-9 of the Tourism Code uses the general term 'seller', which can be either an organiser or a retailer.

(2) Time for providing information

The majority of national laws require that pre-contractual information duties be fulfilled before conclusion of the contract. Variations exist in AUSTRIA and GERMANY, where the information has to be provided before the statement of intent (e.g. the booking). Under DUTCH law, the point at which the travel agreement is concluded is key in terms of providing the information. In ITALY, the consumer must be provided with information during negotiations and, in any event, prior to the conclusion of the contract.[357] HUNGARIAN legislation stipulates that, if a brochure has not been made available, all the information normally provided in a brochure has to be given in writing before the contract is concluded.[358]

Table: Time for providing information

Before conclusion of the contract	BE, CY, CZ,[359] DE, DK, EE, EL, FI, FR, HU, IE, IT,* LT, LV, LU, MT, PL, PT, SE, SK, SL, UK *(21)*
Before statement of intent (booking)	AT, DE *(2)*
When the travel agreement is concluded	NL *(1)*
During negotiations (in any event prior to conclusion of the contract)	IT* *(1)*
Not transposed	ES *(1)*

* *more than once*

(3) Method for providing information

About half of the member states have transposed the method for providing pre-contractual information as per the Directive ("in writing or in any other appropriate form"). Certain member states (e.g. FINLAND, POLAND[360]) have opted to require exclusively a written format. Moreover, no special formal requirements exist in GERMANY or DENMARK. CZECH[361] and SLOVAK[362] law similarly require a brochure or some other written form ('proved (established) form' in the Czech Republic / "as the case may be" in the Slovak text), whereas HUNGARIAN[363] law states that the information shall be provided in writing if it is not included in any brochure.

---

357 Article 87(1) of the Consumer Code.

358 § 4(1) of the Government Decree No. 214/1996.

359 The Czech CC does not use the term "pre-contractual information" and refers only to prerequisites for the travel contract (sec. 852b); i.e. a draft (offer) of the travel contract has to be presented by the travel agency (sec. 852a(2)). However, Act 159/1999 requires the travel agency to provide information prior to the conclusion of the travel contract in a brochure or some other demonstrable form (sec.10).

360 Article 13(3a) of the Act on Tourist Services.

361 § 10(1) of the Act No. 159/1999 on conditions of business operation in the tourism industry.

362 § 8(1) of the Act No. 281/2001 on Package Travel.

363 § 4(1) of the Government Decree No. 214/1996.

Table: Method for providing information

In writing or any other appropriate form	AT, CY, EL, IE, LU, LV, MT,[364] NL, PT, SL, UK *(11)*
Written form	BE, FI, FR, IT, LT, PL *(6)*
Format which can be reproduced in writing	EE *(1)*
In a brochure or in other written form	CZ, HU, SK *(3)*
In an appropriate manner	SE *(1)*
No special form	DE, DK *(2)*
Not transposed	ES *(1)*

Such differences in formal requirements very probably hinder the marketing and performance of travel contracts for consumers in different member states. The organiser has to examine carefully which national law is applicable and, if it is foreign law, which formal requirements are relevant. Moreover, it must be admitted that the wording of the Directive is unclear with regard to the question of what is meant by "any other appropriate form". In the course of the review of the Directive, consideration should be given to clarifying this – possibly with reference to a definition of the "durable medium" along the lines of Art. 2(f) of Directive 2002/65.

(4) Content of pre-contractual information

(a) Information requirements in the Directive

The transposition of the Directive's pre-contractual information requirements is inconsistent across EU member states. For example, FRANCE[365] has implemented the information duty on passport and visa requirements, though neither the duty regarding the period for obtaining the documents nor that on health formalities. About one third of member states, having implemented the obligation to provide information about passport and visa requirements, refrain from demanding further information on the period for obtaining the relevant documents (e.g. DENMARK, LUXEMBOURG, SLOVENIA *inter alia*). BELGIAN legislation requires general information on passports and visas, which does not necessarily include the deadlines for their receipt. In HUNGARY, passport and visa requirements are described in general terms.[366] French law shifts away from the terminology of 'passport and visa requirements' by demanding information on conditions for crossing borders.[367] Slovenian law uses the term 'border formalities'. Under DUTCH law, the organiser has to provide any relevant general information on travel documents and health formalities necessary for the journey and stay.[368] Such wording leaves it to national courts to determine whether, for instance, the organiser also has to provide information about the period for obtaining the necessary documents. Finally, the Danish and LATVIAN legislators chose to use different terminology when intro-

364 Until now, there has been no interpretation in the courts as to what is meant by "some other appropriate form". The duty to pass on the information to the consumer is ultimately incumbent on the organiser. If he fails to do so, it constitutes a breach of the regulation .

365 Article L 211 – 9 of the Tourism Code.

366 § 3(1)(k) of the Government Decree 214/1996.

367 « Conditions de franchissement des frontières » in Art. L 211-9 of the Tourism Code.

368 Article 1(c) of the Decree of 15 January 1993 containing rules concerning information that organisers of package travel must notify in the interest of travellers.

ducing the duty to provide information about health formalities in their legislation.[369] In SLOVAKIA and the CZECH REPUBLIC, information requirements exist concerning the period for obtaining details on health formalities.

Especially with regard to travel documents, different national legislation varies on one point: the citizen's nationality according to which the information on passports and visas may differ. The Directive stipulates that information on passport and visa requirements for nationals "of the Member State or States concerned" must be made available. This implies that travellers from all EU countries should be informed about the requirements applicable. ITALIAN, MALTESE and SWEDISH law explicitly mention the requirements for EU citizens (the latter two also for European Economic Area nationals). The CZECH REPUBLIC, on the other hand, only includes the formalities for its own citizens, while CYPRUS adds residents. GERMANY and AUSTRIA have adopted regulations only applying to nationals / citizens (Austria) of the country in which the trip is offered. These regulations might be deemed to be too narrow and therefore to infringe Community law.

In GERMANY, the Federal Supreme Court (BGH)[370] ruled recently that a travel agency was not liable for damages resulting from the fact that the claimant had not been allowed to travel on the grounds that he did not have a valid passport. The court held that it was not up to the travel agency to provide information about passport and visa requirements. On the other hand, it is possible that the organiser must inform the traveller in this respect. Another case was heard before the Audiencia Provincial de Barcelona in March 2001. The court reasoned that it was the consumer's duty and not that of the agency to ensure that he was in possession of a valid passport. The requirement for valid travel documents was regarded as general knowledge. The information duty on passports, visas and health formalities must, however, be complied with in the mandatory brochure.[371]

Table: Information requirements in the Directive

Passport and visa requirements	AT, BE, CY,[372] CZ, DE, DK, EE, EL, ES*, FI, FR, HU, IE, IT, LT, LU, LV, MT, NL, PL, PT, SE, SK, SL, UK *(25)*
Period for obtaining a passport and visa	AT, CY, CZ, DE, EE, EL, IE, IT, LT, LV, MT, PL, PT, SK, UK *(15)*
Health formalities	AT, BE, CY, CZ, DE, DK, EE, EL, ES*, FI, HU, IE, IT, LT, LU, LV, MT, NL, PL, PT, SE, SK, SL, UK *(24)*

* *as part of the mandatory brochure*

369 Denmark (§ 6 of Act No. 472/1993 on Package Travels): "information on requirements as regards (...) vaccination and similar prerequisites"; Latvia (Art. 5 of Cabinet Regulation No. 163): "other requirements (health insurance, vaccination and other issues related to medicine)".

370 BGH judgment of 25 April 2006, NJW 2006, 2321.

371 Article 3(1)(e) of the Law 21/1995 regulating package travel.

372 Article 7(a) of the The Package Travel, Holidays and Tours Law of 1998 also includes information concerning the time the consumer will need to obtain a suitable passport or visa.

(b) Additional information requirements

Some member states have introduced additional requirements for information to be provided before conclusion of the contract. The following table shows some examples:

Table: Additional information requirements

Parties to the contract	FI, FR *(2)*
Optional insurance	AT, BE, CZ, EL,[373] PL, SK *(6)*
Details of minimum insurance cover where consumer is required to take out insurance	IE *(1)*
General terms and conditions	AT, BE,[374] FI, HU *(4)*
Content of the package	CZ, FI, FR, HU, PT, SK *(6)*
Price of the package	CZ, FR, HU, LT, NL, PT, SK *(7)*
Security for money paid over in the event of insolvency	CY, EL, IE, MT, UK *(5)*
Repatriation in the event of insolvency	CY *(1)*
Specific threats to life or health	PL[375] *(1)*
Documentation for medical or hospital assistance	PT *(1)*
Currency exchange conditions	LT *(1)*
Procedure and terms for performing travel contract	LT *(1)*
Contractual penalties for the consumer in the case of cancellation	CZ, SK *(2)*
Programme in situ	CZ, HU, PT, SK *(4)*
Period for the consumer to provide information about a substitute replacing him in the package	CZ, SK *(2)*
Other	SL[376] *(1)*

(c) Exemptions from information requirements

Some countries have adopted exemptions from the requirements where the information has already been made available to the consumer in some way and is not subject to subsequent changes: AUSTRIA (in advertisement or confirmation document), ESTONIA (brochure),

373 According to Art. 4(1) of the Decree 339/96, the organiser/retailer is obliged to inform the consumer in writing or in any other appropriate manner before conclusion of the contract of his/her (the consumer's) obligation to cover the risk of improper or non-performance of his/her contractual obligations by taking out a liability insurance.

374 Article 7(1)(b) of the Act of 16 February 1994 regulating package travel contracts and travel intermediation contracts.

375 Article 13(2) of the Act on Tourist Services.

376 According to Art. 884(2) of the Code of Obligations, the travel information must contain detailed information, e.g. place and date of issue, the travel organiser's logo and title, the traveller's name, the location and dates of the beginning and end of the travel package, the number of days of accommodation, the necessary information on timetables, prices and conditions for transport and the quality of the means of transport, the necessary information on the accommodation (including the location of the accommodation and type and category of the accommodation facilities), and information on the number of meals (e.g. full board, half board, bed and breakfast).

FINLAND[377] (brochure), GERMANY (brochure), the NETHERLANDS (brochure or any other publication), SLOVENIA[378] (travel itinerary).

Exemptions also exist in the case of last-minute contracts in the following member states: DENMARK (derogation possible if the contract is entered into shortly before the package tour is due to begin), FINLAND[379] (some other suitable form), HUNGARY (at the latest at the time of conclusion), ITALY (information at the same time as conclusion if the contract is concluded just before departure), the NETHERLANDS[380] (if the travel agreement is made less than 72 hours before the trip begins).

None of these exemptions is mentioned in SPANISH law. As such, according to legal doctrine, the information duties to be fulfilled in the brochure (cf. points above) must also be performed in the case of last-minutes contracts in order to enhance consumer protection.

It is questionable whether such exemptions for last-minute contracts are in line with the Directive. As Art. 4(2)(c) of the Directive only allows for exceptions from the formal requirements in the case of a last-minute contract, it could be concluded, by an *argumentum e contrario,* that such exemptions from the duties stipulated in Art. 4(1)(a) are contrary to the Directive. In the course of the planned review, it could be clarified whether exemptions from information duties in the case of last-minute contracts should also be allowed with regard to Art. 4(1).

c. Information before the start of the journey

Art. 4(1)(b) of Directive 90/314 details the information to be provided in good time before the start of the journey, i.e. details of transport connections, contact details for the organiser's or retailer's local representatives and, as the case may be, an emergency telephone number, special information for minors staying abroad and information on the option of taking out an insurance policy (no. i-iv).

Seemingly all member states have transposed the Directive's rules concerning the information to be provided in good time before the start of the journey, though with some variations.

---

377 The information (terms of a contract) must be given in writing, unless they have been published in a brochure to which the traveller has access (§ 7(1) of the Package Travel Act of 28 November 1994/1079).

378 Article 884(3) of the Code of Obligations.

379 If a contract is entered into immediately before the journey and it would therefore be unreasonably inconvenient to provide the contract conditions in written form, they may be supplied to the traveller in some other suitable form (§ 7(2) of the Package Travel Act of 28 November 1994/1079).

380 CC Art. 7:501(3).

aa. The obligated party

Again, the majority of member states impose information duties on the organiser and/or the retailer. Despite the use of different terms in national legislation (e.g. AUSTRIA: 'professional', CYPRUS and the UNITED KINGDOM: 'the other party to the contract', LUXEMBOURG: 'travel agent', PORTUGAL: 'travel agency', SLOVAKIA: 'travel bureau'), if you interpret these terms according to the Directive, then they must be treated as equivalents.[381] SPANISH legislation states that the duty lies first with the retailer and only "as the case may be, with the organiser".[382] ITALIAN law imposes pre-journey information duties on both the organiser and the retailer.[383] ESTONIA and SWEDEN only state that the information shall be provided, without naming any obligated party. The information has to be provided by the organiser in DENMARK, GERMANY, the NETHERLANDS, POLAND and SLOVENIA. In MALTA, the organiser has to provide the information, either directly or through a retailer.[384]

Table: The obligated party

Organiser and/or retailer	AT, BE, CY, EE, EL, ES, HU, IE, IT, LT, LU, PT, SE, SK, UK *(15)*
Organiser	DK, DE, FI, MT, NL, PL, SL *(7)*
Travel agency	CZ *(1)*
No specific transposition	FR,[385] LV *(2)*

bb. Timeframe for providing information

Half of the member states chose to require that the information be supplied "in good time before the start of the journey", as per the Directive. 7 countries (see table below) only require that the information be provided "before the start of the journey", without further specifying the time period. This can, however, be so close to departure that consumers are not really fully aware of the information or able to react to it. Therefore, such a transposition cannot possibly be considered in line with the Directive. Only three countries, BELGIUM, the CZECH REPUBLIC and SLOVAKIA, specify the last point at which information is provided "in good time before the start of the journey" as 7 calendar days prior to departure. Similarly, in HUNGARY[386], the information has to be provided "at least seven calendar days" before the start of the journey or at the time the contract is concluded if this occurs less than 7 days before departure. LATVIA does not provide for any specific transposition measures in its legislation. Nevertheless, Latvian law includes all the information duties in Art. 4(1)(b) of the Directive in the requirements to be fulfilled before the contract is concluded.[387] FRANCE also requires that some of the information due under Art. 4(1)(b) be given prior to concluding the contract (for the content cf. III. 1. d.).

---

381 Cf. Part 2.B.III.1.b.bb.(1).

382 Article 6 of the Law 21/1995 regulating package travel.

383 Article 87(2) of the Consumer Code.

384 Article 7.1 of the Package Travel Regulations, 2000.

385 Article L 211-11 of the Tourism Code specifies that the information shall be provided in the contract between the 'seller' and the 'buyer'.

386 § 5 of the Government Decree No. 214/1996.

387 Article 5 of the Cabinet Regulation No. 163.

Table: Timeframe for providing information

In good time before the start of the journey	AT, CY, DE, EE, EL, ES, FI, IE, LT, MT, PL,[388] SE, UK *(13)*
Before the start of the journey	DK, FR,[389] IT, LU, NL, PT, SL *(7)*
7 calendar days[390]	BE, CZ,[391] HU, SK *(4)*
No specific transposition (but information duties to be fulfilled before conclusion of contract)	LV *(1)*

cc. Method for providing information

The majority of member states have adopted the formal requirement that the information be provided "in writing or any other appropriate form" or at least "in writing". The SPANISH transposition law specifies that it must be "in writing or any other documentary form".[392] SWEDEN has opted for the wording "in an appropriate manner".[393] The Directive's wording "any other appropriate form" implies that the information must be either in writing or in a form equivalent to the written form. Based on this interpretation, the Swedish transposition law should be understood as "an appropriate form equivalent to a written form". In the NETHERLANDS, the information must be given "in writing or in any other understandable and accessible way" before an agreement is reached.[394] The CZECH REPUBLIC, ESTONIA and GERMANY have not introduced any formal requirement governing the format in which the information should be provided. This could be considered as a shortcoming in transposition. However, the wording of the Directive ("in writing or any other appropriate form") is rather vague. In the course of a review, the Directive could make clearer what is meant by the "other appropriate form". In this context, use might be made of the definition of a "durable medium" in other directives, in particular in Art. 2(f) of Directive 2002/65.

Table: Method for providing information

In writing or any other appropriate form	AT, CY, DK, EL, ES,[395] IE, MT, NL, PT, SL, UK *(11)*
In written form	BE, FI, HU, IT, LT, LU, PL, SK *(8)*
In an appropriate manner	SE *(1)*
No special form	CZ, DE, EE *(3)*
No specific transposition	FR, LV *(2)*

[388] Article 13(3) of the Act on Tourist Services states "in good time before the start of the tourist event".

[389] Article L 211-11 of the Tourism Code specifies "before start of the journey or stay".

[390] Calendar days.

[391] CC sec. 852d(1).

[392] Article 6 of the Law 21/1995 regulating package travel.

[393] § 6(2) of the Package Tours Act 1992:1672.

[394] CC Art 7:501(2) refers to the formal requirement for information, which are listed in a separate government decree. Art. 3 of the 'Decree of 15 January 1993 containing rules concerning information that organisers of package travel must notify in the interest of travellers' lists the information to be given without mentioning a formal requirement.

[395] Taken literally, there is no requirement for a 'documentary form', but a written form "or any other form that gives evidence", e.g. a recorded voice message.

dd. Content of the information requirements

(1) Items of information listed in Art. 4(1)(b)

The majority of member states have transposed the information items as listed in Art. 4(1)(b) of the Directive. In some cases, member states have deviated with regard to the point of time at which certain information has to be provided. For instance, with regard to the information about the option to take out an insurance policy (No. iv), AUSTRIA, BELGIUM, the CZECH REPUBLIC (partially), LATVIA, POLAND and SLOVAKIA stipulate that this information must be provided before conclusion of a contract. Furthermore, the Czech Republic requires that transport details be provided before conclusion of the contract, but not details of the place to be occupied by the traveller. This may be seen as an infringement of the Directive. In FRANCE, the relevant information requirement (before conclusion of the contract) is even more general, as the consumer must only be given information pertaining to the transport services provided.[396]

There are many further examples of deviations from the Directive's text. With respect to the details of transport connections, ITALIAN law does not require any information on the place to be potentially occupied by the traveller; LUXEMBOURG law requires a reservation reference for boat or train travel and SWEDISH law uses the general term 'travel arrangements'. Most legislation does not refer to the examples listed in the Directive, "e.g. cabin or berth on ship, sleeper compartment on train".

Moreover, SWEDEN also opted for a general transposition of the provisions requiring information on the organiser's or retailer's local representatives and on the local agencies by simply requiring information enabling the traveller to contact the organiser or retailer during the tour. Thus, the transposition law adopts the aim of the Directive's provisions, though leaves it up to the organiser or retailer to decide on the level of detail they will provide in order to enable possible contact. ESTONIAN law explicitly mentions the address and phone number of a local agency that can be contacted, but not the name of the local agency. In PORTUGAL, the law requires information on the "means of contacting the local representative of the agency or the bodies that may assist the customer in the event of difficulties or, failing that, the means of contacting the agency itself".[397] In ITALY, the organiser's or retailer's telephone number is to be given for use in the event of difficulties and in the absence of local representatives.[398] In the case of minors abroad, the Italian transposition law refers to "journeys overseas", which would imply a trip to another continent. However, the Directive aims to ensure adequate information and protection for minors travelling to foreign countries, even within Europe. With respect to insurance contracts, SPANISH law includes repatriation in the event of death.[399]

---

396 Article L 211-9 of the Tourism Code.

397 Article 23 of the Decree-Law No. 198/93.

398 Article 87(2)(c) of the Consumer Code.

399 Article 6 of the Law 21/1995 regulating package travel.

Table: Information requirements

Details of transport connections (incl. place to be occupied by the traveller)	AT, BE, CY, (CZ), DE, DK, EE, EL, ES, FI, FR, *(HU)*, IE, IT, LT, LU, *LV*, MT, NL*, PL, PT, SE, SK, SL, UK *(25)*
Contact details for the organiser's / retailer's local representatives	AT, BE, CY, CZ, DE, DK, EE, EL, ES, FI, HU, IE, IT, LT, LU, LV, MT, NL, PL, PT, SE, SK, SL, UK *(24)*
Contact details for local agencies	AT, BE, CY, CZ, DE, DK, EE, EL, ES, FI, HU, IE, IT, LT, LU, *LV*, MT, NL, PT, SK, UK *(21)*
Emergency telephone number	AT, BE, CY, CZ, DE, DK, EE, EL, ES, FI, HU, IE, IT, LT, *LV*, MT, NL, SK, SL, UK *(20)*
Special information in the case of minors abroad	AT, BE, CY, CZ, DE, DK, EE, EL, ES, FI, HU, IE, IT, LT, LU, LV, MT, NL*, PL, PT, SE, SK, SL, UK *(24)*
Option to take out an insurance policy	*AT*, *BE*, CY, (CZ), DK, EL, ES, FI, *(HU)*, IE, IT, LT, LU, *LV*, MT, NL, *PL*, PT, SE, *SK*, SL, UK *(22)*

Member states in italics stipulate that information must be provided before conclusion of the contract
Member states in italics and brackets stipulate that information must be provided in the brochure
* if necessary

(2) Additional information requirements

BELGIUM, ESTONIA, MALTA, PORTUGAL and SLOVAKIA introduced additional requirements for information to be provided before departure. In Estonia and Slovakia, detailed information on the package must be given (e.g. in Estonia, when (dates, times) and where the package will begin and end). Maltese law additionally requires the e-mail address of local representatives or local agencies.

Table: Additional information requirements

Fax number	BE *(1)*
Details of the package	EE, HU, SK[400] *(3)*
Information about provision of security	HU *(1)*
E-mail address	MT *(1)*
Documentation for medical or hospital assistance	PT *(1)*
Procedure to follow in the specific case of illness or accident	PT *(1)*
Documents for additional services	HU, SK *(2)*
Insurance contract in the case of withdrawal	CZ *(1)*
Contact details for the consulate office	CZ *(1)*

(3) Exemptions from information requirements

AUSTRIA, ESTONIA and GERMANY provide for exemptions from the information requirements if the information has already been made available in a brochure or travel confirmation and no changes have subsequently taken place. SLOVAKIAN law states that the information has to be provided unless already contained in the contract or the brochure given to the traveller.

400 E.g. when and where the package will begin and end, new § 8(1)(d) of Package Travel Act 281/2001, as amended by Act 186/2006 (entry into force 1 January 2006).

The time limit of seven days before departure for providing the information does not apply to last-minute bookings in BELGIUM,[401] the CZECH REPUBLIC[402] and Slovakia[403]. The latter two then require that the information be provided when the contract is concluded. In ITALY, general information must be supplied at the same time as the contract is concluded when this takes place just before departure.[404]

d. Elements to be included in the contract

Art. 4(2)(a) of the Directive states that the contract shall contain at least the elements in the annex, depending on the particular package.

aa. Inclusion of the elements

According to the Directive, the contract must contain the elements listed in the annex. The AUSTRIAN, ESTONIAN, GERMAN and SLOVENIAN legislators have adopted a different approach. The organiser is obliged to provide the traveller with a confirmation document for the travel contract, which must contain all the necessary information. In Slovenia, if the confirmation is not issued, the contract must be in writing and contain the same information as the confirmation. The duty is considered to have been fulfilled in Austria if the professional makes reference to an advertising document available for the consumer that includes all the elements.[405] In BELGIUM, the same list of obligations applies to both the organiser and the retailer.[406]

Table: Where the elements are to be included

Travel contract	CY, CZ, EL, ES, FI,[407] FR, HU, IE, IT, LT, LU, LV, MT, PL, PT, SE, SK, SL, UK *(19)*
Travel confirmation document	AT, DE, EE, SL[408] *(4)*
Travel contract and order form	BE *(1)*
Brochure or any other publication available	NL *(1)*
Description of the package in brochure or other similar material made available to travellers	EE *(1)*

401 Article 7 of the Decree of 16 February 1994 regulating package travel contracts and travel intermediation contracts.

402 CC sec. 852(2).

403 If the contract is concluded less than 7 days before departure.

404 Consumer Code, Art. 87 sec. (3) and sec. (1).

405 § 4(3) of the Regulation on travel agencies.

406 Article 10 (organiser) and Art. 23 (travel intermediary) of the Act of 16 February 1994 regulating package travel contracts and travel intermediation contracts. A slightly different list of obligations applies when the travel organiser is not acting as a retailer (Art. 23 of the same Decree).

407 Written travel contract or brochure.

408 Equally possible in a travel programme.

bb. Timing for inclusion of the elements

Art. 4(2)(b) of Directive 90/314 states that the terms and conditions of the contract must be communicated to the consumer before its conclusion. However, AUSTRIAN and GERMAN law stipulate that, "at or immediately after conclusion of the contract", a confirmation document including certain elements must be handed over to the traveller. This approach contradicts the above-mentioned provision in the Directive.

The SLOVENIAN Code of Obligations states that the travel organiser must issue the traveller with a travel confirmation at the latest by the point at which the contract is concluded. Alternatively, he must conclude a contract in written form that contains all the mandatory components of the travel confirmation.

cc. Elements of the contract

(1) Elements in the annex (and some variations in detail)

The elements in the annex have been implemented as obligatory elements of the contract by most member states. Some amendments have, however, been introduced. In AUSTRIA, the name and address of the organiser, but not of the retailer, have to be provided. This is similar in the NETHERLANDS (where the organiser's phone number also has to be provided). The BELGIAN legislator has specified a time limit for cancellation by the organiser where the minimum number of participants is not reached (15 days before departure). LUXEMBOURG even requires a period of 21 days before departure. Moreover, in Belgium, where there is a travel mediation contract relating to a travel organisation contract, the name and address of the travel agent and his role as agent acting on behalf of the travel organiser have to be stated. In CYPRUS, the number of meals not included in the agreed package price and the excursion programme must be mentioned, as well as the name and address of the licensed insurer or the financial institution underwriting the security if required by the consumer. ESTONIAN law only requires the travel destination to be included in the contract and not the relevant periods and dates where a stay is involved. Furthermore, the contract must state only the operator's right to cancel the contract if the minimum number of participants has not been reached. In this case, the tour operator must have previously and explicitly reserved this right and must not have informed the consumer after the deadline. In ITALY, there is no requirement to give the insurer's name, but the name, address, telephone number and business licence details of the organiser or retailer signing the contract must be supplied. In the context of accommodation information, the accommodation's suitability for disabled people, if appropriate, must be detailed. In addition, the balance payment must not, under any circumstances, exceed 25 % of the price to be paid upon booking. In Luxembourg, the contract term concerning any instalment must also include reference to the fact that the last partial payment by the buyer may not be less than 30 % of the overall price and is payable upon delivery of the travel documents. PORTUGUESE law not only requires details of the deadlines for lodging a complaint concerning failure to perform the contract or improper performance thereof, but also the procedure to be followed. SWEDISH law only uses headings to describe the elements to be included in the contract.

The LITHUANIAN transposition provision does not stipulate the inclusion of the following elements in the contract: travel destination, means, characteristics and categories of transport, details of accommodation, the meal plan, the deadline for informing the consumer in the event of cancellation where a minimum number of participants is not reached or special requirements which the consumer communicated to the organiser or retailer when making the booking (and which both accepted). However, Lithuanian law requires the contract to include personal details and the traveller's place of residence, what happens in the event of amendments to the contract or the cancellation thereof, health insurance formalities and financial guarantees, the contract number and the date of its conclusion.

In HUNGARY, certain information elements in the table below already have to be contained in the brochure, which automatically becomes an integral part of the contract via a reference in the contract and following signature by the traveller.

Table: Information to be included

Travel destinations and relevant periods	AT, BE, CZ, CY, DE, DK, EE, EL, ES, FI, *(HU)*, IE, IT, LU, LV, MT, NL*, PL, PT, SE, SK, SL, UK ***(23)***
Transport details	AT, BE, CY, CZ, DE, DK, EE, EL, ES, FI, *(HU)*, IE, IT, LU, LV, MT, NL*, PL, PT, SE, SK, SL, UK ***(23)***
Dates, times and points of departure and return	AT, BE, CY, CZ, DE, DK, EE, EL, ES, FI, HU, IE, IT, LT, LU, LV, NL*, PL, PT, SK, SL, UK ***(22)***
Accommodation details	AT, BE*, CY, CZ, DE, DK, EE, EL, ES, FI, *(HU)*, IE, IT, LU, LV, MT, NL*, PL, PT, SE, SK, SL, UK ***(23)***
Meal plan	AT, BE*, CY, CZ, DE, DK, EE, EL, ES, FI, *(HU)*, IE, LU, LV, MT, NL*, PL, PT, SK,[409] SL,[410] UK ***(21)***
Minimum number of participants; deadline for information in the event of cancellation because the minimum number is not reached	AT, BE*, CY, CZ, DE, DK, EE, EL, ES, FI, *(HU)*, IE, IT, LU, LV, MT, NL*, PL, PT, SK, SL, UK ***(22)***
Itinerary	AT, BE*, CY, CZ, DE, DK, EE, EL, ES, FI, *(HU)*, IE, IT, LT,[411] LU, LV, MT, PL, PT, SE, SK, SL,[412] UK ***(23)***
Services included in the package price	AT, BE*, CY, CZ, DE, DK, EE, EL, ES, FI, FR,[413] *(HU)*, IE, IT, LT, LU, LV, MT, NL*, PL, PT, SE, SK, SL, UK ***(25)***
Name and address of the organiser, retailer and, where appropriate, the insurer	BE, CY, CZ, DE, DK, EE, EL, ES, FI, FR,[414] *(HU)*, IE, IT, LT, LU, LV, MT, NL, PL, PT, SL,[415] UK ***(22)***
Package price	AT, BE, CY, CZ, DE, DK, EE, EL, ES, FI, FR, *(HU)*, IE, IT, LT, LU, LV, MT, PL, PT, SE, SK, SL, UK ***(24)***

409 If the meal plan is a component of the package.

410 Information on the number of meals (e.g. full board, half board, bed and breakfast).

411 CC Art. 6.749(2) 3rd indent includes the places or countries to be visited as well as the dates of arrival and departure.

412 A detailed itinerary is required.

413 Article L 211-9 of the Tourism Code requires information on the transport and accommodation services before conclusion of the contract.

414 Article L 211-11 of the Tourism Code states that the names and addresses of the organiser, seller, guarantor and insurer have to be provided in the contract before the start of the journey or the stay.

415 Only the name and address of the organiser.

Possibility of price revision	AT, BE, CY, CZ, DE, DK, EE, EL, ES, FI, FR, IE, IT, LT, LU, LV, MT, PL, PT, SE, SK[416], UK *(22)*
Additional fees not included in the package	CY, CZ, DE, DK, EE, EL, ES, FI, HU, IE, IT, LU, LV, MT, PL, PT, SK, UK *(18)*
Schedule and method of payment	AT, BE, CY, CZ, DE, DK, EE, EL, ES, FI, FR, IE, IT, LT, LU, LV, MT, NL, PL, PT, SE, SK, UK *(23)*
Special requests from the consumer which have been accepted	AT, BE*,[417] CY, CZ, DE, DK, EE, EL, ES, FI, HU, IE, IT, LU, LV, MT, PL, PT, SE, SK, UK *(21)*
Deadlines for lodging a complaint because of improper or non-performance	AT, BE, CY, CZ, DE, DK, EE, EL, ES, FI, HU, IE, IT, LT, LU, LV, MT, NL, PL, PT, SE, SK, SL, UK *(24)*

* *if relevant to the particular contract*

Member states in italics and brackets provide for the information duty in the brochure

(2) Additional elements

Additional elements to be included in the contract have, for example, been introduced by the following member states:

- BELGIUM (1. place and date of signature; 2. name and address of traveller or other beneficiaries; 3. conditions for cancellation by the traveller or organiser and/or retailer; 4. conditions for cancellation insurance, medical assistance insurance and/or any other insurance; 5. differences in accommodation classifications and current standards in the member states; 6. special requirements communicated by the traveller when making the booking);
- CYPRUS (indication of whether there is a stop-over in another city);
- the CZECH REPUBLIC (1. names of the contract parties; 2. amount of compensation for the organiser if the consumer cancels the contract);
- FRANCE (1. possibility of withdrawing from the contract; 2. possibility of assigning the contract to a third party; 3. information to be conveyed to the purchaser before the journey or stay);
- GREECE (1. number of kilometres travelled per day; 2. operating permit for the accommodation; 3. other services (besides meal plan) offered in the accommodation; 4. insurance policy number and amount of insurance cover; existence of other guarantees);
- HUNGARY (1. deadline for the traveller to cancel without any requirement to reimburse the costs incurred; 2. name and address of traveller; 3. name of insurance company or financial institution responsible for financial security; 4. premium for any insurance policy included in the package; 5. traveller is liable for cancellation costs if contract is concluded within 35 days of departure or within a given contractual period);
- IRELAND (nominated agent with an address in the case of packages sold by an organiser (whether dealing directly with the consumer or through a retailer) who has no place of business in the State);
- ITALY (1. any costs arising for the traveller in the case of contract transfer; 2. requirements and procedures for use of the guarantee fund; 3. details of insurance cover and any additional policies agreed with the traveller);

416 Contract parties may entitle the travel bureau to increase the price of the package, though not within 20 days of departure.

417 The provision relating to the organiser does not state explicitly that special requests must have been accepted.

- LATVIA (1. the deadline for opting out of services and the percentage sum consequently forfeited; 2. the type of insurance chosen by the client; 3. right of withdrawal for the consumer in the case of a distance contract or contract concluded outside the company's usual business premises);
- LITHUANIA (1. name and address of traveller; 2. details of permissible contract alterations or cancellation; 3. health insurance formalities; 4. financial guarantees; 5. contract number and date of conclusion);
- LUXEMBOURG (1. rights and duties of the travel agent and traveller in the case of price revision, cancellation or transfer of the package; 2. assignor has to inform the travel agent via a letter sent by recorded delivery at least 21 days before departure; 3. signature of the travel agent and purchaser; 4. guarantee certificate (details of potential repatriation costs must be attached to the contract));
- MALTA (indication of whether there is a stop-over in another city);
- the NETHERLANDS (visa and passport requirements, health formalities);
- POLAND (1. legal basis of the agreement and legal consequences; 2. deadline for informing the client about procedures for assigning rights and assuming obligations);
- PORTUGAL (1. maximum amounts for any possible claims from the agency; 2. optional services to be paid for by the consumer; 3. copy of the insurance policy or policies sold by the travel agency as part of the contract);
- SLOVAKIA (1. identification of the contractual parties; 2. amount of compensation for the organiser if the consumer cancels the contract; 3. conditions a participant must meet and a notification period if a substitute takes the package);
- SLOVENIA (1. place and date of issue of the travel confirmation; 2. name of the traveller; 3. conditions under which the traveller may demand annulment of the contract; 4. necessary information on border and customs formalities, health, financial and other administrative regulations, 5. other information deemed to be useful if included in the travel confirmation);
- SPAIN (1. consumer's duty to give notice in writing or any other demonstrable form in the event of improper or non-performance; 2. cut-off date for these claims; 3. period in which the consumer may request confirmation of the reservation; 4. means of contacting organiser or retailer during the tour).

The broad spectrum of provisions shows that it will be very difficult for organisers to fulfil the information obligations where the law of another member state is applicable. This may constitute a barrier to trade.

(3) Exemptions

In BELGIUM, the contract may simply refer to a programme, brochure or voucher which contains the necessary elements and then only highlight any subsequent changes. Equally, provided that there is a precise reference to the relevant page in the brochure where the name and address of the insurance company are detailed, the organiser or retailer is no longer bound to indicate them in the contract. In GERMANY, the organiser may also fulfil his duties by referring to the information contained in the brochure.[418] Similar rules exist in

418 § 6(4) of the Regulation on duties to supply information in civil law.

DENMARK, where the information in brochures and other marketing material[419] as well as the contractual confirmation[420] constitute part of the contract. These exemptions seem to be problematic as the Directive does not provide for any such derogations. In HUNGARY, it is sufficient to refer to the brochure in the contract if such a brochure was prepared for the traveller. AUSTRIAN law states that, in the case of a booking made within 7 days of departure, a travel confirmation document with the obligatory elements only has to be provided if it is reasonable to expect this of the professional. The traveller, however, has to be informed about deadlines for lodging complaints for inadequate or non-performance and further details must be provided at the latest by the time of departure.[421] SLOVAKIAN law rules that the description of the package may be replaced by the package reference number or other reference in the brochure if relevant and provided that the brochure has been handed over to the consumer. In SLOVENIA, if a travel itinerary with the necessary information is delivered before the travel confirmation, it is sufficient for the confirmation document simply to refer to the itinerary.[422]

e. Information requirements with regard to all terms of the contract

Art. 4(2)(b) of Directive 90/314 imposes on the member states the obligation to ensure that all contract terms are set out in writing or such other form as is comprehensible and accessible to the consumer. These terms must be communicated to the consumer before conclusion of the contract and he must be given a copy of these terms. It is clear from the wording ("all the terms of the contract") that this obligation does not only refer to the standard terms and conditions, but includes all particulars of the contract. Most member states have transposed this provision.

POLAND, however, has not fulfilled its duty because, in the relevant Act, there is no provision regulating the communication of the terms before conclusion of the contract. Only the obligation to provide a copy of the written contract is regulated. SLOVENIAN law does not require the contract terms according to the Directive's annex to be communicated to the traveller prior to the conclusion of the contract, since it states that the travel confirmation with this information shall be issued upon conclusion of the contract at the latest; otherwise, there must be a written contract containing all the mandatory components of the travel confirmation.

IRELAND transposed the relevant article almost literally. SWEDISH law substitutes the Directive's term "in writing" with the expression "in an appropriate matter". CYPRUS added that the traveller must receive the copy in good time. MALTA has provided for an exemption where a consumer makes a proposal to the organiser or the retailer not more than 14 days before the date of departure. DANISH law lists passports, visas and vaccinations as examples of the information required. In the UNITED KINGDOM, the obligation is deemed to be an im-

---

419 § 6-8 of the Act 472/1993, Annex I and II of Regulation No. 776/1993.

420 § 5 subs. 2 of the Act 472/1993, Annex I no. 11 of Regulation No. 776/1993.

421 As laid down in § 31e(2) of the Consumer Protection Act.

422 Article 884(1), (3) of the Code of Obligations. For the relationship between the contract and travel confirmation, cf. Art. 885 et seq.

plied condition with the effect that a failure to comply with it permits the consumer to terminate the contract.

Several countries have stipulated that the contract must be in writing (e.g. ITALY), going beyond the Directive's provisions. In SPAIN, for example, any information and the contract itself must be provided in written form. The sanction for non-compliance with such formal requirements need not lead to the contract's being declared null and void. In Spain, case law states that the absence of a contract in written form does not render the contract invalid if its existence can be proved in some other way. The Directive itself does not stipulate that the consequence of non-compliance with the formal requirement must necessarily be that the contract is null and void. Such a sanction may be laid down in national law, but other sanctions are possible as well. LUXEMBOURG has devised an intermediary solution. Violation of the relevant provisions leads to the contract's being declared null and void, though the traveller is not entitled to lodge a claim.

Some member states (e.g. BELGIUM, FRANCE, HUNGARY,[423] LATVIA, LITHUANIA, LUXEMBOURG) also omitted the alternative in the Directive of providing the contract in another form that is comprehensible and accessible to the consumer as per the Directive. In French law, the requirement for the contract to be a written document arises from other legal duties.[424] GREEK law likewise contains such a rule. There is some controversy over whether this is a mandatory condition for legal transactions which may lead to the contract's being declared null and void or not, in accordance with the legislator's intention to simply guarantee that information is provided. ITALY has an even stricter formal requirement because the contract must be in writing and a copy of the contract has to be signed or stamped by the organiser/retailer.

Several member states have made use of Art. 4(2)(c) and allow exemptions in the case of last-minute bookings. For instance, in the UNITED KINGDOM and CYPRUS, when the period between the booking and departure is so short that it is impracticable to provide written terms, it is not necessary to provide the essential terms of the contract. In SLOVAKIA, confirmation with the relevant information also has to be provided up to 7 days before the beginning of the package travel. Otherwise, it must be provided upon conclusion of the contract. AUSTRIAN law prefers not to apply the rules when the booking is made less than 7 days before departure. This is because it would be unreasonable to do so and the information is of little importance given the nature of the trip. In that case, the consumer must be given notice only at the time of departure. Under GERMAN law, the organiser is also disavowed of any duty to provide a written contract and to hand it to the consumer if the booking is made less than 7 working days before departure. Nevertheless, in such an instance, some core information must be given to the consumer by departure at the latest.

---

423 § 2(4) of the Government Decree No. 214/1996 rules that the contract must be in writing.

424 Cf. Art. 98 of the Decree No. 94-490 of 17 June 1994. This principle was reinforced in a CA Paris ruling that the traveller cannot be asked to pay for services provided in the agreement if there is no written contract (Judgment of 29 June 2001, *Petites affiches* of 1 July 2003).

f. General prohibition of misleading information

Art. 3(1) of Directive 90/314 states that, as a rule, "any descriptive matter concerning a package and supplied by the organiser or the retailer to the consumer, the price of the package and other conditions applying to the contract must not contain any misleading information".

It should be noted that such an unspecified ban on misleading information could be considered superfluous because the general rules on unfair commercial practices in member states should prohibit misleading practices anyway. There are manifold general rules outlawing misleading advertising and other misleading commercial practices in EC law. As such, the law would not change if this Directive provision were omitted. Thus, the grouping of 'no legal definition' in this regard does not necessarily mean that the provision has not been (correctly) transposed.

Nevertheless, several member states did explicitly transpose this provision. In ITALY, the provision of any misleading information about services offered, the price and other elements of the contract is always prohibited, irrespective of the method used to communicate such information to the consumer.[425] LATVIAN as well as LUXEMBOURG law only stipulate that the information given must be accurate, complete, clear and precise. The same can be found in SLOVAKIAN and CZECH law where there is a requirement that the organiser provide the consumer with exact, clear, correct and truthful information before the contract is concluded (in the brochure as well). SWEDISH law is less detailed than the Directive's text as the information must purely be clear and understandable. Several countries (e.g. AUSTRIA, DENMARK, FINLAND,[426] GERMANY,[427] the NETHERLANDS, SPAIN) have not specifically transposed this provision, but provide for a general rule in their contract law.

Table: No misleading information

Substantively as per the Directive	BE, CY, CZ, EL, HU, IE, IT, LT, MT,[428] PL, PT, UK *(12)*
Variations	EE, LU, LV, SE, SK *(5)*
Not specifically transposed	AT, DE, DK, ES, FI, FR, NL, SL *(8)*

g. Sanctions for non-compliance with information duties

Directive 90/314 does not contain many provisions on sanctions for non-compliance with the various information duties stipulated in Art. 3 and Art. 4(1) and (2). The only explicit provision can be found at the end of Art. 3(2). This states that the particulars contained in the brochure are binding on the organiser or retailer, unless changes have been clearly communicated to the consumer or agreed between the parties to the contract. However, it could be argued that this provision just states the obvious. If a brochure has been made available to

425 Article 87(4) of the Consumer Code.

426 The general clause in the Consumer Protection Act (*lex generalis*) applies.

427 Especially unfair trade practices law.

428 In the case of any infringement of this provision, the organiser or retailer is liable to compensate the consumer for any loss due to false or misleading information and is obliged to pay a (criminal) fine, cf. Art. 4.1, 4.2 and 16.1 of the Package Travel Regulations.

the consumer and subsequently a package travel contract is concluded on the basis of this brochure, the general rules on the conclusion and interpretation of a contract should already mean that the particulars contained in the brochure become part of the contract. Thus, the effect of this provision is rather limited. It is a mere reminder that the rules of general contract law provide for sanctions in many cases of non-compliance with information obligations.

A further sanction provided for in EC law follows from the Injunctions Directive (98/27/EC). Directive 90/314 is listed in the annex to this Directive. Therefore, consumer protection instruments in national laws transposing the Injunctions Directive apply to the law on package travel. This means that qualified entities ensure that consumers' collective interests are also met by the law on package travel.

Finally, the general rule of "effet utile" obliges member states to provide for effective sanctions. In this respect, member states have considerable leeway to determine which sanctions they provide for. Besides private law sanctions, such as remedies covered in the contract, member states may equally lay down various public law sanctions. Examples are fines or other administrative sanctions, which are found, for instance, in AUSTRIA, BELGIUM, CYPRUS, FRANCE, GREECE, SPAIN and SWEDEN. In many countries (GREECE, HUNGARY and MALTA, *inter alia*), the competent authorities can also revoke an operator's licence to run a travel agency. On the other hand, under CZECH law for example, there are no special sanctions, though the general system governing improper performance and damages applies.

The broad variety of sanctions provided for by member states does not seem to constitute a barrier to trade. The differences might even be regarded as having a positive effect on organisers' and retailers' compliance with information duties in cross-border cases, because such differences make it more difficult to calculate the costs of infringements committed abroad. Therefore, it should suffice to tackle the more substantial differences in the material information obligations applicable in member states. This would indeed facilitate compliance when packages are marketed and performed under the laws of different member states.

Nevertheless, EC law must also ensure that member states provide for effective sanctions. Although, under the principle of "effet utile", member states already have such a duty, consideration might be given to inserting a general reminder into the Directive, which could follow the model of Art. 11(1) of the Distance Selling Directive (C 97/7/EC).[429]

2. Restrictions on price revision

Art. 4(4) of Directive 90/314 regulates the circumstances under which it is permissible to agree a price revision in the package travel contract. The prices laid down in the contract can only be subject to revision if the contract explicitly provides for the possibility of upward or downward revision and states precisely how the revised price is to be calculated. Besides, only variations in transport costs, fees, taxes or fees chargeable for certain services and the exchange rates can be taken into account.

---

429 "Member States shall ensure that adequate and effective means exist to ensure compliance with this Directive in the interests of consumers."

a. Legislative transposition technique

The transposition of the rules in Art. 4(4) of Directive 90/314 into national law differs throughout the member states.

Table: Transposition laws for Art. 4(4)

Special act on package travel	BE,[430] CY,[431] DK,[432] EL,[433] ES,[434] FI,[435] FR,[436] IE,[437] LU,[438] MT,[439] PL,[440] PT, SE,[441] UK[442] *(14)*	
General regulation	Civil Code	CZ,[443] DE,[444] HU,[445] LT,[446] NL,[447] SK[448] *(6)*
	Consumer Code	AT,[449] IT[450] *(2)*
	Law of Obligations	EE,[451] SL[452] *(2)*
Government decree	HU,[453] LV[454] *(2)*	

b. Transposition in particular

aa. Increase "and" decrease in price

Art. 4(4)(a) of the Directive provides for a revision of the prices laid down in the package travel contract. According to the wording, the prices laid down in the contract shall not be

430 Article 11 of the Act of 16 February 1994 regulating package travel contracts and travel intermediation contracts.

431 Article 11(1)-(3) of the Package Travel, Holidays and Tours Law of 1998.

432 Article 13 of the Act No. 472/1993 on package travel.

433 Article 4(4) of the Decree No. 339/96 on package travel.

434 Article 7(1)-(3) of the Law 21/1995 regulating package travel.

435 Article 14 of the Package Travel Act of 28 November 1994/1079.

436 Article L 211-13 of the Tourism Code, Article 99 of Decree No. 94-490.

437 Article 17 of the Package Holidays and Travel Trade Act, 1995.

438 Article 13 of the Package Travel Act.

439 Article 11(1)-(2) of the Package Travel, Package Holidays and Package Tours Regulations, 2000.

440 Article 17 sec. (1) - sec. (2) of the Act on Tourist Services.

441 Article 11 of the Package Tours Act 1992:1672.

442 Regulation 11 of the Package Travel, Package Holidays and Package Tour Regulations 1992.

443 CC Art. 852c.

444 CC § 651a(4).

445 §§ 415-416 of the CC constitute general provisions on travel contracts.

446 CC Art. 6.752(3).

447 CC Art. 7:506.

448 CC § 741c(1).

449 § 31c(1) of the Consumer Protection Act.

450 Article 90(1), (4) of the Consumer Code.

451 § 871(1)-(3) of the Law of Obligations.

452 Article 900 of the Code of Obligations.

453 Article 8 of the Government Decree No. 214/1996.

454 Article 10, 11 of Cabinet Regulation No. 163.

subject to revision unless the contract explicitly provides for the possibility of upward or downward revision. While all member states restrict an increase in the price, only the transposition laws of AUSTRIA, BELGIUM, CYPRUS, DENMARK, FINLAND, FRANCE, GREECE, IRELAND, ITALY, LATVIA, LUXEMBOURG, MALTA, PORTUGAL, SLOVENIA,[455] SPAIN, SWEDEN and the UNITED KINGDOM contain provisions governing the possibility to decrease prices where a term on downward revision is laid down in the package travel contract. In contrast, the national laws of the CZECH REPUBLIC,[456] ESTONIA,[457] GERMANY,[458] HUNGARY,[459] LITHUANIA,[460] the NETHERLANDS,[461] POLAND[462] and SLOVAKIA[463] cover only price increases. Moreover, Hungarian law only allows a price increase if a term governing a price increase is part of the package travel contract. On the basis of the wording of the Directive, it is unclear whether transposition dealing only with the possibility of a price increase is an infringement of EC law. Art. 4(4) requires explicit provision in the contract for the possibility of upward "or" downward revision. There is good reason to assume that the "or" must be read as an "and" because otherwise it makes no sense that both upward and downward revisions are explicitly mentioned.[464] In this case, transposition in these countries is not in line with EC law. This should be clarified when reviewing the Directive.

Table: Increase and decrease in price

Regulations for price increase and decrease	AT, BE, CY, DK, EL, ES, FI, FR, IE, IT, LU, LV, MT, PT, SE, SL, UK *(17)*
Only increase covered	CZ, DE, EE, HU, LT, NL, PL, SK *(8)*

bb. Conditions for price revision

Art. 4(4)(a) of the Directive states that a price revision is possible only for variations in transportation costs (including the costs of fuel), dues, taxes or fees chargeable for certain services (such as landing taxes or embarkation or disembarkation fees at ports) and the exchange rates applied to the particular package.

Almost all member states transposed these provisions literally or almost literally. In DUTCH law, the transportation costs, such as fuel, tax and exchange rates may justify a price increase.[465] Only the FINNISH legislator used a significantly broader form of words for the transposition of Art. 4(4)(a) 2nd indent. A price revision is possible if "changes in transport costs beyond the tour

---

455 Slovenian law similarly allows for an increase or decrease in the price if the changes take place after conclusion of the contract and the calculation method was set out in the travel confirmation.

456 CC Art. 852c.

457 Article 871(1) of the Law of Obligations.

458 CC § 651a(4).

459 Article 8(1) of the Government Decree No. 214/1996.

460 CC Art. 6.752(3).

461 CC Art. 7:505(3).

462 Article 17 of the Act on Tourist Services.

463 CC § 741c(1).

464 *Howells/Wilhelmsson*, EC Consumer Law, 238 (see also note 35).

465 CC Art. 7:505(3).

organiser's control or which he could not have taken into account when the contract was concluded" have to be offset.[466] A literal interpretation of the transposition laws in the CZECH REPUBLIC and SLOVAKIA indicate a narrower form of words than in EC law. In the Czech Republic, an increase in the package price is possible only as a result of an increase in "payments connected with transportation, e.g. airport and port taxes, included in the price of the package".[467] Furthermore, a price increase due to variations in the exchange rate of the Czech crown is solely possible if the exchange rate increases by more than 10 % on average.[468] No alterations are possible less than 21 days before the package begins. Additionally, an agreement between the parties may state that the travel agency is entitled to increase the package price unilaterally if the revision method is precisely set out.[469] A similar provision can be found in the Slovakian transposition law, which states that a change in the exchange rate of the Slovak crown can only be taken into account if the exchange rate increases by more than 5 % on average.[470] As a restriction, this increase in the exchange rate must equally be registered at least 21 days before departure. The customer has to be notified in writing about the price increase at least 21 days before departure. Otherwise, the travel bureau does not have any right to claim the difference in price. In SLOVENIA, only changes in the currency exchange rate or changes in the carriers' tariffs affecting the price of the tour are mentioned. In ITALY, alongside the possibility of a price revision, detailed calculation methods for the different variations mentioned in the Directive must be provided.[471]

Table: Conditions for price revision

Similar to the Directive	AT, BE, CY, DE, DK, EE, EL, ES, FI, FR, HU, IE, IT, LT, LU, LV, MT, NL, PL, PT, SE, SL, UK *(23)*
Deviations	CZ, SK *(2)*

cc. Period

According to Art. 4(4)(b) of the Directive, the price stated in the contract must not be increased less than 20 days prior to departure. While most member states transposed this 20-day period, some national laws provide for a longer period. Whereas the CZECH[472] legislator established a period of 21 days, the transposition laws in FRANCE[473] and the UNITED KINGDOM[474] lay down a period of 30 days.

466 Article 14 of the Package Travel Act.

467 CC § 852c(2).

468 CC § 852c(2)(c).

469 CC § 852c(1).

470 CC § 741c(2)(c).

471 Article 90(1) of the Consumer Code.

472 CC Art. 852c(2).

473 Article L 211-13 of the Tourism Code.

474 Regulation 11(3) of the Package Travel, Package Holidays and Package Tour Regulations 1992.

dd. Other deviations

Furthermore, the transposition laws in CYPRUS[475] and the UNITED KINGDOM[476] provide for an additional restriction on any price revision. According to the laws in these member states, there may be no price increase for an individual consumer liable under the package travel contract where such an increase would be less than 2 % or greater than the percentage laid down in the package travel contract. ITALIAN law stipulates that a price increase may never exceed 10 % of the original price.[477] In SLOVENIA, if the increase in the agreed price exceeds 10 %, the traveller may withdraw from the contract without being obliged to reimburse any damages and retaining the right to a refund of all payments made.

3. Consumer Rights

a. Right to transfer the booking

Art. 4(3) of Directive 90/314 entitles the consumer to transfer his booking if he is prevented from proceeding with the package. Member states again chose different techniques to transpose this provision, as the following table shows.

Table: Transposition method

Special act on package travel	BE,[478] CY,[479] DK,[480] EL,[481] ES,[482] FI,[483] FR,[484] IE,[485] LU,[486] MT,[487] PL,[488] PT, SE,[489] UK[490] ***(14)***	
General regulation	Civil Code	CZ,[491] DE,[492] HU,[493] LT,[494] NL,[495] SK[496] ***(6)***

475 Article 11(3) of the Package Travel, Holidays and Tours Law.

476 Regulation 11(3)(ii) of the Package Travel, Package Holidays and Package Tour Regulations 1992.

477 Article 90(2) of the Consumer Code.

478 Article 12 of the Act of 16 February 1994 regulating package travel contracts and travel intermediation contracts.

479 Article 10 sec. (1)-(2) of the Package Travel, Holidays and Tours Law of 1998.

480 Article 12 of the Act No. 472/1993 on Package Travel.

481 Article 4(3) of the Decree No. 339/96 on package travel.

482 Article 5 sec. (1)-(3) of the Law No. 21/1995 regulating package travel.

483 Article 10 of the Package Travel Act of 28 November 1994/1079.

484 Article L 211-12 of the Tourism Code, Art. 99 of Decree No. 94-490.

485 Article 16 sec. (1)-(2) of the Package Holidays and Travel Trade Act, 1995.

486 Article 12 of the Package Travel Act.

487 Article 10(1)-(2) of the Package Travel, Package Holidays and Package Tours Regulations, 2000.

488 Article 16(1)-(3) of the Act on Tourist Services.

489 Article 9, Art. 10 of the Package Tours Act 1992:1672.

490 Regulation 10 of the Package Travel, Package Holidays and Package Tour Regulations 1992.

491 CC Art. 852b.

492 CC § 651b.

493 CC §§ 415-416.

494 CC Art. 6.753(1)-(2).

	Consumer Code	AT,[497] IT[498] *(2)*
	Law of Obligations	EE,[499] SL[500] *(2)*
Government decree	HU,[501] LV[502] *(2)*	

With regard to the content of national transposition laws, the following aspects may be highlighted.

aa. Party to which notice must be given

Art. 4(3) of the Directive stipulates that notice of the transfer has to be given to the package organiser or retailer. The national laws in BELGIUM, DENMARK, ESTONIA, GREECE, IRELAND, ITALY, MALTA,[503] SPAIN and SWEDEN stipulate that notice has to be given to the organiser or the retailer. According to the national laws of CYPRUS[504] and the UNITED KINGDOM,[505] notice to "the other party" is required. Other member states' laws make a choice, indicating whether notice has to be given to the organiser or the retailer. In AUSTRIA,[506] FINLAND,[507] GERMANY,[508] HUNGARY,[509] LITHUANIA,[510] the NETHERLANDS[511] and POLAND,[512] notice has to be given to the package organiser. On the other hand, FRANCE,[513] LUXEMBOURG[514] and PORTUGAL[515] require notice to be given to the retailer. In SLOVAKIA,[516] notice has to be given to the travel bureau and, in the CZECH REPUBLIC,[517] to the travel agency. SLOVENIAN[518] law does not contain any provision stating explicitly that notice is required.

---

495 CC Art. 7:506 contains a special rule for travel agreements, whereas Book 6 contains a general rule.

496 CC § 741f(1), § 741d(2).

497 § 31c(3) of the Consumer Protection Act.

498 Article 89 sec. (1)-(2) of the Consumer Code.

499 § 873 sec. (1)-(2) of the Law of Obligations.

500 Article 899 of the Code of Obligations.

501 Government Decree No. 214/1996.

502 Article 9 of Cabinet Regulation No. 163.

503 Regulation 10.1 of the Package Travel Regulations states that notice has to be given to the organiser or retailer acting on the instructions of the organiser.

504 Article 10(1) of the Package Travel, Holidays and Tours Law.

505 Regulation 10 sec. 1 of the Package Travel, Package Holidays and Package Tour Regulations 1992.

506 § 31c(3) of the Consumer Protection Act.

507 Article 10 of the Package Travel Act of 28 November 1994/1079.

508 CC § 651b.

509 Article 9(1) of the Government Decree No. 214/1996.

510 CC Art. 6.753(2).

511 CC, Art. 7:506.

512 Article 16(2) of the Act on Tourist Services.

513 Article 99 of the Decree No. 94-490.

514 Article 12 of the Package Travel Act.

515 Article 24 (1) of the Decree-Law 198/93.

516 CC § 741f(1).

517 CC Art. 852b (f).

518 Article 899 of the Code of Obligations.

Table: Party to which notice must be given

Organiser or retailer	BE, DK, EE, EL, ES, IE, IT, MT, SE *(9)*
The other party	CY, UK *(2)*
Organiser	AT, CZ, DE, FI, LT, NL, PL *(7)*
Retailer	FR, LU, PT *(3)*
Travel agency	CZ *(1)*
Travel bureau	SK *(1)*
Travel company	HU *(1)*
No specific provision on notice	SL *(1)*
Transposition not entirely clear	LV *(1)*

The Directive is unclear at this point because the wording in Art. 4(3) ("having given the organiser 'or' the retailer reasonable notice") can have two different meanings with regard to the addressee of the notice:
(1) Member states are free to decide to whom the consumer must address the notice – either the organiser or the retailer, or both. If the consumer addresses the notice to the wrong person, then no notice is deemed to have been given (unless the wrong person is regarded as an agent of the other person).
(2) The consumer may give notice to either the organiser or the retailer, and, in either case, has complied with the notice requirement.

It is obvious that the latter interpretation would be more consumer-friendly. If this interpretation is correct, several member states are in breach of the Directive. The question should therefore be clarified in the course of the review.

bb. Timeframe for giving notice

Art. 4(3) of the Directive states that the consumer has to give the organiser or the retailer "reasonable notice" of his intention to transfer the booking. The national laws in AUSTRIA, BELGIUM, DENMARK, ESTONIA, GERMANY, IRELAND, LUXEMBOURG, MALTA, the NETHERLANDS, SWEDEN and the UNITED KINGDOM do not lay down a specific period. They merely require that notice be given within a reasonable time before departure and some even allow notice to be given by departure (e.g. German law). Dutch law clarifies that notice given 7 days before departure is to be considered early enough. The CZECH REPUBLIC, LATVIA, POLAND and SLOVAKIA[519] stipulate that notice has to be given within the period agreed in the package travel contract. In CYPRUS, the transposition law stipulates that notice has to be sent within the period specified in the contract or in the advertising material or, where no such period is specified in either of the documents, within a reasonable time before departure. In contrast, the transposition laws in FRANCE, GREECE and PORTUGAL set a fixed period of time, whereby the length of the period may depend on the type of the package. In France, the normal period covers 7 days.[520] In the case of a cruise, this period is extended to 15 days. In Greece, the transferor has to give notice 5 working days before departure.[521] In the case of

519 The Package travel contract has to include a notice period if a substitute takes a package.

520 Art. 99 of Decree 94-490.

521 Article 4(3) of the Decree 339/96 on package travel.

sea journeys, the period for giving notice increases to 10 days. Under Portuguese[522] law, information has to be given at least 7 days before departure. If the trip involves long-haul flights and sea cruises, the period is extended to 15 days. Other member states' legislators provided for a specific period in their transposition laws without drawing any such distinction. In FINLAND, notice of the transfer has to be given no later than 48 hours before departure.[523] In HUNGARY, notice has to be given without delay as soon as there is an intention to transfer the contractual rights.[524] In ITALY, this period is 4 working days.[525] SPANISH[526] law sets a period of 15 days before the start of the package, unless the parties have agreed to a shorter period in the contract. In LITHUANIA, where no specific period is set, the tourist is entitled to transfer the trip to a third person who must agree to all the terms of the contract.[527] As already mentioned above, under SLOVENIAN law, no notice is required.

The meaning of "reasonable notice" is unclear. In the course of a review of the Directive, it could be clarified that it is really a reasonable period and not reasonable notice that is meant, and this period could perhaps be specified. It should also be decided whether the fixed periods provided for by member states are in line with EC law. The longer periods might plausibly deprive consumers of their right to transfer the booking.

Table: Timeframe for giving notice

(Within a reasonable time) Before departure	AT, BE, DE, DK, EE, IE, LU, MT, NL, SE, UK *(11)*	
Other solutions	Specific period before departure	ES, FI (48h), HU (without delay), IT (4 working days) *(4)*
	Differentiation	CY, EL, FR, PT *(4)*
	Contractual agreement	CZ, ES, LV, PL, SK *(5)*
	No specific period	LT *(1)*
No notice required	SL *(1)*	

cc. Form for giving notice

Art. 4(3) of the Directive does not require the transferor's notice to appear in a specific form. In AUSTRIA, BELGIUM, CYPRUS, DENMARK, ESTONIA, FINLAND, GERMANY, GREECE, HUNGARY, IRELAND, LATVIA, LUXEMBOURG, MALTA, POLAND, SWEDEN and the UNITED KINGDOM, the transferor does not have to meet any formal requirement for his notice. As already mentioned, SLOVENIAN law does not require notice in order to transfer the rights of the package. In contrast, the transposition laws in the CZECH REPUBLIC, ITALY,[528] LITHUANIA,[529] the NETHERLANDS,[530] PORTUGAL,[531] SLOVAKIA[532] and SPAIN[533] stipulate that notice has to be

---

[522] Article 24 sec. (1)-(2) of the Decree-Law 198/93.

[523] Article 10 of the Package Travel Act of 28 November 1994/1079.

[524] Article 9(1) of the Government Decree 214/1996.

[525] Article 89(1) of the Consumer Code.

[526] Article 5(2) of the Law 21/1995 regulating package travel.

[527] CC Art. 6.753(1).

[528] Article 90(1) of the Consumer Code.

[529] CC, Art. 6.753(2).

[530] CC, Art. 7:506(2).

given in writing. FRENCH[534] law even requires a letter sent by recorded delivery. It is questionable whether these formal requirements are in line with the Directive. In the course of the review, it could be clarified that the consumer does not need to meet any formal requirement for the notice.

Table: Form for notice given by traveller

No specific form	AT, BE, CY, DE, DK, EE, EL, FI, HU, IE, LU, LV, MT, PL, SE, UK *(16)*
Written form	CZ, ES, IT, LT, NL, PT, SK *(7)*
Recorded delivery	FR *(1)*
No notice required	SL *(1)*

dd. Liability

According to Art. 4(3) of the Directive, the transferor of the package and the transferee shall be jointly and severally liable to the organiser or retailer who is party to the contract for the balance due and for any additional costs arising from the transfer of rights. Most member states transposed this provision almost literally into their national laws (AUSTRIA, BELGIUM, CYPRUS, DENMARK, ESTONIA, FINLAND, FRANCE, GERMANY, GREECE, IRELAND, ITALY, LATVIA, LITHUANIA, LUXEMBOURG, MALTA, the NETHERLANDS, POLAND, PORTUGAL, SLOVAKIA, SPAIN, SWEDEN and the UNITED KINGDOM). Similarly, under HUNGARIAN law[535], the transferor and the transferee are jointly liable for contractual obligations and additional costs arising in the period before the transfer. In SLOVENIA,[536] it seems that only the transferor is liable.

Table: Liability of transferor and transferee

Joint and several liability	AT, BE, CY, DE, DK, EE, EL, ES, FI, FR, HU, IE, IT, LT, LU, LV, MT, NL, PL, PT, SE, SK, UK *(23)*
Deviations	SL (transferor) *(1)*
Transposition not entirely clear	CZ *(1)*

b. Consumer rights in the case of significant alterations

aa. Legal environment for consumer rights granted under the Directive

Directive 90/314 does not provide for a general rule governing cancellation of the booking by the consumer. The Directive only deals with consumer rights in the case of a significant alteration to the essential terms by the organiser (Art. 4(5)). For the sake of clarification, it

531 Article 24(1) of the Decree-Law 198/93.

532 CC, § 741f(1).

533 Article 5(2) of the Law 21/1995 regulating package travel.

534 Article 99 of the Decree No. 94-490.

535 Article 9(1) of the Government Decree 214/1996.

536 Article 899 of the Code of Obligations.

should be noted that the rights granted to the consumer under the Directive are embedded in other rules of national law concerning the consequences in the event of cancellation by the consumer. As such, a consumer may have different rights with regard to cancelling the booking. Firstly, the applicable national law may allow the consumer to cancel the contract without any reason. This is the case in GERMANY, HUNGARY, SPAIN and many other member states. It goes without saying that, in such a case, the consumer is liable to compensate the organiser. National laws may stipulate rules for the calculation of compensation if the consumer cancels without reason.[537] For instance, recent Spanish case law had to deal with this very question[538], i.e. of how to calculate a different percentage of compensation depending on the timing of cancellation if a consumer cancels without due reason.[539] In Hungarian law, compensation must not exceed the price paid. The right of cancellation can be exercised for reasons other than price increase or alteration to the terms or to the programme.

There is a second type of cancellation right under national laws, allowing the consumer to terminate the contract when there is a good reason even if this reason is beyond the organiser‘s control. According to FINNISH law, for example, the consumer may cancel the contract if he has sufficient reasons for not participating in a trip to a dangerous region – even if the organiser is not going to cancel it.[540] SPANISH law sometimes even excludes compensation if the consumer cancels for compelling reasons.[541] GERMAN law allows the consumer to cancel the booking if the trip is endangered by unforeseen *force majeure*. In this case, the consumer is partly freed from the obligation to pay the price. Additional costs must be partially shared by the parties, i.e. they are to be borne partially by the consumer (e.g. cost for return travel).[542]

A third type of cancellation right – very probably – exists in all national laws when the organiser is in (usually severe) breach of contract. This case is partially regulated by Art. 5 of the Directive, so will not be dealt with here in the context of Art. 4.

bb. Consequences of an alteration to the terms by the organiser

Art. 4(5) sent. 1 of Directive 90/314 sets out the organiser‘s obligations in the case of significant alterations to the essential terms and the rights of the consumer. The organiser must notify the consumer as quickly as possible about any important change in order to enable the consumer to either cancel[543] the contract without penalty (1st indent) or to accept a rider to the contract specifying the alterations made and their impact on the price (2nd indent). The consumer may therefore choose between these two possibilities. Should he opt to cancel,

537 Spain: Art. 9(4) of Law 21/1995 regulating package travel; Hungary: Art. 11(3) Government Decree No. 214/1996.

538 A.P. Jaén judgment of 4 March 2002; A.P. Pontevedra judgment of 29 October 2001.

539 Cf. Art. 9(4) of Law 21/1995 regulating package travel.

540 § 15(1) of the Package Travel Act.

541 A.P. Malaga judgment of 29 September 2004: consumer depression; A.P. Salamanca judgment of 7 September 2001: NATO bombing in Yugoslavia.

542 CC § 651j.

543 Although Directive 90/314 uses the term “withdrawal”, “cancellation” is used here instead in order to avoid confusion with the withdrawal rights granted in Directives 85/577, 97/7 and 94/47.

Art. 4(5)(a) and (b) of the Directive again offers two possibilities for the consumer: he may either take a substitute package of equivalent or higher quality or be refunded with respect to all sums paid under the contract. In this case, the consumer may be compensated according to the applicable law of the relevant Member State, unless the trip is cancelled due to an insufficient number of participants or *force majeure* (Art. 4(6)(b) no. i and ii).

With regard to the terms used, the Package Travel Directive consistently uses "withdrawal" when referring to the consumer's right to terminate the contract and "cancellation" when the organiser terminates. Nevertheless, consideration should be given to avoiding the notion of "withdrawal" in this context, because this may be confused with the very different 'cooling off periods' provided for in other Directives, which are commonly known as "withdrawal rights". As such, in this study, "withdrawal" is only used for cooling-off periods, while "cancellation" is used for both termination of the contract by the consumer and termination of the contract by the organiser. In the German version of the Directive, this linguistic problem does not occur.

The vast majority of member states have transposed the provisions in Art. 4(5) and (6) by closely following the system in the Package Travel Directive. LITHUANIA is the only country not to have explicitly transposed these provisions; rather, it simply grants the tour organiser a right to waive the contract for compelling reasons, though he is still obliged to inform the tourist of this decision.[544]

(1) Requirements for the right of cancellation

(a) Significant alteration to the essential terms

The Directive requires a significant alteration to the essential terms by the organiser and gives as an example a price increase. Member states have transposed this prerequisite with only slight variations. For instance, GERMAN law regards any price increase of more than 5 % as a significant alteration to the essential terms.[545] HUNGARIAN law sets a threshold of 10 %. It cannot be argued that such variations, which aim at clarifying whether an alteration is "significant", constitute a shortcoming in transposition. Further variations are displayed in the following table.

Table: Alteration to terms

Significant alteration to the essential terms	AT, BE, CY, DE, DK,[546] EE, EL,[547] ES, FI, FR,[548] HU, IE, LV, MT, NL, SL,[549] UK *(17)*

---

544 CC Art. 6.751(1).

545 CC § 651a(5).

546 § 16 of the Act 472/1993 refers to an 'anticipated significant breach of contract'.

547 The only regulatory gap in the Directive commented on in Greek legal literature is that no rules exist where the consumer is compelled to cancel the trip after conclusion of the contract, but before the beginning of the trip. In Greek law, those who identify the travel contract as a service contract apply CC Art. 700, which stipulates that the traveller may cancel the contract at any time,

Alteration to the essential terms	SK *(1)*
Significant alteration to any term	IT *(1)*
Alteration to essential terms for reasons beyond the organiser's control	PL *(1)*
Impossible to perform an essential term due to incidents beyond the organiser's control	CZ,[550] FR,[551] LU, PT *(4)*
Impossible to fulfil the contractual obligations	SE *(1)*
Not explicitly transposed	LT *(1)*

(b) Obligation to notify the consumer

Art. 4(5) of the Directive places obligations on the 'organiser' as the party who, where essential terms are notified, must notify the consumer as quickly as possible.

In the transposition laws, variations in the wording exist: e.g. the CZECH REPUBLIC (travel agency), FRANCE (seller), ITALY (organiser and retailer), LATVIA (undertaking), LUXEMBOURG (travel agent), PORTUGAL (travel agency) and SLOVAKIA (travel bureau). Although in some cases not very clear, such a choice of wording leads to the conclusion that both the organiser and the retailer are obliged to inform the consumer. If this is correct, the consumer's position is strengthened in comparison with the Directive, which places obligations only on the organiser. SLOVENIAN law does not contain any specific provision, but only a general provision stipulating that the organiser must provide the traveller with the services described in the contract, as well as a confirmation or travel itinerary, and act in accordance with the traveller's rights and best interests.

There is another feature particular to CZECH law. There is no obligation specified, but only a provision stipulating that the travel agency may suggest a contractual change without any time limit.[552]

Table: Party obliged to inform the consumer about the need for alteration

As per the Directive	AT, BE, CY, DE, DK, EE, EL, ES, FI, HU, IE, LV, MT, NL, PL, SE, UK *(17)*
Variations	CZ, FR, IT, LU, PT, SK *(6)*
Not explicitly transposed	LT, SL *(2)*

Moreover, the organiser must notify the consumer "as quickly as possible" in order to enable him to take appropriate decisions. SLOVENIA has not transposed this notification duty for

though he remains obliged to pay the agreed price, minus the amount saved as a result of non-performance of the contract.

548 Article 101 of the Decree No. 94-490.

549 Article 903 of the Code of Obligations refers to 'significant changes in the travel itinerary'.

550 CC sec. 852e(1) states that, as a result of reasons beyond the organiser's control, the terms of the travel contract may be changed before departure if necessary.

551 Article L 211-14 of the Tourism Code.

552 CC sec. 852e(1).

the organiser at all. FRANCE[553] and ITALY, on the other hand, go beyond the Directive's requirements by demanding that the consumer receives written notification from the organiser. As to the timeframe for giving notice, the majority of member states have adopted the same formulation as the Directive. Whereas LUXEMBOURG grants the organiser a three-day period for fulfilling his obligation, CZECH and SLOVAKIAN law do not have any regulations with regard to the timeframe for notifying the consumer. This no longer seems to be in line with the Directive's formulation "as quickly as possible". The Italian regulation uses the term 'immediately'.[554]

The majority of member states require information about any significant alteration to the essential terms. Additionally, the organiser must inform the consumer about a price increase in ESTONIA. In PORTUGAL, the organiser has to inform the consumer if the contractual obligations cannot be met. In HUNGARY, no notification duty is laid down in any special law, but the general rules of civil law apply, demanding immediate notification if it appears that it might be impossible to perform the contract.

Table: Time period for notification duty

As quickly as possible	AT, BE, CY, DE, DK, EE, EL, ES, FI, FR, IE, MT, NL, PT, SE, SK, UK *(17)*
Immediately	IT *(1)*
Without delay	LV, PL *(2)*
3 calendar days	LU *(1)*
No time limit	CZ, HU *(2)*
Not explicitly transposed	LT, SL *(2)*

Table: Content of notification

Information about any alteration	AT, BE, CY, DE, EE, EL, ES, FI, FR, IE, IT, LU, LV, MT, PL, SE, UK *(17)*
Information about right to choose	AT, FR, LU, PL *(4)*
Information about right of cancellation	BE, DK, SE *(3)*
Suggestion of alteration to contract	CZ, SK *(2)*
Information about any price increase	EE *(1)*
Cancellation of the journey	EE *(1)*
Information if contractual obligations cannot be fulfilled	PT *(1)*
Not explicitly transposed	LT, SL *(2)*

(2) Consumer rights after notification of a significant alteration

The consumer may subsequently either cancel the contract without penalty or accept a rider to the contract specifying the alterations made and their impact on the price. Some member states only grant the consumer the right of cancellation without explicitly mentioning the possibility of accepting a rider to the contract, e.g. DENMARK, ESTONIA, FINLAND, GERMANY

---

553 Cf. Art. L 211-134 of the Tourism Code and Art. 101 of Decree 94-490.

554 Article 91(1) of the Consumer Code.

and SWEDEN. The reason for this may be the fact that the parties can, as a matter of course, agree on a contract amendment.

Table: Consumer rights after notification of an alteration

Right of cancellation	AT, BE, CY, CZ, DE, DK, EE, EL, ES, FI, FR, HU, IE, IT, LU, LV, MT, NL, PL, PT, SE, SK, SL, UK *(24)*
Not explicitly transposed	LT *(1)*

The possibility for the consumer to "accept a rider to the contract specifying the alterations made and their impact on the price" has not been transposed into GERMAN law as such. Instead, the traveller has a right to another journey or equivalent if there is an essential alteration to the services and the organiser is able to offer an alternative trip.[555] Thus, Art. 4(5), 2nd indent of Directive 90/314 has probably not been correctly transposed. Moreover, in HUNGARY, the traveller is allowed to demand an equivalent or higher standard service. If the organiser is not able to offer such a service or the traveller does not accept such an offer, the price can be reduced by 20 % where the organiser's decision to cancel the contract does not stem from the traveller.[556]

In BELGIUM, if the consumer accepts amendments to the initial agreement, the change must be laid down in a rider or a new contract. The parties are, however, free to decide which method is appropriate.

Alteration of contract	Rider	BE*, CY, EL, ES, FR, IE, LV, MT, NL, UK *(10)*
	Acceptance of alteration to contract	AT, CZ, FI, HU*, IT, LU, PL, PT, SK *(9)*
	New contract	BE* *(1)*
Replacement with equivalent or higher standard services		DE, DK,[557] EE,[558] HU*, LV *(5)*
Transposition not entirely clear		SE, SL *(2)*

* *more than once*

(3) Duty of the consumer to give notice of his decision

Generally, all member states have transposed this duty for the consumer to give notice of the remedy he/she wishes to select. There are variations in the deadline by which this information has to be notified to the other contract party. This period varies from "as soon as possi-

555 CC § 651a(5), sent. 3.

556 § 10(2) of Government Decree 214/1996.

557 § 16 of Act 472/1993 gives the consumer the right to withdraw from the contract or to choose a substitute package without causing disproportionate costs or loss to the organiser where it is anticipated that there will be a significant breach of contract before departure.

558 According to § 872(2) of the Law of Obligations, the traveller may, instead of withdrawing, demand a substitute package of equivalent or higher cost (if the tour operator is able to offer such a substitute), or a substitute package of lower cost and a refund of the difference in price between the packages.

ble" (or similar) in most member states to a fixed period of differing length in the CZECH REPUBLIC,[559] ITALY,[560] LUXEMBOURG, PORTUGAL and SPAIN. Moreover, Portuguese law even demands written acceptance of any change to the contract and of any potential price revision.

Table: Time limit

As soon as possible	BE, CY, DE, EE, EL, FR, HU, IE, MT, UK *(10)*
2 working days	IT *(1)*
3 calendar days	ES *(1)*
5 calendar days	CZ *(1)*
7 calendar days	LU *(1)*
8 calendar days	PT *(1)*
Without delay	FI, PL, SL[561] *(3)*
Established by the travel bureau	SK *(1)*
Reasonable time	DK, SE *(2)*
Not explicitly transposed	LT *(1)*

(4) Effects of the cancellation by the consumer or by the organiser

If the consumer withdraws from the contract pursuant to Art. 4(5) or if the organiser cancels the package for reasons other than the fault of the consumer, Art. 4(6) of Directive 90/314 gives the consumer the right either to take a substitute package (a) or to be repaid as soon as possible (b).

Overall, member states have adopted these provisions, although, in some cases, have supplemented them with additional rules (e.g. rules about other reasons for cancellation, cf. above under point III.3.b.aa.). In most member states, the consumer is entitled to take a substitute package as stated in the Directive, as the following table shows.

Table: Consumer's entitlement to take a substitute package

Substitute package of equivalent or higher quality	AT, BE, CY, CZ, DE, EL, EE, ES, HU, IE, IT, LT, LU, MT, NL, PL, PT, SE, SK, UK *(20)*
Refund of the difference in the case of lower quality package	AT, BE, CY, CZ,[562] DK, EE, EL, ES, FI, HU, IE, IT, LU, MT, PL, PT, SE, SK, UK *(19)*
Substitute package	FR *(1)*
Another package without any undue expense or financial loss for the organiser	DK *(1)*

559 CC sec. 852e(2).

560 Article 91(2) of the Consumer Code states that the consumer shall inform the organiser or retailer of his decision within two working days from the date on which he received notice concerning the alteration.

561 No specific transposition exists, but the general rules governing contract avoidance require that a creditor cancelling a contract due to the non-performance of a debtor's obligation must notify the debtor without delay.

562 The special regulation on travel contracts specifies an obligation to pay the price difference between the original and substitute package, CC Art. 852g(3).

Substitute package at the original price, compensation for unnecessary costs incurred	FI *(1)*

Some member states have also specified a deadline for refunding the difference if the substitute package is cheaper (for instance, BELGIUM ("as soon as possible"), CZECH REPUBLIC ("with undue delay") and SLOVAKIA ("forthwith")).

Where the consumer is not offered, or does not take, a substitute package, most member states explicitly regulate the reimbursement of all sums paid.

Table: Obligation to reimburse all sums paid

Reimbursement of all sums paid	AT, BE, CY, CZ,[563] DE,[564] DK, EL, ES, FI, FR, IE, IT, LT, LU, MT, NL, PL, PT, SE, SK, SL, UK *(22)*
Immediate repayment of the full price paid	HU *(1)*

FINLAND additionally stipulates that the consumer must be compensated for any unnecessary costs incurred.

Several member states also explicitly transposed the provision on the timeframe for repayment ("as soon as possible").[565] FRENCH[566] law requires, for instance, the "immediate" refund of all sums paid if the buyer does not take the substitute package.

Table: Time of repayment of all sums paid under the contract

As soon as possible	BE, EL, IE, MT, SE, UK *(6)*
Immediately	FR, HU, PL, PT *(4)*
Upon cancellation of contract	CY *(1)*
Without delay	FI *(1)*
When contract is cancelled	ES *(1)*
7 working days after cancellation by the consumer or the organiser	IT *(1)*
10 days after cancellation by the consumer	LU *(1)*
No time limit	CZ *(1)*

Some national laws also contain cancellation penalties for the organiser if he cancels the package. If the organiser cancels less than 20 days prior to the date on which the package begins, he is obliged to pay the consumer 10 % of the package price in the CZECH REPUBLIC and to reasonably compensate any damages suffered by the consumer in SLOVAKIA. In HUNGARY, the organiser must pay interest of 20 % per annum on the price to be repaid.

---

563 General provisions governing unjust enrichment apply without any time limit.

564 CC § 346.

565 As an example for the other member states, LATVIA does not provide for any particular deadline for repayment of all sums.

566 Article 101 of the Decree 94-490.

(5) Compensation under member states' laws governing non-performance

Article 4(6) of the Directive also states that the consumer shall be entitled to compensation for non-performance of the contract, except in one of the cases listed in i) (minimum number not reached) or ii) *(force majeure)*.

Most member states have explicitly transposed the duty to compensate the consumer. The others seem to rely on their general rules on compensation in the case of a breach of contract. Again, CZECH law differs in imposing on the travel agency a penalty of 10 % of the package price in the consumer's favour if the trip is cancelled within 20 days of departure.[567] In addition, the customer is entitled to damages.[568]

Table: Compensation for non-performance

As per the Directive	AT, BE, CY, CZ,[569] DE, DK, EL, ES, HU, IE, IT, LT,[570] LU, LV,[571] MT, NL, PL, PT, SE, SK,[572] SL, UK *(22)*
Cancellation penalty	CZ[573] *(1)*
Not explicitly transposed	EE, FI, FR *(3)*

There are some variations with regard to the two exemptions from the duty to compensate the consumer (i.e. if the minimum number is not reached (n° i) or in the case of *force majeure* (n° ii)).

Some member states have introduced a time limit for cancellation where the minimum number of participants is not reached. For instance, in SLOVENIA, the organiser must cancel at the latest 5 days before the scheduled departure. In BELGIUM, the period is 15 days and in ITALY 20 days.

With regard to exemptions on the grounds of *force majeure*, the definition of this notion seems to differ across member states. For instance, under FINNISH law, the organiser is entitled to cancel the package because of an act of war, a natural catastrophe, a strike or similar situation at or near the package destination, or because, on the grounds of other unforeseen circumstances, the package cannot be performed without risk to the traveller's life or health.[574] *Force majeure* is not defined in GERMAN legislation, though it has been more closely defined in a number of rulings in the German courts as an "external event that is not in any way connected to the company and could not, even with due care and attention, have been

567 CC § 852g(4).

568 CC § 852g(4) last sent.

569 CC Art. 852j.

570 CC Art 6.751(3) 1st indent explicitly transposed a compensation duty for the organiser who, on waiving the contract, must compensate the tourist for any material damage and reimburse the money already paid by the consumer.

571 As compensation for non-performance, any monies paid must be reimbursed, and, additionally, the customer has a right to claim losses under Civil law on the grounds of a breach of contract.

572 If the organiser cancels less than 20 days prior to departure, he is obliged to pay the consumer reasonable compensation .

573 CC § 852g sec. (4), (5).

574 Article 12 of the Package Travel Act of 28 November 1994/1079.

avoided".[575] In contrast, the Directive's definition is wider, covering internal events rooted in the company's business operations, such as staff strikes affecting the travel agency/trip organiser, where such an event was not foreseeable or its consequences could not have been avoided. Since the definition adopted by German courts limits the opportunities for the trip organiser to cancel, German case law actually works in the consumer's favour.

Some differences also exist in SPAIN as regards the exemption on the grounds of *force majeure*. These differences exist in various administrative rules that some Autonomous Communities (Catalonia, the Balearic Islands etc.) have enacted to bring their rules into line with the Directive. The administrative (though not civil) liability of retailers (travel agencies) is therefore slightly different depending on the Spanish region in which they operate.

In FRENCH law, there are no explicit exemptions.[576] In the CZECH REPUBLIC, exemptions from liability for damages (not for compensation) are similar to the provisions in the Directive.[577]

The following table indicates further variations across member states.

Table: Exemptions from the obligation to compensate the consumer

As per the Directive	AT, BE, CY, CZ, DK, EL, ES, HU, IE, IT, LT, LU, MT, NL, PL, PT, SE, SL, UK *(19)*	
Examples of variations with regard to i) (minimum number)	Explicit right to cancel	EE, FI, SK *(3)*
	Not explicitly transposed	DE, FR *(2)*
Examples of variations with regard to ii) (*force majeure*)	Explicit right of cancellation	DE, EE, FI *(3)*
	Not explicitly transposed	FR *(1)*
	Definition of *force majeure*	EE,[578] FI *(2)*
	No explicit use of the term '*force majeure*'	CY, CZ, DK, MT[579] *(4)*
	No explicit exclusion of over-booking	CY, CZ, DK, HU, IE, LT, MT, PL, SE, SK *(10)*
Transposition not entirely clear	LV *(1)*	

4. Additional duties for the organiser

a. Obligation to make alternative arrangements

The first sentence in Art. 4(7) of Directive 90/314 lays down an obligation for the organiser to make alternative arrangements without extra cost and to compensate the consumer, where

[575] Cf. BGH judgment of 16 April 2002, X ZR 17/01.

[576] Neither in Art. L 211-15 of the Tourism Code nor in Art. 102 of the Decree 94-490.

[577] CC sec. 852g(5)(b). This is a technical problem as the regulation in CC sec. 852g(5) duplicates the provision in sec. 852j(1).

[578] Article 103(2) of the Law of Obligations.

[579] Regulation 13.3.2 of the Package Travel Regulations uses the wording "on the grounds of unusual and unforeseeable circumstances beyond the control of the organiser, the retailer or other supplier of services, the consequences of which could not have been avoided even if all due care had been exercised" instead of the term '*force majeure*'.

appropriate, should a significant proportion of the services not be provided after departure. It is unclear whether the duty to compensate the consumer "where appropriate" constitutes an independent specific liability rule or – more plausibly – merely refers to the general rule in Art 5(2) of the Directive.[580] According to the latter scenario, the organiser could cite the reasons provided for in Art. 5(2), e.g. force majeure. This question could be clarified when reviewing the Directive.

Many member states have transposed these provisions by closely following the Directive. The following table shows the general picture.

Table: Obligation to make alternative arrangements

Substantively as per the Directive	BE, CY, EL, FR, HU, IE, IT, LT, MT, NL, PL, PT, SE, SK, UK *(15)*
Variations	AT, CZ, DE, DK, EE, ES, FI, LU *(8)*
Additional requirements	FR, HU, PL, PT *(4)*
Not explicitly transposed	SL[581] *(1)*
Transposition not entirely clear	LV *(1)*

There is a relatively broad spectrum of – in most cases slight – variations across member states. For instance, in AUSTRIA, although the travel agent is obliged to assist the traveller in any possible way, the Austrian Consumer Protection Act does not mention any obligation for the travel agent to compensate the traveller where alternative arrangements are impossible. As such, Austria relies on the general provisions in the Austrian Civil Code concerning compensation (e.g. § 1042). In LUXEMBOURG, the transposition law does not oblige the travel agent to make alternative arrangements when due justification is provided that it is impossible to meet the contractual obligations.

The FINNISH legislator, in the first instance, provides for any defect in performance to be remedied. If, however, the traveller suffers material inconvenience, he may refuse such a remedy. If it is not possible to remedy the defect or if it is not remedied without delay, the traveller is entitled to a price reduction in accordance with the scale of the defect. CZECH law obliges the travel agency to provide a consumer in difficulty with prompt assistance if damage was caused by a third party or unforeseeable circumstances.[582] Where all services or a significant part are not provided or the travel agency perceives that it will be unable to provide the services laid down in the contract, the travel agency must take appropriate measures without undue delay and free of charge.[583]
The Directive lays down a duty to compensate for the difference between the services offered and those supplied "where appropriate". CZECH law and FRENCH law[584] clarify that compensation is appropriate when the service supplied is of lower quality.

Some countries (for instance DENMARK) provide for a right of cancellation in the situation regulated in Art. 4(7) of the Directive. In the event of cancellation, the operator has to re-

580 Cf. *Howells/Wilhelmsson*, EC Consumer Law, 243 (see also note 55).

581 Article 903 of the Code of Obligations only regulates when changes in the travel programme are permitted.

582 CC sec.852k(1).

583 CC § 852k(2).

584 Article L 211-16 of the Tourism Code.

fund any payments made, but is therefore entitled to a sum corresponding to the value which the package tour may be considered to have had for the customer. Cancellation or alternatively a price reduction is excluded if the operator offers to remedy the shortcoming without extra cost or significant inconvenience and within a reasonable period of time. Besides, compensation is granted both for any shortcoming and – unlike ordinary rules on damages – for any subsequent significant inconvenience, such as a "ruined holiday", unless the breach is due to *force majeure*.

ESTONIAN law offers the traveller the right to cancel the contract if an essential travel service is changed significantly. Instead of cancelling, the traveller may demand a substitute package of equivalent or higher cost if possible. Otherwise, the difference in price between the packages must be refunded. A replacement service can be provided in HUNGARY and LUXEMBOURG, too. In ESTONIA, the consequences of breaching a contractual obligation are also specified in detail. Firstly, the traveller has to notify the tour organiser or retailer who must then take all reasonable steps in order to provide immediate assistance to a traveller in difficulty – unless the traveller has caused the breach himself. In SLOVAKIAN law, the travel bureau is liable to the customer and must take action without undue delay in order to ensure that the tour may begin and to refund the customer in accordance with the price difference between the services offered and provided.

There is no right to compensation in POLAND if the reason it is impossible to make alternative arrangements is due either solely to the actions or failings of third parties not involved in the alternative arrangements (if their conduct was not foreseeable and preventable), or to *force majeure*. Moreover, the client may seek a proportional price reduction provided that the replacement service is of lower quality than the service described in the tourist event programme.

GERMAN law offers the traveller a wide range of remedies. Compared to the Directive, there is a higher standard of liability. One special feature relates to what is termed a travel defect, meaning that when the trip does not meet the specifications or necessary quality standards, German law regards it as unsatisfactory. In the case of an infringement, the organiser may, in the first instance, either rectify the defect or provide an equivalent replacement service. If he fails to do so, the traveller is entitled to a price reduction in line with the duration of the inconvenience, provided that he has informed the organiser about the defect. If there is a fundamental breach, the consumer may also cancel the contract. It is important to note that these remedies do not depend on establishing the organiser's fault. This is only a requirement when the consumer additionally seeks damages, including recompense for wasted holiday time.

SPANISH law adds that when the consumer continues the trip under the alternative arrangements, this is deemed tantamount to acceptance of the proposal. PORTUGAL includes an obligation to communicate to the agency any deficiency in the performance of the contract in respect of services provided by third parties within the period stipulated in the contract or, failing that, as soon as possible, either in writing or another appropriate form.

SLOVENIAN law does not contain any specific provision. The substance of Art. 4(7) of the Directive can rather be found in several different articles of the Code of Obligations. It is stated that the agreed accommodation may only be replaced with accommodation facilities of the same category or of a higher category at the travel organiser's expense, and only in the agreed location. This seems stricter than the Directive's "suitable alternative arrangements". In the event of substantial alterations without justified reasons, the organiser must return everything obtained from the traveller, who is allowed to cancel the contract.

b. Duty to provide equivalent return transport and compensation

If an alternative arrangement according to Art. 4(7) sent. 1 of the Directive is either impossible or not accepted by the consumer for good reasons, the organiser has to provide equivalent return transport to the place of departure or to another return point to which the consumer has agreed. He must also compensate the consumer where appropriate (Art. 4(7) sent. 2).

Once again, most member states, (e.g. BELGIUM, CYPRUS, FRANCE, GREECE, ITALY, LITHUANIA, LUXEMBOURG, MALTA, PORTUGAL, SPAIN, SWEDEN and the UNITED KINGDOM) have implemented this provision in a similar way or even word-for-word.

Examples of variations or more detailed provisions can be found in several member states. For instance, AUSTRIA does not have a specific provision on compensation. Nevertheless the consumer is entitled to compensation under the general rules in the Austrian Civil Code. Whereas SLOVAKIA omits the term "for good reasons" as per the Directive, IRISH law replaces it with "on reasonable grounds" and the ITALIAN legislator chooses the term "in good faith".

The CZECH REPUBLIC regulates the question of transport in detail. The return journey includes any necessary replacement accommodation and catering. Furthermore, if there is any price difference, this has to be reimbursed.[585] In SLOVAKIA, return transport to the point of departure or such other point of return as agreed by the consumer also includes any necessary replacement board and lodging. In HUNGARY, if an alternative arrangement is either impossible or not accepted by the consumer for good reasons, the organiser has to arrange equivalent transport back to the place of departure, cover its costs and reimburse the fees minus the price of services already provided.[586] ESTONIAN law also clarifies that all additional expenses are to be borne by the operator.

According to DANISH, ESTONIAN and GERMAN law, the consumer must be returned, free of charge, to his point of departure or to another location specified in the contract using a means of transport corresponding to that specified in the contract if he *cancels* the contract and not if he *does not accept* the organiser's arrangements as per the Directive. In POLAND, the rules apply if he *either* cancels *or* does not accept the replacement service.

SLOVENIAN law has only very indirectly implemented the EU provision as it contains a general provision requiring the organiser to do everything to safeguard the traveller's interests.[587]

Similarly, in the NETHERLANDS, there is a general rule stating that help and assistance must be provided, though "return transport and compensation" are not specifically mentioned.[588]

---

585 CC sec. 852k(4).

586 Article 12(3) of Government Decree 214/1996.

587 Cf. Art. 890 of the Code of Obligations covering the organiser's general liability for damages.

Table: Duty to provide equivalent return transport and compensation

Substantively as per the Directive	BE, CY, EL, ES, FI, FR, HU, IT, LT, LU, LV, MT, PT, SE, UK *(15)*
Variations	AT, CZ, DE, DK, EE, IE, SK, PL *(8)*
Indirectly transposed	NL, SL *(2)*

c. Duty to make prompt efforts in cases of complaint

According to Art. 6 of Directive 90/314, in cases of complaint, the organiser and/or retailer or his local representative (if there is one) must make prompt efforts to find appropriate solutions.

The BELGIAN, DUTCH, FRENCH, LATVIAN, LITHUANIAN, POLISH and SLOVENIAN legislators have not transposed this provision. This may be due to the fact that the obligation is considered to be part of general contract duties in these countries.[589]

Table: Explicit transposition of the duty to make prompt efforts in case of complaints

Substantively equivalent to the Directive	As per the Directive	CY, DK, ES, HU, IE, MT,[590] PT, SE, SK, UK *(10)*
	In relation to the consumer‘s rights	AT *(1)*
	Following the consumer's duty	EE, IT *(2)*
Possibility to refuse in the case of unreasonable expense or inconvenience	DE, FI *(2)*	
Indirectly transposed	EL *(1)*	
No specific legislative transposition	BE, FR, LT, LV, NL, PL, SL *(7)*	
Transposition not entirely clear	CZ, LU *(2)*	

In some member states, the national laws use a slightly different wording or legislative technique than the Directive. For instance, in AUSTRIA, ESTONIA, GERMANY, FINLAND and HUNGARY, the organiser must make prompt efforts to help not in the case of complaints, but in the case of a failure in performance. In CYPRUS, ITALY[591] and the UNITED KINGDOM, the national regulations refer to complaints about failures in performance. The SWEDISH regulation refers to a "justified complaint". In IRELAND, the organiser must help if the consumer is in difficulty. According to the GREEK regulation, a written complaint is needed. Where the organiser, retailer or local representative receives such a complaint or is called upon by the supervisory authorities, he must be able to provide explanations and show that he is endeavouring to find appropriate solutions. Thus, a duty to give prompt assistance is not explicitly mentioned, but covered by the obligation to document attempts to find a so-

588 CC Art. 7:507(3).

589 With regard to the Netherlands cf. CC Art. 6:248.

590 See Reg. 8.3 Package Travel Regulations, which states that, in cases of complaint, the organiser or his local representative shall make prompt efforts to find appropriate solutions.

591 The consumer shall inform the organiser or retailer of his decision within two working days from the date on which he received notice about the alteration to the contractual conditions.

lution. A peculiarity in Italy[592] is that the duty to help the consumer is "hidden" in a regulation that obliges the consumer to make complaints about failures in performance. In ESTONIA, the duty to try immediately to find suitable solutions is also connected to the consumers' duty to notify the travel provider in the case of a failure in performance. In FINLAND[593] and GERMANY,[594] the consumer's counterparty is not obliged to take measures which cause unreasonable inconvenience.

Table: Cases in which the organiser/retailer must make prompt efforts to find a solution

Complaints	ES, DK, IE, MT, PT *(5)*
Complaints about failure in performance	CY,[595] HU, IT, UK *(4)*
Justified complaint	SE *(1)*
Written complaint	EL *(1)*
Failure in performance	AT, DE, EE, FI *(4)*
Called upon by supervisory authority	EL *(1)*
No specific legislative transposition	BE, FR, LT, LV, NL, PL, SL *(7)*
Transposition not entirely clear	CZ, LU *(2)*

The provision in Art. 6 is often integrated into the regulations governing consumers' rights. Consequently, some member states place obligations on the consumer's counterparty, whether the organiser or retailer. The local representative is mentioned in CYPRUS, GREECE, ITALY, MALTA, PORTUGAL, SWEDEN and the UNITED KINGDOM. In HUNGARY, the traveller must inform the representative of a problem without delay who, in turn, is obliged to act and inform the travel company without delay. If there is no representative, a travel agency previously indicated by the travel company must be informed.

Table: Obligated party

Organiser	AT, DE, EL, ES,[596] FI, IE, IT, MT, SE *(9)*
Retailer	EL, ES, IE *(3)*
Agency	HU,* PT *(2)*
Other party to the contract	CY, UK *(2)*
Organiser and service provider in question	DK[597] *(1)*
Representative	HU* *(1)*
Local representative mentioned	CY, EL, IE,[598] IT, MT, PT, SE, UK *(8)*

* *more than once*

592 Article 98(1) of the Consumer Code.

593 § 19 of the Package Travel Act of 28 November 1994/1079.

594 CC § 651c.

595 Art 15(8) of the Package Travel, Holidays and Tours Law of 1998 refers not to 'failures in performance' but to 'deficiencies' in contractual performance.

596 Article 10(3) of Law 21/1995 regulating package travel refers to the "retailer or, depending on the case, the organiser".

597 § 25 of Act 472/1993.

598 Article 14(4) of the Package Holidays and Travel Trade Act, 1995 states that, in the case of complaints, either the 'organiser' or the 'local representative' shall make prompt efforts in order to find appropriate solutions.

5. Liability

a. Liability of organiser and/or retailer

Art. 5(1) of the Directive obliges member states to ensure that the organiser and/or the retailer is liable to the consumer for the proper performance of any obligations under the package travel contract, irrespective of whether the organiser, the retailer or other service suppliers were to fulfil the relevant obligations. The provision therefore does not specify possible remedies. Its main function is to make the organiser and/or retailer liable where another supplier is responsible for improper performance. In particular, this provision reveals the overriding problem of the Package Travel Directive, i.e. that it did not clearly decide whether the organiser, the retailer or both are liable to the consumer. This decision is left to member states' discretion. They have to ensure that at least one of the two is liable in all cases.

In the course of a review of the Directive, consideration might be given to clarifying this rather vague situation. The most consumer-friendly solution would be joint and several liability for both the organiser and the retailer.[599] However, this could be a rather radical solution for some member states, where travel agencies are commonly just small retailers with low profit margins. A less invasive solution could be to make the organiser liable in all cases and to leave to member states' discretion whether the retailer should be jointly liable.

IRELAND has transposed the provisions in the Directive concerning the liability of the retailer and the travel organiser almost literally. In MALTA, LITHUANIA, LUXEMBOURG and PORTUGAL, the rules concerning liability are also the same as in the Directive. Thus, the organiser and/or the retailer can be either separately or jointly responsible.

In FRANCE, this system of broad liability, which includes liability for other suppliers of services, is regarded as a new departure. It is explicitly stated in French law that "each natural or legal person who organises or sells package travel...is strictly liable to the buyer for proper performance thereof ...".[600]

In AUSTRIA, the Consumer Protection Act exclusively uses the term 'organiser'[601], comprising, on the one hand, a travel organisation providing the services itself or through an auxiliary and, on the other hand, a travel agency brokering contracts between the travel organisation and the traveller. Thus, the question of separate or joint liability for the travel organisation and travel agency depends on each individual case. If the travel agency commits to providing the travel services (i.e. it acts as an intermediary for the travel organisation[602]), both are jointly liable.[603] If the travel agency only pledges to broker a corresponding travel contract with the travel organisation, it is only liable where it infringes a contractual duty (e.g. by knowingly commissioning an unreliable organisation). Otherwise, claims arising from improper performance of the contract can only be made against the travel organisation. Any claim lodged by a consumer on the grounds of loss of enjoyment as a result of non-per-

599 Suggested by *Howells/Wilhelmsson*, EC Contract Law, 242.
600 Article L 211-17 of the Tourism Code.
601 Definition in § 31b(2)(2) of the Consumer Protection Act.
602 According to CC § 1313a.
603 Joint liability is regulated in CC § 1302.

formance of a considerable part of the contract must be underpinned by clear evidence that the organiser is at fault. It is also based on the degree, gravity and duration of the defect, the purpose of the trip and the price.[604]

CZECH legislation imposes liability on the travel agency. One particular feature is that the consumer has to enforce his rights without undue delay, and at the latest within three months. Moreover, in SLOVAKIA, the travel bureau (the 'organiser') is liable to the consumer for proper performance of the contract. In POLISH law, the organiser is liable for non- or improper performance of the contract for tourist services.[605]

As FINNISH law only refers to the concept of 'organiser', the latter is solely liable, even for other persons he uses when providing services. The traveller is entitled to compensation for personal injury and material and property damage caused by a defect in performance if the organiser acted negligently.[606] According to DUTCH law, the organiser is liable.[607] In LATVIA, the undertaking (company) is liable for the provision of services in line with the contract.

In BELGIUM, both are also liable for non- or improper performance, irrespective of whether they, their agents, assignees or representatives are at fault. This is similar in CYPRUS and SLOVAKIA. In GREECE, any service provider (i.e. the organiser as well as the retailer) is generally liable for faults to the detriment of the consumer. The legislators in Cyprus and the UNITED KINGDOM decided to hold the consumer's contractual partner responsible for the whole performance of the contractual obligations.

A different legislative technique is used in HUNGARY, achieving the same result. The organiser is liable for every person he uses to fulfil his duties, irrespective of fault. Moreover, a retailer who sells trips on behalf of a foreign organiser, is liable in the same way as the organiser. Price reduction applies where performance is not in line with the Directive. Besides, the consumer is entitled to compensation for damages unless the organiser acted with the intention of correctly performing the services and in a manner, which, under the circumstances, would generally be expected of him.

In ITALY, both the organiser and the retailer have to pay damages according to their respective liabilities unless it is impossible to perform the services due to circumstances beyond their control. Liability can be avoided when the tour is cancelled because of *force majeure* or an insufficient number of participants, though overbooking does not constitute a good reason. SWEDEN has also included a possibility for the organiser or retailer to escape liability. They are liable for any faults unless they can prove that the damages were caused by circumstances beyond their control. Another exception can be found in SLOVENIA, where the organiser is essentially responsible. He is also liable for damages caused by third persons involved in any travel services unless the organiser proves that he chose the service provider concerned with due diligence. The Slovenian legislator specifically refers only to non- or partial performance. However, under the general principle of liability for non-performance/improper performance, the organiser is liable for improper performance. In DENMARK, the

---

604 CC § 31e(3), § 31f.

605 Article 11a of the Act on Tourist Services.

606 § 23(1) of the Package Travel Act of 28 November 1994/1079.

607 CC Art. 7:507(2).

concept of joint liability applies. The retailer is liable to the consumer for all his financial claims against the organiser. In SPAIN, although the wording of the legislative regulations provides for separate liability as a rule (i.e. the organiser and the retailer are only liable for faults they committed themselves), joint liability applies exceptionally if there are several retailers and organisers. However, in order to enhance consumer protection, case law tends to assume that the organiser and retailer are jointly liable.

In contrast to the Directive, which uses the terms "non-performance", "failure to perform", and "improper performance", GERMAN law, reflecting the peculiarities of the German system, prefers the more general term "travel defect". As a consequence of this broad definition, liability and guarantees are extended, so that the traveller is afforded a higher level of protection. The trip organiser (though not the retailer) is liable for the trip's success (irrespective of who is at fault) and essentially carries the risk. Thus, remedial action (§ 651c BGB), price reduction (§ 651d BGB) and cancellation on the grounds of an unsatisfactory trip (§ 651e BGB) do not require the trip organiser to be at fault. According to case law, these rules apply to any cases where the service has been disrupted even if this does not impinge directly on the traveller. With regard to compensation claims, the German Civil Code is broadly aligned with the Directive.

b. Liability for damages and exemptions

According to Art. 5(2) of the Directive, the organiser and/or retailer is/are not liable for damages if
(1) the failures are attributable to the traveller,
(2) the failures are unforeseeable, unavoidable and attributable to a third party with no relation to the performance of any contractual services and provisions,
(3) the failures are due to a case of force majeure, or
(4) the failures are due to an event that the organiser and/or retailer or the supplier of services could not foresee and forestall with all due care.

Up to a certain degree, it remains unclear whether this provision regulates a classic 'culpa liability' or follows the more modern pattern of 'strict liability' with some exceptions.

The four reasons for excluding liability listed in Art. 5(2) of the Directive are transposed by BELGIUM, CYPRUS, the CZECH REPUBLIC, DENMARK, FRANCE, GREECE, IRELAND, ITALY, LATVIA, LITHUANIA, LUXEMBOURG, MALTA, the NETHERLANDS, PORTUGAL, SLOVAKIA, SPAIN and the UNITED KINGDOM. POLAND[608] has only transposed numbers (1), (2) and (3).

Instead of adopting the four exceptions, GERMANY preferred to refer to its general rules.[609] The organiser is not liable if he is able to prove that he acted neither intentionally nor negligently ('culpa liability').[610] Under FINNISH law, the travel agent also has to prove that he did

608 Article 11a, 1st - 3rd indent of the Act on Tourist Services.

609 CC § 651f(1), § 276.

610 For case law, see BGH judgment of 11 January 2005, X ZR 118/03, BGH judgment of 9 November 2004, X ZR 119/01, BGH judgment of 15 October 2002, X ZR 147/01, OLG Munich judgment of 24 January 2002, 8 U 2053/01.

not act carelessly. It is unclear if transposition using the 'culpa liability' model constitutes a false implementation of Art. 5(2) of the Directive. In principle, there is a difference between the exceptions listed in the Directive and culpa liability, but it is difficult to find cases that illustrate different results. In particular, if the burden of proof lies with the organiser/retailer who has to prove that he did not act negligently, legal practice will very probably come to the same results.

In SLOVENIA, the organiser is exempted from any contractual liability in circumstances that the organiser was not able to prevent, remedy or avoid.[611] In SWEDEN, the organiser is not liable only if he can prove that non-performance is due to circumstances beyond his control, which he cannot reasonably be expected to have foreseen and/or to have avoided.[612] In AUSTRIA, ESTONIA and HUNGARY, there seems to be no explicit transposition of Art. 5(2) sent. 1 part 2 of the Directive. In Hungarian law, exemptions cover failures in performance of the contract that are attributable to the consumer or to a third person who is not connected to the performance of the contractual obligation. Furthermore, there is an exemption if the company could not have foreseen or avoided the defect with due care, as well as in cases of *force majeure*, which is defined as an unforeseeable, unusual circumstance that runs counter to the travel company's intentions and the consequences of which cannot be foreseen with due care.

Table: Exemptions from liability

As per the Directive	BE, CY, CZ, DK, EL, ES, FR, IE, IT, LT, LU, LV, MT, NL, PT, SK, UK *(17)*
Deviations	DE, FI, PL, SE, SL *(5)*
Not explicitly transposed	AT, EE, HU *(3)*

c. Limitation on amount of damages to be paid

aa. According to international conventions

Under Art. 5(2) sent. 3 of the Directive, member states may provide for limitations on the organiser's and/or retailer's liability in accordance with international conventions governing such services. Most member states have made use of this option. In BELGIUM, CYPRUS, the CZECH REPUBLIC,[613] DENMARK, ESTONIA, FINLAND,[614] GERMANY, GREECE, HUNGARY,[615]

---

611 Article 240 of the Code of Obligations.

612 § 16 sec. (2), (3) of the Package Tours Act 1992:1672.

613 The two possible limitations on damages covered in Art. 5(2), sent. 4 and 5 of the Directive are transposed in CC sec. 852j(3), i.e. damages (including personal) can be limited if an international convention provides for such a limitation and it is included in the travel contract.

614 Article 24 of the Package Travel Act of 28 November 1994/1079. This article also refers directly to national statutes like the Maritime Act (674/94), the Act concerning Transportation in an Aircraft (289/37), the Air Transportation Contracts Act (45/77) or Air Transportation Act (387/86), the Railway Transport Act (1119/00), which seem to reflect the conventions, and to Regulation 2027/97 on Air Carrier Liability in the Event of Accidents.

615 Since 13 May 2005.

IRELAND, ITALY, LUXEMBOURG, MALTA, the NETHERLANDS, PORTUGAL,[616] SLOVAKIA, SPAIN, SWEDEN[617] and the UNITED KINGDOM, liability is limited according to international conventions. Although LITHUANIAN law has not directly transposed this provision, this principle follows from general contract law. As a rule, the parties are free to determine the terms and conditions of a contract, except when they are set by mandatory rules of law.[618]

AUSTRIA has signed various international conventions on flight liability (the Warsaw Convention 1929/1955, the Guadalajara Convention 1961 and the Montreal Convention 1999) though the legislator did not transpose this provision into Austrian law. Furthermore, FRANCE, LATVIA and SLOVENIA have equally not transposed Art. 5(2) sent.3 of Directive 90/314.

Table: Option to allow limitations on liability according to international conventions

Use of Option	Member States
Yes	BE, CY, CZ, DE, DK, EE, EL, ES, FI, HU, IE, IT, LT, LU, MT, NL, PL, PT, SE, SK, UK *(21)*
No	AT, FR, LV, SL *(4)*

bb. Limitations on damages other than personal/physical damages

Except for personal injury, Art. 5(2) sent. 4 of the Directive permits member states to provide for contractual limitations on compensation for damages that result from the non-performance or improper performance of services included in the package, provided that the reduction is not unreasonable.

Most member states (AUSTRIA, BELGIUM, CYPRUS, the CZECH REPUBLIC,[619] DENMARK, ESTONIA, FINLAND, GERMANY, GREECE, IRELAND, ITALY,[620] LITHUANIA, LUXEMBOURG, MALTA, the NETHERLANDS, POLAND, PORTUGAL,[621] SLOVAKIA,[622] SLOVENIA[623] and the UNITED KINGDOM[624]) have made use of this option, while FRANCE, HUNGARY, LATVIA, SPAIN and SWEDEN have not. Furthermore, such a contractual term limiting compensation for damages other than personal damages would be invalid under French law.

---

616 Article 40(1) of the Decree 209/97.

617 § 18 of the Package Tours Act 1992:1672. This refers to the Maritime Act, the Air Transport Act, the Rail Transport Act and the International Rail Transport Act.

618 CC Art. 6.156(4).

619 The two possible limitations on damages covered in Art. 5(2), sent. 4 and 5 of the Directive are transposed in CC sec. 852j(3), i.e. damages (including personal) can be limited if an international convention provides for such a limitation and it is included in the travel contract.

620 Article 94 and 95 of the Consumer Code.

621 See also Art. 40 of Decree 209/97.

622 This rule existed before transposition of Directive 90/314.

623 Article 894(2), (3) of the Code of Obligations.

624 Regulation 15(4) of the Package Travel, Package Holidays and Package Tour Regulations 1992.

Even in those countries which do generally allow limitations on compensation as per Art. 5(2) sent. 4 of the Directive, the individual solutions vary considerably. For instance, DENMARK has a special regulation concerning this case. Under Danish law, an agreement limiting compensation can only be made if it is in accordance with rules in international conventions applicable to travel contracts.[625]

In AUSTRIA,[626] the tour organiser cannot limit his liability for death or personal injury, nor his liability for intentional and gross negligence. In BELGIUM,[627] the organiser can limit his compensation to double the travel costs, but only where the organiser does not provide the services himself. However, in Belgium, the tour organiser cannot limit his liability for death or personal injury, nor his liability for intentional and gross negligence. This is the same in ESTONIA,[628] where compensation in other cases may be limited to three times the price of the package. There can also be no limitation in the event of death or personal injury, or in cases of intentional and gross negligence. Under GERMAN[629] law, non-material damages can also be limited by agreement between the organiser and the traveller to three times the price of the package, either in the case of minor negligence or if a service provider is solely responsible for the damage. In IRELAND,[630] it is double the amount of the fully inclusive package price for adults and an amount equal to the inclusive price for a minor. Again, there can be no limitation in the event of death or personal injury, or in cases of intention and gross negligence. In POLAND,[631] it is double the price of the package with respect to each customer.

The PORTUGUESE[632] legislator implemented a minimum scheme for damages. The sums applicable to travel organisers vary from ESC 220.000[633] for damage to baggage arising from damage to a motor vehicle up to ESC 88.5000.000 in the event of death or personal injury. Travel agencies' liability for damage to, or destruction or removal of, baggage or other articles can be limited to ESC 280.000 in all, or ESC 90.000 per article.

In HUNGARY, there is no provision for any limitation on compensation for damages other than personal damages. However, two general provisions concerning limitations are applicable instead. There can be no limitation on compensation for death and physical damages, or for any damages caused intentionally or by gross negligence. There can be a limitation on compensation for property damages and physical damages caused by normal negligence if this limitation can somehow be offset by another benefit.

---

625 § 24 of Act 472/1993.

626 § 31f(1) of the Consumer Protection Act.

627 Article 19 sec. (2), (4), (5), Article 28 of the Act of 16 February 1994 regulating package travel contracts and travel intermediation contracts.

628 § 878(3) of the Law of Obligations.

629 CC § 651h(1).

630 S. 20(3), (4) of the Package Holidays and Travel Trade Act.

631 Article 11b(3), (4) of the Act on Tourist Services.

632 Article 40 sec. (2), (3), (5) of the Decree-Law 198/93.

633 1€ = 200.482 ESC.

The FINNISH[634] and CYPRIOT[635] legislators introduced the option to reduce damages as long as the reduction is not unreasonable. Moreover, such a reduction is only possible if the package is not booked for private purposes. In SLOVAKIA,[636] the court is entitled to limit compensation. GREEK[637] law contains a regulation similar to the one in the Directive allowing a contractual limitation on liability for non-physical damages. The scope, however, is narrow because several other regulations apply. The organiser's or retailer's liability for intentional and gross negligence cannot be excluded or limited. Liability for third party service providers appointed by the organiser or the retailer and acting with intentional or gross negligence cannot be excluded or limited in advance. Liability for minor negligence cannot be limited if this limitation is not negotiated individually. Above all, according to the Greek Consumer Protection Act, any agreement with a consumer that excludes or limits the liability of the service provider towards the consumer is null and void.

In ITALY,[638] the parties to the contract can agree in writing to limit compensation for damages other than physical injuries. If there is no such agreement, compensation for damages is permitted within the limits laid down in Art. 13 of the 1970 International Convention on Travel Contracts. In LITHUANIA,[639] there is no explicit reference to any possibility to contractually limit compensation for damages other than physical damages, though this can justifiable be provided for.

Such differences in national laws concerning the possibility to limit compensation in the case of damages resulting from non-performance or improper performance of services included in the package show the difficulties inherent in agreeing on a limitation that is valid in several or all member states. Organisers and retailers who want to market package tours in several member states are compelled, in practice, to refrain from agreeing any limitation on compensation if they want to act lawfully. Depending on your political point of view, this may be seen as a barrier to trade or as a – not undesirable – incentive for businesses to offer a high standard of consumer protection.

Table: Use of option provided for in Art. 5(2) 4th indent of the Directive

Use of Option	Member States
Yes	AT, BE, CY, CZ, DE, DK, EE, EL, FI, IE, IT, LT, LU, MT, NL, PL, PT, SK, SL, UK *(20)*
No	ES, FR, HU, LV, SE *(5)*

634 § 25 of the Package Travel Act of 28 November 1994/1079.

635 Article 15(4) of the Package Travel, Holidays and Tours Law of 1998.

636 CC § 450.

637 Article 5(2)(d) of the Decree-Law 339/96.

638 Article 95 of the Consumer Code.

639 CC Art. 6.755(2).

d. Loss of enjoyment

The ECJ made clear in case C-168/00 – *Simone Leitner*[640], that Art. 5 of the Directive is to be interpreted as, in principle, conferring on consumers a right to compensation for non-material damage resulting from the non-performance or improper performance of the services constituting a package holiday. In particular, such compensation for non-material damage can arise from the loss of enjoyment the consumer has suffered as a result of improper performance of the travel contract.

Only some member states (e.g. AUSTRIA, BELGIUM and ESTONIA) explicitly provide for compensation for loss of enjoyment. The DANISH Act – contrary to ordinary rules on damages – allows the customer to be compensated for "considerable inconvenience" (which should include a "ruined holiday"). In the NETHERLANDS and HUNGARY, the organiser may need to compensate for non-material damages as well. GERMANY only awards damages if the trip has been *significantly* disrupted. In view of the ECJ case C-168/00, it could be argued that this additional pre-requisite may result in an infringement of EU law. In SPAIN, according to general law and specific case law on package travel covering all 'damages', the organiser/retailer is also liable for non-material damages.

Most member states have not explicitly regulated compensation for non-material damage in their package travel laws. Member states that have literally transposed Art. 5(2) of the Directive will have to apply their law in the light of the C-168/00 judgment. Other member states, where the calculation of damages in the case of travel contracts follows general rules on damages must also take the ruling into account when applying these general rules. It will have to be seen whether all member state courts also award non-material damages to consumers in the case of non-performance or improper performance of travel contracts.

e. Communication of any shortcomings in performance

According to Art. 5(4) of Directive 90/314, the consumer has to communicate any perceived failure in the performance of a contract to the supplier of the services concerned *in situ*, and to the organiser and/or retailer in writing or any other appropriate form at the earliest opportunity. It should be noted that this provision is one of the few exceptional cases where the Directive seeks to impose an obligation on the consumer. Thus, because of the minimum clause, the member states are free to define a notification duty that is more favourable to the consumer or not to transpose this provision at all (e.g. SPAIN). However, it is questionable whether they may impose a notification duty that is stricter with regard to formal requirements or time limits than the Directive's provisions dictate.

Some member states, such as IRELAND, LATVIA, MALTA and the UNITED KINGDOM, have transposed the provision almost literally. In DENMARK,[641] FINLAND[642] and SWEDEN,[643] similar provisions can be found, except that no specific period has to be complied with where the

---

640 ECJ judgment of 12 March 2000, C-168/00 – *Simone Leitner*.

641 § 26, § 27 of Act 472/1993.

642 § 18 of the Package Travel Act of 28 November 1994/1079.

643 § 19 of the Package Tours Act 1992:1672.

organiser is guilty of dishonest or grossly negligent behaviour. Furthermore, in Denmark,[644] a complaint has to be filed in the case of personal injury. GREEK[645] law also contains a provision comparable to Art. 5(4) of the Directive, but, in Greece, the communication has to be given in writing, so that there is a stricter formal requirement than the Directive provides for. Under PORTUGUESE[646] law, only the travel agency has to be informed. In POLAND, the organiser and the service provider ought to be informed by the 'client' without delay about any defects in the performance of the contract. Furthermore, the form in which such information should to be given depends on the kind of service involved.[647] The wording is more favourable to the consumer ("ought") as it does not indicate an obligation, but rather a recommendation. As indicated above, in making use of the minimum clause, such a formulation does not contradict the Directive's provision.

The laws in AUSTRIA[648] and the CZECH REPUBLIC[649] state that the traveller is obliged to give notice to the provider immediately after any shortcomings are detected. Furthermore, according to Czech legislation, the contract must set out how the consumer has to lodge his claim that the travel agency is in breach of its legal duties.[650] In HUNGARY,[651] an official complaint must be made immediately to the tour guide and to the organiser's local representative. ESTONIAN law lays down a notification duty for the traveller, who must inform the immediate provider of the travel services and the tour operator or retailer of any breach of contract.[652] CYPRUS has indirectly imposed a notification duty on the consumer by obliging the supplier or the other party to the contract to include information concerning the conditions for compensation in the contract. The contract must stipulate that the supplier or the other party to the contract is bound to provide a clear indication that, in order for a compensation claim to be processed, the supplier of the relevant services or the other party to the contract must be notified of any problem, either in writing or any other appropriate manner.[653]

In BELGIUM,[654] the traveller has to complain immediately about shortcomings and, additionally, has to send the complaint to the organiser or the travel agent by recorded delivery within one month of the end of the trip at the latest. A similar regulation can be found in

---

644 § 26, § 27 of the Act No. 472/1993 on Package Travels.

645 Article 5(4) of the Decree 339/96 on Package Travel.

646 Article 30 sec. (4), (5) of the Decree-Law 198/93.

647 Article 16b of the Act on Tourist Services states that the client should give notice "in a manner appropriate for this type of service".

648 § 31e(2) of the Consumer Protection Act.

649 CC Art. 852b.

650 CC sec. 852b(2)(a).

651 § 12(5) of the Government Decree 214/1996.

652 § 875(1) of the Law of Obligations.

653 Article 15(9) of the Package Travel, Holidays and Tours Law of 1998.

654 Article 20 and Art. 29 of the Act of 16 February 1994 regulating package travel contracts and travel intermediation contracts.

SLOVAKIAN law.[655] Initially, the traveller has to inform the local travel agent and also has to give written notification at the earliest opportunity after detecting the shortcoming. The traveller subsequently has to inform the organiser in writing about the failure no later than three months after departure and produce the written notification (first step). In ITALY,[656] the consumer must complain about partial or total failures to the organiser (or his local representative or the group guide) without delay to allow these problems to be remedied. The consumer can also send the organiser or retailer a letter of complaint (by recorded delivery) within 10 days of returning to the place of departure. Such formal requirements (e.g. letter sent by recorded delivery, in writing) may be contrary to the Directive, which only requires notification in writing or any other appropriate form.

GERMAN[657] law even lays down a second obligation to communicate any shortcomings after the end of the trip, in addition to the primary duty to inform the tour operator or his local representative. This requirement may not be in line with EC law.

According to FRENCH law,[658] the purchaser may lodge a claim against the seller for non- or improper performance of the contract by sending a letter by recorded delivery as soon as possible.

In LITHUANIA and LUXEMBOURG, there is no reference to a need to lodge a formal complaint, but simply to the general principle of due performance of a contract. In the NETHERLANDS, there is no duty to notify under statutory law. If the organiser stipulates such a duty in the contract, he must inform the traveller about any deadline for exercising it.[659] In SLOVENIA, no specific provision exists, therefore the general rule governing the notification of defects applies.[660]

Table: Registering complaints about shortcomings

As per the Directive	IE, LV, MT, UK *(4)*
Deviations	AT, BE, CY, CZ, DE, DK, EE, EL, FI, FR, HU, IT, PL, PT, SE, SK *(16)*
Not explicitly transposed	ES, LT, LU, NL, SL *(5)*

f. Assistance to consumer in difficulty

According to Art. 5(2) sent. 2 of Directive 90/314, the organiser is obliged to give prompt assistance to a consumer in difficulty in cases referred to in Art. 5(2) 2nd and 3rd indent of the

655 CC § 741i sec. (1), (2). According to § 19 of the Consumer Protection Act, the organiser is obliged to ensure that the representative (agent) is available and qualified to deal with complaints throughout the whole excursion.

656 Article 98 sec. (1), (2) of the Consumer Code.

657 CC § 651d(2), § 651g(1).

658 No explicit transposition, but covered in Art. 98 of Decree No. 94-490.

659 Article 1(e) of the Decree of 15 January 1993 containing rules concerning information that organisers of package travel must notify in the interest of travellers.

660 Article 461 of the Code of Obligations, applicable to all types of contracts (Art. 100 of the same Code).

Directive. The legislators in GREECE, IRELAND, PORTUGAL, SLOVAKIA, SPAIN and the UNITED KINGDOM transposed this provision. In SWEDEN, a similar provision can be found as well.[661]

In AUSTRIA,[662] BELGIUM,[663] ESTONIA[664] and MALTA,[665] the tour operator must take all reasonable steps in order to provide immediate assistance to a traveller in difficulty. In Austria, Estonia and Malta, this duty does not exist if the traveller has caused the difficulties himself. However, according to Belgian law, the tour operator is still obliged to provide assistance in this case, but may charge the traveller for the costs of assistance. The POLISH[666] legislator makes clear that the tourism organiser is never free from his or her duty to provide assistance to a client in difficulty during the trip, even though he has duly excluded liability.

Moreover, in FINLAND,[667] the obligation to assist the consumer is wider and more detailed than in the Directive. It also applies if the consumer has caused the difficulties himself. It is argued that, in a foreign country, it is very difficult to get the right treatment or help without assistance from the organiser. In LITHUANIA[668] and the NETHERLANDS,[669] the tour organiser is equally obliged to give help and support to the consumer even if the tourist is ultimately responsible for the improper performance. In that case, it is possible that the costs for providing assistance are charged to the consumer. ITALIAN[670] law states that the organiser or retailer must make every effort to help the customer in continuing his journey, though the consumer must compensate for damages where he is responsible for improper performance of the contract.

In DENMARK,[671] the organiser only has to provide assistance to the consumer if the consumer suffers personal injury. In SLOVENIA, Art. 887 of the Code of Obligations only lays down a very broad obligation for the organiser to safeguard the rights and interests of the passengers in accordance with good customs. The GERMAN legislator has not explicitly transposed this provision of the Directive. However, under § 651c Civil Code (BGB), the organiser must remedy any defects in performance. In practice, this should lead to the same results as the Directive requires.

In FRANCE,[672] the contract must give contact details for the seller's local representative or, where there is no representative, for the local authorities which are likely to assist the con-

---

661 § 16(4) of the Package Tours Act 1992:1672.

662 § 31e(1) of the Consumer Protection Act.

663 Arts. 18(3), 27 of the Act of 16 February 1994 regulating package travel contracts and travel intermediation contracts.

664 § 877(4) of the Law of Obligations.

665 Article 15(7)(2) of the Package Travel, Package Holidays and Package Tours Regulations.

666 Article 11a(2) of the Act on Tourist Services.

667 § 16 Package Travel Act of 28 November 1994/1079.

668 CC Art. 6.754(3) 1st indent stipulates that the tour organiser, depending on the specific circumstances, has a duty to give all possible help and support to the tourist if the contract does not meet his expectations.

669 CC Art. 7:507(3).

670 Article 96(2) of the Consumer Code.

671 § 23(2) of the Package Travel Act.

672 Article 98(19) of the Decree 94-490.

sumer in the case of difficulty or, failing that, an emergency telephone number. In CYPRUS, the organiser is still obliged to assist a consumer in difficulty in the case of *force majeure* (Art. 5(2), 4th indent of the Directive).

Table: Assistance to consumer in difficulty

As per the Directive	CZ, EL, ES, HU, IE, PT, SK, UK *(8)*
Deviations	AT, BE, CY, DK, EE, FI, FR, IT, LT, LV, MT, NL, PL, SE, SL *(15)*
Not explicitly transposed	DE *(1)*
Transposition not entirely clear	LU *(1)*

6. Security in the event of insolvency

According to Art. 7 of Directive 90/314, "the organiser and/or retailer party to the contract shall provide sufficient evidence of security for the refund of money paid over and for the repatriation of the consumer in the event of insolvency".

Most member states have adopted the Directive's wording and oblige the organiser and/or retailer to provide security in the event of insolvency. Again, different wording exists. FRANCE, for example, uses the term "agent de voyage" and IRELAND "package provider", which could be either the retailer or the organiser as per the Directive. SPAIN is slightly different insofar as all the Autonomous Communities have developed a security system with detailed regulations and, to some extent, with varying requirements.[673]

Table: Obligated party

Organiser	AT, CZ, DE, FI, LT, LV,[674] PL, SL *(8)*
Retailer	*(0)*
Organiser and/or retailer	BE, CY, DK, EE, EL, ES, FR, HU, IE, IT, LU, MT, NL, PT, SK, UK *(16)*
Transposition not entirely clear	LV, SE *(2)*

The formulation "sufficient evidence in the case of security" is quite open and leaves it up to member states to choose appropriate measures. Nevertheless, the goal of the provision has been clearly explained by the ECJ in several cases. In the *Dillenkofer* case[675], the court applied its rulings on state civil liability to the field of consumer law for the first time. The case hinged on damages owing to the claimant because of Germany's incomplete transposition of Directive 90/314. The central question was whether Art. 7 of Directive 90/314 grants a qualified right to the traveller insofar as it meets the first requirement of state liability. The ECJ ruled that this was the case, on the grounds that consumer protection is an independent goal

---

673 Et al: Art. 46(4) of Law 6/2003 of 27 February on Tourism in Aragón (and Art. 13 of the Regulation on travel agents in Aragón), Art. 163 of the Regulation on Tourism in La Rioja (Decree 111/2003 of October 10), Arts. 11 and 12 of Decree 301/2002 of December 17 on Travel Agents in Andalucia, Art. 31 of Law 2/1999 of March 24 on Tourism in the Balearic Islands (and Art. 13 of Decree 60/1997 of May 7).

674 Undertakings that market package tourism services shall provide a safety guarantee.

675 ECJ judgment of 8 October 1996, C-178/94 – *Dillenkofer*.

of the Directive.[676] Furthermore, the court argued that any regulation allowing the tour organiser to require an unsecured deposit payment would contradict the purpose of Art. 7. Thus, it was evident that there should be a third party, independent from the organiser and responsible for maintaining sufficient funds, to act as guarantor.

In this context, it is questionable whether DUTCH transposition is in line with the Directive. Art. 7:512 of the Dutch CC states that the organiser shall take the necessary measures to ensure that, in the event of insolvency, his debts are covered by a third party or that the price under the travel agreement will be repaid or other specific measures taken in line with this article. The organiser is also bound to make these measures public. This regulation does not state the requirements governing the appointment of a guarantor who himself is not exposed to the risk of insolvency because of his internal structures and policies.

Table: Evidence of security

Financial guarantee	AT, DE, DK, EE, EL, ES, FI, FR, HU, LU, LV, PL, PT, SK, SL[677] *(15)*
Insurance policy	AT, BE, CY, CZ, DE, EE, EL, ES, FI, FR, HU, IE, IT,[678] LT, LU, MT, PL, PT, SE, SK,[679] UK *(21)*
Security fund	DK, EL,[680] HU, IE, IT,[681] LU, MT, NL,[682] SK, UK[683] *(10)*
Bond provided by authorised institution or insurance company	CY, IE, UK *(3)*
Necessary measures[684]	NL *(1)*

In the ECJ case *Verein für Konsumenteninformation*[685], the court held that all risks possibly arising from insolvency of the tour organiser must be fully covered. In this regard, member states have a variety of regulations. The vast majority stipulate that any money paid or repatriation costs must be refunded as per the Directive. Additionally, in FRANCE, equivalent services are to be reimbursed if the consumer agrees to this. DANISH law provides for reimbursement of the intermediary who paid the customer's claims on behalf of the insolvent organiser. ITALIAN law also ensures that immediate financial help is available if tourists are forced to return from non-EU countries in the event of an emergency, for which the organ-

676 Line 39 of Judgement C-178/94.

677 Or security. It is unclear whether this means an insurance policy or a security fund.

678 Article 99(1) of the Consumer Code.

679 The organiser is obliged to conclude an insurance contract with an insurer and to provide the consumer with an insurance certificate together with one copy of the contract.

680 Only if the organiser or retailer is a travel agency. According to Art. 5(5)(b) of Decree 339/96, the organiser/retailer (i.e. travel agencies for general national tourism, shipping charter companies, tourist accommodation) is obliged to conclude an insurance contract concerning professional indemnity insurance for faults and omissions in exercising his profession. The insurer has to be a properly registered insurance company authorised to operate in Greece or in a member state of the EU.

681 The Ministry of Productive Activities is responsible for this. On financing, see Art. 100 of the Consumer Code on the total compulsory insurance premium paid into the national budget.

682 On a voluntary basis only (repeats only the wording in the Directive).

683 Trustee for the consumer.

684 Either his debts are covered by a third party, or the price under the travel agreement will be repaid or other specific measures taken.

685 ECJ judgment of 5 May 1998, C-354/96 – *Verein für Konsumenteninformation.*

iser may or may not be responsible. In SLOVAKIA, the difference between the package prices in the case of a substitute package or the difference in the case of a package only partially provided may be refunded. PORTUGUESE law explicitly states that any medical assistance and medicines necessary in the event of accident or illness may be refunded.

Table: Refund

Payments (including partial payments) made	AT, BE, CY, CZ, DE, DK, EE,[686] EL,[687] ES, FR, HU, IE, IT,[688] LT, LU, LV, MT, PT, SK, SL,[689] UK[690] *(21)*
Repatriation costs	AT, BE, CY, CZ, DE, DK, EE, EL,[691] ES, FR, HU,[692] IE, IT, LT, LU, LV, MT, PT,[693] SK, SL, UK[694] *(21)*
Accommodation	DK, EE *(2)*
Equivalent service	FR *(1)*
Other needs resulting from non-performance	DK, EL,[695] HU, PT, SL[696] *(5)*
Others	DK, IT, PT, SK *(4)*

The European Court of Justice further had to rule on Art. 7 of Directive 90/314 in the *Rechberger*[697] and *Ambry* [698] cases. In the *Rechberger* case, the court found no indication in the Directive's text that the guarantee mentioned in Art. 7 might be limited. Therefore, it seems problematic that some European legislators have opted for a certain limitation on the insurance sum. According to GERMAN law, the guarantor may limit his liability to 110 million euro per year for all potential refunds. Should refunds exceed this maximum amount, individual refund claims diminish in line with the proportion of the total individual sum to the maximum amount.[699] PORTUGUESE law sets a 50-million euro limit.[700]

686 Or compensation for the cancelled part of the tour.

687 Generally, the third party (traveller/consumer) has a direct claim against the insurer (Art. 26 of the Act 2496/1997) if the insurance contract has been stipulated in law. There is a valid claim up to the indemnity limit for compulsory insurance, irrespective of the real insurance sum. The insurer is not allowed to raise an objection against the third party on the basis of anything contained in the insurance contract.

688 "To reimburse consumers in the event of financial failure".

689 The refund obligation comes into force two years after the entry into force of the Promotion of Tourism Development Act on 30 January 2004.

690 The sum must be reasonably expected to cover all monies paid by consumers.

691 According to Art. 7(2) of Decree 339/1996, the insurance contract must state the method for immediate reimbursement of repatriation costs.

692 "Actions to be taken in the interest of travellers who face an emergency after starting the tour" (e.g. return trip) and costs of the enforced stay abroad.

693 And assistance.

694 The sum must be reasonably expected to cover all monies paid by consumers.

695 Or improper performance; cf. Art. 5(5)(b) of Decree 339/1996.

696 Damage caused to consumers as a result of a breach of contract.

697 ECJ judgment of 15 June 1999, C-140/97 – *Rechberger*.

698 ECJ judgment of 1 December 1998, C-410/96 – *Ambry*.

699 CC § 651k(2).

700 Article 45(2) of Decree-Law 198/93.

In AUSTRIA, BELGIUM, CYPRUS, DENMARK, ESTONIA, HUNGARY, IRELAND, LITHUANIA and the UNITED KINGDOM, legislation sets a minimum insurance sum. For example, in Austria, the minimum amount depends on the different elements of a package and is approximately 10 % of the company's annual turnover.[701] In Belgium, it is 15 % of assets.[702] Cypriot law sets a minimum insurance sum if the 'other party to the contract' opts for a bond provided by an authorised institution or insurance company, instead of an insurance policy. This minimum sum is equivalent to 20 % or more of the payments received by the other party to the contract during the 12-month period preceding the start date of the bond or equivalent to the maximum amount of all payments "which the other party to the contract expects at any moment to be in his possession, pursuant to contracts which have not yet been fully performed, or whichever amount is greater".[703] In Denmark, the regulation only applies to foreign organisers who have set up a business in Denmark and the minimum sum depends on the business's turnover.[704] Hungarian law specifies a sum of at least 12 % of the travel company's net revenue.[705] LITHUANIAN law[706] distinguishes between cases where the tour organiser's annual revenue is over/under LTL 4 million. In the first case, the sum insured ranges from LTL 100.000 to LTL 200.000, while, in the second instance, it constitutes 5 % of the tour organiser's annual revenue. In LATVIAN law, the security must cover the money the customer has paid over a period of not less than one year and a sum of 50 % of the forecast turnover for the following year, but not less than 20.000 lats. In the *Rechberger* case, the ECJ did not express a view as to whether a national system that stipulates a "minimum insurance sum" can be considered in line with the Directive. An argument in favour would be that such a regulation is designed to effectively support consumers by ensuring that the guarantor maintains sufficient funds.

In GERMANY, LUXEMBOURG and SLOVAKIA, a guarantee certificate has to be provided before payment. This can be requested by the consumer. In BELGIUM, it is compulsory to publish a list of organisers who provide insurance, thus enabling the consumer to collect necessary information. MALTESE law stipulates that information on insurance has to be provided in the travel brochure, whereas POLISH law demands written confirmation.

In the *Ambry* case, the court held that any national legislation requiring the insurer to have a registered office or branch on its territory pursues a legitimate aim insofar as it ensures immediate payment in the event of repatriation. Nevertheless, it was regarded as contrary to the EC Treaty. It does not seem that any member state has adopted or maintained any such regulation.

---

701 § 4 Regulation on travel agencies implementing Art. 7 of the Package Travel Directive.

702 At least the equivalent of 1 000 000 BEF. Art. 3 of the Royal Decree of 25 April 1997 implementing Art. 36 of the Act of 16 February 1994 regulating package travel contracts and travel intermediation contracts.

703 Article 18(4) of the Package Travel, Holidays and Tours Law of 1998.

704 Between 300 000 DKK and 30 million DKK.

705 Article 8(2) of Government Decree 213/1996.

706 Article 7(3) of the Law on Tourism. The calculation must take the previous year into account and cover all contracts concluded for the supply of tourist services abroad.

Table: Special requirements

Limitation on insurance sum	DE, PT *(2)*
Minimum insurance sum	AT, BE, CY, DK, EE, HU, IE, LT, LV, PT, UK *(11)*
Guarantee certificate	DE, LU, SK *(3)*
Information duty	BE, MT, PL *(3)*
Security as condition for licence	CZ, FR, HU, PL, PT, SK, SL *(7)*

Some member states provide for exemptions from the obligation to guarantee security in the event of insolvency. The GERMAN provisions do not apply if the organiser only operates occasionally and not within his professional capacity, if the trip does not last longer than 24 hours, does not include an overnight stay and does not cost more than 75 euro and, finally, if the tour organiser is a public legal entity that cannot be subject to insolvency proceedings.[707] In DANISH law, exemptions exist where a not-for-profit association operates travel activities that constitute only a minor part of its activities and an intermediary acting on behalf of a foreign organiser complies with the scheme approved by another EU member state. Finally, the UNITED KINGDOM provides for exemptions from the requirements to provide security where the person with whom the consumer has concluded a contract is established in a member state other than the United Kingdom and the package is subject to the rules implementing Art. 7 in that member state. The same applies where the contract party is subject to specific civil aviation regulations.[708]

In the light of the ECJ rulings in *Centros*[709], *Überseering*[710] and *Inspire Art*[711], one might wonder whether, for example, an organiser headquartered in member state A may transfer the security system established under its rules to member state B, where it may not comply with B's laws. A preliminary assessment of this question suggests that the organiser will have to comply with the rules of member state B. However, this question may need further (empirical) research. This requirement to transfer into a new security system may constitute a barrier to trade. This would be particularly true if an organiser wishing to set up branches or offices in several member states had to comply with each of the respective national rules governing security systems.

Bibliography

Working Document on the Council Directive 90/314/EEC of 13 June 1990 on package travel, package holidays and package tours, **http://ec.europa.eu/consumers/rights/commission_working_document_final26-07-2007.pdf**; Working Document of the Commission Responses to the consultation on the Council Directive 90/314/EEC of 13 June 1990 on package travel,

707 CC § 651k(6).

708 The Civil Air Regulations 1995 require a person (not acting as 'retailer') who sells a package involving flights to hold an Air Travel Organiser's Licence (ATOL), issued by the Civil Aviation Authority (CAA). ATOL holders must lodge a bond with the CAA to protect their customers against insolvency.

709 ECJ judgment of 9 March 1999, C-212/97.

710 ECJ judgment of 5 November 2002, C-208/00.

711 ECJ judgment of 30 September 2003, C-167/01.

package holidays and package tours, **http://ec.europa.eu/consumers/rights/summary_responses_publication_final_30012007.pdf**; Report on the Implementation of Directive 90/314/EEC on Package Travel and Holiday Tours in the Domestic Legislation of EC Member States, SEC(1999) 1800 final;

Ajani, Gianmaria / Rossi, Piercarlo, *Codice del consumatori, 2005,* ***Biroóvá, Emese***, *Ochrana spotrebiteľa v zmluve o obstaraní zájazdu, Bratislava 2002,* ***Bläumauer, Ingrid***, *Reiserecht, Verhältnis Reiseveranstalter – Kunde, 2004,* ***Bruun-Nielsen, Anne-Dorte***, *Forbrugeret, Copenhagen 1999,* ***Bydlinski, Michael***, *Verbraucherschutz in Österreich und in der EG, Reisevertragsrecht,* ***Cambier, Veronique / Dulák, Anton / Karsten, Jens / Tonner, Klaus***, *Timeshare and Package Travel Legislation in Central and Eastern Europe: Approximation, Harmonisation and Compatibility with European Union Law, Louvain, 2000,* ***García Rubio, María Paz***, *La responsabilidad contractual de las agencias de viaje (en el contrato de viaje combinado), Madrid 1999,* ***Howells, Geraint / Weatherill, Stephen,*** *Consumer Protection Law, Aldershot 2005,* ***Hulva, Tomáš***, *Ochrana spotřebitele, Praha 2005,* ***Ilie, Elena***, *Protectia Consumatorilor in Dreptul Comercial Roman-Lucrare de Licenta, Bucarest 2005,* ***Jarner Torrens, Joan David / Torres Lana, José Ángel / Tur Faúndez, M. Nélida,*** *La protección del turista como consumidor, Valencia 2003,* ***Kaller, Paul***, *Reiserecht, Munich 2005,* ***McDonald, Marc***, *European Community Tourism Law and Polic, Dublin 2003,* ***Nesterowicz, Miroslaw***, *Prawo turystyczne, Kraków 2003,* ***Psychomanis, Sp.,*** *Dikaio Tourismou, 2003,* ***Rambousek, Jan***, *Cestovní smlouva (Travel contract), 2003,* ***Tassoni, Giorgia***, *Il contratto di viaggio, Milano 1999,* ***Tonner, Klaus,*** *Reisevertrag (§§ 651a – § 651m BGB), in: Gebauer/Wiedmann, Zivilrecht unter europäischem Einfluss, Kap.13, Stuttgart 2005.*

C. Unfair Contract Terms Directive (93/13)

Drafted by Martin Ebers

Executive Summary

I. Transposition deficiencies

Even though most member states did endeavour to accommodate the requirements of Directive 93/13 and the case law of the ECJ, some shortcomings in the member states can be noted. Examples of most importance are

- Some member states (esp. CZECH REPUBLIC, LATVIA and the NETHERLANDS) act on the proviso that unfair clauses are binding unless the consumer invokes unfairness. This legal consequence contradicts the requirements of the ECJ, which in *Océano*,[712] *Cofidis*[713] and *Mostaza Claro*[714] explicitly emphasised, that unfairness is to be determined on the court's own motion. In other member states, the legal situation is unclear, so it remains

---

[712] ECJ judgment of 27 June 2000, Joined Cases C-240/98 to C-244/98 – *Océano Grupo Editorial SA v. Murciano Quintero* [2000] ECR I-04941.

[713] ECJ judgment of 21 November 2002, C-473/00 – *Cofidis v. Fredout* [2002] ECR I-10875.

[714] ECJ judgment of 26 October 2006, C-168/05 – *Elisa María Mostaza Claro v. Centro Móvil Milenium SL* [2006] ECR I-10421.

to be seen whether national case-law will bring the relevant provisions in line with European Community Law.[715]

- According to Art. 3 and recital (15) of Directive 93/13, the member states are obliged to fix the criteria in a general way for assessing the unfair character of contract terms. Although this requirement also applies to pre-formulated individual contracts for single use, the general clauses in AUSTRIA and in the NETHERLANDS only relate to standard terms. Even though in these member states other legal instruments are available to monitor such types of terms, this legislative technique gives rise to the danger that the requirements of the Directive will go unheeded.
- For those member states which only transposed certain parts of the Annex, it remains unclear whether this legislative technique can be accepted through applying the decision of the ECJ in C-478/99,[716] since in those countries the danger exists, that the consumer will be misled about his rights.[717]
- The principle of transparency prescribed in Art. 5, sent. 1 of the Directive 93/13 has not been explicitly transposed in the CZECH REPUBLIC, ESTONIA, GREECE, HUNGARY, LUXEMBOURG and in SLOVAKIA. Therefore it is doubtful whether the requirements of the Directive have been sufficiently adhered to.[718]
- The requirements articulated by the ECJ in C-70/03[719] (concerning the transposition of Art. 5 and Art. 6 of the Directive 93/13) have thus far not been implemented in SPANISH law, but a draft is currently being discussed in the Spanish parliament.[720]
- In ESTONIA pre-formulated ambiguous terms must be interpreted to the detriment of the party supplying the term. Directive 93/13, in contrast, goes beyond the mere interpretation to the detriment of the user, since in Art. 5, sent. 2 it requires not only an interpretation favourable to the consumer, but the "most" favourable interpretation.[721]
- If one assumes, that the member states are obliged by Art. 7(2) of Directive 93/13, to provide consumer associations with standing to bring collective proceedings against the user of unfair terms, then in LITHUANIA and MALTA an infringement of the Directive can be affirmed, since in both countries consumer associations do not have the right to proceed directly against the user of the clause, but merely to proceed against a measure of the relevant public body or to bring an action before a court for an order requiring the public body to make a compliance order.[722]

---

715 See *infra*, Part 2 C.IV.4.

716 ECJ judgment of 7 May 2002, C-478/99 – *Commission of the European Communities v. Kingdom of Sweden* [2002] ECR I-04147.

717 See *infra*, Part 2 C.IV.3.b

718 See *infra*, Part 2 C.V.1.b

719 ECJ judgment of 9 September 2004, C-70/03 – *Commission v. Kingdom of Spain* [2004] ECR I-7999.

720 See *infra*, Part 2 C.II.23.

721 See *infra*, Part 2 C.V.2.b.

722 See *infra*, Part 2 C.VI.3.b.

2. Enhancement of Protection

a. Extension of scope

Many member states have broadened the scope of application of their national laws on reviewing contract terms, for instance by

- Broadening the notion of consumer;[723]
- Monitoring contractual terms which reflect mandatory provisions;[724]
- Monitoring individually negotiated terms.[725]

b. Use of options

The member states have made different use of the options offered by the Directive:

- The Directive largely leaves the member states the choice of collective proceedings which must be put in place in order to prevent the continued use of unfair terms, Art. 7(2). The member states have chosen different enforcement mechanisms based on administrative measures, collective court proceedings and criminal proceedings.[726]

c. Use of minimum clauses

Most of the member states have made use of the minimum clause (Art. 8). Some examples of major importance are

- Directive 93/13 is essentially concerned with the establishment of a very pronounced system of control of the content of contractual clauses and of the principle of transparency. The Directive does not prescribe requirements for the incorporation of clauses into the contract (apart from recital 20, according to which the consumer must have the opportunity to become acquainted with all the terms of the contract). A number of member states do, in contrast, provide for a review of incorporation of the term into the contract, which in some circumstances can bring about a more advantageous position for the consumer (e.g. by way of establishing a duty to bring the terms to the consumers' attention or even a duty to give out the terms).
- Art. 3(1):
  - Whereas according to the Directive, unfairness only exists if a term causes an imbalance and this imbalance is furthermore contrary to the principle of good faith, seven countries make direct reference to "significant imbalance" without mentioning the additional criterion "good faith". This tends to lead to a lowering of the burden of proof for consumers.[727]
- Art. 3(3) in conjunction with the Annex:
  - Many member states have blacklisted Annex No. 1 of the Directive and therefore provide a higher level of consumer protection. Moreover, the blacklist in some

---

723 See *infra*, Part 2 C.III.1.b. and Part 3 A.III.

724 See *infra*, Part 2 C.III.3.a.

725 See *infra*, Part 2 C.III.3.b

726 See *infra*, Part 2 C.VI.

727 See *infra*, Part 2 C.IV.2.

member states such as BELGIUM, ESTONIA, MALTA, PORTUGAL and SPAIN, contains more clauses than the Annex of Directive 93/13.[728]
- While Annex No. 2 of Directive 93/13 establishes certain exceptions with regard to clauses used by suppliers of financial services, many member states provide a higher level of consumer protection by having not transposed Annex No. 2.[729]

- Art. 4(1):
  - In some member states, while assessing the fairness of contractual terms regard is to be paid not only to the circumstances prevailing at the time of conclusion of the contract (as the Directive provides), but also to conditions following conclusion of the contract.[730]
- Art. 4(2):
  - In many member states the review of terms also encompasses the subject matter of the contract and the adequacy of price.[731]
- Art. 6(1):
  - If a clause is unfair, then Directive 93/13 basically only requires removal or amendment of the offending term and the contract as such remains in force. However, in some member states the contractual rights and obligations can generally be adjusted, not only concentrating on the specific unfair term. Furthermore, in some member states public bodies can request the incorporation of new terms in order to prevent a significant imbalance between the rights and obligations.[732]
- Some member states (esp. POLAND, PORTUGAL and SPAIN) provide for a Standard Terms Register, whose aim is to increase the protection of consumers by publicising standard terms and judgments on unfair terms, with some effects towards Notaries, Registrars and judges.[733]

3. Inconsistencies or Ambiguities

Some major inconsistencies or ambiguities of the Directive are:
- Definition of consumer (regarding mixed contracts).
- Although the Directive is basically applicable to all types of contracts, the Directive uses the terms "seller and supplier" and "goods and services".
- The wording of the general clause (Art. 3) has caused problems in some language versions of Directive 93/13.[734]

With regard to the fairness test (Art. 3) and consequences of unfairness in individual proceedings (Art. 6 (1)) the following inconsistencies and ambiguities can be detected:
- The relationship of the principle of good faith to the criterion of "imbalance" remains unclear. Are these criteria to be understood cumulatively, as alternatives, or in the sense that any clause which generates a significant imbalance is always contrary to the principle of good faith?

---

728 See *infra*, Part 2 C.IV.3.b.

729 See *infra*, Part 2 C.IV.3.b.

730 See *infra*, Part 2 C.IV.2.

731 See *infra*, Part 2 C.IV.2.

732 See *infra*, Part 2 C.IV.4.

733 See infra, Part 2 C.II.19, 20 and 23.

734 See *infra*, Part 2 C.IV.2.

- The expression "significant" imbalance has caused some problems, since it is difficult to determine whether this term means that the imbalance is gross (extremely significant with a substantive evaluation) or evident (with an evaluation of its external perception).
- The Directive alone does not reveal the legal nature of the Annex. Clarification in relation to this point became evident with the decision of the ECJ in C-478/99.[735]
- The wording of Art. 6(1) (consequences of unfairness) does not reflect the ECJ case-law (C-240/98 to C-244/98 – *Océano*[736]; C-473/00 – *Cofidis*[737]; C-168/06 – *Mostaza Claro*).[738]

The principle of transparency laid down in Art. 5 of the Directive 93/13 suffers from some significant ambiguities:

- Transparency is required in Art. 5 "in the case of contracts where all or certain terms offered to the consumer are in *writing*". This formulation raises the question of whether the requirement of transparency, likewise applies to orally concluded contracts (see thereto recital 11).
- The Directive does not explicitly state whether the business has the duty of delivering or making the document available with the terms in the cases where the contract is normally written.
- The Directive does not specify (with the exception of the *contra proferentem* rule) what the consequences of lack of transparency are. Therefore, it is unclear whether the requirement of transparency is a condition for the incorporation of terms, whether clauses that lack transparency are to be assessed according to Art. 3 and whether this lack of transparency per se results in nullity/non-binding effect.

Certain issues in relation to collective proceedings also appear to be in need of regulation:

- From the wording of Art. 7(2) it is not entirely clear whether consumer associations must be given the right of standing in any event.
- The notion "persons and organisations" moreover does not sufficiently explain if a single person or a group of persons, which is not organised could take actions under Art. 7.

Finally, the international scope of application of the unfair terms provisions in Art. 6(2) is not clearly defined, since the Directive does not define the notion of "close connection with the territory of a Member State".

4. Gaps in the Unfair Contract Terms Directive

The analysis reveals some important gaps in the Directive. Examples of this are:

- As the legal consequences for unfairness of a contractual term are only rudimentarily regulated in the Directive, the danger exists that the requirements of the Directive are not transposed with sufficient effectiveness in the member states. This applies especially in those member states which do not provide for courts/authorities to monitor terms on their own motion. The particular problem in these cases is that the consumer cannot

---

735 ECJ judgment of 7 May 2002, C-478/99 – *Commission of the European Communities v. Kingdom of Sweden* [2002] ECR I-04147. See *infra*, Part 2 C.IV.3.a.

736 ECJ judgment of 27 June 2000, Joined Cases C-240/98 to C-244/98 – *Océano Grupo Editorial SA v. Murciano Quintero* [2000] ECR I-04941.

737 ECJ judgment of 21 November 2002, C-473/00 – *Cofidis v. Fredout* [2002] ECR I-10875.

738 ECJ judgment of 26 October 2006, C-168/05 – *Elisa María Mostaza Claro v. Centro Móvil Milenium SL* [2006] ECR I-10421; see *infra*, Part 2 C.IV.4.a.

defend himself against unfair terms because he is either not aware of his rights (and that he has to exercise these rights) or is deterred from asserting them by limitation periods or the costs entailed with bringing a court action.

- The Directive is silent (with the exception of the *contra proferentem* rule) on the consequences of lack of transparency. This gap leads to considerable legal uncertainty and at the same time jeopardises the effectiveness of transposition of the Directive.
- Court decisions in the context of collective proceedings are in the vast majority of member states only binding on the business who is party to the case. Furthermore decisions in collective proceedings are generally restricted to the clause in question in its particular wording. These legal consequences are particularly disadvantageous in those member states which do not have an administrative procedure to monitor unfair terms. Therefore how these can avoid the negative consequences of *res judicata* should be considered.

5. Potential Barriers to (Cross Border) Trade

Obvious barriers to trade in the field of the Directive are

- The different benchmarks in member states when reviewing contractual terms.
- The different standards in member states when reviewing the transparency of contractual terms and the (not harmonised) consequences of lack of transparency.

The case law of the ECJ has not prompted harmonisation in this respect, since the ECJ stressed in C-237/02[739] that the court would not decide whether a contractual term is in breach of good faith in a concrete case. Accordingly, traders cannot use a contractual clause which is valid across the EU, but must instead formulate different clauses for each member state. Hence, considerable obstacles to the functioning of the internal market exist. Providers can only perform pre-formulated contracts across borders with considerable transaction costs.

6. Conclusions and Recommendations

In order to remove inconsistencies and ambiguities, the following issues could be tackled:

- Definition of consumer (esp. with regard to mixed purpose cases).
- In place of the terms "seller/supplier" a uniform term should be used for all consumer protecting directives, to denote the contractual partner of the consumer. Conceivable formulations are "business" or "professional".
- The Directive should clearly express that it is applicable to all types of contracts.
- Clarification of the wording of Art. 3(1) (amendment of misleading wording in some language versions; clarification whether the criteria "good faith"/"imbalance" are to be understood cumulatively, alternatively or in the sense that any clause which generates a significant imbalance is always contrary to the principle of good faith; definition of "significant" imbalance).
- Provisions clarifying the legal nature of the Annex.

---

[739] ECJ judgment of 1 April 2004, C-237/02 – *Freiburger Kommunalbauten GmbH Baugesellschaft & Co. KG v Ludger Hofstetter et Ulrike Hofstetter* [2004] ECR I-3403.

- The consequences of unfairness should also be clarified, in that the unfairness of a term can be assessed on the court's own motion (as referred to in the cases of *Océano*, *Cofidis* and *Mostaza Claro*).[740]
- Clarification whether the requirement of transparency applies to orally concluded contracts.
- Provisions on whether the business has the duty to deliver or make the document available with the terms in cases where the contract is normally written. Moreover, it should be considered whether the Directive should be amended to expressly incorporate the prohibition of "surprising terms", in the same way as the proposals of directives of 1990 and 1992.
- The consequences of lack of transparency should be expressly regulated.
- Certain issues in relation to collective proceedings also appear to be in need of regulation: Clarification whether consumer associations must be given right of standing in any event and whether a single person or a group of persons which have not been organised could take actions under Art. 7. Moreover, it should be considered how the negative consequences of *res judicata* can be avoided.
- Definition of the notion of "close connection with the territory of a member state" in Art. 6(2).

Moreover, in order to remove at least the most obvious barriers to trade, whether application of the minimum clause should be excluded to some of the provisions of the Directive 93/13 thereby bringing about maximum harmonisation in these areas must be considered. In this respect it would be desirable if at least some of the terms listed in Annex no. 1 could be formulated not only in terms of an indicative, illustrative list, but as a blacklist.

A complete harmonisation of the law on unfair terms however, in the present state of development of the law, appears neither possible nor desirable, as the fairness of a clause can only be determined by comparison to (hardly harmonised) dispositive law and full harmonisation would bring about a marked reduction in consumer protection in those countries where it is particularly high.

I. Introduction: Policy reasons for monitoring pre-formulated terms

1. The law in the Member States prior to transposition of the Unfair Contract Terms Directive

If one enquires into the policy reasons for monitoring pre-formulated contract terms, two primary lines of argument come to the fore.[741]

The first theory is based on a consideration of transaction costs: A party using pre-formulated terms is usually better informed about the content of the terms than the other party (whether a consumer or business). By drafting terms just once for several transactions, the user can spread costs an infinite number of times, whereas for the other party it is often too expensive to obtain the information required for negotiating the conditions of the trans-

---

740 See Part 2 C.IV.4.

741 See e.g. *Kötz*, Europäisches Vertragsrecht I, 211 et seq.; *Tenreiro/Karsten*, in: Schulte-Nölke/Schulze (eds.), Europäische Rechtsangleichung, 225 et seq.

action. Informational asymmetries – disparities in the level to which each party is familiar with the terms of the contract – and the uneven distribution of transaction costs therefore have to be balanced by reviewing pre-formulated terms.

A series of legal systems, especially GERMAN, DUTCH and PORTUGUESE law, were based on this model even before transposition of Directive 93/13. Characteristic of these countries is that in principle only standard terms are subject to review, i.e. terms pre-formulated for a multitude of contracts, but not individual agreements. This is due to the fact that an uneven distribution of transaction costs regularly results only where standard terms are used, and not with individually negotiated clauses. At the same time, however, standard terms are capable of endangering not only the consumer, but any contractual partner against whom they are used. Therefore, the protection afforded by monitoring of terms in the aforementioned countries extends not only to B2C transactions, but also to B2B and P2P transactions.

According to the second model ("abuse theory") the control of pre-formulated contract terms is based, in contrast, upon the notion that unfair terms are often used against weaker parties. The main catalyst for control of terms is not the danger of standard terms, but rather the protection of a specified class of persons. In view of the economic, social, psychological and intellectual superiority of the business the customer has no choice other than to submit to the clauses in question. A review of validity shall accordingly counter an imbalance in bargaining power and knowledge.

This fundamental notion underpinned the laws of some countries, namely FRANCE, BELGIUM, LUXEMBOURG, even prior to the transposition of Directive 93/13. Characteristic of these countries is that in principle they only protect the consumer, as the inferior party (and especially in FRANCE[742] those persons concluding contracts which are not directly related to his or her profession). Consequently, this protection does not only cover standard terms, but rather all clauses, whether pre-formulated or individually negotiated.

Alongside both these models many other mixed systems exist as well as the model of the NORDIC STATES, where according to the general clause (Contract Acts, sec. 36), it is possible even in B2B contracts to review individually negotiated standard terms.

2. Model of the Unfair Contract Terms Directive

The first proposals for Directive 93/13 initially followed the French system, in which the rules were limited to consumer contracts, although individually negotiated terms were subject to the fairness test as well. Since the Common Position of the Council in 1992, however, a compromise between the French and the German models emerged: According to Art. 3(1) and (2) of Directive 93/13 individually negotiated terms – in contrast to FRANCE – are excluded from the scope of the Directive, however – in contrast to GERMANY – it is unnecessary for the contract terms to be pre-formulated for a multitude of contracts, so that in addition to standard terms also pre-formulated individual contracts for single use, but not individually negotiated terms, are subject to control of the Directive. This mixture of both systems is particularly emphasised in recital 9 of Directive 93/13, which refers both to the need

[742] See Part 3 A.III.2.

of protection from abuse of power – as in FRANCE – as well as to the danger for the consumer of unfair exclusion of essential rights – an allusion to the GERMAN model – particularly present in one-sided standard contracts.

The ECJ in its case law on Directive 93/13 primarily applies the "abuse theory". According to the ECJ,[743] the system of protection introduced by Directive 93/13 "is based on the idea that the consumer is in a weak position vis-à-vis the seller or supplier, as regards both his bargaining power and his level of knowledge. This leads to the consumer agreeing to terms drawn up in advance by the seller or supplier without being able to influence the content of the terms."

3. The law in the Member States following transposition of the Unfair Contract Terms Directive

Most member states, which prior to enactment of Directive 93/13 already had a developed system of monitoring the content of contractual clauses, limited their transposition of the Directive to minor adaptations to the rules whilst retaining the old system. Those member states, which prior to transposition of the Directive had no extensive system of monitoring of contract terms, by and large followed the model of the Directive. The ten new member states of the European Union which acceded in April 2004 have as far as possible adopted one of the existing systems.

The system of monitoring the fairness of terms in all 25 member states can be classified into four different models:

- In the Nordic States (DENMARK, FINLAND, SWEDEN) review of content relates to all contracts (B2B, B2C, P2P), also individually negotiated terms are subject to review.
- In other States, which traditionally follow the "transaction costs theory", control of content likewise extends to all contracts (B2B, B2C, P2P), however, according to the model only standard terms are subject to review. A review of "terms not individually negotiated" in contrast – in accord with the Directive – is only possible for B2C contracts. This model is followed by GERMANY, PORTUGAL, AUSTRIA and the NETHERLANDS. Also the new member states HUNGARY, LITHUANIA and SLOVENIA have adopted this model.[744] To a certain extent ESTONIA also counts amongst this group, as according to the Estonian Law of Obligations Act review of all contracts is possible, however with the difference that this primarily (and not only, as in the aforementioned member states, for B2C contracts) relates to "terms not individually negotiated".
- All member states, who restrict the monitoring of content to B2C contracts, but thereby also subject individually negotiated terms to review fall into the third group. These are FRANCE, BELGIUM and LUXEMBOURG as well as the CZECH REPUBLIC, LATVIA and MALTA.
- Finally a number of member states follow the concept of Directive 93/13, in which the content review is restricted to B2C contracts and only terms not individually negotiated

---

[743] ECJ judgment of 27 June 2000, Joined Cases C-240/98 to C-244/98 – *Océano Grupo Editorial SA v. Murciano Quintero* [2000] ECR I-04941, para. (25). See as well ECJ judgment of 26 October 2006, C-168/05 – *Elisa María Mostaza Claro v. Centro Móvil Milenium SL* [2006] ECR I-10421, para. (25).

[744] However, with the peculiarity that in SLOVENIA in B2C contracts even individually negotiated terms are subject to review.

can be controlled. These are UNITED KINGDOM, IRELAND, SPAIN, GREECE and ITALY (although some of these member states provide a black list for certain individually negotiated clauses). Amongst the new member states CYPRUS, POLAND and SLOVAKIA have opted for this model.

II. Legal framework in the Member States

1. Austria (AT)

Since its inception the AUSTRIAN Civil Code has contained a provision against immorality (CC Art. 879(1)) and general rules on formation of contract. In addition, since 1979 the Austrian Civil Code has prescribed special rules on the incorporation and applicability of contractual clauses: According to CC Art. 864a, unusual standard terms, disadvantageous to the other contractual party, can only form part of the contract if the other party's attention has specifically been drawn to them.

According to CC Art. 879(3), a contractual term contained within the general conditions of business or contractual forms, which does not make clear one of the party's ancillary performance duties, is void, if, in consideration of all the circumstances of the case, it grossly disadvantages one party. Whereas the rules of the CC do not only apply to B2C contracts, but also to B2B and P2P transactions, the Consumer Protection Act which also came into force in 1979 contains special provisions to monitor the content of clauses, which apply only to B2C contracts.

The only changes within this statutory framework so far have been limited to the details. With the Amendment Act of 1 January 1997 the pre-existing "black lists" in Art. 6(1) and (2) of the Consumer Protection Act were slightly extended. Furthermore breach of the transparency imperative in Art. 6(3) of the Consumer Protection Act was recognised as an independent ground of nullity in its own right for the first time.

2. Belgium (BE)

Prior to 1991, there was no explicit protection in the field of unfair contract terms. Thus consumers had to have recourse to general contract law. The Act of 14 July 1991 on Trade Practices and Consumer Protection (hereinafter TPA) was the first general regulation on unfair contract terms. The provisions were enacted in anticipation of the Directive, directly inspired by its content. However, the European Commission notified a reasoned opinion on 8 March 1994 pointing out that a significant number of the provisions of the Act of 1991 did not conform to the Directive. It was perceived as particularly problematic that the TPA does not apply to services provided by liberal professions. The BELGIAN legislator therefore opted to pass a separate Act on unfair clauses in contracts between consumers and practitioners of liberal professions (Liberal Professions Act – LPA).[745] Also the TPA was amended on

[745] Act of 3 April 1997, replaced by the Act of 2 August 2002 on misleading and comparative advertising, unfair contract terms and distance marketing in respect of liberal professions – Liberal Professions Act – LPA.

several occasions (Act of 7 December 1998 and the Act of 25 May 1999) in order to meet the Directive's requirements. The reforms expanded the personal and substantive scope and transposed the interpretation rule and transparency requirement of Art. 5 of Directive 93/13 into the TPA. Moreover, the reform changed the effects of unfair clauses. Whereas according to the earlier version of the Act unfair terms first became ineffective through judicial declaration, since 1998 they have been declared void from the start.

The TPA goes beyond the scope of the Directive in also bringing within its ambit, terms which were negotiated by the parties, whereas the LPA for liberal professions is confined to unfair standard terms which were not individually negotiated by the parties. However, the LPA contains an exception to this principle since the unfair clauses enumerated in the 'blacklist' in the annex to the Act are prohibited and void, even if they were individually negotiated (Art. 7(4) of the Liberal Professions Act).

Art. 34 of the TPA empowers the King to impose or prohibit by Royal Decree certain clauses in contracts applicable to certain commercial sectors or to specific products or services. The King has also the power to impose type-contracts on the seller – consumer relationship. The power of the King is restricted in two ways. On the one hand the King is only empowered to take action if inevitably to guarantee the balance between the rights and obligations of the parties or to assure the fairness of commercial transactions. On the other hand the King must primarily consult the Unfair Contract Terms Commission and the High Council of Tradespeople (Hoge Raad voor de Middenstand). At present only one Royal Decree has been issued: the Royal Decree of 9 July 2000 on the Essential Data and the Terms and Conditions to be Mentioned on The Order Form of New Cars. A Royal Decree on the contract terms in broker contracts of real estate agents is in preparation.

3. Cyprus (CY)

Prior to 1996 in CYPRIOT legislation there were no express rules regarding the monitoring of standard contract terms. Instead the general rules of conclusion of contract applicable to all persons of the General Contract Law, Cap 149, were applied. Moreover, the Sale of Goods Law of 1994[746] contains a provision which renders null and void those terms excluding the supplier's obligations implied by the aforesaid law. In 1996 the House of Representatives passed the Unfair Terms in Consumer Contracts Act.[747] The Act was amended in 1999 to transpose Directive 93/13.[748] This Law applies to any term in a contract concluded between a seller or supplier and a consumer where it has not been individually negotiated.

4. Czech Republic (CZ)

Prior to implementation of Directive 93/13 there were no specific provisions regarding unfair terms in the Civil Code of Czechoslovakia of 1964. Also the Consumer Protection Act 634/1992, which was passed in December 1992 by the Federal Assembly and subsequently

746 Law 10(I) of 1994.
747 Law 93(I) of 1996.
748 Law 69(I) of 1999.

(after separation of the state) further developed by the CZECH REPUBLIC and SLOVAKIA separately, did not (and does not) contain any specific provisions to monitor contract terms for the Czech Republic. Moreover, the Consumer Protection Act 634/1992 only specified obligations for the provision of information to consumers, prohibition of misleading advertising and discrimination, and further obligations in the sale of products and provision of services, as well as principles for co-operation and the rights of organisations created for consumer protection. Directive 93/13 was transposed into the Civil Code in 2000 with Act 367/2000. The Czech Republic transposed the Directive almost literally by inserting its provisions into CC Art. 52, 55, 56. The relevant rules only apply in the B2C context. In contrast to the Directive the definition of consumer (Art. 52(3)) in Czech law is not limited to natural persons. Furthermore, terms individually negotiated come within its ambit. Unfair terms are considered valid unless the consumer invokes nullity (Art. 55(2), 40a).

5. Denmark (DK)

The DANISH system of consumer protection law is comparable to that of the other Nordic countries (FINLAND and SWEDEN, see 7. and 24.). A key feature of those countries is the vast usage of the general clause, laid down in sec. 36 of the Contracts Acts. This clause makes it possible to wholly or partly disregard an (even individually negotiated) agreement, if the term is unfair/unreasonable with respect to the contract's content, the position of the parties and the circumstances prevailing during and after the conclusion of the contract. The general clause is not limited to B2C contracts, but applies to contracts in general. But it must be noted, that in the context of non consumer contracts, the threshold of unreasonableness is higher. A further characteristic of the Scandinavian states consists of the administrative control of clauses through the Consumer Ombudsman, whose task in Denmark is to monitor compliance with the Danish Marketing Practices Act in the interest of consumers. Directive 93/13 was transposed into Danish law in 1994 by means of amendments to the Contracts Act. Through the transposition an even higher degree of flexibility was achieved, making it possible not only to disregard an agreement in whole or in part, but also to amend it. In addition to approximating the general clause, additional special rules for consumer contracts were inserted into Danish Contract Law (ss. 38a-38d). The definition of consumer corresponds with the Directive, but gives a broader consumer protection by covering not just natural persons, but also legal persons, provided that they are not acting within the course of a business. In the case of consumer contracts, the general clause in sec. 36 of the Contracts Act applies with two modifications. Firstly, in applying the general clause, account may not be taken of circumstances to the detriment of the consumer arising at a later date if this means that a contractual term may not be amended or overridden. Secondly, even if a contract contains terms which are incompatible with proper business practice and cause a significant imbalance to the parties' rights and obligations to the detriment of the consumer, the consumer may ask to have the remainder of the contract retained without amendment, if this is feasible.

6. Estonia (EE)

Before the transposition of the Directive there were no special rules in national law explicitly covering unfair contract terms. All consumer law questions were regulated by the Civil Code of the ESTONIAN Soviet Socialist Republic of 12 June 1964 (in force from 1 January 1965). On 15 December 1993 the Parliament passed the Consumer Protection Act (hereinafter CPA) which came into force on 1 January 1994. The CPA contained general provisions concerning responsibilities of and restrictions upon the seller (sec. 7 and 8) but did not provide similar special rules as prescribed by the Directive. The Directive had to be implemented into Estonian law after the European Agreement Establishing an Association between the European Communities and their member states and the Republic of Estonia came into force on 1 February 1998. The legislator transposed the Directive in sec. 35-44 of the Law of Obligations Act which includes rules on the non-incorporation of surprising (uncommon or unintelligible) terms (sec. 37(3)) the priority of individual agreements over standard terms (sec. 38) the "*contra proferentem*" rule of interpretation (sec. 39(1)) and the "battle of forms" (sec. 40). The scope of application is broader than that defined in the Directive. All kinds of persons are covered including consumers, non commercial legal persons and commercial legal persons. Specific consumer protection provisions are included in a black list (sec. 42(3)) covering a total of thirty seven terms. If a blacklisted term is used in B2B-contracts, the term is presumed to be unfair (sec. 44).

7. Finland (FI)

The FINNISH system of consumer protection law is comparable to that of other NORDIC COUNTRIES (DENMARK and SWEDEN, see 5. and 24.). As in the other Scandinavian states, the central features are the general clause of Contracts Act (CA) sec. 36 and administrative protection measures and means of control, which in Finland are enforced by the Consumer Ombudsman and the Consumer Agency on the basis of the Act of Consumer Agency (1056/1998) respectively. In contrast to other Scandinavian states, since 1978 a Consumer Protection Act (CPA) has also existed, which in Chapter 3 lays down a general clause which gives the court the power to adjust or disregard express terms of the contract in B2C-contracts, whether individually negotiated or non-negotiated. Directive 93/13 was transposed in 1994 by amendments to a few points in the CPA. In contrast to Directive 93/13 the CPA also relates to individually negotiated terms. Moreover, in contrast to Art. 4(2) of the Directive 93/13, Chapter 4, section 1 CPA expressly provides for adjustment of the price. At the end of 1998 there was a further amendment Act to transpose Art. 6(2) of Directive 93/13.

8. France (FR)

The control of unfair contractual terms was initially developed through case law. There were also certain widespread, fragmented rules concerning unfair terms in the Code Civil. The first comprehensive legislative approach was law 78-22 of 10 January 1978,[749] the provisions of which were later transferred in 1993 into Art. L-132-1 et seq. of the new Consumer Code. Originally the law 78-22 was enacted in order to set up an administrative system of control of unfair terms before the *commission des clauses abusives*. The commission can only issue recommendations, on the basis of which the executive may prohibit certain clauses by decree. However, this procedure remained practically unused, since only two decrees banning the

749 Law on Protection and Information for Consumers; so-called "*loi scrivener*".

use of certain terms (black list) had been enacted.[750] Against this background, the Cass. civ. established in 1991 the principle of judicial review of unfair contractual terms in order to spread the control.[751] In addition to control through administrative bodies and judicial review of content in individual cases, since 1998 it has also been possible for consumer associations to institute legal actions (Art. L-421-1 et seq. of the Consumer Code).

Directive 93/13 was transposed through the enactment of law 95-96 of 1 February 1995 which slightly modified the Consumer Code. The general clause of Art.L-132-1 of the Consumer Code provides benchmarks for assessing unfairness albeit without explicitly mentioning the requirement of good faith as stated in Art. 3(1) of Directive 93/13. The French provisions still apply solely to terms used in B2C contracts but, in contrast to the Directive, individually negotiated terms are covered as well.

9. Germany (DE)

Since 1977 the GERMAN legislator had already comprehensively regulated the use of unfair contract clauses in the Act Concerning the Regulation of the Law of Standard Business Terms (Gesetz zur Regelung des Rechts der Allgemeinen Geschäftsbedingungen, hereinafter AGBG). Not only was (and is) the consumer protected, but every natural or legal person, against whom standard contract terms are used. Therefore contracts between private parties and commercial transactions are also, in principle, within its scope. In this respect the scope of protected persons is considerably wider than in the Directive. Prior to implementation of the Directive however it was only possible to review contractual terms pre-formulated for a multiplicity of contracts, unilaterally made by one party. Clauses which were pre-formulated for a one-off contract or contracts which were incorporated on the initiative of a third party (such as notary, agent etc.) thus laid outside of the ambit of the AGBG. The "grey" list of suspicious clauses (clauses whose validity depends on an appraisal) in § 10 of the AGBG (now: CC § 308) as well as a black list of wholly void clauses (clauses whose invalidity is not subject to any appraisal) in § 11 of the AGBG (now: CC § 309) serve as benchmarks for the control of contractual content. Clauses not catalogued in these lists, were judged according to the most important norm (in practice), the general clause § 9(1) of the AGBG (now CC § 307(1)). This provision declares that clauses are void if, contrary to the requirement of good faith, they place the contractual partner of the user at an unreasonable disadvantage.

In transposing the Directive in 1996 the legislator opted for a minimalistic solution. § 12 of the AGBG (international scope) was merely modified and a new provision was introduced in § 24a of the AGBG (now CC § 310(3)), which extends the scope for consumer contracts and also enables a review of clauses, which were formulated for one-off use and introduced into the contract on the initiative of a third party (notary, agent). Within the framework of the reform of the law of obligations, with effect from 1 January 2002 the legislator repealed the AGBG and its substantive provisions were integrated into the CC with minor, mainly draft-

---

750 See Art. R. 132-1, 132-2 and 132-2-1 of the Consumer Code.

751 Arrêt du 14 mai 1991, Bulletin des arrêts de la Cass. civ. I, no. 153 and Receuil Dalloz Sirey 1993, jurisprudence, 568.

ing changes (CC § 305-310). To meet the requirements of the ECJ (C-144/99[752]), CC § 307(1) made clear that clauses which lack transparency are void.

10. Greece (EL)

Even in the 1970s the GREEK academic and judicial communities had begun to intensively address the ever increasing practice of conclusion of contracts through the use of standard terms. This protection was provided in three levels of review (incorporation, interpretation, and reviewing the content of the clause). In 1991 a comprehensive consumer protection act was passed, which for the first time provided rules expressly for protection against unfair terms, but whose scope of application was limited to consumer contracts (B2C). This act was repealed in 1994 and replaced with a new Consumer Protection Act. The requirements of Directive 93/13 were transposed in Art. 2 of this Act, further amendments followed in 1999. The scope of the Greek provisions extended according to Art. 1(4) to all natural and legal persons, who are the end recipients of goods or services, irrespective of the purpose/nature of the transaction; it thus goes considerably further than the Directive.

11. Hungary (HU)

In socialism general conditions of business were practically irrelevant, it was only at the end of the 1960s that pre-formulated contract terms started to appear. Case law developed special benchmarks for the incorporation of standard contract terms,[753] consumer law provisions specifically however were still unknown. With the amendment act of 1978 the HUNGARIAN Civil Code (Act IV of 1959) was comprehensively reformed. Henceforth CC Art. 209 provided that unilaterally formulated standard contract terms used by legal persons, which conferred an unjustified advantage on one party, were rescindable. The party entitled to rescind was the "other" contractual party confronted with the clause (in which case the nullity was declared with effect *inter partes*) as well as certain state or community organs (here the nullity applied *erga omnes*).

In 1997 Directive 93/13 was transposed into the Hungarian Civil Code in the part "Law of Obligations", Title "Contract", Chapter XVIII. The provisions of the CC have been amended numerous times in recent years to take account of the case law of the ECJ (C-240/98 to C-244/98;[754] C-372/99;[755] C-473/00;[756] C-70/03[757]). The last amendment occurred with the Act III of 2006, in force since 1 March 2006.

752 ECJ judgment of 10 May 2001, C-144/99 – *Commission v Kingdom of the Netherlands* [2001] ECR I-03541.

753 See the 37th opinion of the economic council of the Supreme Court.

754 ECJ judgment of 27 June 2000, Joined Cases C-240/98 to C-244/98 – *Océano Grupo Editorial SA v. Murciano Quintero* [2000] ECR I-04941.

755 ECJ judgment of 24 January 2002, C-372/99 – *Commission of the European Communities v. Italian Republic* [2002] ECR I-00819.

756 ECJ judgment of 21 November 2002, C-473/00 – *Cofidis v. Fredout,* [2002] ECR I-10875.

757 ECJ judgment of 9 September 2004, C-70/03 – *Commission v. Kingdom of Spain* [2004] ECR I-0799.

The CC contains general provisions applicable to all persons on the incorporation and interpretation of standard contract terms (CC Art. 205a et seq.). A content review is likewise available in all contractual relationships, although in stages. According to CC Art. 209(1) (new version), a standard contract term is unfair if, contrary to the requirement of good faith, it causes a considerable and unjustified disadvantage to the other party. Furthermore, with consumer contracts, terms not individually negotiated can be reviewed; a review of individual agreements on the other hand has no longer been possible since 1 March 2006. In respect of B2C contracts, the rules of the CC are complemented with a *black* and a *grey list* by the government regulation 18/1999 (II.5.). Since Act III of 2006 came into force, the legislator has changed the consequences of unfairness. CC Art. 209a(2) provides that unfair terms in consumer contracts are void and that unfairness can only be asserted to the advantage of the consumer. The scope of application of the *actio popularis* has been limited to B2C contracts since 1 March 2006.
Further changes are expected with the planned "big" reform of the CC, including *inter alia* limiting the definition of consumer to natural persons and regulation of the concurrence of standard contract terms (battle of forms).

12. Ireland (IE)

Before transposition of the Directive, there was no protection in IRISH law comparable to that of the Directive. Instead 'fairness' was addressed by a number of contract law doctrines, such as the doctrines of duress and undue influence, mistake and misrepresentation. Moreover, the extent to which a supplier could exclude his liability for breach of the statutory implied terms in contracts for the sale of goods and supply of services was regulated by the Sale of Goods Acts 1893 and 1980 (for sale of goods) and Part IV of the Sale of Goods and Supply of Services Act 1980 (for the supply of services). As regards the sale of goods, any attempt to exclude liability for breach of the statutory implied terms against a consumer was considered void (see e.g. sec. 55 of the Sale of Goods Acts 1893), whereas, in relation to services an express exclusion would be valid if fair and reasonable and if it had been specifically brought to the consumer's attention (sec. 40 of the Sale of Goods Acts 1980).

Related provisions in the Sale of Goods and Supply of Services Act 1980 allowed a Minister to make orders on various matters, such as: required particulars in contracts; notice on the use of standard form contracts; font size in printed contracts and contracts required to be in writing (sec. 51-54, 1980 of the Act), but they were never implemented.
The Directive was transposed by the European Communities (Unfair Terms in Consumer Contracts) Regulations, 1995. Like in the UNITED KINGDOM, the content and structure of the implementing provisions remained quite close to the Directive, limiting the scope of the Regulations to B2C transactions.

It was not until 2000, that the European Communities (Unfair Terms in Consumer Contracts) (Amendment) Regulations 2000 (SI No. 307 of 2000) were introduced to extend enforcement powers under Regulation 8 of the 1995 Regulations to 'consumer organisations'.

13. Italy (IT)

In ITALIAN law there were no special separate regulations on unfair terms before the implementation of the Directive. However in 1942, within the Italian Civil Code certain general provisions on incorporation (Art. 1341(1), 1342) and interpretation of standard terms applicable to all persons already existed, for instance, CC Art. 1370 (*contra proferentem* rule). In addition, according to CC Art. 1341(2) pre-determined and pre-formulated clauses were void, if they were not individually accepted in writing, especially limitations of liability. Special rules on the review of content of clauses on the other hand were not introduced into the CC until 1996: In order to transpose the Directive, the legislator produced a new chapter in the Civil Code (ex CC Art. 1469-bis to 1469sexies). The scope of these rules was restricted to consumer contracts. Meanwhile the rules have been amended many times. In 1999, in response to pressure from the European Commission, the Italian legislator extended the scope of review of clauses to all contractual relationships (whereas thus far the only contracts to which it applied were contracts for the sale of goods and the supply of services). A further amendment occurred in 2003 with Art. 6 of the Act 14/2003: After the ECJ made it clear in C-372/99,[758] that Art. 7(3) of Directive 93/13 requires "the setting up of procedures of a deterrent nature and a dissuasive purpose which may also be directed against conduct confined to the recommending of the use of unfair contract clauses, without actually using them in specific contracts", the Italian legislator refined the relevant provision (CC Art. 1469sexies) according to these guidelines. With the passing of the consumer code, on 22 July 2005 which came into force by legislative decree of 23 October 2005, the provisions on unfair clauses of the CC (ex CC Art. 1469bis-1469sexies) were carried over to the consumer code. This instrument changed the legal consequences of the use of unfair terms by introducing the concept of relative nullity (*nullità di protezione*) in Art. 36(3): Henceforth the consumer can rely on the validity of the contract so long as it suits him, as only he (or the court which is obliged to take into account his interests) can claim nullity and no limitation period looms.

14. Latvia (LV)

In LATVIA the first normative act in the field of consumer protection came into force on 28 October in 1992 – law "On Consumer Rights Protection". This normative act did not stipulate specific provisions regarding unfair contract terms. However, from 1992 to 1999 (when the new Consumer Rights Protection Act came into force) consumer rights protection developed intensively. In 1999, the Consumer Rights Protection Act was modified in order to transpose Directive 93/13. The provisions only apply to B2C-Contracts, however, the concept of consumer has been extended by the Latvian legislator, since the notion "consumer" encompasses all transactions which are not directly related to his or her entrepreneurial activity, sec. 1(3). Sec. 5(1) provides that contracts between a consumer and a business shall provide for equal rights of both contracting parties. According to sec. 5(2) contract terms (even though they have been individually negotiated) shall be deemed to be contradictory to the principle of legal equality of the contracting parties if the terms put the consumer in a disadvantageous position and are contrary to the requirements of good faith, while sec. 6(3) adopts the wording of Art. 3(1) of Directive 93/13, blacklisting twelve clauses of the Annex.

---

758 ECJ judgment of 24 January 2002, C-372/99 – *Commission of the European Communities v. Italian Republic* [2002] ECR I-00819.

A key feature of Latvian law is the administrative control of contractual clauses by the Consumer Rights Protection Centre, whose competences are laid down in sec. 25 of the Consumer Rights Protection Act.

15. Lithuania (LT)

Consumer protection is a relatively new sphere of law in the Republic of LITHUANIA. Before the transposition of Directive 93/13, consumer law issues were regulated by the 7 July 1964 Civil Code (soviet times code) and since 1994 by the Consumer Protection Act, but Lithuanian law did not provide for a level of protection comparable to the Directive. In 2000, the legislator replaced the Civil Code of 1964 with the new Civil Code of Lithuania (in force since 1 July 2001), closely mirroring the Unidroit Principles and the Principles of European Contract Law. Parallel to this the Act on Consumer Protection (entry into force 1 January 2001) was amended. Both the Civil Code as well as the Consumer Protection Act serve to implement the provisions of Directive 93/13. In contrast to the Consumer Protection Act the Civil Code, however, does contain general rules on standard conditions which are applicable to all kinds of contracts. According to CC Art. 6.185(2), standard conditions prepared by one of the parties shall be binding on the other only if the latter was provided with an adequate opportunity to become acquainted with said conditions. Moreover, the Civil Code provides special rules on surprising terms (CC Art. 6.186(1) and (2)), the battle of forms (CC Art. 6.187) and the interpretation of standard terms (CC Art. 193(4)). CC Art. 6.186(3) also provides that all kinds of parties being confronted with standard terms have the right to claim for dissolution or modification of the contract in the event where, even though the standard conditions of the contract are not contrary to the law, they exclude the party's rights and possibilities that are commonly granted in a contract of that particular class, or exclude or limit the civil liability of the party who prepared the standard conditions, or establish other provisions which violate the principle of equality of parties, cause imbalance in the parties' interests, or are contrary to the criteria of reasonableness, good faith and justice. These rules were complemented with special provisions for the review of terms not individually negotiated in consumer contracts (CC Art. 6.188). The provisions of the Consumer Protection Act correspond with these rules almost word for word. At present, courts apply both acts simultaneously.

16. Luxembourg (LU)

The Consumer Protection Act which was enacted on 25 August 1983 provided comprehensive regulations on unfair contract terms. Structurally very similar to the Directive, the provisions contained a general clause defining criteria for assessing unfairness as well as a non-exhaustive black list of unfair clauses. Therefore the transposition of the Directive by the Law of 26 March 1997[759] lead only to slight modifications to the domestic law as four clauses were added to the black list. Parallel to this, provisions on the distinction between individual agreements and pre-formulated clauses were introduced into CC Art. 1135-1 and a new rule on the incorporation of standard terms was adopted: According to CC Art. 1135-1 standard terms are only binding, as long as the other party has had the possibility to acquaint himself

759 Law of 26 March 1997 (Memorial A No. 30 of 29 April 1997).

with the terms at the time of signing, and if in the prevailing circumstances he is to be treated as having accepted them. Whereas the review of content provided in the Consumer Protection Act is only applicable in the context of B2C relationships, the incorporation rules of CC Art. 1135-1 apply to all persons.

17. Malta (MT)

Before the transposition of Directive 93/13, there were no express legal norms dealing with the use of unfair terms in consumer contracts. However, in practice, the provisions of the Civil Code were utilised by the MALTESE Courts as a legislative tool for regulating the use of unfair terms by traders especially with respect to the exemption of liability clauses.
In 1994 the legislator passed the Consumer Affairs Act. Among other things the Act created (and conferred powers upon) the post of Director of Consumer Affairs, and provided for the establishment of the Consumer Affairs Council, the Consumer Claims Tribunal and the regulation of the role of consumer associations. Directive 93/13 was transposed in 2000, by amending the Consumer Affairs Act 1994,[760] especially Art. 94 which empowers the Director on his initiative or at the request of a qualifying body to require the deletion or alternation of unfair terms in a consumer contract. The Maltese Consumer Affairs legislation goes beyond the minimum requirements, since the Maltese law extends the protection of consumers to all contractual terms without making any distinction as to whether the term was individually negotiated or not. A characteristic of the Maltese system are the far reaching powers of the Director of Consumer Affairs. If a trader is considered to have acted in breach of the Consumer Affairs Act, the Director of Consumer Affairs can request the initiation of criminal proceedings before the Court of Magistrates (Criminal Jurisdiction). If the trader is found to be in breach of the requirements of the Consumer Affairs Act, a maximum fine of Lm 2000 (4658 Euros) can be imposed by the aforesaid court.

18. Netherlands (NL)

Before 1992, the DUTCH Civil Code did not contain specific provisions on unfair contract terms. Those terms used in consumer contracts were dealt with by the courts by means of the general doctrine. Also, general terms excluding or limiting the legal liability of the seller or supplier were deemed void as being contrary to good morals or public order.[761] Furthermore, general terms were interpreted in favour of the consumer in case a term was not very clear. The courts often applied the principle of "good faith" in order to fill in gaps and to nullify unacceptable terms.

The new Dutch civil code which came into force on 1 January 1992 contains special provisions on unfair contract terms (Art. 6:231-6:247). The provisions were inspired by the German act on unfair contract terms.[762] The scope of the provisions also extends to B2B transactions, however, contractual parties who employ more than 50 staff cannot seek review of

---

760 Article 44-47 in Part VI ("Unfair Practices") and Art. 94-101 in Part IX ("Compliance Orders").

761 Article 1373 in conjunction with Art. 1371 of the Old Dutch Civil Code.

762 GERMAN Act Concerning the Regulation of the Law of Standard Business Terms, see above Part 2 C.II.9.

either incorporation or content (Art. 6:235 BW). The black list and the grey list (Art. 6:235, 6:236 BW) on the other hand relate only to consumer contracts. After the ECJ (C-144/99[763]) criticised that Dutch Law does not contain explicit provisions on the principle of transparency, the legislator amended CC Art. 6:231 and 6:238 and clarified moreover, that in case of doubt about the meaning of a term, the interpretation most favourable to the consumer shall prevail. A further amendment occurred in 2004. As Dutch law on unfair terms, in contrast to the Directive, only applied to written contracts, the word "written" was removed.[764]

19. Poland (PL)

In 1933 Art. 71, 72 of the POLISH law of obligations already contained provisions on unfair terms. Although Polish civil law was familiar with the concept of review of contractual clauses, the level of protection for consumers was very different to the one prescribed by the Directive, especially up until 1990. Since 1990 certain mechanisms for consumer protection have been established in the Civil Code. By virtue of CC Art. 384 the Council of Ministers could, by means of a regulation, specify particular conditions for concluding and executing contracts with consumers (normative 'standard forms'), if it was justified by the aim of protecting consumer interests. In fact, the Council adopted only one regulation with a limited scope of application on 30 April 1995 (*on the conclusion and execution of contracts of sale of movable goods with consumers*). CC Art. 385.2 (as per the amendment of the Civil Code of 28 July 1990) stipulated that if contractual clauses, contractual forms or rules secured significantly unjustified benefits for the party who used them, the other party (unless a businessperson) could apply to court to have them declared ineffective *inter partes*, i.e. there was no possibility for abstract control of contractual clauses.

The Directive was transposed by the Act *on the protection of some consumer rights and liability for damage caused by a dangerous product* of 2 March 2000 amending the Polish Civil Code of 1964 – Arts. 384-385.4. The new concept distinguishes between forms used in all contracts, those used in contracts between professionals (traders) and those used in contracts with consumers. A review of the incorporation of standard terms is according to CC Art. 384 in principle not confined to B2C relationships, but yet stronger provisions on incorporation apply to consumer contracts. The battle-of-forms rule in Art. 485, modelled on Art. 2:209 PECL, on the other hand, relates only to B2B contracts. A review of the content of standard terms is limited to B2C transactions. The notion of "consumer" differs from the Directive, since a person can also be regarded as a consumer when he is concluding a contract for a purpose not directly related to his business.

Since transposition of Directive 93/13 Polish law also contains in Art. 479[36] et seq. of the Polish Civil Procedure Code rules on the abstract review of terms in collective proceedings for the first time. Standing is enjoyed not only by consumer associations, local consumer ombudsmen as well as the President of the Office for Competition and Consumer Protection, but every person, who could have concluded the contract following an offer by the user. If the designated consumer court in Warsaw prohibits the use of a certain contractual clause,

---

763 ECJ judgment of 10 May 2001, C-144/99 – *Commission v. Kingdom of the Netherlands* [2001] ECR I-03541.

764 By the Act of 13 May 2004, Stb. 2004, 210.

the decision is published in the Economic and Court Journal and entered in a register with the President of the Office of Competition and Consumer Protection. Once the judgment has been published in the Register it has general effects. The Register is open to the public, and at present it contains more than 1000 clauses.

20. Portugal (PT)

The PORTUGUESE legislator had already established provisions for the protection against standard contract terms in 1985 with the Decree-Law 446/1985 of October 25. It followed the German Act Concerning the Regulation of the Law of Standard Business Terms of 1976 very closely, i.e. it was also applicable to contracts concluded between businesses (B2B) and amongst private parties (P2P). Conversely the scope of application was limited to standard terms pre-formulated for frequent use. The content review was carried out according to the general clause of Art. 15 (contradiction against good faith). Additionally, in Art. 18 et seq. and Art. 21 et seq. the act contains four different catalogues of forbidden clauses, whereby the first two (black and grey list) apply generally, whereas the other two (also a black and a grey list) are only applicable to consumer contracts.

Directive 93/13 was transposed by means of legislative decree 220/1995 of August, in which the decree merely made some minor amendments, above all a correction of the prohibited lists and an extension of some procedural provisions. In the course of transposition the legislator began to compile a register of those judgments, as a consequence of which the use of clauses was prohibited or declared ineffective. As far as substantive scope is concerned, with the repeal of the old Art. 3(1)(c) it enabled a review of clauses that were imposed or approved by legal persons of public law. Only through a further amendment in 1999 (Decree-Law 249/1999 of July 7) on the other hand did pre-formulated individual contracts come within the purview of the act.

21. Slovakia (SK)

Prior to transposition of Directive 93/13 there were no specific provisions in the Civil Code of 1964 or in the Consumer Protection Act 1992 which had the protection of the consumer from unfair terms as their aim (see above, 4.). Public control and market surveillance authority in the field of consumer protection were regulated by the Act 274/1993 on Jurisdiction of Bodies in Matters of Consumer Protection, which defined the powers of individual authorities in matters of consumer protection (Ministry of Economy and other ministries and other institutions of state administration, Trade Inspection, county offices, district offices, municipalities).

In order to transpose the Directive, the SLOVAKIAN legislator amended the Civil Code in 2004,[765] inserting the provisions of the Directive almost literally. These rules were complemented by the Consumer Protection Act, also adopted in 2004,[766] whereby the notion of

---

765 Amendment No 150/2004 Fifth head: Consumer contracts: Art. 52-54, date of coming into force 1 April 2004.

766 Last amendment 616/2004, date of coming into force: 25 November 2004.

consumer contract was more closely defined, Art. 23a of the Consumer Protection Act, and general provisions for public control and market surveillance authorities as well as the rights of consumer organisations were laid down. The scope of application of the domestic provisions is broader than the one prescribed by the Directive since legal persons are also regarded as consumers, provided they are acting for purposes outside their trade, business or profession. One key feature of Slovakian Law is the co-operation between the government and non-government organisations in promoting consumer protection and policy. According to Slovakian Law, Consumer organisations have a legal right to work with public authorities in both creating and monitoring consumer policy, and in improving the effectiveness of its administration. Their representatives sit on the government's advisory Consumer Policy Council (the Vice-Chairman is the representative of the Association of Slovak Consumers).

22. Slovenia (SL)

Before the transposition of Directive 93/13 into SLOVENIAN law, the Code of Obligations of 1978 contained two articles regarding general terms and conditions of the contract. Neither of them included a detailed description or definition of unfair terms. Art. 143 provided that any provisions of general terms and conditions that oppose the actual purpose for which the contract was concluded or good business customs shall be null and void, even if the general terms and conditions in which they are contained were approved by the relevant authority. In addition, the court could reject the application of individual provisions of general terms and conditions that remove another party's right to object or appeal, or provisions based on which a party loses contractual rights or deadlines or that are otherwise unjust or too strict for the party.

The Slovenian legislator transposed the Directive in February 1998, amending Arts. 22-24 of the Consumer Protection Act. The new provisions came into force on 28 March 1998. Compared with the Directive Slovenian law provides greater protection for consumers because individually negotiated terms can equally well be declared unfair and therefore null and void. Terms used in other contracts (B2B or P2P) can be reviewed under Art. 121 of the new Code of Obligations (in force since 2002). Art. 121 of the Code of Obligations provides that general terms and conditions that oppose the actual purpose for which the contract was concluded or good business customs shall be null and void.

23. Spain (ES)

Although in SPAIN there was not a separate Law on unfair contract terms, there did exist a concise regulation on the topic with protection to some extent comparable to that of the Directive. In 1980 *Law 50/1980 of October 8 on the insurance contract* was passed, whose Art. 3 deals with standard terms and unfair terms in contracts of insurance. Apart from that branch of the Law, taking a more general approach, Law 26/1984 of July 19 on Consumer Protection created a full regime on unfair contract terms in contracts concluded by consumers. Art. 10 of the Law 24/1986 contained (mixing to some extent the notions of standard terms and unfair terms, with some confusion) a definition on standard contract terms and the formal requirements for them to be considered part of the contract, a general rule on equity in contractual clauses and a list of 12 sections on forbidden terms, a rule on the interpretation *contra stipulatorem*, the priority of particular clauses over general clauses and the sanction of nullity. This regulation on unfair contract terms was inspired by Comparative Law, with a particular influence of the GERMAN Law on standard terms in contracts.[767]

Directive 93/13 was transposed in 1998 by the enactment of Law 7/1998, 13 April 1998, on Standard Terms in Contracts and Law 26/1984 of July 19 on Consumer Protection, in which the list of unfair clauses was extended by a further 29 clauses. Both acts are different in terms of scope and content. The act on standard contract terms deals with standard terms in contracts in general, its provisions apply equally to B2C contracts and B2B contracts. This act however only regulates the incorporation and interpretation of standard terms, and does not review content. The General Consumer Protection Law on the other hand contains (for consumer contracts) provisions on content review.

One of the main characteristics of the domestic system of preventive control of unfair terms is the Spanish Standard Terms Register, listing terms that have been declared unfair by final court decisions. The Notaries and Registrars of the Land Registry and the Commercial Registry must adhere to this Register and refuse to authorise contracts containing any of the listed terms. The public Register enables anybody to invoke the unfairness of these terms before the courts.

The requirements articulated by the ECJ in C-70/03[768] (concerning the transposition of Art. 5 and Art. 6 of Directive 93/13) have thus far not been implemented in Spanish law, but there is currently a draft being discussed in the Spanish parliament, modifying not only the wrong transposition, but also some other questions on unfair terms (e.g. round-off clauses against the consumer, unfair practices in service contracts, unfair clauses on requisites for termination).

24. Sweden (SE)

In 1971 SWEDEN issued an Act on Contract Terms in consumer relationships (Contract Terms Act, CTA) which contained mainly market law rules, enabling the Consumer Ombudsman to negotiate with suppliers' organisations and issue prohibitions against the use of unreasonable terms and conditions. Measures could be taken to fend off the use of certain contract clauses which were considered unreasonable. Such cases are tried separately via the Consumer Ombudsman and the Swedish Consumer Agency and before the Market Court as the only and final court, since Market Court's judgments cannot be appealed. Furthermore, since 1976 all contractual clauses (in B2C, B2B and P2P relationships) can also be subjected to a content review under sec. 36 of the Contracts Act – as also in the other SCANDINAVIAN COUNTRIES (DENMARK and FINLAND, see 5. and 7.). With the accession of Sweden to the EU the CTA 1971 was repealed and replaced with the CTA of 15 Dec 1994 (1994:1512). The Act (covering only B2C relations) contains not only marketing law, but also civil law provisions, that essentially refer to sec. 36 of the Contracts Act. However, the general clause in sec. 36 of the Contracts Act applies with two modifications. Firstly, circumstances that occurred after conclusion of the contract can only be considered if this would not be to the disadvantage of the consumer (CTA Art. 11(2)). Secondly, the possibility of amendment of

767 GERMAN Act Concerning the Regulation of the Law of Standard Business Terms of 1976, see above I.9.

768 ECJ judgment of 9 September 2004, C-70/03 – *Commission v. Kingdom of Spain* [2004] ECR I-0799.

unreasonable contract terms is limited; in the case of unfair terms which have not been individually negotiated, the consumer can request that the remainder of the contract shall remain unchanged i.e. the court does not amend the remaining clauses.

25. United Kingdom (UK)

Even before legislative regulations came into force case law had developed a series of protective mechanisms to review standard contracts. According to the case law, standard terms would only then form part of the contract, if the user had given the other contractual party reasonable opportunity to become acquainted with the terms (reasonable notice test[769]). An additional role was played by the interpretation of contracts according to the *contra proferentem* rule and even a review of content was possible within limits. The first piece of legislation was the *Unfair Contract Terms Act 1977* (UCTA). UCTA is not limited to consumer contracts; it applies to B2B contracts, and also, in limited circumstances, to P2P contracts. However, it only covers a narrow range of terms, since it is designed to control exclusion clauses, where one party attempts to exclude or limit their normal liability for negligence or breach of contract or tries to "render a contractual performance substantially different from that which was reasonably expected". UCTA remained unaffected in transposing the Directive and remains in force.

The Directive was initially transposed in 1994 via a statutory instrument (Unfair Terms in Consumer Contracts Regulations, UTCCR) resembling the Directive almost word for word. Since the implementation of the Directive, the Office of Fair Trading (OFT) has been the leading regulator in this field. However, contrary to Art. 7 of Directive 93/13, the UNITED KINGDOM did not introduce a general right of standing for consumer associations, since this had been opposed by the privity of contract doctrine. The Queen's Bench Division of the High Court therefore asked the ECJ whether the Directive allowed private persons or organisations having a legitimate interest in protecting consumers to take action before the courts or before competent administrative bodies for a decision as to whether contractual terms drawn up for use are unfair. However, the question was withdrawn: as a result of political change, the government gave right of standing to consumer associations in the Consumer Contracts Regulations 1999 and granted the Claimant Consumers' Association the right to litigate.

The dual applicability of UCTA 1977 and UTCCR 1999 results in a particularly complex legal framework, since the two laws contain inconsistent and overlapping provisions, using different language and concepts to produce similar but not identical effects. The Law Commission and Scottish Law Commission in February 2005 therefore published a draft Unfair Terms in Contracts Bill and proposed in its final report to clarify and unify the legislation on unfair terms presently contained in UCTA 1977 and UTCCR 1999.[770] The report also recommends improved protection for small businesses and to allow them to challenge any standard term of the contract that has not been altered through negotiation, and is not the main subject matter of the contract or the price.

---

[769] Parker v. South Eastern Railway Co Ltd. [1877] 2 CPD 416; Thornton v. Shoe Lane Parking Ltd [1971] 2 QB 163.

[770] See the final report of the Law Commission and the Scottish Law Commission on unfair terms in contracts, LAW COM No. 292/SCOT LAW COM No. 199.

III. Scope of application

1. Consumer, Seller and Supplier, Public-sector undertakings

a. B2C, B2B and P2P Contracts

Directive 93/13 is applicable to terms in contracts concluded between a seller or supplier and a consumer (B2C). Most member states have, in the course of transposition of the Directive, introduced special B2C rules to review pre-formulated clauses.

In addition to this, in a number of member states a review of B2B and P2P contracts is possible at different levels.

In the NORDIC STATES (DENMARK, FINLAND, SWEDEN), due to the general clause of sec. 36 Contracts Act, a content review of unfair terms (even if they are individually negotiated) has always been possible in all manner of contractual relationships, thus also in B2B and P2P contracts. However, according to sec. 36 Contracts Act, in determining what is unfair, regard shall not only be paid to the content of the contract and to the circumstances prevailing at and after the conclusion of the contract, but also to the positions of the parties. This means that in B2B contracts, very strict requirements must be overcome to render a clause unfair.

In GERMANY, PORTUGAL and ESTONIA as well as in AUSTRIA, HUNGARY, LITHUANIA, NETHERLANDS and SLOVENIA there are general clauses which provide for a content review of standard terms, which do not merely apply to B2C contracts, but also to B2B and P2P contracts. A further special feature of Germany, Portugal and Estonia is that in relation to B2B contracts a grey list and black list are also employed:

- The GERMAN provisions for monitoring of standard terms (CC § 305 et seq.), in principle, protect all contractual parties against whom standard terms are used. So far as standard terms are being used against a business, certain specific provisions do not have any direct application, especially the grey list (CC § 308) and black list (CC § 309), which apply to B2C contracts (CC § 310(1)). However, where the use of a particular clause against consumers would be prohibited according to CC §§ 308, 309, in a B2B situation the judge must examine whether the clause is also to be considered void in the business sphere. According to the case law of the BGH, the black list especially (CC § 309) has an indicative effect of whether the relevant rule leads to a disproportionate imbalance to the detriment of the business.
- PORTUGUESE Law, in addition to the general clause applying to all transactions (Art. 15 of the Decree-Law 446/1985), also has a grey and a black list, which are applicable to all contractual relationships (Art. 18, 19 of the Decree-Law 446/1985).
- In ESTONIA, the general clause for standard terms (Art. 42 of the Law of Obligations Act) is applicable to both B2C and P2P contracts alike. The black list, which applies to B2C contracts (Art. 42(3) of the Law of Obligations Act) is, pursuant to Art. 44, to be considered as a grey list in respect of B2B contracts.[771]

---

[771] Cf. Art. 44 of the ESTONIAN Law of Obligations Act: "If a standard term specified in subsection 42(3) of this Act is used in a contract where the other party to the contract is a person who entered into the contract for the purposes of that person's economic or professional activities, the term is presumed to be unfair".

In the UNITED KINGDOM, a review of standard contract terms for both B2B and P2P contracts is possible, since UCTA 1977 also applies to contracts between businesses and certain "private" contracts for the sale of goods where neither of the two parties is a business. However, UCTA applies only to exclusion and limitation of liability clauses and indemnity clauses.

In contrast, there are no special general clauses providing for a content review of preformulated terms in BELGIUM, CYPRUS, CZECH REPUBLIC, FRANCE, GREECE, IRELAND, ITALY, LATVIA, LUXEMBOURG, MALTA, POLAND, SLOVAKIA and SPAIN.

It is nevertheless worth noting, that in some of these member states a content review is possible indirectly: many member states regulate the incorporation of standard terms, which have a general application to all kinds of contractual parties.[772] In the course of reviewing incorporation (and interpretation) this often represents a hidden form of content review, in which not only formal aspects are examined. Thus for example, in a number of member states the incorporation of standard terms does not merely depend upon whether the other party has had the opportunity of becoming acquainted with the contractual terms (such formal requirements are e.g. the duty of the user to inform the other party of its use of standard terms; the duty of the user to give the other party the opportunity to become acquainted with the terms; duty of the user to communicate the standard terms; the duty of the user to draft the terms in plain intelligible language). Rather, in some of the member states the content of the clause (and its fairness) are considered as well, when deciding whether or not a term has been incorporated into the contract.

Finally it should be noted, that many member states (e.g. BELGIUM and SPAIN[773]) apply general concepts, which can be used to correct an extremely disproportionate imbalance in the main performance duties, also in B2B contracts, such as on the basis of the *laesio enormis* or the benchmark of "public policy/good morals". In FRANCE, the Cass. civ. has sporadically allowed a review of clauses between two businesses (via the doctrine of *cause*, CC Art. 1131), although the French provisions on content review are in principle limited to consumer contracts.[774]

b. Definition of consumer[775]

Art. 2 lit. (b) of Directive 93/13 defines consumer as any natural person who is acting for purposes which are outside his trade, business or profession. The member states have only partly followed this definition. In a number of member states one finds deviating definitions

---

772 See *supra*, Part 2 C.II.1.-25.

773 SPANISH courts quite often use "indirect control" by applying the general theory on vices of consent (mistake, fraud, etc.). Moreover, the Civil law of Navarre and Catalonia admits a *laessio enormis* (but not the Spanish Civil Code).

774 Cass. civ. 22 October 1996 D. 1997, 121 *Société Banchereau v. Société Chronopost*. In later decisions however the Cass. civ. did place limitations on the extent of the principles developed in *Chronopost*, see Chambre mixte 22 April 2005, pourvoi n° 02-18326 and 03-14112; Chambre commerciale 21 February 2006, pourvoi n° 04-20139.

775 See thereto in detail Part 3 A. of the study.

of consumer. In SPAIN, GREECE and HUNGARY all "final addressees" are protected as consumers. In most cases, this concept offers wider protection than Directive 93/13, since it also encompasses atypical transactions, which are not related to a further transfer. In FRANCE, POLAND and LATVIA businesses concluding contracts which are not directly related with his or her profession are also protected as "consumers" or "*non-professionnels*".[776] In AUSTRIA, BELGIUM, CZECH REPUBLIC, DENMARK, FRANCE, GREECE, HUNGARY, SLOVAKIA and SPAIN (controversial), legal persons are treated as a consumer, provided that the purchase is for private use or (in GREECE, HUNGARY and SPAIN) the legal person is the final addressee. HUNGARY is presently planning to limit the notion of consumer to natural persons. In PORTUGAL, it is unclear whether legal persons can be protected as "consumers", however, a draft of a new Consumer Code acknowledges that legal persons may, in certain circumstances, benefit from the protection conferred to consumers.

In MALTA, any other class or category of persons whether natural or legal may, from time to time, be designated as "consumers" for all or any of the purposes of the Consumer Affairs Act by the Minister responsible for consumer affairs after consulting the Consumer Affairs Council. Furthermore, in Malta the notion of "consumer" includes any other individual not being the immediate purchaser or beneficiary, whether or not a member of the consumer's household, who, having been expressly or tacitly authorised or permitted by the consumer, may have consumed, used or benefited from any goods or services provided to the consumer by the trader.

c. Definition of seller or supplier[777]

According to Art. 2 lit. (c) "seller or supplier" means any natural or legal person who is acting for purposes relating to his trade, business or profession, whether publicly or privately owned. The notion of business in Art. 2 lit. (c) of Directive 93/13 is autonomous to European law and is to be interpreted widely. The Directive states that the term seller/supplier encompasses all natural and legal persons in the course of their business or profession, thus including farmers and freelancers.

Most member states have transposed the terms "seller" and "supplier" (in part under the generic term "professional/business") in accordance with Directive 93/13. In some member states on the other hand, there are no express definitions, above all in FRANCE and LUXEMBOURG. In BELGIUM, there is the peculiarity that separate rules are enacted concerning contracts between consumers and practitioners of liberal professions; instead of broadening the scope of the TPA the legislator preferred to pass a separate Act dealing with unfair contract terms in consumer contracts with practitioners of liberal professions. In MALTA any category or class of persons can be designated as a "trader" by Order of the Minister responsible for consumer affairs after consulting the Consumer Affairs Council, and publication in the Gazette.

---

776 As to the situation in the UNITED KINGDOM see in detail Part 3 A.III.2.

777 See thereto in detail Part 3 B. of the study.

d. Public Sector Undertakings

For detailed information on the domestic legislation of the 15 "old" member states with regard to unfair terms used in contracts for public services please refer to the study "*Application de la Directive 93/13 aux prestations de service public, Rapport de synthèse*" conducted by Harriet Hall and Claire Tixador.[778]

2. Exclusion of specific contracts

a. Contracts in the area of succession rights, family, employment and company law

According to recital 10, contracts relating to employment, succession rights, rights under family law and contracts relating to the incorporation and organisation of companies or partnership agreements are excluded from the Directive, as such contracts, as a rule, are not consumer contracts. For contracts relating to employment, succession rights and rights under family law this is uncontroversial as there is hardly a case imaginable, in which such a contract could at the same time be a consumer contract. Whether member states can exclude contracts relating to the incorporation and organisation of companies or partnership agreements from a review of clauses on the other hand is doubtful, as according to the wording and the preparatory works[779] the exceptions named in recital 10 shall only apply in the absence of a consumer contract. With company contracts concerning the acquisition of company rights as a capital investment without a business function, however, a consumer contract can be present.

Contracts relating to employment, succession rights, rights under family law and to the incorporation and organisation of companies or partnerships are above all in CYPRUS and IRELAND expressly excluded from the scope of application of the national provisions. The DUTCH provisions do not relate to contracts of employment, in ESTONIA company law contracts are excluded. Since the modernisation of the law of obligations, contracts of employment in GERMANY are also in principle subject to review of standard terms (CC § 310(4)); company law contracts on the other hand are excluded, although according to the case law of the BGH company law contracts remain subject to content review under CC § 242, 315. In the UNITED KINGDOM contracts in the areas of family law, succession law, employment law and company law were expressly excluded from the scope of application by UTCC 1994, Schedule I a)-d); this limitation was however abolished in 1999.

b. Real property contracts

The Directive is basically applicable to all types of contracts. However, there is the view in academic literature that real property contracts are not included, as according to recital 5,

---

[778] Online at: http://europa.eu.int/comm/consumers/cons_int/safe_shop/unf_cont_terms/uct02_fr.pdf. See as well Part 3 B.I.4 and Part 3 B.III.3. of this study.

[779] See the common position of the council of 22 September 1992.

Directive 93/13 refers only to "goods and services". This is also confirmed by the English language version of Art. 4(1) of Directive 93/13, as its term "goods" only encompasses movable objects. But a difficulty with this view is already presented by the French language version, which with the term "*biens*" does not contain any limitation to moveable objects.

Accordingly in the UNITED KINGDOM, the CA correctly clarified in *Khatun & Others v. Newham LBC*,[780] that both the Directive and the English implementing act apply to contracts relating to land. The court reasoned that to exclude contracts relating to land from the scope of "goods and services" would go against the grain of the aim and purpose of the Directive, which is to provide a high level of protection. There can thus be no justification for doing so. Although English common law distinguishes between real and personal property, other language texts of the Directive use terminology that can just as readily apply to immovable goods as to movables. Furthermore, the text and preparatory works of the Directive indicate that the drafters attached no significance to the distinction between land and other transactions and proceeded on the basis that the Directive would apply to both. Such materials powerfully suggest that if they were to be excluded from the scope of the Directive, then this would have been specifically provided for. Similar arguments have been made in IRELAND about the application of the regulations to contracts relating to land. However, there is no Irish authority on this point although the United Kingdom case *Khatun & Others v. Newham LBC* would represent persuasive authority.

BELGIAN law did not originally encompass contracts for real property, it was only clarified with the Act of 7 December 1998, that such contracts are included.

3. Exclusion of specific contractual terms

a. Contractual terms based on mandatory provisions

According to Art. 1(2) of Directive 93/13 contractual terms which reflect mandatory statutory or regulatory provisions and provisions or principles of international conventions, particularly in the transport area, are excluded from the scope of the Directive. Roughly half of the member states have implemented this exclusion, namely BELGIUM (in the Liberal Professions Act), CYPRUS, CZECH REPUBLIC, GERMANY, ESTONIA, HUNGARY, IRELAND, ITALY, LATVIA, PORTUGAL, SLOVAKIA, SPAIN (in the law 7/1998 on standard terms) and the UNITED KINGDOM. Under SLOVAKIAN law only legislative rules on the creation of legal instruments are excluded; however, according to Art. 7(5) of the Slovakian Constitution certain international conventions take priority over laws of the Slovak republic. In GERMANY, CC § 307(3) excludes mandatory provisions from content review (via the general clause assessing unfairness and the black and grey lists). Nevertheless, clauses repeating mandatory legislative provisions may be reviewed in terms of incorporation and transparency.

The remaining member states, i.e. AUSTRIA, BELGIUM (Trade Practices Act), DENMARK, FINLAND, FRANCE, GREECE, LITHUANIA, LUXEMBOURG, MALTA, NETHERLANDS, POLAND, SLOVENIA and SWEDEN have decided not to transpose Art. 1(2) of Directive 93/13 at all. To some extent the exclusion of mandatory provisions may nonetheless be established as an

---

780 CA judgment of 24 February 2004 – *Khatun & Others v. Newham LBC* [2004] EWCA Civ 55.

unwritten principle through case law and/or legal literature, for example in the Nordic countries (DENMARK, FINLAND, SWEDEN) and also in AUSTRIA, GREECE and LITHUANIA. In FRANCE clauses in contracts with companies in public control e.g. contracts for gas, oil, electricity, telecommunications as well as contracts for public transport or the provision of public services, are capable of review. In any event it is uncertain whether these are in the jurisdiction of the administrative courts (according to the Cass. civ.) or of the ordinary courts (the academic view).

b. Individually negotiated terms

Art. 3 of Directive 93/13 excludes contractual terms which have been individually negotiated by the consumer. 15 member states have adopted this exclusion: AUSTRIA, CYPRUS, ESTONIA, GREECE, GERMANY, HUNGARY, IRELAND, ITALY, LITHUANIA, NETHERLANDS, POLAND, PORTUGAL, SLOVAKIA, SPAIN and the UNITED KINGDOM.

The remaining 10 member states, by not having transposed this exclusion, allow their courts/authorities to monitor individually negotiated terms. This is the case in the NORDIC COUNTRIES (Denmark, Finland, Sweden) and also in BELGIUM (Trade Practices Act), CZECH REPUBLIC, FRANCE, LATVIA, LUXEMBOURG, MALTA and SLOVENIA. The BELGIAN Liberal Professions Act opts for the middle way. The unfair contract terms, mentioned in Annex n° 1 of the Directive are sanctioned with relative nullity even when individually negotiated (Art. 7(4) LPA). The principle of Art. 3 of Directive 93/13 (Art. 7(2) LPA) applies to other contractual terms.

According to Art. 3(2), sent. 3 of Directive 93/13, where any seller or supplier claims that a standard term has been individually negotiated, the burden of proof in this respect shall be incumbent on him. This provision has been transposed faithfully by nearly all member states.

In GERMANY "individually negotiated terms" are excluded from review, but this is counterbalanced through a very narrow definition of the aforementioned notion. The BGH held that for a term to be individually negotiated the customer has to fully understand the content of the contract and be aware of its legal consequences.[781]

Although 10 countries generally provide for a review of individually negotiated terms, of those only FRANCE and SLOVENIA have decided not to transpose Article Art. 3(2)(3). It can be concluded that in the remaining countries which allow the monitoring of individually negotiated terms (BELGIUM, CZECH REPUBLIC, DENMARK, FINLAND, LUXEMBOURG, LATVIA, MALTA, SWEDEN) the distinction between standard and negotiated terms remains relevant for assessing unfairness i.e. that different benchmarks apply. However BELGIAN practice doesn't show such a different approach.

781 BGH judgment of 19 May 2005, NJW 2005, 2543.

IV. Assessing the fairness of contract terms according to Art. 3

1. Concept of the Unfair Contract Terms Directive

The most important provision of the whole Directive in practical terms, the general clause in Art. 3(1) defines the standard of the unfairness test:

> *A contractual term which has not been individually negotiated shall be regarded as unfair if, contrary to the requirement of good faith, it causes a significant imbalance in the parties' rights and obligations arising under the contract, to the detriment of the consumer.*

The general clause according to its wording requires an "imbalance in the parties' rights and obligations". This does not relate to the main performance duties, as these are not subject to the fairness test according to Art. 4(2) of Directive 93/13. Therefore, it only relates to the remaining rights and duties arising out of the contract. An imbalance can, above all, be present if the respective contractual positions are structured differently by the terms with regard to one and the same question. The issue of whether an imbalance is present in a given case however, cannot be assessed in isolation from the surrounding legal context. Rather, the position of the consumer has to be compared to the position in which he would have been but for the term in question. Therefore, the term must be judged in its regulatory context, arising by virtue of the respective member state law. An imbalance only then exists "to the detriment of the consumer", if the dispositive statutory law is more advantageous to the consumer than the clause in question. Furthermore, according to the principle *minima non curat praetor,* this imbalance must be significant.

In addition to these criteria the Directive also requires that the imbalance is "contrary to the requirement of good faith". The relationship of the principle of good faith to the criterion of "imbalance" remains unclear. The wording of the Directive suggests that a clause is unfair only if it causes an imbalance *and* this imbalance is furthermore contrary to the principle of good faith. Following this reading, a clause can therefore cause an imbalance without simultaneously being contrary to good faith. Others however, assume that any clause which generates a significant imbalance is always (automatically) contrary to the principle of good faith.[782] It is ultimately worth considering whether the criteria "significant imbalance" and "good faith" are to be understood as alternatives in the sense that the two criteria operate independently of one another, so that a clause is unfair if it results in a significant imbalance, *or* if it is contrary to the requirement of good faith. In view of these multifarious interpretation possibilities it is not surprising that the member states have constructed their general clauses very differently.[783]

According to Art. 4(1) the unfairness of a contractual term shall be assessed (1) by taking the nature of the goods or services for which the contract was concluded into account, and (2) by referring, at the time of conclusion of the contract, to all the circumstances attending the conclusion of the contract and (3) in relation to all the other terms of the contract or of

---

782 Cf. *Tenreiro,* ERPL 1995, 273, 279.

783 See *infra,* under Part 2 C.IV.2.

another contract upon which it is dependent. Additionally, the annex to Directive 93/13 has a certain indicative effect in the assessment of the fairness of a clause.[784]

2. The form which the general clause has taken in the Member States

The member states are obliged by Art. 3 of Directive 93/13 in conjunction with recital 15 to fix the criteria for assessing the unfair character of contract terms in a general way. All member states prescribe such general clauses to monitor terms. However, although Art. 3 of the Directive applies to pre-formulated individual contracts for single use, the general clauses in AUSTRIA and in the NETHERLANDS only relate to standard terms. Even though in these member states other legal instruments are available to monitor such types of terms, this legislative technique gives rise to the danger that the requirements of the Directive will go unheeded.

A word for word transposition of Art. 3(1) of Directive 93/13 has admittedly only occurred in seven member states, namely CYPRUS, CZECH REPUBLIC, HUNGARY, IRELAND, ITALY, SPAIN and the UNITED KINGDOM. Most notably in Italy, the verbatim transposition of the Italian language version of the Directive led to the term "*malgrado la buona fede*" in the Italian Consumer Protection Act (*Codice del Consumo*). This formulation obviously is based on a translation error, as the expression "*malgrado il requisito della buona fede*" in the directive does not mean "contrary to good faith", but rather "despite good faith".

The other member states, in contrast, have not transposed the criteria in Directive 93/13 word for word, but either retained the general clauses of their respective national laws or adopted principles deviating from, or even going further than that prescribed in the Directive for the review of terms:

- In AUSTRIA the principle of good faith is not mentioned, instead CC Art. 879 applies a test of whether the relevant term grossly disadvantages the other contractual party, taking account of all circumstances of the case.
- BELGIAN law applies the principle of good faith indirectly. The key feature of the Belgian domestic legislation on unfair contract terms is the existence of two slightly different general clauses. According to TPA Art. 31(1), an unfair term is a clause or a condition which creates a "manifest"[785] imbalance between the parties' rights and obligations. By contrast, in respect of the liberal professions LPA Art. 7(2) defines an unfair term as a clause or a condition which has not been individually negotiated and which creates a "significant" imbalance between the parties' rights and obligations arising under the contract, "to the detriment of the consumer". At present BELGIAN practice does not show any distinction between the application of both criteria (manifest imbalance versus significant imbalance).
- The vast usage of classic general clauses is a key feature of DANISH law. The most important one is laid down in Art. 38c(1), 36 of the Consolidated Act 781/1996 on Contracts

---

784 On the legal nature of the Annex and its transposition in the Member States see *infra*, under Part 2 C.IV.3.

785 The term "manifest" may also refer to the legal concept of marginal control by the judge, which means that the powers of the judge are confined to the assessment of whether the contract is in conformity with the requirements of good faith.

Act. It refers to the criterion "significant imbalance" and the characteristic of "*stridende mod hæderlig forretningsskik*" (literal translation; "violating honest business practices"). However, the Danish legislature did not use the wording of the Directive ("*god tro*"), since according to Danish legal language the expression that a person is in "*god tro*" means that this person did not know and could not have been aware of a certain fact. Against this background the expression used in Art. 38c(1) seems to many authors to be a more adequate way of expressing the criterion of "good faith". In order to meet the requirements of the Directive, the legislator included a special provision (Art. 38c(2)) which explicitly states that circumstances arising after the contract has been concluded cannot be taken into consideration to the detriment of the consumer. Furthermore, in contrast to the Directive (Art. 4(2)) adequacy of price, and subject matter of the contract are not beyond its scope. Overall the Danish approach, although not referring to the principle of good faith, offers a higher level of protection than the Directive.

- In ESTONIA, pursuant to Art. 42(1) of the Law of Obligations Act, a standard term is deemed void if the term causes "unfair harm" to the other party, particularly if it causes a "significant imbalance in the parties' rights and obligations" arising from the contract to the detriment of the other party or if the standard term is "contrary to good morals". Additionally, according to para. (2) "unfair harm" is presumed if a standard term derogates from a fundamental principle of law or detrimentally affects the rights and obligations of the other party in a manner inconsistent with the nature of the contract in such a manner that it becomes questionable as to whether the purpose of the contract can be achieved. However, this does not necessarily indicate that results differ from those that would be achieved under the Directive.
- In FINLAND, Chapter 3 Section 1 of the Consumer Protection Act (CPA) states that a business offering consumer goods or services shall not make use of a contract term which, in view of the price of the good or service or other relevant circumstances, is to be deemed unfair from the consumer's point of view. The principle of good faith, although known in general contract law, is not applied when it comes to assessing unfairness. Besides, in contrast to the Directive the review of terms also encompasses the subject matter of the contract and the adequacy of price.
- In FRANCE clauses in consumer contracts are unfair according to Art. L 132-1(1) of the Consumer Code whose object or effect is to achieve a significant imbalance in the rights and obligations of the contractual parties to the detriment of the consumer („*un déséquilibre significatif entre les droits et obligations des parties au contrat*"). Whilst the concept of good faith in France exists as a general principle of interpretation (CC Art. 1134(3)), it does not however play a role in the review of contract terms. It was deliberately not adopted, as the view was held that a business which endeavours to achieve a significant imbalance cannot, by definition, be acting in good faith. Furthermore, the French legislator did not take over the definition "*bonne foi*" as the French language version of the Directive (like the Italian, *ante*) is regarded as misleading.
- GERMAN law by contrast in CC § 307 attaches significant emphasis to the principle of good faith. The "significant imbalance in the parties' rights and obligations arising under the contract" on the other hand is not named. According to the general clause of CC § 307(1) standard contract terms are invalid, if they "place the contractual partner of the user at an unreasonable disadvantage contrary to principles of good faith". CC § 307(2) lists examples of where this is presumed (incompatibility with the essential basic principles of the statutory rule from which it deviates, restriction of essential rights or

duties resulting from the nature of the contract in such a manner that there is a risk that the purpose of the contract will not be achieved).

- In GREECE, Art. 2(6), sent. 1 of the Consumer Protection Act provides that standard contract terms which lead to a disturbance in the balance of the contractual rights and duties to the detriment of the consumer may not be used and are invalid. The concept of good faith was not adopted. One also observes that the general clause not only serves the review of terms in individually negotiated transactions, but also – by mentioning the "use" of terms – as a basis for collective proceedings. A further characteristic is that owing to the non-transposition of Art. 4(2) of Directive 93/13 the main subject matter of the contract and the adequacy of price are also subject to review.
- In LATVIA, Art. 6(1), sent. 3 of the Consumer Rights Protection Law clarifies that a manufacturer, seller or service provider may not offer such contractual terms as are in contradiction with the "principle of legal equality of the contracting parties". Additionally, pursuant to para. (3) "a contractual term which has not been mutually discussed by the contracting parties shall be deemed to be unfair, if to the disadvantage of the consumer and contrary to the requirements of good faith, it creates a substantial disparity with respect to the rights and duties of the contracting parties provided for by the contract". Thus Latvia combines the principle of "good faith" and the broad new emerging principle of "legal equality". Moreover, the scope of review is broader than envisaged in the Directive, since Latvia has not transposed Art. 4(2) of Directive 93/13.
- In LITHUANIA, CC Art. 6.188(2) (Peculiarities of conditions in consumer contracts) only provides a brief definition of unfairness: "Conditions of a consumer contract which have not been individually negotiated shall be regarded as unfair if they cause a significant imbalance in the parties' rights and duties to the detriment of consumer rights and interests...". There is no reference to the principle of good faith, but the provision is supplemented by a comprehensive list of forbidden terms as a black list, which is a verbatim translation of the Annex of Directive 93/13. Moreover, Art. 11(2) of the Lithuanian Law on Consumer Protection provides that contractual terms (other than those in the black list) may also be regarded as unfair, provided that they are contrary to the requirements of "good will" and cause inequality of mutually enjoyable rights and obligations between the seller or service provider and consumer.
- In LUXEMBOURG, Art. 1 Consumer Protection Act provides a definition of unfairness very similar to the French concept (see above). The provision solely refers to an imbalance in the rights and obligations to the detriment of the consumer (*déséquilibre des droits et obligations au préjudice du consommateur*). In contrast to France and most other member states, price adequacy and subject matter of the contract are not excluded from review since Luxembourg has decided not to transpose Art. 4(2) of Directive 93/13.
- MALTA has developed quite a unique system for monitoring the unfairness of terms. Art. 44-45 of the Consumer Affairs Act contain a combination of different concepts: Firstly, the provisions refer to "a significant imbalance between the rights and obligations of the contracting parties to the detriment of the consumer" (Art. 45(1) lit. (a)), a verbatim transposition of the Directive. Secondly, the legislator adopted the principle of good faith ("or is incompatible with the requirements of good faith", Art. 45(1) lit. (d). Additionally, a term may be regarded unfair if "it causes the performance of the contract to be unduly detrimental to the consumer" (Art. 45(1) lit. (b)); or causes the performance of the contract to be significantly different from what the consumer could reasonably expect" (Art. 45(1) lit. (c)). All these definitions are applied as alternatives, i.e. it is sufficient for a term to fulfil one of the criteria to be considered as unfair.

- Pursuant to Art. 6-233 lit. (a) of the DUTCH Civil Code, a standard contract term is considered voidable, if it is "unreasonably disadvantageous" (*onredelijk bezwarend*) to the other party. In addition to the possibility for the other party to annul a specific unfair clause, they can also argue that the stipulation – although valid – is not applicable in the sense that, in the given circumstances, this would be unacceptable according to the criteria of reasonableness and justice. There is no reference to good faith, significant imbalance or other related concepts.
- In POLAND, CC Art. 385/1(1), sent. 1 states that contractual clauses do not bind the consumer if they shape his/her rights and obligations in a manner contrary to good faith, strikingly (distinctly, disproportionately) (*rażąco*) infringing his/her interests (referred to as "prohibited contractual clauses"). It has to be noted that the principle of "good faith" has been introduced into the Civil Code with the aim of gradually replacing another general clause – the principle of social cooperation which has been used throughout the Socialist period and is still in existence at present.
- In PORTUGAL, the general clause Art. 9(2) of Consumer Protection Act 24/96 refers to the elements of significant imbalance (*desequilíbrio nas prestações gravemente*) and good faith (*atentatório da boa fé*). Another formulation taken from the Directive, to the detriment of the consumer (*significativo desequilíbrio em detrimento do consumidor*), can be found in Art. 9(2) lit. (b).
- In SLOVAKIA, CC Art. 53(1) states that a consumer contract may not include contract terms, which cause a significant imbalance in the parties' rights and obligations arising under the contract, to the detriment of the consumer (unacceptable condition in the contract). CC Art. 54 provides, that the terms of the consumer contract may not deviate from the provisions of Civil Code to the disadvantage of the consumer. The consumer may not waive the rights conferred on him by law (as these provisions are mandatory). According to the general provision CC Art. 39 an agreement shall be invalid if its content or purpose contradicts or circumvents the law, or contravenes proper morals.
- In SLOVENIA, according to the general clause Art. 24(1) of the Consumer Protection Act, the terms of the contract are considered unfair (1) if they bring about a significant imbalance in the contractual rights and obligations of the parties to the detriment of the consumer or (2) if they cause the fulfilment of the contract to be detrimental to the consumer without good reason or (3) if they cause the fulfilment of the contract to differ substantially from what the consumer rightly expected or (4) if they go against the principles of fairness and good faith. The Slovenian approach combines the benchmarks prescribed by the Directive ("significant imbalance", "to the detriment of the consumer", "good faith") with the principle of fairness. Finally Slovenia has not transposed Art. 4(2) of the directive.
- SWEDISH law contains no precise definition of unfairness. There is Art. 11 of the Act on contract terms in consumer relations (CTA) (1994:1512) which makes reference to Art. 36 of the Contracts Act (CA) which has been in force and unchanged since 1976. CA Art. 36(1), sent. 1 states very broadly: "A contract term may be adjusted or held unenforceable if the term is unreasonable with respect to the contract's content, circumstances at the formation of the contract, subsequent events or other circumstances". Good Faith, imbalance or other concepts do not form part of the law as far as unfair terms are concerned. Circumstances that occurred after conclusion of the contract can only be considered if this would not be to the disadvantage of the consumer (CTA Art. 11(2)). The overall level of consumer protection is considered to be higher than that prescribed by the Directive, since the Courts are entitled to adjust payment.

The above overview illustrates that the general clause has taken a number of very different forms in the member states. The requirement of "good faith" is only explicitly mentioned in thirteen member states in total, namely in CYPRUS, CZECH REPUBLIC, GERMANY, HUNGARY, IRELAND, ITALY, LATVIA, MALTA, POLAND, PORTUGAL, SLOVENIA, SPAIN and UNITED KINGDOM.

The following countries make direct reference to "significant imbalance" in their general clauses: BELGIUM, CYPRUS, DENMARK, ESTONIA, GREECE, FRANCE, HUNGARY, IRELAND, ITALY, LITHUANIA, LUXEMBOURG, MALTA, POLAND, PORTUGAL, SLOVAKIA, SLOVENIA, GREECE, SPAIN and the UNITED KINGDOM. However seven of these countries do not mention (explicitly) the additional criterion "good faith": BELGIUM, DENMARK, FRANCE, GREECE, LITHUANIA, LUXEMBOURG and SLOVAKIA. This legislative technique tends to result in a lowering of the burden of proof for consumers.

A final point to note is that there is no uniform understanding of the concept of good faith, even in those countries which adopt the exact wording of the directive. In the UNITED KINGDOM, it is understood as a concept of procedural fairness,[786] whereas other countries also look at the substantive fairness of the transaction.

Another issue treated differently in the member states is whether the fairness test encompasses the subject matter of the contract and the adequacy of price. In AUSTRIA, DENMARK, GREECE, LATVIA, LUXEMBOURG, SLOVENIA, SPAIN and SWEDEN Art. 4(2), (1st alternative) has not been transposed, so that in principle, the monitoring of the main subject matter of the contract and the adequacy of price is possible. However, in some member states (for example, Greece and Spain), this silence has produced uncertainty in interpreting national law with the result that academia and case law use different approaches to solve the problem with contradictory solutions.[787]

3. Transposition of the Annex in the Member States

a. Legal nature of the Annex

According to Art. 3(3) of Directive 93/13, the "Annex shall contain an indicative and non-exhaustive list of the terms which *may* be regarded as unfair." Therefore, a contractual term corresponding to the Annex is not automatically unfair. In contrast to the preliminary drafts of Directive 93/13,[788] the Annex does not contain a so-called "black list" of terms which are always (per se) ineffective. Rather, the Annex – as the ECJ emphasised in C-478/99[789] – "is of indicative and illustrative value". As stated in the opinion of advocate general *Geelhoed*[790] – "The list thus offers the courts and other competent bodies, affected groups and individual

786 House of Lords, judgment of 25 October 2001 – *Director General Fair Trading v. First National Bank plc* [2002] All ER 97; Micklitz, ZEuP, 865.

787 For a comparative law perspective in this regard see *Cámara Lapuente*, El control.

788 See COM 90, 322 final and COM 92, 66 final.

789 ECJ judgment of 7 May 2002, C-478/99 – *Commission of the European Communities v. Kingdom of Sweden* [2002] ECR I-04147 at para. (22).

790 At para. (29).

consumers, sellers and suppliers – including those from another member state – a criterion for interpreting the expression unfair terms. Thus by giving concrete form to the open provision contained in Art. 3(1), that is to say, the first criterion for determining whether a contractual term is unfair, their certainty is reinforced."

In this respect the Annex to Directive 93/13 is usually referred to as a "grey list".

b. Transposition of the Annex in the Member States

The following table indicates whether the provisions of No 1 lit. (a)-(q) of the Annex have been transposed (1) by a *black letter rule* according to which clauses are always considered per se unfair, (2) by a *grey letter rule* according to which clauses may be considered unfair, or, (3) whether the respective provisions of the Annex have not been transposed at all.[791]
The table cannot claim to mirror member states' law exclusively as it reflects mainly written law, and not case law, which can have wide ramifications and is difficult to outline. In certain circumstances it can therefore be the case that rules indicated in the table as "grey letter rules" have to all intents and purposes become "black letter rules" through the member state case law. However, reference to case law of the database is provided in footnotes wherever possible.

In AUSTRIA, BELGIUM, CZECH REPUBLIC, ESTONIA, GREECE, LATVIA, LITHUANIA, LUXEMBOURG, MALTA, SLOVENIA[792] and SPAIN the clauses in the Annex – insofar as they have been transposed – are always regarded as unfair (black list). In MALTA, the Minister responsible for consumer affairs after consultation with the Consumer Affairs Council is empowered to amend, substitute or revoke any of the terms in the black list. GERMANY, HUNGARY, ITALY, NETHERLANDS and PORTUGAL in contrast, have opted for a combination of both black and grey lists. The blacklist in some member states, for instance, those of BELGIUM,[793] ESTONIA, MALTA, PORTUGAL and SPAIN, contains more clauses than the Annex of Directive 93/13.

In CYPRUS, FRANCE, IRELAND, POLAND, SLOVAKIA and the UNITED KINGDOM on the other hand there are only non-binding grey lists. In special cases, however, other legislation (such as in the UNITED KINGDOM through the UCTA 1977) can result in certain clauses being rendered unfair per se. In FRANCE, the Annex is by contrast only a "light" grey, as the list is not binding on the judge. The clauses contained in the Annex have an indicative function, as according to Art. L 132-1(3), sent. 2 of the Consumer Code, a consumer involved in a dispute is not relieved of the burden of proving a term is unfair. Moreover, the judge must decide whether the criteria of unfairness are fulfilled on a case by case basis.

---

791 This is to be distinguished from the question of whether the consumer must assert that a clause is non-binding, see on this point Part 2 C.IV.4.b.

792 The wording of the Slovenian Consumer Protection Act ("contract terms are regarded as unfair") indicates a black list, however, until now there is no case-law or literature confirming this interpretation.

793 See Art. 32 Trade Practices Act. The Liberal Professions Act on the other hand only blacklists the unfair contract terms mentioned in the Annex n° 1 of the Directive.

In DENMARK, FINLAND and SWEDEN, no part of the Annex is explicitly transposed, but the Annex to Directive 93/13 was reproduced in the preparatory work for the Act implementing the Directive and, according to well established legal tradition common to the Nordic countries, preparatory work constitutes an important aid to interpreting legislation. This legislative technique was accepted by the ECJ in C-478/99.[794] However, for member states in which certain parts of the Annex are transposed and others are not, it remains unclear whether this decision applies to them as well, since in those countries there is a danger that the consumer may be mislead about his rights.

1st Table: Transposition of the Annex No 1 lit. a-q of the Unfair Contract Terms Directive

Article of Unfair Contract Terms Directive	Black letter rule	Grey letter rule	Annex not transposed
ANNEX No 1a Death or personal injury	AT,[795] BE, CZ, DE,[796] EE, EL, ES,[797] HU, IT,[798] LV, LT, LU, PT,[799] SL, UK[800]	CY, FR, IE, NL, PL,[801] SK	DK, FI, SE, MT[802]

794 ECJ judgment of 7 May 2002, C-478/99 – *Commission of the European Communities v. Kingdom of Sweden* [2002] ECR I-04147.

795 See cases OGH 22 February 2001 6 Ob 160/00y; OGH 19 November 2002 4 Ob 179/02f; OGH 7 October 2003 4 Ob 130/03a; OGH 25 April 1995 4 Ob 522/95.

796 In contrast to the Directive the German provisions (CC §§ 309 No 7a, 276(3)) require fault/negligence of the user.

797 Instead of "death of a consumer or personal injury", the Spanish rule mentions "damages, death or injuries" („por los daños o por la muerte o lesiones"), without any mention of "personal" or "physical" injury, therefore including non-pecuniary damages or non-material injuries („daño moral") and patrimonial damages.

798 The IT black letter rule applies as well to individually negotiated terms.

799 See case STJ 6 May 1993 P. 83348.

800 Despite the adoption of the Unfair Terms in Consumer Contracts Regulations 1999 (UTCCR), the Unfair Contract Terms Act (UCTA) 1977 which is also applicable to B2B contracts and deals mainly with exclusion and limitation clauses, remains in force. Section 2(1) of the UCTA 1977 renders ineffective a contract term which restricts liability for death or personal injury caused by negligence. Moreover, UCTA 1977 sections 10 and 23 make it impossible to use a secondary contract to exclude/restrict liability which could not be excluded/restricted under the main contract. Therefore although the official transposition Act UTCCR 1999 contains solely a grey list identical to that of the Directive, on the basis of the UCTA any restriction of liability for death or personal injury is black-listed (i.e. automatically considered void).

801 CC Article 385.3 1st indent contains no express mention of death.

802 No direct reference – The list under Article 44 of terms that may be unfair is not exhaustive and includes terms which are not listed in the Annex to the EU Directive.

Article of Unfair Contract Terms Directive	Black letter rule	Grey letter rule	Annex not transposed
ANNEX No 1b Total or partial non-performance or inadequate performance	AT,[803] BE,[804] CZ, DE,[805] EE, EL,[806] ES, IT,[807] LV, LT, LU, MT,[808] NL,[809] SL, UK[810]	CY, FR,[811] HU,[812] IE,[813] NL, PL, SK	DK, FI, PT, SE
ANNEX No 1c Condition whose realisation depends on the seller's own will alone	AT,[814] BE, CZ EE, ES, LT, LU, MT, SL[815]	CY,[816] DE, FR, HU, IE, IT, NL, PL, SK, UK	DK, EL, FI, LV, PT, SE
ANNEX No 1d Permitting the seller or supplier to retain sums paid by the consumer where the latter decides not to conclude or perform the contract, without providing for the consumer to receive compensation of an equivalent amount from the seller or supplier where the latter is the party cancelling the contract;	AT, BE, CZ, DE,[817] EE, ES, LV, LT, LU, MT,	CY, FR, DE, HU, IE, IT, NL, PL, SK, UK	DK, EL, FI, PT, SL, SE

803 OGH 6 September 2001 2 Ob 198/01h; OGH 22 February 2001 6 Ob 160/00y; OGH 19 November 2002 4 Ob 179/02f; OGH 7 October 2003 4 Ob 130/03a; OGH 25 April 1995 4 Ob 522/95.

804 The TPA and LPA prohibit in a more detailed manner unfair terms which relate to specific consumer rights as a consequence of total or partial non- or inadequate performance.

805 Partly transposed in CC Art. 309 No 7, 309 No 8, 307(2), 475; see case OLG Saarbrücken 29 August 2001 1 U 321/01.

806 This clause is transposed through numerous rules in the Consumer Protection Act (Art. 2 of Statute No. 2251-1994).

807 The IT black letter rule also applies to individually negotiated terms.

808 Cf. Qorti Civili Prim' Awla (MT) 13 November 1995 Silvana wife of Raymond Camillerivs. Alfred Pisani noe et; Qorti tal-Kummerc 22 November 1985 Carmelo Grima noe vs Carmel Vella Brincat noe.

809 Transposed in a black letter rule (CC Art. 6: 236 c-d) and in a grey letter rule (CC Art. 6: 237 lit. (f)).

810 UCTA 1977 Section 3(2) lit. (b) prohibits the use of a contractual term allowing the seller/supplier to perform in a considerably different manner from that which was reasonably expected of him or not to perform at all, respectively. The classification as black letter rule is again based on the UCTA 1977 as already explained above.

811 Long before the transposition of the Directive the State Council (*Conseil d'État*) had enacted 2 decrees prohibiting particular types of contract terms; some parts of those decrees are still effective. According to Art. 2 of Decree 78-464 of 24 March 1978 in a sales contract any term which restricts the purchaser's rights in case of non-performance is considered void.

812 Terms which exclude or limit the legal rights of the consumer are usually regarded as unfair (Art. 2 lit. (h) of the Government Decree 18/1999, II.5.). The right of the consumer to set-off can never be excluded (Art. 1 (1) lit. (f) Government Decree 18/1999, II.5.

813 Cf. HC 20 December 2001 Sp. 229 Applicant – The Director of Consumer Affairs.

814 See case OGH 26 January 1994 9 ObA 361/93.

815 A vague (inaccurate) transposition: Contract term is unfair if the seller may unilaterally alter the fundamental provisions of the contract.

816 Instead of referring to "making an agreement binding on the consumer", the domestic provision refers to "excluding the right of a consumer to cancel a contract".

Article of Unfair Contract Terms Directive	Black letter rule	Grey letter rule	Annex not transposed
ANNEX No 1e Disproportionately high sum in compensation	AT, BE,[818] CZ, DE, EE, EL, ES, LV, LT, MT, SL	CY, FR, HU, IE, IT,[819] NL, PL, PT,[820] SK, UK	DK, FI, LU, SE
ANNEX No 1f Right to dissolve the contract on a discretionary basis and retain the sums paid for services not yet supplied in case of dissolving the contract by the seller	AT,[821] BE,[822] CZ, DE,[823] EE, EL, ES, HU, LV, LT, LU, SL[824]	CY, FR, DE, IE, IT, NL, PL,[825] PT, SK, UK	DK, FI, MT, SE
ANNEX No 1g Termination of a contract of indeterminate duration without reasonable notice	AT, BE (LPA), CZ, EE, EL, ES, HU, LV, LT, SL	CY, FR, IE, IT, NL, PL, PT,[826] SK, UK	BE (TPA), DE, DK, FI, LU, MT, SE
ANNEX No 1h Automatically extending a contract of fixed duration	AT,[827] BE,[828] CZ, DE,[829] EE, EL,[830] ES, LV, LT, LU, NL, SL	CY, FR, HU, IE, IT, PL, PT, SK, UK	DK, FI, MT, SE

817 Transposed in a black letter rule (CC Art. 309 No 5) and in a grey letter rule (CC Art. 308 No 7).

818 CC Art. 1231 gives the court the possibility to reduce the amount of compensation. The provisions of the TPA on unfair contract terms form a 'lex specialis' of the general provisions in the Civil Code; see cases: Hof van Beroep Gent 3 March 2004 Algemeen ziekenhuis Sint-Lucas v.z.w. / I. Bruynooghe; Hof van Beroep Gent 8 October 2003 Immostad b.v.b.a. / Van Ammel G.; Hof van Beroep Gent 4 March 2003 Algemeen Ziekenhuis St-Lucas VZW / R. Jonckheere.

819 See Tribunale Ivrea judgment of 11 July 2005.

820 Cf. STJ 6 October 1998 855/98.

821 See OGH 20 November 2002 5 Ob 266/02g.

822 In this regard it should be noted that the blacklist of the TPA considers a clause unfair if the seller were permitted to retain sums paid by the consumer where the latter decides not to *conclude* the contract, without providing for the consumer to receive compensation of an equivalent amount from the seller where the latter decides not to conclude the contract. Hence, the requirement of reciprocity referred to in the annex was not transposed in the TPA as such.

823 Transposed in a black letter rule (CC Art. 309 No 5) and grey letter rules (CC Art. 308 No 3).

824 A vague transposition: Contract term is unfair if the seller may unilaterally dissolve the contract at any time.

825 Not following the text of the Annex precisely – the Code (indent 14) refers somewhat to clauses where only the consumer is deprived of the right to dissolve or withdraw from the contract. Indent 13 refers to dissolving the contract by either of the parties.

826 See case STJ 23 November 1999 99A796.

827 Cf. OGH 25 August 1998 1 Ob 176/98h.

828 See case Hof van Beroep Gent 3 March 2004 Algemeen ziekenhuis Sint-Lucas v.z.w./I. Bruynooghe.

829 The term „unreasonably early "in the Directive has been defined by the German legislator as "more than three months prior to the expiration of the initial or tacitly extended period of the contract".

830 Greece classifies as unfair all clauses, the consequences of which consist of the extension or renewal of the contract for a disproportionately long period of time, if the consumer has not cancelled the contract before a specified point in time. (Art. 2(7) lit. (d) of Statute 2251-1994).

Article of Unfair Contract Terms Directive	Black letter rule	Grey letter rule	Annex not transposed
ANNEX No 1i Irrevocably binding the consumer to terms with which he had no real opportunity of becoming acquainted	AT, BE, CZ, DE, EE, EL,[831] ES, HU,[832] IT,[833] LV, LT, LU, MT, SL	CY, FR, IE, NL, PL,[834] PT, SK, UK	DK, FI, SE
ANNEX No 1j Unilateral alteration of the terms of the contract	AT, BE, CZ, EE, EL,[835] ES, LV, LT, LU,[836] MT, SL	CY, FR,[837] HU, IE, IT, NL, PL, PT, SK, UK	DE,[838] DK, FI, SE
ANNEX No 1k Unilateral alteration of characteristics of the product or service to be provided	AT,[839] BE,[840] CZ, EE, EL,[841] LV, LT, LU, MT, PT, SL	CY, FR, DE, HU, IE, IT, NL, PL,[842] SK, UK	DK, ES,[843] FI, SE
ANNEX No 1l Determination or increase of price	AT,[844] BE,[845] CZ, DE, EE, ES, EL,[846] LV, LT, LU, MT, NL, SL	CY, FR, IE, HU, IT, PL, PT, SK, UK	DK, FI, SE

831 The requirement to ensure that the consumer has a genuine possibility to become acquainted with the content of the clauses *before the* conclusion of the contract has been recognised in Greek law as a condition, precedent for the incorporation of such terms into the contract.

832 See CC Art. 205/B: "Standard contract terms will become part of a contract, only if they have previously been made available to the other party for perusal and if the other party has accepted the terms explicitly or through conduct that implies acceptance."

833 The black letter rule also applies to individually negotiated terms.

834 The Code refers to terms being merely included in the contract, and not to those, which 'irrevocably bind the consumer'.

835 See cases A.P. 16 February 2001 A.P. 296/2001; A.P. 1219/2001; A.P. 4 May 2001 A.P. 1030/2001.

836 See case CA Luxembourg 27 February 1996.

837 Pursuant to Art. 3 of the Decree 78-464 of 24 March 1978 enacted by the State Council (*Conseil d'État*), a contractual term in a contract for sale, tenancy, services or manufacturing enabling the seller/supplier to unilaterally modify the terms or conditions of the contract is considered void.

838 Covered by general clause in CC Art. 307(2), sent. 1.

839 Cf. OGH 17 April 2002 7 Ob 287/01h.

840 The Trade Practices Act blacklists solely those clauses which allow the unilateral alteration of characteristics which in the eyes of the consumer are *essential* (or under specific circumstances are essential for the product's or service's intended use). The Liberal Professions Act does not contain such limitation.

841 Not directly transposed. CC Art. 361 prescribes the principle of party autonomy, according to which every contractual amendment requires a new agreement of both parties. See also case A.P. 4 May 2001 A.P. 1030/2001.

842 Instead of 'characteristics' the Code refers to the 'crucial characteristics'.

843 But probably encompassed in the broad wording of Additional Disposition number 1 of LGDCU 1984, part I, rule 2 (where rules g), j) and m) of Annex I of the Directive are transposed.

844 See cases OGH 17 November 2004 7 Ob 207/04y; OGH 24 June 2003 4 Ob 73/03v; OGH 17 December 2002 4 Ob 265/02b; OGH 20 November 2002 5 Ob 266/02g; OGH 22 March 2001 4 Ob 28/01y.

845 The TPA considers contracts with an open price unfair, when the determination of the price is dependant solely on the seller's will, whereas the Directive (Annex l) also considers open price contracts unfair when the determination of the price is dependant on other events.

846 Greece classifies as unfair all clauses, which without important reason leave the consideration undetermined and do not allow for their determination according to criteria specially provided for in the

Article of Unfair Contract Terms Directive	Black letter rule	Grey letter rule	Annex not transposed
ANNEX No 1m Right to determine whether the goods or services supplied are in conformity with the contract, or right to interpret any term of the contract;	AT, BE, CZ, EE, EL,[847] ES, HU, LT, LU, MT,[848] NL, PT, SL	CY, FR, IE, IT, PL,[849] SK, UK	DE,[850] DK, FI, LV, SE
ANNEX No 1n Limiting of commitments undertaken by agents	AT,[851] BE, CZ, DE,[852] EE, ES, EL, HU, LV, LT, LU, MT, SL	CY, FR, IE, IT, NL, PL, PT, SK, UK	DK, FI, SE
ANNEX No 1o Obliging the consumer to fulfil all his obligations where the seller or supplier does not perform his	AT,[853] BE, CZ, EE, EL, ES, HU, LT, LU, MT, NL, PT, SL	CY, DE, FR, IE, IT, PL, SK, UK	DK, FI, LV, SE
ANNEX No 1p Possibility of transferring his rights and obligations under the contract	AT,[854] BE, CZ, DE, EE, EL, ES,[855] HU, LV, LT, LU, MT, NL, PT,[856] SL[857]	CY, FR, IE, IT,[858] PL,[859] SK, UK	DK, FI, SE
ANNEX No 1q Excluding or hindering the consumer's right to take legal action; restricting the evidence available or imposing a burden of proof.	AT,[860] BE,[861] CZ, DE, EE, EL,[862] ES, HU, LV, LT, LU, MT, NL, PT, SL	CY, FR, IE, IT,[863] PL,[864] SK, UK	DK, FI, SE

contract which are also reasonable for the consumer. Also considered unfair are those clauses, which hinder the consumer from rescinding the contract, whereby the increase in price according to the terms of the contract is disproportionate for the consumer (Art. 2(7) cases k and r of Statute 2251-1994).

847 Only the first indent has been transposed.

848 See case CA Kummercjali 22 January 1992 Mario Bezzinavs Albert Mizzi et noe.

849 See cases Sąd Antymonopolowy (PL) 30 September 2002 T XVII Amc 47/01 Head of the Office for the Protection of Competition and Consumers, Defendant – Powszechna Kasa.

850 Annex No 1m has not been transposed, but CC § 307(2), No 1 can be applied.

851 See case OGH 28. Apr 1999 3 Ob 246/98t.

852 Covered by general clause and various specific rules in commercial and insurance law (Art. 307(2) No 1 in conjunction with CC Art. 164(1), CommC Art. 56, Art. 43-47 of the Insurance Contract Act.

853 See case OGH 23 February 1999 1 Ob 58/98f.

854 See cases OGH 28 April 1999 3 Ob 246/98t;OGH 4 November 1997 10 Ob 367/97m.

855 The Spanish rule declares unfair, with different initial wording, "the freedom from liability following transfer of rights and obligations under the contract." Therefore, a mere transfer ("cesión") is not deemed unfair in itself. It is only caught by the rule when it encloses the limitation of liability for that transfer.

856 See case STJ 6 May 1993 P. 83348.

857 Possibility of transferring the rights and obligations to a third person, whose name is not specifically mentioned in the contract. The absence of the consumer's consent is not a requirement under the Slovenian Consumer Protection Act.

858 See Tribunale Rome judgment of 18 June 1998 Movimento Federativo Democratico v. A.B.I. e altri.

859 No mention of the reduction of guarantees for the consumer.

860 See case OGH 27 May 2003 1 Ob 244/02t.

861 Partly transposed since the Trade Practices Act does not prohibit arbitration clauses and only prohibits restriction of evidence but not the heightening of the burden of proof.

862 See case A.P. 1219/2001.

2nd Table: Transposition of Annex No 2 of the Unfair Contract Terms Directive

Annex No. 2 of Directive 93/13 establishes certain exceptions with regard to clauses used by suppliers of financial services. The following table indicates whether the member states explicitly made use of these exceptions or whether they provide a higher level of consumer protection by having not transposed Annex No. 2.

Article of Unfair Contract Terms Directive	Annex transposed	Annex not transposed
ANNEX No 2a Exception from No 1g for suppliers of financial services	BE (LPA), CY, CZ, EE, ES, FR, IE, IT, SK, UK	AT, BE (TPA),[865] DE, DK, EL,[866] FI, HU, LV, LT, LU, MT, NL, PL, PT, SL, SE
ANNEX No 2b sent. 1 Exception from No 1j for suppliers of financial services	BE, CY, CZ, EE, ES, FR, IE, IT, PT, SK, UK	AT, DE, DK, EL,[867] FI, HU, LV, LT, LU, MT, NL, PL, SL, SE
ANNEX No 2b, sent. 2 Exception from No1j where the consumer is free to dissolve the contract	BE,[868] CY, CZ, EE, ES, FR, IE, IT, PT, SK,[869] SL, UK	AT, DE, DK, FI, EL,[870] HU, LV, LT, LU, MT, NL, PL, SE
ANNEX No 2c Exception from No 1g, No 1j and No 1l in case of products or services where the price is linked to fluctuations in a stock exchange and in case of contracts for the purchase or sale of foreign currency	BE,[871] CY,[872] CZ, ES, FR, IE, IT, LT, PT, SK, UK	AT, DE, DK, EE, EL, FI, HU, LV, LU, MT, NL, PL, SL, SE

863 Cf. Cass. 29 September 2004 n. 19591/2004 Credito Emiliano S.p.A. v. Pugliese Vincenzo; Cass. 20 August 2004 no. 16336/2004 Soc. Tegola Canadese v. Concato Lida; Cass. 21 June 2004 11487 Vitali v. Assitalia S.p.a.; Cass. 28 November 2003 no. 18290/2003 Gianmarco Achille v. Autoberardi s.r.l.; Cass. 1 October 2003 14669 Abrescia v. Consultur S.r.l.; Cass. 9 December 2002 17475 C. Larato v. Axa Assicurazioni S.p.a. and Isvap.

864 The reduction of evidence or burden of proof have not been mentioned.

865 The Trade Practices Act does not contain specific rules on this subject: the general rules of the Code Civil regarding termination of the contract when the other party does not fulfill his obligations apply. In the courts' interpretation of those rules, clauses on the right of termination of the contract without prior notice may be allowed, dependent on the circumstances. TPA Art. 32, No 22 prohibits the termination of a contract because of the introduction of the Euro.

866 Greek courts have rejected an application of the exception rule to achieve a high level of consumer protection (cf. Polimeles Protodikeio Athinon 1208/98).

867 Greek courts have rejected an application of the exception rule of Annex No. 2b to achieve a high level of consumer protection (cf. Efeteio Athinon 6291/2000). See also A.P. 1219/2001.

868 The exception in the TPA is confined to financial services contracts the price, which is unilaterally changed by the provider.

869 Reasons for alternation of terms have to be listed in the contract.

870 Greek courts have rejected an application of the exception rule of Annex No. 2b to achieve a high level of consumer protection (cf. Efeteio Athinon 6291/2000).

871 Completely transposed in the Liberal Professions Act. Partly transposed in the Trade Practices Act since this act does not exclude contracts for the purchase or sale of foreign currency.

872 The phrases "financial instruments" as well as "or index or a financial market rate" are omitted in the particular domestic provision.

Article of Unfair Contract Terms Directive	Annex transposed	Annex not transposed
ANNEX No 2d Exception from No 11 in case of price-indexation clauses	AT, BE, CY, CZ, ES, FR, IE, IT, PT, SK, UK	DK, EE, FI, DE, EL, HU, LV, LT, LU, MT, NL, PL, SL, SE

4. Legal consequences of unfairness

a. Concept of the Unfair Contract Terms Directive

Art. 6(1) of the Directive 93/13:
Member States shall lay down that unfair terms used in a contract concluded with a consumer by a seller or supplier shall, as provided for under their national law, not be binding on the consumer and that the contract shall continue to bind the parties upon those terms if it is capable of continuing in existence without the unfair terms.

Art. 6(1) envisages that unfair clauses are not binding, whereas the remainder of the contract is usually preserved.

aa. Non-binding nature of unfair terms

The open wording of the Directive does not clarify how the member states shall establish the form of the non-binding nature. There are several possibilities, e.g.:

- The national legislators can declare the ineffectuality or absolute nullity of an unfair term *ex officio* or provide that the contractual term is regarded as not being written in civil law (fiction of non-existence) and does not give rise to any legal consequences.
- In some member states, however, there also exists the more flexible concept of relative nullity, according to which the unfair term initially remains in force, so long as this suits the contractual partner of the user (i.e. generally the consumer), who alone can unilaterally assert its nullity.
- Other member states follow different concepts of nullity providing that the nullity of a clause can only occur to the advantage of the consumer, whereby the court has jurisdiction to declare the term void on its own motion (so called "protective nullity" – "*nullità di protezione*").

The ECJ first addressed the legal consequences of unfairness in *Océano.*[873] The case concerned the procedural issue of the reviewability of a jurisdiction clause, disadvantageous to the consumer. In this decision the ECJ held, that

> "the protection provided for consumers by the Directive entails the national court being able to determine of its own motion whether a term of a contract (...) is unfair when making its preliminary assessment as to whether a claim should be allowed to proceed before the national courts".

[873] ECJ judgment of 27 June 2000, Joined Cases C-240/98 to C-244/98 - *Océano Grupo Editorial SA v. Murciano Quintero* [2000] ECR I-04941, para. (29).

In *Cofidis*[874] the ECJ extended the competence to review further and stated that the protection of the consumer precludes *any* national provision which prohibits the national court, on expiry of a limitation period, from finding that a term of the contract is unfair. In contrast to the *Océano* case, the dicta of the ECJ is related not only to the issue of whether the member state court can review its jurisdiction "on its own motion", but on the nullity of clauses generally. It is therefore to be assumed, that according to the view of the ECJ, national courts must have the power to review the fairness of a clause on their own initiative generally (and not only for the special case of jurisdiction clauses).

In *Mostaza Claro*[875] the court clarified that Art. 6(1) is a mandatory provision:

> "The nature and importance of the public interest underlying the protection which the Directive confers on consumer justify, moreover, the national court being required to assess of its own motion whether a contractual term is unfair, compensating in this way for the imbalance which exists between the consumer and the seller or supplier."

The concept of absolute nullity is in line with the requirements of the ECJ, whereas the concept of relative nullity as described above does not comply with *Océano, Cofidis* and *Mostaza Claro*. Other legal consequences – such as the concept of protective nullity – seem to be in accordance with ECJ case-law, provided that a consumer is protected even if he fails to raise the unfair nature of the term, either because he is unaware of his rights or because he is deterred from enforcing them.

Additionally, *Océano, Cofidis* and *Mostaza Claro* raise the question whether national courts are obliged to take evidence on their own initiative. The German and the French versions of the judgments use the expressions "*Befugnis von Amts wegen zu prüfen, ob die Klausel missbräuchlich ist*" and "*pouvoir du juge d'examiner d'office le caractère abusif d'une telle clause*". Both language versions suggest that, not only does the court decide about the issue on its own initiative but also takes evidence on its own initiative, based on the alleged facts. In contrast, the English language version ("to determine of its own motion") sounds rather neutral and does not seem to affect the evidence itself. Therefore, it remains unclear whether Art. 6 of Directive 93/13 in conjunction with the concept of effectiveness (*effet utile*) changes the national rules on burden of proof.[876]

bb. Consequences for the contractual term and the contract as a whole

The possibility of a so-called partial retention, i.e. a preservation of the unfair clause with content which is still permissible, is not mentioned in the Directive. One argument against a partial retention is that the clause would thereby, contrary to the prescription in recital 21 and in Art. 6(1) of Directive 93/13, not be rendered "non-binding" but merely "partly bind-

---

874 ECJ judgment of 21 November 2002, C-473/00 – *Cofidis v. Fredout*, [2002] ECR I-10875.

875 ECJ judgment of 26 October 2006, C-168/05 – *Elisa María Mostaza Claro v. Centro Móvil Milenium SL* [2006] ECR I-10421, para. (38).

876 Directive 93/13 explicitly allocates the burden of proof only regarding the question whether the term in issue has been individually negotiated, see Art. 3(2), sent. 3. But it is silent with respect to other issues. Cf. *Bruder*, ERPL 2007, 205.

ing". Additionally, such a possibility would reduce the risk of use of unfair terms from the point of view of the business and thereby run contrary to consumer protection. It nonetheless remains unclear whether a partial retention is admissible.

The whole contract remains binding on both parties, so long as this is possible without the offending clause according to the purpose and legal nature of the contract. The nullity is thus as a rule limited to the unreasonable term. In *Ynos*[877] the ECJ was asked whether the hypothetical consideration of whether the business/user would have concluded the contract without the corresponding term, is to be taken into account in Hungarian law, but as the facts occurred prior to Hungary's accession to the European Union, the ECJ stated it lacked jurisdiction, without giving an opinion. However, it seems to be fairly clear from the Directive that the contract stays in force, and the trader has to live with the fact that the particular clause is no longer available.

b. Transposition in the Member States

aa. Absolute nullity

When transposing Art. 6(1) of Directive 93/13, many member states have decided to adopt or maintain the concept of absolute nullity. In ESTONIA, GERMANY, IRELAND, PORTUGAL, SLOVAKIA, SLOVENIA and SPAIN, a contractual term considered unfair will be automatically deemed null and void. In MALTA, FRANCE and LUXEMBOURG, unfair clauses are regarded non-existent or "*non écrites*", respectively. Apart from the wording and creation of a legal fiction, no significant practical differences between nullity and non-existence can be identified.

bb. Relative nullity

The aforementioned concept of relative nullity can be found in the CZECH REPUBLIC, LATVIA and the NETHERLANDS with different specifications. According to CC Art. 55 in the CZECH REPUBLIC, an unfair term is only relatively ineffectual, i.e. ineffectual only upon assertion thereof by the consumer. According to the LATVIAN Consumer Rights Protection Law Section 6(8), unfair terms included in a contract entered into between a seller or service provider and a consumer shall be declared null and void upon the consumer's request. As seen, actually, the consumer is the one who needs to initiate particular actions in order to trigger the procedure that could ensure that the Consumer Rights Protection Centre (State Institution) or the court will declare the contractual term in question is unfair. Also in the Netherlands CC Art. 6:233 provides that an unfair term is merely voidable (*vernietigbaar*). As explained above, this legal consequence contradicts the requirements of the ECJ.

---

877 ECJ judgment of 10 January 2006, C-302/04 – *Ynos Kft v. János Varga* [2006] ECR I-00371.

cc. Unclear legal situation

In many member states it remains controversial whether or not the domestic provisions can be interpreted in such a way as to provide for relative nullity. In AUSTRIA, it is recognised that the jurisdiction of the relevant court is in principle to be exercised on its own motion. The unfairness of other (substantial) clauses by contrast is in principle not assessed ex officio, but rather only on a plea raised by the consumer. Indeed it is unclear whether the principles from the *Cofidis* case can also apply. As to BELGIUM, prior to the amendments of the Act of 7 December 1998 the clauses listed in the black list of Art. 32 of the Trade Practices Act (TPA) were prohibited and void whereas the clauses which violated the general prohibition on unfair terms of TPA Art. 31 *could* be declared void by the judge. The formulation created the impression that nullity was optional. Now after the amendment in both cases the nullity is compulsory. The TPA has stimulated a discussion on the nature of nullity. In a case concerning an infringement of the general clause of former TPA Art. 31, the CA Mons[878] pointed out that given the relative nullity it did not have the competence to assess the unfair character of terms on its own motion. Then again in a judgment of 3 March 2003 the CA Ghent[879] stated that although most of the provisions on unfair contract terms only concerned private interests, and consequently are sanctioned by relative nullity, there are some provisions which do concern public policy and are therefore sanctioned by absolute nullity. There are also legal scholars who proclaim absolute nullity as a general consequence of unfairness.

In CYPRUS, the transposition law copies the Directive, thereby stating that an unfair term shall not bind the consumer. In POLAND, Art. 385.1(1) of the Civil Code stipulates that "prohibited contractual clauses" do not bind the consumer and no absolute nullity is expressly provided. Therefore, it remains controversial in both countries whether or not the domestic provisions can be interpreted in such a way as to provide for relative nullity.

According to Art. 2(8) of the GREEK Consumer Protection Act (Law 2251/1994), the supplier cannot claim nullity of the contract as a whole if one or more terms are unfair and therefore considered void. Some authors regard this provision as an argument for relative nullity, others argue that due to the public law character of the provisions and the lack of an explicit claim for damages of use of unfair terms then solely absolute nullity would match the intention of the domestic legislator. In HUNGARY, the legislator changed the consequences of unfairness in 2006, however, without clarifying whether the consumer can influence the validity of the term in question. Art. 209a(2) of the Hungarian Civil Code provides that unfair clauses in consumer contracts are void. On the other hand CC Art. 209a(2), one sentence later, states that the unfairness of a clause can only be *asserted* to the advantage of the consumer. In ITALY, the new Consumer Code changed the legal consequences of the use of unfair terms by introducing the concept of protective nullity (*nullità di protezione*) in Art. 36(3). This provides that nullity of a clause can only occur to the advantage of the consumer, whereby the court has jurisdiction to declare the term void on its own motion (Art. 36(3): "*La nullità opera soltanto a vantaggio del consumatore e può essere rilevata d'ufficio dal giudice*"). Against this background it remains unclear in Hungary and Italy whether, according to the present state of the law, the court can also declare nullity if the consumer expressly wishes to be bound by the clause.

---

878 CA *Mons*, judgment of 29 March 1999, Journal des Tribunaux 1999, 604.

879 *Hof van Beroep Gent*, judgment of 3 March 2003, Algemeen Ziekenhuis St-Lucas VZW/R. Jonckheere, Tijdschrift voor Gentse rechtspraak 2003, 162.

As explained above, the concept of protective nullity seems to be in accordance with ECJ case-law, provided that a consumer is protected, even if he fails to raise the unfair nature of the term, either because he is unaware of his rights or because he is deterred from enforcing them. In other words *Océano*, *Cofidis* and *Mostaza Claro* do not completely outlaw the consumer's decision whether nullity of the unfair term will serve his interest.

dd. Alteration, amendment and adjustments of terms and contracts

The Nordic countries DENMARK, FINLAND and SWEDEN traditionally apply a more flexible approach based on the vast usage of general clauses. The Courts are entitled not only to declare an unfair term null and void, but also to alter, amend and adjust the particular term, other terms or the entire contract, thereby taking into account circumstances that have arisen after the contract was entered into. Although there is no relative nullity in the strict sense, this discretionary power allows the Courts to decide in the interests of the consumer. In the course of the implementation of the Directive, DENMARK introduced a special provision enabling the consumer to demand that the remaining part of the contract is upheld without any amendment if it is possible.[880] Similarly in PORTUGAL, the consumer may choose to keep the contract itself in force, in accordance with the principle of conservation. Under LITHUANIAN Law, the consumer is entitled to apply to court for invalidation or alteration of any unfair term.[881] In MALTA, the Director of Consumer Affairs of his own initiative or at the request of a "qualifying body", may issue a compliance order on any person requiring that person to delete or alter a term if the Director considers the term to be unfair to consumers. The Director may also require the incorporation of terms in a consumer contract if he considers that this is necessary "for the better information of consumers, or for preventing a significant imbalance between the rights and obligations of the parties, and this to the benefit of consumers" (Art. 94(1) lit. (a) of the Consumer Affairs Act).

ee. Splitting terms into a valid and unfair part

The question whether it is admissible – if possible – to split a contract term into a valid and an unfair part i.e. to reduce an unfair term to its legally permitted core, has been regulated and discussed only in a few member states. In SLOVAKIA, the Civil Code establishes partial nullity of the contract, thus it is possible to split a contractual term into valid and void parts, in order to keep the valid parts. In ESTONIA, Art. 39(2), sent. 2 of the Law of Obligation Act states that if a term can be divided into several independent parts and one of them is void, the other parts remain valid. Similarly, under Art. 3:42 of the DUTCH Civil Code a contractual, invalid (annulled) term can be legally replaced by a contractual term that would have been agreed on by the parties. In AUSTRIA and the UNITED KINGDOM the legitimacy of such a "reduction" of an unfair term is still being controversially discussed in legal literature, whereas in GERMANY it is acknowledged case law[882] and established in legal literature that a reduction is inadmissible for it would stimulate the use of unfair terms and weaken consumer protection. The latter legal attitude also applies to GREECE.

---

[880] Article 38c(1) referring to the general clause Art. 36(1) of the Formation of Contracts Act.

[881] Vid. Art. 12(1) of the Law on Consumer Protection; CC Art. 6.188(6).

[882] BGHZ 114, 342; BGHZ 120, 122 and NJW 2000, 1110.

ff. Consequences for the contract as a whole

As far as the consequences for the contract as a whole are concerned, virtually all member states followed the prescriptions of the Directive upholding the entire contact if it is capable of a continuing existence without the unfair terms. Minor differences relate to the exact legal techniques applied. Some countries achieve the result via general contract law while others have inserted a specific provision in the relevant Act or Chapter dealing with unfair contract terms. Because of their more flexible approach as described above, FINLAND and SWEDEN have not explicitly regulated the consequences for the contract. Under ESTONIAN Law the remaining part of the contract is valid unless the party supplying the term proves that the party would not have entered into the contract without the standard term which is void or deemed not to be part of the contract. The same hypothetical assumption can be found in SLOVENIA.

c. Compensation and/or punitive damages

The Directive does not prescribe any further sanctions for the use of unfair terms such as damages, fines and criminal penalties. Nevertheless, a number of member states in using the minimum harmonisation (Art. 8 of the Directive 93/13) have provided for compensation for the use of unfair contract terms. In BELGIUM, CZECH REPUBLIC, ESTONIA, HUNGARY, GERMANY, ITALY, LATVIA, LITHUANIA, MALTA, PORTUGAL, SLOVAKIA, SLOVENIA, SPAIN and UNITED KINGDOM damages/compensation is available under general civil law/contract law (via breach of a contractual duty, tort or related concepts). Punitive damages, however, cannot be imposed under civil law in the member states, indeed there may be such provisions in competition law which are not examined within this study.

V. Requirement of transparency according to Art.5

The requirement of transparency laid down in Art. 5 of Directive 93/13 constitutes – alongside the control of unfair terms in Art. 3 – the second primary pillar of Directive 93/13. The principle of transparency is an essential part of the European information model and is closely related to the other consumer-protecting information requirements prescribed by Community law.[883]

1. Drafting of terms in plain and intelligible language

a. Requirements of the Unfair Contract Terms Directive

According to Art. 5, sent. 1 of Directive 93/13 terms must always be drafted in plain, intelligible language. Recital 20 additionally makes clear, that the consumer should be given a genuine opportunity to examine all the terms.

---

883 See on this point, Part 3 D. of this study as well as *Grundmann/Kerber/Weatherill*, Party Autonomy and Information; *Schulze/Ebers/Grigoleit*, Information Requirements and Formation of Contract in the Acquis communautaire; *Howells/Janssen/Schulze*, Information Rights and Obligations.

The criteria "plain" and "intelligible" complement each other and are difficult to distinguish. Contractual terms are "plainly" drafted, when no ambiguities, misunderstandings or doubts exist in relation to the content of the terms. A contractual clause is "intelligible", when the consumer can understand the essential substance of the rules.

The general view is that the requirements of "plain and intelligible" drafting encompass both formal as well as substantive criteria: In terms of *formal requirements* the user has to ensure the drafting style of the terms is such that the consumer can comprehend the essential rights and duties. This is unlikely to be the case when the outward appearance of the document makes it difficult to get an overview of the terms or recognise a structure (e.g. frequent cross-referencing), is printed in a type face that is difficult to read or is disproportionately long in relation to the significance of the transaction. Furthermore, there is a *substantive, linguistic aspect* to the requirement of plain, intelligible language. In this respect technical jargon, long convoluted sentences or imprecise, fragmentary statements are to be avoided as far as possible. To some extent it is furthermore inferred from the requirement of transparency, that terms must be drafted in comprehensible language from the consumer's point of view.

b. Transposition of Art. 5, sent. 1 in the Member States

The vast majority of member states have transposed Art. 5, sent. 1 word for word. After the ECJ in its judgment C-144/99[884], clarified that, to implement the principle of transparency in full, "it is essential that the legal position under national law is sufficiently precise and clear that individuals are made fully aware of their rights" and that "even where the settled case-law of a member state interprets the provisions of national law in a manner deemed to satisfy the requirements of a Directive, that cannot achieve the clarity and precision needed to meet the requirement of legal certainty", the principle of transparency was explicitly anchored in DUTCH and GERMAN law.

By contrast Art. 5, sent. 1 of Directive 93/13 was not explicitly transposed in the CZECH REPUBLIC, ESTONIA, GREECE, HUNGARY, LUXEMBOURG and in SLOVAKIA. These countries do of course have rules on the incorporation and/or interpretation of pre-formulated terms, in the context of which the issue of whether the clause is formulated in plain, intelligible language also has a role to play. Whether this sufficiently accommodates the requirements of the ECJ is doubtful however, since in those countries the danger exists that consumers and consumer associations do not know that they can take actions against clauses which lack transparency.

The difficulty in transposing the requirement of transparency exists above all in the qualification in Art. 5, sent. 1 of Directive 93/13, that the requirement of transparency only applies in the case of contracts where all or certain terms are in *writing*. This formulation stands in contradiction to the recitals of the Directive: Apart from the fact that recital 20 does not contain any such limitation, it is expressly emphasised in recital 11, that consumers bound

---

884 ECJ judgment of 10 May 2001, C-144/99 – *Commission v Kingdom of the Netherlands* [2001] ECR I-03541, para. (17); ECJ judgment of 7 May 2002, C-478/99 – *Commission of the European Communities v. Kingdom of Sweden* [2002] ECR I-04147, para. (18) and ECJ judgment of 9 September 2004, C-70/03 – *Commission v. Kingdom of Spain* [2004] ECR I-0799, para. (15).

by an oral contract should be granted the same level of protection as consumers bound by a written contract. This inconsistency cast doubt on the applicability of the transparency principle in those member states, which – for example BELGIUM – included this qualification.

c. Interpretation of the requirement of transparency in the Member States

The issue of whether a term is formulated in plain and intelligible language is assessed by reference to how it is understood. Directive 93/13 does not contain any clear guidelines in this regard. It is also unclear, whether and to what extent the benchmark of the average consumer who is reasonably well informed and reasonably observant and circumspect, developed in the ECJ's case law on the fundamental freedoms and interpreting directives of trade practices law,[885] also applies in the context of control of unfair terms.

In this regard it is not surprising that the various benchmarks of the consumer in the individual member states (a detailed exposition of which is beyond the scope of this study) deviate considerably from one another.

Clear differences in practice are above all evident in the extent to which legal terminology is permissible. In the UNITED KINGDOM, there is a clear tendency towards the fact that clauses must always be formulated in everyday layman's terms. In the guidance on unfair terms in consumer contracts issued by the Office of Fair Trading it is laid down that expressions such as "indemnity" must always be avoided, since such references can have onerous implications of which consumers are likely to be unaware.[886] In place thereof terms like "pay damages" are preferred. In GERMANY, by contrast, case law in this respect is more generous; the BGH emphasises in a number of judgments, that the duty of the user to formulate the content of the clause clearly and intelligibly only exists within the bounds of what is actually possible. Should various kinds of legal and factual difficulties exist for the drafter, the terms shall nonetheless be binding even if the other party has to make a certain effort in order to understand them rather than being able to understand immediately.[887]

Uncertainties in the application of the requirement of transparency also relate to the extent to which the principle of transparency must reflect the individual prevailing circumstances at the time of conclusion of the contract. This concerns not only the general problem of whether the particular consumer in question is better or less informed than the average consumer, but also the issue of whether clauses lacking transparency can be "healed" by making specific reference to them. In GERMANY, case law assumes that an objective lack of transparency in an individual case can be overcome if the user informs the customer (which may even be only orally, dependent upon the circumstances).[888] Whether this interpretation is compatible with the Directive appears doubtful, as the Directive aims not only at transparency in the individual case, but also at the guarantee of the internal market through comparability of contractual conditions of domestic and foreign providers (market transparency).

---

885 See also recital 18 of the Directive 2005/29.

886 See 19.5 and 19.7 of the guidance, available at http://www.oft.gov.uk/Business/Legal/UTCC/guidance.htm.

887 BGH NJW 1998, 3114.

888 BGH WM 1997, 518 with further references.

Contractual documents must therefore in principle be intelligible in themselves and not only after specific reference by the user upon conclusion of the contract.

2. Consequences of lack of transparency

a. Requirements of the Unfair Contract Terms Directive

The wording of the Directive does not specify the legal consequences that apply where the transparency requirement has been breached in the individual case. The sole legal consequence of failure to fulfil the requirement of transparency to be explicitly provided is the interpretation rule in Art. 5, sent. 2 of Directive 93/13. This interpretation rule, however, only applies to clauses not drafted in plain language and which are capable of interpretation. However, the legal consequences for plain, but unintelligible clauses are not regulated (an example would be where, due to legal terminology or insufficient command of the language in which the terms are drafted, the clause is unintelligible to the consumer).

Accordingly there are widely differing views on the legal consequences of a breach of the transparency imperative. Some assume that the member states are free to decide on the legal consequences. However, others see the requirement of transparency, by reference to recital 20, as a condition for the incorporation of terms. Finally there is the view that clauses which lack transparency are to be assessed according to Art. 3. If one follows this latter view, it is furthermore doubtful, whether lack of transparency *per se* results in the term being rendered unfair or non-binding according to Art. 3(1) in conjunction with Art. 6(1) of Directive 93/13 or whether there is a further condition in that the content of the clause is disadvantageous, i.e. causes a considerable and unjustified imbalance in the contractual rights and obligations contrary to the principle of good faith.

In this aspect the judgment of the ECJ in *Cofidis*[889] has not brought any clarification. The case under dispute concerned an offer of credit with the words "Free application for money reserve" in large letters on the front, while the references to the contractual interest rate and a penalty clause were in small print on the reverse. The *Tribunal d'instance Vienne* was of the opinion, that "the financial clauses lack legibility", which was likely to mislead the consumer. Accordingly, the conclusion was reached that "the financial clauses may be regarded as unfair". The ECJ by contrast explained that[890]

> "To fall within the scope of the Directive, however, those terms must satisfy the conditions set out in Art. 3(1) of the Directive 93/13, that is, they must not have been individually negotiated and must, contrary to the requirement of good faith, cause a significant imbalance in the parties' rights and obligations arising under the contract, to the detriment of the consumer. Although the national court has not provided any information on the latter point, it cannot be excluded that that condition is satisfied."

---

889 ECJ judgment of 21 November 2002, C-473/00 – *Cofidis v. Fredout*, [2002] ECR I-10875.

890 ECJ judgment of 21 November 2002, C-473/00 – *Cofidis v. Fredout*, [2002] ECR I-10875, para. (23).

However, with this judgment the ECJ is giving an opinion only in relation to the admissibility of the complaint and not to the fundamental question of which legal consequences lack of transparency gives rise to.

b. Transposition of the *contra proferentem* rule in the Member States

The interpretation rule laid down in Art. 5, sent. 2 of Directive 93/13, according to which any doubt on the meaning of a clause is always to be resolved in the manner most favourable to the consumer, has been transposed by all member states.

The implementation of the requirements of the Directive in ESTONIA however seems problematic. According to Art. 39(1), sent. 2 of the Law of Obligations Act, "in the case of doubt, standard terms shall be interpreted to the detriment of the party supplying the standard terms." Directive 93/13 however goes beyond a mere interpretation to the detriment of the user, in that it requires not only an interpretation favourable to the consumer, but an interpretation "most" favourable to the consumer.

In AUSTRIA, unclear contract terms are ineffectual according to Art. 6(3) of the Consumer Protection Act. This rule has resulted in certain confusion, as some authors assume that clauses lacking transparency are to be assessed according to this rule alone, so that the consumer cannot rely on the *contra-proferentem* rule in CC Art. 915, 2nd alternative. The majority view, by contrast, holds that the consumer, even in the case of mere lack of transparency, can rely on an interpretation favourable to him.

According to Art. 5, sent. 3 of Directive 93/13 the *contra proferentem* rule applies only in individual proceedings, not in collective actions. This should prevent the rule on interpretation from allowing parties to evade orders to cease and desist using particular terms by simply stating that the clause cannot be regarded as unfair when interpreted in favour of the consumer. SPAIN has as yet not transposed Art. 5, sent. 3, but is required to do so according to the judgment of the ECJ in C-70/03.[891]

c. Further legal consequences according to Member State law

aa. Non-incorporation of terms which lack transparency

In many member states, the transparency of a clause can only be assessed within a review of incorporation of terms. The review of incorporation of terms is based upon the notion that a contractual clause can in principle only become part of the contract through a legally binding declaration of consent by the other party. The aim and purpose of the review of incorporation of terms is to establish minimum conditions for a valid, legally binding declaration of consent. Accordingly, most cases of review of incorporation of terms only apply formal requirements of transparency with a "broad brush approach", in which it is assessed whether the consumer, in general terms, had the opportunity of becoming acquainted with the clause

891 ECJ judgment of 9 September 2004, C-70/03 – *Commission v. Kingdom o Spain* [2004] ECR I-0799 (paras 16-22); see Part 2 C.II.23.

or could have reckoned with its true content. As a rule, only especially clear-cut cases of lack of transparency attract any sanction, i.e. when even a minimal measure of intelligibility, certainty or readability is lacking.

bb. Assessment of transparency within a content review

An assessment of transparency within a content review by contrast occurs in very few member states: Besides the aforementioned rule in AUSTRIA (*ante*), GERMAN law, since the modernisation of the law of obligations, provides in CC Art. 307(1), sent. 2 that an unreasonable disadvantage may also result from the fact that the provision is not clear and comprehensible. This should make clear that, in the context of a content's review, clauses lacking transparency are *per se* regarded as non-binding, without an additional criterion of unreasonable disadvantage to the contractual partner. Legal consequences of a breach of the transparency imperative therefore include not only an interpretation favourable to the consumer and non-incorporation into the contract, but also the ineffectuality of the clause within the content review. In relation to this point the German BGH has clarified that a clause declared unfair according to CC Art. 307(1) (Art. 6(1) of Directive 93/13) cannot be replaced by one with identical content.[892] As Directive 93/13 contains no rules on how to replace non-binding terms, then it is – according to the BGH – for the national law to decide by means of judicial interpretation, how to fill a gap in a contract if the removal of a non-binding term without substitution thereof would cause inequity. If the customer, in reliance on the binding nature of the non-binding clause suffers financial loss, then, according to German case law, he additionally has the possibility of a claim for damages in an action for breach of pre-contractual duty of care culpa in contrahendo.

cc. Unclear legal situations

The state of the law remains unclear in ITALY. Whereas some authors assume that lack of transparency implies nullity *per se*, for some commentators the infringements of the principle of transparency must be evaluated under Art. 36(2) lit. (c) of the Consumer Code (binding the consumer to terms with which he had no real opportunity of becoming acquainted before the conclusion of the contract).

In LATVIA, although the legal consequences are not regulated in the Consumer Protection Act, general norms of civil law could be nevertheless applied, particularly Art. 1506 of the Law of Obligations stating that absolutely disreputable and unintelligible and also contradictory terms shall not be interpreted at all, but deemed null and void.

In MALTA, there are no express rules on the consequences of a lack of transparency for individual cases. However under general civil law rules, if the lack of transparency is such as to amount to fraud or bad faith on the part of a party to the contract, then that contract may be annulled by the choice of the other party. Moreover, the Director of Consumer Affairs in accordance with his powers under Art. 94 of the Consumer Affairs Act may issue a compliance order under that article if he considers that the term used is unfair to consumers and is

---

[892] BGHZ 164, 297.

in breach of Art. 47 which requires that terms in a consumer contract are written in plain and intelligible language "which can be understood by the consumers to whom the contract is directed."

The legal consequences in SPAIN are also unclear, as the principle of transparency has been transposed into two different Laws with different consequences. Art. 10(1)(a) of the Law 26/1984 of July 19 on Consumer Protection prescribes very generally the principle of transparency, without laying down specific consequences. In Art. 5(5) of the Law 7/1998 (standard terms) the consequences of lack of transparency are by contrast positively regulated within two articles. These have been criticised in academia because the respective sanctions partly contradict each other: In Art. 7(2) the sanction against standard terms that are "illegible, ambiguous, obscure and incomprehensible" is non-incorporation into the contract, whereas Art. 8 declares standard terms that infringe any rule of this Law null and void (i.e. including the principle of transparency). Both laws can be applied simultaneously, when an unfair term in contracts concluded with consumers is at the same time a standard term. Case law, in a pragmatic (but not clarifying) approach, tends to use any of the cited norms to achieve a fair outcome in favour of the consumer; frequently through declaring the term null and void.

In the UNITED KINGDOM, it is unclear whether a term is capable of being found to be unfair *principally* or *solely* because it is not transparent, but the Law Commission and the Scottish Law Commission recommend in their final report on unfair contract terms that it should be possible for a contract term to be found to be unfair principally or solely because it is not transparent.[893]

3. Conclusions

The requirements of Directive 93/13 in respect of the imperative of transparency have been transposed in most of the member states (with the exception of the CZECH REPUBLIC, ESTONIA, GREECE, HUNGARY, LUXEMBOURG and SLOVAKIA). It is doubtful whether a breach of the transparency imperative is sufficiently and effectively sanctioned. As Directive 93/13 contains no explicit guidelines on this point, the vast majority of member states have also declined to regulate the consequences for breach of the transparency requirement in individual actions. In a reform of Directive 93/13 the Community legislator should clearly lay down the legal consequences.

VI. Collective proceedings according to Art. 7(2)

1. Overview

According to Art. 7(1) of Directive 93/13, member states shall ensure that adequate and effective means exist to prevent the continued use of unfair terms in contracts concluded with consumers by sellers or suppliers. The Directive largely leaves the choice of means to the

---

893 See the final report of the Law Commission and the Scottish Law Commission on unfair terms in contracts, LAW COM No. 292/SCOT LAW COM No. 199, para. 3098-3102.

member states which must be put in place. Community law aims to accommodate appropriately the existing systems which had already developed in the member states even before Directive 93/13 came into force. Art. 7(2) of Directive 93/13 thus only provides in general terms, that

> "the means (...) shall include provisions whereby persons or organizations, having a legitimate interest under national law in protecting consumers, may take action according to the national law concerned before the courts or before competent administrative bodies for a decision as to whether contractual terms drawn up for general use are unfair, so that they can apply appropriate and effective means to prevent the continued use of such terms."

This rule is supplemented by Directive 98/27 on injunctions for the protection of consumer interests (see esp. Annex 7 to the Directive).[894]

All member states provide for collective court procedures, by which the use or recommendation of unfair terms in legal agreements shall be prohibited. In a number of member states, the emphasis is on administrative proceedings (see 2.), in almost all member states it is furthermore possible to pursue collective court actions against unfair clauses (3.).

Some member states, e.g. FRANCE and SLOVAKIA, make additional provisions for criminal proceedings to prohibit unfair terms. It appears however, that such kinds of proceedings play a subordinate role in practice, so a more detailed examination is not required here. In MALTA, where a person does not abide with a compliance order issued by the Director of Consumer Affairs, then such non-compliance is considered a criminal offence and punishable as such. However, it has been suggested that these consequences should be re-evaluated and substituted by a more effective regime of administrative fines since the initiation of criminal proceedings is invariably time-consuming and the burden of proof in such instances is that required in criminal cases – namely of proving beyond reasonable doubt.

Alongside the aforementioned collective proceedings, in respect of certain types of contracts, especially financial services contracts in the banking and insurance sector as well as dealings in stocks and shares, many member states make provision for specific monitoring by industry regulators governed by public law. The use and recommendation of unfair terms can in relevant cases be additionally regulated through antitrust measures. Since such proceedings only concern specialised questions, their relevant characteristics will not be addressed more closely either.

2. Administrative control of unfair terms

a. The role of public bodies in the Member States

Many member states use an administrative law based system for monitoring contract terms. These systems are characterised by the dominant position of public bodies responsible for protecting the collective interests of consumers. Such bodies exist especially in the Nordic

---

894 On the transposition of this Directive cf. the report in this study, Part 2 G.

countries (DENMARK, FINLAND, SWEDEN) with the Consumer Ombudsman, in CYPRUS with the Director of Competition and Consumers' Protection Service, in ESTONIA with the Consumer Protection Board, in HUNGARY with the General Inspectorate for Consumer Protection, in IRELAND with the Director of Consumer Affairs,[895] in LATVIA with the Consumer Rights Protection Centre, in LITHUANIA with the National Consumers' Rights Protection Board, in MALTA with the Director of Consumer Affairs, in POLAND with the Director of the Office for the Protection of Competition and Consumers, in SLOVAKIA with the Slovak Trade Inspectorate as well as in the UNITED KINGDOM with the Office of Fair Trading.

Administrative elements can also be found in other countries, which admittedly do not have an extensive system of public control of contract terms, but administrative bodies do however at least have standing to apply for injunctions in court, e.g. in BELGIUM (Minister of Economic Affairs), PORTUGAL (Public Prosecutor) and SPAIN (National Consumer Institute and the corresponding bodies or entities of the Autonomous Communities and their local authorities dealing with consumer protection; Public Prosecutor or Attorney General).

In BELGIUM, the King is empowered to impose or prohibit by Royal Decree certain clauses applicable to certain commercial sectors or to specific products or services.[896] In FRANCE, a special administrative body, the "*Commission des clauses abusives*" has the power to issue statements on terms contained in standard contracts, but those statements are not legally binding.[897] In ITALY, the National Council of Consumers and Users ("*Consiglio Nazionale dei Consumatori e degli Utenti* – CNCU") represents the consumers' and users' associations nationwide. The Council is attached to the Ministry for Production Activities and its main duties are those of expressing opinions, where requested, on preliminary draft legislation produced by the Government or draft legislation produced by the members of parliament and on draft regulations that affect the rights and interests of consumers and users. In addition to its advisory function vis-à-vis the Parliament (at hearings), and vis-à-vis the Government (consultation sessions), the CNCU participates in other regular consultation processes with other authorities and bodies by being a signatory to memorandums of understanding as well as by attending hearings on specific topics. In POLAND, PORTUGAL and SPAIN, the Standard Terms Register contains a list of clauses which are declared as unfair; the register has binding effects for administrative authorities, e.g. registrars.

b. Investigatory powers of public bodies

The administrative law's power to monitor terms differs considerably between the member states. In many member states, the competence of the public bodies far exceed the ability to bring an action in court. Moreover, through special legal provisions, the public bodies generally have a duty to investigate a complaint or examine whether a term is unfair on their own initiative. This corresponds with the power in many member states for the public body to demand that traders submit the relevant documents and information.

---

895 On 24 August 2006, a new draft legislation, the Consumer Protection (National Consumer Agency) Bill, has been announced which will, inter alia, replace the office of Director of Consumer Affairs with a new administrative body, the National Consumer Agency.

896 See Part 2 C.II.2.

897 See Part 2 C.II.8.

c. Negotiation and guidelines

On this basis many public bodies work towards reasonable contractual conditions through negotiation. This procedure is above all characteristic in DENMARK, FINLAND and SWEDEN as well as in the UNITED KINGDOM: In the NORDIC STATES, according to the principle of negotiation, the Consumer Ombudsman shall endeavour by negotiation to induce persons carrying on a trade or business to act in accordance with the principles of good trade practices. One of the ways in which the Consumer Ombudsman may try to influence business is by issuing guidelines within specified areas on the basis of negotiations with the relevant business and consumer organisations. In the UNITED KINGDOM, any complaints about unfair terms are usually resolved through negotiation with the trader concerned. The Office of Fair Trading, in particular, has been very active in approaching traders about terms which may be unfair and has successfully persuaded them to change their terms. It regularly publishes an "Unfair Contract Terms" Bulletin in which it provides details of the terms it has dealt with in this way.[898]

In BELGIUM, the legislator created a Commission on Unfair Contract Terms in 1993. It is an advisory organ that not only makes recommendations about clauses in contracts between businesses and consumers but also may give advice upon request and has the competence to submit proposals to the Minister of Economic Affairs. On a regular basis the Commission's advice has been obtained by Ministers on a number of diverse subjects. The reports holding the Commission's recommendations may be consulted on the internet.[899] The Commission can act on its own initiative, or at the request of the competent minister, a consumer organisation or an association of traders.

d. Power of public bodies to issue orders

In some member states, the powers of the public bodies are particularly extensive. They encompass not only the right to litigate in court, but also the power to issue a compliance order.

In DENMARK, the Consumer Ombudsman may issue orders in respect of conduct which is in clear contravention of the Marketing Practices Act and cannot be changed by negotiation. The party against whom an order is made may demand that the Consumer Ombudsman ensures that the order is brought before the courts. Non-observance of a prohibition or injunction imposed by a court/Ombudsman is punishable by a fine or imprisonment of up to four months. In SWEDEN, where negotiations fail in cases of lesser significance, the Ombudsman may likewise make a prohibitory order. If a prohibition is not observed or if the case is one of significant public interest, then the Ombudsman can apply for an injunction before the Market Court. Similar to this, in FINLAND, the Consumer Ombudsman may impose an injunction in cases that are not of significant importance. The injunction becomes void in case the addressee objects to the injunction within 8 days. The Consumer Ombudsman may also impose a conditional fine, but the Market Court decides whether or not it is payable.

---

898 See http://www.oft.gov.uk.

899 See http://mineco.fgov.be.

In ESTONIA, supervisory authorities engaging in consumer protection may issue a precept in which it demands that the offence desists and, if possible, that the initial situation is restored; the precept shall set out the penalty fine to be imposed upon failure to comply with the precept; contestation of a precept does not release the trader from the obligation to comply unless the court decides otherwise. The upper limit for a penalty payment is 10.000 kroons.

In HUNGARY, the General Inspectorate for Consumer Protection is empowered by the Consumer Protection Act to make an order to remedy the unlawful situation and prohibit the continuance of such conduct and impose a financial penalty (consumer protection fine). If the conduct of the user simultaneously constitutes unfair trading practice, the competition authority can also prohibit the use of standard terms and impose a fine.

In LATVIA, the Consumer Rights Protection Centre can require businesses to make changes in draft contracts and prohibit further use of unfair or ambiguous contract terms, both in respect of draft contracts and in contracts which have already been entered into. The requirements set and instructions given by officials of the Consumer Rights Protection Centre are binding on the business. If a violation of consumer rights has been found, which affects individual or group consumer interests (consumer association interests) and which may cause harm or loss to particular consumer rights, the Consumer Rights Protection Centre is entitled (1) to make an order requiring a business to cease the violation, and to perform specific activities to rectify the impact thereof and imposing a time limit for implementation of such measures and (2) to publish the decision taken either fully or partially in the official Gazette of the Government of Latvia.

In MALTA, the Director of Consumer Affairs, either of his own initiative or at the request of a 'qualifying body', may issue a compliance order on any person requiring: (1) the deletion or alteration of terms in consumer contracts which the Director considers to be unfair to consumers, and/or (2) the incorporation of terms in consumer contracts which the Director considers to be necessary to ensure that consumers are better informed or to counter a significant imbalance between the rights and obligations of the parties, and this to the benefit of consumers, and/or (3) require a person to comply with any measures specified in the order to ensure compliance. The trader against whom such an order is made then has the right to contest such an order before the Court of Magistrate (Civil Jurisdiction). If the order is not contested, or unsuccessfully contested by the trader and accordingly confirmed by the Court, and the trader notwithstanding fails to abide by the order, then the failure to comply is considered as a criminal offence.[900]

In POLAND, the Director of the Office for the Protection of Competition and Consumers likewise has the right to issue an injunction and set a fine for non-compliance. A precondition for such a measure, however, is that not only is the individual interest of a particular consumer affected, but that the general consumer interest so requires.

In SLOVAKIA, consumers have the right to file a complaint to the public control and market surveillance authority (Slovak Trade Inspectorate). The Slovak Trade Inspectorate is a state administrative body subordinate to the Slovak Ministry for the Economy. The Public Con-

900 See *supra*, Part 2 C.VI.1.

trol and Market Surveillance Authority is empowered to impose financial penalties for infringements, but it can not intervene in decision-making about rights and duties of contracting parties. Only the court has authority to make a decision.

3. Judicial review of unfair terms

Court proceedings for prohibiting unfair clauses also vary across the member states.

a. Types of actions in the Member States

As a minimum standard almost all member states allow injunctions against persons who use or recommend unfair clauses. By and large it is also possible to obtain an interlocutory/interim injunction where urgent action is required.

An injunction generally aims to ensure that the business ceases the infringement and does not engage in similar conduct in the future. Most member states also provide for all or part of the relevant decision of the court or of a corrective announcement to be published, with the aim of terminating any continued effects of the use of the unfair term in question.
Alongside injunctions some member states also allow actions for damages: In FRANCE, consumer associations have a right to collective damages where a misfeasance by a user of standard terms has caused damage to the collective consumer interest (Art. L. 422 et seq. of the Consumer Code). In GREECE, consumer associations also can bring actions for damages. The quantum of damages is determined by the court, taking account of the circumstances of the case and especially the intensity of the unlawful conduct, the size of the respondent company, its annual turnover and the necessity of a general or specific precedent. This sum is made available for the public benefit. In HUNGARY, if the consumer protection authorities issue an *actio popularis* pursuant to Art. 39 of the Consumer Protection Act, the infringer is required to compensate the consumer in accordance with the judgment; this is however without prejudice to the right of the consumer to bring an action according to the general civil law.

In SPAIN, consumer associations have the right to claim damages under Art. 12 of the Law 7/1998 on standard terms in contracts. Moreover, the Spanish Civil Procedure Act 1/2000 allows consumer associations to claim damages on behalf of unidentified classes of consumers.

In so far as the use of unfair terms also represents a breach of fair trading provisions, in certain circumstances additional sanctions can apply in the member states: Thus for instance, in GERMANY, according to the Act against Unfair Competition of 2004, competitors are entitled to claim damages, if the violating party has acted negligently. According to Art. 10 of the Act against Unfair Competition 2004, there is the further possibility of claiming restitution for the profits that a violating party has wilfully achieved by injuring a multitude of customers.

In ITALY, a new proposal of 26 June 2006 plans to introduce into the Consumer Code a provision providing that consumer associations are entitled to recover damages on behalf of one or more consumers.

b. Standing to apply for an injunction

The persons who may bring an action varies between the member states. Those member states which primarily prescribe administrative forms of control (see 2.), also give standing to the relevant public bodies.

Furthermore, consumer associations in all member states have standing to bring collective proceedings. The exceptions are two member states: The LITHUANIAN implementing provisions do not provide that private organisations can employ appropriate and effective means to prevent the continued use of such terms. Only individual consumers whose interests have been infringed are entitled to apply to the board (see above) or to bring an action in an individual proceeding. In MALTA, under Art. 94 of the Consumer Affairs Act, a "qualifying body" (i.e. a registered consumer association and any other body whether constituted in Malta or otherwise as the Minister may, after consulting the Consumer Affairs Council, designate by notice in the Gazette) can only file a written application to the Director to issue a compliance order. According to Art. 95, it shall be at the discretion of the Director whether or not to issue a compliance order after a written request by a qualifying body has been made to him. If the Director decides not to issue a compliance order after an application has been made to him by a qualifying body, he shall, within seven days from the date of his decision, notify, in writing, the qualifying body and the persons against whom the compliance order was requested of his decision stating his reasons therefore. A qualifying body may, within fifteen days from the date of service of the decision of the Director not to issue a compliance order, bring an action before the Court of Magistrate (civil jurisdiction) for an order requiring the Director to make a compliance order. If one assumes, that the member states are obliged by Art. 7(2) of Directive 93/13, to provide consumer associations with standing to bring collective proceedings against the user of unfair terms, then in LITHUANIA and MALTA, an infringement of the Directive can be affirmed, since in both countries consumer associations do not have a right to proceed *directly* against the user of the clause.

In all other countries, by contrast, the right of consumer associations to litigate has been introduced, even though in some countries (IRELAND und UNITED KINGDOM), there was some delay in doing so.[901] Alongside consumer associations, many countries have also extended the right to seek injunctions against unfair clauses to trade and professional associations. Such types of claim exist above all in AUSTRIA, BELGIUM, GERMANY, GREECE, HUNGARY, ITALY, NETHERLANDS, POLAND, PORTUGAL, SLOVENIA and SPAIN.
Finally, in some member states, the right has been conferred on an individual consumer to seek an injunction, most notably in POLAND.

---

901 See relevant country reports under Part 2 C.II.12 and 25.

c. Effects of collective actions: Relativity of *res judicata*

Court or administrative decisions in the context of collective proceedings are in the vast majority of member states only binding on the businesses who are party to the case. The decision has no effect on other businesses who use identical terms. In derogation from these principles though, the relativity of court decisions has been eroded in some member states: In POLAND, a legally binding decision, which prohibits the use of unfair terms, is published in the economic and court journal and entered into a register. With the registration the judgment acquires, according to Art. 479[43] of the civil procedure rules, *erga omnes* effect – a legal consequence, which is questionable on principles of constitutional law in Poland. Court decisions, which, in HUNGARY, according to CC Art. 209/B are handed down in relation to the *actio popularis*, likewise have *erga omnes* effect; only contracts, which have already been fulfilled before the action was lodged, are excluded. In SLOVENIA, only a sustaining judgment has a general *erga omnes* effect, such that any person may refer to a final judgment by which certain contracts, individual provisions of those contracts or the general terms and conditions of business incorporated in those contracts were declared null and void. However, a judgment of refusal only affects the parties concerned and does not prevent a new action in respect to the same claim. In SPAIN, the Law on Standard Terms[902] in contracts did originally prescribe in Art. 20 a rule according to which decisions of the Supreme Court have precedent value; this rule however was repealed and not replaced with the new civil procedure rules (Law 1/2000).[903]

Decisions in collective proceedings are generally confined to the cases that have arisen before them. But if the legal effect of a court judgment is restricted to the clause in question in its particular wording, then the judgment does not prohibit the user of the clause from replacing the term in question with other terms that are just as unfair but that are not covered by the judgment.

Some member states have introduced safeguards for this very eventuality in the interests of consumer protection: In the UNITED KINGDOM, according to UTCCR Art. 12(4) an "injunction may relate not only to use of a particular contract term drawn up for general use but to any similar term, or a term which has a similar effect, used or recommended for use by any person." Similarly, in CYPRUS, injunctions can be filed against more than one seller or supplier of the same or different business domain who uses or recommends for general use, the same or similar contract terms. Accordingly, in these countries, provision is made to prevent businesses from circumventing the judgment by replacing the offending term by terms that have a similar effect.

It must finally be borne in mind that the associated disadvantages to the consumer of the principle of relativity of *res judicata* can be *de facto* avoided if public bodies, on the basis of a relevant judgment, proceed against other businesses and thus extend the effect of the judgment far beyond the particular proceedings.

---

902 Law 7/1998 of April 13 on Standard Terms in Contracts.

903 The Law 1/2000 on civil procedure now states in Art. 221.2 that in case of successful injunction, the judgment shall indicate "whether it will produce procedural effects not limited to the parties in the procedure".

4. Conclusions

The implementation of Directive 93/13 has not led to an approximation of enforcement mechanisms in the member states. Completely different systems of collective forms of action continue to exist, which place varying emphasis on administrative measures or collective court proceedings by consumer associations or other persons who have the right to make a claim. With the accession of the ten new member states administrative proceedings have assumed greater significance in the European Community. This may be above all attributable to the fact that in the former communist-socialist countries, now as then, only a few private consumer organisations exist, which in turn increases the need for administrative control.

VII. Practical impact of the Unfair Contract Terms Directive

1. Impact on the level of consumer protection

The practical effects of Directive 93/13 have been differently assessed by national rapporteurs. In some of the "old" member states, and, above all, in the Nordic States (DENMARK, FINLAND, SWEDEN) and also in AUSTRIA, GERMANY and PORTUGAL, it has been stressed that the Directive has not led to any noticeable increase in the level of consumer protection, since, in these countries, there was already far reaching legislation in place prior to transposition of the Directive and the (minimal) changes brought about by the Directives primarily consisted of inserting provisions in order to avoid possible gaps. For FRANCE, LUXEMBOURG and the NETHERLANDS it has been emphasised how difficult it is to assess the effects of the Directive, as an established system of monitoring terms already existed and very few changes were carried out as a result of the Directive. The transposition and application of the Directive in BELGIUM is subject to considerable criticism because of the great number of sector-specific Acts which each contained a number of unfair clauses which made it very difficult for legal practitioners to gain an overview of the rules applicable and also, more generally, because it undermines the coherence of the law. In IRELAND, there is only one court case involving the Regulations and so it is arguable that their impact to date has been minimal. However, there is consistent evidence of soft enforcement by the Office of Director of Consumer Affairs, which each year reports of amendments to contractual terms, following dialogue with relevant interested parties. These relate to, for example, mobile 'phone contracts, airline ticket contracts, car hire contracts, house alarm contracts and buildings' insurance contracts. For the UNITED KINGDOM it has been stressed that consumers have clearly benefited by being able to challenge a greater range of terms than has previously been the case. Also for GREECE, ITALY and SPAIN it is accepted that the level of consumer protection has been improved, even though in the case of Spain it is emphasised, that this is attributable not only to the Directive, but also because a new comprehensive regulation on standard terms (beyond the scope of the Directive) was approved.

The situation is different in the ten new member states. As all of the newly acceded States had no comparable system of monitoring terms in place prior to transposition of the Directive, many rapporteurs have emphasised, that the new rules concerning unfair contractual terms have undoubtedly been beneficial, even though many also point out that the practical effects cannot yet be assessed, as hardly any case law exists and no national reports have recently been made.

A fundamental problem that is seen in many member states, especially in BELGIUM, POLAND and MALTA, is that many traders have problems complying with the law on unfair terms. According to a recently conducted investigation by the POLISH Office for the Protection of Competition and Consumers, that above all concentrated on the business practices of organisers of tourist events und language schools, around 95% of the examined brochures, leaflets and contracts used by the 'organisers' contained prohibited clauses.

Finally, many correspondents complain that the limited success of the unfair terms provisions is caused by the ignorance of the consumers in the first place, and maybe also that of their lawyers. Another explanation might be that these lawyers prefer to combat unfair contract terms on the basis of the well-known concepts of general contract law with which they are more familiar, but – as emphasised by the Belgian Rapporteur – there is no evidence to support this statement.

2. Additional burdens or costs for traders

In those countries which prior to transposition of Directive 93/13 did not have a comparable system for monitoring contract terms, i.e. especially in the new member states, it is partly assumed that traders have incurred additional burdens and costs as a result of the implementation of this Directive in that their business dealings may have to be cancelled as a result of imposing a term that is considered unfair under the current legislation but which was not regulated under the previous legal system. However, for other countries it is stated that traders do not incur additional burdens because of the lack of awareness among the business community of the applicable provisions and a lack of pro-active enforcement.

3. Particular difficulties with transposing the Unfair Contract Terms Directive

The transposition of Directive 93/13 has evoked a series of problems in the member states, which are in part attributable to the fact that the legal orders of the member states have been confronted with unfamiliar rules and concepts (this concerns, for example, the concept of "good faith", alien to the common law system and therefore causing uncertainty as to its meaning), but also partly due to an inconsistent legislative technique in transposition.

So, for example, in BELGIUM, the law on Unfair Terms is regulated in both the Trade Practices Act and (for freelancers) in the Liberal Professions Act. This separate treatment of contracts concluded by practitioners of liberal professions was criticised, not only because of the adoption of a separate Act but most of all because of discrepancies between both Acts. Such inconsistencies are also present in SPANISH law. When a contract with standard terms is concluded with consumers, both the Law on General Consumer Protection and the Law on Standard Terms in contracts apply, with the indicated conflict of consequences. In IRELAND, it has been noted that there may be an incompatibility between the Unfair Terms in Consumer Contracts Regulation and the rules on exclusion clauses under the sale of goods legislation. Under sale of goods legislation, a clause which excludes/limits liability for breach of the statutory implied terms is void – completely prohibited. Whereas, if such a clause passes the 'fairness' test, it would appear to be enforceable under the Regulations. It is assumed that the consumer would be protected by the superior protection in this regard, i.e. the sales legislation. In CYPRUS, the same kind of difficulties exist, since the Sales of Goods Law renders null and void any term excluding or rendering ineffective any of the statutory implied terms whereas the Unfair Terms in Consumer Contracts Regulation requires that such a term should pass the unfairness test. In the UNITED KINGDOM, as the UTCCR are now almost a "cut-and-paste" implementation of the Directive, there are no shortcomings in that sense. However, the retention of the parallel regime in UCTA 1977 has caused some confusion, and affected legal certainty. The Law Commission and Scottish Law Commission in February 2005 therefore published a draft Unfair Terms in Contracts Bill and proposed in its final report to clarify and unify the legislation on unfair terms presently contained in UCTA 1977 and UTCCR 1999.[904]

Bibliography

Report from the Commission on the implementation of Council Directive 93/13/EEC of 5 April 1993 on unfair terms in consumer contracts, COM(2000)248; Material from the conference "The Unfair Terms Directive – Five Years on – Evaluation and future perspectives, Conference Material," http://europa.eu.int/comm/consumers/cons_int/safe_shop/unf_cont_terms/event29_en.htm; CLAB Database, https://adns.cec.eu.int/CLAB; **Alfaro Aguilareal, Jesús / Díez-Picazo, Luis / Menéndez, Aurelio**, Comentarios a la Ley sobre condiciones generales de la contracion, Madrid 2002, **Andersen, Lennart Lynge**, Aftaleloven med kommentarer, Copenhagen 2005, **Ajani, Gianmaria / Rossi, Piercarlo**, Codice del consumatori, 2005, **Basedow, Jürgen**, Vorbemerkung zu § 305 BGB paras. 18-67, in: Münchener Kommentar zum Bürgerlichen Gesetzbuch, Band 2, 5. Aufl., München 2007, **Bernitz, Ulf**, Standardavtalsrätt, Stockholm 1995, **Cámara Lapuente, Sergio**, El control de las 'cláusulas abusivas' sobre elementos esenciales del contrato. ¿Incorrecta transposición, opción legal legítima o mentís jurisprudencial? Navarre 2006, **Fazekas, Judit**, Fogyastóvédelmi Jog, Komplex Kiadó Kft. Budapest, 2007, **Grundmann, Stefan / Mazeaud, Denis** (eds.), General Clauses and Standards in European Contract Law. Comparative Law, EC Law and Contract Law Codification, den Haag, 2006, **Hulva, Tomá** , Ochrana spotřebitele, Praha 2005, **Jamin, Christophe / Mazeaud, Denis** (eds.), Les clauses abusives entre professionnels, Paris 1998, **Nebbia, Paolisa**, Unfair Contract Terms in European Law. A Study in Comparative and EC Law, Oxford/Portland 2007, **Nieto Carol, Ubaldo**, Condiciones generales de la contración y cláusulas abusivas, Volladolid 2000, **Nobis, Steffi**, Mißbräuchliche Vertragsklauseln in Deutschland und Frankreich zur Umsetzung der Klauselrichtlinie 93/13/EWG des Rates, Baden-Baden 2005 **Pfeiffer, Thomas**, in: Eberhard Grabitz/Meinhard Hilf, Das Recht der Europäischen Union, Kommentar, Stand: Mai 1999, Band III, Sekundärrecht, A 5 Klauselrichtlinie, Vorbem. Rn.47 et seq., **Ribeiro, Joaquim de Sousa**, O Problema do Contrato: As Cláusulas Contratuais Gerais e o Principio da Liberdade Contratual, Coimbra 1999, **Sá Almeno de,** Cláusulas Contratuais Gerais e Directiva sobre Cláusulas Abusivas, Coimbra 2001, **Tilmann, Irene**, Die Klauselrichtlinie 93/13/EWG auf der Schnittstelle zwischen Privatrecht und öffentlichem Recht – eine rechtsvergleichende Untersuchung zum Europarecht, München 2003, **Wilhelmsson, Thomas**, Standardavtal, 2nd edition, Helsingfors 1995, **European Review of Private Law 5-2 (1997)** – Special Issue on the Transposition of the Unfair Terms Directive.

904 See the final report of the Law Commission and the Scottish Law Commission on unfair terms in contracts, LAW COM No. 292/SCOT LAW COM No. 199.

D. Timeshare Directive (94/47)

Drafted by Hans Schulte-Nölke, Andreas Börger and Sandra Fischer

Executive summary

1. Transposition deficiencies

Although Directive 94/47[905] has been transposed in all member states, analysis has revealed some transposition deficiencies with regard to details. The following examples could constitute a transposition deficiency of at least some importance:

- The information document does not have to contain information on the right of withdrawal in LITHUANIA.
- The information stated in lit. (j)[906] of the Annex is lacking in the transposition laws in the CZECH REPUBLIC and SLOVAKIA.
- No transposition of the language requirements of Art. 4 in LATVIA and LITHUANIA (only the national language).
- No language requirements for the information document, e.g. in the CZECH REPUBLIC and SLOVAKIA.
- 90 days withdrawal period (instead of three months plus 10 days) in LATVIA in case of lack of information (Art. 5, 2nd indent of the Directive).

2. Enhancement of protection

a. Extension of scope

Some national laws provide a wider scope of application in the field of timesharing, for example:

- Definition of "purchaser": inclusion of legal persons;
- Extension of the scope of application to contracts where timeshare rights are resold by another consumer through a professional agent;
- Definition of "contract relating directly or indirectly to the purchase of the right to use one or more immovable properties on a timeshare basis":
  - No minimum duration of three years;
  - No minimum duration for the annual use of the immovable property;
  - Inclusion of timeshare objects other than buildings (caravans, camping grounds);
- Extension of the scope of application to legal constructions which do not relate to a certain building or a group of specified buildings, but simply promise special rates on tourist services ("holiday clubs").

---

905 Directive 94/47/EC of the European Parliament and the Council of 26 October 1994 on the protection of purchasers in respect of certain aspects of contracts relating to the purchase of the right to use immovable properties on a timeshare basis, OJ L 280, 29 October 1994, p. 83.

906 A clause stating that acquisition will not result in costs, charges or obligations other than those specified in the contract.

b. Use of minimum clause

Most member states made use of the minimum clause. Major examples of such findings are:

- Additional requirements concerning the information document in Art. 3(1) (e.g. manifold additional information to be included, some taken from the Directive's Annex, others additionally introduced by member states).
- Additional information items to be included in the contract.
- Additional formal requirements for the information on the right of withdrawal (standard form, graphic accentuation, etc.).
- Prolongation of the regular withdrawal period.
- Extension of the list of information duties stated in Art. 5(1) 2nd indent (i.e. those information duties which lead to a prolongation of the withdrawal period, if infringed).
- Stricter language requirements
  - Also languages of EEA contracting states.
  - More languages than stated in the Directive.
- Additional right of withdrawal in situations other than those granted in the Directive, e.g. in case of non-delivery of the information document or non-compliance with the formal and language requirements, or even if the vendor has received any advance payments.
- No costs for exercising the right of withdrawal can be burdened on the consumer.
- More favourable provisions concerning the cancellation of related credit agreements.

c. Other instruments

Some member states have introduced protection instruments which are not stated in the Directive, e.g.

- Introduction of licensing procedures for vendors;
- Specific provisions for timeshare objects under construction;
- Requirement of a financial guarantee to be provided by the vendor securing the performance of the contract.

3. Use of options

- Article 4, 2nd indent, sent. 2 (language requirement of the member state where purchaser is resident): About half of the member states made use of this option.
- Introduction of formal requirement for the exercise of the right of withdrawal by consumers: About two thirds of the member states have made use of this option.

4. Inconsistencies or ambiguities

- It is unclear whether "in writing" means text on paper or also includes, e.g., electronic text on a durable medium.
- Different language versions of the Directive concerning the prohibition of advanced payment (the German version of the Directive refers to the regular withdrawal period of

10 days; other language versions might also refer to the prolonged withdrawal period in case of lack of information).

5. Potential barriers to (cross-border) trade

The following examples could be likely causes of barriers to trade in the European market:

- Additional elements to be included in the brochure (Art. 3(2)) or the contract (Art. 4(2)) diverging within the different member states.
- Different beginnings, lengths and computation methods of withdrawal periods and formal requirements for exercising the right of withdrawal (also influencing the duty to inform consumers of their right of withdrawal).

6. Conclusions and recommendations

In order to remove ambiguities, incoherencies or barriers to trade, the following issues could be considered:

- Definition of 'consumer': adaptation to a coherent definition in EC consumer law;
- Definition of 'vendor': adaptation to a coherent definition of 'business' in EC contract law;
- Extension of the scope of application to contracts where timeshare rights are resold by another consumer through a professional agent;
- Dropping or lowering the requirements of the minimum duration of three years and the minimum annual period of 7 days;
- Inclusion of timeshare objects other than buildings, for example, camping grounds, caravans, boats, mobile homes and other movables, which can be used for the purpose of accommodation;
- Inclusion of holiday clubs;
- Reducing the detailed lists of information to be provided by using a general clause with an indicative list of core information, in particular, on costs, including maintenance;
- Provision of a standard form for information on the withdrawal right;
- Clarification of whether "in writing" means text on paper or also includes, e.g., electronic text on a durable medium;
- Provision of some rules on computation of the withdrawal period (or – perhaps better – a reference to Regulation 1182/71)[907];
- Prolongation of the regular withdrawal period to 14 days (perhaps considering a longer period for up to three months or at least leaving it to the member states' discretion to fix a longer period);
- Prohibition of any formal requirement for the exercise of the withdrawal right;
- Clarification in Art. 5(1) 2nd indent, that the information must be provided in writing;
- Clarification of whether the dispatch rule is also applicable when the consumer dispatches the declaration of withdrawal in time, but it does not reach the vendor;
- Introduction of a prolonged period of one year (instead of three months plus 10 days) in case information duties are not fulfilled;

---

907 Regulation (EEC, Euratom) No 1182/71 of the Council of 3 June 1971 determining the rules applicable to periods, dates and time limits, OJ L 124 of 8 June 1971, 1-2.

- Clarification of whether the prohibition of advance payments is only applicable during the regular withdrawal period (10 days) or also during the prolonged period;
- Prescription of highly effective sanctions in order to enforce the prohibition of advance payments (penalties) on Community level;
- In the case the planned Rome I Regulation deals with the issue, Art. 9 could be deleted.

In order to ensure that the member states can no longer introduce or maintain additional protection instruments and thereby create barriers to trade, full harmonisation in the most sensitive areas could be considered, e.g. pre-contractual information duties, in particular with regard to the prospectus and information about the withdrawal right.

I. Member state legislation prior to the adoption of the Timeshare Directive

Before Directive 94/47 was transposed, there were no specific provisions on timeshare contracts in most of the member states' laws. Some basic protection of purchasers of timeshare rights was provided, primarily by general contract law and laws on unfair competition. Therefore, in the field of timeshare contracts, mainly general contract law applied, e.g. in AUSTRIA[908], BELGIUM[909], CYPRUS[910], DENMARK[911], ITALY[912], the NETHERLANDS[913], POLAND[914], SLOVAKIA[915] and SPAIN[916].

In GERMANY[917] and PORTUGAL[918], consumers were protected by the general regulations of good faith and wilful deceit and by the rules concerning the review of standard business

---

908 Offence against public policy (*Sittenwidrigkeitsregel*) CC § 879(1); rescission of the contract because of error CC § 871 et seq.; in case of doorstep selling: rights provided in KSchG (Consumer Protection Act) § 3 and § 4.

909 General rules of contract law and the law of property in the Belgian CC applied.

910 Contract Law, Cap 149. The Hotel and Tourist Dwellings Law of 1969 (revoked in 2000) dealt with the licensing of immovable property intended to be used for residential purposes.

911 General clause of the Contract Act (principle of reasonableness or fair conduct). In addition, the general clause of the Marketing Practices Act (principle of good marketing practice) applied.

912 CC. Drafts of a ministerial commission in 1989 and a parliamentary bill of 1987 on the topic of timeshares have never been enacted.

913 E.g. general principle of good faith, CC Art. 6:2 and 6:248.

914 General principles of the law of contract as regulated in the CC.

915 CC.

916 Application of Law 26/1984 of July 19 on Consumer Protection and the common law rules of the Spanish CC with respect to contracts (mainly vices of consent and actions of nullity and termination); norms on information in cases of sale and lease of immovable goods (Royal Decree 515/1989).

In some cases, Spanish courts drew on the rules of the Directive before its transposition into national law for an interpretation in conformity with the Directive (e.g. Judgments of CA Castellón of 4 May 2001. *Fernando R. M. and Jacinta F. P. v "Mundivac, S. A."* and *"Aqualandia S. A."*, CA Valencia of 16 July 2001, *Hermann T. and Imgard T. v "Oliva Beach Title Limited", "Amapola Holiday Marketing Ltd."*).

917 E.g. CC § 134, § 138; § 123, § 142. Review of contract terms according to the Act concerning the Regulation of Standard Business Terms.

terms and conditions if the vendor made use of these. In HUNGARY[919], some regulations of competition acts were applicable. Various member states, having recently joined the European Union, for example, ESTONIA[920], HUNGARY[921], LATVIA[922], LITHUANIA[923] and SLOVENIA[924], had Consumer Protection Acts partially applying to timeshare contracts.

PORTUGAL[925] and SPAIN[926] had additional specific rules on timesharing with, in the latter case, the regional administrative rules of the Autonomous Communities Canary and Balearic Islands. A FRENCH law from 1986[927] regulated the functioning of the timeshare companies rather than protecting the consumers. Nevertheless, it obliged the seller to provide the purchaser of the immovable property with a description of the immovable property including the various parts of the building, information on the period within which the right that was the subject of the contract may have been exercised and information on the conditions of the use of the common facilities. In the UNITED KINGDOM, the Timeshare Act 1992[928] existed, which remains in force supported by the introduction of statutory instruments.[929]

---

918 Decree-Law 275/93 of August 5. It also applied the 1966 Civil Code rules on good faith (e.g. 227 – pre-negotiation duty of care) and the unfair terms legislation.

919 Competition Act. The public administrative body (Hungarian Competition Authority) has been dealing with several complaints regarding this area of law, where case handlers have been applying the relevant section of the Competition Act (Act LVII of 1996 on the Prohibition of Unfair and Restrictive Market Practices).

920 The Consumer Protection Act (in force since 1 February 1994) contained general provisions concerning responsibilities and restrictions of the seller.

921 Act CLV of 1997 on Consumer Protection. The public administrative body, responsible for the enforcement on deceptive practices, namely the Hungarian Competition Authority has been dealing with several complaints regarding this area of law, where case handlers have been applying the relevant section of the Competition Act.

922 Consumer Rights Protection Law.

923 Law on consumer protection.

924 The Consumer Protection Act of 26 February 1998. The Act (prior to its amendment according to the Directive) already included two provisions regulating the field of the Directive, however, only regarding the substance of the contract and withdrawal from it.

925 Decree-Laws: 130/89 of 18 April 1989 regulating some contractual forms of "timeshare" and 275/93 of 5 August 1993 regulating timeshares.

926 Related to the requisites of the commercial activity and insurance duties. With regard to civil aspects, the norms only refer to some advertising rules. Order of 25 August 1988, Law 7/1995 on Tourism in Canary Islands (Art. 46), Decree 272/1997 of November 27 on timesharing, Order of 15 January 1990 and Decree of 6 September 1997.

927 Loi du 6 janvier 1986 relative aux sociétés d'attribution d'immeubles en jouissance partagée.

928 In force since 12 October 1992.

929 Timeshare (Cancellation Notices) Order 1992, SI 1992/1942, regulating the requirements of appearance and content of a cancellation notice to be given to consumers; Timeshare (Repayment of Credit on Cancellation) Order 1992, SI 1992/1943, regulating the form that can be used to request the repayment of credit following notice of cancellation; Timeshare (Cancellation Information) Order 2003 regulating additional cancellation rights introduced as a result of the implementation of the Timeshare Directive.

II. Scope of application

1. Personal scope

a. Purchaser

Directive 94/47 protects the purchaser of timeshare rights (rights to use immovable properties on a timeshare basis). A purchaser is defined by the Directive as "any natural person who, acting in transactions covered by this Directive, for purposes which may be regarded as being out of his professional capacity, has the right which is the subject of the contract transferred to him or for whom the right which is the subject of the contract is established".

aa. Transposition technique

Nearly half of the member states have introduced a special definition in the field of timeshare (e.g. BELGIUM[930], GREECE[931], ITALY[932] and SWEDEN[933]) whereas about the same number of member states made reference to a general consumer definition (e.g. the CZECH REPUBLIC[934], FINLAND[935], GERMANY, HUNGARY[936], LATVIA[937] and PORTUGAL[938]).

No legal definition exists in FRANCE, SPAIN and the UNITED KINGDOM. French legislation uses the notion of consumer („consommateur"[939]), which is not defined by statutory provisions, but frequently used in French consumer law. Spanish law does not provide an express transposition. However, in the Law 42/1998, different terms such as "titleholder of the right"[940], the "final consumer"[941] and "purchaser"[942] are used synonymously but not clarified further. Spanish caselaw has considered the purchaser of timeshare rights as a "consumer" in the sense of general legislation, and, therefore, deems applicable the Law 26/1984 of July 19 on Consumer Protection. In the United Kingdom, the person acquiring timeshare rights is introduced as the "offeree", i.e. the "person on whom timeshare rights are conferred, or purport to be conferred". Some provisions of the Timeshare Act only apply when the "offeree" is an individual not acting in the course of a business.[943]

---

930 Article 2(5) of the Act of 11 April 1999 on the Purchase of the Right to Use Immovable Properties on a Timeshare Basis.

931 Article 2(1)(d) of the Decree 182/1999.

932 Article 69(1)(b) of the Consumer Code uses the term "consumer" in the definition of the purchaser.

933 Section 2, 1st indent of the Timeshare Contracts (Consumer Protection) Act 1997:218.

934 CC Art. 52(3)

935 Chapter 1 sec. 4 of the Consumer Protection Act of 20 January 1978/38.

936 CC Art. 685(d).

937 Article 1(3) of the Consumer Rights Protection Law.

938 CC Art. 874, Art. 2(1) of the Consumer Protection Act 24/96 of July 31.

939 Code de la Consommation, Art. L. 121-60(1).

940 Article 1(1), Art. 15-16 of the Law 42/1998.

941 Article 1(4) of the Law 42/1998.

942 Article 9(1)(9)(c), Art. 10-13 of the Law 42/1998.

943 E.g. sec. 1A(4) of the Timeshare Act 1992.

Table: Transposition technique

Specific definition	BE, CY, DK, EL, IE, IT, LU, MT, NL, PL, SE *(11)*
Reference to a general consumer definition	AT, CZ, DE, EE, FI, HU, LV, LT, PT, SK, SL *(11)*
No legal definition	ES, FR, UK *(3)*

Within the member states providing a definition, most have chosen to make use of the term 'consumer' whereas only some rest with the term 'purchaser' of the Directive. In MALTESE legislation, the notion of 'buyer' is recognised. In DENMARK, LUXEMBOURG, the NETHERLANDS and SWEDEN, a special definition for purposes of timeshare provisions exists, however, using the term 'consumer'. Thus, confusion is likely to emerge as to other 'common' definitions of 'consumer' in different fields of consumer law.

Table: Use of terms

Purchaser	BE, CY, EL, ES*, IE, IT, NL, PL *(8)*
Consumer	AT, CZ, DE, DK, EE, ES*, FI, FR, HU, LT, LU, LV, PT, SE, SK, SL *(16)*
Buyer	MT *(1)*
Offeree	UK *(1)*

* *more than once*

The transposition throughout the member states shows that nearly half of the national legislators opt for the solution of providing one general consumer definition, applicable in the field of consumer law. A general notion of 'consumer' on the level of Community law would allow for this development and not only contribute to greater legal certainty but also to a coherent use of terminology.

bb. Content of the definitions

As prescribed in Directive 94/47, the vast number of transposition laws limits the scope of application to natural persons not acting within their professional capacity. Some national legislators have extended it to legal persons as well, provided that they do not act in their professional capacity. Among them, AUSTRIA, HUNGARY and LATVIA resort to general consumer definitions. In SPAIN, despite lacking legislative transposition, the preponderant opinion in doctrine seems to also extend the scope of application to legal persons.

While the DUTCH definition of 'purchaser' applies – according to its wording – only to natural persons, it could possibly be applied per analogy to small businesses by case-law. In Dutch case-law, some examples of analogous application of comparable consumer protection measures exist, such as protection against unfair contract terms.

In GREECE, the definition of the purchaser includes all natural persons, regardless of whether they act in their professional capacity or not. This extension of the scope may be unintended by the legislator as it seems unreasonable to exclude legal persons from the scope of application but to include natural persons acting in their professional capacity.

Under GERMAN law, companies coming into existence without further requirements if two or more persons pursue a common purpose[944], are not treated as legal persons[945] and may thus profit from the provisions of Directive 94/47 provided they do not act in their professional capacity.

Table: Content of the definitions

Limitation to natural persons	BE, CY, DE, EE, EL, FI, IE, IT, LT, LU, LV, MT, NL, PL, SE, SL *(16)*
Natural and legal persons	AT, CZ, DK, ES, FR, HU, PT, SK *(8)*
No requirement of acting within professional capacity	EL *(1)*

b. Vendor

The notion of 'vendor' in Directive 94/47 is defined as "any natural or legal person who, acting in transactions covered by this Directive and in his professional capacity, establishes, transfers or undertakes to transfer the right which is the subject of the contract". Again, similar to the definition of 'purchaser', more or less half of the member states have inserted a special definition of 'vendor' in the course of transposing the Directive (e.g. CYPRUS[946], DENMARK[947] and MALTA[948]). In contrast, a little less than the other half resort to a general definition (e.g. AUSTRIA[949], LATVIA[950], POLAND[951] and SLOVAKIA[952]).

Table: Legislative techniques

Special definition	BE, CY, DK, EE, EL, ES, HU, IE, IT, LU, MT, NL[953], SE *(13)*
Reference to a more general definition	AT, CZ, DE, FI, LT, LV, PL, PT, SK, SL *(10)*
No legal definition	FR, UK *(2)*

Most of the member states with a general definition do not, in consequence, make use of the term 'vendor' but rather employ the terms of 'professional' (e.g. POLAND), 'seller' (e.g.

944 «Gesellschaft bürgerlichen Rechts» CC § 705 et seq.

945 BGH judgment of 23 October 2001, XI ZR 63/01, NJW 2002, 368.

946 Article 2 of the Timeshare Contract Law of 2001, L.113(I)/2001.

947 Section 3(1), sent. 1 of the Act 234 of 2 April 1997 on Consumer Contracts Relating to the Purchase of the Right of Use to Real Estate on Timeshare Basis (the Timeshare Act).

948 Article 2(1) of the Protection of Buyers in Contracts for Timesharing of Immovable Property Regulations 2000.

949 § 1(1) of the Timeshare Act.

950 Article 1(1) sec. 5 of the Consumer Rights Protection Law.

951 Article 4(1) of the Act on the Freedom of Economic Activity.

952 CC sec. 52(2) and sec. 55(1), sent. 1.

953 The definition of vendor is partly included into the definition of timeshare contract. Dutch CC 7:48a defines a contract of sale within the scope of chapter 7.1.10A as "any contract or group of contracts, concluded for the duration of at least three years, to the effect that one party – the vendor – shall, for the payment of a price, give or undertake to give to the other party – the purchaser – a right *ad rem* or a right *ad personam* to the use of one or more immovable properties, or parts thereof, for at least one week during each year."

MALTA) or 'entrepreneur' (e.g. GERMANY). FRENCH legislation does not provide a special definition but mentions the term 'professional'[954] which is neither concretised by statutory provisions nor seemingly specified by case-law. Moreover, in the UNITED KINGDOM, reference is made to a "person who proposes in the course of a business to enter into a timeshare agreement ... as offeror", sometimes abbreviated as "operator". SPANISH law provides a similar content of the definition, but using different terminology, such as "owner", "developer" (promoter) or "any natural or legal person who participates professionally in the transmission or commercialisation of rights to use on a timesharing basis".[955] Under PORTUGUESE law, rights may be exercised against the 'vendor' or the 'owner' of timeshare rights.

Table: Use of terms

Vendor	BE, CY, DK, EE, EL, HU, IE, IT, LU, NL, PT*, SK *(12)*
Professional	FR, SE *(2)*
Trader	FI, PL, *(2)*
Undertaking	SL *(1)*
Offeror/operator	UK *(1)*
Seller	MT, LT, LV *(3)*
Supplier/entrepreneur	AT, CZ, DE *(3)*
Others	ES, PT* *(2)*

* *more than once*

Generally, the personal scope of the national provisions, as regards the counterpart of the consumer, is in accordance with the provisions of the Directive.

Under LATVIAN[956] and LITHUANIAN[957] law, the definitions of 'seller' include persons "selling or offering goods" which does not directly match to the field of timeshare, as here the seller may assign rights to immovable property.

Some countries, however, have extended the scope of application to contracts where timeshare rights are resold by another consumer through a professional agent (DENMARK[958], ITALY[959], PORTUGAL). Italy[960] and Portugal have consequently extended the purchaser's rights and allow an exercise of all rights against professional agents who conclude a timeshare contract on behalf of a non-professional. The GERMAN statutory provisions on timeshare contracts do not extend the scope in such a way. However, it is being discussed whether a consumer who establishes or transfers a timeshare right to another consumer can be treated as a vendor if he makes use of an agent who acts in his professional capacity (e.g. a broker). In legal literature, it is argued that the party acquiring the timeshare right should be granted a right of withdrawal which can be exercised against the person (consumer) who establishes or

954 Code de la Consommation, Art. L. 121-60(1).

955 Article 1(5) of the Law 42/1998.

956 Article 1(5) of the Consumer Rights Protection Law.

957 Article 2(2) of the Law on Consumer Protection.

958 Article 3(2) of the Timeshare Act.

959 Article 70(2) of the Consumer Code.

960 Article 69(1)(c) of the Consumer Code.

transfers the right (not the agent).[961] In IRELAND, the regulations impose obligations on vendors which would, according to the law of agency, include both the vendor himself and his agent.

Following such models, tackling the phenomenon of consumers reselling their timeshare rights with the aid of professional agents or resale companies on a European level in order to grant a certain consumer protection against the selling methods of these agents, which are often identical to timeshare companies could be considered. In this context, extending the application of the Directive's regulations to such cases could be considered, however, without fully neglecting the protection of the selling consumer. A possible solution for the conflicting consumer interests might be to only impose sanctions, like penalties, on the (professional) agent or resale agency, and to allow the purchaser a right of withdrawal against the consumer who sells the timeshare right.

2. Situations falling in the scope

a. Contracts

According to Art. 2, 1st indent of Directive 94/47 a 'contract relating directly or indirectly to the purchase of the right to use one or more immovable properties on a timeshare basis`, hereinafter referred to as 'contract`, shall mean any contract or group of contracts concluded for at least three years under which, directly or indirectly, on payment of a certain global price, a real property right or any other right relating to the use of one or more immovable properties for a specified or specifiable period of the year, which may not be less than one week, is established or is the subject of a transfer or an undertaking to transfer.

It should be borne in mind that this bulky definition intends to cover a broad variety of rights allowing the rotating use of immovable property (including connected services) for the purpose of accommodation. The reason is that member states have developed very different legal constructions to allow for timeshare rights, namely real property rights (shared rights *in rem*), but also personal rights arising from various legal grounds (e.g. tenancy, partnership in a civil law association or shareholder of a company) and different sorts of trusts.

Some member states, namely IRELAND, ITALY and MALTA have literally adopted the definition of timeshare contracts given in the Directive. The definition is substantially in line with the Directive in GREECE[962], SLOVENIA[963] and the NETHERLANDS[964].

In several member states, contracts, which grant an annual use of the property for less than one week, are also included into the scope. In BELGIUM[965], the minimum duration of use

961 *Martinek*, in: Staudinger, Teilzeit-Wohnrechtegesetz, § 1 no. 19; *Saenger*, in: Erman, BGB I, § 485 no. 3.

962 Article 2(1)(a) Decree No 182/1999: GREECE has omitted "real property".

963 Article 59(1) of the Consumer Protection Act.

964 CC Art. 48a(a).

965 Article 2(1), sent. 1 of the Act of 11 April 1999 on the Purchase of the Right to Use Immovable Properties on a Timeshare Basis.

must be two days. In AUSTRIA[966], CYPRUS[967], the CZECH REPUBLIC[968], ESTONIA[969], FINLAND[970], FRANCE[971], GERMANY[972], HUNGARY[973], LUXEMBOURG[974], POLAND[975], SWEDEN[976] and the UNITED KINGDOM, there is no minimum duration for the annual use of the building at all.

In PORTUGAL, the definition of timeshare right prescribes that the period of time in which such a right can be established may vary from 7 days to 30 days per year. As a consequence, it is not possible for the parties to create a timeshare right in Portugal with an annual use of more than 30 days. The purchaser seems to be then protected insofar as he is not obliged by such an agreement due to invalidity. Furthermore, the timeshare right in Portugal is perpetual but a limit of no less than 15 years can be fixed.[977]

Spanish law only differs on one essential point: it establishes two ways of creating the right: a right *in rem*, or as rent of a house for some seasons under some special conditions.[978]

Several member states have not transposed the minimum duration of the contract of three years, which is provided by the Directive. In CYPRUS, FINLAND and HUNGARY, there is no minimum duration of the contract at all. In BELGIUM, the scope includes contracts of duration of more than one year and also contracts with duration of one year or less if they contain a taciturn prolongation.[979] In LUXEMBOURG[980], a contract with a duration of less than three years is included if it contains a clause which determines a taciturn extension and / or the conditions for an extension of the contract. SPAIN and PORTUGAL have laid down provisions that the owner of the immovable property has to reserve a period of at least seven days per year for repairs, maintenance and cleaning.

In the definitions of timeshare contracts in the transposition laws of the CZECH REPUBLIC, DENMARK, FINLAND, LATVIA, LITHUANIA, SLOVAKIA[981] and SWEDEN, there is no requirement of a global price.

---

966 § 1(1), § 2 (1) of the Timeshare Act.

967 Article 2, 9th indent of the Timeshare Contract Law of 2001, L.113(I)/2001.

968 CC § 58(1), at least once a year .

969 Article 379(1) of the Law of Obligations Act.

970 Chapter 10 § 1 of the Consumer Protection Act of 20 January 1978/38.

971 Code de la Consommation, Art. L.121-60.

972 CC § 481(1).

973 § 2(a) of the Government Decree 20/1999 (II. 5.) on Contracts for the Purchase of the Right to Use Immovable Property on a Timeshare Basis.

974 Article 1(1) of the Timeshare Act of 18 December 1998.

975 Article 1(1)) of the Act of 13 July 2000 on the Protection of Purchasers in Respect of the Right to Use Buildings or Dwellings During Certain Time Each Year.

976 Article 1(1) of the Timeshare Contracts (Consumer Protection) Act 1997:218.

977 Article 3(1) of the Decree-Law 180/99.

978 Article 1(6) of the Law 42/1998; the latter for a period of at least three and up to a maximum of 50 years.

979 Article 2(1), sent. 2 of the Act of 11 April 1999 on the Purchase of the Right to Use Immovable Properties on a Timeshare Basis.

980 Article 1(1), sent. 2 of the Timeshare Act of 18 December 1998.

981 CC §55(1), sent. 1, sent. 2, 1st part.

Contracts falling in the scope	Member States
Literally adopted	IE, IT, MT *(3)*
Substantially equivalent as in the Directive	EL, NL, SL *(3)*
Deviations concerning:	
• Shorter or no period of use of property per year	AT, BE, CY, CZ, DK, DE, EE, FI, FR, HU, LU, PL, SE, UK *(14)*
• Shorter or no minimum duration of the contract	BE, CY, FI, HU, LU *(5)*
• No need for global price	CZ, DK, ES, FI, LT, LV, SE, SK *(8)*

In order to prevent escaping from the Directive by offering contracts with a duration of less than 36 months or with an annual period shorter than seven days, following the model of several member states and dropping, or lowering, the requirements of the minimum duration of three years and the minimum annual period of seven days could be considered. However, such an amendment must avoid simple rental agreements (in particular if repeatedly concluded in advance) falling under the definition.

b. Immovable property

Directive 94/47 defines the notion of immovable property as "any building or part of a building for use as accommodation to which the right which is the subject of the contract relates". This definition of immovable property has been literally transposed in CYPRUS, IRELAND, MALTA and LUXEMBOURG. It is transposed closely to the Directive in AUSTRIA, ESTONIA, ITALY[982] and SPAIN.

The BELGIAN[983] definition only mentions buildings for accommodation, but leaves out "part of a building". In the CZECH REPUBLIC[984] and SLOVAKIA, the term "immovable property or part thereof" is defined as a building intended for habitation and accommodation. FINLAND has two definitions, firstly "timeshare housing", being a building or an apartment whose possession rotates among shares at defined or definable intervals, and, secondly, the "timeshare object", defined as an entity comprising timeshare housing and the common rooms available to the shareholders, as well as the services connected to it.

The PORTUGUESE[985] legislator has created the term "accommodation units", which are parts of apartment hotels, holiday resorts or holiday apartments. Moreover, the Portuguese transposition law contains a specific chapter on "holiday accommodation systems", defined as accommodation rights in holiday developments which do not constitute timeshare rights, and contracts under which, by means of an advance payment, such accommodation rights are transferred. Thus, the aforementioned chapter broadens the scope of application to rights not covered by the Directive in order to make some of the protective instruments of the Directive also applicable to such rights.[986]

---

982 Article 69(1)(d) of the Consumer Code ("immovable property shall mean any building, also used as a hotel ...").

983 Article 2(3) of the Act of 11 April 1999 on the Purchase of the Right to Use Immovable Properties on a Timeshare Basis.

984 CC § 59(2).

985 Article 1 of the Decree-Law 275/93 of August 5.

986 Article 45 of the Decree 180/99 of May 22.

In several member states, there is no specific legislative transposition of immovable property. In DENMARK, FRANCE, GERMANY, HUNGARY, LITHUANIA[987] and the NETHERLANDS[988], the general definitions of immovable property are used. In the UNITED KINGDOM, there is no specific transposition of the definition of immovable property. As the British definition of the contract is based on the term of "timeshare accommodation" the content of the Directive's definition can partly be found in the British definition of accommodation, which means accommodation in a building or – insofar going beyond the Directive – in a caravan. In SLOVENIA[989] the immovable property can be land, a building, a part of a building or a piece of land and must be destined for use as accommodation constantly or temporarily and be in legal commerce according to the law of the country where it lies. The mentioning of "land" could be interpreted as an inclusion of, for instance, camping grounds. If this understanding is correct, the Slovenian law goes beyond the Directive which is only applicable to buildings.

Table: Notion of immovable property

Literally transposed	CY, IE, LU, MT *(4)*
Substantially equivalent as in the Directive	AT, EE, ES, IT *(4)*
Small deviations	BE, CZ, EL, FI, SK *(5)*
Inclusion of obligatory holiday accommodation rights ('holiday clubs')	PT *(1)*
Inclusion of caravans, camping grounds	SL, UK *(2)*
No specific legislative transposition, but general definitions or concepts used	DK, DE, FR, HU, LT, LV, NL, PL, SE *(9)*
No restriction of accommodation	EE *(1)*

The definitions of "contract" and "immovable property" provided by the Directive in principle seem to cover perfectly not only an *ius in rem*, but also the personal rights and trust constructions, as long as the right in question relates closely to a certain building or to a specified group of buildings, in the latter case combined with an exchange or point system. Only very few member states have extended their definitions to objects other than buildings, e.g., caravans or camping grounds. Nevertheless, including camping grounds, caravans, boats mobile homes and other movables, which can be used for the purpose of accommodation could be considered.

Other legal constructions which do not give rights to repeatedly use a certain building or a group of specified buildings, but simply promise special rates on tourist services ('travel discount clubs') do not fall under the definition of the Directive. Seemingly only one member state, PORTUGAL, has broadened its transposition of the Directive to such timeshare-like constructions.

---

987 Article 4.2(2) of the Civil Code.

988 CC Book 3 Art. 3, Book 7 Art. 48a(a).

989 Article 59(2) of the Consumer Protection Act. The Slovenian definition of the Directive's "immovable property" is not clear, but since the title already includes the words "dwelling building" and since, according to Slovenian law a building is only a part/a component of land (land is immovable and a building on it is its part), it can nevertheless be deduced that the definition is in accordance with the Directive.

III. Consumer protection instruments

1. Information duties, Art. 3

a. Information document (prospectus)

According to Art. 3 of the Directive, the vendor must be required to provide any person requesting information with a document, which contains a general description of the immovable property along with at least brief and accurate information on certain details listed in the Annex[990] of the Directive, and on how further information may be obtained.

All member states have used the list of information duties provided in Art. 3 of the Directive as a model for their transposition legislation and have created a similar list. Some member states (e.g. CYPRUS, DENMARK, GREECE, IRELAND, MALTA, the NETHERLANDS[991] and the UNITED KINGDOM) have used the same technique as in the Directive by implementing an annex containing all the information obligatory for both, the information document and the contract. These member states refer to the Annex when laying down the obligatory details for the information document and the contract. The other member states have split up the information for the information document and the contract by using two different lists of information duties for the contract and the information document, e.g. ESTONIA, GERMANY, ITALY.

Many member states have added further information obligatory for the prospectus. Such additional information has been partially taken from the list in the Annex of the Directive (i.e. the items from the list that are to be included in the contract under Art. 4, but not in the prospectus under Art. 3 like lit. (h) or lit. (k)). In CYPRUS[992] and in the NETHERLANDS[993], the information to be provided in the prospectus is the same as the information in the contract document. The following table shows which additional information duties the other member states have stated for the prospectus:

Additional information duty	Member States
Lit. (h) of the annex of the Directive[994]	CZ, EE (partially), LT *(3)*
Lit. (k) of the annex of the Directive[995]	AT, BE, CZ, DE, EE, ES, FI, HU, LU, PL, SE, SK, SL *(13)*

990 Litera (a), (g), (i) and (l) of the Annex.

991 A separate decree: Decree of 25 June 1997 containing rules concerning information that sellers of timeshare rights must mention in the contract in the interest of the buyer.

992 Annex I of the Timeshare Contract Law of 2001, L.113(I)/2001.

993 In Dutch law, the vendor has to provide any person requesting information a draft of the purchase contract, cf. CC Book 7, Art. 48f.

994 Litera (h): The exact period within which the right which is the subject of the contract may be exercised and, if necessary, its duration; the date on which the purchaser may start to exercise the contractual right.

995 Litera (k): Whether or not it is possible to join a scheme for the exchange or resale of the contractual rights, and any costs involved should an exchange and/or resale scheme be organised by the vendor or by a third party designated by him in the contract.

Additional information duty	Member States
Information on whether the consumer becomes the owner of the building or not	EE, DE, HU *(3)*
Information on the prohibition of advanced payments	HU, SE *(2)*
Information on the distance to the next means of transport	DK *(1)*
Information that the written information shall become part of the contract	HU *(1)*
Information that joining an exchange system does not guarantee that an exchange can be realised	BE, LU *(2)*
Information on the payment method	CZ, SK *(2)*

The transposition in LITHUANIA, where the information document does not have to contain information on the right of withdrawal, is rather problematic. FRENCH law refers only to the information the offer has to contain but does not regulate anything about a possible prospectus.[996] The reason seems to be that under French law a prospectus would be considered as an offer anyway.

aa. Information provided in the information document (prospectus) forms an integral part of the contract

Article 3(2), sent. 1 of the Directive states that the information provided in the information document forms an integral part of the contract. Except for FRANCE, all the member states have transposed this rule according to the Directive. In France, there has not been a specific legislative transposition of Art. 3(2), sent. 1 of Directive 94/47, but because of general rules a written offer as the information document becomes part of the contract. Therefore, the effect that Art. 3(2), sent. 1 is supposed to achieve is reached in France as well.

	Member States
As in the Directive	AT, BE, CY, CZ, DK, DE, EE, EL, ES, FI, HU, IE, IT, LT, LU, LV, MT, NL, PL, PT, SE, SK, SL, UK *(24)*
Variations	FR *(1)*

bb. Changes resulting from circumstances beyond the vendor's control

Article 3(2), sent. 2, sent. 3 and sent. 4 of the Directive state that, unless the parties expressly agree otherwise, only changes resulting from circumstances beyond the vendor's control may be made to the information provided in the information document. Any changes to that information shall be communicated to the purchaser before the contract is concluded. The contract shall expressly mention any such changes.

More than half of the member states have transposed the rule similarly to the Directive. Additionally, in AUSTRIA and LITHUANIA, no specific transposition measure was used, but general law principles apply and cover this gap. Therefore, the same result is reached as if Art. 3(2), sent 1, sent. 2 and sent. 3 of the Directive were legislatively implemented. Nevertheless, it is questionable whether this way of transposition complies with the requirements

[996] Consumer Protection Act, Art. L.121-61.

of the ECJ rulings in the cases C-144/99 – *Commission v Netherlands* and C-478/99 – *Commission v Sweden*. According to these rulings, it is essential that the legal situation resulting from national implementing measures is sufficiently precise and clear and that individuals (also from other member states) are made fully aware of their rights so that, where appropriate, they may rely on them before the national courts.

The transposition laws of several countries vary from the rule laid down in the Directive. In the CZECH REPUBLIC, POLAND, SLOVENIA and the UNITED KINGDOM, the vendor is obliged to inform the consumer about the changes in writing. In SLOVAKIA and the Czech Republic, the consumer has to be informed of any changes at least 10 days before the conclusion of the contract. Also the FINNISH law is stricter than the Directive, as it does not only set the requirement that the changes were outside the vendor's scope of control, but in addition to that, the vendor must not have been able to reasonably foresee the changes.

In AUSTRIA[997], the contract may only deviate from the information document if the consumer and the vendor expressly agree upon it. There is no requirement that the changes result from circumstances beyond the vendor's control. The situation is similar in ESTONIA and GERMANY, where the transposition laws also do not fully comply with the Directive since they do not require that the changes must result from circumstances beyond the vendor's control. On the contrary, in POLAND[998], the document may only be changed if the amendment results from circumstances beyond the trader's control. Due to the estimation that the parties are not in an equal position, the document may not be changed just by the agreement of the parties.

Moreover, in the CZECH REPUBLIC, GERMANY, SLOVAKIA, SLOVENIA, POLAND and SPAIN, there is no rule that the deviation from the information document has to be expressly mentioned in the contract. FRANCE did not transpose Art. 3(2), sent. 2, sent. 3 and sent. 4 at all.

	Member States
As in the Directive	BE, CY, DK, EL, HU, IE, IT, LU, LV, MT, NL, PT, SE *(13)*
Variations	AT, CZ, DE, EE, ES, FI, LT, PL, SK, SL, UK *(11)*
Not transposed	FR *(1)*

cc. Advertising shall indicate the possibility of obtaining the information document

All member states seem to have transposed the obligation stated in Art. 3(3) of Directive 94/47 that advertising shall indicate the possibility of obtaining the information document referred to in Art. 3(1) of the Directive. The SPANISH provisions[999] refer to the duty of the vendor to inform the purchaser of how to obtain general information on rights and to inform the purchaser on organisations and professionals that may help him (instead of how to achieve the document).

---

997 § 4(2) of the Timeshare Act.

998 Article 3(2) of the Act of 13 July 2000 on the Protection of Purchasers in Respect of the Right to Use Buildings or Dwellings During Certain Times Each Year.

999 Mainly Art. 8(3) of the Law 42/1998.

Advertising	Member States
As in the Directive	AT, BE, CY, CZ, DE, DK, EE, EL, FI, FR, HU, IE, IT, LT, LU, LV, MT, NL, PL, PT, SE, SK, SL, UK *(24)*
Variations	ES *(1)*

It has been criticised that the Directive does not regulate the time when the document should be given to a possible purchaser.[1000] As a consequence, it might happen that the consumer does not receive the information document far enough in advance of signing the contract, so that he cannot take note of the information. This could be avoided by inserting a provision similar to Art. 4(1) of Directive 97/7[1001] ("in good time prior to the conclusion of any contract"), perhaps clarified along the model of Directive 2002/65.[1002]

b. Information duties in the contract

Article 4 , 1st indent of Directive 94/47 states that the contract must include the items referred to in the Annex. Again, the vast majority of member states has transposed this provision closely to the Directive. GREECE, MALTA, the NETHERLANDS, IRELAND and the UNITED KINGDOM have used the copy and paste method. Member states, e.g., FINLAND, GERMANY, ITALY, LATVIA, POLAND and SLOVENIA have transposed this provision and the items listed in the Annex with some slight variations in the wording.

Some member states have stated – besides the information provided in the Annex of the Directive – additional information duties which have to be part of the contract. This additional information is often the same as that which these member states already regulate in the provisions for the information document according to Art. 3(1) of the Directive (cf. above under III.1.a.). The following chart gives a short overview on some of these additional information duties:

Additional information duty to be included in the contract	Member States
Information on whether the consumer becomes the owner of the building or not	EE, DE, HU *(3)*
Information on the prohibition of advanced payments	HU *(1)*
Information on the distance to the next means of transport	DK *(1)*
Information that the written information shall become part of the contract	HU *(1)*
Information that joining an exchange system does not guarantee that an exchange can be realised	BE, LU, PT[1003] *(3)*
Information on the payment method	CZ, SK *(2)*

1000 *Howells/Wilhelmsson*, EC Consumer Contract Law, 252.

1001 Directive 97/7/EC of the European Parliament and of the Council of 20 May 1997 on the protection of consumers in respect of distance contracts; OJ L144 of 4 June 1997, 19-27.

1002 Directive 2002/65/EC of the European Parliament and of the Council of 23 September 2002 concerning the distance marketing of consumer financial services and amending Council Directive 90/619/EEC and Directives 97/7/EC and 98/27/EC; OJ L 271 of 9 October 2002, 16-24.

1003 Article 11(2)(g) of the Decree-Law 180/99.

Further additional information duties are only regulated with regard to the contract. For instance, the AUSTRIAN[1004] provisions concerning the list of information that has to be given, also include the year of construction of the building, reserves for maintenance and repair or restrictions concerning the conveyance of the right. In PORTUGAL, the vendor is obliged to provide the purchaser with additional information concerning the administration, the value of the immovable property, a description of the furniture and confirmation that the immovable property is in conformity with the national building laws. In BELGIUM, the contract has to state all the particulars on the mortgage situation of the immovable property or on any existing rights *in rem* that might directly influence its use. Furthermore, in Belgium, the information about the right of withdrawal and the text of provision stating the right of withdrawal must be given in bold letters and in a separate frame on the first page of the contract.[1005] Also in LUXEMBOURG, this information has to be provided in bold.[1006] According to CYPRIOT law, the purchaser has to receive a form for the notification of withdrawal and an information document containing the purchaser's rights and the vendor's obligations.[1007] Also, the GERMAN Regulation on duties to supply information in civil law[1008] contains in its Annex 2 a standard form, which suppliers can use in order to fulfil the obligation to inform the consumer on the existence, the exercise and the effects of the right of withdrawal.

Some member states have not transposed all items of the Annex. In LITHUANIA, the information stated in lit. (j), (k) and (l) of the Directive's Annex has not been transposed, neither for the prospectus nor for the contract. The seller is only obliged to inform the consumer more generally of his rights. It is questionable whether this transposition is sufficient, especially with regard to the information on the right of withdrawal. In the CZECH REPUBLIC, SLOVAKIA and SPAIN[1009], the contract also does not have to contain the information referred to in lit. (j)[1010] of the Annex. However, the impact of this lack of transposition may be rather limited as the information needs to be provided in the information document anyway, which then, finally, becomes part of the contract.

The overall picture shows extremely detailed information obligations, which are probably rather burdensome to the vendor. At the same time it can be doubted whether such catalogues lead to effective consumer protection instead of simply overloading the consumer with more information than he can make use of sensibly. It might be rethought whether it really is useful to give the consumer most of the information twice.

From the viewpoint of a vendor who wants to undertake cross-border business lawfully, the actual situation in the member states must be seen as a substantive barrier to trade. As most member states have made use of the minimum clause, it is rather costly to find out what

---

1004 Section 3(1), No. 1 of the Timeshare Act.

1005 Article 7(1) of the Act of 11 April 1999 on the Purchase of the Right to Use Immovable Properties on a Timeshare Basis.

1006 Article 7(1)(3) of the Timeshare Act of 18 December 1998.

1007 Annex II Part A and B of the Timeshare Contract Law of 2001, L.113(I)/2001.

1008 BGB-Informationspflichten-Verordnung (BGB-InfoV).

1009 Article 9(1) of the Law 42/1998 which, nevertheless, states expanded information duties. Most of them have a more detailed structure than those stated in the Directive.

1010 A clause stating that acquisition will not result in costs, charges or obligations other than those specified in the contract.

information has to be given under the law of a certain member state (as to the formal and language requirements to be fulfilled see below in the next chapter).

In the course of the review of the Directive, identifying some items of core information which must in any case be provided could be considered. The starting point could be a general clause, saying that the vendor has to provide such information concerning the goods or services to be provided as the average consumer can reasonably expect and as he needs in the given context to take an informed transactional decision. Such a general clause could be supplemented by an indicative list of core information which must be provided, if appropriate, in the case of timeshare contracts.

2. Requirements with regard to form and language of the information document and the contract

a. Formal requirements for the contract

Article 4, 1st indent of Directive 94/47 states that the contract must be concluded in written form. Almost all member states have implemented this obligation very closely to the Directive. Only GREECE sets out a stricter requirement in the written form, namely the deed. In POLAND, the contract does not have to be in written form whenever a different specific form for the conclusion of a contract has been laid down. Regarding this different specific form, there is no explicit requirement that it must be stricter than the written form. But this should follow from the rule that member state law has to be interpreted in the light of the Directive.

In ESTONIA and GERMANY, the transposition laws conform to the Directive, but also set out the possibility that more stringent requirements concerning the form of a contract can be provided by law. In Germany, for example, it does often not suffice that the contract is in writing (CC § 126). It also requires authentication by a public notary in accordance with CC § 128 and § 311b. This applies, for instance, to timeshare contracts through which the purchaser acquires joint ownership of a property. In SPAIN, the purchaser has the right to demand the conclusion of the contract in a notarial deed and he has to be informed of this option.[1011]

Formal Requirements	Member States
As in the Directive	AT, BE, CY, CZ, DK, ES, FI, FR, HU, IE, IT, LT, LU, LV, MT, NL, PT, SE, SK, SL, UK *(21)*
Variations	DE, EE, EL, PL *(4)*

b. Language of the contract and the information document, Art. 4, 2nd indent

According to Art. 4, 2nd indent of the Directive, the contract and the information document must be drawn up in the language or in one of the languages of the member states in which the purchaser is resident or in the language or one of the languages of the member state of

1011 Article 9(1)(11)(b) of the Law 42/1998.

which he is national which shall be an official language or official languages of the Community, at the purchaser's option.

Most of the member states have transposed this provision. The provisions in LATVIA and LITHUANIA are rather problematic, where the contract has to be drawn up in the official language of the state, thus in Latvian and Lithuanian respectively.

MALTA[1012] offers the consumer an even wider choice than the Directive requires. It is possible to choose between the language of the member state where the purchaser is resident, the language of the member state of which he is national and any official language of the Community that he understands. In ESTONIA, the purchaser can choose between the language of the state where he is resident, the language of the state of which he is a national and the Estonian language. In DENMARK, FINLAND[1013] and SWEDEN (only for the information document), the consumer can choose not only one of the official languages of the EEC, but also Norwegian or Icelandic. SLOVENIAN law rules that a contract or an information document referring to a property in the Republic of Slovenia, or one given to a citizen of the Republic of Slovenia or an individual with permanent residence in the Republic of Slovenia must also be available in the Slovene language.[1014] The CZECH REPUBLIC and SLOVAKIA have not stated language requirements for the information document. Finnish law only rules that for promotional events the information document shall be at least available in the language used in the invitation.[1015] This seems to be an infringement of the Directive. However, according to the preparatory works, this provision (Chapter 10 sec. 6(2) of the Consumer Protection Act) is meant to correctly transpose the language requirements also with regard to the information document. This might be at least partially true because of an indirect effect of the Finnish provisions on the language of the contract. According to these provisions in Chapter 10 sec. 7 of the Consumer Protection Act, the prospectus automatically becomes part of the contract. The effect is that a trader cannot enter into contracts at all unless complying with the language provisions in the information document.

In SPAIN, foreign purchasers may request a translation in an EC language of their choice. Furthermore, consumer organisations and tourist bodies can require a translation.

Language	Member States
As in the Directive	AT, BE, CY, DE, EL, ES, FR, HU, IE, IT, LU, NL, PL, PT, UK *(15)*
Variations	CZ, DK, EE, FI, MT, SE, SK, SL *(8)*
Not transposed	LT, LV *(2)*

It is evident, that the language provisions can become very burdensome for the vendor. This can become even more so, because the necessary content of the information document also depends on the applicable law. In theory, a vendor could be obliged to provide up to 25 different types of information documents (one for each jurisdiction) and to translate these documents in all the (not only official) languages a consumer may be entitled to choose

1012 Regulation 6(1)(3) of the Protection of Buyers in Contracts for Time Sharing of Immovable Property Regulations 2000.

1013 Chapter 10 sec. 6(2) of the Consumer Protection Act of 20 January 1978/38.

1014 Article 60(4) of the Consumer Protection Act.

1015 Chapter 10 sec. 6(2) of the Consumer Protection Act of 20 January 1978/38.

from. However, it has to be considered that timeshare contracts are complicated and that the timeshare objects are often located in a country other than the consumer's home country and frequently sold to tourists during their holiday. It would invalidate the information duties if the consumer did not have the possibility to obtain a version in a language he could understand. It follows from the idea of an EU-wide internal market that all possible consumers should be enabled to participate. Therefore, it would be difficult to find reasons for lowering the language requirements. The solution should be sought by simplifying the long lists of the information items to be given. If, for instance, the EU legislation provides for a standard form for the information on the withdrawal right, it would be easy for the vendors to provide it in all official languages.

c. Option stated in Art. 4(1) 2nd indent, sent. 2

Article 4(1) 2nd indent, sent. 2 of Directive 94/47 states that the member state in which the purchaser is resident may, however, require that the contract has to be drawn up in any case in its language or languages. 9 countries have made use of this option, whereas 8 member states did not (cf. the table enclosed). Some member states' legislation have also laid down some provisions varying from the Directive. In GREECE, LATVIA, LITHUANIA and PORTUGAL, the contract has to be written in the official language of the respective state in any case. The FRENCH 'Code de la Consommation' states that the contract has to be drawn up in French if the purchaser is resident in France or if the immovable property is situated in France.[1016] In IRELAND, the seller is required to provide a version of the contract in English, or in English and Irish (which has become an official language)[1017] at the purchaser's request, in the case of a purchaser residing within Ireland. MALTA goes further because the seller shall provide the buyer with a certified translation of the contract in Maltese or in English if the buyer so requests, irrespective of whether the buyer's residence is in Malta.[1018] In SPAIN, the contract has to be drawn up in Castilian or any other of the official Spanish languages as chosen by the purchaser. These can be languages other than the official languages of the Community.[1019] SLOVENIAN law rules that a contract or an information document referring to a property in the Republic of Slovenia, or one given to a citizen of the Republic of Slovenia or an individual with permanent residence in the Republic of Slovenia must also be available in the Slovenian language.[1020]

Option stated in Art. 4 (1), 2nd indent	Member States
Option used	CY, CZ, FR, HU, IT, LU, PL, SK, UK *(9)*
Option not transposed	AT, BE, DE, DK, EE, FI, NL, SE *(8)*
Variations	EL, ES, IE, LT, LV, MT, PT, SL *(8)*

1016 Consumer Protection Act, Art. L121-68.

1017 Regulation 6(1)(d) European Communities (Contracts for Time Sharing of Immovable Property – Protection of Purchasers) Regulations 1997 and 2000.

1018 Regulation 6(2) of the Protection of Buyers in Contracts for Time Sharing of Immovable Property Regulations 2000.

1019 According to Spanish doctrine, this deviation is deemed to be legitimate; Lete *Achirica*, La configuración de la multipropiedad en España, 125, 149 ; Munar *Bernat*, La regulación española de la "multipropiedad":, 205.

1020 Article 60(4) of the Consumer Protection Act.

d. Certified translation of the contract in the language of the member state in which the immovable property is situated

A great majority of member states has transposed the vendor's obligation to provide a certified translation of the contract in the language of the member state in which the immovable property is situated (cf. the enclosed table). There are only a few deviations in some member states. MALTESE law states that the seller shall provide the buyer with a certified translation of the contract in Maltese or in English as the buyer so requests, but in the language of the country where the immovable property is located.[1021] In GERMANY[1022], SLOVENIA[1023] and HUNGARY[1024], the obligation to give the consumer a certified translation of the contract in the language of the country where the residential property is located, does not apply if subjects of a timeshare contract are parts of residential properties located in two or more countries. In FINLAND[1025], the translation has to be authenticated by a licensed translator, in POLAND by a "sworn translator".[1026] In some member states, the official version of the Directive does not request a "certified translation" and, subsequently, the national legislation does not contain this requirement, e.g. ITALY, SPAIN.

Certified translation	Member States
As in the Directive	AT, BE, CY, CZ, DK, EE, EL, FR, IE, LT, LU, LV, NL, PT, SE, SK, UK *(17)*
Variations	DE, ES, FI, HU, IT, MT, PL, SL *(8)*

e. Sanctions for non-compliance with the form and language requirements

Most transposition laws lay down sanctions for not complying with the Directive regarding the written form and the language obligation. Hereby nullity of the contract, a right of the consumer to cancel or withdraw from the contract or fines are popular sanctions.

Regarding non-compliance with the obligation to conclude a timeshare contract in written form, in AUSTRIA, BELGIUM, CYPRUS, FRANCE, GERMANY, GREECE[1027], ITALY, LUXEMBOURG, the NETHERLANDS and POLAND, for instance, the contract is void. In the CZECH REPUBLIC, DENMARK, ESTONIA, FINLAND, SPAIN and SWEDEN, for example, if the contract is not set up in writing, the consumer is not bound by that agreement and can terminate the contract or withdraw from it within specified periods.

In CYPRUS, for instance, administrative fines can additionally be imposed on the vendor. In BELGIUM, a vendor can only be sanctioned by a fine from EUR 150 up to EUR 10 000, if he

1021 Article 6(2) of the Protection of Buyers in Contracts for Time Sharing of Immovable Property Regulations 2000.

1022 CC § 484(2)(3).

1023 Article 60a(3) of the Consumer Protection Act.

1024 § 5(3) of the Government Decree 20/1999 (II. 5.) on Contracts for the Purchase of the Right to Use Immovable Property on a Timeshare Basis.

1025 Chapter 10 sec. 6(2) of the Consumer Protection Act of 20 January 1978/38.

1026 Article 5(3), sent. 2 of the Act of 13 July 2000 on the Protection of Purchasers in Respect of the Right to Use Buildings or Dwellings During Certain Times Each Year.

1027 Deed as formal requirement.

did not respect any of the provisions in the Timeshare Act. Furthermore, his registration can be revoked. In SLOVENIA, vendors who do not meet the obligation of concluding contracts in written form are sanctioned by fines. The law distinguishes between different kinds of vendors. Whereas a natural person can be sanctioned by a fine between SIT 1.000.000 – 5.000.000, a fine between SIT 3.000.000 – 10.000.000 can be imposed on a legal person and, additionally, on the person accountable for the undertaking of this figure between SIT 300.000 – 1.000.000. In IRELAND, a vendor or his agent who fails to comply with Regulation 4, 5 (on information), 6 (on withdrawal) or 8 (prohibition on advance payments) is guilty of an offence and liable on summary conviction to a fine not exceeding £1,500 [€1,904.61], to be prosecuted summarily by the Director of Consumer Affairs.[1028]

Concerning the obligation to set up the contract in a specific language, the same kinds of sanctions as mentioned above have been chosen to punish the vendor for not complying with the Directive. For instance, in AUSTRIA and FRANCE, the timeshare contract is void, if it is not set up in the required language. In Austria, the purchaser has to claim nullity of the contract within two years of the beginning of the contract. In the CZECH REPUBLIC, ESTONIA, FINLAND, SPAIN and SWEDEN, if the timeshare contract has not been set up in the required language, the consumer has the right to terminate or withdraw from the contract. BELGIUM, CYPRUS and DENMARK, for instance, lay down that the vendor shall be fined. In HUNGARY, the withdrawal period is prolonged up to 30 days if the information document was not provided in the correct language.[1029] In GERMANY, the withdrawal period is one month, if the information document is not provided at all or not provided in the correct language.[1030]

3. Right of withdrawal

a. Information duty

According to lit. (l) of the Annex in conjunction with Art. 3 and 4 of the Directive, the information document and the contract must include information on the right to withdraw from the contract and must indicate the person to whom any letter of withdrawal should be sent [...]. Thus, the information document and the contract have to contain information on the right of withdrawal and how to exercise it. This provision has been transposed closely to the Directive by most of the member states. In contrast to all the other member states, LITHUANIA does not oblige the vendor to indicate the right of withdrawal to the consumer, neither in the information document nor in the contract.

Many member states have additionally laid down precise provisions on how to inform the purchaser, e.g. by standard forms or precise wordings to be used. Such countries are, e.g., BELGIUM, CYPRUS, FRANCE, GERMANY, GREECE, LATVIA, LUXEMBOURG, MALTA and the

---

1028 Regulation 16 of the European Communities (Contracts for Time Sharing of Immovable Property – Protection of Purchasers) Regulations 1997 and 2000.

1029 § 8(2) of the Government Decree 20/1999. (II. 5.) on contracts for the purchase of the right to use immovable property on a timeshare basis.

1030 CC § 485 (3).

UNITED KINGDOM[1031]. In Malta[1032], a clause with the following wording must be included in the contract:

> "You as the buyer have the right to withdraw or cancel such a contract in accordance with 'The Protection of Buyers in Contracts for Time Sharing of Immovable Property Regulations, 2000'. These Regulations provide that a buyer may withdraw, without giving any reason, from such a contract within ten days from when the parties sign the contract."

If the clause is missing, the buyer may claim that the contract is null and void.

In BELGIUM[1033] and LUXEMBOURG, the information about the right of withdrawal must be given in bold letters and in a separate frame. GERMAN law also prescribes that the vendor must formally inform the consumer about the right of withdrawal. For this purpose, the vendor can use an information form of withdrawal designed by the legislator. This information does not necessarily have to be in written form, but must be sufficiently provided in text form (email, fax, CD-ROM). Some authors assume that this is an infringement of EC law because Art. 4 states that the contract with the information referred to in the Annex including the information on the right of withdrawal needs to be in writing.[1034] In the course of a review of the Directive, it could be made clear whether "in writing" means text on paper or also includes, e.g., electronic text on a durable medium.

In CYPRUS[1035] and LATVIA, traders also have to inform consumers about their right of withdrawal by a separate written notice and, in FRANCE[1036], the vendor must provide the consumer with a special form which the consumer can use for exercising his right of withdrawal. In GREECE, the consumer also has to be given a separate form containing information about the right of withdrawal and its exercise and a specimen/sample of the explanation of withdrawal.

As already said, it might really be helpful for improving cross-border trade if a standard form for the information about the withdrawal right were provided on a European level.

b. Withdrawal period

aa. Right of withdrawal within 10 calendar days of both parties signing the contract

The Directive states in Art. 5(1) 1st indent a period of withdrawal of 10 calendar days after the signature of the contract by both parties or the signature of a binding preliminary con-

[1031] Article 3(5) of the Timeshare (Cancellation of Information) Order 2003.

[1032] Regulation 4.4 of the Timeshare Regulations.

[1033] Article 7 § 1 in fine TA.

[1034] *Kelp*, Timesharing-Verträge, 63; *Mankowski*, VuR 2001, 364.

[1035] Article 6(a) of the Timeshare Contract Law of 2001, L.113(I)/2001.

[1036] Article L. 121-63.

tract. If the last day of the period is a Sunday or a holiday, the period is prolonged to the next working day.

The 10 calendar days period has been adopted by DENMARK, ESTONIA, FINLAND, FRANCE, GREECE, IRELAND, LITHUANIA, LUXEMBOURG, MALTA, the NETHERLANDS, POLAND, SLOVAKIA, SPAIN and SWEDEN. Many member states have used the minimum clause to prolong the withdrawal period. The period lasts for 10 working days in ITALY and PORTUGAL, 14 calendar days in AUSTRIA, LATVIA and the UNITED KINGDOM, two weeks (in some cases one month) in GERMANY, 15 calendar days in CYPRUS, the CZECH REPUBLIC, HUNGARY and SLOVENIA and even 15 working days in BELGIUM.

Withdrawal Regular Period	Member States
10 calendar days	DK, EE, EL, ES, FI, FR, IE, LT, LU, MT, NL, PL, SE, SK *(14)*
10 working days	IT, PT *(2)*
14 calendar days	AT, LV, UK *(3)*
Two weeks	DE (one month, if the necessary information is provided after conclusion of contract) *(1)*
15 calendar days	CY, CZ, HU, SL *(4)*
15 working days	BE *(1)*

In CYPRUS, FINLAND, IRELAND, LUXEMBOURG, MALTA and SPAIN (Finland, Spain and LITHUANIA not referring to the preliminary contracts), the beginning of the withdrawal period is regulated as in the Directive. Many member states do not refer to the signing of the contract but to the conclusion of the contract. They are: the CZECH REPUBLIC, DENMARK, ITALY, LATVIA, LITHUANIA, PORTUGAL, SLOVAKIA, SLOVENIA and the UNITED KINGDOM. In BELGIUM and SWEDEN, the period begins the day after the signature of the contract by both parties. In FRENCH law, the 10 day period starts when the purchaser sends the accepted offer to the professional. In addition to that, France attempts to improve the protection of the consumer by requiring that the offer should be maintained for at least 7 days.[1037] However, this provision just regulates the period during which the vendor is bound by his offer.[1038] The consumer is not detained from accepting the offer before the 7 day period expires.

In AUSTRIA, GERMANY, GREECE, ESTONIA, HUNGARY, the NETHERLANDS and POLAND, the withdrawal period starts running from the day when the contract document is delivered to the purchaser. In Germany, the period does not start running before the vendor was additionally informed the purchaser on the right of withdrawal and provided some further information.[1039] These provisions improve the position of the consumer and are therefore in accordance with the Directive.

Only some member states have seen the necessity to include an explicit provision on the signature of a binding preliminary contract in their national law, e.g., CYPRUS, GREECE, HUNGARY, IRELAND, LUXEMBOURG, MALTA and SLOVENIA.

1037 Code de la Consommation, Art. L. 121-63.

1038 Cf. *Calais-Auloy*, *Steinmetz*, Droit de la Consommantion, no. 483.

1039 Stated in § 2 BGB-InfoV.

Table: Start of the withdrawal period

After the signature of the contract	CY, ES, FI, IE, LU, MT *(6)*
After the conclusion of the contract	CZ, DK, IT, LT, LV, PT, SK, SL, UK *(9)*
Day after the day of signature of the contract	BE, SE *(2)*
Delivery of the contract copy	AT, DE,[1040] EE, EL, HU, NL, PL *(7)*
Day of sending the offer to the vendor	FR *(1)*

Article 5(1) 1st indent, sent. 2 of Directive 94/47 states the extension of the period in case of Sundays or public holidays. This is an odd provision because the EEC-Regulation 1182/71 determining the rules applicable to periods, dates and time limits, regulates the rule in its Art. 3(4) that, where the last day of a period is a public holiday, Sunday or Saturday, the period shall end with the expiry of the last hour of the following working day. Therefore, the only function of Art. 5(1) 1st indent, sent. 2 of Directive 94/47 is to amend the general rule in Art. 3(4) of Regulation 1182/71 in the sense that periods shall end on Saturdays. It is doubtful that this was meant. The issue should be clarified, preferably by striking out Art. 5(1) 1st indent, sent. 2 of Directive 94/47 and referring to Regulation 1182/71. This would also make clear that the period has to be calculated according to the rules laid down in this Regulation. Several member states, for instance, GERMANY, ITALY, LITHUANIA, MALTA, POLAND and SLOVENIA, have transposed Art. 5(1) 1st indent, sent. 2 of Directive 94/47 by referring to pre-existing provisions in their civil law. In ITALY and PORTUGAL, the withdrawal period is 10 working days, in BELGIUM 15 working days, thus the period always expires on a working day.

The overall picture shows a great variety between the member states. It is obvious that the differences of the length and the beginning (also of the rules on calculation) of the withdrawal period can make cross-border business difficult and therefore may amount to a barrier to trade. This is in particular true with regard to the information of the consumer about his right of withdrawal. For this reason a (full) harmonisation of the regular period seems desirable. A 14 day period would not substantially deprive consumers from the rights they currently enjoy under the national laws.

But it should be borne in mind that the period of withdrawal provided for in Directive 94/47 may be considered as being too short for fulfilling its purpose. This might be the case, especially, when a consumer signs a contract at the beginning of his holidays, and may need to exercise his right of withdrawal during the holidays, but has no possibility to speak to a lawyer in his home country. Moreover, timeshare contracts are often rather complicated and difficult to compare; in particular in cross-border cases it may also be difficult and time consuming to get competent legal advice. Much more than in the case of the withdrawal periods granted under Directives 97/7[1041] and 85/577[1042], it could be considered as problematic to prohibit longer periods the member states may want to provide. Therefore, leaving some discretion to the member states might also be considered. Potential barriers to trade could perhaps be avoided by prescribing a maximum (regular) period. It is a political decision as to

1040 The period does not start running before the vendor has additionally informed the purchaser of the right of withdrawal and provided some further information stated in § 2 of the Regulation on BGB – Information Duties.

1041 Directive 97/7 on distance selling.

1042 Directive 85/577 on doorstep selling.

how long such a regular maximum period could be. The considerations made here would lead to a duration of the withdrawal period from one month up to about three months.

bb. Right of withdrawal in case of lack of information

According to Art. 5(1) 2nd and 3rd indent of Directive 94/47, the member states shall make provisions in their legislation to ensure that:

"in addition to the possibilities available to the purchaser under national laws on the nullity of contracts, the purchaser shall have the right:

- [...]
- if the contract does not include the information referred to in points (a), (b), (c), (d) (1), (d) (2), (h), (i), (k), (l) and (m) of the Annex, at the time of both parties signing the contract or of both parties signing a binding preliminary contract, to cancel the contract within three months thereof. If the information in question is provided within those three months, the purchaser's withdrawal period provided for in the 1st indent, shall then start,
- if by the end of the three month period provided for in the second indent the purchaser has not exercised the right to cancel and the contract does not include the information referred to in points (a), (b), (c), (d) (1), (d) (2), (h), (i), (k), (l) and (m) of the Annex, to the withdrawal period provided for in the 1st indent from the day after the end of that three month period;".

The provisions of Art. 5(1) 2nd and 3rd indent of Directive 94/47 have not been transposed at all in FRANCE. The French legislator only transposed a right of withdrawal within 10 days. In addition to that, it is stipulated in the French transposition law that, in consequence of a failure to give the necessary information in the contract, the contract shall be null and void.[1043]

In the other member states, non-compliance with information duties leads to a prolongation of the withdrawal period. However, the lists of information duties which have this effect in case of non-compliance by the vendor, vary considerably in the member states. For the general transposition of Art. 4 of the Directive, which regulates the information to be included in the contract, see above under point D III 1 b.

It should be noted that non-compliance with information duties does not lead in any case to a prolongation of the withdrawal period. The Directive and several member states distinguish between information duties which, if infringed, have the effect of prolongation of the withdrawal period, and others, which do not have this effect (but may lead to other sanctions if breached).

For instance, GREECE, IRELAND, MALTA and the UNITED KINGDOM make the same distinction as the Directive, i.e. only the information items listed in Art. 5(1) 2nd and 3rd indent have the effect of prolongation. In contrast to this, many other member states do not differentiate between the information items they prescribe to be included in the contract and grant a

---

[1043] Code de la Consommation, Art. L. 121-76, L.121-61.

prolonged right of withdrawal if any of the obligatory information is lacking in the contract, e.g., AUSTRIA, BELGIUM, the CZECH REPUBLIC, ESTONIA, FINLAND, GERMANY, LATVIA, LITHUANIA, LUXEMBOURG, the NETHERLANDS, PORTUGAL, SLOVAKIA, SLOVENIA, SPAIN and SWEDEN.

Some member states differentiate between the information duties, but they also grant a prolongation of the withdrawal period for some information items other than those stated in Art. 5(1) 2nd indent of the Directive, but not for their whole catalogue of information duties. Such countries are, e.g., CYPRUS and HUNGARY (information on prohibition of advanced payments), DENMARK (information about the guarantee regarding the completion of the immovable property and the person where the consumer may address complaints) and POLAND (lit. (j) of the Directive's Annex).

ITALIAN law seems to infringe the Directive, because a breach of the information duties listed in lit. (d)(2) and lit. (m) (concerning the parties) of the Directive's Annex does not lead to a prolongation of the withdrawal period.

Table: Information duties sanctioned by a prolongation of the withdrawal period

Incomplete transposition of Art. 5(1) 2nd and 3rd indent	IT (lit. (d)(2), and lit. (m) are missing) *(1)*
Substantially equivalent to Art. 5(1) 2nd and 3rd indent	EL, IE, MT, UK *(4)*
All information items to be included in the contract (NB: differing in the member states)	AT, BE, CZ, DE, EE, ES, FI, LT, LU, LV, NL, PT, SE, SK, SL *(15)*
Other additional information	CY, DK, HU, PL *(4)*
No prolongation of withdrawal period at all	FR (but contract is void) *(1)*

Some variation could also be observed with regard to the length of the prolonged period. Most of the member states have adopted a period of three months in line with the Directive. In LITHUANIA, the period is prolonged to 4 months. In GERMANY, in case of missing information, the purchaser is entitled to revoke the contract even up to 6 months after the conclusion of the contract. The withdrawal period of two weeks does not start until the purchaser has received all the necessary information in written form. In the event of an ongoing lack of information concerning the right of revocation the withdrawal period is unlimited. The transposition in LATVIA, where the period is 90 calendar days instead of three months is problematic. The FRENCH legislator has not specifically transposed these provisions (see above).

Table: Withdrawal period in case of lacking information (Art. 5(1) 2nd indent)

Period of three months	AT, BE, CY, CZ, DK, EE, EL, ES, FI, HU, IE, IT, LU, MT, NL, PL, PT, SE, SK, SL, UK *(21)*
Period of 4 months	LT[1044] *(1)*
Period of 90 calendar days	LV *(1)*
Period of up to 6 months; if information on withdrawal is incomplete or missing, even unlimited	DE *(1)*
No period, contract is void	FR *(1)*

1044 Article 22(2), sent. 2 of the Law on Consumer Protection.

cc. Withdrawal period, if the information is provided within the three months

Article 5(1) 2nd indent, sent. 2 of the Directive states that, if the information in question is provided within those three months, the purchaser's "regular" withdrawal period shall then start. It should be borne in mind that the length of the regular period is different in the member states (for details see above). In GERMANY, an extended withdrawal period of one month starts to run if the missing information is provided subsequently.

Regarding the beginning of the period, most member states have adopted the starting point as prescribed by the Directive. DUTCH and POLISH law extends the regular period of withdrawal by the period between the provision of a copy of the contract and the provision of the missing data. Some member states lay down explicitly that the missing information must be provided in writing, e.g. in DENMARK, GERMANY, HUNGARY, the NETHERLANDS, POLAND and SLOVENIA. This could be clarified in the Directive. In BELGIUM and SWEDEN, the period starts on the day following the day on which the missing information was provided. In AUSTRIA and FINLAND, the purchaser has to receive a corrected version of the contract. FRANCE has not stated any provisions similar to that in the Directive because the contract is void if the offer does not contain all obligatory information.

Table: Start of regular period after provision of missing information

After the provision of the information	CY, CZ, DE[1045], DK[1046], EE, EL, ES, HU[1047], IE, IT, LT, LU, LV, MT, NL, PL, PT, SK, SL, UK *(20)* Explicitly in writing: DE, DK, HU, NL, PL, SL *(6)*
Day following the day on which information is provided	BE, SE[1048] *(2)*
Delivery of a copy of the contract	AT ("Ergänzungsurkunde"), FI[1049] ("rectified contract") *(2)*
No specific legislative transposition	FR *(1)*

dd. Withdrawal period, if missing information is not provided within three months

According to the Directive, if by the end of the three month period the purchaser has not exercised the right to cancel and the contract does not include the information referred to in points (a), (b), (c), (d) (1), (d) (2), (h), (i), (k), (l) and (m) of the Annex, the consumer has the right to withdraw from the contract within the regular withdrawal period (in the Directive: 10 days) from the day after the end of that three month period.

1045 In GERMANY, instead of the regular 2 week period, an extended period of one month starts running when the information is provided subsequently.

1046 Section 9(2) of the Timeshare Act.

1047 The day when information is provided in written form and becomes part of the contract by agreement, cf. § 8(3) of the Government Decree 20/1999 (II. 5.) on Contracts for the Purchase of the Right to Use Immovable Property on a Timeshare Basis.

1048 Article 12(2), sent. 2, Art. 11(3) of the Timeshare Contracts (Consumer Protection) Act 1997:218.

1049 Chapter 10 sec. 9 of the Consumer Protection Act of 20 January 1978/38.

The transposition in the member states varies considerably, partially also because the length of the regular withdrawal period is different in the member states. For instance, in LITHUANIA, the period is 4 months counting from the conclusion of the contract. In BELGIUM, the period of withdrawal is one year, counting from the day following the day on which the contract was signed, if the missing information has not been provided within three months. In GERMANY, the length of the period depends on the type of information that is lacking. If the information about the right of withdrawal is lacking or incomplete, there is no period for the withdrawal at all. In this case, the consumer has in effect an eternal right of withdrawal. If other necessary information is lacking, the extended withdrawal period is 6 months.[1050] Also in AUSTRIA, the withdrawal period does not begin before the purchaser is informed of his right of withdrawal.

Table: Period of withdrawal if information is not provided

Three months plus 10 days	DK, EE, EL[1051], ES, FI, IE, IT[1052], LU, MT (working days), NL[1053], PL, PT (working days), SE, SK, UK *(15)*
Three months plus 14/15 days	CZ, CY, HU, SL *(4)*
90 calendar days plus 14 days	LV *(1)*
4 months	LT[1054] *(1)*
One year	BE[1055] *(1)*
Three months plus 14 days or unlimited	AT[1056] *(1)*
6 months or unlimited	DE[1057] *(1)*
No specific legislative transposition	FR *(1)*

In general, the Directive's provisions on the prolongation of the withdrawal period in case of lacking information are rather intricate. Regarding the case where information about the right of withdrawal is lacking, they are not in coherence with the ECJ case C-481/99 – *Heininger*. It can also be doubted whether a three month plus 10 day period is long enough. A possible way to simplify the provisions could be to follow BELGIUM'S model and introduce a prolonged period of one year, starting from the point when the contract is concluded. It would then have to be considered, whether this period shall also be applicable in *Heininger* cases.

ee. Additional right of withdrawal

Some member states have additionally granted a right of withdrawal in situations not regulated in the Directive. Many member states grant a right of withdrawal if the form and lan-

---

1050 CC § 355(3)(1).

1051 Article 4(1)(c) of the Decree 182/1999.

1052 Article 73(2) and (4) of the Consumer Code.

1053 CC Book 7 Art. 48c(1), sent. 2.

1054 Article 22(2), sent. 1 of the Law on Consumer Protection.

1055 Article 9(1)(3) of the Act of 11 April 1999 on the Purchase of the Right to Use Immovable Properties on a Timeshare Basis.

1056 § 6(2) of the Timeshare Act.

1057 CC § 355(3) and § 485(3).

guage requirements have not been observed. In POLAND[1058], the consumer can withdraw within three months from delivery of the contract document if the prospectus was not delivered to the purchaser or if the prospectus or the contract were not written in the correct language. In SLOVENIA[1059], withdrawal is also possible within a maximum of three months and 15 days, if a prospectus was not presented, or if the contract was drawn up in a language not compliant with the provisions of the Consumer Protection Act. In HUNGARY[1060], the consumer can exercise the right of withdrawal within 30 calendar days it the information form is missing or if the latter does not meet the language requirements. In ESTONIA[1061], the consumer has the right to withdraw within one month after receipt of the signed contract, if an information document is not submitted to the consumer before entry into a contract or if the document is not submitted in the prescribed language. In SWEDEN[1062], the right to withdraw within a period of three months also applies if the provisions concerning the language of the contract are not fulfilled.

In the CZECH REPUBLIC[1063], the consumer can additionally withdraw from the contract within three months counting from the date of the agreed completion of the building, if it is not properly completed by that date. In SPAIN, the purchaser has a right of withdrawal if the prohibition of the label *multipropiedad* ("shared property", "joint ownership") [1064] has been disregarded.[1065]

c. Formal requirements for exercising the withdrawal

The Directive does not stipulate any formal requirements for the exercise of the right of withdrawal and only states in its Art. 5(2) that the consumer has to notify the recipient appearing in the contract by a means that can be proven. The result is that it is left to the member states' discretion to regulate formal requirements for the exercise of the withdrawal.

1058 Article 6(3) of the Act of 13 July 2000 on the Protection of Purchasers in Respect of the Right to Use Buildings or Dwellings During Certain Times Each Year.

1059 Article 60c(2) of the Consumer Protection Act.

1060 § 8(2) of the Government Decree 20/1999 (II. 5.) on Contracts for the Purchase of the Right to Use Immovable Property on a Timeshare Basis.

1061 Section 383(3) of the Law of Obligations Act.

1062 Article 11(1) of the Timeshare Contracts (Consumer Protection) Act 1997:218.

1063 CC § 63(1)(d).

1064 Article 10(2) and Article 8(1) of the Law 42/1998.

1065 See also the CA Alicante judgment of 19 September 2002 No. 545/2002, *"Sain 333 S. L." v Francisco Javier G. B. and Amparo M. G.* The Court sanctioned the use of this label with the nullity of the contract due to the infringement of a mandatory rule (CC Art. 6(3)).

AUSTRIA, CYPRUS, FINLAND[1066], GREECE[1067], HUNGARY[1068], LATVIA, LITHUANIA[1069], POLAND, SLOVENIA[1070] and the UNITED KINGDOM[1071] have regulated that the withdrawal must be notified to the vendor by a written notice. In Slovenia, the purchaser can also implicitly express his withdrawal. In IRELAND[1072], the notice can, but need not be in writing. In Cyprus[1073], the consumer must complete and send written notification of withdrawal which has to contain the purchaser's decision to withdraw, the date at which the notice is given and the name and address of the recipient of the notice according to the recipient named in the contract. In SLOVAKIA[1074], the notice of withdrawal needs to meet the form in which the contract was agreed. As the contract has to be concluded in writing, the notice of withdrawal must be in writing, too.

In AUSTRIA[1075], the withdrawal can be exercised by a written notice to which the fax is equated. Additionally, the consumer can return the contractual document with a notation that indicates that the consumer does not want to draw up or to maintain the contract.

In BELGIUM, MALTA[1076] and LUXEMBOURG[1077], the notification of the withdrawal must be in writing and sent as a registered letter. In FRANCE, ITALY[1078] and PORTUGAL, the consumer has to send a signed registered letter with return receipt. In ITALY, it is also possible to use telegram, telex or fax to meet the period of withdrawal, if they are confirmed by a registered letter with return receipt within the following 48 hours.

In FRANCE[1079], the vendor is also obliged to fix a withdrawal form to the contractual document given to the consumer. The consumer can use this form to exercise his right of withdrawal. In CYPRUS, the purchaser can also use the notification form.[1080]

1066 10:11 CPA stipulates that a written informal notice must be sent and that there is no need to use a means which can be proved.

1067 Although the wording "declaration in writing" is unambiguous, in GREEK legal literature Art. 4(2) of Decree 182/99 is seen as a burden of proof provision only. As a consequence, the purchaser could also withdraw from the contract by other means if the purchaser can prove it. The jurisprudence is inconsistent in this point but tends to interpret this provision as a formal regulation.

1068 § 10(1) of the Government Decree 20/1999 (II. 5.) on Contracts for the Purchase of the Right to Use Immovable Property on a Timeshare Basis.

1069 CC Art. 6.370(1)(1).

1070 Article 60c(1) of the Consumer Protection Act.

1071 Regulation 12(6) of the Timeshare Act 1992.

1072 Article 8 of the European Communities (Contracts for Time Sharing of Immovable Property – Protection of Purchasers) Regulations 1997 and 2000.

1073 Article 9 (1), sent. 1 of the Timeshare Contract Law of 2001, L.113(I)/2001.

1074 CC § 55(1)(o), § 48 para. (1) and (2), § 49.

1075 § 6(3), sent. 1 and sent. 2 of the Timeshare Act.

1076 Article 8(1) of the Protection of Buyers in Contracts for Time Sharing of Immovable Property Regulations 2000.

1077 Article 10(2), sent. 1 of the Timeshare Act of 18 December 1998.

1078 Article 73(5) of the Consumer Code.

1079 Article L. 121-63.

1080 Article 9(3) provides that the purchaser can use any other written form that satisfies the requirements of Art. 9(1) and (2) of the Timeshare Act No 113(I)/2001.

In the CZECH REPUBLIC, the consumer has to indicate the reason for exercising the right of withdrawal in case of the prolonged withdrawal period because of lack of information.[1081]

Withdrawal Formal Requirements	Member States
None	CZ, DK, EE, ES,[1082] IE, NL *(6)*
In writing	AT,[1083] CY,[1084] EL, FI,[1085] HU, LT, LV, PL, SL, UK *(10)*
Text form	DE *(1)*
As agreed in contract	SK[1086] *(1)*
Registered letter	BE, LU, MT *(3)*
Registered letter with return receipt	FR[1087], IT[1088], PT *(3)*
Transposition not entirely clear	SE *(1)*

Such formal requirements for the exercise of the withdrawal right might cause a barrier to trade, because, if the vendor is also obliged to inform the consumer about formal requirements, it is impossible to draft such information which can be used in all member states. Therefore, harmonising the national laws in the way that formal requirements must not be introduced by the member states could be considered.

d. Dispatching rule

According to Art. 5(2), sent. 2 of the Directive, the deadline of withdrawal is observed if the consumer dispatches the notification before the deadline expires.

This provision has been transposed by the vast majority of member states. Only the CZECH REPUBLIC, FRANCE, HUNGARY, LATVIA and SLOVAKIA have no specific legislative transposition. Some of these member states may achieve the same result acquired by the Directive with the application of their general rules on the computation of periods. ITALY has not laid down a dispatch rule, but the purchaser has to send a registered letter with advice of delivery and may therefore prove that the notice was sent within the withdrawal period. The legislator in the UNITED KINGDOM has chosen a different wording. If the notice is sent by post in a properly addressed and pre-paid letter, it is to be treated as given at the time of posting.

1081 CC § 63(1) lit. (b) and (c).

1082 By any means which guarantee the proof of the communication, the reception and the date of sending.

1083 Fax is equated. Additionally the consumer can return the contractual document with a notation that indicates that the consumer does not want to draw up or to maintain the contract.

1084 Or by any other means which can be proved.

1085 Informal written notice, 10:11 CPA.

1086 Unless agreed otherwise, the notice of withdrawal must be written in case of written contract.

1087 Article L. 121-64(1) of the Code de la Consommation states that if the consumer does not send a letter with a return receipt, he can use any other means that provide for the same guarantees as to the determination of the date.

1088 Registered letter with advice of delivery. It is also possible to use telegram, telex or fax to meet the period of withdrawal, if they are confirmed by a registered letter with advice of delivery within the following 48 hours, cf. Art. 73(5) of the Consumer Code.

Substantially equivalent as in the Directive	AT, BE, CY, DE, DK, EE, EL, ES, FI, IE, IT, LT, LU, MT, NL, PL, PT, SL, UK *(19)*
No specific legislative transposition	CZ, FR, HU, LV, SK *(5)*
Transposition not entirely clear	SE *(1)*

It is unclear whether the dispatch rule is also applicable, if the consumer dispatches the declaration of withdrawal in time, but it never reaches the vendor. This could be clarified.

e. Costs

aa. Art. 5(3)

According to Art. 5(3) of Directive 94/47, the purchaser may, where he exercises the right of withdrawal provided for in the 1st indent of paragraph (1), be required to defray, where appropriate, only those expenses which, in accordance with national law, are incurred as a result of the conclusion of and withdrawal from the contract and which correspond to legal formalities which must be completed before the end of the period referred to in the 1st indent of paragraph (1). Such expenses shall be expressly mentioned in the contract.

Member states like the CZECH REPUBLIC, GREECE, LUXEMBOURG[1089] and SWEDEN have transposed Art. 5(3) of the Directive by using nearly exactly the Directive's wording. Furthermore, GREECE has stated that the costs must not exceed 3 % of the purchase price.

A remarkable number of member states has increased the consumer protection level by ruling that no costs and damages can be charged on the consumer, e.g. BELGIUM[1090], CYPRUS[1091], DENMARK[1092], the NETHERLANDS[1093], PORTUGAL[1094], SPAIN[1095] and the UNITED KINGDOM[1096]. ITALIAN[1097], HUNGARIAN, POLISH[1098] and the SLOVENIAN[1099] law only allow the imposition of the costs of entering into the contract on the purchaser, but not of the costs of withdrawal. Contrary to these countries, in SLOVAKIA, the vendor can only request reimbursement of "demonstrably expended unavoidable costs connected with withdrawal from the contract" .[1100] Some member states have specified which costs the purchaser has to

1089 Article 10(3) of the Timeshare Act of 18 December 1998.

1090 Article 9(2), sent. 3 of the Act of 11 April 1999 on the Purchase of the Right to Use Immovable Properties on a Timeshare Basis.

1091 Article 10 of the Timeshare Contract Law of 2001, L.113(I)/2001.

1092 Section 10 of the Timeshare Act.

1093 CC Art. 48c(3).

1094 Article 16(1) of the Decree-Law 275/93 of August 5.

1095 Article 10(1), sent. 3 of the Law 42/1998.

1096 Section 5(8) of the Timeshare Act 1992.

1097 Article 73(1) of the Consumer Code.

1098 Article 7(2) of the Act of 13 July 2000 on the Protection of Purchasers in Respect of the Right to Use Buildings or Dwellings During Certain Time Each Year.

1099 Article 60c(3), sent. 3 of the Consumer Protection Act.

1100 CC § 59(3), sent. 1.

defray, e.g. AUSTRIA[1101] (the costs of a notarisation or necessary translation of the contract and the duties and taxes that result from agreeing on the contract, if the purchaser has been informed of this possibility in the contract), ESTONIA[1102] (the costs for notarisation and attestation of the contract), FINLAND[1103] (costs that must be paid before the end of the cooling-off period and because of formal requirements "or are otherwise of a public nature"), GERMANY[1104] (the costs for a necessary notarisation of the contract) and HUNGARY[1105] (costs for preparation and translation of the contract). In Austria, Germany, Hungary and Slovenia, the legislator explicitly stated that the vendor cannot demand interest for use of the immovable property.

In IRELAND and MALTA, this provision has not been transposed. In Malta, the intention was to maintain the more favourable rights the purchaser has under the general rules.

Table: Costs in case of withdrawal within cooling-off period

Cost Provisions	Member States
Substantially equivalent to the Directive	CZ,[1106] EL,[1107] LU, SE[1108] *(4)*
Expressly: no costs for use of the residential property	AT, DE, HU, SL *(4)*
No costs and damages	BE, CY, DK, ES, LT, NL, PT, UK *(8)*
Costs and defrayal specified	AT, DE, EE, FI, HU *(5)*
Unavoidable costs connected with conclusion of the contract necessary to enter into the agreement	IT, PL, SL[1109] *(3)*
Unavoidable costs connected with withdrawal	LV,[1110] SK *(2)*
Fees necessarily incurred	FR[1111] *(1)*
No specific legislative transposition	IE, MT *(2)*

bb. Art. 5(4)

According to Art. 5(4) of the Directive, the purchaser shall not be required to make any defrayal where he exercises the right of cancellation provided for in the 2nd indent of paragraph 1 (in case of missing information).

AUSTRIA, the CZECH REPUBLIC, GREECE, IRELAND, ITALY, LUXEMBOURG, POLAND, SLOVAKIA, SPAIN and SWEDEN have transposed Art. 5(4) of the Directive. In the GERMAN and

1101 § 6(4) of the Timeshare Act.

1102 Section 383(5) of the Law of Obligations Act.

1103 Chapter 10 Section 14 of the Consumer Protection Act of 20 January 1978/38.

1104 CC § 485(5), sent. 1 and sent. 2.

1105 § 10(2) of the Government Decree 20/1999 (II. 5.) on Contracts for the Purchase of the Right to Use Immovable Property on a Timeshare Basis.

1106 CC § 63(2), sent. 1.

1107 As in the Directive, but costs may in any case not exceed 3 % of the price.

1108 § 14(2) of the Timeshare Contracts (Consumer Protection) Act 1997:218.

1109 Article 60c(3), sent. 2 of the Consumer Protection Act.

1110 Article 12(4) of the Consumer Protection Act. Only costs for the return of goods, general rule for all rights of withdrawal.

1111 Consumer Protection Act, Art. L.121-64(2).

HUNGARIAN national law, it is additionally stated that the consumer can claim damages from the vendor. In BELGIUM, CYPRUS, DENMARK, LITHUANIA, MALTA and the NETHERLANDS, the general rule on costs for every case of withdrawal is applicable (see above). In PORTUGAL and the UNITED KINGDOM, the Directive's provision is transposed indirectly, as all sums paid by the consumer must be refunded by the vendor. Thus, in consequence, no costs are left with the consumer.

In SLOVENIA, the provision is not explicitly transposed, but can be deducted from the general provision.[1112] According to the LATVIAN regulation, the consumer shall not pay any costs except those for returning the goods to the vendor. In FINLAND, the provision, which also transposes Art. 5(3) of the Directive, applies. According to this provision, the costs which must be paid before the end of the cooling-off period are imposed on the consumer. In FRANCE, the provision is not specifically transposed, but as the contract is void anyway, the result should be the same.

Table: Costs in case of withdrawal within prolonged period

Substantially equivalent to the Directive	AT,[1113] CZ,[1114] EE,[1115] EL,[1116] ES,[1117] IE,[1118] IT,[1119] LU,[1120] MT, PL,[1121] SE,[1122] SK[1123] *(12)*
General exclusion of costs and damages for all rights of withdrawal granted in Art. 5 of the Directive	BE, CY,[1124] DK,[1125] LT, NL *(5)*
Refund all sums received from the consumer	PT,[1126] UK *(2)*
Expressly mentioned that consumer can claim damages	DE,[1127] HU[1128] *(2)*
Deviances	FI , LV[1129] *(2)*
Not expressly transposed	FR *(1)*

1112 Article 60 c(3)(2) of the Consumer Protection Act.
1113 Section 6(4), sent. 3 of the Timeshare Act.
1114 CC § 63(2), sent. 2.
1115 Section 383(5) of the Law of Obligations Act.
1116 Article 4(4) of the Decree 182/1999.
1117 Article 10(2) *in fine* of the Law of the Law 42/1998.
1118 Article 9 European Communities (Contracts for Time Sharing of Immovable Property – Protection of Purchasers) Regulations 1997 and 2000.
1119 Article 73(2) of the Consumer Code.
1120 Article 10(4) of the Timeshare Act of 18 December 1998.
1121 Article 7(1) of the Act of 13 July 2000 on the Protection of Purchasers in Respect of the Right to Use Buildings or Dwellings During Certain Time Each Year.
1122 § 14(1) of the Timeshare Contracts (Consumer Protection) Act 1997:218.
1123 CC § 59(3) sent. 2.
1124 Article 10 of the Timeshare Contract Law of 2001, L.113(I)/2001.
1125 Section 10 of the Timeshare Act.
1126 Article 16(7) of the Decree-Law 275/93 of August 5.
1127 CC § 485(5), sent. 3.
1128 § 10(3) of the Government Decree 20/1999 (II. 5.) on Contracts for the Purchase of the Right to Use Immovable Property on a Timeshare Basis.
1129 Article 12 (1) and (4) of the Consumer Rights Protection Law.

4. Prohibition of advance payments before the end of the withdrawal period

According to Art. 6 of the Directive, the member states shall make provision in their legislation to prohibit any advance payments by a purchaser before the end of the period during which he may exercise the right of withdrawal. Although not entirely clear, this wording probably also covers the prolonged three months plus 10 day period provided for in Art. 5(1) 2nd and 3rd indent of the Directive. If so, the German version of the Directive has a different content as it only refers to the 10 day period prescribed in Art. 5(1) 1st indent. This discrepancy should be clarified, preferably in the sense of the English version as understood here.

a. Prohibition of advanced payments

All member states have transposed the prohibition of advanced payment provided in Art. 6 of the Directive.

In BELGIUM[1130], FINLAND, FRANCE[1131] and PORTUGAL[1132], the prohibition only applies to the regular period of withdrawal (which is 15 days in BELGIUM and 10 days in the other countries mentioned), but not to the longer periods (e.g. three months plus X days) in the case of non-compliance with information duties. According to the wording of the ESTONIAN[1133] regulation, payments must not be received within 10 days after the submission of the signed contract to the consumer. In SLOVENIAN[1134] law, any contract clause stipulating that the consumer must pay a partial amount of the price or costs before the expiry of the cancellation period (usually 15 days) is void.[1135]

In SWEDEN[1136], advanced payments are prohibited during the normal period of withdrawal and in the time until a surety is provided in the case that the property is still under construction.

In AUSTRIA[1137], CYPRUS[1138], the CZECH REPUBLIC[1139], DENMARK[1140], GREECE[1141], HUNGARY[1142], IRELAND[1143], ITALY[1144], LATVIA[1145], LUXEMBOURG[1146], MALTA, the NETHER-

---

1130 Article 9(3) of the Act of 11 April 1999 on the Purchase of the Right to Use Immovable Properties on a Timeshare Basis).

1131 Consumer Rights Protection Act, Art. L121-66.

1132 Article 53 and 14 of the Decree-Law 275/93 of August 5.

1133 Section 385 of the Law of Obligations Act.

1134 Article 60č of the Consumer Protection Act.

1135 Article 60c(3), sent. 1, Art. 45d of the Consumer Protection Act.

1136 § 13(1) of the Timeshare Contracts (Consumer Protection) Act 1997:218.

1137 § 7(1) of the Timeshare Act.

1138 Article 11 of the Timeshare Contract Law of 2001, L.113(I)/2001.

1139 Article 61 of the Act of 15 April 2002 amending the Act 40/1964 (CC).

1140 Section 12 of the Timeshare Act.

1141 Article 5 of the Decree 182/1999.

1142 § 11(1) of the Government Decree 20/1999 (II. 5.) on Contracts for the Purchase of the Right to Use Immovable Property on a Timeshare Basis. Cf. also the CA Budapest (Fővárosi Ítélőtábla)

LANDS[1147], POLAND[1148], SLOVAKIA[1149], SPAIN[1150] and the UNITED KINGDOM[1151], payments are prohibited for the duration of the normal and of the prolonged period of withdrawal in the case of missing information, which can amount up to three months and 10 days. In LITHUANIA[1152] and GERMANY[1153], the prohibition also applies within the whole period of withdrawal, which can, in the case of missing information, be up to 4 months in Lithuania and up to 6 months in Germany. In GREECE, the prohibition of advanced payment does not apply to the costs of the contract, the costs of withdrawal and the cost of acts which have to take place within the cooling-off period of 10 days (which may be a maximum 3 % of the agreed price). In SPAIN[1154], the parties can make appropriate agreements to guarantee the payment. These must not be contrary to the prohibition of advanced payments and not mean a direct or indirect compensation for the vendor in case of withdrawal.

b. Table: Prohibition of advanced payments

Prohibition for normal period of withdrawal	BE (15), EE (10), FI (10), FR (10), PT (10), SE (10; cooling-off period) *(6)*
Prohibition also for prolonged period of withdrawal (three months plus 10 days, if not agreed otherwise)	AT,* CZ, CY, DE (up to 6 months), DK, EL, ES, HU, IE, IT, LT (up to 4 months), LU,* LV,* MT, NL, PL,* SK, SL,* UK *(19)* *The transposition laws just read „withdrawal period". It is assumed that this has to be interpreted in line with the Directive and therefore means for the full duration of the withdrawal period, even if prolonged.
Prohibition also for a period until a surety is provided in case of property under construction	SE *(1)*
Exemption: costs of the contract and withdrawal	EL *(1)*
Exemption: appropriate agreement to guarantee payment, provided it is not contrary to the prohibition	ES *(1)*
Also no payment on credit agreement	FI *(1)*

judgment of 1 December 2004, 2.Kf.27.379/2003/3. The Court held that the vendor must not claim any payments – even payments held in trust – within the withdrawal period.

1143 Article 10(1) of the European Communities (Contracts for Time Sharing of Immovable Property – Protection of Purchasers) Regulations 1997 and 2000.

1144 Article 74 of the Consumer Code.

1145 Article 11(3) of the Consumer Rights Protection Law.

1146 Article 10(6) of the Timeshare Act of 18 December 1998.

1147 CC Book 7 Art. 48d.

1148 Article 8(1) of the Act of 13 July 2000 on the Protection of Purchasers in Respect of the Right to Use Buildings or Dwellings During Certain Time Each Year.

1149 CC § 57(b).

1150 Cf. also the CA Cantabria judgment of 24 May 2004 No. 196/2004, *Sergio and Carmela v "Free Enterprise S. L."*. The CA held that the prohibition of advanced payment also applies to the prolonged withdrawal period. Furthermore, the Court ruled that it does not suffice to make general references to appendices since that information has to be inserted in the contract.

1151 Article 5B(1) of the Timeshare Act 1992.

1152 Article 22(5), sent. 1 of the Law on consumer protection.

1153 CC § 486.

1154 Article 11(1) of the Law 42/1998.

Such differences show that the Directive has been understood differently within the member states and, therefore, clarification is still required on this point.

c. Refund of sums paid

It goes without saying, that, if any advanced payments have been made by the consumer, the vendor has to return the sum. Many member states rely on their general rules (e.g. GERMANY, where the refund has to be made immediately). Others have specific rules, for instance, LITHUANIA (refund within a period of 10 days) or SLOVENIA.[1155]

In some member states, the obligation to return the amount, which has already been paid, is aggravated. In AUSTRIA[1156], the vendor is obliged to pay interest on the sum amounting to 6 percentage points above the base rate (which means a total of about 8 % at the moment).[1157] In HUNGARY[1158], the vendor has to pay additional default interest, too. The interest on the sums starts with the day of their payment. In SPAIN[1159], the vendor is obliged to return double the amount of the sum which the consumer has paid in advance.[1160] In addition, the consumer is given a period of three months within which he can choose, if he wishes, to terminate the contract or claim its performance.

Some member states have established fines, if the vendor infringes upon the interdiction of demanding and receiving any advanced payment. In SWEDEN[1161], a person is liable to a fine in case of a deliberate infringement of the prohibition of advanced payment. In AUSTRIA[1162], the obligation to pay the interest described above is combined with a fine because of an administrative offence amounting up to EUR 7.260. In FRANCE, Art. L. 121-71 of the 'Code de la consommation' states that if the seller asks for or receives any payment before the 10 day withdrawal period ends, he will have to pay a fine of EUR 30.000. GREECE states fines between EUR 1.467 and EUR 5.694 and other public law sanctions. In PORTUGAL[1163], the fine is between ca. EUR 10.000 and ca. EUR 100.000. In the ITALIAN[1164] law, a penalty between EUR 500 and EUR 3.000 is foreseen. In case of repeated infringements an additional administrative penalty or a suspension of pursuit of business between 15 days and

---

1155 Article 60c(3), sent. 1, referring to Art. 43d of the Consumer Protection Act.

1156 Interdiction of advanced payment in § 7(1) of the Timeshare Act.

1157 § 7(2) of the Timeshare Act.

1158 § 11(2) of the Government Decree 20/1999 (II. 5.) on Contracts for the Purchase of the Right to Use Immovable Property on a Timeshare Basis.

1159 Article 11(2) of the Law 42/1998.

1160 See also the CA Las Palmas judgment of 22 November 2003, no. 682/2003, Benedicto and Margarita v "Palm Oasis Maspalomas S. L.". The Court ruled that the refund of double the amount of the sum that was paid in advance constitutes the legal compensation for the purchaser for the abuse of rights carried out by the seller. Therefore, Article 11(2) of the Law 42/1998 can also be applied to contracts which are invalid due to the omissions and negligence of the vendor.

1161 Article 13(2) of the Timeshare Contracts (Consumer Protection) Act 1997:218.

1162 § 12(2) of the Timeshare Act.

1163 Article 54(1), Art. 55 of the Decree-Law 275/93 of August 5.

1164 Article 81 of the Consumer Code.

three months can be imposed. In the UNITED KINGDOM[1165], the infringement constitutes a criminal offence, as well as in IRELAND[1166], where the fine amounts to EUR 1.904,61 (1500 pounds). In MALTA[1167], any violation of the regulation that prohibits advanced payment is also an offence. A person who has committed an offence will be liable on conviction to a fine (*multa*) of not less than MTL 100 but not exceeding MTL 1.000, and to a fine (*multa*) of not less than MTL 25 and not exceeding MTL 50 for every day during which the offence continues.[1168] In LUXEMBOURG[1169], in the case of infringement the vendor is fined with a sum between FLUX 10.001 and FLUX 1.000.000. In BELGIUM[1170], a similar regulation exists with fines between EUR 150 and EUR 10.000.

In CYPRUS[1171], it is the Competition and Consumers' Protection Service in the Ministry of Commerce, Industry and Tourism that can take measures, for example, confirm a contravention, recommend the offender to cease the infringement, impose an administrative fine (up to 10 % of the offender's annual turnover; or in case of repetitive infringement 50 to 1.000 pounds per day of continuation of the infringement) or apply to the Court and ask for a prohibitory, mandatory or interim order.

As the prohibition of advance payments seems to be a rather effective consumer protection instrument, prescribing certain sanctions, in particular criminal sanctions, on Community level could be considered.

5. Credit agreements

According to Art. 7 of the Directive, the member states shall make provisions in their legislation to ensure that:

- if the price is fully or partly covered by credit granted by the vendor, or
- if the price is fully or partly covered by credit granted to the purchaser by a third party on the basis of an agreement between the third party and the vendor,

the credit agreement shall be cancelled, without any penalty, if the purchaser exercises his right to cancel or withdraw from the contract as provided for in Art. 5. The member states shall lay down detailed arrangements to govern the cancellation of credit agreements.
These provisions have been closely transposed to the Directive by AUSTRIA[1172], BELGIUM[1173], CYPRUS[1174], the CZECH REPUBLIC[1175], DENMARK[1176], ESTONIA[1177], FINLAND[1178], GERMANY[1179],

---

[1165] Article 5B(2) of the Timeshare Act 1992.

[1166] Article 16(1) and 2 of the European of the Communities (Contracts for Time Sharing of Immovable Property – Protection of Purchasers) Regulations 1997 and 2000.

[1167] Regulation 10(1) and 10(2) of the Protection of Buyers in Contracts for Time Sharing of Immovable Property Regulations, 2000.

[1168] Regulation 13(1) Protection of Buyers in Contracts for Time Sharing of Immovable Property Regulations, 2000

[1169] Article 12 of the Timeshare Act of 18 December 1998.

[1170] Article 17 Act of 11 April 1999 on the Purchase of the Right to Use Immovable Properties on a Timeshare Basis.

[1171] Article 18(2) of The Timeshare Contract Law of 2001, L.113(I)/2001.

[1172] § 8 of the Timeshare Act.

GREECE[1180], HUNGARY[1181], IRELAND, ITALY[1182], LATVIA[1183], LITHUANIA[1184], LUXEMBOURG[1185], MALTA[1186], the NETHERLANDS[1187], POLAND[1188], PORTUGAL[1189], SLOVENIA[1190], SPAIN[1191], SWEDEN[1192] and the UNITED KINGDOM[1193].

In FRANCE[1194], it seems that only a credit agreement which has been announced to the vendor can be cancelled with the timeshare contract. In SLOVAKIA[1195], the purchaser is obliged to inform the third party about the withdrawal. In AUSTRIA[1196] and GERMANY[1197], the purchaser also has the possibility to withdraw from contracts concluded with a third party which are related to the timeshare contract. This can be more favourable to the consumer, as there does not need to be an "agreement" (cf. Art. 7, 2nd indent) between the third party and the vendor.

6. Provisions transposing this Directive shall be binding

All member states have regulated in their national law that the provisions transposing Directive 94/47 are binding.

1173 Article 10 of the Act of 11 April 1999 on the Purchase of the Right to Use Immovable Properties on a Timeshare Basis.

1174 Article 12(1) of the Timeshare Contract Law.

1175 CC Article 58, 62, 63.

1176 Section 11 of the Timeshare Act.

1177 Section 384 of the Law of Obligations Act.

1178 Chapter 10 sec. 12 of the Consumer Protection Act of 20 January 1978/38.

1179 CC § 358.

1180 Article 6 of the Decree 182/1999.

1181 § 12 of the Government Decree 20/1999 (II. 5.) on Contracts for the Purchase of the Right to Use Immovable Property on a Timeshare Basis.

1182 Article 77 of the Consumer Code.

1183 Cabinet Regulation 325.

1184 10 November 1994 Law No. I-657 of the Republic of Lithuania "On Consumer Protection".

1185 Article 11 of the Timeshare Act of 18 December 1998.

1186 Article 11(1) of the Protection of Buyers in Contracts for Time Sharing of Immovable Property Regulations 2000.

1187 CC Book 7, Art. 48e(2).

1188 Article 8(2) of the Act of 13 July 2000 on the Protection of Purchasers in Respect of the Right to Use Buildings or Dwellings During Certain Time Each Year.

1189 Article 16 (6), Art. 49 (2) of the Decree-Law 275/93 of August 5.

1190 Article 60d (1)(2) of the Consumer Protection Act.

1191 Article 12 of Law 42/1998 forbids the imposition of clauses containing sanctions or penalties on the purchaser in case of withdrawal or termination.

1192 § 16 of the Timeshare Contracts (Consumer Protection) Act 1997:218.

1193 Section 6A of the Timeshare Act 1992

1194 Consumer Protection Act, Art. L. 121-67. This regulation is seen as a possible breach of EC Law.

1195 CC § 58. Termination of the loan contract cannot be connected with any sanctions exerted by the supplier or third party.

1196 § 9(1) of the Timeshare Act.

1197 CC § 358.

7. Private International Law

Article 9 states that, regardless of the law that is applicable to a specific contract, if the immovable property is situated within the territory of a member state, each country must take the necessary measures in order to ensure that the consumer is not deprived of the protection afforded by Directive 94/47.

Because of the overlaps with the general rules on International Private Law, the transpositions found in the member states vary considerably. However, at least BELGIUM, CYPRUS, the CZECH REPUBLIC, HUNGARY, IRELAND and ITALY have transposed the provision closely to the Directive.

Many other countries have tried to reach the aims of the Directive by other means. As the number of possible constellations is very high, the following reference concentrates on some significant examples. For instance, AUSTRIA, ESTONIA and POLAND, require that the timeshare contract is somehow linked to the territory of these countries. The required relation between the country and the contract can result from the fact that, for example, an offer was made by an entrepreneur to a consumer or vice versa in that specific member state. Furthermore, concerning Estonia and Poland, the timeshare contract shall be deemed as linked to the country, if the purchaser is a resident of that country or if the immovable property is located in that member state.

In SLOVENIA, domestic law is applicable to a contract concluded on the basis of business activity managed by a Slovenian enterprise, and if the consumer is a current resident of Slovenia, the immovable property does not even have to be situated within the territory of a member state of the European Union. The laws of MALTA, PORTUGAL and SPAIN require that the building concerned is located within the territory of their countries in order for the respective Maltese, Portuguese or Spanish consumer protection law to be applicable.

DENMARK, the NETHERLANDS, SWEDEN and the UNITED KINGDOM have expressly regulated that the immovable property does not necessarily have to be situated within a member state of the European Union, but can also be located within the territory of a member state of the EEA. In order for the consumer protection laws of the UNITED KINGDOM to apply, either the parties of the timeshare agreement must to some extent be subject to the jurisdiction of any court in the United Kingdom in relation to the agreement or the offeree must ordinarily reside in the United Kingdom. SWEDISH law, however, sets out that consumers will only be granted protection by Swedish rules, if the law which is actually applicable to the contract, is the law of a country which is not a member of the EU or the EEA. Similarly, in FINLAND, if the immovable property is located in an EEA state and the law of a non-EEA state would apply, Finnish consumer protection law applies to timeshare contracts insofar as it offers more effective consumer protection than the law that would be applicable otherwise.

GERMANY applies its domestic consumer protection laws to cases where the law applicable is not one of an EU member state or EEA contracting state and the immovable property is situated either within the territory of the EU or of the EEA.[1198] This is considered to be

---

1198 Article 29a(3) of the Introductory Act to the CC (EGBGB); for more details see also Art. 29 and Art. 29a(1) of the same Act.

contrary to the Directive, because the obligatory application of German law may deprive the consumer of a more favourable law. In other cases, German International Private Law makes the law of the member state which is the most closely related to the case, applicable, if there is a relation between the timeshare contract and one of the member states. Such a specific relation is deemed to be given, if the contract is concluded due to business activities in a member state of the EU or within the EEA. Furthermore, the contract is linked to the member states, if the consumer is a resident of one of these states.

In FRANCE and LUXEMBOURG, domestic consumer protection rules are also applicable to contracts where the building concerned is situated in a non-EU member state. But in this case, the consumer will only be granted protection, if the timeshare contract was concluded in a country, in which he is normally a resident or if the contract was preceded in that country by a specially drawn up offer or by an advertisement or action carried out by the consumer. Furthermore, the consumer protection law of France and Luxembourg will apply if the contract has been concluded in a country that the consumer has travelled to on the grounds of an offer of travel or accommodation made to him by the professional with the intention to induce him to sign the contract.

Under AUSTRIAN law, the application of Austrian consumer protection law to timeshare contracts is restricted to certain Articles if the immovable property is situated in another EEA-State. The consumer is only provided with protection measures that are regulated in Art. 6, Art. 7(2), Art. 8 and Art. 9 of the Timeshare Act. These Articles deal with the right of withdrawal from the timeshare contract (Art. 6) and from any relating agreements (Art. 9). Furthermore, it contains rules regarding the effect of the exercised right of withdrawal of Art. 6 on other contracts (Art. 8) and regarding the right to reclaim payments that the vendor has already taken illegally.

In LATVIA, Art. 9 has been transposed in a way that is not quite clear. It is laid down that when a timeshare contract is concluded and the immovable property is located in a foreign country, then the law in force in that particular state shall apply insofar as it complies with the provisions of the Latvian Consumer Rights Protection Law. This regulation neither states whether the building needs to be situated within the territory of a member state of the European Community, nor does it say how the case, that the law of the foreign state does not comply with Latvian law, should be handled. LITHUANIA does not seem to have transposed Art. 9 of Directive 94/47 at all.

It is highly questionable whether such a punctual provision on International Private Law should be located in individual consumer protection directives like Directive 94/47. This may lead to interferences and confusion with the Rome Convention and the planned Rome I Regulation.[1199] Therefore, leaving the question to the Rome I Regulation could be considered. It should also be borne in mind that the lines of the C-381/98– *Ingmar*[1200] ruling of the ECJ could lead to the result that a choice of law clause which deprives the consumer from his rights granted under the Directive is contrary to mandatory law and, therefore, void.

1199 See the Greenbook COM (2002) 654 final, 17.

1200 ECJ judgment of 9 November 2001, C-381/98 – *Ingmar GB Ltd and Eaton Leonard Technologies Inc.*

8. Other consumer protection instruments

Some member states provide for further consumer protection instruments. Only some instructive examples shall be pointed out here. For instance, in MALTA, the seller (and any salespersons acting on his behalf) is obliged to hold a license and to use a distinctive identification document. There are also stringent provisions prohibiting the excessive selling techniques and harassment of prospective timeshare buyers.[1201] The seller has to ensure that a period of at least 7 consecutive days in a calendar year is reserved for repairs, maintenance, cleaning and other purposes related to the upkeep of the property; a person who fails to abide with this requirement is guilty of an offence. BELGIUM and SPAIN also require a licence.

In ITALY[1202], the vendor is required to provide a bank or insurance guarantee for the execution of the contract, if it is not a company with share capital, or if it is a company without capital of at least EUR 5 164 569 and where the head office is not registered, or which has no offices in a member state. In any case the vendor is required to provide a bank or insurance guarantee for the completion of the property, when the property is under construction. If the guarantees are not expressly mentioned in the contract, the contract is void. In SPAIN, the creator of a timeshare right that needs to be registered has to conclude an insurance contract to cover the risks until the transfer of the right is completed. The owner of the building is obliged to conclude an insurance contract to cover the liability for torts caused by the titleholders of the timeshare rights. Additionally, Spanish law states a duty for the seller to terminate any contracts with suppliers of the services in case of non-performance of the services related to the right.

Some member states stipulate more specific provisions for the marketing of timeshare contracts. In BELGIUM, advertising for timesharing contracts has to be presented in a clear way, that it is a direct or indirect promotion for the sale of rights concerning the use of immovable property on a timesharing basis. Assuming that timeshare objects are often promoted by inviting consumers to sales promotion events by sending marketing letters or by giving leaflets in the streets, often strengthened with promises of free gifts, FINNISH law stipulates that if the timeshare housing is to be offered to a consumer in person at a promotion or sales event, the business shall clearly indicate the nature of the event in the invitation and supply the most significant information on the nature of the timeshare right, the selling prices the other costs and the timeshare object. The marketing document shall be available to the consumer at any time during the event, at least in the language used in the invitation to the event.

Bibliography

Proposal for a Directive of the European Parliament and of the Council on the protection of consumers in respect of certain aspects of timeshare, long-term holiday products, resale and exchange, COM(2007) 303 final; Consultation Document on revision of the Timeshare Directive, http://ec.europa.eu/consumers/rights/timeshare_en.htm; Report on the application of

---

1201 See Regulation 6 of the Timeshare and Timeshare-like Products Promotion (Licensing of OPC Representatives) Regulations.

1202 Article 76(1), Art. 76(2), Art. 76(3) of the Consumer Code.

Directive 94/47/EC of the European Parliament and Council of 26 October 1994, on the protection of purchasers in respect of certain aspects of contracts relating to the purchase of the right to use immovable properties on a timeshare basis, SEC(1999) 1795 final; **Ajani, Gianmaria / Rossi, Piercarlo**, Codice del consumatori, 2005, **Arrivas, Fabio**, La multipropiedad, Análisis de los derechos nacionales y del Derecho comunitario, Valencia 1998, **Cambier, Veronique / Dulák, Anton,** Timeshare Consumer Protection in Slovakia, Louvain-la-Neuve 2000, **Cambier, Veronique / Dulák, Anton / Karsten, Jens / Tonner, Klaus,** Timeshare and Package Travel Legislation in Central and Eastern Europe: Approximation, Harmonisation and Compatibility with European Union Law, Louvain, 2000, **Cañizares Laso, Ana / Ruiz-Rico Ruiz, José Manuel,** Multipropiedad y aprovechamiento por turno: comentarios sistemáticos a la ley sobre derecho de aprovechamiento por turno, Madrid 2000, **Caringella, Francesco**, Codice del consumo Studi di diritto civile, 2006, **D'Alessandro, Roma**, Timeshare in the E.U. and in Malta – The Impact of Directive 94/47/EC , University of Malta Doctor of Laws thesis 2002, **Efthimiatou – Poulakou, A.,** To Time-sharing ston Tourismo. Simbasi xronomeristikis misthosis, 2003, **Gam, Henrik**, Timeshare, Copenhagen 1998, **Hildenbrand, Thomas,** Vertragsgestaltung und Verbraucherschutz im Timesharing-Vertragsrecht, Frankfurt a.M./Berlin/Bern/New York/Paris/Wien 1997, **Howells, Geraint/ Weatherill, Stephen**, Consumer Protection Law, Aldershot 2005, **Hulva, Tomáš**, Ochrana spotřebitele, Praha 2005, **Kelp, Ulla**, Time-Sharing-Verträge, Baden-Baden 2005, **Łętowska, Ewa**, Europejskie prawo umów konsumenckich, Warszawa 2004, **Martinek, Michael**, Teilnutzung an Immobilien, in: Grabitz / Hilf, Das Recht der Europäischen Union, Band III, Sekundärrecht, A.13 , München 1999, **Matias, Maria Judite**, Do Direito Real de Habitação Periódica, 1997, **Munar Bernat, Pedro A.,** La regulación española de la "multipropiedad": la Ley de Derechos de aprovechamiento por turnos de bienes inmuebles de uso turístico y normas tributarias, 2003, **Nesterowicz, Miroslaw**, Prawo turystyczne, Kraków 2003, **Sorsa, Kaisa** Timeshare-matkailupalvelun tuotteistamisen lainsäädännölliset puitteet: Espanjan, Iso-Britannian ja Suomen Timeshare-lainsäädäntöä koskeva oikeusvertaileva tutkimus The Legal Framework of Productisation of Timeshare Travel Services: Comparative Study concerning Spanish, British and Finnish Legislation, 2003, **Staudinger, Ansgar,** Teilzeitwohnrechteverträge (§§ 481-487, 355 ff.), in: Gebauer/Wiedmann (Hrsg.), Zivilrecht unter Europäischen Einfluss, Kap.10, Stuttgart 2005,·**Tichý, Lubos**, Pojem spotřebitele jako smluvní strany v evropském a českém právu, Spotřebitelská legislativa EU a její implementace do práva členského a kandidátského státu (např. do Francie a České republiky (Spotřebitelská legislativa EU) 2001, 131-161,·**Toader, Camelia**, Contractul de time-sharing, acum reglementat si in Romania, Revista Romana de Drept Comunitar 2004.

E. Distance Selling Directive (97/7)

Drafted by Hans Schulte-Nölke and Andreas Börger

Executive summary

1. Transposition deficiencies

Despite many variations of the wording in the national transposition laws, the number of substantial transposition deficiencies to be found throughout the EC does not seem to be very high. Examples of at least some importance are:

- The total (as opposed to only partial) exemption of contracts in the sense of Art. 3(2) 1st indent (regular roundsmen) or 2nd indent (accommodation, transport, catering or leisure services) from the scope of application of the Directive by some member states.
- No general obligation to confirm the prior information according to Art. 5(1) sent. 1 in the CZECH REPUBLIC, LITHUANIA and SPAIN.
- The withdrawal period of seven "jour francs" in FRANCE (cf. Art. 6(1)).[1203]
- The lack of duty to inform the consumer that goods or services ordered are unavailable (Art. 7(2)) in GERMANY, GREECE and LITHUANIA.

2. Enhancement of protection

a. Extension of scope

Some member states have broadened the scope of application of their national laws on distance selling, for instance, by:

- Broadening the notion of consumer (e.g. legal persons);
- Broadening the notion of distance selling contract (e.g. no organised distance selling scheme required);
- Not transposing exceptions provided in Art. 3.

b. Use of options

The member states have made different use of the options the Directive offers:

- Article 7(3) (allowance to deliver goods or services of equivalent quality and price) has been transposed by about half of the member states.
- Article 11(3)(a) (burden of proof concerning the existence of prior information, written confirmation, compliance with time-limits or consumer consent) has also been transposed by about half of the member states.

1203 The Commission seems to be uncertain with regard to the withdrawal period in France, cf. the Commission's report COM (2006) 514 final on the implementation of Directive 97/7/EC, Annex IV; http://ec.europa.eu/consumers/cons_int/safe_shop/dist_sell/comm_21092006_en.pdf.

- Article 11(4) (self-regulatory bodies) has only been transposed by 6 member states.
- Article 14, sent. 2 (ban of marketing of certain goods or services, particularly medicinal products) has only been transposed by 2 member states.

c. Use of minimum clause

Most member states have made use of the minimum clause. Some examples of major importance are:

- Article 4: additional pre-contractual information duties (e.g. suppliers address, telephone number; non-existence of withdrawal right)
- Article 5(1):
  - Additional information to be confirmed in good time during the performance of the contract;
  - Fixing an earlier point in time when this confirmation is due;
  - Additional formal requirements: not transposing the term "another durable medium available and accessible to the consumer" and thereby obliging the supplier to always provide confirmation of the information in written form;
  - Duties to use a certain wording or form to inform the consumer (in particular a standard notice on the right of withdrawal);
  - Language requirements.
- Article 6(1):
  - Prolongation of withdrawal period;
  - Introduction of formal requirements for the exercise of the withdrawal right by the consumer;
  - Not transposing exceptions provided in Art. 6(3).

3. Inconsistencies or ambiguities

Some major inconsistencies or ambiguities of the Directive are:

- It is unclear whether mixed purpose cases fall under the notion of 'consumer' (Art. 2(2)).
- It is unclear whether non-profit organisations can fall under the notion of 'supplier' (Art. 2(3)).
- It is unclear whether the so-called 'Ebay auctions' fall under the notion of 'auction' (Art. 3(1) 5th indent).
- The requirement that certain information has to be provided 'in good time' (Art. 4(1)); Art. 5(1) seems to have created some ambiguities.
- The length of the withdrawal period (7 working days) is difficult to handle (in particular in cross-border cases where different days may be public holidays) and not in coherence with the withdrawal periods provided for in other directives.
- It is unclear whether Art. 6(1), sent. 3 and 4 prolong the withdrawal period up to three months or up to three months plus 7 working days.

- The prolongation of the withdrawal period up to the three months (probably plus 7 working days) maximum period is not in coherence with other Directives and the ECJ *Heininger*[1204] ruling.
- Article 7(1) does not mention the – necessary – prerequisite that the obligation created there only comes into force if the contract is concluded.
- The Directive does not contain any rules on the computation of time, which leaves some ambiguities, e.g. with regard to the notion of 'working day' or to time limits ending on a Sunday, other public holidays, or Saturdays.

4. Gaps in the Directive

The analysis did not reveal many gaps in the Directive. Examples of at least some importance are:

- The absence of provisions on whether it suffices for the consumer to dispatch the notice of withdrawal before the end of the withdrawal period.
- An express provision clarifying to what extent the Directive applies to digital content, such as computer software, music or games, supplied online.

5. Potential barriers to (cross-border) trade

Obvious barriers to trade in the field of the Directive are:

- The differences of the information obligations, also the differences with regard to formal requirements for the provision of information.
- The different withdrawal periods, the formal requirements imposed on the consumers when exercising their withdrawal rights, and the differences with regard to the unravelling of the contract after withdrawal (because such differences hamper the information of consumers on their withdrawal right).

6. Conclusions and recommendations

In order to remove ambiguities, the following issues could be tackled:

- Definition of consumer (with regard to mixed purpose cases);
- Definition of supplier (with regard to non-profit organisations);
- New definition of goods (with regard to digital content);
- (New) Definition of auction (with regard to Ebay auctions);
- Clarification of 'in good time' (Art. 4(1); Art. 5(1)) along the model of Directive 2002/65, perhaps also following the example of some member states;
- Provision of some rules on computation of time (or – perhaps better – a reference to Regulation 1182/71);
- Clarification whether Art. 6(1), sent. 3 and 4 prolong the withdrawal period up to three months or up to three months plus 7 working days;

1204 ECJ judgment of 13 December 2001, C-481/99 – *Georg Heininger et Helga Heininger v. Bayerische Hypo- und Vereinsbank AG.*

- Clarification in Art. 7(1) that this obligation only comes into force if the contract is concluded;
- Introduction of a dispatch rule, which also clarifies its applicability in case the consumer dispatches the declaration of withdrawal in time, but it never reaches the supplier.

Moreover, in order to at least remove the most obvious barriers to trade the following measures could be considered:

- At least the pre-contractual information (Art. 4) duties could be brought in line with Directive 2002/65 and the law of those member states which made use of the minimum clause (e.g. supplier's address, non-existence of withdrawal right).
- Provision of a (EC law) standard notice informing the consumer of his right of withdrawal.
- The withdrawal period could be changed into 14 (calendar) days, also following Directive 2002/65.
- Any formal requirement for the exercise of the withdrawal right could be prohibited.
- The (3 month) prolongation of the withdrawal period in case of non-fulfilment of information duties could be reviewed in the sense that the lack of information about the withdrawal right is exempted. For this type of information, a more intensive sanction could be envisaged, be it the eternal period along the lines of the *Heininger*[1205] case, or a much longer maximum period (e.g. one year, as is the case in FINLAND).

In particular, it will have to be considered whether at least some of these provisions could be exempted from the minimum clause and thereby maximised in order to avoid member states creating new barriers to trade.

I. Member state legislation prior to the adoption of the Distance Selling Directive

Prior to the adoption of Directive 97/7, consumer protection in the field of Directive 97/7 was rather different. This may be illustrated by three groups of examples:

1. Some member states had already enacted consumer protection legislation comparable to the protection provided by the Directive. For instance: BELGIUM in the Trade Practices Act of 1971 and the Act of 14 July 1991 on trade practices and consumer information and protection which both contained a provision on inertia selling, DENMARK with its Act No. 137 of 29 March 1978 on consumer contracts, which included provisions on distance selling, PORTUGAL with its Decree-Law 272/87 of July 3, which imposed duties of information on the trader and gave the consumer a right of withdrawal comparable to that in the Directive, and FRANCE with its "Law of 6 January 1998" which stated some rules for home shopping and had established a rather high level of consumer protection in the area of distance selling at a relatively early stage. Other member states like GREECE and SPAIN adopted legislation on the background of the Commission's proposals for a Directive on distance selling in the early 1990s.

1205 ECJ judgment of 13 December 2001 C-481/99 – *Georg Heininger and Helga Heininger v. Bayerische Hypo- und Vereinsbank AG.*

2. Member states like FINLAND, IRELAND, ITALY, the NETHERLANDS, SWEDEN and the UNITED KINGDOM had no specific legislative acts dealing with distance selling, except for some provisions on inertia selling, as in Ireland[1206] and the United Kingdom, and selling via telephone and post in Finland. Nevertheless, consumers were protected by codes of conduct and other self-regulatory instruments.

3. A third group of member states had no comparable protection in the field of distance selling before the transposition of the Directive. In AUSTRIA and GERMANY, no specific legislative protection of consumers existed in civil law. Only a small selection of commercial practices were considered unfair and, thus, sanctioned by the UWG (Act against Unfair Competition). Furthermore, in the new member states (e.g. CYPRUS, the CZECH REPUBLIC, ESTONIA, HUNGARY, LITHUANIA, MALTA, SLOVAKIA, SLOVENIA, POLAND) no comparable protection existed.

II. Scope of application

1. Consumer

In Article 2(2) of the Directive, a consumer is defined as a "natural person who, in contracts covered by this Directive, is acting for purposes which are outside his trade, business or profession".

a. Legislative techniques

Some member states have implemented a general definition of a consumer, applicable to many consumer contracts. They are e.g. AUSTRIA, BELGIUM, the CZECH REPUBLIC, ESTONIA, FINLAND, GERMANY, GREECE, ITALY, LATVIA, LITHUANIA, MALTA, the NETHERLANDS, POLAND[1207], SLOVENIA and SPAIN.

DENMARK[1208], PORTUGAL[1209], SLOVAKIA[1210] and SWEDEN have established the same definitions for doorstep and distance selling contracts. Other member states have transposed Directive 97/7 in a separate legislative act and, therefore, stipulated a separate definition in the corresponding acts, e.g. CYPRUS, IRELAND, LUXEMBOURG and the UNITED KINGDOM. In FRANCE, case-law has developed a notion of consumer because there is no explicit transposition of this definition in the national law.[1211] In HUNGARY, the transposition law of Directive 97/7 does not contain an express definition. It is unclear whether the definition of the Hungarian CC § 685(d) or the definition in § 2(e) of the Consumer Protection Act is applicable. With the planned integration of the distance selling regulation into the Civil Code in the future, this question could be cleared up.

[1206] Grabitz Hilf/*Micklitz*, Haustürwiderrufsrichtlinie, „Nach A3", Rn 17.

[1207] The POLISH CC Art. 22 (applicable to doorstep and distance selling and to unfair terms).

[1208] § 3(1) of the Act No. 451 of 9 June 2004 on certain consumer contracts.

[1209] Article 1(3)(a) of the Decree-Law 143/2001 of April 26.

[1210] § 1 of the Act No. 108/2000 on Consumer Protection in Doorstep Selling and in Distance Selling.

[1211] See for example Cass. civ., chambre civile 1, judgment of 5 March 2002, Bulletin 2002 I no. 78, 60.

Transposition of Art. 2(2) of Directive 97/7: Definition of Consumer

Reference to a more general definition	AT, BE, CZ, DE, EE, EL, ES, FI, HU, IT, LT, LV, MT, NL, PL, SL *(16)*
Definition for purposes of both doorstep and distance selling provisions	DK, PT, SE, SK *(4)*
Definition for purposes of distance selling provisions	CY, IE, LU, UK *(4)*
Not transposed expressly	FR[1212] *(1)*

b. Content of the definitions

Though generally the member states have implemented the definition of a consumer set by the Directive properly, a huge number of variations is noticeable. This is due to the fact that most member states did not transpose the definition word for word. As a result, the differences mainly consist in details only. A broad overview is given in the general chapter on the notion of consumer.[1213] With regard to distance selling, some major variations can be outlined as follows:

aa. Inclusion of certain legal persons

As in the Directive, the CYPRIOT, DUTCH, ESTONIAN, FINNISH, GERMAN, IRISH, ITALIAN, LATVIAN, LITHUANIAN, LUXEMBOURGIAN, MALTESE, PORTUGUESE, SLOVENIAN, SLOVAKIAN, SWEDISH and UK Regulations are expressly limited in the scope of distance selling and only apply to natural persons. In LATVIA, there has recently been a reform, so that from now on legal persons are excluded from the notion of consumer.[1214]

In some countries, however, certain legal persons (e.g. private associations) are treated as consumers on the condition that they act for private purposes. Such member states are AUSTRIA, BELGIUM[1215], the CZECH REPUBLIC, DENMARK, FRANCE, GREECE[1216], HUNGARY, IRELAND, POLAND and SPAIN.

Overview: Inclusion of legal persons

Limitation to natural persons	CY, DE, EE, FI, IE, IT, LT, LU, LV, MT, NL, PT, SE, SL, SK, UK *(16)*
Inclusion of certain legal persons	AT, BE, CZ, DK, EL, ES, FR, HU, PL *(9)*

1212 Case-law has developed a notion: See for example Cass. civ., chambre civile 1, judgment of 5 March 2002, Bulletin 2002 I no. 78, 60.

1213 See Part 3. A.

1214 Amendment of the Consumer Protection Law, which came into force on 11 November 2005.

1215 Article 1 No.7° of the TPA: "act for exlusively private purposes".

1216 In GREECE, legal persons are treated as consumers even if they act for professional purposes, provided that they are the end recipients of the products or services.

bb. Clarification of 'mixed' purpose cases

The definition of consumer in Art. 2(2) of Directive 97/7 does not clarify expressly whether a person who concludes a contract intended for a 'mixed' purpose falls under the notion of consumer (e.g. a purpose which is in part within and in part outside his trade or profession, for example, the purchase of a car for both private and professional use). In applying the rather similar definition in Art. 13 of the Brussels (I) Convention, the ECJ (C-464/01 – *Gruber*) has held that in such a case the person may not rely on the special rules of jurisdiction laid down in Articles 13 to 15 of the Convention, unless the trade or professional purpose "is so limited as to be negligible in the overall context of the supply". The fact that the private element is predominant has been considered to be irrelevant in that respect. It is an open question whether this ruling is also applicable in the field of distance selling.

Some member states have tried to clarify when a person concluding such a contract for a 'mixed' purpose is a consumer. DENMARK, FINLAND[1217] and SWEDEN[1218] have expressly stated that in such cases the preponderant purpose prevails. According to the preparatory works, in Finland, as a guideline, the professional purpose is at question when a person is accountable according to the Accounting Act.[1219] In GERMANY, the courts would probably also focus on the question of whether the private or business purpose is predominant.[1220] In ITALY, the definition is rather similar to the Directive in this respect. But in the case where a small tobacconist concluded a contract for the hire of a vehicle, which was for both private and business use, he was held to be a consumer.[1221] It is not clear from that decision whether the private use was predominant. Mixed purpose transactions are not a problem in GREECE, as according to the notion of consumer, a professional might also be treated as a consumer. In Greece, the only criteria is whether the consumer is the end recipient of the product or service or not.

In AUSTRIA[1222] and BELGIUM[1223], the consumer needs to acquire or use goods or services for purposes which fall outside his professional activity. As a consequence, a person is considered to be a consumer only if he or she has concluded the contract for a purely private purpose. Although the definition of some other member states reads rather similarly, it cannot be discerned how the courts would decide on the matter.

1217 Chapter 1 sec. 4 of the Consumer Protection Act of 20 January 1978/38.

1218 Chapter 1 sec. 2 of the Law (2005:59) on Consumer Protection on Distance Contracts and Doorstep Selling Contracts.

1219 Kirjanpitolaki 1336/1997.

1220 Cf. OLG Naumburg, judgment of 11 December 1997, NJW-RR 1998, 1351 (concerning consumer credit).

1221 Giudice di pace Civitanova Marche, 4 December 2001, Gius 2002, 1188.

1222 § 1(1)(1) and § 1(1)(2) of the Consumer Protection Law: § 1(1) Dieses Hauptstück gilt für Rechtsgeschäfte, an denen

1. einerseits jemand, für den das Geschäft zum Betrieb seines Unternehmens gehört, (im folgenden kurz Unternehmer genannt) und

2. andererseits jemand, für den dies nicht zutrifft, (im folgenden kurz Verbraucher genannt) beteiligt sind.

1223 Article 1 No. 7 of the Act of 14 July 1991 on Trade Practices and Consumer Information and Protection and Art. 2(2) of the Act of 2 August 2002 on Misleading and Comparative Advertising, Unfair Contract Terms and Distance Marketing in Respect of Professional Services.

Overview: 'mixed' purpose transactions as consumer contract

Purely private purpose	AT, BE *(2)*
Also 'mixed' purpose, preponderant purpose prevails	DE, DK, FI, SE *(4)*
Also 'mixed' purpose – unclear whether private purpose must preponderate	IT *(1)*
No clear rule on 'mixed' purpose transactions discernible	CY, CZ, EE, EL, ES, FR[1224], HU, IE, LT, LU, LV, MT, NL, PL, PT, SK, SL, UK *(18)*

cc. Extension to certain professionals

Some member states have broadened the notion of consumer in a way that it also covers certain professionals. This is the case in FRANCE, where, according to well-established case-law, a consumer is a (natural or legal) person concluding contracts which are not directly related to his or her profession.[1225] Hence, a business will be protected like a consumer if an atypical contract is concluded. In such a case the business will be considered as non-professional.[1226] In POLAND, the seemingly rather similar definition of the CC is applicable so that a person who is acting indirectly for his professional purposes is also considered to come under the definition of consumer. Also the LATVIAN[1227] law provided for a similar definition: a natural or legal person who expresses a wish to purchase, purchases or might purchase goods or utilises a service for a purpose which is not directly related to his or her entrepreneurial activity. In GREECE, where in contrast to other member states a limitation to private purposes does not exist, a consumer is any individual or legal entity for whom goods or services on the market are intended, or who makes use of these goods or services, provided that this individual or legal entity constitutes the end recipient of the goods or services. The recipient of advertisements is equally regarded as a consumer. In practice, such a broad definition can lead to difficulties in applying the law, so that in academic literature a necessity for a teleological reduction is considered. The condition for being qualified as an end consumer is a need for protection which must be verified in each case. MALTESE law refers to the general definition of the consumer in the Consumer Affairs Act, which contains the most detailed rule of all member states. Under the relevant law a consumer is:

(i) any individual who in transactions and other matters is acting for purposes which are not related to his trade, business, craft or profession; and

(ii) any other individual, not being the immediate purchaser or beneficiary, and whether or not a member of the consumer's household, who having been expressly or tacitly authorised or permitted by the consumer, may have consumed, used or benefited from any goods or services provided to the consumer by a trader acting in the course of a trade, business, craft or profession, including goods or services provided as part of gift schemes and similar or analogous inducements; and

---

1224 In lower jurisdictions' case-law, some examples of application of the unfair terms' legislation in cases of mixed purpose can be found, where private purpose preponderates.

1225 See for example Cass. civ., chambre civile 1, judgment of 5 March 2002, Bulletin 2002 I no. 78, 60.

1226 See the general chapter on the notion of consumer, Part 3.A. for more details.

1227 Since 27 October 2005 when the changes in Consumer Rights Protection Law were made, the definition of consumer applies only to any natural person.

(iii) any other class or category of persons whether natural or legal as may, from time to time, be designated as "consumers" for all or for any of the purposes of the Consumer Affairs Act by the Minister responsible for consumer affairs after consulting the Consumer Affairs Council.

At least no. iii also allows professionals to fall under the Maltese definition of consumer.[1228]

SPANISH law does not use the terms of the Directive but instead – partly – introduces the notion of a "buyer". Nevertheless, in other articles the "consumer" is mentioned. The notion includes legal persons and focuses on the concept of "final addressee". This term seems to include any buyer, that is the public in general, and not necessarily the "consumer", as Spanish law does not refer to the terms "acting for purposes outside of his trade". The scope of application of Spanish law is much broader than in the Directive on the one hand. On the other hand it could be doubted that Spanish law covers a buyer who wants to use a good for a private purpose but who intends to resell it afterwards. It is disputed in Spanish legal literature whether this can be brought in line with the Directive.

In GERMANY, the relevant definition of the term consumer clarifies that an employee who concludes a contract for a purpose in relation to his job is protected as a consumer (e.g. a worker buying workwear). Accordingly, the German Bundesarbeitsgericht (Federal Labour Court) considers an employee to be a consumer.[1229] It is possible that, to some extent, some other member states also protect professionals as consumers.

Overview: extension to certain professionals

Extension to certain professionals	EL, FR, MT, LV, PL *(5)*
Clarification that employees are consumers	DE *(1)*

dd. Examples for variations in wording

The variety of national transpositions can be exemplified by some further national laws. Most follow the wording of Directive 97/7 rather closely. Examples are, besides many others, CYPRUS, PORTUGAL or LUXEMBOURG (e.g. *« toute personne physique qui, dans les contrats relevant de la présente loi, agit à des fins qui n'entrent pas dans le cadre de son activité professionnelle »*). In ESTONIA, the term is much the same ("purposes not related to his or her business or professional activities"). This also applies to the NETHERLANDS, where a consumer constitutes a natural person who is acting for purposes which are outside his trade, business or profession. In the UK, it is any natural person who, in contracts to which these Regulations apply, is acting for purposes which are outside his business. A similar definition is given by CZECH legislation: Consumer means any person who, when concluding and performing a contract, does not act in his commercial or entrepreneurial capacity. SLOVAKIAN law considers a natural person as a consumer when he or she buys the goods or a material performance or deed

---

1228 It is to be noted that the Minister has to date not specifically designated professionals as a class or category to be included within the definition of consumers.

1229 Bundesarbeitsgericht, judgment of 25 May 2005, 5 AZR 572/04, NJW 2005, 3305; cf. also Part 3. A. of the study "Definition of consumer".

from the service provided and they are not used to perform that person's trade, profession or business. The SLOVENIAN definition resembles the following; a consumer is any natural person who acquires or uses goods or services for purposes which are outside his professional or profit-making activity. Likewise in LITHUANIA, where a consumer means a natural person, who expresses the intention to buy, buys and uses goods or services for a purpose that can be regarded as outside his trade or profession to meet his own personal or household needs. AUSTRIAN law approaches the notion of a consumer in a negative way: a consumer is someone who is *not* a trader. A trader is in turn someone for whom the transaction belongs to the business of his enterprise. Although different in wording, such definitions seem to transpose the Directive properly or can at least be interpreted in accordance with the Directive.

2. Supplier

Under the terms of Directive 97/7, a supplier is "any natural or legal person who, in contracts covered by this Directive, is acting in his commercial or professional capacity". The wording of this definition slightly varies from the respective definitions in the other consumer protection directives.[1230] Nevertheless, it can be assumed that these definitions are generally to be interpreted in a similar way.

It might be useful to bear in mind that the main purpose of the definition of the supplier is simply to clarify that the Directive is only applicable for B2C situations, but not in C2C relations. Therefore, variations in the transposition laws of the member states are not very relevant for the proper functioning of the law, as long as the definition of consumer is precise and the respective definition of its counterpart does not exclude persons who come under "supplier" in the sense of the Directive.

From this starting point, the differences to be found in the member states do not seem to be far-reaching. Some member states have used the copy and paste technique transposing the definition into their national law, e.g. DENMARK, IRELAND, ITALY, the NETHERLANDS and PORTUGAL. However, not all member states have explicitly adopted this definition. In the CZECH REPUBLIC the general definition of supplier also applies to distance selling situations.[1231] In ESTONIA, FINLAND, MALTA, POLAND and SWEDEN, the term "trader" is used, whilst in ITALY and LUXEMBOURG, it is the "professional"[1232] against whom the consumers can exercise their rights. In SLOVENIAN legislation, the term "undertaking" is used, whilst in GERMANY, it is "entrepreneur". Many member states have tried to clarify details or give examples. LATVIAN[1233] and LITHUANIAN[1234] law list the "seller" of goods and the "service pro-

---

[1230] For more details see Part 3.B.

[1231] CC § 52(2) applicable for all consumer contracts: "... a person who concludes and fulfils a contract within the framework of his commercial or other business activity".

[1232] In LUXEMBURG "professionel", in ITALY "professionista".

[1233] Article 1 CRPL defines "service provider" as a natural or legal person who provides a service to a consumer. The definition does not include any reference to the entrepreneurial or professional activity of person

[1234] Under the terms of the Law on Consumer Protection **seller** means a person who sells the goods on the premises intended for business purposes or outside them, and **service provider** means a person who supplies services to the market.

vider". BELGIUM uses the notion of "seller", focusing on the activity of selling goods or services[1235] and not – slightly different from the Directive – on the contract itself. This seems to be similar in ESTONIA and FINLAND, where – besides selling – offering and marketing of goods and services are enumerated. Moreover, the BELGIAN legislator has explicitly included traders and artisans.[1236] The HUNGARIAN legislator has enumerated certain business enterprises in its transposition law.

Further examples of additions are revealed in GERMAN legislation, where partnerships with legal capacity (meaning those who are capable of acquiring rights and entering into engagements) are expressly mentioned (CC § 14), or in the CYPRIOT notion, where the supplier acts "either personally or through his representative".[1237] MALTA expressly makes reference to corporate and incorporated bodies as well as to commercial partnerships. Among others, AUSTRIA, FINLAND, GREECE and MALTA have made clear that legal persons of public law are also covered. In other member states, Germany for example, the same would follow from the general definition of legal person.

Some member states have tried to clarify whether a person who does not intend to make a profit is included. In AUSTRIA, the legal transaction has to belong to the undertaking of the business. The term 'business' is defined as an organisation of independent commercial activity, even if it does not have the aim of making a profit. In GREECE, non-profit-making organisations or institutions as well as public corporations and local authorities can also act as suppliers.[1238] The GERMAN courts also seem to interpret the definition in a way that an intention to make a profit is not a prerequisite to qualify a person, who regularly and steadily sells goods, as an entrepreneur.[1239] In contrast to that, SLOVENIAN and FINNISH law expressly regulate that the purpose of making a profit or other economic gain is necessary in order to qualify as a professional.

In two member states though, no explicit definition of "supplier" exists. The SPANISH implementing legislation relates to the term "retail trade" (in Art. 1(2) of the Law 7/1996) and sometimes characterises the supplier as an "enterprise of distance selling" while other provisions refer to the "seller". It cannot be assessed to what extent such a variety of terms causes difficulties in the application of Spanish law. In FRANCE, however, where also no explicit definition exists, a considerably wide application has been favoured by the legal literature[1240] and the courts.

1235 Only the provision of services which constitute acts of commerce (as referred to in Art. 2 - 3 Commercial Code) or artisanal activities fall under the scope of the Act of 14 July 1991 on Trade Practices and Consumer Information and Protection.

1236 Article 1(6) of the Act of 14 July 1991 on Trade Practices and Consumer Information and Protection.

1237 Article 2 of the Law for the Conclusion of Consumer Distance Contracts of 2000.

1238 Article 1(4)(ß) and Art. 1(3) of the Consumer Protection Act.

1239 BGH judgment of 29 March 2006, VIII ZR 173/05, NJW 2006, 2250.

1240 *Calais-Auloy, Steinmetz,* Droit de la consommation, 4, propose to include all kinds of professionals such as private or public institutions/ co-operations, irrespective of a purpose of gaining profit and stress the organised and customary character which creates an imbalance between the professional and the consumer.

3. Contracts falling within the scope of the Directive

a. Definition of "distance contract"

According to Art. 2(1) of the Directive, the term 'distance contract` means any contract:

- concerning goods or services,
- under an organised distance sales or service-provision scheme run by the supplier,
- that, for the purpose of the contract, makes exclusive use of one or more means of distance communication up to and including the moment at which the contract is concluded.

AUSTRIA, BELGIUM, CYPRUS, DENMARK, FRANCE, GERMANY, IRELAND, ITALY, LUXEMBOURG, MALTA, PORTUGAL, SLOVENIA and the UNITED KINGDOM have, verbatim or almost verbatim, transposed the definition of a distance contract given in Art. 2(1) of Directive 97/7. FINLAND, the NETHERLANDS and SWEDEN have used some different terms which seem to have the same meaning as the definition in the Directive. ESTONIA[1241] and LATVIA[1242] have added that the supplier must have made an offer or a proposal to the consumer to make an offer. Among others, CZECH[1243], DANISH[1244], ESTONIAN[1245], GREEK[1246], POLISH[1247] and SPANISH[1248] law clarify the definition by stating that there is no distance contract if the supplier and the consumer are present together in the same place at the time the contract is concluded.

Some member states have not implemented the – restrictive – precondition that the contract must be concluded "under an organised distance sales or service-provision scheme". This can be observed for the CZECH REPUBLIC, HUNGARY, LATVIA, LITHUANIA and SLOVAKIA. Consequently, such member states have extended the scope of application of their distance selling laws to contracts concluded without such a system, e.g. cases where the supplier uses means of distance communication, merely exceptionally, for the conclusion of a contract.

b. Definition of "means of distance communication"

Article 2(4), sent. 1 of Directive 97/7 defines "means of distance communication", being one of the elements of the distance contract, as "any means which, without the simultaneous physical presence of the supplier and the consumer, may be used for the conclusion of a contract between those parties".

1241 § 52 (1)(2) of the Law of Obligations Act.

1242 Article 10(1) of the Consumer Rights Protection Law.

1243 § 53(1) of the CC.

1244 § 10a(1) of the Consumer Contracts Act.

1245 § 52(1)(3) of the Law of Obligations Act.

1246 Article 4(1) of the Consumer Protection Act 2251/94.

1247 Article 6(1) of the Act of 2 March 2000 on the Protection of Certain Consumer Rights and Liability for an Unsafe Product.

1248 Article 38(1) of the Law 7/1996 of January 15 on retail trade.

Most of the member states have transposed this definition literally or with only some deviations in the wording, e.g. AUSTRIA[1249], BELGIUM[1250], CYPRUS[1251], the CZECH REPUBLIC[1252], DENMARK[1253], ESTONIA[1254], FINLAND[1255], FRANCE[1256], GERMANY[1257], IRELAND[1258], ITALY[1259], LITHUANIA[1260], LUXEMBOURG[1261], MALTA[1262], the NETHERLANDS[1263], PORTUGAL[1264], SLOVENIA[1265] and the UNITED KINGDOM[1266].

POLISH[1267] and SLOVAKIAN[1268] legislation have incorporated the definition of "means of distance communication" into the definition of a distance contract. GREEK[1269] and SPANISH law[1270] use the term, but do not define it. LATVIAN[1271] law does not give a theoretical definition of "means of distance communication", but lists possible and more frequently used means of communication. Also in SWEDEN, the term "means of distance communication" is not defined. The Swedish Law on Consumer Protection on Distance Contracts and Door-

---

1249 § 5a(2) of the Consumer Protection Act.

1250 Article 77(1)(2) of the Act of 14 July 1991 on trade practices and consumer information and protection; Art. 2(7) of the Act of 2 August 2002 on Misleading and Comparative Advertising, Unfair Contract Terms and Distance Marketing in Respect of Professional Services.

1251 Article 2, 6th indent of the Law for the Conclusion of Consumer Distance Contracts of 2000.

1252 CC § 53(1), also including "means ..., operated by an entrepreneur whose activity involves provision of one or more means of distance communication".

1253 § 4 of the Consumer Contracts Act.

1254 § 52(2) of the Law of Obligations Act.

1255 Chapter 6 § 4 of the Consumer Protection Act of 20 January 1978/38.

1256 Consumer Protection Act, Art. L. 121-16.

1257 CC § 312b(2).

1258 Article 2(1) 7th indent of the Protection of Consumers in Respect of Contracts made by Means of Distance Communication Regulation.

1259 Article 50(1)(b) of the Legislative Decree of 6 September 2005, No. 206 "Consumer Code".

1260 Article 2(10) of the Law on consumer protection.

1261 Article 1(4) of the Distance Contracts Act of 16 April 2003.

1262 Article 2, 6th indent of the Distance Selling Regulations, 2001.

1263 CC Book 7 Art. 46a(e).

1264 Article 2(b) of the Decree-Law 143/2001 of April 26.

1265 Article 43(2) of the Consumer Protection Act.

1266 Regulation 3(1) 16th indent of the Consumer Protection (Distance Selling) Regulations 2000.

1267 Article 6(1) of the Act of 2 March 2000 on the Protection of Certain Consumer Rights and Liability for an Unsafe Product.

1268 According to § 9 para. 1 of the Act No. 108/2000 on Consumer Protection in Doorstep Selling and in Distance Selling (as amended by Act No. 118/2006 Z.z. (date of coming into force 1 April 2006) 'distance contract' means a contract on goods or services concluded between a supplier and a consumer with the use of one or more means of distance communication, as mainly; addressed letter, addressed book-post, unaddressed book-post, offering catalogue, book-post advertisement with order form, automatic telephone set, telephone, videophone, fax, videotext (microcomputer with TV monitor) with keyboard or touch-sensitive display , radio, teleshopping or electronic mail .

1269 Article 4(1), sent. 1 and 2 of the Law 2251/94 on Consumer Protection.

1270 Article 38(6) of the Law 7/1996 of January 15 on retail trade.

1271 Article 10 (1) of the Consumer Rights Protection Law.

step Selling Contracts uses a verbal construction instead, which reads as "communication takes place exclusively at a distance".[1272]

Article 2(4), sent. 2 of the Directive refers to Annex I which contains a rather detailed indicative list of examples of means of distance communication. Seemingly, the member states have different legislative cultures to deal with such detailed lists of examples. Some have left it out completely (e.g. BELGIUM, DENMARK, FRANCE, LUXEMBOURG, the NETHERLANDS, PORTUGAL and SPAIN). ITALY had originally had such a list but recently adopted its new Consumer Code[1273], which had it removed.[1274] However, CYPRUS, the CZECH REPUBLIC, GREECE, HUNGARY[1275], IRELAND, MALTA, SLOVENIA[1276], LITHUANIA and the UNITED KINGDOM ("letter" instead of "standard letter") have basically adopted the examples of the Annex. Other national legislators have been inspired to omit or to add some examples in order to improve the list. The CZECH REPUBLIC exempts correspondence.[1277] ESTONIA, FINLAND and SLOVAKIA have the notion "telephone" for both cases "telephone with or without human intervention" of the Annex. GERMANY has shortened the list to some core techniques and incorporated it into the definition of 'means of distance communications'. POLISH[1278], LITHUANIAN[1279] and SLOVAKIAN[1280] law have added further examples to their list. As the list is only indicative, such examples should not infringe EC law, in particular when the definition is transposed properly, which anyway has to be interpreted in accordance with the Directive.

c. Definition of "operator of a means of communication"

Article 2(5) of Directive 97/7 defines an 'operator of a means of communication' as "any public or private natural or legal person whose trade, business or profession involves making one or more means of distance communication available to suppliers". It should be noted that the term 'operator of a means of communication' is rather self-explanatory and is used in the Directive only in two cases, namely in Art. 5(2) and in Art. 11(3)(b). The first being a small exception from a general rule, the second being a rather general task assigned to the member states which can be implemented in many ways. Therefore, it is easily possible to transpose these two articles of the Directive without an explicit definition of the term 'operator of a means of communication' or even without using it at all.

1272 Chapter 1 Section 2 of the Law (2005:59) on Consumer Protection in Distance Contracts and Doorstep Selling Contracts.

1273 Legislative decree of 6 September 2005, No. 206 "Consumer Code".

1274 Legislative decree of 22 May 1999, No. 185 "Implementation of the Directive 97/7/EC concerning distance contracts between consumers and suppliers".

1275 § 1(5) of the Government Decree No. 17/1999 (II.5.) on Distance Contracting.

1276 Under SLOVENIAN law in particular, the following are means of distance communication: standard letter and other printed matters, catalogues, telephone conversations, press advertising with order form, teleshopping, facsimile machine, electronic mail, internet.

1277 CC § 53(1).

1278 "Electronic advertising ... or other electronic means of communication within the meaning of the Act of 18 July 2002 on the provision of electronic services (Official Gazette No 144, item 1204)".

1279 "Telegraph".

1280 "Address list".

Thus, it is not a surprise that many member states have not transposed this notion at all, such as AUSTRIA, the CZECH REPUBLIC, FRANCE, GERMANY, GREECE, HUNGARY, LATVIA, SLOVENIA, SLOVAKIA and SWEDEN. DANISH law does not contain a specific definition of a *provider* of communication technique, corresponding with Art. 2(5) of Directive 97/7. A specific definition is not deemed necessary since the definition of a provider in the Directive already corresponds with the generally applicable understanding of "a provider" under Danish law.

However, BELGIUM, CYPRUS, ITALY, LUXEMBOURG and PORTUGAL have transposed the term by copy and paste technique. Some national legislators deviate slightly from the wording of the Directive, e.g. the NETHERLANDS. SPANISH law replaces "whose trade involves making available" with "who are titleholders of the means of communication".[1281] Others do not distinguish in regard to the specific nature of the entrepreneur between natural and legal (UNITED KINGDOM[1282]) or public and private (IRELAND[1283] and LITHUANIA[1284]). This may be due to the respective national meaning of the term 'person' which often includes legal persons or public law persons.[1285]

FINLAND[1286] abstains from its own definition of an operator of a means of communication. POLAND refers to the Directive's definition for the transposition of Art. 5(2) of Directive 97/7 ("invoiced by a natural or legal person who within the framework of his enterprise makes at least one means of distance communication available, to which the consumer and the contractor have access"[1287]). The ESTONIAN Electronic Communication Act uses the term of an "electronic communications undertaking", which is defined as "a person who provides a publicly available electronic communications service to the end user or to another provider of a publicly available electronic communications service".[1288] Such variations seem to be deviations of the wording only and not of the substance.

1281 Article 48(2) of the Law 7/1996.

1282 Regulation 3(1) of the Consumer Protection Regulations 2000.

1283 Article 2(1) of the Protection of Consumers in Respect of Contracts made by Means of Distance Communication Regulation.

1284 Article 2(11) of the Law on Consumer Protection.

1285 E.g. MALTA where the Interpretation Act Cap. 249 of the Laws of Malta applies – more specifically Article 4(d) which states that the express 'person' shall include a body or other association of persons, whether such a body or association is corporate or not.

1286 Chapter 6 § 4 (1) the Consumer Protection Act.

1287 Article 9(4) of the Act of 2 March 2000 on the Protection of Certain Consumer Rights and Liability for an Unsafe Product.

1288 § 2(5) of the Electronic Communications Act.

d. Exemptions provided by Art. 3 of the Distance Selling Directive

aa. Contracts concluded by means of automatic vending machines or automated commercial premises

Exemption (Art. 3(1) 2nd indent)	Member States
As in the Directive	AT, CY,CZ, DE, DK, EL, ES, FI, FR, IE, IT, LV, LU, MT, NL, PL, PT, SE, SK, UK *(20)*
Variations	EE, HU, LT, SL *(4)*
Not transposed	BE *(1)*

The exemption concerning contracts concluded by means of automatic vending machines or automated commercial premises has been adopted by a great majority of member states, with the exception of BELGIUM. AUSTRIA has, in general, transposed this exemption, but the specific protection with regard to fraudulent use of credit cards according to Art. 8 of the Directive has been transposed in a way that it is also applicable to contracts concluded by means of automatic vending machines.[1289] ESTONIA[1290], HUNGARY[1291], LITHUANIA[1292] and SLOVENIA[1293] did not implement the exemption for "automated commercial premises", but for "automatic vending machines". LITHUANIA exempts these contracts from the application of Articles 4 (prior information), 5 (confirmation), 7(1) (obligation to execute the order within a maximum of 30 days) and Article 11(3)(a) of the Directive.[1294]

bb. Contracts concluded with telecommunications operators through the use of public payphones, Art. 3(1) 3rd indent

Exemption (Art. 3(1) 3rd indent)	Member States
As in the Directive	CY,CZ, DK, ES, FI, FR, HU, IE, IT, LV, LU, MT, NL, PL, PT, SE, SK, SL, UK *(19)*
Variations	DE, EE, LT *(3)*
Not transposed	AT, BE, EL *(3)*

This exemption has been transposed in all countries except for AUSTRIA, BELGIUM and GREECE. The LITHUANIAN legislator did not restrict the provision to the use of public payphones, but excludes all contracts concluded with telecommunications operators. In ESTONIA[1295] and GERMANY[1296], the transposition law only exempts the contracts concluded with telecommunications operators through the use of public payphones insofar as they concern the use of those payphones.

1289 § 31a of the Consumer Protection Act.

1290 § 53(2)(1) of the Law of Obligations Act.

1291 § 1(3)(b) of the Government Decree 17/1999 (II.5.) on Distance Contracting.

1292 Article 17(3) 5th indent of the Law on Consumer Protection.

1293 Article 43a(1)(5) 1st indent of the Consumer Protection Act.

1294 Article 17(3) of the Law on Consumer Protection; CC Art. 6.366(3).

1295 § 53(2)(2) of the Law of Obligations Act.

1296 CC § 312b(3)(7)(b).

cc. Contracts concluded for the construction and sale of immovable property, Art. 3(1) 4th indent

Exemption (Art. 3(1) 4th indent)	Member States
As in the Directive	AT, CY,CZ, DE, DK, FR, HU, IE, IT, LU, MT, PL, PT, SK, SL, UK *(16)*
Variations	BE, EE, ES, FI, NL, SE *(6)*
Not transposed	EL, LT, LV *(3)*

Only GREECE, LATVIA and LITHUANIA did not make use of this exemption. In BELGIUM, the exemption is not transposed in the Act of 2 August 2002 on Misleading and Comparative Advertising, Unfair Contract Terms and Distance Marketing in Respect of Professional Services (Liberal Professions Act, LPA). The Act of 14 July 1991 on Trade Practices and Consumer Information and Protection (Trade Practices Act, TPA) on the other hand does not apply to the sale of immovable goods. But according to well-established case-law, the TPA applies to all service contracts relating to immovable property, including e.g. contracts for the construction of an immovable property. Whereas ESTONIA did not implement the part "except for rental", SPAIN did not include the entire part relating to "other immovable property rights, except for rental". The NETHERLANDS[1297] and SWEDEN[1298] only exempt contracts for the construction of immovable property. In contrast, FINNISH legislation does not refer to the construction of immovable property. Swedish law also mentions, besides the construction of buildings, "other fixed plants on land or in water"[1299]. Member states like GERMANY, Finland and SLOVENIA explicitly exempt timeshare contracts besides contracts concluded for the construction and sale of immovable property.

dd. Contracts concluded at an auction, Art. 3(1) 5th indent

Exemption (Art. 3 (1) 5th indent)	Member States
As in the Directive	AT, CY, CZ, HU, IE, IT, LT, LU, MT, NL, PL, PT, UK *(13)*
Variations	DE, DK, EE, ES, FI, FR, LV, SE, SK, SL *(10)*
Not transposed	BE, EL *(2)*

Except for GREECE and BELGIUM, this exemption has been transposed by every member state. However, BELGIUM has not totally exempted auctions, as the Trade Practices Act[1300] and the Liberal Professions Act[1301] only contain provisions that empower the King to lay down specific provisions for public auctions organised by means of distance communication.

1297 CC Book 7 Art. 46i(2)(b).

1298 SWEDEN exempts contracts that are concluded for the construction of buildings or other fixed plants on land or in water.

1299 Chapter 2 Section 1 of the Law (2005:59) on Consumer Protection in Distance Contracts and Doorstep Selling Contracts.

1300 Article 83undecies(1) No. 6 of the TPA.

1301 Article 11, sent. 3 of the Act of 2 August 2002 on Misleading and Comparative Advertising, Unfair Contract Terms and Distance Marketing in Respect of Professional Services.

Again, there are a significant number of member states who have deviated from the Directive. In LATVIA, the supplier is disburdened from any duties of information and from a right of withdrawal, when the contract has been concluded at an auction[1302], whereas the other provisions of the distance selling law seem to be applicable. GERMANY and ESTONIA have not completely exempted auctions. In ESTONIA, auctions are only exempted from the right of withdrawal. This is similar in GERMANY, where the rules on distance contracts in principle apply to auctions, but the consumer does not have the right of withdrawal.[1303] The Federal Supreme Court has held in this context that an Ebay 'auction' is not to be considered as an 'auction' in this sense.[1304] Consequently, Ebay auctions fall under the distance selling laws.

The same result with regard to Ebay auctions should be reached in the following countries. DENMARK exempts auctions where "a significant number of bidders is normally present at the place of the auction". The FINNISH Consumer Protection Act does not apply to contracts concluded at an auction, "if participation in the auction is also possible without using a means of distance communication"[1305]. In SPAIN, auctions are generally exempted from the scope of application, but the Law 7/1996 of January 15 on retail trade[1306] is, according to its Art. 38(3) (b), applicable to auctions concluded by electronic means. SWEDISH law does not apply to contracts concluded at auctions where the bidding could be made by means other than at a distance.[1307] In FRANCE,[1308] SLOVAKIA[1309] and SLOVENIA,[1310] only public auctions are exempted.

ee. Partial exemption of contracts for the supply of foodstuffs etc. supplied by regular roundsmen, Art. 3(2) 1st indent

Partial Exemption (Art. 3(2) 2nd indent)	Member States
As in the Directive	AT, DE, DK, ES, FR, IT, LU, MT, NL, PL, PT, SE, UK *(13)*
Variations	CY, CZ, EE, EL, FI, HU, IE, LV, LT, SK, SL *(11)*
Not transposed	BE *(1)*

1302 Sections 8.3 and 15.9 of the Regulation regarding Distance Contracts.

1303 CC § 312d(4)(5).

1304 BGH judgment of 3 November 2004, VIII ZR 375/03, NJW 2004, 53-56.

1305 Chapter 6 sec. 6(5) of the Consumer Protection Act 20.1.1978/38.

1306 Ley 7/1996, de 15 de enero, de ordenación del comercio minorista.

1307 Chapter 2 Section 1(2)(4) of the Law (2005:59) on Consumer Protection in Distance Contracts and Doorstep Selling Contracts.

1308 A "vente aux enchères publiques" is a classical auction where movable or immovable goods are sold openly to the public. The auction is mostly driven by a "commissaire priseur" who is a public official.

1309 The Act on Voluntary Public Auction 527/2002 provides provisions on public auctions. The Act applies to the sales initiated by the owner of the unsecured assets, as well as to the sales of pledged assets initiated by the secured creditor on behalf of the pledgor.

1310 The public auction is regulated in the Execution of Judgments in Civil Matters and Insurance of Claims Act; the Ministry of Justice is empowered to regulate the procedure of the public auction in detail by regulation. The public auction is basically a way of selling certain seized movables (of higher value and is expected that they will be sold for a higher price than the estimated value).

According to Art. 3(2) 1st indent of Directive 97/7, Articles 4 (prior information), 5 (confirmation), 6 (right of withdrawal) and 7(1) (obligation to execute the order within a maximum of 30 days) do not apply to contracts "for the supply of foodstuffs, beverages or other goods intended for everyday consumption supplied to the home of the consumer, to his residence or to his workplace by regular roundsmen". This exemption is said to be designed for the traditional English dairy man, but its scope is, of course, broader.

All the member states, except for BELGIUM, have implemented provisions transposing this exemption. AUSTRIA, DENMARK, FRANCE[1311], GERMANY, ITALY, LUXEMBOURG, MALTA, the NETHERLANDS, POLAND, PORTUGAL, SPAIN, SWEDEN and the UNITED KINGDOM have transposed this partial exemption more or less literally. In principle, FINLAND has also implemented the exemption for the supply of foodstuff by regular roundsmen, but has narrowed it slightly.[1312] If the supplier offers those goods and services by way of "cold calling", the provisions on prior information, the confirmation and the right of withdrawal all apply.[1313] According to LITHUANIAN law, no reference to the supply by regular roundsmen is made. Furthermore, the provisions transposing Art. 11 (3)(a) of the Directive do not apply to these contracts.[1314]

By contrast, some member states, such as the CZECH REPUBLIC, GREECE, SLOVAKIA and SLOVENIA, have widened the exemption and completely excluded these contracts from the scope of application of their transposition laws. This may constitute an infringement of the Directive, as, for instance, Art. 8 (Payment per Card) and Art. 9 (Inertia Selling) are applicable to such contracts and, therefore, must be transposed. Contrary to the Directive, ESTONIA has broadened the exemption by also excluding the provisions transposing Art. 7(2) of Directive 97/7.[1315] The IRISH transposition law states that Regulations 4, 5, 6 and 7(1) shall not apply to the contracts for the supply of foodstuff etc. supplied by regular roundsmen. Regulation 7(1) of the Irish Protection of Consumers in Respect of Contracts made by Means of Distance Communication Regulation does not contain the obligation to execute the order within a maximum of 30 days. This is a wrong transposition – probably a drafting mistake - because this obligation is stated in Reg. 9(1) of Irish transposition law.

Some member states have stated differences concerning the place of the supply of the goods. HUNGARIAN law only refers to the "foodstuff and contracts concerning the regular delivery of everyday consumer goods". Also, the GREEK legislator did not explicitly lay down the consumer's residence or workplace as places that the food could be supplied to.[1316] In CYPRUS, the scope has been widened for the supply of the said goods by regular roundsmen at all places other than the supplier's workplace.[1317]

1311 Not transposing "foodstuffs and beverages", only referring to goods for everyday consumption.

1312 Using the term „regular delivery system" in Chapter 6 sec. 7(1)(1) of the Consumer Protection Act of 20 January 1978/38.

1313 Chapter 6 sec. 7(2) of the Consumer Protection Act 20.1.1978/38.

1314 CC Art. 6.366(3): "The provisions of this **Article** shall not apply ...".

1315 § 53(3) of the Law of Obligations Act.

1316 Article 4(13)(γ) of the Consumer Protection Act 2251/94.

1317 Article 4(2)(a) of the Law for the Conclusion of Consumer Distance Contracts.

ff. Partial exemption of contracts for the provision of accommodation, transport, catering or leisure services, Art. 3(2) 2nd indent

Partial Exemption (Art. 3(2) 2nd indent)	Member States
As in the Directive	CY, PT, UK *(3)*
Variations	AT, BE,[1318] CZ, DK, DE, EE, EL, ES, FI, FR,[1319] HU, IE, IT, LT, LU, LV, MT, NL, PL, SE, SK, SL *(22)*
Not transposed	*(0)*

Article 3(2) 2nd indent provides that Articles 4, 5, 6 and 7(1) shall not apply:

- to contracts for the provision of accommodation, transport, catering or leisure services,
- where the supplier undertakes, when the contract is concluded, to provide these services on a specific date or within a specific period.

Exceptionally, in the case of outdoor leisure events, the supplier can reserve the right not to apply Article 7(2) in specific circumstances.

Until now, this Article is the only provision of Directive 97/7 which had to be applied by the ECJ (C-336/03 – *Easycar*).[1320] The Court held that Art. 3(2) of the Directive is to be interpreted as meaning that 'contracts for the provision of transport services' includes contracts for the provision of car hire services. The reasoning offers some guidance for the future application of this provision. The Court stated that the exemption has the purpose of protecting the interests of suppliers of certain services in order that they should not suffer the disproportionate consequences arising from the cancellation at no expense and with no explanation of services. An example of this would be a booking which is made and then cancelled by the consumer at short notice before the date specified for the provision of that service. In the view of the ECJ, car hire undertakings carry out an activity which, against such consequences, the legislature intended to protect by means of the exemption. The reason is that those undertakings must make arrangements for the performance on the date fixed at the time of booking, of the agreed service and, therefore, suffer the same consequences in the event of cancellation as other undertakings operating in the transport sector or in the other sectors listed in the exemption.

Only three member states have transposed Art. 3(2) 2nd indent of the Directive faithfully. Many other member states have chosen different methods of transposing this exemption. For instance, the CZECH REPUBLIC, GREECE, LITHUANIA, SLOVAKIA and SLOVENIA have completely exempted the contracts regulated in Art. 3(2) 2nd indent. As this provision allows only a partial exemption, such member states are in breach of EC law. This may also be the case with ESTONIA, which has broadened the exemption by also excluding the provisions transposing Art. 7(2) of Directive 97/7.[1321]

[1318] The Royal Decree of 18 November 2002 only states an exemption for Art. 4 and 5 of Directive 97/7 and additionally requires that the contract may not exceed 350 Euro.

[1319] Article L. 121-20-4, 2°, of the Consumer Protection Act, however, states that articles L. 121-18 and L. 121-19 (information and written confirmation to be provided) do nonetheless apply to **electronic contracts** for the provision of accommodation, transport, catering etc.

[1320] Judgment of 10 March 2005 C-336/03 – *EasyCar (UK) Ltd v. Office of Fair Trading*; see in particular n° 28, 29.

[1321] § 53(3) of the Law of Obligations Act.

One core element of the partial exemption in Art. 3(2) 2nd indent of Directive 97/7 is that the date of execution must be fixed at the time of the conclusion of the contract. AUSTRIA, BELGIUM, CYPRUS ("upon conclusion of the contract"), DENMARK, ESTONIA ("upon conclusion of the contract"), FINLAND, GERMANY, GREECE, IRELAND, ITALY, LUXEMBOURG, MALTA, the NETHERLANDS, PORTUGAL, SPAIN ("upon conclusion of the contract"), SWEDEN ("in the contract") and the UNITED KINGDOM have implemented this clause. Others, for example, the CZECH REPUBLIC, FRANCE, HUNGARY, LATVIA, LITHUANIA, POLAND, SLOVAKIA and SLOVENIA have extended the exemption to contracts where the date of execution is fixed after the conclusion of the contract.

The majority of the member states has not transposed the second part of the exemption in Art. 3(2) 2nd indent ("exceptionally, in the case of outdoor leisure events..."), namely AUSTRIA, BELGIUM, the CZECH REPUBLIC, DENMARK, ESTONIA, FINLAND, FRANCE, GERMANY, GREECE, HUNGARY, IRELAND, ITALY, LATVIA, LITHUANIA, LUXEMBOURG, MALTA, the NETHERLANDS, SLOVAKIA, SLOVENIA, SPAIN[1322] and SWEDEN. On the contrary, CYPRUS, PORTUGAL and the UNITED KINGDOM[1323] have transposed this part as it is in Directive 97/7. POLISH law limits the exemption to leisure events, however it does not refer to "specific" circumstances, but to circumstances stipulated in the contract.[1324]

III. Consumer protection instruments

1. Information duties

a. Pre-contractual information

Article 4(1) of the Directive obliges the supplier to provide the consumer with the following information in good time prior to the conclusion of the contract:

a) the identity of the supplier and, in the case of contracts requiring payment in advance, his address;
b) the main characteristics of the goods or services;
c) the price of the goods or services including all taxes;
d) delivery costs, where appropriate;
e) the arrangements for payment, delivery or performance;
f) the existence of a right of withdrawal, except in the cases referred to in Art. 6(3);
g) the cost of using the means of distance communication, where it is calculated other than at the basic rate;
h) the period for which the offer or the price remains valid;
i) where appropriate, the minimum duration of the contract in the case of contracts for the supply of products or services to be performed permanently or recurrently.

According to Art. 4(2), the information must be provided in a clear and comprehensible manner in any way appropriate to the means of distance communication used. Paragraph 3

1322 1st Additional Disposition para. 1(2) of the Law 7/1996 of January 15 on retail trade.

1323 Regulation 19(8) of the Consumer Protection Regulations 2000.

1324 Article 16(2)(2) of the Act of 2 March 2000 on the Protection of Certain Consumer Rights and Liability for an Unsafe Product.

additionally clarifies that in the case of telephone communications, the identity of the supplier and the commercial purpose of the call must be made explicitly clear at the beginning of any conversation with the consumer.

All member states have used the list of pre-contractual information duties provided in Art. 4 of the Directive as a model for their transposition legislation and have created a rather similar list. For the purpose of this study, the following aspects shall be pointed out:

aa. "In good time" prior to the conclusion of the contract

A certain ambiguity can be seen in the requirement that the information must be provided to the consumer "in good time" prior to the conclusion of the distance contract. The member states have incorporated this requirement into their national law with some variations of the wording (some examples on the basis of translations which may be inaccurate: CYPRUS: "in time" instead of "in good time"; CZECH REPUBLIC: "sufficiently in advance"; ESTONIA: "within a reasonable period of time before a contract is concluded"; LITHUANIA: "prior to concluding the contract" LATVIA: "offers expressed to consumers" (no indication as to the point in time); POLAND: "at the latest, at the time of the proposal to conclude a contract being submitted"; SLOVAKIA: "before the distance contract is concluded"; SLOVENIA: "within a reasonable time period depending on the means of communication used but before the consumer is bound by the contract or by the offer"; SPAIN: "before the beginning of the contractual process and with the necessary anticipation"). BELGIAN law is more restrictive than the Directive as the information duty must be fullfilled at the time of the offer, which is interpreted broadly including advertisements which imply the seller's willingness to supply.[1325] As such provisions have to be interpreted and applied in accordance with the Directive, the courts responsible should not come to results which breach EC law. Nevertheless, clarifying this requirement might be considered when reviewing the Directive. A model could be the wording of the parallel article of Directive 2002/65: "in good time before the consumer is bound by any distance contract or offer" whereby – following the example of some member states – the word "reasonable" instead of "good" could be used. This would make clearer that the courts shall judge on the question of whether the period was sufficient in order to allow the consumer to reflect on the information before concluding a contract.

bb. Additional pre-contractual information obligations

Many member states have added further information to the list. The bulk of such additional pre-contractual information obligations introduced by the member states is related to the identity of the supplier. In AUSTRIA[1326], CYPRUS, the CZECH REPUBLIC[1327], DENMARK[1328],

---

1325 Article 78 and Art. 2 of the TPA.

1326 Article 5c(1)(1) of the Consumer Protection Act. See also the OGH judgment of 23 September 2003, 4 Ob 175/03v. The OGH held that a supplier who, in his prior information, only provides a PO box number and the municipality in which the company is based, and fails to give more precise geographical indicators (the street name), is in breach of § 5c(1)(1) of the Consumer Protection Act.

1327 CC § 53(4)(a).

1328 § 11(1)(1) of the Act No. 451 of 9 June 2004 on certain consumer contracts.

FINLAND[1329], FRANCE[1330], GERMANY[1331], LUXEMBOURG, MALTA[1332], POLAND[1333], SLOVAKIA[1334], SLOVENIA[1335], SPAIN[1336] and SWEDEN[1337], the prior information must always include the supplier's address, whereas Art. 4(1) of Directive 97/7 only asks for the address in the case of contracts requiring payment in advance. In FRANCE, LUXEMBOURG[1338] and HUNGARY[1339], suppliers also have to provide their telephone numbers. The SLOVAKIAN transposition law specifies the Directive insofar as the supplier also has to inform the consumer about a trading permit (natural person) or the trade name and registered office (legal person). In the CZECH REPUBLIC, the prior information has to contain information about the supplier's identification number and the body supervising the activity of the supplier.

However, it has to be borne in mind that such additional information obligations might be a generalisation of other, more specific information obligations, such as Art. 3 of Directive 2002/65, applicable only in the case of financial services. Article 3(1)(1)(a) of this Directive expressly obliges to provide information about the geographical address at which the supplier is established; and, according to lit. d, the supplier must give information about the trade register in which it is entered and the registration number, if any. In e-commerce cases, rather similar obligations also arise from Art. 5 of Directive 2000/31 which obliges to provide – among others – information about the geographic address (para. 1(b)), an email address (para.1(c)) or (para. 1(d)) the trade register (if any) and the registration number.

Other additional information obligations relate to the right of withdrawal. In BELGIUM[1340], FINLAND[1341], GERMANY, ITALY,[1342] SLOVENIA and SPAIN[1343], the consumer also has to be

---

1329 Chapter 6(13) of the Consumer Protection Act 20.1.1978/38.

1330 Consumer Protection Act, Art. L121-18.

1331 See also the OLG Karlsruhe judgment of 27 March 2002, 6 U 200/01, GRUR 2002, 730-731; and the OLG Munich judgment of 11 September 2003, 29 U 2681/03, NJW-RR 2003, 913-915 dealing with the requirements of how to provide such information on an internet hompepage, and whether it is sufficient to provide this information below the heading "Impressum" on a special page to which users were directed via the link "contact".

1332 Article 4(1)(a) of the Distance Selling Regulations, 2001.

1333 Article 9(1)(1) of the Act of 2 March 2000 on the Protection of Certain Consumer Rights and Liability for an Unsafe Product.

1334 § 10 (1) lit. a of the Act No. 108/2000 on Consumer Protection in Doorstep Selling and in Distance Selling.

1335 Article 43b(1) of the Consumer Protection Act – a transposition of Art. 4(1)(i) – minimum duration of the contract – is lacking.

1336 Article 40(1)(a) of the Law 7/1996 of January 15 on retail trade.

1337 Chapter 2 Section 6 of the Law (2005:59) on Consumer Protection in Distance Contracts and Doorstep Selling Contracts.

1338 Article 3 (1)(a) of the Distance Contracts Act of 16 April 2003.

1339 Article 2(1)(a) of the Government Decree 17/1999 (II.5.) on Distance Contracting.

1340 Article 78(6) of the TPA and Art. 12(6) of the LPA.

1341 Chapter 6 Section 13 Consumer Protection Act; see also the Consumer Complaint Board judgment of 26 October 2004, 03/36/3370. The Board held that the consumer has a right of withdrawal because the supplier did not inform the consumer about the non-existence of a right of withdrawal in case of delivery of goods that, by their nature, cannot be resold.

1342 Article 52(1)(f) of the Legislative Decree of 6 September 2005, No. 206 "Consumer Code".

informed about the non-existence of the right of withdrawal. This may have been inspired by Art.(1)(3)(a) of Directive 2002/65 which stipulates the obligation to give information about the existence or absence of a right of withdrawal. In LUXEMBOURG[1344] and BELGIUM[1345], the supplier has to inform the consumer in advance of the conclusion of the contract if he aims to charge the cost of the return of goods to the consumer in the case of withdrawal. In ITALY, the pre-contractual information need not only include the existence of a right of withdrawal, but also the conditions and procedures for exercising it.[1346] In SLOVENIA, the description of the right of withdrawal in accordance with Art. 43č is to be included.[1347] In ESTONIA, the prior information has to contain – if the object is acquired or the service is used on credit – the right of the consumer to withdraw from the credit contract pursuant to the provisions of § 57 of the Estonian Law of Obligations Act.

Only a very few further additional information obligations that are not related to the supplier's identity or to the withdrawal right, could be traced. In POLAND, for instance, the supplier has to inform the consumer about the place and procedure for submitting complaints already prior to the conclusion of the contract.[1348] In ESTONIA, the prior information has to contain the estimated time of entry into force of the contract.[1349]

It should be noted that several member states have regulated some e-commerce related duties in very close context to their rules on pre-contractual information duties in cases of distance selling. For instance, LATVIAN law provides some specific information duties for the supplier if the consumer uses the internet for the conclusion of the contract. These information duties are e.g. technical stages, that shall be observed in order to enter into the contract; conditions for the storage of the contractual documents (whether the contractual documents are saved) and availability of such contracts to consumers; technical means for determination and correction of input errors prior to the making of an order and languages offered for entering into the contract.[1350] Also, in SLOVENIA, the supplier has to inform the consumer about details concerning the technical steps leading to the conclusion of the contract; a statement of whether the concluded contract will be kept at the enterprise and the method of access to it; a statement of the technical means for identifying and correcting errors prior to the placing of an order; the languages in which the contract may be concluded.[1351] This is, of course, a (partial) transposition of Art. 10 of Directive 2000/31 and not a 'gold plating' of Directive 97/7.

1343 Spain has laid down further information duties e.g. on "the circumstances and conditions upon which the seller could supply a good of similar quality and price replacing the ordered good by the consumer, whenever this posibility is foreseen" (Art. 40.1.j) and – "In case, indication on whether the seller has or is integrated into any alternative dispute resolution system". (Art. 40.1.k).

1344 Artcile 3(1)(f) of the Distance Contracts Act of 16 April 2003.

1345 Article 78(7) of the Act of 14 July 1991 on Trade Practices and Consumer Information and Protection, but no similar provision exists in the Liberal Professions Act.

1346 Article 52(1)(g) of the Legislative Decree of 6 September 2005, No. 206 "Consumer Code".

1347 Article 43b(1)(6) of the Consumer Protection Act.

1348 Article 9(1)(10) of the Act of 2 March 2000 on the Protection of Certain Consumer Rights and Liability for an Unsafe Product.

1349 § 54(1)(3) of the Law of Obligations Act.

1350 Article 2(10) of the Cabinet Regulation No. 207 "Regulations Regarding Distance Contracts".

1351 Article 43b(2) of the Consumer Protection Act.

Overview: Additional Pre-contractual Information Obligations

Additional Information	Member State	Parallel EC law provisions
Supplier's address (in any event)	AT, CY, CZ, DE, DK, ES, FI, FR, LU, MT, PL, SE, SK, SL *(14)*	Art. 3(1)(1)(a) Dir. 2002/65; Art. 5(1)(b) Dir 2000/31
Supplier's telephone number	FR, HU, LU *(3)*	None (but cf. Art. 5(1)(c) Dir. 2000/31: email address)
Trading permit (natural person) / trade name and registered office (legal person)	SK *(1)*	None (but cf. Art. 5(1)(d) Dir. 2000/31)
Identification number	CZ, HU *(2)*	
Information about a body supervising the activity of the supplier	CZ *(1)*	
Non-existence of the withdrawal right	BE, DE, ES, FI, IT, SL *(6)*	Art. 3(1)(3)(a) Dir. 2002/65
Conditions and procedures for exercising withdrawal right	IT, SL *(2)*	Art. 3(1)(3)(a) and (d) Dir. 2002/65
Costs of the return of goods after withdrawal	BE, LU *(2)*	
Right of the consumer to withdraw from a related credit contract	EE *(1)*	
Estimated time of entry into force of the contract	EE *(1)*	
Place and procedure for submitting complaints	PL *(1)*	

b. Written Confirmation, Art. 5

Art. 5(1), sent. 1 of the Directive obliges the supplier to provide, in good time during the performance of the contract, written confirmation (or confirmation in another durable medium) of some of the information to be given prior to the contract, unless the information has already been given to the consumer in such form.

Most of the member states, such as AUSTRIA[1352], BELGIUM, CYPRUS, FINLAND, FRANCE, HUNGARY, IRELAND[1353], ITALY, LATVIA, LUXEMBOURG, MALTA[1354], the NETHERLANDS[1355], PORTUGAL, SWEDEN and the UNITED KINGDOM have followed the Directive rather closely when transposing this provision. ESTONIA[1356], GERMANY, GREECE, POLAND, SLOVAKIA and SLOVENIA[1357] have widened this duty to confirm the information insofar as all information due to be given prior to the contract has to be confirmed, whereas the Directive regulates in Art. 5(1), sent. 1 such a duty only for some information. In GREECE, written confirmation during the performance of the contract is obligatory, even if the information has already been given to the consumer in such form prior to the contract. However, in the CZECH REPUBLIC,

[1352] § 5d(2) of the Consumer Protection Act.

[1353] Regulation 5(2) of the Protection of Consumers in Respect of Contracts made by Means of Distance Communication Regulation.

[1354] Article 5(2) of the Distance Selling Regulations 2001.

[1355] CC Book 7 Art. 46c(2).

[1356] § 55(1) of the Law of Obligations Act.

[1357] Art 43b of the Consumer Protection Act.

LITHUANUA and in SPAIN[1358], there is - contrary to the Directive - no general obligation to confirm the prior information according to Art. 5(1), sent. 1.

Characteristic variations can be found with regard to the formal requirements (see below under aa.) and to the time of the confirmation (see below under bb.). Noteworthy also is that CYPRUS, GREECE and SPAIN[1359] have introduced a requirement that the language used must be the same one that was prevalent in the offer.

aa. Formal requirements

Formal requirements	Member States
As in the Directive	AT, BE (only in the LPA), CY, EE, FR, IE, LU, PT, UK *(9)*
Not transposed	*(0)*
Variations	BE, CZ, DE, DK, EL, ES[1360], FI, HU, IT, LT, LV, MT, NL, PL, SE, SK, SL *(17)*

Article 5(1) of the Directive states that the consumer has to receive written confirmation, or confirmation in another durable medium available and accessible to him, of some of the information laid down in Art. 4 of the Directive.[1361] The following member states have literally transposed these formal requirements: AUSTRIA, BELGIUM in the Liberal Professions Act (LPA), CYPRUS, ESTONIA, FRANCE, IRELAND, LUXEMBOURG, PORTUGAL and the UNITED KINGDOM. Article 79(1)(2) of the Belgian Trade Practices Act obliges the supplier to present a clause informing about the right of withdrawal with the exact text, written in bold, and on the first page of the contract.

Many member states have implemented variations with regard to the term "another durable medium available and accessible". Such differences seem to be only deviations of the wording, and not of the substance. Some examples, on the basis of the available translations, are: DENMARK (in legible form on paper or another permanent medium available and accessible to the consumer), FINLAND (in writing or electronically so that the consumer can reproduce the information unchanged), GERMANY (text form[1362]), HUNGARY (written information or other documents confirming the verbal information), MALTA (tangible medium[1363]), SLOVENIA (a suitable permanent data storage medium), SWEDEN (in a document or another readable, permanent form which is accessible to the consumer), LATVIA (written confirmation or confirmation that can be perceived and retained in another visual or audio form and is available to consumers[1364]). The Latvian law even lists examples for these other visual or

---

1358 Article 47 of the Law 7/1996 of January 15 on retail trade.

1359 Article 47(2) of the Law 7/1996 of January 15 on retail trade (with regard to the information to be given according to Art. 5(1), sent. 2 of the Directive).

1360 Article 47(2) of the Law 7/1996 of January 15 on Retail Trade (with regard to the information to be given according to Art. 5(1), sent. 2 of the Directive).

1361 Article 4(1)(a)-(f) of Directive 97/7.

1362 Defined in CC § 126(b).

1363 This difference in terminology is arguably somewhat problematic since it is not clear whether electronic mail or contracts should be classified as tangible or intangible.

1364 Article 6(1) of the Cabinet Regulation No. 207 "Regulations Regarding Distance Contracts".

audio forms, e.g. voice mail, audio text, videophone, video text, electronic mail or facsimile and other means of communication.

Some member states have increased consumer protection by not transposing the term "another durable medium available and accessible to the consumer". They oblige the supplier to always provide confirmation of the information in written form. Such member states are the CZECH REPUBLIC[1365], GREECE[1366], LITHUANIA[1367], POLAND[1368] and SLOVAKIA[1369]. The NETHERLANDS have partially done the same by providing that the confirmation of some core information (e.g. main characteristics of the good or service, existence of right of withdrawal) must be given in writing. Only the information about other subjects (e.g. identity of the supplier, price, delivery costs and arrangements for payment, delivery or performance) can alternatively be provided in another durable medium.[1370] In ITALY, the supplier can only use another durable medium if the consumer chooses to do so.[1371] In SPAIN, the supplier can use another durable medium unless the consumer rejects this explicitly.

bb. Time of the confirmation

Formal requirements	Member States
As in the Directive	AT, EL, IE, LU, MT, NL, PT, UK *(8)*
Not transposed	*(0)*
Variations	BE, CY, CZ, DK, DE, EE, ES, FI, FR, HU, IT, LV, LT, PL, SE, SK, SL *(17)*

Article 5(1) of the Directive further provides, with regard to the time when the conformation is due, a rule with two elements. The confirmation must be given:

- in good time during the performance of the contract.
- where goods are concerned, the latest point being at the time of delivery (not applicable when the goods are for delivery to third parties).

Member states like AUSTRIA, GREECE, IRELAND, LUXEMBOURG, MALTA, the NETHERLANDS, PORTUGAL or the UNITED KINGDOM have almost literally implemented this provision.

Some member states have changed the terms "in good time". CYPRIOT law refers to "in due course". In GERMANY, FINLAND and SWEDEN, the supplier has to provide confirmation "at once" or "as soon as possible", at the latest by the time of the performance or delivery. SLOVENIA fixes a "reasonable period of time" for providing confirmation. Other member states have completely left out a formula like "in good time", e.g. the CZECH REPUBLIC ("after the

[1365] § 53(5) of the Act 40/1964, CC. Recently there has been a reform which seems to allow the provison of confirmation by any means of distance communication.

[1366] Article 4(9) of the Consumer Protection Act 2251/94.

[1367] CC Art. 6.366(6); Art. 17(6) of the Law on Consumer Protection.

[1368] Article 9(3) of the Act of 2 March 2000 on the Protection of Certain Consumer Rights and Liability for an Unsafe Product.

[1369] § 10(3) and (4) of the Act No. 108/2000 on Consumer Protection in Doorstep Selling and in Distance Selling.

[1370] CC Book 7 Art. 46c(2).

[1371] Article 53(1) of the Legislative Decree of 6 September 2005, No. 206 "Consumer Code".

conclusion of the contract, but no later than before the performance"), ESTONIA[1372] ("at the latest during the performance"), ITALY ("before or when entering into any contract."), LITHUANIA ("prior to performance of the contract"), SPAIN[1373] ("at the time of the performance of the contract"). Also POLAND and SLOVAKIA determine the moment of the delivery of goods and the provision of services at the latest date when confirmation has to be provided.

As the Directive fixes the latest moment only for goods and not for services, many member states seemingly felt a need to clarify such a moment for services, too. Some examples are already mentioned above; others are: FRANCE ("au plus tard au moment de la livraison"), GERMANY ("at the latest until the complete performance of the contract"), LATVIA ("but no later than at the moment of delivery of goods or provision of services") or SLOVENIA ("no later than by the time of delivery of the goods or the start of the provision of services"). BELGIUM has developed a rather elaborate set of rules. For goods, Belgian law follows the Directive. For the provision of services, confirmation has to be given at the latest before the performance, but if the performance has begun – with the agreement of the consumer – before the end of the withdrawal period, the supplier can also confirm during the performance.[1374] For the liberal professions, however, Belgian law provides a different rule, which is closer to the Directive.[1375]

DENMARK ("when the contract is concluded") has regulated an earlier point of time than the Directive requires. The HUNGARIAN transposition has the same starting point ("in good time before signing the contract"), but also allows for confirmation at "the time of the conclusion of the contract at the latest". Some member states, e.g. BELGIUM, the CZECH REPUBLIC, ESTONIA, FRANCE, GERMANY, HUNGARY, ITALY, LATVIA, POLAND, SLOVAKIA, SLOVENIA and SPAIN have also omitted the reference to goods for delivery to third parties.

Such differences with regard to the point in time when confirmation has to be provided may cause difficulties for suppliers who are active in cross-border trade. Nethertheless, suppliers should be able to overcome most of these difficulties by providing confirmation as early as possible.

cc. Information to be provided in any event, Art. 5(1), sent. 2

Furthermore, the supplier must, according to Art. 5(1), sent. 2, provide certain information in any event, namely:

- written information on the conditions and procedures for exercising the right of withdrawal;
- the geographical address of the place of business of the supplier to which the consumer may address any complaints;

[1372] § 55(1) of the Law of Obligations Act.

[1373] Article 47(1) of the Law 7/1996 of January 15 on retail trade (with regard to the information to be given according to Art. 5(1), sent. 2 of the Directive).

[1374] Article 79(2) of the Act of 14 July 1991 on Trade Practices and Consumer Information and Protection.

[1375] Article 13 of the Act of 2 August 2002 on Misleading and Comparative Advertising, Unfair Contract Terms and Distance Marketing in Respect of Professional Services.

- information on after-sales services and guarantees which exist; and
- the conclusion for cancelling the contract, where it is of unspecified duration or a duration exceeding one year.

Again, most of the member states have correctly transposed this specific information duty (e.g. AUSTRIA, BELGIUM, CYPRUS, the CZECH REPUBLIC, DENMARK, ESTONIA, FINLAND, FRANCE, GERMANY, GREECE, HUNGARY, IRELAND, ITALY, LATVIA, LITHUANIA, LUXEMBOURG, MALTA, the NETHERLANDS, PORTUGAL, SLOVAKIA, SLOVENIA, SPAIN, SWEDEN and the UNITED KINGDOM). Only some deviations could be observed. Additionally, in Belgium, Cyprus and Spain, the supplier has to provide the consumer with a standard notice on the right of withdrawal. The GERMAN Regulation on duties to supply information in civil law[1376] contains a standard form in its Annex, which suppliers can use in order to fulfil the obligation to inform the consumer about the existence, exercise and effects of the right of withdrawal. In Finland the information on the right of withdrawal also has to contain the fact that the consumer cannot withdraw any more if the service has begun with the consent of the consumer.[1377]

The POLISH transposition law does not include a duty to inform about after-sales services and guarantees. Other member states oblige the supplier to provide more detailed information than prescribed by the Directive. Additionally, in ESTONIA, the confirmation has to provide information about the conditions of the supplier's liability.[1378]

dd. Exception from Art. 5(1) for services performed through the use of a means of distance communication

Exception	Member States
As in the Directive	AT, BE, CY, DE, ES, FR, HU, IE, IT, LU, LV, MT, NL, PL, PT, SE, SK, SL, UK *(19)*
Variations	DK, EE, FI *(3)*
Not transposed	CZ, EL, LT *(3)*

Article 5(2) of Directive 97/7 allows for the exemption that the supplier does not have to provide confirmation for services which are performed through the use of a means of distance communication, where they are supplied on only one occasion and are invoiced by the operator of the means of distance communication. Nevertheless, the consumer must in all cases be able to obtain the geographical address of the place of business of the supplier to which he may address any complaints.

The majority of the member states have transposed this exemption, e.g. AUSTRIA, BELGIUM, CYPRUS, FRANCE, GERMANY, HUNGARY, IRELAND, ITALY, LATVIA, LUXEMBOURG, MALTA, the NETHERLANDS, POLAND, PORTUGAL, SLOVAKIA, SLOVENIA, SPAIN, SWEDEN and the UNITED KINGDOM, although many of them do not use the term 'operator of a means of communication' defined in Art. 2(5) of the Directive.[1379] In DENMARK, the exemption only

---

1376 BGB-Informationspflichten-Verordnung (BGB-InfoV).

1377 Chapter 6 Section 14(1)(1) of the Consumer Protection Act 20.1.1978/38.

1378 Article 55(2)(4) of the Law of Obligations Act.

1379 For more details, see above point II. 3 c. Definition of "operator of a means of communication".

applies to services with a maximum price of DKK 75 (approx. EUR 10).[1380] Some member states do not refer to the term 'operator of means of distance communication' and use other terms, e.g. ESTONIA ("provider of telecommunication") and FINLAND ("business whose distance communication service is being used"). These seem to be deviations only of the wording and not of the substance. The CZECH REPUBLIC, GREECE and LITHUANIA have not implemented this exception into their national law.

c. Sanctions for breach of information duties

Most of the provisions of the Directive on sanctions for any breach of information duties are rather general and thereby leave great discretion to the member states. For instance, Art. 11(1) obliges the member states to ensure that adequate and effective means exist to ensure compliance with this Directive in the interests of consumers. Article 11(2) (now practically superfluous because of Directive 98/27 being enacted in the meantime), grants public bodies, consumer organisations and professional organisations the right to take action. A further instrument to secure compliance can be seen in the provision for voluntary supervision by self-regulatory bodies of compliance (Art. 11(4)).

The only concrete rule on sanctions for non-fulfilment of information duties in the Directive is Art. 6(1). This provision leads to a prolongation of the withdrawal period in the case that the information obligations laid down in Art. 5 have not been fulfilled, or fulfilled late. The Directive is somewhat unclear as to the point whether the maximum period in case of no confirmation at all is just three months or – more plausible – three months plus 7 working days. The period begins, in the case of goods, from the day of receipt by the consumer; in the case of services, the period starts from the day of conclusion of the contract. It is worth noting that this sanction only applies for the obligations laid down in Art. 5. Consequently, the information obligations to be fulfilled prior to the conclusion of the contract (Art. 4) are not sanctioned by this mechanism.

Moreover, the prolongation for just three months in the case that the consumer has not been informed about his withdrawal right creates incoherencies with regard to other Consumer Directives. Only the Timeshare Directive provides in Art. 5 a rather similar prolongation rule. By contrast, in the field of the Doorstep Selling Directive, the ECJ has ruled in *C-481/9 – Heininger*[1381] that the withdrawal period does not begin before the consumer has been informed about his right of withdrawal. Thus, the consumer has an eternal right to withdraw if the information has not been given. The Directive on Distance Selling of Financial Services is unclear on this point. In Art. 6(1) 2nd indent, this Directive provides that the withdrawal period does not begin before certain information has been given. But this Directive does not contain an explicit rule on a maximum period during which the consumer is entitled to withdraw. If one applies the rule developed by the ECJ in the *Heininger* decision, the consumer also has an eternal right to withdraw under this Directive, as long as the necessary information is not provided.

[1380] § 12(4) and (5) of the Act on Consumer Contracts.

[1381] ECJ judgment of 13 December 2001, C-481/99 – *Georg Heininger and Helga Heininger v. Bayerische Hypo- und Vereinsbank AG* [2001] ECR I-09945.

The vague and ambiguous rules in Directive 97/7 have lead to a broad variety of sanctions for breach of information obligations provided for by the member states. The following types of sanctions can be observed:

- Prolongation of withdrawal period along Art. 6(1);
- Injunctions (i.e. in most cases transposition of Directive 98/27);
- Right of competitors to claim for damages;
- Fines under criminal or administrative law;
- Other private law consequences.

This variety makes it rather difficult for suppliers to assess the risk of any non-fulfilment of information obligations. But it should be noted that such an uncertainty need not constitute a barrier to trade. The reason is that law-abiding traders remain totally unaffected. It may even be seen as an advantage when the sanctions for breach of information duties are difficult to predict and calculate. Those suppliers who fulfil the information obligation might benefit even more from the internal market in comparison to their competitors, who do not inform properly, thereby also coming into difficulties because of different sanction regimes in the member states.

aa. Prolongation of withdrawal period along Art. 6(1)

Article 6(1), sent. 4 of the Directive provides that if the supplier has failed to fulfil the information obligations laid down in Art. 5, the period shall be three months. The period shall begin:

- in the case of goods, from the day of receipt by the consumer;
- in the case of services, from the day of the conclusion of the contract.

Additionally, Art. 6(1), sent. 5 of Directive 97/7 provides that, if the information is supplied within the three month period, the seven working day period shall begin as from that moment.

Prolongation of withdrawal period	Member States
As in the Directive	AT, BE, DK, EE, ES, FR[1382], HU, IE, LU, MT, PL, PT, SK, SL *(14)*
Variations	CY, CZ, DE, EL, FI, IT, LT, LV, NL, SE, UK *(11)*
Not transposed	*(0)*

Some member states have varied the length of the additional period. Not very substantially, but, nevertheless, in breach of the Directive are the LATVIAN and the ITALIAN transposition laws which prescribe a period of 90 calendar days instead of three months. Other member states have provided for a longer additional period. This can be observed e.g. for GERMANY[1383], where the period is generally extended to 6 months in the case that information duties are not fulfilled. However, if the information about the withdrawal right is not given, the consumer is entitled to withdraw forever. In case this confirmation is given later, the consumer has a prolonged withdrawal period of one month. Instead of extending the withdrawal period, FIN-

1382 In FRANCE, the prolongation rule is as in the Directive, Code de la Consommation, Art. L. 121-20 (although the ordinary withdrawal period is just 7 days and, therefore, too short).

1383 CC § 355.

LAND[1384] has stipulated that, if there is no confirmation at all, the contract is not binding upon the consumer. However, the consumer must inform the supplier within one year from the conclusion of the contract if he wants to claim that the contract is not binding. If the supplier provides the consumer with confirmation before he claims that the contract is not binding, the ordinary (14 days) withdrawal period begins. In case that confirmation is given, but does not fulfil all requirements, the withdrawal period is three months; if confirmation is corrected during that period, the ordinary (14 days) withdrawal period begins. In SWEDEN, the consumer has a withdrawal period of one year if the supplier fails to provide the information foreseen in Art. 5(1), sent. 2 of the Directive. When the failure concerns other information, the withdrawal period is just extended to three months. Also, GREECE has a rather elaborate system of sanctions in case of lack of confirmation. In general, the contract is avoidable, if confirmation is lacking or incorrect. The supplier can only escape the avoidance if he provides the information within a three month period. If the supplier fails to provide the information within this three month period, the consumer is entitled to avoid the contract without any time limit.

Some member states have varied the beginning of the three month period slightly. These are, e.g. LITHUANIA (start of period – also for goods – from the day of conclusion of contract), the CZECH REPUBLIC (start of period for both goods and services from the day of "receipt of contracted performance") or CYPRUS and the UNITED KINGDOM ("the day after the day on which the contract is concluded"). The NETHERLANDS do not seem to have provided a rule on the beginning of the additional period at all.

bb. Injunctions

It goes without saying that – originally because of Art. 11(2) of Directive 97/7, now on the basis of Directive 98/27[1385] – compliance with information obligations can be enforced by injunction proceedings in all member states.[1386]

cc. Right of competitors to claim for damages

In some member states, e.g. AUSTRIA, BELGIUM, GERMANY or HUNGARY, competitors may also claim for damages against suppliers who breach information obligations and thereby achieve an unlawful advantage over the law-abiding market participants. For example, recently, GERMAN law has also allowed the siphoning of profits made from unfair marketing practices. However, the practical relevance of such instruments seems to be very limited until now.

[1384] Sections 15(2) and (3), sec. 20 of the Consumer Protection Act.

[1385] It may be noteworthy that the scope of application of these instruments may differ. In the UNITED KINGDOM, for example, under Reg. 27 of the Consumer Protection (Distance Selling) Regulations 2000, what matters is that there has been a breach – it is irrelevant whether this harms the collective interests of consumers. It is therefore more readily available than the kind of injunction one would seek under the Enterprise Act, which implements the Injunctions Directive (amongst other things) and under which the breach has to harm the "collective interests" of consumers.

[1386] For more detail, see Part 2.G.

dd. Fines under criminal or administrative law

Most of the member states, such as DENMARK, FRANCE, GERMANY, GREECE, HUNGARY, IRELAND, ITALY, LATVIA, MALTA, PORTUGAL, SLOVAKIA, SLOVENIA and SWEDEN, have stated administrative sanctions. Suppliers who fail to provide the information are guilty of an offence and can be sanctioned with a fine.

ee. Other private law consequences

It is difficult to assess to what extent member states foresee the consequences of the infringement of information obligations in general private law. There are not many examples where this is stated expressly in the law. For instance, in IRELAND, a contract is not enforceable against the consumer if the supplier fails to provide the prior information.[1387] The same seems to be the case in MALTA and CYPRUS. In BELGIAN law, the omission to insert the prescribed withdrawal clause into the written document is sanctioned on the basis of Art. 79(1)(2) of the Trade Practices Act. According to this provision, the product is deemed to be delivered without the prior request of the consumer as a consequence of which, the consumer is neither required to pay the price nor send the product back to the seller. Moreover, under BELGIAN law, the consumer has right of withdrawal if the information on the non-existence of the right of withdrawal is not provided. FINLAND also offers the consumer assistance by the Consumer Ombudsman in individual cases.

Besides such express regulations on other sanctions of infringement of information duties, it is more than probable that in most member states the general rules on pre-contractual obligations, on breach of contract or on tort may lead to individual rights or claims of consumers such as right of avoidance from a contract or a claim for damages. This depends very much on the concrete nature of the violated information obligation, the availability of remedies under the general law of obligations, the question of whether a breach of information obligations amounts to a breach of contract under the respective system and whether such a breach leads to concrete damage or disadvantage to the consumer. The possible constellations are so manifold that general conclusions can hardly be drawn.[1388] However, it has to be kept carefully in mind that information obligations heavily interfere with the general remedies under private law available in the member states. Therefore, any full harmonisation of the sanctions of non-fulfilment of information duties would massively intervene into member states' private laws.

1387 Article 4(1) of the Protection of Consumers in Respect of Contracts made by Means of Distance Communication Regulation.

1388 Cf. *Howells/Wilhelmsson*, EC Consumer Law, 182.

2. Right of withdrawal

a. Exceptions to the right of withdrawal

aa. Exception to the right of withdrawal if performance of services has begun before the end of the seven working day period (Art. 6(3) 1st indent)

Exemption (Art. 6(3) 1st indent)	Member States
As in the Directive	AT, BE, CY, CZ, DE, DK, EE, ES, FR, HU, IE, IT, LU, MT, NL, PL, PT, SE, SK *(19)*
Not transposed	EL, LT, SL *(3)*
Variations	FI, LV, UK *(3)*

Most member states have transposed the exception to the right of withdrawal if performance of services has begun before the end of the seven working day period, as stated in Art. 6(3) 1st indent of Directive 97/7. This can be observed for AUSTRIA, BELGIUM, CYPRUS, the CZECH REPUBLIC, DENMARK, ESTONIA, FRANCE, GERMANY, HUNGARY, IRELAND, ITALY, LUXEMBOURG, MALTA, the NETHERLANDS, POLAND, PORTUGAL, SLOVAKIA, SPAIN and SWEDEN. However, GREECE, LITHUANIA and SLOVENIA have not transposed this exception. Some countries have implemented provisions differing from the Directive. FINLAND, LATVIA and the UNITED KINGDOM have supplemented this exemption with a provision which obliges the supplier to inform the consumer that he will not be able to withdraw from the contract if performance of the service has begun. In FINLAND, this information must be given in the confirmation of the information, while in LATVIA and the UNITED KINGDOM, this is to happen prior to the conclusion of the contract. In BELGIUM, the consumer is granted a right of withdrawal if the supplier has not informed him of the absence of the right of withdrawal.

bb. Exception to the right of withdrawal in the case of goods or services, the price of which is dependent on fluctuations in the financial market (Art. 6(3) 2nd indent)

Exemption (Art. 6(3) 2nd indent)	Member States
As in the Directive	AT, BE* (LPA), CY, CZ, DK, FI, IE, IT, LU, MT, NL, PT, SE, SK, SL, UK *(16)*
Not transposed	EE, EL, LT *(3)*
Variations	BE* (TPA), DE, ES, FR, HU, LV, PL *(7)*

* *more than once*

Fifteen member states have transposed this exception. Only in ESTONIA, GREECE and LITHUANIA, there is no provision corresponding to Art. 6(3) 2nd indent of Directive 97/7. It cannot be assessed how these legal systems organise the unravelling of such contracts. In BELGIUM, only the Liberal Professions Act contains this exemption expressly.[1389] The Trade Practices Act however does not apply to stocks[1390], so that the exemption in this Act is also partly used. GERMANY and SLOVENIA have given some examples of goods and services which fall under this exception. In LATVIA, the supplier has to inform the consumer about the

[1389] Article 14(3) No. 2 of the LPA.

[1390] Article 1 of the TPA.

absence of a right of withdrawal prior to the conclusion of the contract. FRANCE and POLAND have omitted the clause "which cannot be controlled by the supplier". HUNGARY has implemented a clause stating that goods or services are exempted where the price cannot be "controlled" by the supplier. Such variations seem to be more a difference in the wording than in the substance. SPANISH law does not refer to services and thereby consequently has limited the exception to goods. In the case of services the position of the consumer is therefore better as foreseen in the Directive, as he is granted a right of withdrawal.

cc. Exception to the right of withdrawal in the case of goods made to the consumer's specifications etc. (Art. 6(3) 3rd indent)

Exemption (Art. 6(3) 3rd indent)	Member States
As in the Directive	AT, BE, CY, DE, ES, FR, HU, IE, IT, LU, MT, NL, PT, SL, UK *(15)*
Not transposed	EE, EL, LT *(3)*
Variations	CZ, DK, FI, LV, PL, SE, SK *(7)*

Once again, most member states have transposed the exception referring to all five alternatives mentioned in the Directive, i.e.:

- goods made to the consumer's specifications;
- goods clearly personalised;
- goods which, by reason of their nature, cannot be returned;
- goods which are liable to deteriorate;
- goods which expire rapidly.

Only ESTONIA, GREECE and LITHUANIA have not implemented any provisions transposing the exception to the right of withdrawal in the case of goods made to the consumer's specifications etc.

For a more detailed illustration of the variations with regard to the different alternatives stated in Art. 6(3) 3rd indent of Directive 97/7, please refer to the table below.

N°	*Alternative of exemption (Art. 6(3) 3rd indent)*	AT	BE	CY	CZ	DE	DK	EE	EL	ES	FI	FR	HU	IE	IT	LT	LU	LV	MT	NL	PL	PT	SK	SL	SE	UK
1	consumer's specifications	X	X	X	X	X	-	-	-	X	X	X	X	X	X	-	X	X	X	X	X	X	X	X	-	X
2	clearly personalised	X	X	X	X	X	X	-	-	X	-	X	X	X	X	-	X	-	X	X	X	X	X	X	-	X
3	cannot be returned	X	X	X	-	X	X	-	-	X	X	X	X	X	X	-	X	X	X	X	X	X	X	X	X	X
4	liable to deteriorate	X	X	X	X	X	X	-	-	X	X	X	X	X	X	-	X	X	X	X	X	X	X	X	X	X
5	expire rapidly	X	X	X	X	X	X	-	-	X	X	X	X	X	X	-	X	-	X	X	-	X	-	X	X	X

The table shows that some countries have not implemented all alternatives regulated in the Directive. DANISH and SWEDISH law does not mention the alternative No. 1 (consumer's specification). However, in Denmark, the parties can agree that the supplier may initiate the production of the good before the expiration of the withdrawal period, in which case, the right of withdrawal also expires at the same date the production of the good is initiated.[1391] FINLAND, LATVIA and SWEDEN have not transposed the alternative No. 2 (clearly persona-

---

[1391] § 18(6) of the Consumer Contracts Act No. 451/2004.

lised). The CZECH transposition law does not refer to products which, by reason of their nature, cannot be returned (No. 3). Latvian, POLISH and SLOVAKIAN law does not mention the criteria "expire rapidly" (No. 5). Latvia instead exempts products which can be "quickly utilised", which is somewhat different to "expire rapidly" and, therefore, may be an infringement of the Directive.

FINLAND[1392] has clarified alternative No. 1 by exempting "goods manufactured to the consumer's specifications so that they cannot be resold without incurring considerable loss or that they cannot be resold at all" and thereby perhaps slightly enhancing consumer protection. Some member states have regulated additional criteria.

The practical relevance of this exemption is illustrated by some case-law of national courts. For instance, the GERMAN Federal Court of Justice stated that the consumer's right of withdrawal is not exempted if the product (in this case a laptop which has been constructed out of prefabricated standard units according to the consumer's wishes[1393]) can be disassembled with minor effort and without interference to its (the standard unit's) functional capability.[1394] The court held that the exemption only covers products which are personalised in a way that they can only be sold to other consumers with a significant reduction of price. CA Brussels judged that plants, flowers, fruit trees and similar products – as a general rule – cannot be considered products that age or deteriorate easily.[1395] Consequently, the withdrawal period provided for by the Act of 14 July 1991 (Trade Practices Act) applies to these products.

dd. Exception to the right of withdrawal with respect to audio or video recordings, or computer software (Art. 6(3) 4th indent)

Exemption (Art. 6(3) 4th indent)	Member States
As in the Directive	AT, BE, CY, DE, DK, FI, FR, HU, IE, LT, MT, NL, SE, SK, SL, UK *(16)*
Not transposed	EE, EL *(2)*
Variations	CZ, ES, IT, LU, LV, PL, PT *(7)*

Most member states have transposed this exemption, namely AUSTRIA, BELGIUM, CYPRUS, DENMARK, FRANCE, GERMANY, HUNGARY, IRELAND, LITHUANIA, MALTA, the NETHERLANDS, SLOVAKIA, SLOVENIA, SWEDEN and the UNITED KINGDOM. However, ESTONIA and GREECE have not incorporated this exemption into their laws. ITALY exempts sealed audiovisual products and software, opened by the consumer.[1396] Some variation can be observed with regard to the term "which were unsealed by the consumer": LATVIA ("the consumer opened the packaging"[1397]) and POLAND ("the consumer has removed the original packag-

[1392] Chapter 6(16)(3) of the Consumer Protection Act of 20.1.1978/38.

[1393] "Built-to-order-system".

[1394] BGH judgment of 19 March 2003, VIII ZR 295/01, NJW 2003, 1665-1667.

[1395] CA Brussels judgment of 21 January 1999; *P. Bakker Hillegom vs. Ets. Gonthier.*

[1396] Article 55(2)(d) of the Legislative Decree of 6 September 2005, No. 206 "Consumer Code".

[1397] Article 15(4) of the Cabinet Regulation No. 207 "Regulations Regarding Distance Contracts".

ing"[1398]) refer to the packaging, which at least comes close to the Directive. Also the CZECH transposition law ("if the consumer damages the original packing"[1399]) may perhaps be interpreted in the same sense. In PORTUGAL, the consumer may not withdraw from the contract if he or she removes a certain kind of seal ("selo de garantia de inviolabilidade"[1400]), which may just be seen as a clarification of the function of the seal referred to in the Directive.

Some member states have broadened the exemption regulated in Art. 6(3) 4th indent of Directive 97/7. LUXEMBOURG, for example, also exempts software that has been downloaded by the consumer.[1401] This is more or less the same in SPAIN, where electronic files supplied via electronic means, able to be downloaded or reproduced immediately to be used permanently, are exempted from the withdrawal right.[1402] It could be argued that Art. 6(3) 4th indent of the Directive only allows the member states to exempt audio or video recordings and software which is sold on a physical data medium and consequently requires that a consumer who buys audio, video etc. data to be downloaded, must have a withdrawal right. If this is true, the LUXEMBOURGIAN and the SPANISH law would infringe the Directive. This may be a point for clarification by the legislator.

ee. Exception to the right of withdrawal with respect to newspapers, periodicals and magazines (Art. 6(3) 5th indent)

Exemption (Art. 6(3) 5th indent)	Member States
As in the Directive	BE, CZ, DE, ES, FR, HU, IE, IT, LT, LU, LV, MT, NL, SK, SL, UK *(16)*
Not transposed	DK, EE, EL *(3)*
Variations	AT, CY, FI, PL, PT, SE *(6)*

Most member states have transposed the exemption stated in Art. 6(3) 5th indent of Directive 97/7 (cf. the table above). However, DENMARK, ESTONIA and GREECE have not transposed this exemption. Some member states have implemented provisions deviating from the Directive. In AUSTRIA, contracts for the supply of periodicals ("Verträge über periodische Druckschriften" (§ 26(1)(1)) are not exempted from the right of withdrawal. FINLAND only excepts these products if they are not offered by the way of cold calling. CYPRUS grants no right of withdrawal for the supply of newspapers and any form of periodicals. POLAND uses the term "the press".[1403] In PORTUGAL[1404] and SWEDEN[1405], the legislator only exempted newspapers and magazines, but

[1398] Article 10(3)(2) of the Act of 2 March 2000 on the Protection of Certain Consumer Rights and Liability for an Unsafe Product.

[1399] § 53(7)(d) of the CC.

[1400] Article 7(d) of the Decree-Law 143/2001 of April 26.

[1401] Article 5(4)(d) of the Distance Contracts Act of 16 April 2003.

[1402] Article 45 (c) of the Law 7/1996 of January 15 on Retail Trade.

[1403] Article 10(3)(6) of the Act of 2 March 2000 on the Protection of Certain Consumer Rights and Liability for an Unsafe Product.

[1404] The Portuguese version of the Directive is different from the English one, and concerns only "jornais e revistas".

[1405] The Swedish version of the Directive is different from the English one, and concerns only "tidningar och tidskrifter".

not periodicals. This may be due to the fact that the two terms “magazine” and “periodical” could be seen as synonyms.

ff. Exception to the right of withdrawal with respect to gaming and lottery services (Art. 6(3) 6th indent)

Exemption (Art. 6(3) 6th indent)	Member States
As in the Directive	AT, BE, CY, CZ, DE, DK, ES, FI, IE, IT, LT, LU, LV, MT, NL, PT *(16)*
Not transposed	EE, EL *(2)*
Variations	FR, HU, PL, SE, SK, SL, UK *(7)*

Most member states have transposed this exception stated in Art. 6(3) 6th indent of Directive 97/7 (cf. the table above). Only ESTONIA and GREECE did not transpose the exemption of gaming and lottery services. Some variations of the wording can be observed, e.g. HUNGARY (exempts gaming agreements, which also includes the lottery), POLAND (games and betting), SLOVAKIA (lottery and other similar games), SLOVENIA (games of chance and lottery services) and SWEDEN (gaming or other lottery services). Also the UNITED KINGDOM adds betting to the services which are exempted. A clear difference can be stated for FRANCE, which only makes authorised lotteries exempt.

b. Formal requirements for the exercise of the right of withdrawal

The Directive does not contain an explicit provision allowing the member states to regulate formal requirements for the exercise of the withdrawal right by the consumer. But as Art. 5(1) 1st indent provides, that the consumer is informed about “the conditions and procedures for exercising the right of withdrawal”, it is generally assumed that the member states are free to regulate formal requirements. This understanding is in line with, e.g. Art. 5(1), sent. 1 of the Doorstep Selling Directive, which expressly allows the member states to lay down the rule on the procedure for the exercise of the withdrawal right.

Nevertheless, most member states have not provided any formal requirements for exercising the right of withdrawal, e.g. AUSTRIA, BELGIUM[1406], CZECH REPUBLIC, DENMARK, ESTONIA, FINLAND, FRANCE, HUNGARY, IRELAND, LATVIA, LUXEMBOURG, MALTA, the NETHERLANDS, PORTUGAL[1407], SLOVENIA, SWEDEN and SPAIN. This means that, in these countries, the consumer can withdraw by any means, including a pure oral declaration. Spain has additionally clarified that sending back the goods is to be seen as a withdrawal.

Other member states have regulated that the consumer must use a certain form of communication when he withdraws from the contract. In CYPRUS, LITHUANIA, POLAND and the

1406 Although the TPA and the LPA lay down no specific requirements, the consumer needs to proof the withdrawal. To avoid all discussions the withdrawal should be proven in writing, so that the burden of proof necessitates a withdrawal in writing.

1407 Article 6(5) of the Decree-Law 143/2001 of April 26 clarifies that a registered letter addressed to the supplier or person for this purpose appointed is to be seen as the exercise of the right of withdrawal. This does not seem to be an obligatory requirement.

UNITED KINGDOM the notice of cancellation must be given in writing. The United Kingdom clarifies that writing also includes text on another durable medium. SLOVENIA has legislated to the effect that sending back the goods also constitutes a valid withdrawal. In SLOVAKIA, the parties are free to find an agreement on the formal requirement for exercising the right of withdrawal. If there is no agreement and the contract is concluded in writing, the notice of cancellation must also be in writing. In GERMANY, the consumer has to inform the supplier about his decision to cancel the contract by a notice in 'text form' (which also allows text on another durable medium). Furthermore, it is possible to withdraw from the contract by sending back the goods. Similar provisions can be found in GREECE, where the consumer can exercise the right of withdrawal in witten form or in another durable medium available and accessible to him.[1408] The ITALIAN Consumer Code[1409] states that the consumer has to send this notice of cancellation in a letter sent by registered mail with return receipt ("lettera raccomandata con avviso di ricevimento") and it has to be signed by the person who concluded the contract or drafted the proposal. It can also be sent by telegram, telex, fax or e-mail within the period, but it must be confirmed by a letter sent by recorded delivery within the following 48 hours. The presentation of the return receipt ("avviso di ricevimento"), however, is not an essential condition for proving the exercise of the right of withdrawal (Art. 64(2), sent. 3 of the Italian Consumer Code).

Table: formal requirements

	AT	BE	CY	CZ	DE	DK	EE	EL	ES	FI	FR	HU	IE	IT	LT	LU	LV	MT	NL	PL	PT	SK	SL	SE	UK
none	X	X		X		X	X		X	X	X	X	X			X	X	X	X		X		X	X	
Written			X					X							X					X		X			X
Text form					X			X																	
Return of goods					X					X													X		
Registered letter														X											

c. Withdrawal period

aa. Length of period

The Directive provides a period of seven working days. Legal literature has remained somewhat unclear as to whether a Saturday counts as a 'working day'. It should be noted that this issue has already been clarified long ago in the Regulation 1182/71 determining the rules applicable to periods, dates and time limits. Article 2(2) of this Regulation expressly defines 'working days' as all days other than public holidays, Sundays and Saturdays. Furthermore, this Regulation contains many provisions on the calculation of periods, which are also applicable for the withdrawal period to be granted by the member states under Directive 97/7. One important example may be the rule in Art. 3(4) which provides that, where the last day

---

[1408] Article 4(10) of the Consumer Protection Act 2251/94.

[1409] Article 64(2) of the Legislative Decree of 6 September 2005, No. 206 "Consumer Code".

of the period is a public holiday, Sunday or Saturday, the period shall end with the expiry of the last hour of the following working day.[1410]

Some member states, e.g. AUSTRIA, BELGIUM[1411], IRELAND, LITHUANIA, LUXEMBOURG, the NETHERLANDS, SLOVAKIA, SPAIN and the UNITED KINGDOM have adopted the 7 working days period. It cannot be assessed, whether 'working day' has the same meaning in all these countries as defined in the Regulation mentioned above, and in particular, whether the term excludes Saturdays. But as the term must be interpreted in accordance with the Directive, there should be no infringement, unless a national court comes to a different result.

Many member states have used the minimum clause to prolong the withdrawal period. The period lasts for 8 workings days in HUNGARY, 10 working days in GREECE and ITALY, 10 (calendar) days in POLAND, 14 (calendar) days in CYPRUS, the CZECH REPUBLIC, DENMARK, ESTONIA, FINLAND, LATVIA, PORTUGAL and SWEDEN, two weeks in GERMANY and even 15 (calendar) days in MALTA and SLOVENIA. In Germany, the period is actually one month if the consumer has been informed about his withdrawal right after the conclusion of the contract.[1412] Only the FRENCH law seems to be problematic because the consumer has a period of only seven days ("jours francs") to withdraw from the contract. "Jour franc" is a one-day-period (0 h to 24 h). The day of the event, in this case the receipt of the good in case the delivery of goods or the day of the conclusion of the contract in case of provision of services, is not included for the computation of the period. Furthermore, for the computation of the withdrawal period it is irrelevant whether the seven "jours francs" include "jours ouvrables" (working days) or "jours feriés" (Sundays and public holidays). This understanding of the notion "jour franc" is supported by the text of Art. L.120-20 para. 4 Code de la Consommation. According to this provision a Sunday or public holidays are not included in the withdrawal period, only if the period expires on such a day. Therefore, the seven "jours franc" period in France is a breach of EC law.[1413]

[1410] Equivalent rules can be found, for instance, in FRANCE or GERMANY.

[1411] The Trade Practices Act contains the following definition of working day: "all days other than Sundays and public holidays. If a period expressed in working days ends on a Saturday, the period is extended till the next working day" (Art. 1 No. 9 of the Trade Practices Act).

[1412] Cf. also the Kammergericht Berlin judgment of 18 July 2006, 5 W 156/06 granting the consumer a withdrawal period of one month according to CC § 355(2)(2) in the case of Ebay auctions. The court held that in Ebay actions the supplier can inform the consumer of his right of withdrawal in text form as a rule after the conclusion of the contract because an internet homepage does not fulfil the requirements of CC § 355(2)(1) stipulating information in text form.

[1413] An explanation is given by *Franck*, Les ventes à distance en droit européen : la directive de 1997 sur les contrats à distance et sa transposition en France, published on the site of the Ministère de l'Économie, des finances et de l'industrie: http://www.minefi.gouv.fr/dgccrf/02_actualite/ateliers_conso/atelier27e.htm. It remains unclear if this is meant seriously: "Le texte communautaire prévoit alors un délai de 7 jours ouvrables, traduits en France, pays travailleur, par 7 jours francs, soit des jours d'une durée de 24 heures, durée journalière légale du travail en France, comme chacun le sait ... Plus sérieusement, jours francs et jours ouvrables seraient donc équivalents. La directive est donc bien appliquée."

Table: Withdrawal period

Withdrawal Period	Member State
7 calendar days	FR[1414] *(1)*
7 working days	AT,[1415] BE, ES,[1416] IE, LT, LU, NL, SK, UK *(9)*
8 working days	HU *(1)*
10 working days	EL, IT *(2)*
10 calendar days	PL *(1)*
14 calendar days	CY, CZ, DK, EE, FI, LV, PT, SE *(8)*
Two weeks	DE *(1)* [one month if information on withdrawal right has been given after conclusion of contract]
15 calendar days	MT, SL *(2)*

bb. Start of period

(1.) Start of period in case of delivery of goods

Begin in case of delivery of goods (Art. 6(1), sent. 3, 2nd indent)	Member States
As in the Directive	AT, BE* (LPA), CZ, DE, DK, EE, EL, ES, FR, HU, IE, IT, LT, LU, LV, MT, NL, PL, PT, SE, SK, SL *(22)*
Not transposed	*(0)*
Variations	BE* (TPA), CY, FI, UK *(4)*

* *more than once*

Article 6(1), sent. 3, 1st indent of Directive 97/7 stipulates the start of the withdrawal period in the case of delivery of goods as the day of receipt of goods by the consumer. Most member states have transposed this provision, e.g. AUSTRIA, BELGIUM (LPA), the CZECH REPUBLIC, DENMARK, ESTONIA, FRANCE, GERMANY, GREECE, HUNGARY, IRELAND, ITALY, LATVIA, LITHUANIA, LUXEMBOURG, MALTA, the NETHERLANDS, POLAND, PORTUGAL, SLOVAKIA, SLOVENIA, SPAIN and SWEDEN.

In BELGIUM and CYPRUS, the period begins on the day following the day of receipt of goods. In the UNITED KINGDOM, the period begins with the day on which the contract is concluded but does not end until 7 days after receipt of the goods, starting on the day after receipt.[1417] In FINLAND, the period begins after the receipt of confirmation or, if the goods are delivered after confirmation, with the delivery of the goods.[1418]

1414 7 "jours francs" according to Code de la Consommation Art. L121-20.

1415 Saturday is no working day.

1416 Spanish law contemplates that "the law of the place where the good has been delivered will determine which days are deemed as working days" – Article 44(1) of the Law 7/1996 of January 15 on Retail Trade.

1417 Regulation 11 of the Consumer Protection (Distance Selling) Regulations 2000.

1418 Chapter 6(15) of the Consumer Protection Act 20.1.1978/38.

(2.) Start of period in case of provision of services

Start in case of provision of services (Art. 6(1), sent. 3, 2nd indent)	Member States
As in the Directive	AT, BE* (LPA), DE, DK, EE, FI[1419], FR, HU, IE, IT, LT, LU, LV, MT, NL, PL, PT, SE, SK, SL, UK *(21)*
Not transposed	ES *(1)*
Variations	BE* (TPA), CY, CZ, EL *(4)*

* *more than once*

Article 6(1), sent. 3, 2nd indent of Directive 97/7 stipulates the start of the withdrawal period in the case of services as, "from the day of conclusion of the contract or from the day on which the obligations laid down in Article 5 were fulfilled if they are fulfilled after conclusion of the contract". Most member states have transposed this provision (cf. the table above).

Some member states have implemented provisions varying from the Directive. In GREECE, the period begins when the consumer receives the documentation informing him that the contract is concluded. In BELGIUM and CYPRUS, the period begins on the day following the day of the conclusion of the contract if the confirmation has already been provided. CZECH law refers to the "receipt of performance" for the beginning of the withdrawal period in the case of provision of services.[1420] In SPAIN, the final indent of the Directive's rule[1421] has not been transposed.

cc. Postal rule / dispatching rule

Contrary to the Doorstep Selling Directive 85/577 or the Financial Services Directive 2002/65[1422], which both contain an explicit dispatching rule, Directive 97/7 does not contain any provision specifying how the consumer can exercise the right of withdrawal on time. Nevertheless, some member states have implemented provisions on this. AUSTRIA[1423], BELGIUM[1424], GERMANY[1425], ITALY[1426] and SLOVENIA[1427] have stated a dispatching rule. In CY-

1419 According to preparatory works HE 2000/79 vp, in the case of services, where there is no need to provide confirmation pursuant to CPA 5:14, the withdrawal period begins from the entry of contract.

1420 CC § 53(6).

1421 "Provided that this period does not exceed the three month period referred to in the following subparagraph".

1422 In GREECE, Art 4a(6)(c)(γ) of the Consumer Protection Act 2251/1994 (transposing the dispatching rule of Directive 2002/65) is also applied for regular distance contracts.

1423 § 5e(1), sent. 2 of the Consumer Protection Act.

1424 Article 80(2) of the Act of 14 July 1991 on trade practices and consumer information and protection.

1425 CC § 355(1), sent. 2.

1426 "The notice of withdrawal by recorded delivery letter shall be understood to have been sent in good time if delivered to a post office accepting the delivery by no later than the term provided for by the Code."cf. Art. 64(2) of the Legislative Decree of 6 September 2005, No. 206 "Consumer Code".

1427 Article 43č(1) of the Consumer Protection Act.

PRUS[1428], LATVIA[1429] and the UNITED KINGDOM[1430], the transposition law contains a postal rule which states that the notice of withdrawal sent by post shall be deemed to have been served at the time of posting, whether it has been received or not. This point could be clarified when reviewing the Directive, also with regard to the question whether such a rule purely ensures the timeliness of the withdrawal (e.g. in Germany) or whether it even makes a withdrawal valid in the case that the declaration never reached the supplier (e.g. because the letter got lost after being dispatched) e.g. in Cyprus.

d. Effects of withdrawal

With regard to the effects of withdrawal, the Directive provides at least some basis principles in Art. 6(1) and (2):

- The consumer must be able to withdraw without any penalty.
- The supplier shall be obliged to reimburse the sums paid by the consumer free of charge; reimbursement must be carried out as soon as possible and in any case within 30 days.
- The only charge that may be made to the consumer because of the exercise of his right of withdrawal is the direct cost of returning the goods.

The obligation to reimburse, free of charge, the sums already paid by the consumer has been transposed in all member states. With regard to the deadline of 30 days at the latest to reimburse the sums, some member states have adopted even stricter rules, e.g. CYPRUS, where the supplier has to reimburse the sum immediately[1431], or LITHUANIA, SLOVAKIA and SLOVENIA, where sums have to be reimbursed within 15 days.[1432] GERMANY has indirectly transposed Art. 6(2) of the Directive. The obligation to reimburse the sums paid has to be fulfilled within 30 days according to CC § 286(3) in conjunction with § 357(1), sent. 2 and 3. If the trader is late in reimbursing the sums already paid, the Slovenian and SPANISH legislators have adopted special sanctions to enforce the Directive's provisions. Spain has established the right of the consumer to claim for double the sum when it has not been paid in that period of time. Slovenian law obliges the trader to pay, in addition to the legal interest on arrears, an additional ten percent of the total value for every 30 days of delay with reimbursement.

With regard to the reciprocal obligation that the consumer has to return the goods received, some member states have specified a time limit for the return. For instance, ITALIAN law obliges the consumer to return the goods within 10 days, if they have already been delivered; SLOVENIAN law stipulates a period 15 of days (Consumer Protection Act, Art. 43d(1) and (2)). In PORTUGAL, after having exercised the right of withdrawal, the consumer must keep

---

1428 Article 7(5) of the Law on the Conclusion of Consumer Distance Contracts of 2000.

1429 Civil Law Rrt. 1537.

1430 Regulation 10(4)(b) of the Consumer Protection (Distance Selling) Regulations 2000.

1431 Article 11(1) of the Law on the Conclusion of Consumer Distance Contracts of 2000.

1432 LITHUANIA: Art. 18(6) of the Law on Consumer Protection; CC Art. 6.367(7); SLOVAKIA: § 12(4)(b) of the Act No. 108/2000 on Consumer Protection in Doorstep Selling and in Distance Selling; SLOVENIA: Art. 43d of the Consumer Protection Act: "as soon as possible and not later than 15 days".

the goods, so that he can return them to the supplier or person for this purpose appointed, in good conditions of utilisation.[1433]

According to Art. 6(2) of Directive 97/7, only the costs of returning the goods can be charged to the consumer. Most member states have used this option allowing the trader to charge the costs to the consumer, some with variations. For instance, in AUSTRIA[1434] and ITALY[1435], the consumer may be obliged to pay the costs for the return of goods, if this has been agreed by the parties. The BELGIAN legislator has limited this possibility, as the consumer may not be charged for the direct cost of returning the products when (1) the product or service did not match the offer, or (2) the seller did not fulfil his information duties.[1436] The POLISH provision is unclear. However, Art. 12(3) and (4)[1437], referring to cases where alternative goods or services were provided, stipulate that in such cases the costs of the return of the goods ought to be borne by the trader. One could, therefore, assume that in other cases such costs are to be borne by the consumer. In FINLAND, the supplier even has to compensate the consumer for the costs of returning the goods or other performances if goods and performances can be returned normally by post (6:17 CPA).

However, in LITHUANIA, the legislator seems not to have transposed the limitation that the only charge that may be made to the consumer is the direct cost of returning the goods. Therefore, theoretically, the consumer may be charged with additional costs, too.

Some member states have stipulated express rules on additional costs, in particular if the consumer has made use of the goods or cannot return the acquired goods in their original state. For instance, in AUSTRIA[1438] and GERMANY, under certain conditions, the consumer has to pay compensation for the use of the good, mainly in case of depreciation in value (KSchG § 5g(1)(2)) or even in German law, according to CC § 357(1), sent. 1, § 346(1), § 347, for any benefits he has gained as well as, in some cases, benefits he has not gained but should have gained. This obligation is in turn restricted by imposing the duty on the seller to inform the consumer about this possible consequence at the latest by the time of the conclusion of the contract (CC § 357(3)). In HUNGARY, the consumer has to compensate the seller if he caused damage due to the improper use of the good (Art. 4(5) of the Government Decree 17/1999 on Distance Contracting). The CYPRIOT and ITALIAN legislators saddle the consumer with the obligation to take good care of the goods while in his possession (Art. 7(6) of the Law for the Conclusion of Consumer Distance Contracts of 2000; Art. 67(2) of the Consumer Code). In GREECE, the same rule applies during the period of withdrawal, whereas the consumer is obliged to take any necessary measures to keep the product in good repair.

1433 Article 8(2) of the Decree-Law 143/2001 of April 26.

1434 § 5g(2) of the Consumer Protection Act.

1435 Article 67(3) of the Legislative Decree of 6 September 2005, No. 206 “Consumer Code”.

1436 Article 81 § 3 of the TPA. This is an exception to the rule of Art. 80 § 1 TPA. The Liberal Professions Act does not contain similar exceptions.

1437 Act of 2 March 2000 on the Protection of Certain Consumer Rights and Liability for an Unsafe Product.

1438 See the OGH judgment of 27 September 2005, 1 Ob 110/05s, charging a consumer, who had used the purchase item (a monitor) for many hours and far in excess of the time one might reasonably take for a product trial, leading to wear and tear and a reduction in the item’s value, a compensation for the use of the monitor.

One could perhaps say that such obligations are not imposed on the consumer "because of the exercise of his right of withdrawal" and therefore do not infringe the Directive. Nevertheless, it has been criticised that such provisions possibly do not all conform with Art. 6(2) of Directive 97/7.[1439]

e. Cancellation of credit agreement

Article 6(4) of Directive 97/7 calls on the member states to regulate the automatic and immediate cancellation of a credit agreement if the credit is either granted by the supplier or by a third party on the basis of an agreement between the third party and the supplier, and in case that the consumer exercises his right to withdraw from the credit financed main contract. As the Directive requires detailed provisions on that question the countries are given leeway, so that a huge variety in regard to the implementation into national law can be found.

All member states except SLOVENIA have implemented provisions transposing Art. 6(4) of Directive 97/7. LUXEMBOURG and MALTA transposed the mentioned article literally using the copy and paste technique. Other member states like FINLAND, GREECE (referring to general civil law provision for the cancellation), LITHUANIA ("without any additional commitments on the side of the consumer"[1440]), PORTUGAL ("automatically and simultaneously") and SPAIN[1441] have implemented variations but these differences seem to be deviations of the wording, but not of the substance.

Whereas in most countries the credit contract is automatically cancelled when withdrawing from the distance contract, in some member states like ESTONIA[1442], LATVIA and the NETHERLANDS the consumer has to withdraw from both agreements, the distance contract and the credit agreement. In BELGIUM, two kinds of solutions can be seen, whereas the credit agreement is automatically cancelled, without any charges or damages for the consumer, in the Liberal Professions Act, the consumer has a right of withdrawal according to the Trade Practices Act.[1443]

AUSTRIAN, ESTONIAN and GERMAN law requires, additionally, the credit contract to be regarded as economically linked with the distance contract. This is e.g. in ESTONIA the case if the third party used the assistance of the supplier in the preparation of or entry into the contract.[1444]

HUNGARY, ITALY and the UNITED KINGDOM state a duty of the supplier to inform the creditor that the consumer has withdrawn from the distance contract.

1439 With regard to German law: *Wendehorst*, in: Münchener Kommentar zum BGB, Band 2a, München 2003, § 312d Rn. 10-11.

1440 Article 18(5) of the Law on consumer protection.

1441 Article 44(7) of the Law 7/1996 of January 15 on retail trade.

1442 § 51 of the Law of Obligations Act.

1443 Article 81(4) of the TPA read in conjunction with Art. 20 bis of the Consumer Credit Act.

1444 § 51 of the Law of Obligations Act.

Most other member states seem to refer to their general civil law for the reimbursement of the money already paid. Some member states have fixed the period for the reimbursement of the money already paid to the supplier or creditor. In LATVIA, the supplier has to reimburse the amount of money, together with interest, that has been paid for the goods or services up to the moment of revocation of the contract[1445] within a period of seven days. In FINLAND and IRELAND, the money has to be repaid "without delay and in any time within 30 days after being informed of the withdrawal of the distance contract".

The Directive states that the credit agreement shall be cancelled without penalty. Most of the member states have transposed this provision, e.g. BELGIUM, ESTONIA, GREECE, ITALY, LATVIA, LITHUANIA, LUXEMBOURG, MALTA, the NETHERLANDS and PORTUGAL. POLISH and SLOVAKIAN law have left out the terms "without penalty".[1446]

In some member states, e.g. IRELAND, the consumer can be obliged to pay interest and other costs if agreed in the contract. In HUNGARY, claims regarding costs and interest from the consumer are expresely excluded.[1447] However, damage related to the conclusion of the contract may be demanded. In AUSTRIA, the consumer can be made to bear the costs of an eventual necessary notarisation of signature and compensation for the discharged expenses of the supplier or third party due to the grant of credit, but solely under the condition that the parties have agreed this. Claims regarding other costs or interest are expressly excluded. In CYPRUS, if prior to the reimbursement, any period of time elapsed from the date that the renunciation notice was granted, the supplier or the consumer shall be liable to pay the interest that has accrued on the sum paid. In the UNITED KINGDOM, no charges can be put on the consumer. Nevertheless, a special rule concerning interest exists. Only if the whole or a portion of the credit is repaid, either before the expiry of one month following the cancellation of the credit agreement, or in the case of a credit repayable by instalments before the date on which the first instalment is due, no interest shall be payable on the amount repaid.

3. Performance

a. Obligation to execute the order within a maximum of 30 days

According to Art. 7(1) of Directive 97/7, the supplier is obliged to execute the order of the consumer within 30 days from the day following the day of the order, unless the parties have agreed otherwise. This provision is incomplete, because it is obvious from para. 2 of the same Article, that the supplier is by no means obliged to accept the order. Therefore, Art. 7(1) must be read in the sense that this obligation only comes into force if the contract is concluded. Hence, it is a useful clarification, if, for instance, AUSTRIAN law expressly states that the obligation to perform the contract within 30 days does not arise if the supplier does not accept the offer. This will also be the case in most other member states.

[1445] Article 31 of the Consumer Rights Protection Law.

[1446] Article 13(2) of the Act of 2 March 2000 on the Protection of Certain Consumer Rights and Liability for an Unsafe Product.

[1447] Article 6(2) of the Government Decree No. 17/1999. (II.5.) on Distance Contracting.

The provisions of Art. 7(1) have been transposed by most of the member states, e.g. AUSTRIA, BELGIUM, CYPRUS, DENMARK, ESTONIA, FRANCE, GREECE, ITALY, IRELAND, LUXEMBOURG, MALTA, PORTUGAL, SLOVAKIA[1448], SPAIN, SWEDEN and the UNITED KINGDOM.

In FINLAND, HUNGARY[1449], LATVIA, LITHUANIA, POLAND and SLOVENIA, the period of 30 days seemingly starts to run from the date of the conclusion of the contract. It cannot be assessed whether this is earlier than required by the Directive, because the general rules on computation of time in some of these countries might contain a rule similar to Art. 3(1), sent. 2 of Regulation 1182/71. This rule reads that, where a period expressed in days is to be calculated from the moment at which an event occurs or an action takes place, the day during which that event occurs or that action takes place shall not be considered as falling within the period in question. GREECE refers to the receipt of the consumer's order by the supplier which is later than foreseen in the directive.

In GERMANY, Art. 7(1) is not transposed expressly since in German general contract law there is a regulation stipulating that the contract must be performed immediately save for unforeseen circumstances or separate agreement of the parties. Moreover, the German regulations on standard terms and conditions would prohibit setting an excessively long or inadequate period in standard terms. This is more favourable to the consumer than the provision foreseen in the Directive. DUTCH law stipulates that the supplier is in default if the contract is not performed within 30 days. The period begins on the day of the order, and not the day after the order. In the CZECH REPUBLIC, there is no period of 30 days, but the contract must be performed within an adequate period.

As in the Directive	AT, BE, CY, DK, EE, EL, ES, FR, IE, IT, LU, MT, PT, SE, SK, UK *(16)*
Period starts on day of conclusion of the contract	FI, HU, LT, LV, NL, PL, SL *(7)*
No express period of 30 days	CZ (adequate period), DE (immediately) *(2)*

b. Obligation of supplier to inform and refund in case of unavailability of the goods or services ordered (Art. 7 (2))

According to Art. 7(2) of Directive 97/7, in the case that the ordered goods or services cannot be delivered because they are not available, the supplier is obliged to inform the consumer and must refund any sums already paid by the consumer as soon as possible, and in any case within 30 days.

Article 7(2) has been transposed as stated in the Directive by CYPRUS, ESTONIA, FRANCE, HUNGARY, IRELAND, LATVIA, LUXEMBOURG, MALTA, the NETHERLANDS, POLAND, PORTUGAL, SPAIN and the UNITED KINGDOM. In the United Kingdom[1450], however, a refund does not have

[1448] § 13(1) and (2) of the Act No. 108/2000 on Consumer Protection in Doorstep Selling and in Distance Selling (as amended by Act No. 118/2006 Z.z. (date of coming into force 1 April 2006).

[1449] According to Article 7(1) of the Government Decree, the supplier is obliged to execute the order of the consumer within 30 days from the day following the day of the order, unless the parties have agreed otherwise.

[1450] Regulation 19(8) of the Consumer Protection Regulations 2000.

to be paid if the contract relates to an outdoor leisure event, which by its nature cannot be rescheduled, and if the parties concur (cf. Art. 3(2) 2nd indent of the Directive). This is rather similar in Cyprus and Portugal[1451], whereas Poland has even extended this exception for other cases. In FINLAND, the period in which the supplier must provide a refund is different in cases where the parties have agreed to a later time of delivery or performance of the contract.

The SLOVAKIAN and SLOVENIAN[1452] regulations stipulate a period of 15 days for the supplier to refund the money already paid by the consumer. In CYPRUS, the supplier must refund as soon as possible but not later than 14 days.

Some member states have supplemented the transposition of this article by more detailed provisions which relate the issue to general contract law. For instance, DENMARK and SWEDEN have clarified that the consumer has the right to cancel the contract if the supplier fails to perform the contract in time. The supplier has to inform the consumer about this right and refund the amount already paid as soon as possible and not later than 30 days. In BELGIUM, according to the adage *res perit debitori*, the consumer has the right to be refunded. The rule *res perit creditori* only applies in contracts related to the sale of species goods. However, in most cases, the consumer sales to which this section applies, concerns genus goods, so that mostly the rule *res perit debitori* applies. In FRANCE, the supplier's responsibility is excluded, if he can prove that the failure of performance is due to the consumer, a third person or force majeure.

Other additional rules deal with the consequences of late payment by the supplier. In FRANCE and LUXEMBOURG, there is an express provision that the supplier has to pay legal interest on the sum which has to be returned, if he does not refund the sum within the 30-day period. In SLOVENIA, the supplier has to pay the legal interest of arrears and, additionally, ten percent of the total value of the received payments for every period of 30 days delay. In SPAIN, the consumer can claim double the amount of the sum he has paid to the supplier. It can be assumed that most other member states also provide for such rules on interest or other consequences of delay in their general contract law.

Many member states have only partially transposed Art. 7(2) of the Directive, because they rely on their general contract law in order to reach results which are – in some cases at least partly – in accordance with the Directive. In AUSTRIA, there is no transposition of the duty to refund as soon as possible or at least within 30 days. The obligation to inform the consumer and to refund any sums paid is also applicable, if the supplier does not accept the order of the consumer. In CZECH and GERMAN law, there is no transposition of the duty to inform that the goods are not available and no express rule with regard to the 30 days period, but it follows from general contract law that the consumer can demand the refund of sums already paid if the supplier fails to perform the contract. However, in Germany, such a right of the consumer may depend on the lapse of an "adequate" time limit to be set by the consumer.[1453] Except in very rare cases, such an adequate period will be much shorter than 30 days. After the period has elapsed, the general rule which states that an obligation must be fulfilled immediately save for unforeseen circumstances or separate agreement of the parties, is applica-

---

1451 Article 3(2)(c) of the Decree-Law 143/2001 of April 26.

1452 "As soon as possible but not later than 15 days", but the consumer must be informed of the situation immediately, the 15 days period is relevant only for the refund.

1453 CC § 323(1).

ble. Thus, with regard to the time limit, the results reached under German law will be in accordance with the Directive in the utmost majority of cases. But a crucial difference which can be seen as breach of the Directive, remains. Under German law, the consumer must realise himself that the contract is not going to be performed and then must actively set the adequate time limit in order to avoid the contract and to obtain a refund of any sums paid.

The ITALIAN legislator even goes beyond the provisions of the Directive since the consumer must be informed in writing or via another durable medium. This is also applicable in the case where the promised performance is temporarily unavailable. On the other hand, the supplier has to inform the consumer of the unavailability of the goods and services ordered within 30 days, but there is no express duty to refund the money which has already been paid within 30 days. The GREEK and the LITHUANIAN legislators have not transposed Art. 7(2) of Directive 97/7. In Greece and Lithuania, the general provisions on impossibility of performance are applicable. According to the Greek Consumer Protection Act 2251/94, Art. 4(7), any payments before the productor service is provided to the consumer are prohibited. The consumer can claim the refund of the already paid sums, if any sums have been paid nevertheless, and in the case of negligence the consumer can, additionally, rescind the contract and claim for damages.

Transposition of Art. 7(2)	Member States
As in the Directive	BE* (LPA), EE, ES, FI,[1454] FR, HU, IE, LU, LV, MT, NL, PL, PT, UK[1455] *(14)*
Right to cancel the contract	DK, SE *(2)*
Shorter period for the refund of sums paid	15 days: SL, SK; 14 days: CY *(3)*
Express exclusion of responsibility of the supplier for some cases	BE* (TPA), FR *(2)*
Express obligation to pay interest or higher amount if sum is not refunded within 30 days	ES, FR, LU, SL *(4)*
Not transposed	CZ, DE, EL, LT *(4)*
No express maximum period specified for refund	AT *(1)*

* *more than once*

c. Use of option granted in Art. 7(3) of the Distance Selling Directive

For the use of the option granted in Art. 7(3) of Directive 97/7 cf. Part 2.E.IV. 1 of this report.

4. Payment by card

Payment per Card	Member States
As in the Directive	AT, BE, CY, DK, EE, EL, IE, MT, PL, SK, SL, UK *(12)*
Not transposed	LT, LV *(2)*
Variations	CZ, DE, ES, FI, FR, IT, NL, PT *(8)*
Transposition not entirely clear	LU, SE *(2)*

1454 Unless a later time of delivery is agreed.

1455 Except outdoor leisure events, cf. text above table.

Most member states seem to have transposed the Directive's provisions on payment by card. In AUSTRIA, BELGIUM[1456], CYPRUS, DENMARK, ESTONIA, GREECE, IRELAND, MALTA, POLAND, SLOVAKIA, SLOVENIA and the UNITED KINGDOM, the consumer is entitled to cancel payment (in the scope of a distance contract) when fraudulent use of his credit card has occurred.

However, LITHUANIA and LATVIA have not transposed Art. 8 of Directive 97/7, but it cannot be excluded that the general private law rules on fraud apply. In FRANCE, there is no specific provision implementing Art. 8 of the Directive in the Code de la consommation. However, according to general private law, professionals are liable in the case of undue payments in the case of distance payments ["règlements à distance", not only by credit card]. The liability will be based on the contract.[1457]

For some countries variations could be observed. For instance, ITALIAN law has clarified that the consumer has to prove that the payment was made due to the fraudulent use of a credit card.[1458] By contrast, in GERMANY[1459], the credit institute cannot claim the reimbursement of expenses[1460] for payments made if the credit card has been used for fraudulent purposes, whereby the credit institute has the burden of proof for the claim. In FINNISH law, the consumer is only liable for the unauthorised use of the credit card if he has given the means of identification to another person, or the passing of the means of identification into the possession of an unauthorised person is due to the negligence of the account holder and this "negligence is not slight"; or the account holder has neglected to notify the creditor without delay.[1461] AUSTRIA[1462] and SPAIN have broadened the scope of application by applying not only B2C situations but also other situations where no consumer is involved. DENMARK has clarified that violations of the provisions regarding payment by card are subject to sanctions, including injunctions, by the Consumer Ombudsman in pursuance of the Payment Act. CZECH law contains general provisions on the distance use of electronic payments means which grant the return of money in case of fraudulent use of the electronic payment means.[1463] In POLAND, the legislator states in case of "improper use of a credit card" the obligation to cancel the transaction (the cost to be borne by the trader) and an obligation to remedy any losses suffered by the consumer.[1464] According to DUTCH law, natural persons

---

1456 Article 83novies of the TPA.

1457 Cf. Réponse ministérielle n° 38375, Journal Officiel de l'Assemblée Nationale, 8 juillet 1996, p. 36750. See also "Délibération de la Commission Nationale de l'Informatique et des Libertés n° 2003-034" of 19 June 2003 recommending some security measures in case of payments made by credit cards.

1458 Article 56 of the Legislative Decree of 6 September 2005, No. 206 "Consumer Code". Former Art. 8 Decreto Legislativo 22 maggio 1999, n. 185 "Attuazione della direttiva 97/7/CE relativa alla protezione dei consumatori in materia di contratti a distanza".

1459 CC § 676(h).

1460 The claim of the credit institute against the cardholder is a claim for the reimbursement of expenses.

1461 Chapter 7(19) of the Consumer Protection Act of 20.1.1978/38.

1462 § 31a of the Consumer Protection Act.

1463 § 18 of the Act on Cross-Border Payments No. 124/2002.

1464 Article 14 of the Act of 2 March 2000 on the Protection of Certain Consumer Rights and Liability for an Unsafe Product.

cannot be obliged to pay any amounts resulting from fraudulent use of the credit card except in case of negligence. Additionally, in PORTUGAL, the credit institute is obliged to refund any payment made within a maximum period of 60 days after the demand was made.[1465]

In IRELAND, the failure to comply is a criminal offence according to Art. 10 of the Protection of Consumers in Respect of Contracts made by Means of Distance Communication Regulation. The Irish regulation states furthermore that "payment card" includes credit cards, charge cards, debit cards and store cards.[1466] HUNGARY has also stated criminal law sanctions.

5. Inertia selling

Art. 9 of Directive 97/7 has been amended by Directive 2005/29, which now obliges the member states to "take the measures necessary to exempt the consumer from the provision of any consideration in cases of unsolicited supply, the absence of a response not constituting consent, given the prohibition of inertia selling laid down in Directive 2005/29". Annex I of the Directive contains a list of commercial practices which shall, in all circumstances be regarded as unfair. Annex I No. 29 prohibits inertia selling as an aggressive commercial practice. The impact of this amendment does not seem to be too far reaching as the scope of application of Art. 9 in its old version was not limited to inertia selling in the case of distance contracts but prohibited inertia selling as an unfair commercial practice.[1467] Therefore, it could be considered as abolishing the provisions on inertia selling contained in Directive 97/7.

a. Prohibition of the supply of goods or services to a consumer without their being ordered

Inertia Selling (Art. 9, 1st indent)	Member States
As in the Directive	AT, BE, CY, DK, EL, ES, FR, IT, LT, LU, NL, PT, SE, SK *(14)*
Not prohibited	CZ, EE, HU, LV, PL, SL *(6)*
Variations	DE, FI, IE, MT, UK *(5)*

Most of the member states have prohibited inertia selling, e.g. AUSTRIA, BELGIUM, CYPRUS, DENMARK, FRANCE, GREECE, ITALY, LITHUANIA, LUXEMBOURG, the NETHERLANDS, PORTUGAL[1468], SPAIN and SWEDEN. FINLAND ("shall not be marketed"[1469]) has not explicitly pro-

1465 Article 10(3) of the Decree-Law 143/2001 of April 26.

1466 Regulation 10(4) of the Protection of Consumers in Respect of Contracts made by Means of Distance Communication Regulation.

1467 Grabitz-Hilf/*Micklitz*, A3, Fernabsatzrichtlinie, no.121 et seqq. With regard to German law *Keßler/Micklitz*: Die Richtlinie 2005/29/EG über unlautere Geschäftspraktiken im binnenmarktinternen Geschäftsverkehr zwischen Unternehmen und Verbrauchern, BB 2005, 1, 19.

1468 It is not included in this prohibition the supply of free samples or commercial offers, and the sendings made with altruistic purpose by "instituições de solidariedade social", since these goods have been produced by them (Art. 29(5)).

1469 Chapter 2(2a) of the Consumer Protection Act of 20.1.1978/38.

hibited inertia selling. Nevertheless, in Finland, in the light of preparatory works (HE 79/2000 vp) this clause prohibits inertia selling.[1470]

In some member states, e. g. IRELAND, MALTA and the UNITED KINGDOM, it is a criminal offence to demand payment, threaten to commence legal action, to add a person to a list of defaulters/debtors, or to threaten or actually use another debt collection procedure, in relation to payment for unsolicited goods or services, where the person making such demands etc. has no reasonable cause to believe that he is entitled to receive payment. In the CZECH REPUBLIC, ESTONIA, HUNGARY, LATVIA, POLAND and SLOVENIA, inertia selling has not been prohibited.

b. Exemption of the consumer from the provision of any consideration in cases of unsolicited supply; absence of a response shall not constitute consent.

Inertia Selling (Art. 9, 2nd indent)	Member States
As in the Directive	BE, CY, DK, EE, FI[1471], FR, HU, IT, LU, LV, PT, SK *(12)*
Not transposed	*(0)*
Variations	AT, CZ, DE, EL, ES, IE, LT, MT, NL, PL, SE, SL, UK *(13)*

Many member states have transposed Art. 9, 2nd indent as stated in the Directive, e.g. BELGIUM, CYPRUS, DENMARK, ESTONIA, FINLAND, FRANCE, HUNGARY, ITALY, LATVIA, LUXEMBOURG, PORTUGAL[1472] and SLOVAKIA.

AUSTRIA has transposed Art. 9 of Directive 97/7 in the Civil Code.[1473] This is an extension of scope because the provision is also applicable to B2B situations. POLAND has stated a provision that the trader bears the risk of the consumer not using the services which were unsolicited and that no obligation can be imposed on the consumer.[1474] In some member states, the consumer benefits from a presumption that if the trader sent unsolicited goods, the consumer may use it as an unconditional gift and refuse all payments, e.g. in CYPRUS, LITHUANIA, MALTA, the NETHERLANDS, SLOVENIA and in the UNITED KINGDOM. In Cyprus, this is presumed when neither the seller nor any other authorised person requires the return of the good after a period of 30 days.[1475] In the CZECH REPUBLIC, the consumer shall neither have to return the goods to the supplier nor inform him about it.[1476] In GREECE, the con-

---

1470 It has also been established in legal practice that provision of unsolicited goods that require consumer action is deemed unfair marketing.

1471 According to preparatory works, it is possible to provide, for example, unsolicited magazines offers or product offers for consumers for testing. However, there should not be any obligations to consumers related to their goods.

1472 When the consumer decides to return unordered goods, he has the right to be reimbursed for all expenses, within 30 days (Art. 29(4)).

1473 CC § 864(2).

1474 Article 15 of the Act of 2 March 2000 on the Protection of Certain Consumer Rights and Liability for an Unsafe Product.

1475 Section 13(2) of the Law for the Conclusion of Consumer Distance Contracts of 2000.

1476 § 53(9) of the CC.

sumer can "do as he pleases with the goods" except there has been an obvious mistake. In this case the consumer shall, if possible, hold the goods at the disposal of the supplier for a reasonable period of time.[1477] In SPAIN, the consumer has no duty to return the goods and can keep them free of charge, and in case of unraveling, the consumer has no duty to compensate for damages or deterioration. In AUSTRIA, the recipient has to inform the trader in this situation and send back the goods. In IRELAND, this provision has been correctly transposed for services.[1478] On the other hand, the recipient of unsolicited goods is required to keep the goods for a period of time to enable the sender to recover the goods.[1479] This requirement to retain the goods for six months could constitute consideration, and is absent from the provision in the Regulations on the inertia selling of services. SWEDEN has not explicitly transposed this Directive's provision because this follows from its domestic general contractual principles.

6. Restrictions on the use of certain means of distance communication

Article 10 of Directive 97/7 states that the use of automatic calling machines and fax machines requires prior consent from the consumer.

Almost all member states have transposed Art. 10 of the Directive by using the copy and paste method. These countries are: BELGIUM, CYPRUS, CZECH REPUBLIC, DENMARK, ESTONIA, FRANCE, GERMANY, HUNGARY, ITALY, LATVIA, LUXEMBOURG, the NETHERLANDS, POLAND, PORTUGAL, SLOVAKIA, SLOVENIA, SPAIN and the UNITED KINGDOM. Estonia, Denmark and Slovenia have also extended the restrictions on the use of email. Poland has chosen the opt-in rule for all means of distance communications.

In IRELAND, the contract is not enforceable against the consumer if the supplier used these means of distance communication.[1480] In MALTA, the trader is liable to compensate the consumer for any inconvenience caused and resultant damages suffered.[1481] AUSTRIA has not transposed this provision expressly, but according to the legislator the same protection of the consumer is granted by the general clauses in the Civil Code[1482], the Unfair Competition Act[1483] and, furthermore, by Austrian case-law in this area. Only LITHUANIA has not transposed Art. 10 of Directive 97/7.

The GREEK and DANISH transposition law in the field of automatic calling systems gives a broader protection than Directive 97/7 because the opt-in provision regarding automatic calling systems and fax applies to *everyone* – and not just to consumers.

1477 Article 4(4) of the Consumer Protection Act 2251/94.

1478 Regulation 11 of the Protection of Consumers in Respect of Contracts made by Means of Distance Communication Regulation.

1479 Section 47 of the Sale of Goods Act 1980.

1480 Regulation 12(1) of the Protection of Consumers in Respect of Contracts made by Means of Distance Communication Regulation.

1481 Article 8 of the Distance Selling Regulations, 2001.

1482 CC § 16.

1483 § 1 of the Unfair Commercial Practises Act.

IV. Use of options provided in the Directive

1. Option of member states to allow the supplier to provide the consumer with goods or services of equivalent quality and price

Article 7(3) of Directive 97/7 contains an option for the member states to stipulate that the supplier can provide the consumer with goods of equivalent quality and price, if this possibility was provided before the conclusion of the contract, or in the contract. The option has been used by CYPRUS, ESTONIA, FINLAND, FRANCE, HUNGARY, ITALY, the NETHERLANDS and the UNITED KINGDOM.

IRELAND and LATVIA have added that the consumer must be informed of the possibility to deliver equivalent goods or services prior to the conclusion of the contract. In POLAND, the possibility to deliver products of an equivalent price and quality, must be included into the contract. The required information must be given to the consumer in writing. PORTUGAL and GREECE have provided that the information on the costs of withdrawal must be given to the consumer in writing. However, in Greece, there is no rule stipulating that the possibility of alternative performance needs to be provided prior to the conclusion or in the contract.

In SLOVAKIA, the supplier has the right and the obligation to deliver goods or services of an equivalent quality and price if the parties agree. There is no special information duty or regulation on the costs. In SPAIN, the supplier of a good has the right to deliver a similar one. This right is not applicable for contracts on services.

BELGIUM, the CZECH REPUBLIC, DENMARK, LITHUANIA, LUXEMBOURG, MALTA and SLOVENIA have made no use of the option. AUSTRIA has not transposed the option either, but a seller's right of choice and a buyer's right of replacement exist in Austrian general contract law. Also SWEDEN has not expressly transposed this option, but the possibility to provide the consumer, in the case that he agrees, with an alternative good or service originates from the principle of private autonomy. GERMANY, too, has not expressly transposed this option. According to general rules, the parties can, of course, agree on such a right of the supplier. However, the rules on unfair terms (CC § 308(4)) define strict limits concerning the use of such clauses (right of amendment) in standard terms. In any case, pursuant to CC § 312c(1) in conjunction with BGB-InfoV, § 1(1)(6), the supplier is required to inform the consumer about the existence of any such term. In the UNITED KINGDOM[1484] and ESTONIA[1485], the supplier has to inform the consumer prior to the conclusion of the contract if he proposes, in the event of the goods or services ordered by the consumer being unavailable, to provide substitute goods or services of an equivalent quality and price.

Option used	CY, EE, FI, FR, HU, IT, NL, SK (only if parties agree), UK *(9)*
Option not used	BE, CZ, DK, LT, LU, MT, SL *(7)*
No express transposition, but general contract law with similar effect	AT, DE, SE *(3)*
Only for goods, not for services	ES *(1)*

[1484] Regulation 7(1)(b) of the Consumer Protection (Distance Selling) Regulations 2000.
[1485] Article 54(1)(10) of the Law of Obligations Act.

Information must be given in writing	EL, PL, PT *(3)*
Possibility must be provided prior to the conclusion of the contract	IE, LV *(2)*

2. Option of member states to place burden of proof on the supplier

Use of Option	Member States
Yes	BE, CY, DE, DK, EE, EL, ES, HU, LT (Only regarding submission of mandatory required information to the consumer), LV (only regarding financial services), LU, MT, PT, SL *(14)*
No use	AT, CZ, FI, FR, IE, IT, NL, PL, SE, SK, UK *(11)*

Article 11(3)(a) of the Directive enables the member states to stipulate that the burden of proof concerning the existence of prior information, written confirmation, compliance with time-limits or consumer consent can be placed on the supplier. Half of the European countries, namely BELGIUM[1486], CYPRUS, ESTONIA, GERMANY, GREECE, HUNGARY, LITHUANIA, LUXEMBOURG, MALTA, PORTUGAL, SLOVENIA and SPAIN have made use of this option. DENMARK has not explicitly made use of this option, since the burden of proof in accordance with general principles of Danish law was already placed with the supplier. Lithuania though has only regulated the submission of mandatory required information to the consumer. German law contains a special arrangement on the burden of proof in terms of the right of withdrawal; the supplier must prove that he has properly informed the consumer of his rights and that all the necessary criteria for the period to begin have been met. AUSTRIA, the CZECH REPUBLIC, FINLAND, FRANCE, ITALY, IRELAND[1487], LATVIA, the NETHERLANDS, POLAND, SWEDEN and the UNITED KINGDOM have decided not to transpose this provision.

3. Option of member states to provide for voluntary supervision by self-regulatory bodies

Article 11(4) of Directive 97/7 grants the member states the option to provide for voluntary supervision by self-regulatory bodies. Most member states have chosen not to implement this option. They are: AUSTRIA, BELGIUM, CYPRUS, DENMARK, FINLAND, FRANCE, IRELAND, ITALY, LITHUANIA, MALTA, the NETHERLANDS, POLAND, PORTUGAL, SLOVENIA, SWEDEN, SPAIN and the UNITED KINGDOM. In the United Kingdom and Ireland, codes of conduct (to be approved by the Office of Fair Trading) are encouraged. Only GERMANY, ESTONIA, GREECE, HUNGARY, LATVIA and SLOVAKIA have made use of this option provided in the Directive.

Table: Use of option provided in Art. 11(4) Distance Selling Directive

Use of Option	Member States
Yes	DE, EE, EL, HU, LV, SK *(6)*
No use	AT, BE, CY, CZ, DK, ES, FI, FR, IE, IT, LT, LU, MT, NL, PL, PT, SE, SL, UK *(19)*

1486 Article 83decies(1) of the TPA.

1487 In Ireland, this reverse burden of proof only operates as regards Regulation 13 (an application by the Director of Consumer Affairs or other consumer organisations for an injunction from the High Court to ensure compliance with the Regulations). In all other regards, e.g. a private action between supplier and consumer, the normal rules of evidence apply.

4. Option of member states to ban the marketing of certain goods or services, particularly medicinal products, within their territory by means of distance contracts

Use of Option	Member States
Yes	DE, FI, HU, LT, PT, SK *(6)*
No use	BE, CY,[1488] CZ, DK,[1489] EE, EL, ES, FR, IE, IT, LU, LV, MT, NL, PL, SE, SL, UK *(18)*
Transposition not entirely clear	AT *(1)*

Article 14, sent. 2 of Directive 97/7 provides the option to ban the marketing of certain goods or services, particularly medicinal products, within their territory by means of distance contracts. Sixteen countries have not made use of this option (cf. the table above). The SLOVAKIAN Act 377/2004 on Non-smoker Protection establishes a prohibition of distance selling of tobacco products.

The LITHUANIAN laws on medicines distinguish the marketing of medicines depending on their nature. DENMARK prohibited any kind of advertisements for medicinal products. In FINLAND distance selling of medicinal products is not allowed. The Medicines Act stipulates strict restrictions for postal import of medicines.[1490] In PORTUGAL, the sale of medicines (in the sense of the Decree-Law 72/91 of February 8, Art. 2(1)(a)) is restricted to pharmacies and other authorised establishments (Art. 62 of the Decree-Law 72/91 and Decree-Law 134/2005 of August 16). HUNGARY has also used the option to ban the marketing of certain goods or services by means of distance contracts.[1491]

In CYPRUS, the conclusion of distance contracts may be prohibited or restricted on grounds of public interest, under the provisions of the legislation in force, for specific goods or services. In BELGIUM, Art. 83 undecies of the Trade Practices Act grants the King the right to adopt specific rules for certain types of distance contracts. The Royal Decree of 11 January 1993 Concerning the Regulation of the Division, the Packing and the Marking of Dangerous Preparations provides an additional information duty towards the consumer in the case of distance selling of such preparations, but medicinal products in ready to use form, are expressly excluded from the scope of this Royal Decree.[1492] The distance selling of prescription medicines is forbidden.[1493] The distance selling of non-prescription medicines falls under the general regime of the TPA.

1488 CYPRUS does not exercise this option. However, it leaves the possibility open for the option to be exercised by other legislative acts dealing with specific products or services.

1489 Denmark has not made use of the option, since detailed rules regarding marketing of medicinal products already exist in Danish medicinal legislation.

1490 VNA lääkevalmisteiden henkilökohtaisesta tuonnista Suomeen 1088/2002 vp.

1491 Cf. Act XXXV of 2000 on pesticides, Decree 43/1996. (XI.29.) on products supplied by pharmacies and the Government Decree 4/1997. (I. 22.).

1492 Article 2(4) Royal Decree of 11 January 1993 Concerning the Regulation of the Division, the Packing and the Marking of Dangerous Preparations..

1493 Article 3(4) of the Drugs Act of 25 March 1965.

Until 1 November 2004 GERMANY prohibited the mail order of medicinal products via chemists. The ECJ stated in C-322/01 – *Doc Morris*[1494] that "a prohibition on the sale by mail order of medicinal products the sale of which is restricted to pharmacies in the member state concerned" is a measure having an effect equivalent to a quantitative restriction for the purposes of Article 28 EC. The ECJ ruled that this prohibition can be justified – relying on Art. 30 EC – for medicinal products subject to prescription, but not to medicinal products which are not subject to prescription in the member state concerned. GERMANY amended its Pharmacies Act (Apothekengesetz) and Medicines Act (Arzneimittelgesetz) thereby allowing the mail order purchases both of over-the-counter and prescription-only medicinal products via chemists. However, chemists that are registered in Germany do require a mail order licence. In SLOVENIA, the Medicinal Products Act states that sale of medicinal products via the internet that is accompanied with professional counselling is allowed if it is performed by someone who has a licence for such pharmaceutical activity and if quality and tracking is guaranteed.

Bibliography

Communication from the Commission to the Council, the European Parliament and the European Economic and Social Committee on the implementation of Directive 1997/7/EC of the European Parliament and of the Council of 20 May 1997 on the Protection of Consumers in respect of Distance Contracts, COM (2006) 514 final; Working Document of the Commission – Responses to the Consultation on Distance Selling Directive 97/7/EC contained in Communication 2006/514/EC, http://ec.europa.eu/consumers/cons_int/safe_shop/dist_sell/sum_responses_consultations_en.pdf; **Ajani, Gianmaria / Rossi, Piercarlo**, Codice del consumatori, 2005, **Alpa, Guido / Rossi Carleo, Liliana,** Codice del consumo, 2006, **Arroyo Aparicio, A.** Los contratos a distancia en la Ley de Ordenación del Comercio Minorista, Cizur Menor 2003, **Badenas Carpio, Juan Manuel/Boldó Roda, Carmen,** Régimen jurídico de la llamada "venta directa" Las ventas domiciliarias y a distanzia, Valencia 2003, **Balan, Ioan I.** Contractele la distanta si protectia consumatorilor, Revista Dreptul 2002, **Bártfai, Judit / Cseke, Dóra / Kertész, Ágnes / Németh, Anita / Wallacher, Lajos,** Szerződési Jog-Fogyasztóvédelem, 2003, **Botana García, Gemma** Comercio electrónico y protección de los consumidores, Madrid 2001, **Correia, Miguel Pupo,** Contratos ŕ distância: uma fase na evolução da defesa do consumidor na sociedade de informação?, Estudos de Direito do Consumidor (Estudos de Direito do Consumidor) 2002, 165-180, **Forsman, Edmar,** Internetpublicering – en juridisk vägledning, Stockholm 2001, **Holberg, Benedikte / Kristensen, Lene Pater/Mřgelvang-Hansen, Peter / Nielsen, Tina Morell / Ře, Henrik,** Forbrugeraftaleloven, Copenhagen 2006, **Howells, Geraint / Weatherill, Stephen,** Consumer Protection Law, Aldershot 2005, **Huhtamäki, Ari / Keskitalo, Petri,** Kuluttajansuojaoikeudellisia kirjoituksia Writings of Consumer Protection Law, Lapin 2003, **Kuusela, Hannu,** Kuluttajien asema ja palvelujen etämyynnin sääntelypyrkimykset The Position of Consumers and Ratio of Distance Selling Pro-visions concerning Services, Tampere 1997, **Łętowska, Ewa,** Europejskie prawo umów konsumenckich, Warszawa 2004, **McMahon, Laurence** Contracts negotiated away from Business Premises and the 1997 Distance Selling Directive, Irish Law Times 1999, 139, **Micklitz, Hans-W.** Kommentar zur Fernabsatzrichtlinie, in:

1494 ECJ judgment of 11 December 2003, C-322/01 – *Deutscher Apothekerverband eV v. 0800 DocMorris NV and Jacques Waterval.*

Grabitz/Hilf Band III, Sekundärrecht, A 3, Loseblatt, Das Recht der Europäischen Union, Band III Sekundärrecht 2004, **Orduńa Moreno, Francisco Javier** Contratación y comercio electrónico, Valencia 2002, **Papaioannou, G.,** H simbasi apo apostasi kata to dikaio tis prostasias tou katanalotik, **Schinkels, Boris**, Fernabsatzverträge (§§ 312b-312d, 241a, 355ff. BGB) in: Gebauer/ Wiedmann, Zivilrecht unter europäischem Einfluss, Kap. 7, Stuttgart 2005, **Sola Teyssiere, Javier,** La venta a distancia en el comercio minorista. Régimen jurídico y control administrativo, Valencia 2002, **Teixeira, Glória,** O Comércio Electrónico Estudos Jurídico-Económicos, Lisboa 2002.

F. Price Indication Directive (98/6)

Drafted by Hans Schulte-Nölke and Leonie Meyer-Schwickerath

Executive Summary

1. Transposition deficiencies

All member states have transposed Directive 98/6. The analysis reveals transposition deficiencies mainly in the use of the options provided in Art. 6 (i.e. the option to be exempt from the obligation to indicate the unit price in cases where it constitutes an excessive burden). Primarily, several member states make permanent use of this option whereas Directive 98/6 just allows a temporary exemption.

2. Enhancement of protection

a. Extension of scope

Some national transposition laws provide a wider scope of application in the field of price indication.

- Some member states have broadened the definition of "consumer" (Art. 2 lit. (e)), e.g. by including legal persons.
- Many member states have extended the scope of application to services (whereas Directive 98/6 applies only to products offered by traders, Art. 1).

b. Use of minimum clause

It should be noted that the minimum clause in Art. 10 of Directive 98/6 must be considered as being only declarative, and not constitutive. This means that Directive 98/6 would continue to be just a minimum harmonisation measure even if its Art. 10 was deleted. The reason is that Directive 98/6 has been enacted on the basis of Art. 129 lit. (a) of the EC Treaty, the predecessor of Art. 153 of the EC Treaty. With regard to measures enacted on that basis, Art. 153(5) of the EC Treaty allows the member states to maintain or to enact measures which are more favourable to consumers than the Community measures.

Except for some clarifications which could be interpreted as an improvement of the consumer protection level, the member states made practically no use of the minimum clause.

3. Use of options

The majority of the member states used the options provided in Directive 98/6:

- Art. 3 (2) 1st indent (option not to apply Art. 3(1) to products supplied in the course of the provision of a service) has been made use of by more than 20 member states.
- Art. 3(2) 2nd indent (option not to apply Art. 3(1) to sales by auction and sales of works of art and antiques) has also been made use of by more than 20 member states.
- Art. 5 (option to waive obligation to indicate the unit price in certain cases) has been made use of by several member states. Although these exceptions from the obligation to indicate the unit price have the fact that they are mainly related to food in common, the particular products excluded differ throughout the member states.
- Art. 6 (option to exclude the obligations to indicate the unit price in cases where it constitutes an excessive burden) has been made use of by nearly 20 member states.

4. Inconsistencies or ambiguities

The notion of "small retail business" in Art. 6 is very vague.

5. Gaps in Directive 98/6

- No regulation of services.

6. Potential barriers to (cross-border) trade

Some of the options, in particular Art. 5 and Art. 6, lead to great differences throughout the member states. In certain cases this may hinder cross-border trade.

7. Conclusions and recommendations

In order to eliminate potential barriers to trade the following steps could be taken:

- Concretisation of the option provided for in Art. 5 (or changing the option into a general clause).
- Establishing a definition of "small retail businesses" with the aim of achieving more coherent national legislation.

I. Member state legislation prior to the adoption of the Price Indication Directive 98/6

Prior to the adoption of Directive 98/6 in the EU member states, consumer protection laws in the field of price indication were rather different.

Most of the member states had already enacted legislative acts stipulating price indication in their national laws long before Directive 98/6 came into existence. In the UNITED KINGDOM, the Prices Act was enacted in 1973. Other examples are POLAND with its "Act on Prices of 26 February 1982", CYPRUS with its "Products and Services (Regulation and Inspection) Law of 1962, L.32/62", DENMARK with its "Price Labelling Act" of 1977 and MALTA with its "Control on the Sale of Commodities Regulations, 1972". Contrary to Directive 98/6, these provisions only obliged the traders to indicate the selling price of the products. Only some member states like AUSTRIA, DENMARK and GERMANY stated an obligation for traders in their national law to indicate the unit price for certain products. Nevertheless, these provisions had nearly no practical impact because of numerous exemptions. In BELGIUM, the unit price had to be indicated on products sold in bulk and pre-packaged products with a variable quantity.[1495]

Some member states had no comparable protection in the field of price indication before the transposition of Directive 98/6, such as IRELAND, where only a number of specific ministerial orders relating to the indication of prices with regard to specific subject-matters existed (e.g. the Retail Price (Diesel and Petrol) Display Order 1997 or the Retail Price (Beverages in Licensed Premises) Display Order 1999).

In some of the new member states (e.g. the CZECH REPUBLIC, ESTONIA, LATVIA, LITHUANIA and SLOVENIA), no comparable protection existed.

II. Scope of application

Directive 98/6 stipulates in its Art. 1 the "indication of the selling price and the price per unit of measurement of products offered by traders to consumers (...)".

1. Consumer

Article 2 lit. (e) of Directive 98/6 defines the notion of 'consumer' as "any natural person who buys a product for purposes that do not fall within the sphere of his commercial or professional activity".

About one third of the member states' laws provide a 'consumer' definition in the context of their specific transposition laws (e.g. CYPRUS[1496], DENMARK[1497] and GREECE[1498]). More than

---

1495 Article 6 and 7 of the Royal Decree of 30 June 1996 Concerning the Price Indication of Products and Services and the Order Form.

1496 Similar to Directive 98/6: Art. 2, 1st definition: definition of trader; 4th definition: definition of consumer, The Selling and Unit Price Indication Law of 2000, L.112(I)/2000.

half of the European countries, however, refer to general 'consumer' definitions (e.g. BELGIUM[1499], the CZECH REPUBLIC[1500], ESTONIA[1501] and MALTA[1502]), thus maintaining a coherent concept within their legal systems.

No express transposition of the definition exists in GERMANY, FRANCE and POLAND. Nevertheless, German law introduces the term 'final addressee' in the regulation covering price information without further concretising it.[1503] It is commonly accepted that the notion of 'final addressee' encompasses persons not passing on goods or services to another user but rather for their own use.[1504] In contrast to the general 'consumer' definition in the German CC[1505] or the UWG (Act against Unfair Competition)[1506], in addition to individual consumers, buyers working in an independent commercial or business capacity as well as in public institutions can also be final addressees. However, in case of offers or advertisements vis-à-vis, final addressees who use the good or service within their professional or official capacity, not all provisions on price indication apply. [1507]

Whereas the POLISH transposition Act, despite its lack of definition for consumer, only excludes C2C situations from its scope of application[1508], FRENCH case-law determines the consumer as a person concluding a contract which does not have a direct connection with his commercial activity.[1509] The ruling of the French Cass. Civ. has been further clarified,

---

1497 Corresponding with the Directive: § 2 para 5 (definition of consumer), § 2 para 4 (definition of trader) Executive Order no. 866 of 18 September 2000 on information on sales price and price per unit for consumer goods.

1498 Article 2(δ) (definition of trader), Art. 2(ε) (definition of consumer) ruling of the Ministry of Economics and Development No Z1-404 – 2001 .

1499 Not the Royal Decree of 30 June 1996 concerning the indication of the price of products and services and the order form but the Trade Practices Act transposes the definitions:
Art. 1 sec. 6, 7 Act of 14 July 1991 on trade practices and consumer information and protection
The general definitions in the Trade Practices Act also serve as the transposition for the terms of consumer and trader of the Doorstep Selling Directive (85/577), the Unfair Contract Terms Directive (93/13) and the Distance Selling Directive (97/7). The Belgian consumer concept extends to legal persons, but applies only to activities engaged in for purposes exclusively outside of the trade or profession.

1500 Consumer Protection Act No. 634/1992.

1501 § 2(1) (definition of consumer), § 2(2) Consumer Protection Act (definition of trader).

1502 Article 2 Consumer Affairs Act of 15 October 2002. The definition of consumer is qualified by the Price Indication Regulation including "any final purchaser" in the concept, Reg. 2(2) Consumer Affairs Act (Price Indication) Regulations of 1 October 2002.
Art. 2(3) also implements the concept of consumer defined in the Consumer Sales Directive (99/44) and, additionally, the definition of trader of the Unfair Contract Terms Directive (93/13).

1503 § 1(1), sent. 1 of the Price Indication Regulation.

1504 BGH, GRUR 1974, 477; GRUR 1977, 264.

1505 CC § 13.

1506 § 2(2) of the Act against Unfair Competition.

1507 § 9(1)(1) Price Indication Regulation.

1508 Article 1.2(1)of the Act on prices of 5 July 2001.

1509 Cour de Cassation, Civ. 1ère 3 January 1996 ; 30 January 1996; 10 July 1996.

including in the ambit of the definition, professionals who conclude a contract which does not constitute a direct connection with their professional activity.[1510]

Table: Legislative techniques

Special definition in transposition law	CY, DK, EL, IE, LU, NL, SE, UK *(8)*
Reference to a more general definition	AT[1511], BE, CZ, EE, ES, FI, HU, IT, LT, LV, MT[1512], PT, SK, SL *(14)*
No specific definition	DE, FR, PL *(3)*

The majority of the national definitions substantively mirror the content of the Directive's definition with only some minor differences in wording or style. For instance, the AUSTRIAN legislator has negatively described the notion of 'consumer' as the person not fulfilling the requirements for being a trader.[1513] The LITHUANIAN legislation prescibes a "consumer" definition similar to Directive 98/6 in the general CC[1514] and recapitulates it in the implementing Law on Consumer Protection.[1515]

For a group of member states it can be perceived as an extension of the scope of application to legal persons in case they act outside their professional activity. The PORTUGUESE definition, in contrast to the restriction to natural persons in Directive 98/6, only states "persons", thus allowing the inclusion of natural and legal persons into its concept. Similarly, in MALTA, the term 'consumer' includes any final purchaser, which means that legal entities can also be considered as consumers.[1516] Explicitly mentioned are legal persons in SPANISH[1517] law.

Further variations exist in Maltese law as other individuals, not being the immediate purchaser or beneficiary who has been authorised by the consumer, are regarded as 'consumers'.[1518] Similarly in SLOVAKIA, according to § 2(1) lit. a of Consumer Protection Act, the consumer is a natural person "that buys products or uses services for direct personal use by natural persons, especially for himself and members of his household".
In Spain, the person has to be the final addressee of the good or service without "the aim of integrating them in production, transformation, commercialization processes".[1519] No explicit reference is made to "purposes outside his trade or profession".[1520]

[1510] Cour de Cassation, Civ. 1ère 17 July 1996 ; 25 November 2002.

[1511] Indirectly transposed in § 1 Consumer Protection Act.

[1512] In the context of the Price Indication Regulations 2002, the term 'consumer' has to be interpreted according to the definition in Art. 2 Consumer Affairs Act.

[1513] § 1 of the Consumer Protection Act.

[1514] CC Art. 6350(1).

[1515] CC Art 2(1).

[1516] Regulation 2 (2) of the Price Indication Regulations.

[1517] Article 1 of the Law 26/1984 of July 19 on Consumer Protection.

[1518] Article 2 of the Consumer Affairs Act (Price Indication) Regulations .

[1519] Article 1(3) of the Law 26/1984 of July 19 on Consumer Protection.

[1520] In the context of the implementation of the Unfair Contract Terms Directive, an explanatory note has been introduced in the Law 7/1998 of April 13 on Standard Terms in Contracts, being a non binding part of (any) law, repeating the formulation, thus serving as an interpretation guideline for the legal "consumer" definition. It is debated whether to protect persons acting outside their business without being the final addressees.

Table: General overview of transposition

Substantially equivalent to Directive 98/6	CY, DK, EE, EL, FI, HU*, IE, IT, LT, LU, LV[1521], NL, SE, SL, UK *(15)*
Extension to legal persons	AT, BE, CZ, ES*, MT[1522]*, PT *(6)*
Final addressee	DE, ES* (compulsory requirement), MT* *(3)*
Extension to addressee of information or offer related to goods or services	HU* *(1)*
No mention of purposes outside trade or profession	ES* *(1)*

* *more than once*

2. Trader

In Art. 2 lit. (d) of Directive 98/6, 'trader' is defined as "any natural or legal person who sells or offers for sale products which fall within his commercial or professional activity".

Some of the member states directly introduce the definitions into their transposition laws (e.g. CYPRUS[1523], DENMARK[1524] and the UNITED KINGDOM[1525]). But the majority of national legislators have opted for the use of a more general definition of 'trader', thus maintaining a coherent scope of application in consumer law. In FRANCE[1526] and SWEDEN, the notion of 'trader' has not been specifically transposed.

In France, as the transposition text does not provide any definition, it is deemed that, following Art. L. 113-3 of the Consumer Protection Act[1527], the obliged party should be sellers and service providers. In SWEDISH law, no direct definition has been given but it is generally stated that the regulations apply when a trader is supplying goods or services in his business to a consumer.[1528]

Table: Legislative technique

Special definition in transposition law	CY, DE, DK, EL, ES, IE, LU, NL, UK *(9)*
Reference to a more general definition	AT, BE, CZ, EE, FI, HU, IT, LT, LV, MT, PL, PT, SK, SL *(14)*
Not specifically transposed	FR, SE *(2)*

1521 Definition of "Consumer" has been changed since 27 October 2005 when a legal person was excluded from the scope of a consumer by adopting changes in the Consumer Rights Protection Law.

1522 The Minister responsible for consumer affairs may designate persons as "consumers" for the purpose(s) of the Consumer Affairs Act after having consulted the Consumer Affairs Council.

1523 Article 2, 1st definition Selling and Unit Price Indication Law of 2000, L.112(I)/2000 as amended by Law 119(I)/2005 and Law136(I)/2005.

1524 § 2(4) of the Executive Order no. 866 of 18 September 2000 on information on sales price and price per unit for consumer goods.

1525 Regulation 1(2) The Price Marking Order 2004.

1526 Article 1(3) of the Decree of 16 November 1999 uses the term "trader" ("*commerçant*") without defining it.

1527 Code de la Consommation.

1528 § 2 of the Price Information Act 1991:601.

About half of the member states' legislations substantively mirror the content of the Directive's definition of 'trader'. However, variations exist in some countries, extending the scope of application to persons providing services (e.g. LUXEMBOURG[1529]) or explicitly including persons dealing with agricultural production as regards plants and animals, gardening, vegetable cultivation, forestry and fishery (not sea fishery).[1530] A deviation in the use of terms, such as 'seller' (e.g. the CZECH REPUBLIC, LATVIA, LITHUANIA) or 'professional' (e.g. ITALY, Luxembourg) could also be detected. HUNGARIAN law makes use of the terms 'distributor' and 'manufacturer'.[1531] The 'distributor' is considered as "the economic organization marketing merchandise or services to consumers". In case the manufacturer's main office is not located in the territory of the Republic of Hungary, the importer of the goods shall be considered to be the 'manufacturer'. In POLAND, the obligations of Directive 98/6 are imposed upon producers as well as sellers.

According to Art. 1(6) of the BELGIAN Trade Practices Act, liberal professions fall outside the scope of the trader concept. Furthermore, the definition of services in Art. 1(2) of the TPA requires the pursuit of commercial activities as defined in Art. 2 and 3 of the Commercial Code.

In MALTESE law, the Minister responsible for consumer affairs may, in co-operation with the Consumer Affairs Council, designate any category or class of persons as a "trader" for the purposes of the transposition law. Moreover, the Maltese law also includes professionals who exercise acts of trade in their own name or in that of any commercial partnership.

In LITHUANIA, the concept of 'trader' includes the definitions of 'seller' and 'service provider'. The first definition identifies the difference that any person selling the goods on the premises intended for business purposes, or outside them, shall be regarded as a 'seller'.[1532]

GERMANY has extended the scope of its transposition law considerably by applying it to everyone, who professionally or regularly (in any other manner) offers goods or services or, as offeree of goods or services, advertises goods or services vis-à-vis the final addressee.[1533]

Table: Transposition method

Substantively equivalent to Directive 98/6	AT, CY, DK, EL, ES, FI, IE, MT, NL, SL, UK *(12)*
No explicit mention of 'natural or legal person'	EE, LU, UK *(3)*
Different use of terms	BE, CZ, DE, IT, LT, LU, LV, NL, SK (9)
Inclusion of the intermediary	BE, IT, MT *(3)*
Explicit inclusion of persons dealing with agricultural products	PL *(1)*
No mention of "within commercial or professional activity"	CZ, LT[1534], LU *(3)*

1529 Article 1(1) of the Decree of 7 September 2001 on price indication.

1530 Article 4(1), Art. 3(1)(8) of the Act on the Freedom of Economic Activity.

1531 § 2 lit. j, lit. k of the Act CLV of 1997 on Consumer Protection.

1532 Article 2(2) of the Consumer Protection Law.

1533 § 1(1), sent. 1 of the Price Indication Regulation.

1534 Only with respect to the definition of 'seller'. See above.

3. Situations falling in the scope of application

Article 1 of Directive 98/6 states that the regulations only apply to products offered by 'traders' to 'consumers'. Many of the member states have, nevertheless, extended the scope of application to services: BELGIUM[1535], the CZECH REPUBLIC[1536], DENMARK[1537], ESTONIA[1538], FINLAND, FRANCE[1539], GERMANY[1540], HUNGARY[1541], LATVIA[1542], LITHUANIA[1543], LUXEMBOURG[1544], POLAND, PORTUGAL[1545], SLOVAKIA[1546] and SWEDEN[1547]. In SPAIN[1548], the general consumer definition introduces service offers and provisions.
As to the option of the member states to exempt products supplied in the course of the provision of a service from the indication duty (Art. 3(2) 1st indent), c.f. IV. 1.

Table: Extension to services

Extension to service providers	BE, CZ, DE, DK, EE, FI, FR, HU[1549], LT, LU, LV, PL, PT, SE, SK, SL ***(16)***

4. Selling price

In Art. 2 lit. (a) of Directive 98/6, 'selling price' is defined as the "final price for a unit of the product, or a given quantity of the product, including VAT and all other taxes".

The majority of the member states have transposed this term in accordance with the definition contained in the Price Indication Directive. In some member states however, the implementation law slightly differs from the Directive's regulations. In MALTA, POLAND and SLOVAKIA, only the term 'price'and not 'selling price' is used. Whereas in Malta, it is regulated that the price must be the 'final retail or unit price' and has to include the value added

1535 Article 1 no. 6, 7 of the Act of 14 July 1991 on trade practices and consumer information and protection.

1536 Article 2 of the Consumer Protection Act No. 634/1992.

1537 Effective from 1 July 2006 the price indication rules were transferred to the Marketing Practices Act (re Act No 1389 of 21 December 2005) and the Price Indication Act (re Consolidated Act No 209 of 28 March 2000) was repealed. Pursuant to the Marketing Practices Act § 13(2), the scope of the price indication rules is extended to services, including electronic services (e.g. on the internet) if the consumer is able to place an order electronically.

1538 § 2 no. 1, 2 of the Consumer Protection Act.

1539 Although not specifically transposed, it is assumed that the obliged party shall be 'sellers' and 'service providers'. See above.

1540 § 1(1), sent. 1 of the Price Indication regulation.

1541 § 2(e) of the Act CLV of 1997 on Consumer Protection.

1542 Article 1(1) section 3, 4-5 Consumer Rights Protection Law.

1543 Article 2(1) of the Law on consumer protection.

1544 Article 1(1) and (2) of the Decree of 7 September 2001 on price indication.

1545 Article 10 of the Decree Law 130/90, of April 26.

1546 § 2(1) lit. a, b of the Act No. 634/1992 on Consumer Protection.

1547 § 2 of the Price Information Act 1991:601, amended by Act 2004:347.

1548 Article 1(2) of the Law 26/1984 of July 19 on Consumer Protection.

1549 With regard to the 'distributor'. See above.

tax and all other taxes, in Poland, it is only stated in the legal text that this price needs to include the value added tax. In the CZECH REPUBLIC, the selling price is the same price as the packaged product.[1550] In LATVIA, no taxes other than the value added tax have to be included in the selling price. Finally, FRANCE did not transpose the definition of 'selling price', but there exist provisions in French law obliging the indication of price, including all taxes.[1551]

Table: Transposition method

Substantively equivalent to Directive 98/6	AT, BE, CY, DE, DK, EE, EL, ES, FI, HU, IE,[1552] IT, LT, LU, NL, PT, SE, SL, UK *(19)*
Variations	FR, CZ, LV, MT, PL, SK *(6)*

5. Unit price

Article 2 lit. (b) of Directive 98/6 defines the 'unit price' as the "final price including VAT and all other taxes, for one kilogramme, one litre, one metre, one square metre or one cubic metre of the product or a different single unit of quantity, which is widely and customarily used in the member state concerned in the marketing of specific products".

Out of the 25 member states, BELGIAN, DANISH, DUTCH, ESTONIAN, ITALIAN, IRISH, SLOVAKIAN, SLOVENIAN and SPANISH law does not substantively deviate from the definition in the sense of Directive 98/6. In most member states, the implementation laws vary from the definition.

In AUSTRIA, the value added tax and all other taxes do not necessarily have to be included in the unit price. Furthermore, in ESTONIA and likewise in SWEDEN, the provision concerning the single different unit of quantity has not been transposed in conformity with Directive 98/6. Besides the specified units, namely kilogramme, litre, metre, square metre and cubic metre, not only one, but any different unit of quantity can be used. However, the requirement, that this different unit of quantity needs to be widely and customarily used in the member state concerned in the marketing of specific goods, is still upheld.

In CYPRUS, FINLAND, GREECE, LATVIA, LUXEMBOURG and the UNITED KINGDOM, the possible indication of the price for one "different single unit of quantity which is widely and customarily used in the member state concerned in the marketing of specific products" is not envisaged at all.

Regarding the transposition law in the UNITED KINGDOM, however, the price for certain products must be indicated by quantities which are different from the ones listed in Directive 98/6. The price for products which are indicated in Schedule 1 of the Price Marking Order 2004 (e.g. food colouring, spices, coffee, fruit juices and soft drinks) must be indicated by a specified amount of grams concerning products sold by weight or for a specified amount

[1550] Article 13(3)(a) of the Act on Prices No. 526/1990.

[1551] Decree of 3 December 1987 on price indication.

[1552] The selling price needs to be indicated in 'Euros'.

of millilitres concerning products sold by volume. Furthermore, in respect of products which are sold by number, the price must be indicated for an individual item of that particular product. Similar provisions exist in CYPRUS.

Regarding the possibility to indicate the price for one different unit of quantity, the HUNGARIAN legislator limited this possibility in such a way that this can only be done for products which are sold by number and where, therefore, the price can be indicated individually for each individual piece of that product.

In LATVIA, the possibility to indicate the price for a unit other than the ones indicated by Directive 98/6 is widened insofar as the requirement, that this different unit has to be widely and customarily used in the marketing of that specific product, has not been implemented.

In MALTA, only the term price, but not the more specific term unit price has been legislatively regulated. However, it has been laid down that the price must be the final retail or unit price which has to include the value added tax as well as all other taxes.

The PORTUGUESE legislator has not directly implemented the definition of the term 'unit price' as stipulated in Directive 98/6 either. In fact, in Portugal, the unit price has been defined as the price applicable to a quantity of 1 kilogramme or 1 litre of foodstuff and 1 kilogramme, 1 litre, 1 metre, 1 square metre, 1 cubic metre, or 1 ton of non-food product. Besides these variations from the regulation laid down in Directive 98/6, the possibility to indicate the price for a different unit quantity has not been laid down.

The POLISH legislator only defined the unit price as a price for a unit of specified goods. The amount or number of these goods has to be expressed in units of certain measurements which have to be in accordance with the provisions on measures. Hence, neither the measurements specified by Directive 98/6, nor the option to apply one different unit quantity, nor the requirement to include all kinds of taxes in the price have been legislatively regulated. FRANCE has not directly transposed a definition of the term unit price.[1553]

Table: Transposition method

Substantively equivalent to Directive 98/6	BE[1554], DK, EE, ES, IE, IT, NL, SK, SL *(9)*
Variations	AT, CY, CZ, DE, FI, FR, EL, HU, LT, LU, LV, MT, PL, PT, SE, UK *(16)*

1553 Article 1(1) of the Regulatory Act of 16 November 1999 on consumer protection in the indication of the prices contains: "le prix de vente au kilogramme, à l'hectogramme, au litre, au décilitre, au mètre, au mètre carré ou au mètre cube » .

1554 Article 1 of the Royal Decree of 30 June 1996 concerning the indication of the price of products and services and the order form which provides a definition of 'unit price' does not expressly mention VAT and all other taxes to be included in the unit price. However, the Royal Decree must be read in conjunction with the Trade Practices Act which lays down the general obligation that advertised prices should include all taxes (cf. Art. 3 TPA).

6. Products sold in bulk

Article 2 lit. (c) of Directive 98/6 specifies 'products sold in bulk' as "products which are not pre-packaged and are measured in the presence of the consumer".

Again, more than half of the member states have transposed the term 'products sold in bulk' substantively mirroring the Directive's content. In MALTA and the UNITED KINGDOM, the definition is slightly different. Their legislation prescribes that the consumer does not necessarily have to be present when the non-pre-packaged products are measured since the implementation law only states that the product has to be measured at the request of the consumer. Similarly, in GERMANY, the products have to be measured alternatively either in the presence of the consumer or at his request. LATVIAN law does not provide a direct definition of the term 'product sold in bulk', but lays down the regulation that only the 'unit price' needs to be indicated concerning 'products sold in bulk' or products which are measured in the presence of the consumer. In SLOVENIA, the definition is substantially equivalent with a slight variation: the presence of the consumer is needed "as long as this is allowed by the nature of the product".[1555] Likewise, in SWEDEN, it is determined that only the 'unit price' needs to be given when the product is not pre-packaged, but measured out in front of the consumer.

In LITHUANIA, although there is no legislative regulation which would be comparable to that in LATVIA or SWEDEN, the term 'products sold in bulk' is understood as laid down in Directive 98/6. Finally, in FRANCE, POLAND and Sweden, the law neither provides any definition, nor does any seemingly common understanding of the term exist.

Table: Transposition method

Substantively equivalent to Directive 98/6	AT, BE[1556], CY, DE, DK, EE, EL, ES, FI, HU, IE, IT, LU, NL, PT, SK *(16)*
Variations	LV, MT, SL, UK *(4)*
No specific legislative definition	CZ, FR, LT, PL, SE (5*)*

III. Consumer protection instruments

1. Formal requirements (transparency) Art. 4

Article 4 para. 1, sent. 1 of Directive 98/6 states that the selling price and the unit price must be unambiguous, easily identifiable and clearly legible.

The national legislators of AUSTRIA, BELGIUM, the CZECH REPUBLIC, DENMARK, ESTONIA, GERMANY, GREECE, HUNGARY, IRELAND, ITALY, LATVIA, LITHUANIA, LUXEMBOURG, MALTA,

---

1555 Article 2(2) of the Rules on Price Indication for Goods and Services.

1556 The TPA contains a similar definition (Art. 7 of the TPA, under the Section dedicated to the indication of quantities on the packaging of products), but not within the scope of the price indication section as such.

the NETHERLANDS, POLAND, PORTUGAL, SLOVAKIA, SLOVENIA[1557] and the UNITED KINGDOM have faithfully transposed this provision of the Directive. Most member states therefore used the copy and paste technique.

Some member states have implemented even stricter provisions. In FINLAND[1558] and SWEDEN[1559], both the selling and the unit price have to be indicated in a clear and individualised way to avoid any confusion. In CYPRUS[1560], the selling and unit price must also be distinct. MALTESE law states that the price on the label or mark must be boldly printed or otherwise indicated in writing. In SPAIN[1561], the price must be "located in the same visual ambit" and "visible for the consumer without the need to request that information". Only the national laws of FRANCE do not contain a specific legislative transposition.

Table: Transposition of Art. 4 (formal requirements)

Transposition	Member States
As in Directive 98/6	AT, BE, CZ, DE, DK, EE, EL, HU, IE, IT, LV, LT, LU, MT, NL, PL, PT, SK, SL, UK *(20)*
Stricter provisions	CY, ES, FI, SE *(4)*
No specific legislative transposition	FR *(1)*

2. Sanctions (Art. 8)

Most of the member states have implemented Directive 98/6 as public law. Therefore, in these countries, the public authorities responsible control the application of the price indication law. As a consequence of this, a majority of the member states have stated public law sanctions. These sanctions range from fines to imprisonment.

Additionally, other member states have chosen to implement provisions that enable every competitor of the trader to take action before the courts, e.g. AUSTRIA[1562], GERMANY[1563], LATVIA et seqq. In Germany, this is only possible in cases of considerable infringement. In MALTA[1564], in cases where the offender is convicted more than once, he may also be liable to have his licence to trade suspended for a period not exceeding one week.

The concrete sanctions can be identified with the help of the following table:

[1557] Article 8, 12 of the Rules on Price Indication for Goods and Services (issued by the Minister for the Economy). The prices for services also have to be indicated in an unambiguous way.

[1558] Article 10(2) of the Regulation on Price Indications in Marketing of Consumer Goods.

[1559] § 9 of the Price Information Act 1991:601.

[1560] Article 7(3)(a) of the the Selling and Unit Price Indication Law of 2000, L.112(I)/2000.

[1561] Article 4(1) of the Royal Decree 3423/2000 of December 15, on the regulation of the indication of prices of the products offered to the consumers and users.

[1562] § 1 of the Act against unfair competition.

[1563] §§ 3, 4 No. 11 of the German Act against unfair competition.

[1564] Article 9(3)(b) of the Consumer Affairs Act (Price Indication) Regulations.

Member State	Sanction
Austria	• fines not exceeding € 1.450 (§ 15 PrAG) • damages and injunctions according to the UWG
Belgium	• fines between 250 and 10.000 € • cease and desist orders can be issued against sellers violating their obligations
Cyprus	• a fine of Cyprus Pounds Ł1.000 (maximum) or imprisonment for a period of not longer than 6 months • for every subsequent conviction a fine of Cyprus Pounds Ł 2.000 (maximum) or imprisonment for a period of 1 year (maximum)
Czech Republic	• fines not exceeding 50.000.000 Czech koruna (Sec.24(1) Act No. 634/1992).)
Denmark	• The price indication rules are now transferred to the Marketing Practices Act (cf. above under F.II.2.) Consequently, the sanction system of the Marketing Practices Act applies. This means that the Consumer Ombudsman supervises the rules. The Ombudsman has a variety of sanctions, including negotiation (in order to make the trader comply voluntarily), injunctions and fines.
Estonia	• a fine of up to 100 fine units; if committed by a legal person, is punishable by a fine of up to 30 000 kroons
Finland	• fines (Chapter 11 section 1 Consumer Protection Act)
France	• fines (Art. R.113-1 Code de la Consommation)
Germany	• fines not exceeding 25.000 €
Greece	• fines and/or imprisonment according to Art. 30 of Agoranomikos Kodikas
Hungary	• fines, prohibition of continuation of the illegal conduct (Arts. 47, 48 Consumer Protection Act)
Ireland	• a fine not exceeding 3.000 € • order (injunction) requiring the trader to act, or refrain from doing anything, to ensure compliance with the Regulations
Italy	• fines from 516, 45 Euro (1.000.000 Lire) to 3098,74 Euro (6.000.000 Lire)
Latvia	• administrative sanctions • competitors can claim
Lithuania	• state inspection of non-food products • consumer has the right to appeal to the State Food and Veterinary Service
Luxembourg	•
Malta	• a fine of not less than fifty liri and not exceeding five hundred liri • suspension of licence to trade • publication of a summary of the judgment in the media (one or more daily newspapers)[1565]
Netherlands	• a fine not exceeding € 16.750 • imprisonment for a maximum of 6 (six) months
Poland	• fines between 1.000 and 5.000 €
Portugal	• administrative sanctions
Slovakia	• Public control and market surveillance authorities • fines up to 2.000.000 Slovak crowns (up to 5.000.000 Slovak crowns in case of repeated infringement within the space of one year) • Right of consumer, consumer organisations to take action before the courts
Slovenia	• administrative sanctions provided for under general administrative law.
Spain	• control by competent bodies of the Autonomous Communities of Spain • fines (the amount is determined by reference to three other Acts: Consumer Protection Act, Retail Trade Act and Royal Decree 1945/1983 on sanctions to protect consumers and food production)
Sweden	• sanctions in the Marketing Act
United Kingdom	• control by local weights and measures authority • fines (UK utilises system of sanctions generally provided in the Prices Act)

[1565] See Reg. 9 (3)(b) of the Consumer Affairs Act (Price Indication) Regulations.

IV. Use of options provided in Directive 98/6

1. Products supplied in the course of the provision of a service

Article 3 para. 2, 1st indent permits the member states not to apply Art. 3 para. 1 to products supplied in the course of the provision of a service.

Most of the member states have made use of this option. In AUSTRIA, BELGIUM, CYPRUS, the CZECH REPUBLIC, ESTONIA, GERMANY, GREECE, HUNGARY, IRELAND, LATVIA, LITHUANIA, MALTA, the NETHERLANDS, POLAND, PORTUGAL, SLOVAKIA, SLOVENIA, SPAIN and the UNITED KINGDOM, the trader is not obliged to indicate the unit price for products supplied in the course of the provision of a service. Also ITALY[1566] and LUXEMBOURG[1567] have made use of the option.[1568] Italy explicitly exempts the provision of food and beverages.[1569]
Some countries have not made use of the option, such as FINLAND, FRANCE, DENMARK[1570] and SWEDEN. With regard to Sweden it should be noted that the Prisinformationslag (SFS 1991:601)[1571] is applicable to goods as well as to services.

Table: Use of option with regard to products supplied in the course of the provision of a service (Art. 3 para. 2, 1st indent)

Use of Option	Member States
Yes	AT, BE, CY, CZ, DE, EE, EL, ES, HU, IE, IT, LT, LU, LV, MT, NL, PL, PT, SK, SL, UK *(21)*
No use	DK, FI, FR, SE *(4)*

2. Sales by auction and sales of works of art and antiques

Article 3 para. 2, 2nd indent of Directive 98/6 grants the member states the option not to apply Art. 3 para. 1 of Directive 98/6 to sales by auction and sales of works of art and antiques.

Again a vast majority of member states have chosen to implement this option. They are: AUSTRIA, CYPRUS, ESTONIA, GERMANY, GREECE, HUNGARY, IRELAND, ITALY[1572], LATVIA,

---

1566 Former Art. 2(5)(a) of the Statute 25/02/2000 n. 84 "Implementation of Directive 98/6/EC on consumer protection in the indication of the prices of products offered to consumers" now stated in Art. 14(5)(a) of the Italian Consumer Code.

1567 Article 3(2)(2) of the Decree of 7 September2001 on price indication.

1568 Different: EIM-Study "Appraisal of Directive 98/6/EC on consumer protection in the indication of unit prices of products offered to consumers", P. 43, table 6.

1569 Article 14(5)(a) of the Italian Consumer Code. "including the provision of food and beverages".

1570 As mentioned above under F.II.2., since 1 July 2006 the price indication rules also apply to services. Thus Denmark no longer makes use of the option in Art. 3, para 2, 1st indent of the Directive.

1571 Price Information Act 1991:601.

1572 Legislative Decree of 25 February 2000 No. 84 "Implementation of Directive 98/6/EC on consumer protection in the indication of the prices of products offered to consumers") Now moved into Art. 14(5)(b) and (c) of the Italian Consumer Code. Different: EIM-Study "Appraisal of Direc-

LITHUANIA, MALTA, the NETHERLANDS, PORTUGAL, SLOVAKIA, SLOVENIA, SPAIN and the UNITED KINGDOM.

BELGIUM[1573] and SWEDEN[1574] have made use of the option, but only exclude auctions. LUXEMBOURG only exempts works of art and antiques if such products carry a clear indication, which allows for their identification on a price list.[1575]

Only FINLAND, FRANCE[1576] and POLAND have not made use of the option provided in Directive 98/6. From 1 July 2006 DENMARK has no longer made use of the option regarding works of art and antiques.[1577]

Table: Use of option with regard to sales by auction and sales of works of art and antiques (Art. 3(2) 2nd indent)

Use of Option	Member States
Yes	AT, BE,[1578] CY, CZ, DE, EE, EL, ES, HU, IE, IT, LT, LU,[1579] LV, MT, NL, PT, SE,[1580] SK, SL, UK *(21)*
No use	DK, FI, FR, PL *(4)*

3. Products for which indication of unit price would not be useful

Article 5 of Directive 98/6 allows the member states to waive the obligation to indicate the unit price for products for which the indication might be not useful because of the product's nature or purpose, or, if it creates confusion. Art. 5(2) allows the member states, in the case of non-food products, to establish a list of the products or product categories to which the obligation to indicate the unit price shall remain applicable.

Seemingly all member states have made use of this option. However, the categories of exempt products vary considerably. For instance, § 6 of the SWEDISH Prisinformationslag[1581] simply

tive 98/6/EC on consumer protection in the indication of unit prices of products offered to consumers", p. 43, table 6.

1573 Article 2(1) of the Act of 14 July 1991 on trade practices and consumer information and protection. Different : EIM-Study "Appraisal of Directive 98/6/EC on consumer protection in the indication of unit prices of products offered to consumers", p. 43, table 6.

1574 § 4 Price Information Act 1991:601.

1575 Article 7(2) of the Decree of 7 September 2001 on price indication.

1576 Regulatory Act of the November 16 on consumer protection in the indication of the prices of certain products per unit and pre-packaged products offered to consumers. Different: EIM-Study "Appraisal of Directive 98/6/EC on consumer protection in the indication of unit prices of products offered to consumers", p. 43, table 6.

1577 § 13(1) of the Marketing Practices Act.

1578 Only auctions are excluded.

1579 Only works of art and antiques are exempt if such products carry a clear indication, which allows for their identification on a price list.

1580 Only auctions are excluded.

1581 Price Information Act 1991:601.

states that the trader only has to provide information about the selling price when the nature of the good is of such character that the unit price is of no interest to the buyer or might create confusion. The LATVIAN transposition law uses the same wording as Directive 98/6 and, furthermore, contains a short list of examples, such as milk, sour cream and eggs.[1582]

Several member states have excluded automatic vending machines from the obligation to indicate the unit price. They are: BELGIUM[1583], the CZECH REPUBLIC[1584], GREECE[1585], HUNGARY[1586], ITALY[1587], IRELAND[1588], LITHUANIA[1589], the NETHERLANDS[1590], PORTUGAL, SLOVAKIA[1591] and SPAIN[1592]. GERMANY only exempts automatic vending machines for food and beverages.[1593] The UNITED KINGDOM excludes only those automatic vending machines which sell bread made up in a prescribed quantity and products which are pre-packaged in a constant quantity.[1594] In CYPRUS, after the amendment effected to the original transposition law by Law 136(I)/2005, the exception for vending machines is no longer applicable.

Many member states have exempted products sold in quantities below certain limits. These limits range from 5g or 5ml in CYPRUS and LITHUANIA[1595], less than 10g or ml in GERMANY, less than 15g or ml in the NETHERLANDS, less than 20g or ml in AUSTRIA, less than 50g or ml in ESTONIA, GREECE, HUNGARY, PORTUGAL[1596], SLOVAKIA and SPAIN to 100g or ml in LUXEMBOURG.

Further exemptions are rather specific. BELGIUM has exempted ice cream and snacks sold for immediate consumption, products consumed on the premises in restaurants, hotels and bars

---

1582 Article 12 of the Cabinet Regulation No 178 "Procedures for Diplaying Prices of Products and Services".

1583 Article 10(2) of the Royal Decree of 30 June 1996 concerning the indication of the price of products and services and the order form.

1584 Article 13(9)(j) of the Act on Prices No. 526/1990.

1585 Article 5 Table I, sent. 3 of the Ruling of the Ministries of Economics and Development Z1-404/2001.

1586 Article 4(2)(b) of the Decree No. 7/2001. (III.29.) on the indication of the prices of products and services offered to consumers.

1587 Article 4(1)(c) of the Legislative Decree of 25 February 2000 No. 84 "Implementation of Directive 98/6/EC on consumer protection in the indication of the prices of products offered to consumers".

1588 Article 5(2)(f) of the Requirements to Indicate Product Prices Regulations.

1589 Article 29.6.3 of the Rules of Labelling of Items (Goods) and Indication of Prices

1590 Annex II lit. D of the Decree of 21 May 2003, containing rules in regard to the indication of prices as replacement for the Decree price-indication on goods 1980.

1591 Article 4 of the Price Indication Decree 545/2002: only in the case of goods sold in vending machines for food and beverages.

1592 Annex I lit. (c) of the Royal Decree 3423/2000 of December 15 on the regulation of the indication of prices of the products offered to the consumers and users.

1593 § 9(4)(5) of the Price Indication Regulation.

1594 Regulation 5(3) lit. c and d of the Price Marking Order 2004.

1595 Article 29.6.2 of the Rules of Labeling of Items (Goods) and Indication of Prices

1596 Or above 10 kg or 10 l. Cf. Art. 4(2)(g) of the Decree-Law 130/90 of April 26.

etc. and, furthermore, wine sold in bottles of 75 cl.[1597] GERMANY excludes beverages, chewing tobacco, cosmetics, perfumes and products sold at a reduced price because the sell-by date is almost at an end. Italy has exempted products of various types included in the same package; pre-cooked, or prepared foodstuffs, or those to be prepared, formed of two or more separate items contained in a single package, requiring additional preparation by the consumer before the finished product is obtained; single-portion ice-creams and non-food products that can only be sold individually.[1598] FINLAND has chosen to exclude chocolate eggs, decorative sweets, pastries and confectionary products.[1599] The SPANISH Annex I of the Royal Decree 3423/2000 also excludes "individual portions of ice cream" (lit. d), "wines with geographic nomination" (lit. e) and "alcoholic drinks with geographic nomination" (lit. f). Other member states, e.g., BELGIUM, the NETHERLANDS, ITALY and SPAIN have exempted "fantasy" packages or products.[1600]

Article 5 para 2 of Directive 98/6 allows the member states to establish a list of non-food products or product categories to which the obligation to indicate the unit price shall remain applicable. Only BELGIUM, FRANCE and LUXEMBOURG have enacted a detailed list on non-food products, France also has a list on food products.

Such variations can make it very difficult to predict the details of the price indication laws of the member states. This may cause traders to indicate unit prices just by way of precaution, if they want to trade abroad. In the case that the indication of unit prices is costly, this necessity could deter the trader from doing business in other member states and therefore constitute a barrier to trade. Therefore concretising this option along the lines of the national transposition laws draw might be considered. Another possibility would be to replace the option in Art. 5 with a general clause which simply reads that there is no obligation to indicate the unit price for products for which it is obvious that such indication is not useful because of the product's nature or purpose or if it creates confusion. This would leave it to the courts (and to the ECJ).

4. Indication if unit price were to constitute an excessive burden for certain small retail businesses

Again, a majority of the member states have made use of the option excluding the obligation to indicate the unit price in cases where it constitutes an excessive burden. Member states

---

1597 Article 11 of the Royal Decree of 30 June 1996 concerning the indication of the price of products and services and the order form.

1598 Article 16(1) of the Consumer Code.

1599 Article 7(1) 3rd indent Regulation on Price Indications in Marketing of Consumer Goods.

1600 BELGIUM: Art. 11(6) of the Royal Decree of 30 June 1996 concerning the indication of the price of products and services and the order form; Netherlands: Annex II A. Decree of 21 May 2003, containing rules in regard to the indication of prices as replacement for the Decree price-indication on goods 1980: fantasy products and packaging which are offered. E.g. Chocolate Santa Claus, where the package is more important for the consumer than the product itself.
Spain: Annex I lit. g Royal Decree 3423/2000 of December 15, on the regulation of the indication of prices of the products offered to the consumers and users of nutritional products.

have implemented different criteria to protect small retail businesses. Only some characteristic examples shall be pointed out here.

Some member states have stated provisions that exempt shops depending on the total sales area. The relevant sales area ranges from less than $50m^2$ in GREECE[1601], less than 150 m^2 in SLOVAKIA[1602], less than $280m^2$ in the UNITED KINGDOM, less than $400m^2$ in LUXEMBOURG and the CZECH REPUBLIC to $500m^2$ in SLOVENIA[1603]. In BELGIUM, the indication of the unit price is not required for pre-packaged products that are sold in pre-determined quantities when they are sold by sellers whose sales area is less than $150m^2$.[1604]

Other member states use a certain number of employees as a criterion. AUSTRIA excludes sole traders with up to 9 employees and enterprises operating with up to 50 employees.[1605] In the NETHERLANDS, businesses with up to five full-time employees are exempt.

Member states like the CZECH REPUBLIC[1606], GERMANY[1607], GREECE[1608], SLOVAKIA[1609] and the NETHERLANDS[1610] distinguish between shops where consumers are served, which are exempt from the obligation, and self-service stores, which are not exempt.

In the UNITED KINGDOM, the option in Article 6 has been utilised in respect of bread made up in a prescribed quantity as well as any product pre-packaged in a constant quantity, offered for sale in a small shop, by an itinerant trader, or from a vending machine.

Some member states have exempted *itinerant traders* from the obligation to indicate the unit price, such as AUSTRIA, ESTONIA and IRELAND. The UNITED KINGDOM has chosen to exclude only those itinerant traders, who sell bread made up in a prescribed quantity and products which are pre-packaged in a constant quantity.[1611] CYPRUS initially excluded both small retail businesses and itinerant traders but after the amendment effected to the original transposition law by Law 136(I)/2005, these exceptions are no longer applicable.

ITALY, PORTUGAL, SLOVAKIA and SPAIN have implemented derogations for a transitional period. These periods expired in Portugal on 14 May 2002[1612], in Italy on 1 March 2002[1613],

---

1601 Article 6 (a) of the Decision of the Ministry of Trade No. Z1-404.

1602 Article 4(a) of the Price Indication Decree 545/2002.

1603 Article 15 Rules on Price Indication for Goods and Services (issued by the Minister for the Economy.

1604 Article 12bis of the Royal Decree of 30 June 1996 concerning the indication of the price of products and services and the order form. This provision has been implemented by an amendment decree of 21 September 2004.

1605 Article 10b(3) of the Price Indication Act.

1606 Article 13(9) lit. b of the Act on Prices No. 526/1990.

1607 § 9(4)(3) of the Price indication regulation.

1608 Article 6(e) of the Ruling of the ministry of economics and development - No. Z1-404-2001.

1609 Article 4 of the of the Price Indication Decree.

1610 Annex I lit. H 1st indent of the Decree of 21 May 2003, containing rules in regard to the indication of price.

1611 Regulation 5(3) lit. (c) and (d) of the Price Marking Order 2004.

1612 Article 2(2) of the Decree-Law 162/99 of May 13.

in Slovakia on the date the Treaty of Accession to the EU came into force[1614] and in Spain on 30 June 2002. In Spain, legislative competence has been delegated to the Autonomous Communities which now have the faculty to establish a transitional period to indicate the unit price for products pre-wrapped in pre-fixed quantities and distributed by small retail businesses where the sale is concluded by a seller who deals personally with the customer and offers the products, and also in the case of itinerant traders.

The CZECH REPUBLIC stated the 1 May 2014 as the expiry date.[1615] The majority of the member states have implemented the exemptions for small retail businesses without a time limit. This is contrary to Directive 98/6.

DENMARK, FINLAND, HUNGARY, LITHUANIA, POLAND and SWEDEN have not made use of the option provided by Directive 98/6.

Use of Option	Member States
Yes	AT, BE, CY, CZ, DE, EE, EL, ES, FR, IE, IT, LV, LU, MT, NL, PT, SK, SL, UK *(19)*
No use	DK, FI, HU, LT, PL, SE *(6)*

The variations of the individual transpositions in the member states can make it very difficult to predict the details of the Price Indication laws of a foreign member state. This could be removed by a more precise definition of small trader, which could be drafted along the criteria already contained in Art. 6.

Bibliography

Communication from the Commission to the Council and the European Parliament on the implementation of Directive 1998/6/EC of the European Parliament and of the Council of 16 February 1998 on consumer protection in the indication of prices of products offered to consumers, COM(2006) 325 final; Working Document of the European Commission - Summary of Responses to the Consultation on the Price Indication Directive (COM (2006) 325 final), http://ec.europa.eu/consumers/rights/pc_sSummary_04102007.pdf; Appraisal of Directive 98/6/EC on consumer protection in the indication of unit prices of products offered to consumers, http://ec.europa.eu/consumers/cons_int/safe_shop/price_ind/disclaimer_en.pdf; **Diaconu, Nicoleta**, Acquis-ul comunitar in domeniul protectiei consumatorilor, Revista Romana de Drept Comunitar 2003, **Dona, Massimiliano**, Il codice del consumo, Regole e significati, Torino 2005, **Enthofer-Stoisser, Ruth,** Sind die Preise ausgezeichnet?: Das Preisauszeichnungsgesetz 2000 in Theorie und Praxis, 2002, **Euroventanilla de la Cámara de Comercio e Industria de Madrid,** Protección del consumidor en materia de indicación de los precios al consumo, 1998, **Hanreich, Hanspeter**, Das neue österreichische Wettbewerbs- und Preisrecht, 3. Teil – Das Preisauszeichnungsgesetz, Österreichische Zeitschrift für Wirtschaftsrecht 1994, 65 ff., **Georgiades, Olga**, Sale of Goods in Cyprus, Following Har-

[1613] Article 7(1) of the Legislative Decree of 25 February 2000 No. 84 "Implementation of Directive 98/6/EC on consumer protection in the indication of the prices of products offered to consumers".

[1614] Article 6 of the Price Indication Decree.

[1615] According to Art. II of the Act on Prices No. 526/1990 as amended by an Act 276/2002 and 124/2003.

monisation with the Acquis Communautaire and Consumer Protection, Nicosia 2005, **Kristoffersen, Sonny**, Forbrugerretten 1, Copenhagen 2006, **Köhler, Helmut**, Preisangabenverordnung (PangV), in: Köhler/Bornkamm/Baumbach/Hefermehl, Wettbewerbsrecht (Kommentar), Munich 2006, **Kuluttaja-asiamiehen oh-jeita (The Consumer Ombudsman: Guidelines)**, Hinnat selkeästi esille, Clear Price Indications, 2002, **Maglio, Valentina**, Tutela del consumatore e indicazione del prezzo per unità di misura, Contratto e impresa/Europa 2000, 390.

G. Injunctions Directive (98/27)

Christian Twigg-Flesner

Executive summary

1. Transposition deficiencies

- MALTA has not adopted legislation that extends to all the Directives listed in the Annex, and there are therefore gaps in the transposition of this Directive.
- The law in HUNGARY requires that "substantial" harm be caused, which adds an additional element and raises the threshold before action can be taken.
- No summary procedure is available in ESTONIA and LITHUANIA (cf. Art. 2(1)(a) of the Directive 98/27).
- CYPRUS and MALTA do not refer to the list in the Official Journal required under Art. 4(3) of the Directive in their domestic law, although in both countries, entities from another Member State appear to have the right to take action in any event.
- IRELAND requires that consumer associations must have a *statutory* function of protecting collective interests, which seems to be narrower than the requirement in the Directive.

2. Enhancement of protection

a. Use of options

- Article 5(1) of the Directive (consultation with the defendant) – used by 13 member states. Out of the 13, 8 require consultation only with the defendant, and 5 require consultation with the defendant and the relevant domestic independent public body.
- The NETHERLANDS and GERMANY do not expressly refer to the two-week period for consultation before action can be taken.

b. Use of minimum clause (i.e. more stringent provisions in the field covered by the Directive)

- Many countries have extended the provisions implementing the Directive to domestic consumer legislation not transposing an EC directive.
- Some countries permit a wider range of orders, such as
  - CYPRUS (corrective measures to be taken by trader);
  - MALTA (correction to unfair contract terms; for other areas, order may specify measures to be taken to ensure compliance).
- There are several countries where collective actions by consumers are available against a single trader who has harmed several consumers (e.g. FRANCE, ITALY and the UNITED KINGDOM).
- In FRANCE and the UNITED KINGDOM, the criminal law is used as a means of enforcing some aspects of consumer protection law.

c. Extension of scope

- No reference to "collective interests" as threshold (may permit broader range of actions) in CYPRUS, LATVIA, and MALTA.
- PORTUGAL and SPAIN also include diffuse interest in the scope of their domestic law.
- Some member states permit action even where an individual consumer has been harmed (CYPRUS, PORTUGAL, ESTONIA, and LATVIA).

d. Other measures enhancing consumer protection (i.e. more stringent provisions in fields not covered by the Directive)

- Competitors have the right to take action under the legislation dealing with unfair competition in some member states (e.g., AUSTRIA and GERMANY).

3. Inconsistencies

Article 2(1)(c) of the Directive (penalty payments where domestic law so provides) has been transposed expressly in 19 countries. In three countries (CYPRUS, DENMARK, UNITED KINGDOM), recourse is had to the general law on contempt of court.

Wide variation in national law determining criteria for recognising consumer associations as qualified entities (cf. Art. 3(b). of the Directive).

Variations in procedural rules make it more difficult to give full effect to requirements of the Directive.

Several of the Directives contained in the Annex also contain provisions requiring the member states to set up procedures to ensure the effectiveness of their transposing law (e.g., Directive 97/7). This is usually done by injunction, but the threshold for taking action under these provisions is lower as it does not refer to the "collective interests" of consumers.

Variation in dealing with the Annex (transposition not required): 12 member states have transposed the Annex into their domestic law; 2 refer to it in the explanatory notes to their implementing legislation; two (CYPRUS and LUXEMBOURG) have amended each domestic law transposing the directives listed in the Annex; and 9 member states have not transposed the Annex.

4. Potential barriers to trade

- Scope of Directive 98/27 only extends to the rights granted under corresponding directives, but many of these are minimum harmonisation measures.
- Financial cost for consumer associations and public bodies to take action in another member state is a deterrent.
- Possible delays in updating list in *Official Journal* could deprive a qualified entity from one member state from taking action in another.

5. Conclusions and recommendations

- A clarification regarding the applicable law in cross-border cases might be desirable. It is noted that this may be resolved through the "Rome II" regulation (Regulation 864/2007 on the law applicable to non-contractual obligations (2007) O.J. L 199/40).
- A related question is whether injunctions obtained in a domestic context ought to have Europe-wide reach, at least where the activities of the trader against whom an injunction has been obtained are not limited to one member state. An analysis as to whether this is already possible within Regulation 44/2001 (Brussels-Regulation) may be desirable .
- The relationship with Directive-specific enforcement mechanisms should be clarified. Thus, Art. 11 of Directive 97/7 and Art. 7 of Directive 93/13 both require that member states put into place adequate and effective means to ensure compliance with these respective Directives. This seems to overlap, to an extent, with this Directive. There is a difference in that the provisions in the specific Directives do not include the "collective interest" criterion, although, at a practical level, this may not matter hugely. It may therefore be possible to consider whether these specific provisions could be deleted.
- The evidence to date shows that the cross-border procedure is not being utilised. One reason may be the question of costs for qualified entities from one member state to take action in another. The Directive is silent on the question of costs; a basic rule giving the qualifying entity the right, if successful in the action, to recover costs (not just of the court action, but the costs incurred in taking the action, such as translation, legal advice etc.) could be considered.
- It may be desirable to consider whether a power to ask for compensation should be introduced. Difficulties in this regard may be establishing the loss caused and identifying beneficiaries (e.g., through creating a central fund to which individual consumers may apply). Linked to this is whether cross-border class-actions ought to be facilitated, too.

I. Member state legislation prior to the adoption of the Injunctions Directive

The situation in the member states before the adoption of Directive 98/27 was rather diffuse, with only some countries having in place a system comparable to that introduced by the Directive 98/27. It should be noted that most member states had introduced procedures for some aspects of consumer law, notably in the context of Directive 93/13.[1616] However, not all the member states had a regime comparable to that in Directive 98/27; moreover, the existing frameworks were generally only accessible to qualified entities from the respective member state, and not those from another member state.

In AUSTRIA, for example, there were provisions dealing with challenges to unfair contract terms in standard form contracts, with standing given to a number of commercial associations, as well as the Association for Consumer Information (Verein für Konsumenteninformation).[1617] BELGIAN law also recognised a right for domestic consumer organisations to seek an injunction.[1618] In DENMARK, there was a possibility of bringing an action, provided that the claimant could demonstrate "a sufficient legal interest" to bring an action, although it was not clear whether this extended to the protection of collective interests. The ESTONIAN Consumer Protection Act of 1994 had empowered the Consumer Protection Board to take action "to demand that a third party terminate activities in violation of consumer rights if the activities of the third party affect the common interests of an unspecified number of consumers".[1619] In FINLAND, the Consumer Ombudsman (CO) had a primary right to bring cases to Market Court. In case the CO did not act, consumer organizations and even labour organizations had a secondary right to bring cases concerning (unfair) marketing practices or (unfair) contract terms. However, authorities from other member states did not have right to bring the case to Market Court. In FRANCE, it had been possible since 1973 for consumer organisations to take action "if there was a direct or indirect disadvantage for consumers collectively";[1620] these provisions were subsequently improved with the introduction of a "collective action" procedure.[1621] The law in the NETHERLANDS was similarly advanced.[1622] GERMANY had also introduced a right of action for consumer associations in the context of unfair competition law,[1623] and also in respect of standard contract terms,[1624] but associations had to establish their standing in every case. PORTUGAL had extensive procedures for the protection of the collective interests of consumers,[1625] as well procedures for individual consumers (whether or not harmed), consumer associations, the public prosecutor (Ministerio Publico) and the Institute of Consumers (Instituto do Consumidor) to take action. In

---

1616 Cf. Art. 7 of the Directive 93/13.

1617 Article 29 and 30 of the Consumer Protection Act 1979.

1618 Article 98(1), (4) of the Trade Practices Act.

1619 Article 12(3) of the Consumer Protection Act 1994.

1620 Ordonnance (Law) of 27 December 1973.

1621 Arts. 411(1) – 422(2) Consumer Protection Law, codifying provisions previously contained in law no. 88-14, "*Actions en justice des associations agréées de consommateurs*", of 5 January 1988. This provides for different types of actions, including the "*action en representation conjointe*", which is the nearest to a collective action procedure.

1622 CC, Art. 3:305a and 3:305b, and Art. 6:240-242.

1623 Article 13 of the Unfair Competition Act 1965.

1624 Article 13(3) of the Law on Standard Terms of Business 1976.

1625 Law 83/95.

SPAIN, the role of consumer associations to represent the collective interests before the courts had been recognised for some time, [1626] and this position was progressively strengthened up to the point of having to implement the Directive.[1627] The position regarding consumer associations was confirmed in the Spanish Law on Civil Procedure,[1628] which also extends the scope of protection beyond collective interests to diffuse interests. GREECE[1629] and SWEDEN also had procedures in place for the protection of collective consumer interests. HUNGARIAN law also recognised a right of action for the General Inspectorate of Consumer Protection, as well as social organisations representing consumers' common interests; moreover, foreign qualified entities could register injunctions through an administrative procedure.[1630] Similarly, in POLAND, a procedure permitting social organisations with a statutory task of consumer protection could initiate proceedings for the protection of consumer interests.[1631] In the UNITED KINGDOM, consumer associations had no right of action; the only entity empowered to act was the then Director-General of Fair Trading.[1632] Action could be taken where there has a persistent course of conduct which was (a) detrimental to the interests of consumers and (b) 'unfair' to consumers (but a conduct would only be unfair if it breached an existing legal rule). Whilst it was possible to seek an injunction in CYPRUS, this procedure was not available to public authorities or other organisations seeking an injunction for the protection of third parties such as consumers. No corresponding provisions existed in the CZECH REPUBLIC, ITALY,[1633] IRELAND, LATVIA, LITHUANIA, MALTA,[1634] SLOVAKIA, and SLOVENIA.

II. General comments

The Directive requires that all member states make it possible for qualified entities to take action before domestic courts to protect the various specific rights given to consumers under the measures implementing the EC directives on consumer law into the domestic legal system. Such action may be taken for purely domestic problems, i.e., an entity from member state A can taken action before the courts in that state to prevent infringements of the relevant legislation by a trader from that state. In addition, the Directive introduces specific provisions on the cross-border enforcement of such rights by allowing qualified entities from one member state to take action against a trader from another member state in the courts of that trader's jurisdiction.

1626 Law 26/1984 of July 19 on Consumer Protection.

1627 See Law of the Judicial Power (1985), and specific laws on advertising (1988), unfair competition (1991) and standard contract terms (1998).

1628 Law 1/2000.

1629 Article10(9) Consumer Protection Act (Law 2251/1994).

1630 Article 39 Consumer Protection Act.

1631 Article 61 of the Code of Civil Procedure 1990.

1632 Fair Trading Act 1973, Part III.

1633 Law 281/1998 is contemporaneous with the Directive and introduced similar rules for the first time.

1634 Although a registered consumer association could request the appointment of a representative during proceedings under relevant consumer protection statutes.

The Directive therefore differs from all of the other directives under consideration in this study, because it does not confer any specific rights on individual consumers. Rather, this measure is concerned with the enforcement of consumer law by "qualified entities". Such entities are empowered to seek an injunction to protect the "collective interests" of consumers. It is not dealing with class actions by consumers against traders.

The structure of this particular analysis therefore adopts a different format from the analyses of the directives covered so far, concentrating on the procedural rules specified in the Directive, and the use of the minimum harmonisation clause in Art. 7 of the Directive. It should be noted that even that clause is not a minimum harmonisation clause as they appear in the other consumer directives, because Art. 7 of the Directive is not concerned with granting *consumers* a higher degree of protection, but rather permits the adoption/ maintenance of more extensive rights to take action at the national level. This section will first turn to the procedural rules contained in the Directive.

In general terms, all the member states have taken steps to give effect to the central provisions of the Directive, although there are some variations, and potential gaps in some member states. It can also be noted that not all of the member states have transposed the Directive simply by adopting one single piece of legislation. In CYPRUS and LUXEMBOURG, provisions based on the Directive 98/27 have been inserted into each piece of legislation on particular aspects of consumer protection.[1635] In MALTA, where the laws transposing the directives listed in the annex to the Injunctions Directive, are administered by different public authorities, the provisions based on the injunctions directive have been implemented in the procedural parts of the various domestic laws.

III. Procedural rules

1. Article 1(2) – Protection of "collective interests" of consumers

Article 1(2) of Directive 98/27 sets out the definition of "infringement" for the purposes of the Directive. There has to be an "act contrary to the Directives listed in the Annex as transposed in the internal legal order of the member states", and this act has to harm the "collective interests of consumers". Such "collective interests" do not, however, include the culmination of the interests of individual consumers harmed by an infringement.[1636] An action for an injunction to protect the collective interests of consumers is therefore not the same as a "class action", representing a group of consumers harmed by an infringement.

The second requirement ("collective interests") does not appear to have been transposed in all the member states. Thus, in CYPRUS, there is no specific reference to "collective interests", although reference is made to "the general interest" and "the interests of consumers in general", which is similar in substance. In addition, however, the relevant provisions can be used also in respect of individual cases. HUNGARIAN law refers to illegal activities causing substantial harm to a wide range of consumers *or* illegal activities affecting the wide range of con-

[1635] For Luxembourg, see Loi du 19 décembre 2003 fixant les conditions d'agrément des organisations habilitées à intenter des actions en cessation (Act on injunctions of 19 December 2003).

[1636] Cf. second recital of the Directive.

sumer[1637] as the threshold criteria. These are based on legislation existing before the adoption of the Directive, and were retained. It is arguable that the requirement that the harm be "substantial" may create a higher threshold than under the Directive. However, the reference to "a wide range of consumers" does not seem to be a significant variation from the notion of "collective interests".

In LATVIA, the legislation extends to individual and group consumer interests, and is therefore broader than collective interests.[1638] In LITHUANIA, the legislation does not list the relevant measures as such, but rather includes a list of areas of consumer law in respect of which an injunction is available.[1639] The law in MALTA is also not restricted to the 'collective interests' of consumers, and provides for the issuing of 'compliance orders' for any breaches of consumer legislation.[1640] In POLAND, the legislation states that the 'collective interests' of consumers are not merely the sum of the individual interests of consumers, and, moreover, that the conduct that harms these collective interests must be illegal.[1641] The scope of the legislation in PORTUGAL extends beyond "collective interests", and also includes individual as well as 'diffuse' interests of consumers. Similarly, the legislation in SPAIN does not define 'infringement' expressly and therefore does not refer expressly to collective consumer interests, but the legislation covers both collective (i.e., an ascertainable group of consumers) and diffuse (the group of affected consumers cannot be determined precisely) interests of consumers.

2. Article 2 – Actions for an injunction

This article requires that the member states designate a court or administrative authority which has the competence to deal with applications for an injunction. The powers of the court/authority concerned must include: (i) to issue an order to stop the continuation, or prohibit, an infringement; (ii) to initiate the publication of the decision in an appropriate format and/or of a corrective statement to deal with the continuing effects of the infringement; and (iii) to make an order for penalty payments for non-compliance, but only if the domestic legal system of the member state would already permit this.

a. Action for an order for the cessation or prohibition of an infringement

Article 2(1)(a) of the Directive requires that it must be possible for qualified entities to seek an order which requires the cessation of, or prohibits, an infringement. This has been transposed in accordance with the Directive in all the member states with the exception of MALTA

1637 Article 39 of the Consumer Protection Act 1997.

1638 Article 25(8) of the Consumer Rights Protection Law.

1639 Chapter X of the Law on Consumer Protection.

1640 Article 94 of the Consumer Affairs Act. In the context of the Consumer Affairs Act, such orders may be issued in relation to breaches of that Act, any regulations made under that Act and any other law relating to consumer protection as the Minister may by order designate in the Government Gazette. There are similar provisions in the other laws implementing the various directives listed in the Annex to the Injunctions Directive.

1641 Article 23a of the Law on the protection of consumers and competition.

and SWEDEN. In Malta, the implementing legislation is the Consumer Affairs Act,[1642] but this only covers the directives on misleading and comparative advertising, unfair terms, consumer credit and distance selling. The Minister has the power to issue orders extending the relevant provision to other consumer protection measures, but the legislation on package travel and timeshare is administered by the Maltese Tourism authority, and therefore beyond the reach of the Consumer Affairs Act. Maltese legislation therefore does not cover all the directives listed in the Annex, either because a ministerial order extending the relevant legislation to cover those directives has not been made, or because the necessary amendments in the laws administered by other public authorities[1643] have not yet been enacted. In SWEDEN, the Market Court the Market Court deals with cases involving marketing cases, and there are two special authorities, the Consumer Ombudsman and the National Board of Consumer Protection, responsible for ensuring compliance by traders with consumer protection legislation.

aa. Availability of summary procedure

Article 2(1)(a) of the Directive also refers to the availability of a "summary procedure". The situation in the member states is rather diverse. A temporary injunction may be obtained in AUSTRIA, which does not require proof of an immediate threat to consumers' rights.[1644] In BELGIAN law, the action for an injunction must be brought before a court by a procedure which is comparable to a summary procedure but imposes even less strict conditions. In CYPRUS, there is a procedure for the issuing a temporary injunction,[1645] which is applicable to injunctions to protect the general interests of consumers, and the provisions introduced to transpose the Directive expressly provide for the power of the court to issue a temporary injunction in accordance with the principles laid down in the Courts Law, Art. 32. DENMARK relies on its general procedures regarding interlocutory injunctions, which are also available in this context. In FINLAND, the Market Court may impose a temporary injunction, which, if necessary, can be accompanied by a conditional imposition of fine.[1646] In FRANCE, there is a general procedure ("référé") for when an urgent decision from a judge is needed; this can be used by a consumer association in order to stop an infringement.[1647]

1642 Arts. 94, 95 and 98 Consumer Affairs Act.

1643 Such as the Malta Tourism Authority in the case of the laws implementing the Timeshare and Package Travel Directives.

1644 Article 30(1) of the Consumer Protection Law.

1645 Article 32 of the Courts Law of 1960, L.14/60.

1646 Article 3 Cross-Border Injunctions Procedure Act.

1647 See e.g. Cass. Civ. [Cour de cassation, chamber civile; France] judgment of 1 December 1987; Recueil Dalloz, 1987, Informations rapides, p. 255.

In GERMANY, it is not necessary to prove the urgency of the order at the time it is issued.[1648] GREECE also provides for temporary injunctions.[1649] SPAIN also offers an accelerated procedure ("juicio verbal").[1650] In ITALY, where there are justified grounds of urgency, a summary procedure is available.[1651] It needs to be shown that: (a) in all likelihood the claimant has a valid right which will be or is being infringed by the defendant (fumus boni iuris); and (b) the claimant has not delayed in seeking the relief; and (c) the matter is urgent because there is a danger of irreparable damage from the defendant's wrongful activity (periculum in mora). An urgent injunction can usually be obtained within one to 4 months from filing the action.

In MALTA, where a compliance order is being contested before a Court, the Director of Consumer Affairs may request that court to issue an interim order if he considers that it is necessary to do so in the public interest, pending the final outcome of the proceedings.[1652] The procedure in PORTUGAL follows a summary procedure, too.[1653]

In POLAND, a summary procedure has been available since 2000.[1654] It is available for claims resulting from contracts the value of which does not exceed 10000 PLN (around 2500 EURO) (increased from 5000 PLN in 2005). In SLOVENIA, a temporary injunction can be obtained in a dispute regarding misleading advertising or comparative advertising.[1655] A court can issue a provisional ruling following an application by a claimant in line with the provisions regulating insurance, by which it shall order the cessation of the misleading advertising or the illegal comparative advertising, or prohibit the publication of misleading advertisements or advertisements containing illegal comparative advertising in the event it has not yet been published and is about to be published in public. Otherwise, there are no special summary procedures available under Slovenian Law.

No summary procedure is available in ESTONIA or LITHUANIA.

b. Order for publication of decision

Article 2(1)(b) of the Directive provides that an order may be sought for the publication of the decision to grant an injunction, and of a corrective statement. There is corresponding legislation in all the member states. For example, in ITALY, a court may order that a decision is published in one or more national newspapers, or in regional/local newspapers, where this

---

1648 Article 940 of the Civil Procedure Code in conjunction with Art. 935 of the Civil Procedure Code and Art. 8 and 12(2) of the Act against Unfair Competition: Art. 940 of the Civil Procedure Code concerns general summary procedure that is applicable to an order for cessation and to an order for prohibition. Art. 12(2) of the Act against Unfair Competition states that – in contrast to general summary procedure – the plaintiff is not required to prove the urgency of the order at the time it is issued.

1649 Article 10(9)(c) of the Consumer Protection Act (Law 2251/1994).

1650 Article 250(1)(12) of the Law of Civil Procedure.

1651 Article 669-bis to 669-quaterdecies of the Civil Procedure Code.

1652 Article 97(3) of the Consumer Affairs Act.

1653 Article 111(1) of the Law 24/96.

1654 Articles 5051 to 50515 were inserted into the Code of Civil Procedure of 1964.

1655 Article 74 of the Consumer Protection Act.

would help in dealing with the consequences of the infringement.[1656] In MALTA, such a publication has to be made in at least to daily newspapers, and at the expense of the trader concerned.[1657]

In POLAND, the publication of the decision has to be funded by the business subject to the proceedings.[1658] In SLOVENIA, the plaintiff can demand that the decision be published at the defendant's expense. It seems that in SWEDEN, publication occurs only in the regular journal published by the Market Court.[1659] LITHUANIA has not directly implemented this rule, but instead relies on the general rule that decisions by a court must be available publicly.

c. Order for payments into the public purse

Article 2(1)(c) of the Directive provides for an order, if permitted under national law, for payments into the public purse or any beneficiary designated under national legislation; this may include daily penalty payments. Legislation based on this provision has been adopted in BELGIUM, CZECH REPUBLIC, ESTONIA, FRANCE, GERMANY, GREECE, HUNGARY, IRELAND, ITALY, LATVIA, LUXEMBOURG, MALTA, NETHERLANDS, POLAND, PORTUGAL, SLOVAKIA, SPAIN and SWEDEN.

In GREECE, a qualified entity from another member state cannot request compensation; this right is restricted to Greek qualified entities. However, as an order for compensation is subject to the rules of domestic law, this will not be a problem under the Directive; it may however, be problematic under the general non-discrimination principle.

ITALIAN courts will set a deadline for compliance with the order. If the defendant fails to do so, the court can require the payment of a lump sum into the public purse, or impose a periodic penalty payment of between 516 and 1032 EURO per day for as long as the infringement continues.[1660] Money collected in this way must be paid into State funds, and these can be re-allocated to a fund to be set up as part of a special basic budgetary section of the Ministry of Productive Activities to finance initiatives for the benefit of consumers.

LITHUANIA has not taken specific steps to transpose this provision; instead, the general principle that court judgments can be enforced, with appropriate sanctions for non-compliance, is relied upon.

In MALTA, a failure to comply with a compliance order is a criminal offence. On conviction, a fine of up to Lm 10,000 (circa 23,000 Euros) and/or a daily fine of up Lm 50 (circa 130 euros) may be imposed for each day of non-compliance with the order.[1661] In POLAND, for example, the fine may be set at the equivalent of between 500 to 10,000 EURO for each

---

[1656] Article 140(1) lit. (c) of the Consumer Code.

[1657] Article 101 of the Consumer Affairs Act.

[1658] Article 23 of the Act on the protection of consumers and competition.

[1659] See correspondent's comment in the Database (SE).

[1660] Article 140(7) of the Consumer Code.

[1661] Article 106 of the Consumer Affairs Act.

day.[1662] In SPAIN, fines range from 600 to 60,000 EURO.[1663] With regard to the third element, in CYPRUS, a failure to comply with a court order puts the defendant into contempt of court and renders him subject to imprisonment, or his property subject to seizure. There is, however, no provision akin to Art. 2(1)(c) of the Directive.

In DENMARK, acting in violation of an injunction is a criminal offence generally; the same is true of the UNITED KINGDOM, where a failure to comply with a court order renders the defendant liable to proceedings for contempt of court, and there is no separate provision for penalty payments.[1664]

d. Private International Law

Article 2(2) of the Directive also requires that the rules of private international law regarding the law applicable to the situation, are not affected by the Directive. Most member states have not implemented this provision expressly. These countries rely on existing provisions in their rules on private international law. Those that have transposed this Article by adding specific provisions are the CZECH REPUBLIC,[1665] ESTONIA,[1666] HUNGARY,[1667] and SLOVAKIA.[1668]

3. Article 3 – Qualified entities

This article defines "qualified entity", which is a body or organisation with a legitimate interest ensuring that the collective interests of consumers, as provided for in the directives listed in the Annex, are complied with. This should include both at least one independent public body (in countries where these exist), and/or other organisations whose purpose it is to protect the collective interests of consumers in accordance with the criteria laid down by their national law.

The implementation of this provision has taken different forms. In many member states, the relevant "qualified entities" are listed expressly in the legislation transposing the Directive, whereas in others, these entities are specified through a separate ministerial order. Furthermore, some member states have included a general provision setting out the criteria to be applied in determining whether a particular body might satisfy the requirements for being recognised as a "qualified entity", whereas others have not done so. Many member states maintain lists of domestic "qualified entities", and a domestic association needs to be on such a list to have standing before the courts. There does not seem to be scope for the courts to admit associations not on such a list to bring an action.

1662 Article 102(1) of the Act on the protection of consumers and competition.

1663 Article 711(2) of the Law on Civil Procedure.

1664 The OFT has recently reported that it has secured the imprisonment of a trader who had failed to comply.

1665 CC Art. 64.

1666 Article 34 of the Private International Law Act.

1667 Article 28/A of the Decree on Private International Law 1979.

1668 Article 10(1)-(3); Art. 11 and 15 of the Code of International Law.

In AUSTRIA, the legislation[1669] mentions those organisations that have the right to take action, which includes the Association for Consumer Information.[1670] BELGIUM had already provided a right of action for domestic entities recognised by the Minister of Economic Affairs or represented in the "Raad van Verbruik" to take action. To this, the right of qualified entities from another member state to act was added in the implementing legislation. In CYPRUS, the Competition and Consumer Protection Authority of the Ministry of Industry, Commerce and Tourism is specified as qualified entity. In addition, any legally constituted organisation which by virtue of any law or their memorandum of association have an interest in the protection of consumers' collective interests may take action. No further criteria are laid down, and there is no approvals procedure which would allow for the exclusion of entities with an insufficient interest from the scope of the implementing provisions.

The DANISH provision authorises the relevant minister to appoint the qualified Danish authorities and organisations.[1671] Moreover, the minister may also appoint Danish authorities which can act on behalf of authorities from another member state in taking action. Similarly, FRANCE requires that qualified entities must be approved,[1672] and that only those entities which have the protection of the collective interests of consumers as an objective will be considered for approval,[1673] as will the Association of Family Unions (*unions d'associations familiales*). However, with the exception of the *Commission des clauses abusives*[1674] (a public body whose task is to monitor the use of unfair terms), French law does not know the kind of independent public body referred to in Art. 3(a) of the Directive and no specific attempt at giving effect to this provision was undertaken. GERMANY requires that associations must be registered with the Federal Administrative Office (Bundesverwaltungsamt), that their membership must comprise at least 75 natural persons and that they have been in existence for at least one year.[1675] However, there is a presumption that Consumer Associations and Centres (Verbraucherverbände und -zentralen) funded by the public purse meet these requirements. In addition, certain trade associations can taken action,[1676] as can the relevant Chambers of Trade and Commerce. In GREECE, there are detailed rules regarding consumer associations. These may only accept natural persons as their members, and the financial sources for their activities are restricted to subscriptions, proceeds from public events and the sale of newsletters/magazines, public funds and EU funds; no private funding is permitted. This should guarantee the association's independence. Associations need to be recognised by court order and entered on a register of consumer associations. In order to be entitled to take action under the rules giving effect to the Directive, an association must have at least 500 members and must have been registered for at least two years.[1677]

[1669] Article 29 of the Consumer Protection Act 1979.

[1670] „Verein für Konsumenteninformation".

[1671] Article 4 of the Act on the protection of consumer interests.

[1672] Article L. 421-6 of the Consumer Code.

[1673] Articles R. 411-1 et seq. of the Consumer Code lists the criteria used to agree an association of consumers.

[1674] See Articles L. 132-2 of the Consumer Code.

[1675] Article 4 of the Injunctions Act.

[1676] Article 3(1) of the Injunctions Act.

[1677] Article 10 of the Consumer Protection Act (Law 2251/1994).

In HUNGARY, there are a number of criteria which an organisation seeking to become a "qualified entity" must satisfy: it must be a social organisation founded on the appropriate legal basis; have consumer protection as one of its declared goals; must have been active for at least two years; and must have a membership of at least 50 persons. It must then apply to be included on the register of qualified entities.

ITALY also maintains a list of those entities which satisfy the criteria laid down in the provisions transposing Art. 3 of the Directive. A list is maintained by the Ministry of Productive Activities. Furthermore, independent public organisations, and organisations recognised in other EU member states, are also qualified entities. In IRELAND, the legislation simply states that a qualified entity is one which protects the collective interests of consumers affected by the infringement concerned, but such an entity must also satisfy the Court that it has a *statutory* function in relation to the protection of consumer interest which are the subject of the infringement concerned. The fact that this function must be "statutory" may exclude associations both from within Ireland and from another member states whose functions may not be statutory, but purely based on the terms of association.

In LATVIA, the qualified entity is the Consumer Rights Protection Centre, a public body, under the supervision of the Ministry of Economics. In LITHUANIA, there is no definition of 'qualified entity' in the domestic legislation, although the term itself is used in this legislation. The National Consumers' Rights Protection Board is referred to as a 'qualified entity'. The Board along with the State Food and Veterinary Service, State Inspection of Non-Food Products, the State Public Health Service or the Public Health Centres in districts under the State Public Health Service controls enforcement of the Law on Consumer Protection.[1678]

In MALTA, "qualified entity" means a consumer association which is registered under the Consumer Affairs Act, or any other body whether constituted in Malta or elsewhere, which is designated as a 'qualified body' by the Minister responsible for consumer affairs after consulting the Consumer Affairs Council.[1679]

The legislation in POLAND mentions the Ombudsman, Insurance Ombudsman, Consumers' Representative and consumer organisations as qualified entities. PORTUGUESE law takes a very wide approach to the notion of 'qualified entity' by granting a right of action to individual consumers (whether or not they have been harmed by the conduct), consumer associations, the public prosecutor (Ministerio Publico) and the Institute of Consumers (Instituto do Consumidor). This is because of the pre-existing legislation in this field, which had adopted a wider approach than the Directive requires.

SLOVAKIA maintains a list of qualified entities which contains approximately 10 different consumer associations. In SLOVENIA, a qualified entity is "any legal person that has been founded for the protection of consumers" as well as an "organisation or independent public body of another member state if the consumer's rights of that State could be endangered"; in

---

1678 Article 29 of the Law on Consumer Protection.

1679 Article 2 of the Consumer Affairs Act. A somewhat different definition exists under other Maltese laws implementing the Injunctions Directive – for example the Distance Selling (Retail Financial Services) Regulations, 2005, which whilst including registered consumer associations, makes a list of the categories of those entities which may be eligible to be considered as a ,"qualified entity".

case of the latter, prior consultation is required (see also below).[1680] The entity must have been operating for at least one year.

The implementation in SPAIN does not include the criteria from the Directive, but instead lists those entities which are qualified to take action under the national legislation implementing the Directive. In addition to relevant consumer associations, this also extends to independent public bodies, including Chambers of Commerce and the professional bars. In the UNITED KINGDOM, there are different categories of 'enforcers': general enforcers, designated enforcers, and Community enforcers. Only those in the latter category have the specific power to take action under the provisions transposing the Directive.[1681] The legislation states who the general enforcers are. In respect of "designated enforcers" there is a power for the Secretary of State to specify by order that a person or body of which he "thinks that it has as one of its purposes the protection of the collective interests of consumers" should be a designated enforcer.

In the CZECH REPUBLIC, however, there is no list of qualified entities at all; moreover, no independent public body has been established responsible for the protection of the collective interests of consumers.

4. Article 4 – Intra-Community infringements

a. Recognising qualified entities from another EU member state

Article 4(1) of the Directive requires that each member state where an infringement originates must permit any qualified entity from another member state where the collective interests of consumers are affected by the infringement, to bring an action for an injunction. The *locus standi* of a qualified entity to launch proceedings may not be questioned if it is included in the list compiled and published by the Commission. To that end, member states are obliged by Art. 4(2) of the Directive to notify the Commission of the qualified entities from their jurisdiction.

The following countries have given effect to this requirement by referring expressly to the list published in the Official Journal under Art. 4(3) of the Directive: AUSTRIA,[1682] BELGIUM, CZECH REPUBLIC, DENMARK, ESTONIA, FINLAND, FRANCE, GERMANY, GREECE, HUNGARY, ITALY, IRELAND, LITHUANIA, LUXEMBOURG, NETHERLANDS, POLAND, PORTUGAL, SLOVENIA, SPAIN, SWEDEN and the UNITED KINGDOM.

In LITHUANIAN law, the Consumer Rights Protection Board has the right to empower other institutions or organisations protecting consumers rights and having a right to protect public interests of the consumers to launch proceedings in the courts or other qualified entity of

---

[1680] Article 75(1)-(3) of the Consumer Protection Act.

[1681] Section 213(1), 213(5), 215(2), 215(4) of the Enterprise Act 2002.

[1682] Extending the scope of Art. 29 of the Consumer Protection Act to the qualified entities in the list published in the Official Journal.

any other EU member state in order to oblige the seller or service provider acting within the member state to cease the infringements of the public interest of Lithuanian consumers.[1683]

No specific transposition of this article can be found in CYPRUS. However, this does not mean that entities from the member states are deprived of a right to take action, as the provisions on the right of a qualified authority to bring an action is not restricted to qualified entities from Cyprus. However, it is not stated expressly that entities from other member states can take action, and no reference is made to the list published in the Official Journal.

MALTA has also not transposed this provision, and does not seem to refer to the list in the Official Journal. There is a general power to recognise non-Maltese entities as "qualifying entities" for the purpose of the Consumer Affairs Act, which would then permit them to take action in the same way as domestic qualified entities.[1684] Under the Maltese laws other than the Consumer Affairs Act, there is a direct reference to those entities operating in other member states which are entitled to be recognized as 'qualified entities' under Maltese law.[1685] LATVIA has also not transposed this provision, although the Law of Civil Procedure theoretically, admits the possibility that an entity from another member state could take action before the Latvian courts.

Member state courts retain the right to consider whether the purpose for which the qualified entity was set up justifies its taking the specific action before them. This has been expressly incorporated into domestic law include AUSTRIA, BELGIUM, GREECE, IRELAND, and POLAND.

However, in respect of IRELAND, it must be noted that any qualified entity must have a *statutory* function of protecting the collective interests of consumers; this seems to restrict the national legislation to a scope which is narrower than the Directive itself. DENMARK relies on a general requirement for standing that a claimant must show "sufficient legal interest" in bringing the action, and this applies to the type of action under the Directive. In FINLAND, a court is also entitled to investigate whether a claimant is entitled to bring an action, in line with the proviso contained in the Directive. In POLAND, the qualified entity from another member state has to show that the purpose of its activities justifies its starting proceedings in the Polish courts, and that these proceedings are aimed at conduct taking place in Poland but harming the collective interests of consumers in the member state where that entity is based.[1686]

1683 Article 28-7(2) of the Law on Consumer Protection.

1684 Article 2 of the Consumer Affairs Act.

1685 Thus, under the Distance Selling (Retail Financial Services) Regulations 2005 and the Advertising, Sponsorship and Teleshopping (Protection of Consumers' Interests) (Television Broadcasitng Injunction) Order, 2005 there is express reference to those qualified entities from another Member State which are included in the list complied by the EU Commission.

1686 Article 100a of the Act on the protection of consumers and competition.

b. List of qualified entities published in the Official Journal

The European Commission is required to publish a list of all the qualified entities notified to it by virtue of Art. 4(2) of the Directive in the Official Journal (see Art. 4(3) of the Directive). A detailed list was published in February 2006 ([2006] O.J. C 39/2). With the exception of MALTA, all member states have notified at least one qualified entity, although the number of entities varies considerably between the member states.

The following diagram (all diagrams are based on the 2006 list) illustrates the distribution of 'qualified entities' between the member states:

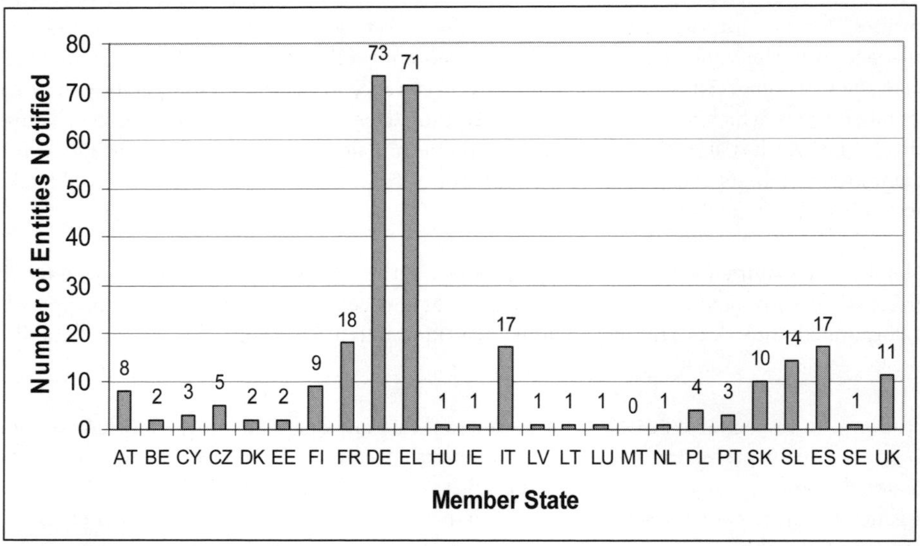

The total number of qualified entities notified to the Commission is 276. GERMANY has notified 26.4% of the total of qualified entities, followed closely by GREECE with 25.7%. This means that more than half of all qualified entities originate in two member states.

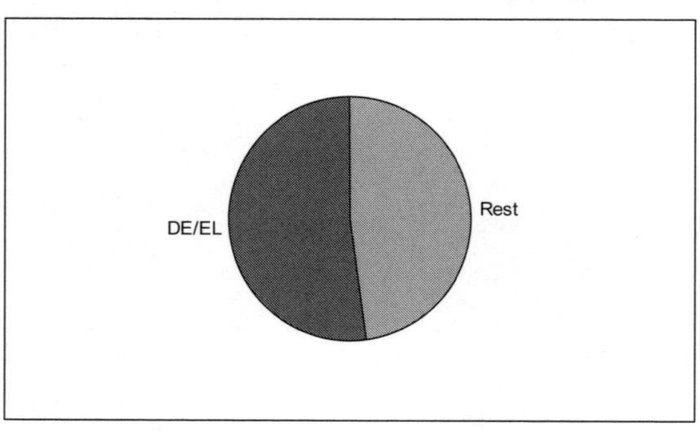

Overall, 235 qualified entities emanate from the pre-2004 member states (EU15), with only 41 entities from new new member states (EU10). The overall distribution is illustrated in the graph below.

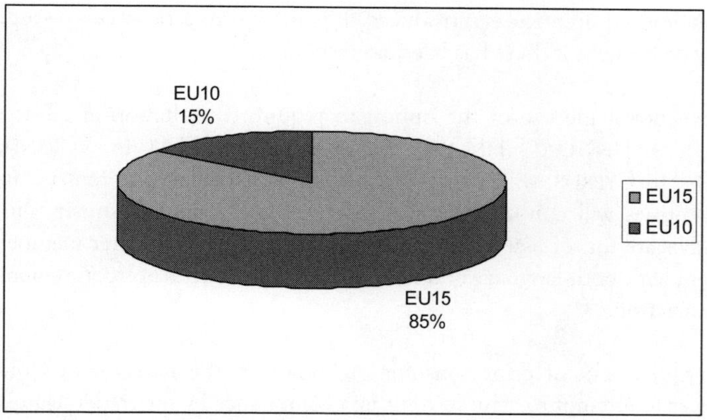

It should be noted that the UNITED KINGDOM has notified 11 entities, although one of them is, in fact, simply a reference to 204 separate entities, i.e., local weights and measures authorities. The analysis above is based on the assumption that only 11 qualified entities exist for the United Kingdom, although if each of the local authorities were treated separately, the position would be different:

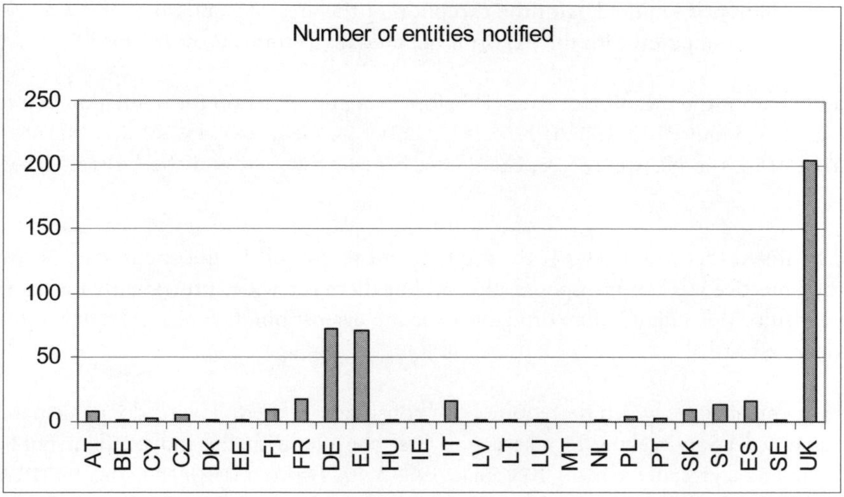

On this view, the total would be 468 qualified entities, of which the UNITED KINGDOM would have 43.4% of the total. It would also mean that the percentage of qualifying entities from the EU 15 States would rise to 91%.

5. Article 5 – Prior consultation

This article grants member states the option to require a qualified entity to consult with the defendant before applying for an injunction. Alternatively, member states may require such consultation to be with both the defendant and the independent public body who is a qualified entity. Even where such a requirement is introduced, it is limited to a two-week period, after which an action may be brought if there has been no response.

Member states which have not made use of the option to require consultation at all are: AUSTRIA, BELGIUM, CYPRUS, DENMARK, FINLAND, FRANCE, GREECE, LATVIA, POLAND, PORTUGAL, and SLOVENIA. In CYPRUS, whilst consultation is not a formal requirement, in practice, most qualified entities will consult voluntarily. In FINLAND, the Consumer Ombudsman can act as an advocate for, or assistant to, qualified entities from another member state, in order to help them with both language and relevant law, but there is no requirement to consult before taking an action.[1687]

In MALTA, there is no requirement of prior consultation; however, the Director of Consumer Affairs has the power to attempt to achieve voluntary compliance by the trader against whom an order might be sought if it is "possible and reasonable to do so".[1688] POLISH law refers to the possibility of an amicable settlement, which would, presumably, bring to an end the need for formal court proceedings.[1689] In SLOVENIA, only a qualified entity from another member state is required to consult the Slovenian consumer protection office before bringing an action, although if no response has been received within two weeks, the action may proceed. In SPAIN, consultation is possible (albeit optional – no consequences flow from not consulting) in respect of specific areas, (medicines, broadcasting and advertising). Beyond that, no consultation is required, with the exception of the area of standard contract terms, where voluntary consultation with the Registrar of Standard Terms is provided for.[1690]

Consultation within the meaning of Art.5(1) before bringing an action for injunction before domestic court is required in: CZECH REPUBLIC, ESTONIA, GERMANY, HUNGARY, IRELAND, ITALY, LITHUANIA, the NETHERLANDS, SLOVAKIA, SPAIN , SWEDEN and the UNITED KINGDOM.

It should be noted that in GERMANY, the requirement to consult in the circumstances covered by the Directive was not transposed directly, but there is a wider principle that a claimant must consult a defendant before bringing an action against him before a court which has the equivalent effect.[1691]

Out of the member states which do require prior consultation, the following do *not* demand that the qualified entity seeking to take action first consults with the independent public body in that member state: CZECH REPUBLIC, IRELAND, ITALY, LITHUANIA, the NETHERLANDS, SPAIN, and SWEDEN.

1687 Article 2(3) of the Act on cross-border injunction procedure.

1688 Article 100 of the Consumer Affairs Act.

1689 Article 100d of the Act on the protection of consumers and competition.

1690 Article 13 of the Law 17/1998.

1691 Article 5 of the Injunctions Act in conjunction with Art. 93 of the Civil Procedure Code establishes the principle that the plaintiff must consult the defendant before bringing an action against him to court. If he fails to do so, the plaintiff may be liable for the costs of litigation if the defendant immediately accepts the claim. However, it is not compulsory for the plaintiff to consult an arbitration board.

No consultation required	Consultation with defendant only	Consultation with defendant and public body
AT, BE, CY, DK, EL FI, FR, LU, LV, PL, PT, SL[1692] *(12)*	CZ, DE, IE, IT, LT, NL, ES, SE *(8)*	EE, HU, MT, SK, UK *(5)*

A specific a reference to the two week period can be found in the laws of the CZECH REPUBLIC, ESTONIA, HUNGARY, IRELAND, ITALY, LITHUANIA, MALTA, SLOVAKIA, SPAIN, and the UNITED KINGDOM. There appears to be some of variation between these countries with regards to the exact time period that needs to elapse before an action may be brought. Thus, in a both Italy and Spain, the entity in question needs to wait for 15 days. In Malta, the 15-day period starts when the qualifying entity is informed by the Director that he has decided not to issue the compliance order requested. Once that period has expired, the qualifying entity may apply to the courts for an order requiring the Director to issue a compliance order.[1693]

ITALY maintains a conciliation procedure, which is available prior to starting legal proceedings, which associations and other qualified entities may bring before the Chamber of Commerce, Industry, Trade and Agriculture competent for the local area as well as some other organisations dealing with out-of-court settlements in relation to consumers. The conciliation report, signed by the parties and the representative of the organisation dealing with out-of-court settlement, shall be filed for approval in the registry of the Court at the place in which the conciliation proceedings were conducted. The Court, having established that it complies with the relevant formal requirements, can order it to be made enforceable, and the approved conciliation report is an enforceable instrument

6. Annex

The Annex to the Directive lists all the directives to which it applies. This Annex has been amended by all the consumer directives adopted since the Injunctions Directive became law. Some member states have chosen to implement the Annex directly into their relevant domestic law, whereas others have not seen the need for this to be done.

Countries which have transposed the Annex as a separate list into their domestic law are: BELGIUM,[1694] DENMARK, ESTONIA, FINLAND, FRANCE, GERMANY, GREECE, HUNGARY, MALTA, PORTUGAL, SLOVAKIA, and the UNITED KINGDOM. Those which have not transposed it into their domestic law are: AUSTRIA, CZECH REPUBLIC, ITALY, IRELAND, LATVIA, LITHUANIA, the NETHERLANDS, SLOVENIA, SPAIN and SWEDEN.

1692 As noted above, Slovenia does require a qualified entity from another Member State to consult the Slovenian public body before taking action.

1693 Article 95 of the Consumer Affairs Act. There is a similar procedure under the Distance Selling (Retail Financial Services) Regulations, 2005 – see reg. 15 thereof.

1694 The Law of 26 May 2002 Concerning Intra-Community Actions for an Injunction in the Field of the Protection of Consumer Interests contains an annex such as the Injunctions Directive. This law however, does not apply to the liberal professions (Art. 3), for whom the Injunctions Directive was transposed in the Liberal Professions Act, which does not contain such list.

In this regard, it must be stressed that there is no obligation to tranpose the Annex itself. What is crucial is that domestic law ensures that an action for injunction is available for all the infringements covered by the Directive. Including the Annex in domestic law could be seen as increasing transparency in that it is easier to identify the collective interests of consumers included in directives listed in the Annex.

In AUSTRIA, Art. 28(a) of the Consumer Protection Act refers to transactions involving those circumstances on which there is a Directive, rather than listing either the directives or implementing legislation themselves. In IRELAND, reference to the Annex is made in the explanatory notes to the implementing legislation. Similarly, in SPAIN, there is no separate list of relevant Directives, although some of these are mentioned in the Exposition of Motives of the Law 39/2002.

CYPRUS and LUXEMBOURG have not transposed the Annex because these countries have chosen to implement the Directive by amending each respective domestic law implementing the consumer directives concerned.

Method of Transposition	Member State
Include Annex in domestic law	BE, DK, EE, FI, FR, DE, EL, HU, MT, PT, SK, UK *(12)*
Reference in explanatory notes	IE, ES *(2)*
No transposition but relevant domestic law amended	CY, LU *(2)*
No transposition	AT, CZ, IT, LV, LT, NL, PL, SL, SE *(9)*

IV. Use of the minimum harmonisation clause

Article 7 of the Directive permits the member states to grant qualified entities, as well as other persons, more extensive rights to take action in their territory. This provision therefore has a two-fold effect: on the one hand, it effectively enables the member states to broaden the ambit of the injunctions scheme by giving *locus standi* to a wider range of persons. On the other hand, a member state remains free to grant qualified entities a right to bring an action in circumstances not covered by this Directive (such as for additional domestic consumer protection rules).

In AUSTRIA, it is possible to challenge standard contract terms even when they are not specifically designed for consumer transactions; moreover, an injunction may be available for a wider range of contracts.

In BELGIUM,[1695] the injunctions procedure can be used to challenge infringements of domestic consumer rules not based on an EC Directive. Such action is also possible in ITALY, HUNGARY, the NETHERLANDS, PORTUGAL and SWEDEN. Similarly, GERMANY applies the implementing legislation to infringements of consumer legislation generally. In the UNITED KINGDOM, the injunctions procedure can also be used for to deal with infringements of

1695 See Art. 95, 97 and 98 of the Trade Practices Act and the Annex of the Law, 26 May 2002 Concerning Intra-Community Actions for an Injunction in the Field of the Protection of Consumer Interests, which includes infringements on the TPA .

other consumer protection legislation, but the right of action excludes the qualified entities from another member state and is restricted to "domestic" and "designated" enforcers.

The law in CYPRUS permits qualified entities to seek a wider range of orders, such as requiring the trader to take corrective measures, or any other order that may be reasonable in the circumstances of the case. Furthermore, it is not necessary that the collective interests of consumers are harmed, and even an infringement affecting a single consumer makes it possible to apply for an injunction, although it is not clear whether an injunction can be sought directly by an affected individual consumer, or whether this should be done by a qualified authority on his behalf. No reference is made to such a right vested on individual consumers. Actions for an injunction to protect individual consumer interests are also possible in LATVIA.

In MALTA, wider orders can be made: where the action is based on the use of unfair contract terms, the order may require the trader to incorporate terms to improve the information of consumers or to prevent a significant imbalance in the rights and obligations of the parties to the contract (if this would benefit consumers); for other actions, the order may specify the measures that need to be taken to ensure compliance. In POLAND, the implementing legislation covers all natural and legal persons providing public services which are not an economic activity as such, as well as professions.

In SPAIN, a qualified entity from another member state may bring an action before the Spanish courts without having to show that the collective interests of the consumers in that State were harmed by the infringement originating from Spain. Moreover, in the fields of advertising, including advertising of medicinal products, and broadcasting, individual consumers also have standing to bring an action for an injunction. Moreover, entities from another member states can intervene in proceedings already pending before a Spanish court. Finally, the procedure for applying for an injunction is a fast-track one, requiring only oral proceedings.

Individual consumers can also take action in ESTONIA.No specific use of this provision was made in the CZECH REPUBLIC, DENMARK, FINLAND (although note that the Consumer Ombudsman has an advisory role for entities from another member state), FRANCE, IRELAND, LATVIA, LITHUANIA, the NETHERLANDS, SLOVAKIA, SLOVENIA, and the UNITED KINGDOM.

V. General comments on adequacy of implementation of the Directive

1. Difficulties encountered during the transposition process

It has been noted that the Directive contains a number of features that may make it weaker than necessary. In particular, there are options given to the member states with regard to the appropriate procedure and competent authority, prior consultation and the criteria for recognising "qualified entities". This creates a risk of different standards and may make it more difficult for a qualified entity from one member state to take action in another member state. Of course, such a flexible approach is needed, to an extent, because of the diversity of the national legal systems.

Moreover, the obligation under the Directive to establish certain procedures which must be in existence in the member states to ensure the full effectiveness of a Directive may be problematic for some states, given the different – and contrasting – legal traditions. For example, in MALTA, the Directive has been implemented on a piecemeal basis (i.e., as part of the legislation transposing specific directives), which now means that different authorities each with their own different appellate tribunals and procedures are charged with the enforcement of these rules.

2. Gaps in the Directive

It has been suggested that it would be beneficial to provide some guidelines on the application of the powers given by this directive. Otherwise, too much discretion may be left to the domestic courts, which will make it more difficult to apply these rules effectively.

Directive only applies to domestic measures giving effect to corresponding EC directives, but most of these directives contain minimum harmonisation clauses. Some traders may therefore be subject to infringement proceedings in one member state, but not in another.

A further question – illustrated by the *Duchesne* litigation by the UK's Office of Fair Trading – is which law should be applied by the court in which the action is brought. In the *Duchesne* litigation, the Belgian commercial tribunal and the Court of Appeal took different views as to whether Belgian or English law applied, although in that case, there was an infringement under both laws.

In several member states, commentators have expressed scepticism about the practical relevance of the Directive in view of the financial difficulties which qualified entities may face when seeking to take action in another member state. Indeed, at the time of writing, there had only been one reported cross-border case.[1696] One suggestion has been to give injunctions granted in one member state immediate EU-wide reach.[1697] However, the Directive is not limited to cross-border injunctions, and at a domestic level, there have been cases where action was taken to combat infringements at a national level.

Concern has also been expressed about the possible delays in notifying the Commission of new qualified entities, and also in publishing a revised list in the Official Journal. Consideration might also be given to extending the right of qualified entities to ask not only for an injunction, but also, in appropriate cases, to bring a claim for compensation on behalf of affected consumers (see, e.g., the French procedure on collective action).

Finally, it may be observed that the Directive 98/27 does not address the relationship with other consumer protection directives which already require that there is a right of action for independent public bodies and other organisations with a legitimate interest in the protection of consumers (see e.g., Art.7 of Directive 93/13; Art.11 of Directive 97/7). This is usually done by permitting such bodies and organisations to seek an injunction, but the threshold for taking action under these provisions is lower as it does not refer to the "collective interests" of consumers.

[1696] The UK's Office of Fair Trading successfully took action in the Belgian courts.

[1697] See *Calais-Auloy* and *Steinmetz*, Droit de la consommation, Dalloz (2003).

3. Other enforcement mechanisms

Correspondents were asked whether there were additional enforcement mechanisms for the protection of collective consumer interests available in the member states.

In AUSTRIA and GERMANY, competitors may be able to take action under the laws on unfair competition; the same applies in LATVIA. Moreover, in Germany, the legislation on investor protection[1698] provides for the possibility of bringing a test case to establish whether incorrect information about investments was published, or whether information was withheld. Provided that there are at least 10 claimants, the action will take evidence only once and a decision for all investors affected will be handed down. In ESTONIA, the Consumer Protection Board can intervene in individual cases. In the CZECH REPUBLIC, an organisation in charge of consumer interests may bring an action for injunction with a civil court.[1699] In FRANCE, a form of collective action is available in circumstances where a number of consumers have been affected by the same conduct of a single trader. Accredited consumer organisations may take up these cases on behalf of the consumers affected, provided that at least two consumers have instructed the organisation to act. Discussions are also underway to introduce the possibility of a class action taken on behalf of consumers directly. HUNGARY also contains provisions in its law on collective actions. FRANCE also involves the criminal law in the enforcement of several of the consumer directives. The same is true of the UNITED KINGDOM, which provides a range of criminal sanctions, e.g., for a breach of the information obligations under Directive 85/577, or Directive 90/314.

In MALTA, registered consumer associations may ask to intervene in proceedings before the Commission of Fair Trading. Moreover such associations have the right to make complaints to the Director of Consumer Affairs in relation to any law which he administers. A representative of the association is entitled to participate and assist in the proceedings undertaken following such reports.[1700] In the case of complaints made by the association under the Trade Descriptions Act, the association may participate in any subsequent proceedings as an aggrieved party.[1701]

ITALY is also considering reform in this area. The "Disegno di legge" no. 679 "Disposizioni per l'introduzione della class action" of 26 June 2006 is before Parliament. It would introduce a new article 141-bis into the Consumer Code to provide that consumers' associations are entitled to recover damages on behalf of one or more consumers.

VI. Conclusions and recommendations

- A clarification regarding the applicable law in cross-border cases might be desirable. It is noted that this may be resolved through the "Rome II" regulation (Regulation 864/2007 on the law applicable to non-contractual obligations (2007) O.J. L 199/40).

1698 Law on Test Cases for the Protection of Investors.

1699 Article 54(2) of the CommC (Act No. 513/1991).

1700 Article 37 of the Consumer Affairs Act.

1701 Article 30 of the Trade Descriptions Act.

- A related question is whether injunctions obtained in a domestic context ought to have Europe-wide reach, at least where the activities of the trader against whom an injunction has been obtained are not limited to one member state. An analysis as to whether this is already possible within Regulation 44/2001 (Brussels-Regulation) may be desirable.
- The relationship with Directive-specific enforcement mechanisms should be clarified. Thus, Art. 11 of Directive 97/7 and Art. 7 of Directive 93/13 both require that member states put into place adequate and effective means to ensure compliance with these respective Directives. This seems to overlap, to an extent, with the Directive 98/27. There is a difference in that the provisions in the specific directives do not include the "collective interest" criterion, although, at a practical level, this may not matter hugely. It may therefore be possible to consider whether these specific provisions could be deleted.
- The evidence to date shows that the cross-border procedure is not being utilised. One reason may be the question of costs for qualified entities from one member state to take action in another. The Directive is silent on the question of costs; a basic rule giving the qualifying entity the right, if successful in the action, to recover costs (not just of the court action, but the costs incurred in taking the action, such as translation, legal advice etc.) could be considered.
- It may be desirable to consider whether a power to ask for compensation should be introduced. Difficulties in this regard may be establishing the loss caused and identifying beneficiaries (e.g., through creating a central fund to which individual consumers may apply). Linked to this is whether cross-border class-actions ought to be facilitated, too.

Bibliography

Commission communication concerning Article 4(3) of Directive 98/27/EC of the European Parliament and of the Council on injunctions for the protection of consumers' interests, concerning the entities qualified to bring an action under Article 2 of this Directive, OJ C 63, 8.3.2008, p. 5-43; **Alexander, Janet C.,** Acciones de defensa de intereses supraindividuales de los consumidores, Estudios sobre Consumo (Estudios sobre Consumo) 2000, 107-124, **Baranovszky, György**, Közérdekű kereset indításának eljárásjogi kérdései, Fogyasztóvédelmi Szemle 2004, **Barona Vilar, Silvia**, Tutela de los consumidores y usuarios en la Ley de Enjuiciamiento Civil, Valencia 2003, **Bassenge, Peter**, Gesetz über Unterlassungsklagen bei Verbraucherrechts- und anderen Verstößen (Unterlassungsklagengesetz UKlaG), in: Palandt, Bürgerliches Gesetzbuch 2005, **Galič, Aleš** Procesni vidiki prava varstva potrošnikov, Podjetje in delo (Podjetje in delo) 2000, 550-562, **Howells, Geraint / Weatherill, Stephen,** Consumer Protection Law, Aldershot 2005, **Hulva, Tomáš**, Ochrana spotřebitele, Praha 2005, **Kristoffersen, Sonny**, RetshÍndhcvelse ved forbrugerklager, Copenhagen 2005, **Łętowska, Ewa**, Europejskie prawo umów konsumenckich, Warszawa 2004, **Méndez Pinedo, Elvira**, La protección de consumidores en la Unión Europea : hacia un derecho procesal comunitario de consumo, Madrid 1998, **Micallef, Paul Edgar**, Making Consumer Redress a Reality: the Consumer Claims Tribunals and the Rights of Consumer Associations under Maltese Law, New Zealand Business Law Quarterly (New Zealand Business Law Quarterly) 2002, 430-451, **Micklitz, Hans-W. / Stadler, Astrid**, Das Verbandsklagerecht in der Informations- und Dienstleistungsgesellschaft, Münster 2005, **Tichý, Lubos**, Pojem spotřebitele jako smluvní strany v evropském a českém právu, Spotřebitelská legislativa EU a její implementace do práva členského a kandidátského státu (např. do Francie a České republiky (Spotřebitelská legislativa EU) 2001, 131-161, **Verardi, C.**, L'accesso alla giustizia e la tutela collettiva dei consumatori, Il diritto privato dell'Unione Europea, Trattato di diritto privato, A. Tizzano (ed.) 2000, 1331.

H. Consumer Sales Directive (99/44)

Drafted by Christian Twigg-Flesner

Executive summary

I. Transposition deficiencies

All the member states have taken the steps necessary to amend their domestic law to give effect to the requirements of Directive 99/44. The Directive is a minimum harmonisation measure and allows member states to adopt or retain legislation which provides a higher level of protection to consumers, and it is possible to identify many such instances where domestic law departs from the standard required by the Directive. In some cases, this has been a deliberate decision by the national legislator, in others it appears to be a side-effect of the failure to transpose particular aspects of the Directive. There are some instances where a member state, in departing from the standard set by the Directive, has fallen below the minimum standard, and there may consequently be transposition deficiencies in this regard. For example:

- Art. 1 para. (4) (partial definition of 'sale' to include contracts for goods to be manufactured) - uncertainty about correct transposition in CZECH REPUBLIC, GREECE, MALTA and UNITED KINGDOM, although likely that this situation is also covered.
- Art. 2 para. (1): no general 'conformity' requirement in UNITED KINGDOM (although functional equivalent exists), or in SLOVAKIA.
- Deviations from conformity standard in GERMANY (by prioritising party agreement); LITHUANIA (reference to sources of public statements), CZECH REPUBLIC (no reference to sample, description, or specific purpose); UNITED KINGDOM (not all aspects of conformity mentioned in domestic law, such as performance, although unlikely to come to different result).
- Art. 2 para. (2) lit. (d). not transposed in CZECH REPUBLIC.
- Art. 2 para. (5) (installation): variations in LITHUANIA, SLOVENIA, SPAIN and UNITED KINGDOM which appear to fall short of what is required.
- Art. 3 – no price reduction where repair/replacement provided with significant inconvenience in GERMANY.
- Art. 3 para. (3): the UNITED KINGDOM and the NETHERLANDS apply the proportionality test in Art. 3(3) to compare repair not only with replacement (or vice versa), but also with the other remedies of price reduction/rescission. No transposition in LATVIA, LITHUANIA, PORTUGAL and SLOVENIA.
- Art. 3 para. (4) ('free of charge'): GERMANY permits deduction to take account of period during which consumer had use of goods before replacement; reference made to ECJ to see if in accordance with Directive.
- Art. 5 para. (3) (reversed burden) not transposed in LATVIA.
- Art. 7 para. (2): incomplete transposition in UNITED KINGDOM.

2. Enhancement of protection

a. Use of options

The Directive provides 4 options in the Articles, as well as two "soft options" via the Recitals. Generally, options have met with a mixed response, and there is no instance where the vast majority of the member states have opted for or against a particular option.

- Art. 1 para. (3) (exclusion of second-hand goods sold at public auction) was exercised only by 8 member states, with 17 not doing so.
- Art. 5 para. (2) grants the option to require notification of a lack of conformity within two months, used by 15 member states, but not by 10.
- The option in Art. 7(1) (reduced period for second-hand goods) was applied by 14 member states, whereas 11 chose not to use it.
- 13 member states have used the option in Art. 6(4) (language of guarantees).
- Some member states have expressly adopted provisions based on Recital 18 (suspension of two-year period), e.g., CZECH REPUBLIC, HUNGARY, MALTA, SPAIN.
- Some have also adopted measures following Recital 15 (period-of-use deduction in case of rescission).

There is therefore a degree of diversity in the use made of these options, with no option being overwhelmingly adopted or rejected.

b. Use of minimum clause (i.e. more stringent provisions in the field covered by the Directive)

The minimum harmonisation clause has featured extensively in the measures transposing the Directive.

- A number of member states have, given a consumer the free choice between the 4 remedies.
- In some countries, there are longer time periods applicable (FINLAND, IRELAND, UNITED KINGDOM).
- A number of legislators took no steps to implement Art. 2(4), which could also be explicable on the basis of minimum harmonisation (CZECH REPUBLIC, LATVIA, LITHUANIA, PORTUGAL and SLOVENIA); others have only transposed some of the exclusions (LUXEMBOURG, FRANCE, GREECE). In ITALY, the consumer must be aware of the correction.
- No transposition of Art. 3(6) (no rescission for minor lack of conformity) in CZECH REPUBLIC, ESTONIA, PORTUGAL, SLOVENIA and UNITED KINGDOM.
- Some of the new member states have retained their system of mandatory guarantees (HUNGARY, SLOVENIA), or have more extensive rules in place (AUSTRIA, ESTONIA, FINLAND, LATVIA, MALTA). Note inadvertent impact in UNITED KINGDOM.

In many instances, the minimum harmonisation clause was relied upon where domestic law already exceeded the standard set by the Directive, making it unnecessary to adopt specific provisions to implement aspects of the Directive. Consequently, there remains a noticeable degree of variation between the member states.

c. Extension of scope

It is possible to identify extensions of scope in the majority of member states. This has generally been achieved either by broadening the definitions of "consumer", "seller" or "consumer goods" in the implementing legislation, or by applying the provisions of domestic law to transactions other than consumer sales.

d. Other measures enhancing consumer protection (i.e. more stringent provisions in fields not covered by the Directive)

- Additional factors to clarify operation of "conformity with the contract" test, such as instructions (HUNGARY), spare parts (CYPRUS), or packaging (DENMARK, ESTONIA, SWEDEN and FINLAND).
- Direct liability of the producer (FRANCE, BELGIUM, PORTUGAL, LATVIA, LITHUANIA).
- The domestic laws of all the member states provide for damages as an alternative or additional remedy in cases of non-conformity.

3. Inconsistencies

Some member states have implemented a "negative presumption" of conformity, i.e., goods are not presumed to be in conformity unless the criteria stated are met (GREECE, NETHERLANDS, PORTUGAL, SLOVENIA). Others do not refer to a presumption at all (FRANCE, MALTA).

The time at which conformity is to be assessed also varies, with some member states relying on the passing of risk as the crucial time, sometimes linked with delivery. The notion of delivery itself is not defined and remains unclear.

The method for calculating a price-reduction is unclear – both a flat-rate and proportionate reduction approach are possible.

Art. 4 (right of redress) is vagueness, leaving a considerable degree of interpretation to the member states in giving effect to its provisions.

4. Consumer protection gaps

One gap identified in this analysis is that the relationship between the remedies in Art. 3 and the right to damages is not made clear, leaving scope for uncertainty. The Directive does not address the position of computer software. There are also no provisions on the need to maintain spare parts (necessary for effective repair), no on after-sales services. There are also no provisions dealing with the particular difficulties of cross-border enforcement.

5. Potential barriers to trade

A number of possible barriers to trade could be identified. The first, a barrier on the consumer-side, may be the lack of any provision on cross-border enforcement. A second possible barrier is the fact that, in some member states, there is direct liability of a producer, whereas in the majority, there is not. Finally, the different interpretation and application of the Directive's provision through national law in the courts of the member states may bring about further barriers, although there is as yet not sufficient evidence of this.

6. Conclusions and recommendations

The following matters could be considered as part of reviewing the Directive:

- Options: It is apparent that all options have been used by some of the member states, but in no instance has there been an overwhelming tendency to use, or to disregard, any of the options given in the Directive. Consequently, no clear recommendation regarding the removal of any of the options can be given.
- Definition of 'consumer' (refer to the general discussion of this matter).
- Definition of 'seller' (refer to the general discussion of this matter).
- Definition of 'goods', in particular whether software and other digital products should be included in the definition. A related question is whether any licenses associated with the supply of software, or other digital products, should be covered by the rules of this Directive, too – for example, when the license is not extensive enough. It may not be possible to address this issue in the context of this Directive, but there may be questions of drawing the line in the correct place if digital products are to be included in the definition of 'goods'.
- Clarification in the text of the Directive that the proportionality criterion should not permit a comparison of repair/replacement with price reduction, to avoid confusion on this matter.
- Clarification of who bears the burden of proof in respect of some of the provisions (e.g., Art. 2 para. (3)).
- Right of redress for the seller: consider whether this could be clarified further, and consider, in particular, whether a clear 'action directe' approach could be adopted.
- The introduction of direct producer liability, and, possibly, distribution network liability, could be considered again. In the context of the internal market, it may be particularly important that a consumer can seek a remedy from somebody based in his own country. The Directive does not address this matter at present, and it should be considered if a system of producer liability, possibly combined with distribution network liability, should be adopted.
- The relationship of the remedies in Art. 3 and the national rules on the award of damages: it may be considered whether the Directive should address this. That would raise the questions which forms of damage should be covered. Broadly speaking, 4 heads of damages can be identified: (i) Equivalence (to the remedies in the Directive); (ii) consequential losses; (iii) loss of profit; and (iv) additional costs incurred as a result of buying replacement. This matter may best be considered once the *Common Frame of Reference* has been completed.
- Related supply transactions: there are other supply transactions, such as hire-purchase or conditional sale, as well as hire and leasing, which are frequently used by consumers

buying more expensive goods. Conditional sale may be included within the scope of the Directive, although the position is not clear. Other supply transactions were explicitly excluded during the legislative process leading up to the adoption of the Directive, but this could bring about the different treatment of similar transactions. The nature of the risk in the context of a hire or leasing arrangement is different from that in sale, or conditional sale; nevertheless, it may be desirable to consider including a wider range of transactions within the scope of the Directive.

I. Member state legislation prior to the adoption of the Consumer Sales Directive

All the current member states (EU25) had legislation applicable to the sale of goods to consumers in place before the adoption of Directive 99/44 in July 1999. However, there was a significant degree of variation in this existing legislation, possibly because of the fundamental nature of sales contracts in the general law of contract in many countries. The following is a brief, and not by any means exhaustive, overview of the situation as it was before the Directive 99/44 was adopted.

At the outset, it needs to be observed that there was a basic difference between countries adhering to the difference between specific and generic goods that stems from ROMAN LAW ("Gattungskauf" vs "Stückkauf") and those, which do not. This distinction was once present, in a moderate form, in the common law but largely lost through developments from the 19th century onwards. The approach to seller liability under these two regimes varied.

In terms of the areas covered by the Directive, a fundamental distinction may be drawn between countries, which had already adopted legislation specifically dealing with consumer sales contracts, and countries that relied upon a general legislative framework covering all types of sales, including consumer sales. General rules applied, for example, in BELGIUM, CYPRUS, FRANCE, GERMANY, HUNGARY, IRELAND, ITALY, MALTA, and the UNITED KINGDOM.

In the Central and Eastern European countries among the new member states (EU10), there were largely only general civil codes, which applied and did not contain specific consumer provisions (e.g., CZECH REPUBLIC, ESTONIA). In LATVIA, an early version of the Consumer Rights Protection Law of 1992 had introduced basic rules on consumer sales, but these fell short of the requirements of the Directive. A similar situation arose in LITHUANIA, where a 1994 law introduced consumer protection provisions that supplemented the Civil Code of 1964. In POLAND, the law contained provisions applicable only in consumer transactions, making the obligations of the seller more precise and indicating to consumers how exactly they could obtain remedies.[1702]

Among those which had adopted consumer-specific rules, some only provided a few additional provisions rather than a detailed separate framework on consumer sales. Thus, in AUSTRIA, the Consumer Protection Law restricted the variations that could be made to the

---

1702 Regulation on the conditions of concluding and executing contracts of sale of movable goods involving consumers of 30 May 1995 (now repealed) which supplemented the Civil Code provisions on legal guarantees.

applicable legal rules by permitting an agreement whereby the seller could (i) avoid termination/price reduction by providing conforming goods within a reasonable time; and (ii) avoid price reduction by repairing the fault. In GREECE, a seller of new durable consumer goods was required to provide a written guarantee to a consumer.[1703] Such guarantees had to be of a duration in proportion to the life expectancy of the product, and for which there were minimum standards. The law in IRELAND[1704] included a specific right for consumers to request a replacement for non-conforming goods. In PORTUGAL, Law 24/9 on Consumer Protection offered some consumer-specific rules in addition to the civil code. The law in SPAIN required mandatory guarantees for durable goods and stipulated the minimum content of guarantees;[1705] moreover, the Spanish civil code had also adopted the Roman law distinction between specific and generic goods. In SLOVENIA, the general sales law rules applied, with only few modifications by the Consumer Protection Act.[1706] Apart from the seller's responsibility for material defects, a parallel regime of mandatory guarantees for the so called "technical goods" was provided for by the general rules[1707] and further specified in the Consumer Protection Act. SWEDEN had also adopted a Consumer Purchase Act, which is a separate and complete piece of legislation.

In the UNITED KINGDOM, modifications had been made to certain provisions of the Sale of Goods Act 1979, e.g., by restricting sec. 15A on slight breaches of contract to non-consumer cases with the effect that consumers could exercise their right of termination even where there had only been a minor non-conformity.

Others had adopted rules, which were broadly similar to those eventually introduced by Directive 99/44, such as DENMARK, FINLAND,[1708] NETHERLANDS,[1709] and SLOVAKIA.[1710]
There were also variations in the standard of conformity that was applied, and the factors that would be relevant in considering whether goods were in conformity with the contract; nevertheless, there were common requirements such as basic fitness for purpose. In some countries, such as FRANCE[1711] (where there were separate provisions on non-conformity with the contract)[1712] or MALTA,[1713] existing rules focused on latent defects.

Moreover, the remedies that were made available in cases of non-conformity varied. Some member states already made available remedies such as repair and replacement in their domestic laws, including DENMARK, FINLAND,[1714] NETHERLANDS,[1715] SLOVENIA,[1716] and SPAIN.[1717]

1703 Article 5 of theLaw 2251/1994 on Consumer Protection.

1704 Section 53(2) of the Sale of Goods Act 1980.

1705 Article 11of the Law 26/1984 of July 19 on Consumer Protection.

1706 Consumer Protection Act 1998.

1707 Obligations Code Art. 481 – 487.

1708 Consumer Protection Act 20.1.1978/38.

1709 Civil Code.

1710 Consumer Protection Act 1998.

1711 Article 1641 et.seq. of the Civil Code.

1712 Article 1604 of theCivil Code.

1713 CC Art. 1424 et seq (Chapter 16 of the Laws of Malta).

1714 Consumer Protection Act 20.1.1978/3.

1715 Civil Code.

Before implementation, therefore, there was a significant difference between the laws of the member states. To some extent, variations continue to exist even after the transposition because of the methods of implementation chosen. Thus, in some instances, changes were made to the existing civil code or sales law, whereas in other instances, specific consumer protection provisions were adopted (perhaps most notably in ITALY, where a new consumer code was adopted in 2005). For example, in MALTA, specific rights in relation to consumer and trader transactions where enacted as part of the Consumer Affairs Act.[1718] These rights were in addition to the rights that already existed under the Civil Code, and prevail over all other laws to the extent that they are more favourable to the consumer.[1719]

II. Scope of application

1. General scope

The Directive applies to contracts for the sale of consumer goods by a seller to a consumer. These definitions determine the scope of the Directive.

It may be observed at the outset that few member states have restricted their implementing legislation to the exact scope specified by the Directive (IRELAND being one of them). Most go beyond its scope in some respects, often because their domestic law makes no clear-cut distinction between consumer and non-consumer sales.

In AUSTRIA, the rules are significantly broader, covering B2B and C2C sales as well as B2C, and there is no restriction to tangible movable items. The CZECH REPUBLIC relies on its civil code that applies to all types of contract, and the implementation of the Directive has been undertaken in a rather haphazard fashion, creating some doubt as to whether it has been transposed adequately. GERMANY took the need to implement the Directive as an impetus for a wider reform to its law of obligations, and contract law in particular. The Civil Code in GREECE was amended and applies rules based on the Directive to all sales transactions, not only to consumer sales. In HUNGARY, the implementation of the Directive resulted in the creation of separate rules for consumer and non-consumer transactions. ITALY has extended the rules to contracts which are similar to contracts of sale, i.e., contracts for exchange and supply, work and materials, and all other contracts for the supply of consumer goods to be manufactured.[1720]

2. Definition of 'consumer'

A consumer is "any natural person who ... is acting for purposes which are not related to his trade, business or profession" (Art. 1(2)(a)). Member states which follow this definition of

---

1716 Obligations Code and Consumer Protection Act 1998.

1717 Article 11 para. (3) of the Law 26/1984 of July 19 on Consumer Protection.

1718 Part VIII Consumer Affairs Act.

1719 Ibid. Art. 92.

1720 Article 128(1) of the Consumer Code.

"consumer" are BELGIUM, CYPRUS,[1721] ESTONIA, IRELAND, ITALY, LUXEMBOURG and NETHERLANDS.

In respect of IRELAND, it should be noted that for the purposes of the general Irish sale of goods legislation, a similar definition to the UNITED KINGDOM's "dealing as a consumer" (mentioned below) is used.[1722]

In many member states, there are variations on the definition of "consumer", which has generally the effect of broadening the overall scope of protection. In AUSTRIA, there is no express definition of "consumer", but instead this notion is defined negatively as someone not a business.[1723] In the CZECH REPUBLIC, a "consumer" is a person not acting within the scope of its commercial and business activity.[1724] DENMARK includes legal persons within the definition.[1725] In FINLAND, the concept is defined in FINLAND as "a natural person who purchases consumer goods primarily for the other purpose than to his/her professional purposes".[1726] GERMANY includes an employee during the course of his employment within the scope of the domestic legislation.[1727] GREECE refers to any individual or legal entity for whom/which goods or services offered on the market are intended, or who/which makes use of these goods or services, provided that this individual or legal entity constitutes the end recipient of the goods or services.[1728] HUNGARY also applies its legislation to both natural and legal persons acting as contracting party outside his/her economic or professional activities.[1729] LATVIA has broadened the definition slightly by including any natural person who is expressing his/her desire to buy, buying or could buy goods or use services for the purposes, which are not related to his/her business or professional activities.[1730] The law in LITHUANIA[1731] does not use the term "consumer" but "buyer" in the Civil Code; in the Law on Consumer Protection, a slightly wider definition of "consumer" can be found: any natural person who expresses an intention to buy, buys and uses goods or services for his personal, family or household needs not related to business or profession.[1732]

MALTA deals with the issue of goods being transferred to another person after they have been bought by including in the definition of consumer a subsequent owner or beneficiary of the goods who has been expressly or tacitly authorized or permitted by the consumer – being the 'original' purchaser of the goods – and who has consumed or benefited from the goods provided to the consumer by the trader. Moreover the Consumer Affairs Act also empowers

1721 Article 2 of the Certain Aspects of the Sale of Consumer Goods and Associated Guarantees Law.
1722 Section (3) of the Sale of Goods Act 1980.
1723 Article1 para. (1)/(2) of the Consumer Protection Law.
1724 CC Art. 52(2).
1725 Article 4 para (a) of the Consolidated Act.
1726 Chapter 1(4) of the Consumer Protection Act.
1727 CC Art.13.
1728 Article 1(4)(a) of the Law on Consumer Protection.
1729 CC Art. 685 lit. (d).
1730 Article 1(1), sent. 3 of the Consumer Rights Protection Law.
1731 CC Art. 6.350(1).
1732 Article 2(1) of the Law on Consumer Protection.

the Minister responsible for consumer affairs after consultation with the Consumer affairs Council to extend the definition of 'consumer' to other classes or categories of persons.[1733]

POLAND does not use the term "consumer" but instead "buyer", which is defined as a physical person buying goods for a purpose not related to professional or economic activity.[1734] In PORTUGAL, a consumer is a person who receives goods or services not for professional use from a person who is professionally or commercially active with a view to economic gain.[1735]

SLOVAKIA also deals with subsequent owners of the goods, albeit in a limited manner, by defining consumer as a "natural person buying products or services for personal use, including for members of that person's household".[1736]

In SLOVENIA, a person has to be acting "outside his profession or profit-making activity".[1737]

SPAIN relies on its general definition, which includes legal persons, but beneficiary has to be the final recipient of the goods; moreover, there is no reference that the person must be acting for purposes not related to his trade; instead, the law excludes from the definition of "consumer" those who are not final recipients of the goods, and acquire or use these with the aim of integrating them in production, transformation, commercialisation processes.[1738] The legislation in SWEDEN applies where goods are purchased mainly for non-professional purposes.[1739]

In the UNITED KINGDOM, there are two definitions: the first is found in the Unfair Contract Terms Act 1977 and provides a definition of consumer for the purposes of the legislation on the sale and supply of goods ("dealing as consumer": person not acting in the course of a business contracting with a person acting in the course of a business; in the case of legal persons, goods must be ordinarily supplied for private use);[1740] the second only applies in respect of the provisions implementing Art. 6 on guarantees ("any natural person who is acting for purposes which are outside his trade, business or profession").[1741] Both definitions are wider than those under the Directive.

FRANCE does not have a specific definition of "consumer", relying instead on case-law developments. The main criterion in order to decide whether a transaction falls within the scope of consumer legislation is that there must be no link between the contract and the professional activity of the buyer.

1733 Article 2 of the Consumer Affairs Act.

1734 Article 1(1) of the Act on detailed terms and conditions of consumer sales and on the amendment of the Civil Code.

1735 Article 1(1) of the Decree-Law 67/2003.

1736 Article 2(1)(a) of the Act on Consumer Protection.

1737 Article 1(2) of the Consumer Protection Act.

1738 Article 1(3) of the Law on guarantees in the sale of consumer goods.

1739 Article 1(4) of the Consumer Purchase Act.

1740 Section 12 of the Unfair Contract Terms Act.

1741 Regulation 2 of the Sale and Supply of Goods to Consumers Regulations 2002.

Definition of "consumer" as in Directive	Variation on definition of "consumer"	No specific transposition
BE, CY, EE, IE, IT, LU, NL *(7)*	AT, CZ, DK, FI, DE, EL, HU, LV, LT, MT, PL, PT, SK,SL, ES, SE, UK *(17)*	FR *(1)*

3. Definition of 'seller'

A seller is "any natural or legal person who, under a contract, sells consumer goods in the course of his trade, business or profession" (Art. 1(2)(c)). No specific transposition was made in AUSTRIA. Those who apply the definition of "seller" are BELGIUM (omitting "under a contract"), CYPRUS, DENMARK, FRANCE, GREECE, IRELAND, LATVIA, LUXEMBOURG, NETHERLANDS, SPAIN and SWEDEN.

In respect of BELGIUM, it should be noted that the Explanatory Note of the Consumer Sales Act cross-refers to the concept of 'seller' in the Trade Practices Act that includes non-profit associations. It remains unclear whether the definition of seller in the Consumer Sales Act also includes such associations, although there is a general tendency in Belgian law to interpret the definition of 'seller' broadly.

Again, variations exist in many countries. In the CZECH REPUBLIC, a "seller" is "a person acting within the framework of its commercial and other business activity".[1742] ESTONIA also uses the term "trader".[1743] FINLAND has a more detailed definition which includes a natural person as well as a private or a public legal person, who, in order to gain income or other economic interest, offers, sells or other provides consumer goods for payment.[1744] GERMANY includes associations etc. not pursuing an activity for economic gain.[1745] In GREECE, the definition also includes public enterprises.[1746]

HUNGARY has not defined "seller", but the definition of "consumer contract" refers to the consumer's contracting party as a person acting within scope of his economic or professional activities.[1747] In ITALY, public legal persons included.[1748] In LITHUANIA, a seller is a person selling goods on premises intended for business purposes or outside them,[1749] or a person engaged in trade.[1750]

1742 CC Art. 52(2).

1743 Article 2(2) of the Consumer Protection Act.

1744 Chapter 1 (5) of the Consumer Protection Act.

1745 CC Art. 14.

1746 Article 1 (3) of the Law 2251/1994.

1747 CC Art. 685(3).

1748 Article 128(2)(b) of the Consumer Code: "any natural or legal, public or private person who, under a contract ... sells consumer goods in the course of his trade, business or profession".

1749 Article 2(2) of the Law on Consumer Protection of Lithuania.

1750 CC Art. 6.350(1).

MALTA also utilises definition of "trader" from the Maltese Commercial Code; moreover, the Minister for Consumer Affairs can designate any other person or category of persons as a "trader".[1751]

In POLAND, there is no specific definition, but legislation applies to sales conducted "in the course of business". PORTUGAL also no express definition, but it follows from the definition of consumer that a seller is a person who is professionally or commercially active with a view to economic gain and provides goods and services.

In SLOVENIA, the contract need not fall within seller's commercial activity.[1752] This is also the case, in some instances, in the UNITED KINGDOM, where any seller (including private individuals) are caught for some purposes; mainly, however, the law applies where a seller is selling in the course of a business, although the goods sold need not be the goods usually sold by that seller.[1753]

In SLOVAKIA the definition of seller (an entrepreneur who sells products or provides services to a consumer),[1754] relies on the general definition of 'entrepreneur' in Art. 2(2) of the Slovakian Commercial Code.

Definition of "seller" as in Directive	Variation on definition of "seller"	No specific transposition
BE,[1755] CY, DK, FR, EL, IE, LV, LU, NL, ES, SE *(11)*	CZ, FI, DE, EE, IT, LT, MT, SK, SL, UK *(10)*	AT, HU,[1756] PL, PT *(4)*

4. Definition of 'consumer goods'

"Consumer goods" are "any tangible movable item, with the exception of goods sold by way of execution or otherwise by authority of law; water and gas where they are not put up for sale in a limited volume or set quantity; and electricity" (Art. 1 para. (2) lit. (b)). Those who apply the same definition of "goods" are BELGIUM, CYPRUS, FRANCE, HUNGARY,[1757] IRELAND, LUXEMBOURG, POLAND, and SWEDEN.

Variations exist in many member states. In particular, a number have not made use of the specific exclusions listed in Art. 1(2)(b): DENMARK, ESTONIA,[1758] FINLAND,[1759] GERMANY (which also includes water and gas supplied through the mains),[1760] LATVIA,[1761] MALTA

1751 Article 2 of the Consumer Affairs Act.

1752 Article1(3) of the Consumer Protection Act.

1753 Section 12 of the Unfair Contract Terms Act, and the CA judgment in *Stevenson v Rogers* [1999] 1 All ER 613.

1754 Article 2 para. (1) lit. (b) and para. (3) of the Act on Consumer Protection.

1755 Omitting only "under a contract".

1756 Definition implicit in notion of "consumer contract".

1757 CC Art. 685(e).

1758 Article 2(3) of the Consumer Protection Act.

1759 Chapter 1 Art. 3 Consumer Protection Act.

1760 CC Art. 90 and Art. 474(1).

1761 Article 1(1), sent. 6 of theConsumer Rights Protection Law .

("any tangible moveable item of property"),[1762] PORTUGAL (which also extends the law to immovables),[1763] and SLOVAKIA (includes electricity and gas supplied to consumers).[1764] Initially, the legislation in ITALY did not include a reference to 'tangible' and therefore the legislation extended to intangible goods, but this was changed and the definition now only applies to tangible goods, whether or not they need to be assembled. [1765] In LITHUANIA, there are no exclusions from the definition of goods itself;[1766] however, the provision of water, electricity and gas is excluded from the relevant parts of the Consumer Protection Act,[1767] and the practical effect is to follow the definition of the Directive. NETHERLANDS defines goods only as tangibles,[1768] although the rules concerning tangible goods can be applied to non-tangible goods to the extent that this is possible.[1769] SLOVENIA has adopted a broader definition of goods and does not define consumer goods separately. SPAIN has added a reference that the goods must be "aimed at the private consumer".[1770] The UNITED KINGDOM relies on the existing general definition of "goods", which is broader.[1771] No specific transposition was undertaken in AUSTRIA, because the relevant law applies to all types of goods. In GREECE, a broader definition can be found.[1772] There also appears to be no definition of "consumer goods" in the law of the CZECH REPUBLIC.

Definition of "consumer goods" as in Directive	Variation on definition of "consumer goods"	No specific transposition
BE, CY, FR, HU, IE, LT,[1773] LU, PL, SE *(9)*	CZ, DK, DE, EE, FI, IT, LV, MT, NL, PT, SK, SL, UK *(13)*	AT, EL, CZ *(3)*

a. Exclusion of goods sold at public auction from the meaning of "consumer goods" (Art. 1 para. (3))

Article 1 para. (3) of the Directive permits member states to exclude from the definition of "consumer goods" second-hand goods sold at public auction which individuals have the opportunity of attending in person. SPAIN has introduced a more limited exclusion, referring only to "administrative auctions".[1774] In the UNITED KINGDOM, this option has been exercised, not by amending the definition of "goods", but rather by modifying the definition of

1762 Article 72(1) of the Consumer Affairs Act.
1763 Article 1(2) of the Decree Law 67/2003.
1764 Article 2(1) (f) of the Act on Consumer Protection.
1765 Article 128(2)(a) of the Consumer Code.
1766 Article 2(5) of the Law of Consumer Protection).
1767 Article 1(2) of the Law of Consumer Protection.
1768 CC Book 7, Art. 5(1) and Book 3, Art. 2.
1769 CC Art. 7:48.
1770 Article 1(2), sent. 2 of the Law on guarantees in the sale of goods for consumers.
1771 Section 61(1) of the Sale of Goods Act 1979.
1772 Article 6(2), sent. 2/3 of the Consumer Protection Law.
1773 Note text above.
1774 Article 2(1), sent. 2 of the Law on guarantees in the sale of goods for consumers.

"dealing as consumer", and a natural person (individual) will now not regarded as dealing as a consumer in these circumstances.[1775]

Other countries, which have made use of this option, are FINLAND, FRANCE, GERMANY, GREECE and HUNGARY. SWEDEN had already established the position that auction sales where the consumer is present would be "as is" sales, giving rise to no conformity obligation, and this position continues to exist. It can therefore be said that Sweden also falls into the category of countries, which provide for this exception.

However, most countries have not exercised this option (AUSTRIA, BELGIUM, CYPRUS, CZECH REPUBLIC, DENMARK, ESTONIA, IRELAND, ITALY (but the prior usage of the goods must be taken into account and faults resulting from the normal use of the goods ('wear and tear') are excluded),[1776] LATVIA, LITHUANIA, LUXEMBOURG, MALTA, NETHERLANDS, POLAND, PORTUGAL, SLOVAKIA, and SLOVENIA)

Option in Art. 1 para. (3) used	Option in Art. 1 para. (3) not used
FI, FR, DE, HU, EL, ES,[1777] SE, UK[1778] *(8)*	AT, BE, CY, CZ, DK, EE, IE, IT, LV, LT, LU, MT, NL, PL, PT, SK, SV *(17)*

5. Definition of 'sale'

There is no complete definition of sale, although contracts involving the "supply of consumer goods to be manufactured or produced" are also treated as contracts of sale for the purposes of the Directive (Art. 1(4)). Many countries have employed the extended notion of "sale" relying on Art. 1(4), and give effect to this in their jurisdiction.

The provision in Art. 1 para. (4) produced specific amendments in DENMARK (previously limited to instances where seller supplied predominant part of materials), FINLAND, and PORTUGAL (work & materials, and hire). In ESTONIA, the definition of "contract of sale" includes contracts for goods to be manufactured or produced, unless the person to whom the finished item is to be supplied provides a substantial part of the materials necessary for the manufacture/production.[1779] In the latter case, the contract will be regarded as one for works. This appears to be narrower than the Directive; however, it should be noted that the Estonian legislation applicable to works contracts (services) contains corresponding provisions on conformity and remedies to those applicable to contracts of sale. The relevant provision of the CZECH legislation also seems narrower, referring only to contracts of sale or work & materials, but not stating clearly that goods to be produced are included;[1780] how-

[1775] Section 12(2) Unfair Contract Terms Act. A legal person will not be regarded as a consumer where the goods in question are sold by auction or competitive tender, irrespective of whether the goods are second-hand or whether there was an opportunity to attend "in person" (presumably by sending a representative).

[1776] Article 128(3) of the Consumer Code.

[1777] Limited use made of this option.

[1778] Option exercised by restricting the definition of "consumer", rather than "goods".

[1779] Article 208 of the Law of Obligations Act.

[1780] CC Art. 52.

ever, no evidence of practical problems resulting from this difference is available.[1781] GREECE appears to have made an oversight in its transposing legislation and has not amended relevant parts of the Civil Code to reflect the requirements of this provision. This provision was not transposed separately in LITHUANIA; however, the general definition of consumer goods already includes goods to be manufactured and there is consequently no gap in Lithuanian law in this regard.[1782] The same is true of LATVIA. In MALTA, there is no specific definition of 'sale', with the Consumer Affairs Act requiring traders to deliver goods in conformity with the contract of sale.[1783] In POLAND, this wider notion of sale posed one of the greatest difficulties in the transposition process; eventually, the Civil Code was amended to ensure that this provision is given adequate effect.[1784] In SLOVENIA, the Consumer Protection Act also applies to consumer services insofar as possible,[1785] and therefore no separate transposition of Art. 1 para. (4) has been made. The UNITED KINGDOM has not changed its definition of sale, but has amended legislation that might apply in the circumstances subject to Art. 1 para. (4) to ensure uniform application of the new rules.

III. Consumer protection instruments

1. Conformity with the contract

In this section, the main aspects regarding the transposition of Art. 2 of the Directive will be examined.

a. "Conformity with the contract" requirement in general (Art. 2)

aa. Requirement to deliver conforming goods

The basic requirement is that the seller must deliver goods which are in conformity with the contract (Art. 2(1)), given effect to accordingly in many member states (BELGIUM, CYPRUS, CZECH REPUBLIC, DENMARK (supplementing existing rules), ESTONIA, FINLAND (relies on existing general test), FRANCE, HUNGARY, IRELAND, ITALY, POLAND, SLOVENIA, SPAIN, and SWEDEN). The UNITED KINGDOM refers to "conformity" only in the context of the new remedies, but also uses a negative expression.[1786] There is, however, no general conformity requirement in UK law (see below).

1781 See also CC Art. 588.

1782 CC Article 6.306(1) provides that things which form the subject matter of a contract of purchase-sale may be "either existing things, owned or possessed by the seller, or things to be manufactured or acquired by the seller in future ...".

1783 Article 73(1) of the Consumer Protection Act. CC Art. 1346 et seq. specifically defines the sale as a contract whereby one of the contracting parties binds himself to transfer to the other a thing for a price, which the latter binds himself to pay to the former.

1784 See Article 14 para. (3)-(5) of the Act on specific terms and conditions in consumer sales.

1785 Article 38 of the Consumer Protection Act.

1786 Section 48F Sale of Goods Act 1979.

bb. Presumption of conformity

The majority of those member states, which have given effect to Art. 2, have adopted the presumption that goods are in conformity if they meet the criteria specified in Art. 2(2). However, a number of countries have chosen to express this requirement in a negative way, i.e., goods are presumed not to be in conformity unless they meet the criteria stated. This is the case in GREECE, NETHERLANDS, PORTUGAL and SLOVENIA.

AUSTRIA does not express its implementing provision in terms of a "presumption", but does otherwise include the factors from Art. 2(2).[1787] The law in FRANCE is also not expressed in terms of a presumption; rather, there is a requirement that in order for goods to be in conformity with the contract, they must be fit for their usual purpose, and correspond to any characteristics individually negotiated.[1788] Rather than stating that there is a presumption that the goods are in conformity with the contract if they comply with the requisites as state in Art. 2(2) of the Directive, the law in MALTA requires the trader to ensure that the goods conform with such requisites.[1789] Similarly, the NETHERLANDS does not use presumptions, and requires a buyer to prove (i) the parties' agreement regarding the goods; (ii) what he could expect from the goods; (iii) what has been shown as a sample or model; and that the goods do not correspond to these matters.[1790]

cc. Criteria for presuming conformity (Art. 2 para. (2) lit. (a)-(d) generally)

Conformity is presumed if the goods correspond with the requirements of Art. 2(2). Again, member states have generally transposed the criteria giving rise to this presumption, although there is greater variation.

GERMANY did not transpose the aspects of "conformity" in Art. 2(2) verbatim, nor did it follow the general approach. Instead, the starting point for establishing conformity is the express agreement as to quality reached between the parties.[1791] Only where there is no express agreement do the criteria corresponding to Art. 2(2) of the Directive come into play. Moreover, in that list, "descriptions" are restricted to those given only by the seller, and sales by sample or model are not listed expressly. Finally, the criteria are not regarded as cumulative, but are ranked in priority instead. This arrangement may conflict with the requirements of the Directive.

In LITHUANIA, there is no reference to the ways how the seller, the producer or his representative could make public statements - particularly in advertising or on labelling. In the CZECH REPUBLIC, no reference is made to sample or model in the national legislation, nor is there any mention of description given by the seller, or the purpose for which the consumer requires the goods, as aspects of conformity.

1787 CC Art. 922.

1788 Article L. 211-5 of the Consumer Code.

1789 Article 73(1) of the Consumer Code.

1790 CC Book 7 Art. 9, Art. 17(1).

1791 CC Art. 434(1), sent. 1.

Whilst IRELAND has implemented Art. 2 para. (2) as per the Directive, under the general sale of goods legislation other factors are enumerated in the legislation, or have been identified by case law. For example, section 14(3) of the Sale of Goods Act 1893 refers to goods being fit for the purpose or purposes for which goods of that kind are commonly bought and as durable as it is reasonable to expect having regard to any description applied to them, the price (if relevant) and all the other relevant circumstances. Based on case law,. "other relevant circumstances' has been held to include resale price, relative incidence of repairs, and cosmetic defects. Further, safety in relation to motor vehicles is expressly addressed by the legislation.[1792] In SLOVAKIA, there appears to be no reference to the "conformity" requirement as such; instead, goods must be of "usual quality".[1793] To this, the Civil Code adds that goods must correspond with the seller's description, and also possess the quality stipulated by the contract or legal regulations.[1794] In SPAIN, all 4 elements are considered except where one is inapplicable in the circumstances of the particular case. In LATVIA, Art. 2(2)(b) has been transposed with the addition of a proviso that this factor will not be relevant where there was not reasonable for the consumer to rely on the specific competence and opinion of the seller.[1795]

Some member states have added additional factors. Thus, in CYPRUS, aspects of the quality of goods include the availability of spare parts, accessories and specialised technicians, where required; safety; reasonable durability in time and use; appearance and finish; and the non-existence of defects. The implementing provision in LUXEMBOURG expressly refers, as an additional criterion, to "characteristics agreed between the parties".[1796] DENMARK includes "durability" and "proper packaging" in the list of relevant factors.[1797] In addition, it provides that there is a lack of conformity if the seller neglected on his own initiative to give the consumer information relevant to the consumer's assessment of the goods and which the seller knew or should have been aware of.[1798] In ESTONIA, "proper packaging" is also a relevant factor, and when goods are not packaged in a way that would be usual for such goods, or in a manner inadequate to preserve and protect the goods, there will be a lack of conformity with the contract.[1799] Packaging which is proper in relation to the goods concerned is also a relevant factor in SWEDEN. FINLAND also makes packaging a relevant factor, if proper packaging is necessary to preserve or protect the goods; in addition, specific requirements imposed by law regarding the characteristics of the goods can be a relevant factor, except where the buyer intended to use the goods for a purpose where such requirements are of no significance.[1800]

HUNGARY provides a more detailed list of factors, and an additional requirement is that the supplier of goods has to mark these suitably for identification, and provide all the necessary information and instructions for proper use, in accordance with the provisions of legal regulations and professional standards.[1801]

1792 Section 13 of the Sale of Goods Act 1980.

1793 Article 3(c) of the Act on Consumer Protection.

1794 CC Art. 496.

1795 Article 14(1), sent. 3 of the Consumer Rights Protection Law.

1796 Article 4 lit. (a) of the Consumer Sales Law.

1797 Article 75a(2) of the Consolidated Act on Sale of Goods.

1798 Article 76(1) of the Consolidated Act on Sale of Goods.

1799 Article 217(1),(2) sub-para. (5) of the Law of Obligations Act.

1800 Article 5:12 of the Consumer Protection Act.

1801 CC Art.277.

In POLAND, a distinction is made between two situations: (i) where qualities of the goods are individually negotiated; and (ii) other transactions. In the first case, a presumption of conformity arises where the goods correspond with the seller's description or a sample shown to the buyer, as well as where the goods are fit for the purposes stated by the buyer before conclusion of the contract (unless the seller explained that this purpose was not possible).[1802] In the latter case, goods are presumed to conform if they are fit for normal purpose and have the qualities common for goods of the same type; they comply with expectations concerning this type of goods based on public statements by the seller, producer or his representative, as well as labeling or advertising.[1803]

The UNITED KINGDOM does not have an identical list of factors, but takes corresponding items into account. There is a requirement that where goods are sold with reference to a description, they must correspond with this description (limited by case-law to essential commercial characteristics which a buyer might rely upon),[1804] and by sample, for this to be relevant. The main test is that "goods must be of satisfactory quality".[1805] There is then a list of factors that may be considered: (a) fitness for all the purposes for which goods of the kind in question are commonly supplied; (b) appearance and finish; (c) freedom from minor defects; (d) safety; and (e) durability. The satisfactory quality test does not make reference to "performance" of the goods, but can be interpreted in line with the Directive. There is also no reference to installation instructions, although, again, case-law indicates that shortcomings in installation instructions could be considered as a relevant circumstance.

dd. Time at which conformity is assessed

Article 2 para. (1) requires that goods must be in conformity with the contract when they are delivered by the seller. The majority of the member states have adopted this provision, but there are variations in some countries.

It is noteworthy that GREEK law assesses whether goods are in conformity with the contract at the time risk passes from seller to buyer.[1806] In POLAND, the relevant time is the time of delivery (i.e., the time of transfer of possession from the seller to the buyer), rather than the time of concluding the contract,[1807] as is the case in LUXEMBOURG.[1808] The position is similar in the UNITED KINGDOM, although the law was amended to equate passing of risk with the time of delivery.[1809] In HUNGARY, the "time of performance" is regarded as the relevant time.[1810]

[1802] Article 4(2) of the Conditions of Consumer Sales.

[1803] Article 4(3) of the Conditions of Consumer Sales.

[1804] Section 13(1) of the Sale of Goods Act 1979.

[1805] Section 14(2) of the Sale of Goods Act 1979.

[1806] CC Art. 522.

[1807] Article 7 Act of 27 July 2002 on specific terms and conditions of consumer sale and amendments to the Civil Code.

[1808] Article 4, sent 2-3 of the Consumer Sales Act.

[1809] Section 20(4) and 32(4) of the Sale of Goods Act 1979.

[1810] CC Art. 305(1).

b. Public Statements and exclusions (Art. 2 para. (2) lit. (d) and Art. 2 para. (4))

A particular factor in the Directive is that public statements regarding the goods can be taken into account in assessing their conformity, although the seller can escape liability in a number of defined circumstances.

This provision was new to many member states. Both the main requirement and the seller's defences have been transposed in accordance with the Directive in most of the member states (although not in the CZECH REPUBLIC). In respect of Germany, which has transposed this provision as required, it should be noted that "public statements" are ranking lower in priority than other factors in establishing conformity with the contract. In the UNITED KINGDOM, these provisions were transposed by making public statements a "relevant circumstance" for considering whether goods meet the statutory standard of "satisfactory quality".

Article 2 para. (4) provides for three circumstances when a seller will not be liable for public statements made by another person in the distribution chain. This has been implemented by most member states.[1811] The implementation of Art. 2(2)(d) and Art. 2(4) in the CZECH REPUBLIC seems to be only partial, and none of the exclusions from Art. 2(4) appear in the legislation.[1812]

Those which have not transposed Art. 2(4) are LATVIA, LITHUANIA, PORTUGAL and SLOVENIA. In LITHUANIA, the justification for this appears to be that it increases consumer protection. Similarly, SLOVENIAN law does not provide an express rule by which the seller could evade liability in these circumstances.

In LUXEMBOURG, only the first situation (seller could not reasonably have been aware of the statement) is mentioned. The two other factors (seller not bound by public statements if, by the time of conclusion of the contract the statement had been corrected, or the decision to buy the consumer goods could not have been influenced by the statement), are not mentioned.[1813] The same is true of FRANCE[1814] and GREECE.[1815] In contrast, DENMARK imposes liability on the seller even when he did not know and could not reasonably have been aware of the statement.[1816] In ITALY, the exclusions may be narrower than under the Directive, because the consumer must have been aware that a public statement had been corrected at the time the contract was made.[1817]

[1811] In SLOVAKIA, this appears to be contained in Art.8 para 4 of the Act on Advertising.

[1812] CC Art. 616(2).

[1813] Article 3, sent. 3 of the Consumer Sales Act.

[1814] Article L. 211-6 of the Code de la Consommation.

[1815] CC Art. 535(4).

[1816] Article 76(1) of the Consolidated Act on Sale of Goods.

[1817] Article 129(4) of the Consumer Code.

c. Exclusion of matters of which consumer is aware (Art. 2 para. (3))

Again, this has been transposed as required in many member states (BELGIUM, CYPRUS, DENMARK, ESTONIA, FINLAND, FRANCE, GERMANY,[1818] GREECE, HUNGARY, IRELAND, ITALY, LATVIA, MALTA, NETHERLANDS, PORTUGAL, SLOVAKIA, SLOVENIA, SPAIN, and SWEDEN[1819]).

This provision has not been transposed expressly in AUSTRIA. In respect of manufacturing contracts, it is provided that where the customer has provided materials that are clearly unsuitable, or has given instructions that are clearly incorrect, the supplier is not liable for the damage provided that he has warned the customer about this problem.[1820] Moreover, the existing provision in CC Art. 928 excludes "obvious shortcomings"[1821] from the scope of the seller's liability, except where there has been fraudulent concealment of the shortcoming, or an express confirmation that this shortcoming is not present in the goods. It has been argued that this should extend to matters known to the buyer before conclusion of the contract.[1822] This provision does not appear to be less favorable to a consumer than the Directive, and so this approach seems unproblematic. In the CZECH REPUBLIC, there is no mention of matters of which the consumer "could not reasonably be unaware", and the final sentence of this paragraph is transposed by stating that the lack of conformity was caused by the consumer.[1823] In HUNGARY, if a recipient of goods (including a consumer) has accepted performance whilst aware of a breach, a subsequent claim based on that breach is precluded except where the right to do so has been expressly retained.[1824]

In LITHUANIA, the reference to a lack of conformity having its origin in materials supplied by consumer has been omitted.[1825] A more restricted exclusion operates in the UNITED KINGDOM, where matters, which would mean that goods are not of "satisfactory quality",[1826] are not considered if the (consumer) buyer inspected the goods and that inspection ought to have revealed the problem, or which were specifically drawn to the buyer's attention before the contract was made. This approach is more favourable towards a consumer. It also only applies with regard to "satisfactory quality", but does not apply to compliance with description or sample, nor fitness for particular purposes.

1818 German law may have a shortcoming: if Art. 2 para. (3) is intended to be applied objectively, then CC Art. 442 para. (1), referring to "unawareness caused by gross negligence" is inadequate for utilising a subjective test. This may, however, not lead to substantial differences in practice.

1819 Article 17(1), Art. 19(3) Consumer Purchase Act.

1820 CC Art. 1168a, sent. 3.

1821 "Mängel, die in die Augen fallen" – transl. roughly as "faults apparent to the naked eye".

1822 M.*Gruber*, "Die Umsetzung der Verbrauchsgüterkaufrichtlinie in Österreich", in M.Schermaier (ed.), Verbraucherkauf in Europa (Munich: Sellier, 2003), p.154.

1823 CC Art.616(3).

1824 CC Art.316.

1825 Article 6.327(2) of the Civil Code.

1826 The "satisfactory quality" criterion is only one of the aspects of conformity, broadly corresponding to Art 2.2(d).

d. Provision on goods to be installed (Art. 2 para. (5))

Under the Directive, the installation of goods is part of a contract of sale and incorrect installation can mean that goods are not in conformity with the contract.

Most member states have transposed these requirements in accordance with the Directive (AUSTRIA, BELGIUM, CZECH REPUBLIC, CYPRUS, DENMARK, ESTONIA, FINLAND, FRANCE, GERMANY, HUNGARY, IRELAND, ITALY, LATVIA, LUXEMBOURG, MALTA, NETHERLANDS, POLAND, PORTUGAL and SWEDEN). In LATVIA,[1827] there is an additional condition regarding installation instructions: goods will also be presumed not to be in conformity with the contract where the installation instructions have not been provided in the official language (i.e., Latvian) and the installation by the consumer has rendered the goods non-conforming. The same is the case in CYPRUS.

LITHUANIA has not introduced a specific rule in this regard, nor have SLOVENIA AND SLOVAKIA. In SLOVENIA, it is possible that the Consumer Protection Act will also cover this situation under the provisions dealing with services, but the situation is insufficiently clear to confirm that this would be so. SPAIN does not include part of Art. 2(5) (product intended to be installed by consumer). In GREECE, incorrect installation itself can give rise to liability on the seller, even if this has not caused a non-conformity.[1828] The UNITED KINGDOM does not refer to inadequate installation instructions (although it is possible that case-law could take this into account when applying the "satisfactory quality" test; there is case-law in respect of safety guidelines and user instructions), and incorrect installation is dealt with under sec. 13 of the Supply of Goods and Services Act 1982, requiring the seller or his representative to have acted without reasonable care before a consumer is entitled to complain of a lack of conformity (see definition of non-conformity in s 11 S).

2. Consumers' rights in cases of non-conformity

a. Consumers' rights in cases of non-conformity in general (Art. 3)

Article 3 states the remedies which are to be available to a consumer where there is a lack of conformity in the goods. Initially, the consumer's choice is between repair and replacement; however, where these are impossible, or cannot be provided within a reasonable time or without significant inconvenience to a consumer, it is possible to ask for price reduction or (in the case of non-minor lacks of conformity) rescission of the contract.

aa. Implementation of the remedies

All the member states now provide for the remedies in Art. 3 of the Directive. That provision has been transposed as required in many member states, although in some countries, there are variations. These are highlighted below.

[1827] Article 28(5) Consumer Rights Protection Act.

[1828] CC Art. 536(1).

bb. Consumer choice between remedies

Art. 3 envisages that a consumer has an initial choice only as between repair and replacement, followed by price reduction or rescission. This approach has been implemented in AUSTRIA, BELGIUM, CZECH REPUBLIC, CYPRUS, DENMARK, ESTONIA, FINLAND, FRANCE, GERMANY, HUNGARY, IRELAND, ITALY, MALTA, NETHERLANDS, POLAND, SLOVAKIA, SPAIN, SWEDEN and the UNITED KINGDOM.[1829] In both IRELAND and the UNITED KINGDOM, a consumer has the choice between invoking the remedies under the national legislation transposing Art. 3, or to rely on the remedies available under general sale of goods legislation.

A different solution was adopted in LATVIA. Here, a consumer has a choice between all 4 remedies initially; however, once 6 months from the date of concluding the contract of sale have elapsed, the hierarchy envisaged under Art. 3 of the Directive is applicable.[1830] In GERMANY, it seems that a consumer is not able to ask for a price reduction where a repair or replacement was provided only with significant inconvenience to the consumer. GREECE does not follow the hierarchical structure of Art. 3, instead making all the remedies available alongside one another. Also, in LITHUANIA and PORTUGAL, a consumer has a free choice among all 4 remedies. Similarly, in SLOVENIA, a consumer can choose between all 4 remedies, although rescission is not available unless a seller has at least had a reasonable time to effect repair or replacement.

b. The "disproportionality" criterion (Art. 3 para. (3))

Article 3(3) applies a proportionality element to consider whether a particular remedy is available. It is not entirely clear whether this applies only to an assessment as between "repair" and "replacement", or also permits a consideration of price reduction/rescission.[1831]

Most countries have transposed the requirement as per the Directive, without further clarifying the scope of this criterion (AUSTRIA, BELGIUM, CYPRUS, DENMARK, ESTONIA, FRANCE, HUNGARY, IRELAND, ITALY, MALTA, SLOVAKIA, SPAIN, and SWEDEN). In CYPRUS, it may be inferred from the national legislation transposing the Directive that it applies this test only between repair and replacement.

The transposition in GERMANY applies the test only as between repair and replacement. In the CZECH REPUBLIC, the test applies only between repair and replacement, but the criteria for establishing whether a remedy is not proportionate have not been included in domestic legislation. The UNITED KINGDOM states expressly that price reduction/rescission can also be comparator remedies. In the NETHERLANDS, a different wording from Art. 3(3) has been used, which does seem to permit a broader comparison. In LUXEMBOURG, a variation to the

---

1829 Note that in the UNITED KINGDOM, provisions to implement Art. 3 were introduced as Part 5A of the Sale of Goods Act 1979, but these operate alongside the existing rules which *int.al.* grant a consumer a right to terminate the contract if he does so within a reasonable time of delivery.

1830 Article 28(1)-(3) of the Consumer Rights Protection Act.

1831 See *Twigg-Flesner*, "English Sales Law After the Implementation of Directive 99/44/EC on Consumer Sales – Back to the Drawing Board?" (2003) 1 Gemeinschaftsprivatrecht 12-21; cf. *Bianca*, "Artikel 3" in Grundmann & Bianca (eds.), EU-Kaufrechtsrichtlinie: Kommentar (Schmidt, 2002).

test has been adopted, according to which a seller is obliged to bring goods into conformity with the contract unless this is impossible or disproportionate.[1832] The consumer has the choice between repair or replacement unless one of them would cause excessive burden to the seller if compared to the other. It is not immediately clear if this is less favourable to consumers than the Directive itself. The transposition in FINLAND does not appear to use the phrase "disproportionate", referring instead to "unreasonable costs" for the seller as a bar to requesting a particular remedy.[1833] However, this is not a serious flaw, because "disproportionality" is defined in Art. 3(3) of the Directive in the terms adopted by the Finnish legislation, and there is consequently no substantive difference from the Directive. POLAND also mentions only the criteria for establishing disproportionality, rather than the term itself.

No express transposition was made in LATVIA and LITHUANIA. PORTUGAL and SLOVENIA do not include the proportionality test, either. There is no transposition in GREECE (following from its decision not to arrange the remedies in a hierarchical order), although this criterion can be inferred from CC Art. 540(1)(1).[1834]

ba. Impossibility

The Member States have generally included the "impossibility" criterion in their domestic legislation. However, in SLOVENIA, the right to either remedy is not restricted at all on the basis of "impossibility".

c. "Free of charge" (Art. 3 para. (4))

A remedy has to be provided free of charge, and the seller has to bear the cost of postage, labour and materials, as well as other relevant costs. This definition has been transposed using the same criteria as the Directive in AUSTRIA, BELGIUM, CYPRUS, DENMARK, ESTONIA, FINLAND, FRANCE, GERMANY, HUNGARY, IRELAND, ITALY, MALTA, POLAND, PORTUGAL, SLOVAKIA,[1835] SPAIN, SWEDEN,[1836] and UNITED KINGDOM. No express transposition was made in LITHUANIA.

In the CZECH REPUBLIC, the reference is only to "free of charge", without further elaboration.[1837] THE NETHERLANDS do not spell out the matters covered by "free of charge". The same is the case in GREECE, where the law uses the phrase "without any cost to the consumer" instead.[1838] FRANCE states that a remedy must be provided "without any cost to the buyer".[1839] In SLOVENIA, the rule is that the consumer is entitled to reimbursement of his

---

[1832] Article 5(2) of the Consumer Sales Act.

[1833] Chapter 5 § 18 of the Consumer Protection Act.

[1834] See *Aitiologiki Ekthesi* II, 5, Mpexlivanis, Dikaio Epixeiriseon kai Etairion 2003, p 625, Fn. 43.

[1835] CC Art. 509(1) and Art. 599(2).

[1836] Article 26(3) of the Consumer Sales Act.

[1837] CC Art. 622(1).

[1838] CC Art. 540.

[1839] Article L. 211-11 of the Consumer Code.

costs.[1840] In LUXEMBOURG, it is also only stated that the remedy must be provided without charge, but the specific elements from Art. 3(4) of the Directive are not transposed.[1841] Similarly in LATVIA, where it is provided as an alternative that the consumer can be compensated for the costs incurred in eliminating the non-conformity.

A controversial issue exists in GERMANY and has become the subject of a preliminary reference to the European Court of Justice under Art. 234 EC. German law provides that a seller is entitled to an allowance for any period of use of the goods which a consumer has had before a remedy was provided ("Nutzungsentschädigung").[1842] Recital 15 admits the possibility of this practice in the case of rescission (see 'f', below). German law, however, applies this also where a consumer is entitled to a replacement. The BGH [Bundesgerichtshof] doubts whether this provision is compatible with Art. 3(4) of the Directive, according to which a remedy should be provided free of charge and has referred this question to the ECJ for a preliminary ruling.[1843]

d. Time limits on seller's liability

aa. Two-year time period

Article 5 para. (1) of the Directive specifies that a seller is liable for a lack of conformity which arises within two years of delivery. This has been transposed as per the Directive in AUSTRIA, BELGIUM, CYPRUS, CZECH REPUBLIC, DENMARK, ESTONIA, FRANCE, GERMANY, GREECE, HUNGARY, ITALY, LATVIA, LITHUANIA,[1844] LUXEMBOURG, MALTA, POLAND, PORTUGAL, SLOVAKIA, SLOVENIA, and SWEDEN.

However, in CZECH law, there is a variation depending on the type of goods being sold: for consumer goods, it is 24 months; for groceries, it is 8 days; for feedstuff, it is three weeks, and for animals it is 6 weeks.[1845]

Not all member states have introduced this particular provision. Those who have introduced different rules are FINLAND, IRELAND and the UNITED KINGDOM. Both IRELAND and the UNITED KINGDOM simply rely on the general limitation period for commencing a legal action for a breach of contract.

BELGIUM has introduced the rule, but there is an extension to this for certain types of defects (all the variations are discussed at IV.1.d, below). Moreover, on 1 September 2006, a proposal to amend the relevant Belgian legislation was presented, according to which the two-year period will start to run from the time of delivery, except where the seller has failed to inform the consumer about his legal rights. If such information is not given until later, then

---

[1840] Article 37c(2) of the Consumer Protection Act.

[1841] Article 5(2) of the Consumer Sales Act.

[1842] CC Art. 439(4), referring to CC Art.346-348.

[1843] BGH [Bundesgerichtshof], decision (Beschluss) of 16 August 2006, VIII ZR 200/05, NJW 2006, 3200.

[1844] Except where a guaranteed quality term is specified.

[1845] CC Art. 620(1).

the two-year period will not start until this information has been provided. Belgian law would therefore impose an information obligation on the seller to ensure that consumers are adequately informed of their legal rights.

SPAIN has also introduced the two-year time period,[1846] although there is also a three year limitation (prescription) period beyond which no action can be brought.[1847] THE NETHERLANDS have not implemented this period, although a general two-year limitation period applies (see IV.1.d, below).

bb. Option: reduced period for second-hand goods

Article 7 para. (1), sent. 2 provides that member states may permit the parties to the consumer sales contract to agree on a shortened period of liability for second-hand goods. This has been given effect to in AUSTRIA,[1848] BELGIUM,[1849] CZECH REPUBLIC,[1850] CYPRUS,[1851] ITALY,[1852] GERMANY,[1853] HUNGARY,[1854] LUXEMBOURG,[1855] POLAND,[1856] PORTUGAL,[1857] SLOVAKIA,[1858] SLOVENIA,[1859] SPAIN,[1860] and SWEDEN (this follows indirectly from the provision concerning the sale of goods as is, which is restricted, but where second hand goods are purchased at auction the situation is different).[1861]

MS using option in Art. 7(1)	MS not using option in Art. 7(1)
AT, BE, CZ, CY, DE, IT, HU, LU, PL, PT, SK, SL, ES, SE *(14)*	DK, EE, FI, FR, EL, IE, LV, LT, MT, NL, UK *(11)*

1846 Article 9(1) of the Law 23/2003 on consumer sales.

1847 Article 9(3) of the Law.

1848 Article 9(1), sent. 1 and 2 of the Consumer Protection Act.

1849 Article 1649*quater* (1) of the Act on the protection of consumers in respect of the sale of consumer goods.

1850 CC Art. 626(3).

1851 Article 13(2) of the the Certain Aspects of the Sale of Consumer Goods and Associated Guarantees Law.

1852 Article 134(2) of the Consumer Code.

1853 CC Art. 475(2).

1854 CC Article 308(4).

1855 Article 6(7) of the Consumer Sales Act.

1856 Article 10.1 of the Act on specific terms and conditions of consumer sale and amendments to the Civil Code.

1857 Article 5(2) of the Decree Law 67/2003.

1858 CC Art. 620(2).

1859 Article 37b(2) of the Consumer Protection Act.

1860 Article 9(1), sent 2 of the Law on Guarantees in the Sale of Goods for Consumers.

1861 Article 17 of theConsumer Purchase Act.

cc. Option: duty to notify lack of conformity within two months

Article 5 para. (2) of the Directive grants member states the option to provide that a consumer must notify a seller of a lack of conformity within a period of two months from the date on which the consumer detected this.

A majority of the member states has chosen to implement this option. They are: CYPRUS, DENMARK, ESTONIA, FINLAND, HUNGARY, ITALY, LITHUANIA, MALTA, THE NETHERLANDS, POLAND, PORTUGAL, SLOVAKIA, SLOVENIA, SPAIN, and SWEDEN.[1862]

In BELGIUM, there is no duty to notify a lack of conformity within the specific period, but the parties are able to specify a notification period, which cannot be less than two months, and may stipulate the consequences where the agreed notification period has not been complied with.[1863] Moreover, the consumer has to act within one year (even where the two-year period would not have expired by then). In DENMARK, the period starts when the consumer has actually discovered the lack of conformity. In FINLAND, the consumer has to notify the trader within a reasonable time, which will be at least two months.[1864] This restriction does not apply where the seller has been grossly negligent or has not acted in good faith.[1865] This is also the case in DENMARK. In HUNGARY, a consumer needs to inform the seller within "the shortest time permitted by the prevailing circumstances", which is deemed to have been so made if it is done within two months.[1866] In MALTA, the period starts from the point when the consumer actually discovered the non-conformity, rather than when he should have discovered it. Furthermore, it is sufficient to demonstrate compliance with this requirement if the notification to the seller is sent by judicial letter or by registered mail. In THE NETHERLANDS, notification is required within a "due period of time" after discovering the defect, which is stated to be "timely" if made within a period of two months. However, there appears to be some flexibility beyond that period in the sense that a "due time" could be more than two months.[1867]

In POLAND, the two-month notification period has been implemented. It further provides that it is sufficient to send a written statement to this effect before this period expires.[1868] In addition, the Minister of Economy together with the Minister of Agriculture, after obtaining an opinion of the Head of the Office for the Protection of Competition and Consumers, has the power to specify shorter periods for food products, considering their durability.[1869] Simi-

---

[1862] Article 23 of the Consumer Purchase Act.

[1863] CC Art.1649 *quarter* (2).

[1864] Chapter 5 Art. 16 of the Consumer Protection Act.

[1865] Chapter 5 Art. 16(2) of the Consumer Protection Act.

[1866] CC Art. 307(1).

[1867] CC Art. 7:23.

[1868] Article 9(1) of the Act of 27 July 2002 on specific terms and conditions of consumer sale and amendments to the Civil Code.

[1869] Article 9(2) of the Act of 27 July 2002 on specific terms and conditions of consumer sale and amendments to the Civil Code.

lar to Belgium, Poland also states that a consumer can only enforce his rights if he takes action within one year of discovering the lack of conformity.[1870]

In SPAIN, no sanction flows from the fact that notification has not been made within the two months required; more significantly, there is a presumption that the consumer did notify within the two-month time period, and the burden is on the seller for demonstrating that notification had, in fact, been made outside this period. In SLOVENIA, the consumer is also required to describe the defect and to enable the seller to examine the goods. In SLOVAKIA, in contrast, the consumer appears to be under an obligation to notify immediately.[1871]

Member states that have chosen not to make use of this option at all are AUSTRIA, CZECH REPUBLIC, FRANCE, GERMANY, GREECE, IRELAND, LATVIA, LUXEMBOURG and the UNITED KINGDOM.

MS using option re notification	MS not using option re notification
CY, DK, EE, FI, HU, IT, LT, MT, NL, PL, PT, SK, SL, ES, SE *(15)*	AT, BE, CZ, FR, DE, EL, IE, LV, LU, UK *(10)*

dd. Recital option: suspension of two-year period[1872]

Recital 18 provides that member states may provide for a suspension of the two-year period in Article 5(1) and any corresponding domestic limitation periods for bringing an action, where the seller attempts to repair or replace non-conforming goods, or is in negotiations with a consumer over a settlement. In BELGIUM, the period is suspended during negotiations over a remedy and whilst repair/replacement is being carried out. In FRANCE, the period is suspended only when the buyer uses the extended guarantee.[1873] In the CZECH REPUBLIC[1874] and SLOVAKIA, the period between claiming a remedy and receiving conforming goods is excluded from the two-year period. In HUNGARY, the period is suspended during the time when the goods are repaired and the consumer is unable to use them.[1875]

Under the law in MALTA, the two-year period is suspended for the duration of negotiations carried on between the trader and the consumer with a view to an amicable settlement.[1876] SPAIN has also introduced provisions to this effect, and the period is suspended where the consumer has asked for repair (from return of goods to seller until redelivery to buyer) or replacement (from requesting this until arrival of replacement goods).[1877]

1870 Article 10.2 of the Act of 27 July 2002 on specific terms and conditions of consumer sale and amendments to the Civil Code.

1871 CC Art. 599(1).

1872 Few national correspondents have reported that domestic law has adopted a specific rule in response to Recital 18.

1873 Article L. 211-16 of the Consumer Code.

1874 CC Art. 627.

1875 CC Art. 308(3).

1876 Article 78 of the Consumer Affairs Act.

1877 Note additional rules on additional periods during which new lacks of conformity may appear, as set out at IV.1.c, below.

In LATVIA, no provision has been introduced, although the practice is that the period is extended proportionally when a problem arises. In ESTONIA, there is no provision on the suspension of the two-year period; there is, however, a provision suspending the period during which a guarantee is applicable whilst a remedy is being sought under the guarantee.[1878]

ee. Presumption of non-conformity during first 6 months

Article 5(3) introduces a presumption of non-conformity at the time of delivery where a latent non-conformity manifests itself within 6 months of delivery. Most member states have transposed this rule correctly (AUSTRIA, BELGIUM,[1879] CYPRUS, CZECH REPUBLIC, DENMARK, ESTONIA, FRANCE, GERMANY, GREECE, HUNGARY, ITALY, LATVIA, LUXEMBOURG, MALTA, NETHERLANDS, SLOVAKIA, SLOVENIA, SPAIN, SWEDEN and the UNITED KINGDOM).

No transposition was undertaken in LITHUANIA. In FINLAND, the 6-month period starts with the passing of risk, rather than the time of delivery.[1880] As risk generally does not pass until delivery, this is not problematic in most cases; however, a delay in delivery for reasons attributable to a consumer may result in risk passing to him if the seller has done everything necessary to be in a position to effect delivery.[1881]

In LUXEMBOURG, POLAND and SLOVENIA, there is no mention of the restriction in Art. 5(3) that the presumption does not apply where this would be incompatible with the nature of the goods or the nature of the lack of conformity. In the UNITED KINGDOM, the presumption only applies to consumer contracts and only in respect of the new remedies introduced in Part 5A of the Sale of Goods Act 1979[1882] (implementing Art. 3). For the existing remedies, which remain available, the presumption does not exist and the burden of proof falls on the consumer even during this initial 6-month period. A similar problem exists in IRELAND, where the existing Sale of Goods legislation remains in force alongside the implementation of the Directive.

The approach adopted in PORTUGAL is very generous towards consumers: here, the reversed burden of proof applies throughout the two-year period from delivery, rather than merely the 6-month period envisaged under the Directive.[1883]

In GERMANY, there have been several decisions by the Federal Supreme Court on the application of the reversed burden of proof. Thus, it has been held that this reversal applies even where a lack of conformity was identifiable at the time of purchase, except where it was so obvious that a consumer not knowledgeable in respect of the particular subject matter would

---

1878 Article 230(1) of the Law of Obligations Act.

1879 Note that the proposal of 1 September 2006 would delay the start of this 6 month period if the consumer was not given information about it at the time of delivery until such information has been provided.

1880 Chapter 5 Art. 15(2) of the Consumer Protection Act.

1881 Chapter 5 Art. 16 of the Consumer Protection Act.

1882 And Part 1B of the Supply of Goods and Services Act 1982.

1883 Article 3(2) of the Decree Law 67/2003.

have discovered the defect.[1884] Moreover, the fact that a third part has installed the goods does not negate the applicability of the reversed burden.[1885]

e. No rescission for 'minor' lack of conformity (Art. 3 para. (6))

This provision has been implemented in most member states, although some member states have chosen not to transpose Art. 3(6) of the Directive (no rescission where lack of conformity is minor). They are CZECH REPUBLIC, ESTONIA, PORTUGAL, SLOVENIA, and the UNITED KINGDOM. The effect of this is that in these countries, a consumer could rescind the contract where the seller has not repaired/replaced the goods even where the lack of conformity is minor. However, in Slovenia, according to Art. 458(3) Obligations Act, a minor defect is not regarded as a defect at all and the relevant legislation would also not be triggered. The effect is therefore akin to that pursued by Art. 3(6). In the United Kingdom, existing provisions of the Sale of Goods Act 1979 had preserved a right of termination in cases of minor defects where the buyer is a consumer,[1886] and the government adhered to its policy of not reducing existing levels of consumer protection by not transposing Art. 3(6). In contrast, IRELAND excludes the right of rescission under the national legislation implementing the Directive where the non-conformity is minor, but the consumer retains a right of termination under general sales law, which extends to a minor lack of conformity.

In DENMARK, the general rule is that the consumer has no right of rescission if the lack of conformity is minor.[1887] An exception is made if the seller does not complete a repair or replacement within reasonable time, free of charge and without any significant inconvenience for the consumer; in such a case the consumer is entitled to rescind the contract even if the lack of conformity is minor.[1888]

The law in LATVIA, provides that a non-conformity will be deemed to be minor if this has been confirmed by an expert-examination organized according to the procedures specified in regulatory enactments.

The question of when a non-conformity is minor has already been considered by the courts in several of the member states. Thus, the AUSTRIAN Supreme Court has held that the accumulation of several defects - which would be minor if looked at individually – means that the lack of conformity is no longer 'minor'.[1889] A further decision by that court stated that in order to consider whether a non-conformity is 'minor' it was not just the severity of the defect itself but also the proportionality of the consequences of rescinding the contract compared to the lack of conformity that had to be considered.[1890]

[1884] BGH (DE) VIII ZR 363/04, 14 September 2005.

[1885] BGH (DE) VIII ZR 21/04, 22 November 2004.

[1886] Section 15A of the Sale of Goods Act 1979 – no right to reject and terminate where breach is minor and buyer is not dealing as a consumer.

[1887] Article 78(1) of the Consolidated Act on Sales of Goods.

[1888] Article 78(4) of the Consolidated Act on Sales of Goods.

[1889] OGH [Oberster Gerichtshof; AUSTRIA], 7 Ob 194/05p, 28 September 2005.

[1890] OGH [Oberster Gerichtshof; AUSTRIA], 8 Ob 63/05f, 21 July 2005.

In GERMANY, it has been held that, in the case of a used car, a lack of conformity would be regarded as minor if the cost of removing the lack would be less than 3% of the purchase price.[1891] Furthermore, it has been held that where a seller has deliberately concealed the defect, it will also generally not be regarded as minor.[1892]

f. Rescission and period-of-use allowance[1893]

Recital 15 states that member states may provide that where a consumer is entitled to a reimbursement of the purchase price, a deduction may be made to take account of the use the consumer has had of the goods since delivery to him. This has been transposed in a number of member states, including GERMANY, ITALY,[1894] and the UNITED KINGDOM (only in respect of rescission under Part 5A).

In GERMANY, the literature has debated an apparent conflict between the fact that a remedy has to be provided free-of-charge and that it is possible to make a deduction to take account of the use the consumer has had of the goods. This deduction may also be made where the consumer is given a replacement, which effectively means that the consumer has to make a payment in addition to the contract price when non-conforming goods are replaced (see also comments regarding Germany at 'c' above).[1895]

In ESTONIA, where a seller provides a replacement, the consumer (and any other buyer) is required to return the non-conforming goods to the seller.[1896] This is made subject to the general rules in the Law of Obligations Act regarding the return of items provided under the contract in the case of withdrawal.[1897] Perhaps of only significance in this context is Art. 189 para. (4), which provides that "if a thing subject to return or delivery has deteriorated and such deterioration is not the result of the regular use of the thing, the decrease in the value of the thing shall be compensated for". This suggests that a consumer is not required to pay a period-of-use allowance to the seller, but if there has been deterioration above and beyond that to be expected from normal use, the consumer may have to compensate the seller.

g. Calculation of price reduction[1898]

A difficult question that has arisen in the wake of the Directive is which method of calculation should be applied to price reduction. It seems that there are various approaches, which may lead to different results in practice (although in monetary terms, these differences will generally be small). If the CISG were to serve as a model, then the so-called 'proportionate

---

1891 OLG Düsseldorf ZGS 04, 197.

1892 BGH [Bundesgerichtshof] NJW 2006, 1960.

1893 Not all national correspondents have reported whether domestic law has or has not adopted a specific rule in response to Recital 18.

1894 Article 132(8) of the Consumer Code.

1895 CC § 439(4).

1896 Article 222(3) of the Law of Obligations Act.

1897 Article 189-191 of the Law of Obligations Act.

1898 Only limited information about this issue was available at the time of writing.

reduction' of the purchase price model would apply. According to this approach, the price would be reduced by the same ratio as the value of the goods as delivered is in relation to the value they would have had if they had been in conformity with the contract. A simpler calculation would be to reduce the price according to the difference between the value of the goods as delivered and the value they would have had if there had been no lack of conformity.

In GERMANY, the price reduction is calculated by multiplying the value of the non-conforming goods and the price, and dividing the result by the value which conforming goods would have had. The NETHERLANDS also apply a proportionate reduction of the purchase price, as does HUNGARY.[1899] SLOVENIA also applies the proportionate reduction approach; the relevant moment for comparison is the time of conclusion of the contract (the ratio is the relation between value of the goods without defect and goods with defect at the time of conclusion). SPAIN is a further country using proportionate price reduction.[1900]

Many countries do not provide specific rules (these include MALTA, UNITED KINGDOM).

3. Guarantees

The provisions on guarantees in Art. 6 require that guarantees must be legally binding, that certain information is provided, and that guarantees remain binding even where the rules in Art. 6 have not been complied with.

These provisions have generally been implemented in identical or very similar format in all the member states. Guarantees generally take effect as a form of contractual obligation. No transposition of Art. 6(2)-(5) was undertaken in LITHUANIA.

MALTESE law goes beyond the requirements of Art. 6 by providing further substantive rules on guarantees.[1901] HUNGARY and SLOVENIA continue to use mandatory guarantees (see below, IV.1.e). Slovenian law does not provide direct transposition measures for Art. 6(1), but the binding nature of a voluntary guarantee (as opposed to the mandatory guarantees) is covered by existing legislation.[1902] Voluntary guarantees have to be in writing, and must contain information about the name and place of business of the seller/producer, the guarantee statement, the minimum duration of the guarantee.[1903] The requirement to include a reference to the consumer's legal rights is missing, which can cause problems because of the existence of mandatory guarantees. In respect of the consumer's remedies under a guarantee, the hierarchy of consumer's remedies under a guarantee resembles that under the Directive: first repair and replacement, then (if the latter are not effected within reasonable time), rescission or price reduction. There is also a right to damages.

1899 CC Art. 306(1)(b).

1900 Article 8 of the Law 23/2003 on consumer sales.

1901 See section IV.1.e, below.

1902 See by Art. 481 of the Obligations Code and Art. 15b-21 of the Consumer Protection Act.

1903 Article 18 of the Consumer Protection Act.

The UNITED KINGDOM has transposed most aspects of Art. 6 in new legislation, except the first indent of Art. 6(2), on which there is already longstanding legislation which makes it a criminal offence to fail to mention a consumer's legal right under sale of goods legislation.[1904] In respect of guarantees given by a seller, the law in FINLAND provides that a seller will not be liable if the fault was the result of an accident, or the inappropriate handling of the goods or another circumstance attributable to the buyer.[1905]

Article 6 para. (4) permits member states to require that guarantees are provided in a particular language. This option has not been exercised by AUSTRIA, CZECH REPUBLIC, FINLAND, FRANCE, GERMANY, IRELAND, LATVIA, NETHERLANDS (believing this provision to be "too complicated"), POLAND and SLOVAKIA.

It has been implemented in CYPRUS (official language, provided that also an official language of the EU), DENMARK (Danish), ESTONIA, GREECE (Greek) HUNGARY (Hungarian), ITALY (Italian), LUXEMBOURG (choice between French and German), MALTA (one of the official languages, i.e., English or Maltese), PORTUGAL (Portuguese), SLOVENIA (Slovenian), SPAIN (at least Spanish) and the UNITED KINGDOM (English). LITHUANIA has not transposed this provision, relying instead on its general law requiring all commercial documents to be in Lithuanian. SWEDEN has not made use of the option in Art. 6 (4).[1906] In BELGIUM, a rule applies according to which the language of the region where goods marketed must be used in guarantee documents, as well as labeling.[1907] A similar situation arises in POLAND.[1908] In ITALY, the law provides additionally that the font-size of the Italian text must not be smaller than the font size of the text of any other language.[1909]

Option on language used	Option on language not used	Other language rule applicable
BE, CY, DK, EE, EL, HU, IT, LU, MT, PT, SL, ES, UK *(13)*	AT, CZ, FI, FR, DE, IE, LV, NL, SK, SE *(10)*	LT, PL *(2)*

Article 6 para. (5) has not been transposed in SPAIN. In the UNITED KINGDOM, special enforcement powers have been given to the Office of Fair Trading and Weights and Measures Authorities for a failure by a person giving a guarantee to comply with the rules on guarantees in Regulation 15 of the Sale and Supply of Goods to Consumers Regulations 2002 (implementing Article 6).[1910] In AUSTRIA, a failure to comply with the rules on guarantees can give rise to a claim for damages.

1904 Article 4-5 of the Consumer Transactions (Restrictions on Statements) Order 1976.

1905 Chapter 5 Art. 15a of the Consumer Protection Act.

1906 During the implementation process in Sweden it was, however, held by the Government that a requirement to provide guarantees in a particular language (i.e. Swedish) already followed from Art. 6 (2) ("plain intelligible language").

1907 Article 13 of the Act on trade practices and consumer information and protection.

1908 It should be noted that although no express requirement for guarantees to be provided in the Polish language is provided in the Act on detailed terms and conditions of consumer sales and on the amendment of the Civil Code., according to Article 3 para. (1) of the Act the seller is obliged to provide the buyer with the information needed to correctly and fully use the product. This information should be clear, understandable and unambiguous, and it should be in Polish language.

1909 Article 133(4) of the Consumer Code.

1910 Regulation 15(6)/(7) of the Sale and Supply of Goods to Consumers Regulations 2002.

4. The Right of redress

Art. 4 envisages that a final seller can in turn bring a claim against the person or persons liable in the contractual chain. This may either require the final seller to bring a claim against his immediate contractual supplier, or it might permit the seller to claim directly against the person liable (i.e., responsible for the defect).

Steps to include a specific provision to reflect the requirements of Art. 4 where taken in CYPRUS, ESTONIA, FINLAND, GREECE, FRANCE, HUNGARY, ITALY, LATVIA, MALTA, [1911] and POLAND.

In FRANCE, general contract law should apply to these claims ("selon les principes du code civil"), [1912] and it is up to the courts to develop the circumstances in which such a claim should succeed. In FINLAND, the final seller has a claim against a business at an earlier level in the supply chain. This is subject to a number of exclusions: (i) the defect is the result of circumstances which arose after the earlier business had already supplied the goods; (ii) the final seller bases his claim on a statement made by someone other than the business; or (iii) an amount exceeding the price reduction/refund which the final seller could have claimed from the business on the same grounds.[1913]

In ITALY, it seems that an action may be brought directly against the person responsible, although this is subject to a time-limit of one year from providing a remedy to the consumer.In MALTA, the final seller normally has to exercise his right of action within 6 months.[1914] In the NETHERLANDS, a seller has a claim against the immediately previous seller. It is possible to claim compensation, except where the claimant was aware of shortcomings in the goods. These rights cannot be excluded. In PORTUGAL, a claim must be brought within 5 years of supply, and also no later than two months after providing a remedy to the consumer. A previous supplier will not be liable for matters, which only arose after the goods had been supplied to the seller. In SPAIN, the final seller must take action within one year from completing the remedy for the consumer and can claim against the person actually responsible for the lack of conformity. It should be noted that this course of action is similarly open to a producer (there is direct producer liability in Spain), who might claim against a seller if the latter is actually responsible for the non-conformity.

Many member states take the view that a claim should follow generally applicable contractual principles: AUSTRIA, BELGIUM, CZECH REPUBLIC, CYPRUS, DENMARK, IRELAND, LITHUANIA, SLOVENIA and UNITED KINGDOM. Some of these (Czech Republic, Denmark, Ireland, Lithuania, Slovenia, Sweden, United Kingdom) have therefore taken no steps to transpose this provision.

In AUSTRIA, a claim by a final seller or intermediary has to be brought within two months of providing a remedy towards the consumer/subsequent buyer, and is limited to the value of the purchase price. There is an absolute limitation period of 5 years. In BELGIUM, any terms

---

1911 Article 77 of the Consumer Affairs Act.

1912 Article L. 211-14 of the Consumer Code.

1913 Chapter 5 Art. 31 of the Consumer Protection Act.

1914 CC Art. 1431.

restricting the liability towards the seller who is liable to a consumer for a lack of conformity resulting from an act/omission by a previous seller in the contractual chain, are ineffective in relation to the consumer.[1915] In GERMANY, the final seller has a claim against his supplier for compensation, although this provision is restricted to "new goods", rather than all the consumer goods subject to the Directive.

In IRELAND and the UNITED KINGDOM, where no specific implementation of this provision was made, the claim may follow the contractual chain, but there are difficulties with this approach: the ground which may have given rise to the final seller's liability towards the consumer may not be available to the seller in bringing a claim against his contractual supplier, and the seller may therefore be left without a basis of claim. Moreover, reasonable exclusion/limitation clauses could further restrict the seller's attempt to obtain redress.

LITHUANIA also did not expressly transpose this rule, but general rules of civil law apply. There also does not appear to be a clear rule for SLOVAKIA. Nothing was done to implement this rule in SLOVENIA.

5. Mandatory nature of the provisions

Article 7 para. (1) states that any contract term excluding or restricting a consumer's rights under this Directive before a lack of conformity is drawn to the seller's attention will be ineffective. All the member states, except LATVIA, have adopted provisions giving effect to this provision, or rely on existing provisions, which have this effect.

Moreover, Article 7(2) makes the provisions of this Directive mandatory, i.e., the choice of the law of a non-EU member state must not deprive consumers of the protection under this Directive. This has been given effect in most member states, but there are some variations in respect of this provision. Thus, in CYPRUS, a proviso has been added according to which the choice of a non-member state law will only then be void if that law provides a lower level of protection than under the law implementing the Directive, and/or the consumer had, at the time of the conclusion of the contract, his habitual residence in Cyprus or another member state and the contract was concluded or performed in Cyprus or another member state.[1916] In GREECE, if a case involving a sale of goods to consumers is brought before a Greek court, Greek provisions must be applied irrespective of any choice of law clause, if Greek law would provide a higher level of protection.[1917]

In a number of countries, no specific steps towards implementing this provision have been taken (FINLAND, LATVIA, LITHUANIA, and SLOVENIA), although it seems that there are equivalent rules already in place coming to a similar result.

1915 CC Art. 1649 *sexies*.

1916 Article 14 of the Certain Aspects of the Sale of Consumer Goods and Associated Guarantees Law of 2000.

1917 Article 5(5), sent 3 of the Law 2251/1994.

The only country in respect of which there are serious shortcomings is the UNITED KINGDOM. It relies on existing provisions in the Unfair Contract Terms Act 1977,[1918] but these only have the effect that this Act will apply notwithstanding a choice of law clause. The Act only prevents the use of a choice of law clause to evade its application. Consequently, a choice-of-law clause selecting a non-Member State law would render ineffective a term seeking to exclude the controls under the Unfair Contract Terms Act. However, the same clause *would* have the effect of excluding the legislation implementing the Directive. UK law therefore does not ensure the application of the legislation implementing the Directive where a non-EU law is chosen. Moreover, even this provision does not apply where the contract is an international supply contract (i.e., where goods to be carried across borders; or offer & acceptance occur in different countries; or goods to be delivered to a state other than where offer and acceptance took place).

IV. Use of the minimum harmonisation clause (Art. 8 para. (2))

1. Higher level of protection for consumers

Some member states have relied on Art. 8(2) in order to retain existing rules which are more generous towards consumers than those in the Directive (CYPRUS, DENMARK, FRANCE, HUNGARY, UNITED KINGDOM). In GERMANY, the implementation of the Directive initiate an extensive reform of the entire law of obligations ("Schuldrechtsreform"), and the conformity requirement is applicable to all contracts of sale. Other provisions introduced to comply with the Directive also extend to other contracts, which may result in a general increase of the level of protection outside the field of consumer sales, although this may depend on the extent to which the provisions are interpreted in accordance with the Directive in a non-consumer case. In IRELAND, the consumer can rely on the rules implementing the Directive as well as other legislation applicable to the sale of goods; it is possible that existing rules may provide better protection to consumers although no case-law to support this is available at the time of writing.[1919] In the United Kingdom, some changes were made in respect of contracts of hire, hire-purchase, and other contracts involving the supply of goods, but only in respect of the rules corresponding to the conformity requirement.

a. Scope of application

The AUSTRIAN legislation extends the rules in the Directive significantly beyond its scope, and applies these also to purely private ("consumer-to-consumer" sales) and business-to-business sales. Moreover, the limited definition of "goods" in Art. 1(2)(b) has not been transposed and the Austrian legislation applies not only to goods, but also to immovables.[1920] In DENMARK, the definition of "goods" has also not been restricted and it includes all the matters listed as exclusions in Art. 1(2)(b);[1921] moreover, the Danish law applies to all types of

---

[1918] Section 26 and 27 of the Unfair Contract Terms Act 1977.

[1919] Regulation 3(1) and 3(3) of the ECR SI 11/2003.

[1920] CC Art. 922.

[1921] Article 76(1),(3) of the Sales of Goods Act.

sales with the exception of real estate. HUNGARIAN law extends beyond the sale of goods and also includes the provision of services.

In PORTUGAL, immovables are included in the scope of the implementing legislation. In SLOVENIA, the objective scope of application of the legislation has not been limited to consumer goods as defined in the Directive, and the exclusions in Art. 1(2)(b) have not been transposed. SPAIN excludes only goods sold through "judicial sales", rather than all sales "by way of execution or otherwise by authority of the Law", and the option to exclude goods sold at public auction (Art. 1 (3)) is limited to "administrative auctions".

As discussed above, there are variations in the definition of "consumer". This is wider e.g., in GERMANY, and can include activities during a person's employment;[1922] also, some companies are treated as consumers in some instances.[1923] Legal persons can also be consumers in SPAIN insofar as the goods are not to be used for production and the recipient is the final user of the goods. Similarly, in the UNITED KINGDOM, a professional or a company may be treated as a consumer provided that the goods in question are of a type ordinarily supplied for private use or consumption.[1924]

In the NETHERLANDS, the rules extend to contracts of barter,[1925] and there is an extension also to intangible goods.[1926] Some provisions are available to non-consumers.[1927] Similarly, in SLOVENIA, the rules on consumer sales are also applied to contracts for services.[1928]

aa. Liability of the producer

Some countries extend liability towards the consumer for a lack of conformity beyond the immediate seller and impose this on the producer.

In FRANCE ('action directe') and BELGIUM[1929] (kwalitatieve rechten/droits qualitatifs), the courts, in case-law developed under the Civil Code, have created the possibility for a buyer to sue any previous supplier in the chain of distribution in contract, thereby permitting a consumer to sue not only the final seller, but also a distributor or producer. All the parties in the distribution chain are jointly liable towards the buyer, but there is a possibility for the seller actually sued to seek an indemnity from the party actually responsible for the loss.[1930]

1922 CC Art. 13.

1923 It had been thought that those founding a new business may also be covered, but this has now been rejected by the Federal Suprement Court: BGH [Bundesgerichtshof] NJW 2005, 1273.

1924 Section 12 of the Unfair Contract Terms Act [UK].

1925 CC Art. 7:50.

1926 CC Art. 7:47.

1927 CC Art. 7:17, 7:21(1)-(3) and 7:23(2).

1928 Article 38 of the Consumer Protection Act.

1929 CC Art. 1615; Cass. 5 December 1980, *Arr. Cass.* 1980-81, 382 en *Pas.* 1981, I, 398.

1930 See e.g., S.*Whittaker*, Liability for Products, Oxford: Oxford University Press, 2005, p. 96-98.

In PORTUGAL, liability can also be imposed on the producer or the producer's representative in the area where the consumer lives.[1931] This is subject to a range of defences, some of which appear to resemble those found in Directive 85/374.[1932] A claim against a producer is also possible in LATVIA (at the consumer's choice)[1933] and LITHUANIA. SPAIN also permits a consumer to claim directly against a producer for repair or replacement of non-conforming goods, where it would be impossible or excessively costly for the consumer to pursue the seller (but the consumer cannot claim price reduction or rescission as against the producer). Case law appears to accept a degree of joint and several liability of seller and producer.

In SLOVENIA, the producer is not liable for a non-conformity of the goods as such. However, as noted earlier, there is a parallel regime of mandatory guarantees for the "proper functioning" of so-called "technical goods". The list of the goods, which must be sold with a guarantee, is very extensive. The minimum time-limit of a guarantee is one year. Both the producer and seller are liable under such guarantees.

b. Conformity requirement

DENMARK has retained a rule requiring the seller to disclose to the consumer any information relevant to the consumer's assessment of the goods of which the seller was aware or ought to have been aware.[1934] The duty of disclosure developed in the law in FRANCE is also very strong, particularly in the consumer context. POLAND has a general rule requiring a seller to provide all the required information to a buyer;[1935] moreover, a seller must confirm in writing all the important contract terms where the contract is a sale by instalments, to order, based on a sample, involving a trial period or in excess of PLN 2,000.[1936] For other sales, the consumer can ask for written confirmation of the contract.[1937] The seller must provide user instructions in Polish, and the goods must feature information about the name of the goods, producer or importer, country of origin, safety and compliance marks, and information about relevant licenses.[1938]

1931 Article 6 Decree Law 67/2003.

1932 These are: the non-conformity is based on statements about the goods or their fitness for purpose made by the final seller; the goods have not been used for their normal purposes; the producer did not put the goods into circulation; taking account of all the circumstances, it was not possible to identify the non-conformity before putting the goods on the market; the goods were not made for sale or with a view to financial gain; the goods were not made in the course of the producer's professional activity, or were put on the market more than 10 years previously.

1933 Article 28(1) of the Consumer Rights Protection Law.

1934 Correspondent's Report, page 4.

1935 Article 2.1 of the Act of 27 July 2002 on specific terms and conditions of consumer sale and amendments to the Civil Code.

1936 Article 2.2 of the Act of 27 July 2002 on specific terms and conditions of consumer sale and amendments to the Civil Code.

1937 Article 2.3 of the Act of 27 July 2002 on specific terms and conditions of consumer sale and amendments to the Civil Code.

1938 Article 3.1 and Art. 3.5 of the Act of 27 July 2002 on specific terms and conditions of consumer sale and amendments to the Civil Code.

Additional factors which can render goods non-conforming have been introduced or retained in several countries. In FINLAND and CYPRUS, incorrect user instructions and a failure of the goods to correspond with applicable regulations can result in the goods being deemed defective.

In the NETHERLANDS, there are specific provisions regarding the use of samples or models; where this is done, it is presumed that the goods delivered should conform with the sample, unless the seller can prove that what had been shown to the consumer was a mere indication.[1939] Moreover, it is not necessary for the seller to have "accepted" the particular purpose, but also where that purpose was foreseen in the contract.[1940]

In MALTA, if the goods are of a nature which makes it likely that maintenance or the replacement of parts may be required, then the trader is required to make available for "a reasonable time" such replacement parts and appropriate repair services. The trader or producer can escape from this obligation if he expressly and in writing informs the consumer before the conclusion of the contract that he does not supply such replacement parts or repair service.[1941]

In SLOVENIA, there appears to be no possibility for the seller to avoid his liability for public statements (as per Art. 2(4) of the Directive), which has the effect of increasing consumer protection, but it is assumed that this was rather the result of poor implementation. However, as noted, several other countries have also not implemented Art. 2(4) (LATVIA, LITHUANIA, PORTUGAL). Note also that LUXEMBOURG, GREECE and FRANCE only include the first of the three defences for the seller.

The UNITED KINGDOM relies on its pre-existing rules regarding the notion of conformity, although there is also a special definition of conformity for the purposes of the new remedies introduced for consumer transactions only. That definition is broader than the Directive, referring to the "implied terms in sec. 13, 14 or 15" of the Sale of Goods Act 1979 and any *express term of the contract*. This could significantly broaden the circumstances that could give rise to a lack of conformity. It also seems to be the case that in respect of particular purposes made known by the buyer, UK law is more favourable than the Directive by allowing a purpose to be made known by implication as well as expressly, and not requiring acceptance by the seller, but rather reasonable reliance on the seller's skill or judgment. There is also a more detailed list of factors to be considered in establishing the goods' conformity with the contract.

The exclusion in Art. 2(3) of the Directive is only given a limited effect in respect of the UNITED KINGDOM's requirement that goods must be of satisfactory quality, and only covers matters specifically drawn to the buyer's attention. In GREECE, the exclusion applies only where the consumer had actual knowledge of the lack of conformity.

1939 CC Art 7:17(4).

1940 CC Art 7:17(2).

1941 Article 93 of the Consumer Protection Act.

c. Remedies

GREECE did not adopt the two-stage hierarchy of remedies, and all 4 remedies are available, subject to restrictions. This is also the case in LITHUANIA and PORTUGAL.

As noted above, some member states have chosen not to transpose Art. 3(6) of the Directive, which would deprive a consumer of the right to rescind the contract where the lack of conformity is minor (CZECH REPUBLIC, ESTONIA, PORTUGAL, and the UNITED KINGDOM). In these countries, the right to rescind the contract is therefore available in a wider range of circumstances. SLOVENIA has also not implemented this provision, but under national legislation in that country, a minor defect is not regarded as a defect at all, and the end result is in line with Art. 3(6).

In most member states, it remains possible to bring a claim for damages/compensation instead of, or as well as, a claim under the provision implementing Art. 3. Thus, in AUSTRIA, a claim in damages is possible, in particular for consequential losses arising from a lack of conformity in the goods. In BELGIUM, there is a right to claim compensation for any losses suffered as a result of the defective performance of the contract.[1942] It remains unclear whether the distinction as to the scope of the compensation operated by CC Art. 1645 and 1646, based on whether the seller at the time of the sale was aware of should have been aware of the latent defect, also applies in case of consumer sales. In that regard, it must be submitted that the Belgian Court of Cassation, in presence of a professional seller, applies the presumption that he was or should have been aware of the defects.[1943] A right to damages is also stated explicitly in FRANCE.[1944] In GERMANY, damages remain available, but this depends on a degree of fault on the part of the seller.

Compensation for losses or payment of a contractual penalty is also available in LATVIA. In MALTA, damages are available for consequential losses suffered as a result of the lack of conformity in the goods; moreover, compensation for 'moral' damages (capped at one hundred Maltese liri) may be claimed for any 'pain, distress, anxiety and inconvenience'.[1945]

In the CZECH REPUBLIC, the consumer is entitled to replacement of goods or termination (rescission) of the contract even if the goods are repaired, should the consumer not be able to use the goods properly due to the occurrence of defects following repair, or due to a greater number of defects.[1946]

In HUNGARY, a consumer is entitled to withhold a proportion of the purchase price until repair or replacement has been completed.[1947]

In the NETHERLANDS, a consumer is also entitled to demand delivery of any missing parts.[1948]

1942 CC Art.1649 *quinquies*.

1943 Cass. 19 September 1997, *Arr. Cass.* 1997, 840 en *Pas.* 1997, I, 883.

1944 Article L. 211-11 of the Consumer Code.

1945 Article 21(2) of the Consumer Protection Act.

1946 CC Art. 622(2).

1947 CC Art. 306(4)-(5).

Furthermore, if a seller in the Netherlands fails to repair the goods within a reasonable time, the consumer can ask a third party to do so and hold the seller liable for the costs.[1949] The same is the case in FINLAND, SWEDEN and DENMARK.

SPAIN permits a consumer to opt for rescission/price reduction where *either* of repair/replacement is not available, rather than where *both* are unavailable. A failure to cure the lack of conformity using repair or replacement grants the consumer the choice of all three remaining remedies.[1950] Moreover, damages are also available as a further remedy.

SLOVENIA gives the seller 8 days within which to implement a remedy (or a written reply if there is a dispute regarding the consumer's claim), rather than relying on the notion of "reasonable time".

In IRELAND and the UNITED KINGDOM, a consumer can exercise the general right available in all contracts of sale to reject goods that do not comply with the implied terms and terminate the contract, provided that the consumer is not deemed in law to have accepted the goods. In addition, the consumer can rely on the general provisions to claim damages, which includes both the loss of value in the non-conforming goods and reasonably foreseeable consequential losses.

d. Time limits

In BELGIUM, the two-year period in Art. 5 para. (2) has been introduced and applies both to identifiable and latent defects. Once the two-year period has expired, the existing Belgian rules regarding latent defects remain applicable, and these are not subject to a specific time-limit.[1951]

In FINLAND, the liability of a trader is without time-limit, rather than being restricted to two years.[1952] Similarly, in the NETHERLANDS, the two-year period has not been implemented; however, the starting point for the limitation period (which is two years) is the moment of notification of the non-conformity to the seller, and not that of delivery.

HUNGARY appears to permit an extension of this time limit if there is an "excusable reason", especially where the lack of conformity, due to its character or the nature of the goods, does not appear until later. If goods are to be used on a long-term basis (durable goods), the time period is three years.[1953]

1948 CC Art.7:21(1).

1949 CC Art. 7:21(6).

1950 Article 6 and 7 of theLaw 23/2003 on consumer sales.

1951 CC Art.1649 *quater* para. (5) CC.

1952 It is argued in the preparatory works that if one for example buys a car, there could be a hidden defect that appears after two years. Nevertheless, there may be procedural rules which can limit the liability of the seller.

1953 CC Section 308/A.

As noted above, SPAIN suspends the two-year period whilst the goods are being repaired or replaced. In addition, goods, which have been repaired/replaced, are subject to 6-month period during which a seller will be liable for any further lack of conformity.[1954]

IRELAND and the UNITED KINGDOM have not introduced a specific time limit, and instead relies on the general limitation period for a breach of contract, which is currently 6 years.

As already noted above, PORTUGAL has extended the reversed burden of proof from the 6 months required by the Directive to the full period of two years, and is therefore significantly more generous to consumers than required.

e. Guarantees

In AUSTRIA, the transparency obligation in Art.6 has been extended to cover guarantees for which a consumer has to pay separately (so-called "extended warranties").[1955] SPANISH law also applies to such guarantees; in addition, it imposes slightly more extensive information obligations. Additional rules on guarantees are also found in GERMANY, where there is a general provision on guarantees not limited to consumer transactions,[1956] combined with no-fault liability.[1957]

In ESTONIA, there is a presumption that a guarantee grants the consumer the right to repair or replacement, that a new guarantee of the same duration will be issued for goods replaced under the guarantee, and that the guarantee period is extended where items are repaired, by the time taken to effect this.

In FINLAND, the guarantee must put the consumer into a more advantageous position than under sales law. Moreover, a trader is liable for guarantees given by a producer unless this is expressly excluded at the time of sale.

HUNGARY has retained its system of binding guarantees, which were introduced by government decree and provide a statutory regulation of guarantees going beyond the rules in Art. 6 of the Directive. The prior regime of so-called "binding guarantees" continues to apply. These are "guarantees" which must be given by law and are regulated by a Government decree. [1958]

In LATVIA, a guarantee must provide something in addition to the Consumer Rights Protection Law and other regulatory enactments. A seller must not reduce the scope of a guarantee given by the manufacturer, and to shorten the time period of the guarantee. Moreover, it is prohibited to use the word 'guarantee' or other words of a similar meaning if the guarantee does not conform to he conditions of Art. 16 of the Consumer Rights Protection Law.

[1954] Article 6, rules c and d, re of the Art. 9 of the Law 23/2003 on consumer sales.

[1955] Article 9b of the Consumer Protection Act.

[1956] CC Art. 443.

[1957] CC Art. 276(1), sent. 1.

[1958] Government Decree 153/2003 on binding guarantees of durable goods.

In MALTA, there are more detailed information obligations, including provisions requiring information about transferability to subsequent owners of the goods, and, where this is not provided, an automatic presumption that guarantees are so transferable. Furthermore, no fee for dealing with a consumer claim under a guarantee may be charged unless this is stated expressly in the guarantee.[1959] If there has been a recall of goods by the manufacturer, the guarantee period is automatically extended.[1960] The guarantor is unless stated in the guarantee required to assume the cost of any carriage of goods in the performance of the guarantee.[1961] The duration of the guarantee is automatically extended for period equal to the period during which the goods remain in the possession of the guarantor during the course of the execution of the guarantee.[1962] Furthermore, even where a third party should provide a remedy under the guarantee, the guarantor remains bound to his obligations towards the consumer.[1963] The court may make an order requiring the guarantor to comply with the obligations undertaken in a guarantee, to take remedial action to observe the terms of the guarantee, or to perform his obligations imposing a civil penalty for each day of non-compliance.[1964]

In SLOVENIA, rules of mandatory guarantees continue to exist. There is a considerable overlap with the legal rights made available under the Directive. Guarantees have a minimum duration of one year, and there is an obligation on the producer to keep spare parts beyond that period. A consumer is entitled to compensation for the period during which he could not use the goods.

The method of implementation chosen by the UNITED KINGDOM has had an unexpected effect. If the person giving the guarantee repairs defective goods under the guarantee, then a failure to repair the goods with reasonable care can permit the consumer to claim against the guarantor for up to 6 years (and therefore beyond the expiry of the guarantee). Similarly, any new parts provided during the repair, or goods replaced under the guarantee, have to meet the general rules on conformity (the implied terms), and a consumer may be able to claim for up to 6 years if a latent fault, which existed at the time of the replacement, manifests itself.[1965]

V. General comments on adequacy of implementation of the Directive

1. Difficulties encountered during the transposition process

Correspondents were asked to point out any particular difficulties that, in their view, were encountered during the process of implementing this Directive. The main challenge, identified by several correspondents, has been to absorb the specific rules introduced by the Directive into an existing system of sales law. The use of concepts in the Directive, which were unfamiliar to particular domestic legal systems, posed a significant hurdle in the transposi-

1959 Article 86 of the Consumer Affairs Act.
1960 Article 88 *et. seq.* of the Consumer Affairs Act.
1961 Article 87 of the Consumer Affairs Act.
1962 Article88 of the Consumer Affairs Act.
1963 Article 89 of the Consumer Affairs Act.
1964 Article 91 of the Consumer Affairs Act.
1965 This is the effect of Regulation 15(1) SSGCR 2002, combined with the rules in the Supply of Goods and Services Act 1982.

tion process. A related difficulty has been the drafting style of the Directive: there are some ambiguities (e.g., regarding Art. 3(3) or Art. 4), which caused difficulties during the implementation process.

Some correspondents raised very specific questions of interpretation, some of which might be clarified by amending the Directive, although others may better be left to interpretation by the courts, particularly the European Court of Justice.

Questions were raised about the scope of the various definitions, and where exactly the limits of the terms "consumer", "seller" and "consumer goods" were. The question of the status of computer software is not addressed, for example; nor is the position of animals.

A major difficulty for many member states has been the "right of redress" in Article 4. This has given rise to a significant body of academic literature, with quite divergent opinions regarding the scope of this section. Thus, correspondents have noted that there is an ambiguity in Article 4 regarding the extent of the member states' obligations to introduce a specific right of redress (i.e., can they rely on existing contract law with consequent use of exclusion clauses; must they introduce an absolute right for the final seller, but leaving the nature of his claim and procedural matters only for domestic law?)

In some countries, the hierarchy in the remedies, and the relegation of "rescission" to a remedy of last resort has been the cause of concern. Where a right to terminate the contract is available immediately, this permits a consumer who has lost confidence and wishes to take his business elsewhere to do so, whereas the system in the Directive requires the consumer to give the seller a further opportunity to perform his obligations.

2. Gaps in the Directive

Correspondents were asked for their opinion as to whether they perceive there to be any gaps in the Directive in its current format. Several issues were identified. As noted, there are clear difficulties with the drafting style of the Directive, and there are some ambiguities in the text itself.

The Directive uses the notion of "delivery", but does not address aspects of this concept, such as late delivery and delivery of the wrong quantity. Some member states take the view that "quantity" could be regarded as an aspect of conformity, for example.[1966]

There are also no provisions on the right to claim damages/compensation, which therefore remains a matter for domestic law – and the relationship between such domestic rules and the remedies in the Directive remains unclear. Moreover, the consequences of exercising the right to rescind the contract remain unclear.

The Directive only imposes liability on the final seller. This has been commented on negatively by a number of correspondents. A major criticism is that the Directive is designed to

[1966] But see the views of *Tenreiro*, "La proposition de directive sur la vente et les garanties des biens de consommation", Revue européenne de droit de la consommation, 187 [1996].

encourage consumer participation in the internal market, but then does not promote obtaining redress by widening the parties against whom a consumer might enforce his rights. As a minimum, the liability of the producer is proposed (although there exist arguments in favour of a wider "network liability").

It is also apparent from some country reports that there remains an issue about the treatment of "after-sales" services, with some countries requiring the availability of spare parts for a period of time after sale, and others requiring at least some information about the availability of after-sales services or spare parts.

In this regard, there appears to be a degree of incoherence between the Directive and the Eco-Label Regulation.[1967] In order to qualify for an eco-label, it is often necessary to provide a guarantee of minimum duration. Moreover, spare parts and after-sales services are also often required.

VI. Conclusions and recommendations

The following matters could be considered as part of reviewing the Directive:

- Options: It is apparent that all options have been used by some of the member states, but in no instance has there been an overwhelming tendency to use, or to disregard, any of the options given in the Directive (see table at end of this section). Consequently, no clear recommendation regarding the removal of any of the options can be given.
- Definition of 'consumer' (refer to the general discussion of this matter).
- Definition of 'seller' (refer to the general discussion of this matter).
- Definition of 'goods', in particular whether software and other digital products should be included in the definition. A related question is whether any licences associated with the supply of software, or other digital products, should be covered by the rules of this Directive, too – for example, when the licence is not extensive enough. It may not be possible to address this issue in the context of this Directive, but there may be questions of drawing the line in the correct place if digital products are to be included in the definition of 'goods'.
- Clarification in the text of the Directive that the proportionality criterion should not permit a comparison of repair/replacement with price reduction, to avoid confusion on this matter.
- Clarification of who bears the burden of proof in respect of some of the provisions (e.g., Art. 2 para. (3)).
- Right of redress for the seller: consider whether this could be clarified further, and consider, in particular, whether a clear 'action directe' approach could be adopted.
- The introduction of direct producer liability, and, possibly, distribution network liability, could be considered again. In the context of the internal market, it may be particularly important that a consumer can seek a remedy from somebody based in his own country. The Directive does not address this matter at present, and it should be considered if a system of producer liability, possibly combined with distribution network liability, should be adopted.

[1967] Regulation 1980/2000.

- The relationship of the remedies in Art. 3 and the national rules on the award of damages: it may be considered whether the Directive should address this. That would raise the questions which forms of damage should be covered. Broadly speaking, 4 heads of damages can be identified: (i) Equivalence (to the remedies in the Directive); (ii) consequential losses; (iii) loss of profit; and (iv) additional costs incurred as a result of buying replacement. This matter may best be considered once the *Common Frame of Reference* has been completed.
- Related supply transactions: there are other supply transactions, such as hire-purchase or conditional sale, as well as hire and leasing, which are frequently used by consumers buying more expensive goods. Conditional sale may be included within the scope of the Directive, although the position is not clear. Other supply transactions were explicitly excluded during the legislative process leading up to the adoption of the Directive, but this could bring about the different treatment of similar transactions. The nature of the risk in the context of a hire or leasing arrangement is different from that in sale, or conditional sale; nevertheless, it may be desirable to consider including a wider range of transactions within the scope of the Directive.

Overview: Use of options by the member states

Member State	Art. 1 para. (3)	Art. 5 para. (2)	Art. 7 para. (1)	Art. 6 para. (4)
AT			✓	
BE			✓	✓
CY		✓	✓	✓
CZ			✓	
DK		✓		✓
EE		✓		✓
FI	✓	✓		
FR	✓			
DE	✓		✓	
EL	✓			✓
HU	✓	✓	✓	✓
IE				
IT		✓	✓	✓
LV				
LT		✓		
LU			✓	✓
MT		✓		✓
NL		✓		
PL		✓	✓	✓
PT		✓	✓	
SK		✓	✓	
SL		✓	✓	✓
ES	✓	✓	✓	✓
SE	✓	✓	✓	[1968]
UK	✓			✓

[1968] During the implementation process in Sweden it was, however, held by the Government that a requirement to provide guarantees in a particular language (i.e. Swedish) already followed from Art. 6 (2) ("plain intelligible language").

Bibliography

Commission Communication on the Implementation of the Directive on Sale of Consumer Goods and Guarantees, COM (2007) 210 final; **Ajani, Gianmaria / Rossi, Piercarlo**, Codice del consumatori, 2005, **Cámara Oficial de Comercio e Industria de Madrid,** Nueva normativa sobre garantías en la venta de bienes de consumo, Aplicación en Espańa de la Directiva 1999/44/CE, Madrid 2004, **Ämmälä, Tuula**, Virhe-erityisesti kuluttajankaupassa ja asuntokaupassa, 2002, **Bártfai, Judit / Bozzay, Erika / Kertész, Ágnes / Wallacher, Lajos**, Új szavatossági és jótállási szabályok. Fogyasztóvédelmi jogharmonizáció a polgári jogban és a polgári eljárásjogban, 2004, **Bradgate, Robert / Twigg-Flesner, Christian**, Blackstone's Guide to Consumer Sales and Associated Guarantees, Oxford 2003, **Braga, Armando**, A Venda de Coisas Defeituosas no Código Civil – A Venda de Bens de Consumo, 2005, **Delios, G./ Doris, Phil. / Karassis, M. / Kornilakis, P. / Koumanis, St. / Valtoudis, A.**, To neo dikaio tou pragmatikou elattomatos stin polisi, 2003, **Dikigorikos, Sillogos Kerkiras / Enosi, Astikologon,** H prosfati tropopoiisi tou dikaiou ton pragmation elattomaton stin polisi, 2004, **Faber, Wolfgang**, Handbuch zum neuen Gewährleistungsrecht, 2001, **Gärtner, Anette**, Die Umsetzung der Verbrauchsgüterkaufrichtlinie in Deutschland und Großbritannien, Frankfurt 2005, **Georgiades, Olga**, Sale of Goods in Cyprus Following Harmonisation with the Acquis Communautaire and Consumer Protection, Nicosia 2005, **Herre, Johnny**, Konsumentköplagen, Stockholm 2004, **Howells, Geraint / Weatherill, Stephen,** Consumer Protection Law, Aldershot 2005, **Hulva, Tomáš**, Ochrana spotřebitele, Praha 2005, **Janssen, André**, The Dutch Law After the Incorporation of the Consumer Sales Directive – Much Ado About Nothing? in: Ajani, Gianmaria/Ebers, Martin, Uniform Terminology for European Contract Law, 343-358, Baden-Baden 2005, **Käerdi, Martin**, Abgrenzung der vertraglichen und außervertraglichen Haftungssysteme im deutschen und estnischen Kaufrecht und im Einheitsrechts, Estonia, Baden-Baden 2006, **Kristoffersen, Sonny**, De nye forbrugerkřbsregler og standardvilkĺr, Copenhagen 2002, **Leible, Stefan**, Kaufvertrag (§§ 433-480 BGB), in: Gebauer/Wiedmann, Zivilrecht unter europäischem Einfluss, Kap.9, Stuttgart 2005, **Leitão, Luís Manuel Teles De Menezes**, Caveat venditor? A Directiva 1999/44/CE do Conselho e do Parlamento Europeu sobre a venda de bens de consumo e garantias associadas e suas implicaçőes no regime jurídico da compra e venda, Portugal 2002, **Lete Achirica, Javier**, Garantías en la venta de bienes de consumo, Ponencias de la Conferencia Internacional. Santiago de Compostela, enero 2004, Santiago de Compostela, Santiago 2004, **Łętowska, Ewa**, Europejskie prawo umów konsumenckich, Warszawa 2004, **Možina, Damjan**, Potrošniška prodajna pogodba v evropskem in slovenskem pogodbenem pravu, Podjetje in delo (Podjetje in delo) 2004, 310-330, **Mpexlivani, A.**, H tropopoiisi tou dikaiou tis polisis tou AK – Sxetika me ton n. 3043/2002 gia tin euthini tou politi gia pragmatika elattomata kai elleipsi sinoimologimenon idiotiton, 2003, **Ortí Vallejo, Antonio**, Los defectos de la cosa en la compraventa civil y mercantil: el nuevo régimen jurídico de las faltas de conformidad según la Directiva 1999/44/CE, Granada 2002, **Papanikolaou, P.**, To neo dikaio tis euthinis tou politi, 2004, **Pfeiffer, Thomas**, Kommentierung der Verbrauchsgüterkauf-Richtlinie, in: Dauner-Lieb/Heidel/Lepa/Ring, Anwaltskommentar zum neuen Schuldrecht, Bonn 2002, **Pirker-Hörmann, Renate**, Das neue Gewährleistungsrecht, 2004, **Silva, João Calvão Da**, Venda de Bens de Consumo, Comentário 2.Ş ediçãoDecreto-Lei n.ş 67/2003, de 8 de Abril – Directiva 1999/44/CE, Lisboa 2004, **Tournafond, Olivier**, De la transposition de la directive du 25 mai 1999 ŕ la réforme du code civil, 2002, **Whittaker, Simon**, Liability for Products, Oxford 2005.

Part 3: Common structures in the Directives

A. The notion of "consumer"

Martin Ebers

I. Introduction

1. European Community law

Notion of consumer in Community law

Directive	Notion of consumer
Directive 85/577, Art. 2	"consumer" means a natural person who, in transactions covered by this Directive, is acting for purposes which can be regarded as outside his trade or profession
Directive 90/314, Art. 2(4)	"consumer" means the person who takes or agrees to take the package ('the principal contractor'), or any person on whose behalf the principal contractor agrees to purchase the package ('the other beneficiaries') or any person to whom the principal contractor or any of the other beneficiaries transfers the package ('the transferee')
Directive 93/13, Art. 2(b)	"consumer" means any natural person who, in contracts covered by this Directive, is acting for purposes which are outside his trade, business or profession
Directive 94/47, Art. 2	"purchaser" shall mean any natural person who, acting in transactions covered by this Directive, for purposes which may be regarded as being outwith [sic!] his professional capacity, has the right which is the subject of the contract transferred to him or for whom the right which is the subject of the contract is established
Directive 97/7, Art. 2(2)	"consumer" means any natural person who, in contracts covered by this Directive, is acting for purposes which are outside his trade, business or profession
Directive 98/6, Art. 2(e)	consumer shall mean any natural person who buys a product for purposes that do not fall within the sphere of his commercial or professional activity
Directive 99/44, Art. 1(2)(a)	consumer: shall mean any natural person who, in the contracts covered by this Directive, is acting for purposes which are not related to his trade, business or profession

Notion of consumer in Directives not covered by this study

Directive	Notion of consumer
Directive 87/102, Art. 1(2)(a)	"consumer" means a natural person who, in transactions covered by this Directive, is acting for purposes which can be regarded as outside his trade or profession
Directive 2000/31, Art. 2(e)	"consumer": any natural person who is acting for purposes which are outside his or her trade, business or profession
Directive 2002/65, Art. 2(d)	"consumer" means any natural person who, in distance contracts covered by this Directive, is acting for purposes which are outside his trade, business or profession
Directive 2005/29, Art. 2(a)	"consumer" means any natural person who, in commercial practices covered by this Directive, is acting for purposes which are outside his trade, business, craft or profession

According to the English version of Directive 85/577, a consumer is "a natural person who, in transactions covered by this Directive, is acting for purposes which can be regarded as outside his trade or profession". Directive 87/102 uses literally the same definition.

Slightly deviating from this are Directives 93/13, 97/7, 99/44, 2000/31 and 2002/65, which define a consumer as a natural person who is acting for purposes which are outside his "trade, *business* and/or profession". Also Directive 94/47 follows this definition, even though it does not use the term "consumer", but instead mentions "purchaser", defined as a natural person acting "for purposes which may be regarded as being outside his professional capacity". Finally, Directive 98/6 also defines consumer as a "natural person who buys a product for purposes that do not fall within the sphere of his commercial or professional capacity".

In other language versions of the Directives, the notion of consumer is likewise defined using deviating terms. However, they all share a common core, as they all provide that a consumer is:

- a natural person;
- who is acting for purposes which are outside some kind of business, commercial or trade activity.

These common features can be found not only in most consumer protection EC directives but also in European procedural law (Art. 13-15 of the Brussels I Convention, now Arts. 15-17 Brussels I Regulation No. 44/2001) and European rules on conflict of laws (Art. 5 of the Rome I Convention).

Directive 90/314 by contrast contains a very different definition. It describes a consumer as a person "who takes or agrees to take the package ('the principal contractor'), or any person on whose behalf the principal contractor agrees to purchase the package ('the other beneficiaries') or any person to whom the principal contractor or any of the other beneficiaries transfers the package ('the transferee')". Directive 90/314, accordingly, also protects those who conclude package travel contracts for business related purposes. Business trips are thus also within the scope of the directive.

2. Overview

The following observations address the question of how the notion of "consumer" has been defined in the member states in transposing Directives 85/577, 93/13, 97/7, 94/47, 98/6 and 99/44.

The transposition of Directive 90/314, on the other hand, will not be addressed further here. Since this Directive uses a different notion of consumer from the other directives, many member states have declined to use the term "consumer" and opted instead for the term "traveller" or "purchaser".[1969]

The following expositions initially give an overview of the legislative techniques used by the member states to transpose the notion of consumer and pay particular attention to the question of which member states have implemented a general definition of consumer, being applicable for several consumer contracts (II.). Attention will then turn to the issue of the extent to which the consumer definitions chosen in the member states differ from European law. A series of member states have not transposed the notion of consumer in the aforementioned directives literally, but rather based their notion of consumer on deviating concepts, which extend the protection of the directives to further groups of persons. This concerns above all the notion of the final addressee which is employed in some member states (III.1.), the extension to businesspersons concluding atypical contracts (III.2.), the extension to legal persons (III.3.) as well as the incorporation of employees into the sphere of protection of the Community law provisions (III.4.). Finally, the question of how "dual-use" contracts are treated in Community law and the member states will be addressed (IV.) and whether activities associated with founding a business are covered by the notion of consumer (V.). The study shows that the member state definitions of consumer are in accordance with the requirements of Community law. Many member states go beyond the minimum level of protection required by Community law by adopting a wide definition of consumer and extending the protection to other groups of persons. Nevertheless, at Community level a series of individual questions remain unanswered. In the context of the acquis consumer law review the different definitions of consumer should be harmonised and important issues addressed (VI.).

II. Legislative techniques in member states

Many member states have harmonised the notion of consumer found in the various directives and established a definition in national law, which is equally applicable in various consumer protection acts. A systematic overview produces the following picture:

Overarching consumer definitions in member states' law

Member state	Consumer definitions in member states' law	Transposed consumer definition of directive
Austria	Art. 1(1) no. 2 in conjunction with (2) of the Consumer Protection Act	85/577; 93/13; 94/47; 97/7; 99/44

[1969] See the detailed report on the transposition of Directive 90/314, in this study, Part 2 B.II.1.

Member state	Consumer definitions in member states' law	Transposed consumer definition of directive
Belgium	Art. 1 No. 7 of the Act of 14 July 1991 on trade practices and consumer information and protection	85/577; 93/13; 97/7; 98/6
	Art. 2 No. 2 of the Act of 2 August 2002 on misleading and comparative advertising, unfair contract terms and distance marketing in respect of liberal professions	93/13; 97/7
Czech Republic	Art. 52(3) Civil Code as amended by Act 367/2000	85/577; 93/13; 94/47; 97/7; 99/44
Denmark	Art. 3 (1) of the Act No. 451 of 9 June 2004 on certain consumer contracts	85/577; 97/7
Estonia	Art. 2 No. 1 of the Consumer Protection Act	93/13; 97/7, 98/6; 99/44
	Art. 34 of the Law of Obligations Act	85/577; 93/13; 94/47; 97/7; 99/44
Finland	Chapter 1 Art. 4 of the Consumer Protection Act 20.1.1978/38	85/577; 93/13; 94/47; 97/7; 98/6; 99/44
Germany	CC § 13	85/577; 93/13; 94/47; 97/7; 99/44
Greece	Art. 1(4) lit. (α) of the Consumer Protection Act 2251/94	85/577; 93/13; 97/7; 99/44
Italy	Art. 3(1) lit. (a) and (b) of the Consumer code	85/577; 93/13; 97/7; 98/6; 99/44
Latvia	Art. 1(1) sec. 3 of the Consumer Rights Protection Law	85/577; 93/13; 94/47; 97/7; 98/6; 99/44
Lithuania	Art. 2(1) of the Law on Consumer	85/577; 93/13; 94/47; 97/7; 98/6; 99/44
	CC Art. 6.350(1)	85/577; 93/13; 94/47; 97/7; 98/6; 99/44
Malta	Art. 2 of the Consumer Affairs Act	93/13; 97/7; 99/44
Netherlands	CC Book 7 Art. 5(1)	97/7; 99/44
Poland	CC Art. 22[1]	85/577; 93/13; 97/7
Portugal	Art. 2(1) of the Consumer Protection Act No. 24/96	93/13; 98/6; 99/44
	Art. 1(3)(a) of the Decree-Law 143/2001 of April 26	85/577; 97/7
Slovakia	Art. 1, 2nd part of the Act No. 108/2000 on consumer protection in doorstep selling and in distance selling	85/577; 97/7
	CC Art. 52	93/13; 94/47
Slovenia	Art. 1(2) of the Consumer Protection Act	85/577; 93/13; 94/47; 97/7; 98/6; 99/44
Spain	Art. 1(2)-(3) of the Law 26/1984 of July 19 on Consumer Protection	85/577; 93/13; 97/7; 99/44
Sweden	Art. 2 of the Law on Consumer Protection on Distance Contracts and Doorstep Selling Contracts	85/577; 97/7

The above overview not only makes it clear that many countries recognise a general consumer definition, equally applicable to various consumer protecting legislative acts, but also that in certain countries (BELGIUM, ESTONIA, LITHUANIA, PORTUGAL, SLOVAKIA) several overarching consumer definitions exist. In some countries (DENMARK, PORTUGAL, SLOVAKIA and SWEDEN) a general notion of consumer has emerged from a combined regulation of doorstep and distance selling in a single statute.

The countries not listed in the table (CYPRUS, FRANCE, HUNGARY, IRELAND, LUXEMBOURG, UNITED KINGDOM), on the other hand, do not recognise any overarching legal definition of consumer within the directives, rather they either define the consumer separately in every transposing act and/or abstain from such a definition in whole or in part. In FRANCE the term consumer is not defined in legislation at all, but case-law has developed a notion of consumer. The French legislator meanwhile explicitly abstains from defining the term consumer, as in this way better account can be taken of different situations.[1970]

In MALTA, any other class or category of persons whether natural or legal may, from time to time, be designated as "consumers" for all or any of the purposes of the Consumer Affairs Act by the Minister responsible for consumer affairs after consulting the Consumer Affairs Council.

So long as the term consumer is defined in different legal acts in the member states, this does not necessarily mean that these definitions differ from each other in substance. On the contrary, it can be stated that in most member states, in spite of the scattered rules in separate legislative acts, the definitions by and large accord, as they are orientated on Community law and Community law, for its own part, exhibits a common core. Difficulties in applying consumer protection legislative acts do of course arise when a member state uses differing definitions of consumer and it is not clear whether one or the other is applicable in each individual case. Generally, however, this does not affect the proper transposition of the relevant directives, since those member states go beyond the minimum level of protection. In HUNGARY, the notion of consumer is regulated differently in the CC, the Consumer Protection Act, the Government Decree on Doorstep Selling, the Hungarian Competition Act and the Business Advertising Activity Act, and it is often not clear which definition is applicable. However, the planned modifications of the Hungarian CC could clear up these ambiguities.

III. Extension of the notion of consumer in member states

Overview: Extension of the notion of consumer in member states

Notion of the final addressee	ES, EL, HU, LU *(4)*
Protection of businesspersons concluding atypical contracts	FR, LU, LV, PL, (UK) *(5)*
Protection of certain legal persons	AT, BE, CZ, DK, EL, ES, FR, HU, SK *(9)*
Protection of employees	DE *(1)*
Protection of business founding activities	AT *(1)*

1970 E.g. most recently, in transposition of the Consumer Sales Directive, the Rapport au Président de la République relatif à l'ordonnance n° 2005-136 du 17 février 2005 relative à la garantie de la conformité du bien au contrat due par le vendeur au consommateur, Journal Officiel n° 41 du 18 février 2005, 2777.

1. Notion of the final addressee

In SPAIN it is an essential prerequisite that the consumer or user "acquires, uses or enjoys *as final addressee* some goods", and without "the aim of integrating them in production, transformation, commercialisation processes".[1971] A comparable notion exists in GREECE, although with the difference that Greek law does not have any limitation for private purpose. According to Art. 1(4)(a) of the Consumer Protection Act 2251/1994 a consumer is every "natural or legal person, at whom products or services on a market are aimed, and who makes use of such products and services, so long as the person is the end recipient." Also in HUNGARY the notion of end recipient is applied; according to Art. 2 lit. (i) of the Consumer Protection Act a "consumer transaction" is the supply of goods or the provision of services and, furthermore, the supply of free samples of goods directly to the consumer as final recipient.[1972] The LUXEMBOURG Consumer Protection Act uses the term final addressee (*consommateur final privé*) in some cases as well[1973], without defining what this term means.

The notion of "final addressee" in SPAIN and GREECE is wider than the term "consumer" established in the directives, since it also includes atypical transactions which are not related to a further transfer. However, in both countries it is acknowledged that in practice such a broad definition of "consumer" can lead to difficulties in applying the law. In SPAIN, the "Motives Explanation" of the Law 7/1998 on Standard Terms in Contracts, which in Spain is a non-binding part of the Law, mentions that the consumer is "any natural person who (...) is acting for purposes which are outside his trade, business or profession". Against this background, it is supposed that the General Law for the Protection of Consumers and Users should be interpreted according to those sentences in the Preamble.

Also in GREECE the need for a teleological reduction is stressed in academic literature and the view is propounded that the regulations should not apply to every final addressee. Rather, in each case it should be verified that the relevant person or entity is in need of protection. In order to qualify as being in need of protection, the end consumer must not be acting within a business or commercial capacity in concluding the transactions in question.

2. Extension to businesspersons concluding atypical contracts

In FRANCE, according to well-established case-law, a consumer is a (natural or legal) person concluding contracts which are not directly related (*qui n'ont pas de rapport direct*) with his or her profession. The leading decision in this regard was that of the Cass. civ. of 28 April 1987.[1974] In the case under dispute an estate agency purchased an alarm system for its business premises, which was not in good working order. A clause in the general conditions of business however declared that the buyer may not rescind the contract or claim damages. In the view of the Cass. civ. the French Consumer Code was nonetheless applicable, because the subject matter of the contract did not bear any direct relation to the substance of the

---

[1971] See Art. 1(2) and (3) of the Law 26/1984 of July 19 on Consumer Protection.

[1972] See thereto the decision of the *Magyar Köztársaság Legfelsőbb Bíróság*, Legf. Bír. Kfv. III. 37.675/2003 in the database.

[1973] As for example in Art. 1-2 and Art. 2 No. 20 in relation to the control of unfair terms.

[1974] Cass. Civ. of 28 April 1987 (JCP 1987. II. 20893 Juris-classeur periodique).

business activity and because the technical expertise of an estate agency did not encompass the technology of alarm systems, by reason of which the buyer must be treated just as any other consumer. In later decisions the Cass. civ. has distanced itself from its wide interpretation and pointed out that the decisive criterion for the applicability of the Consumer Code is not the technical competence of the "professional", but rather whether the contract is directly related to the business activity.[1975] This case-law has been affirmed in numerous decisions.[1976]

Protection for businesses which conclude contracts outside of their usual field of business also exists in POLAND and LATVIA. This thinking underlies the LUXEMBOURG Consumer Sales Act; according to its Art. 2 No. 2 a "consommateur" is "une personne physique qui agit à des *fins qui n'ont pas de rapport direct* avec son activité professionnelle ou commerciale". The practical relevance of this group of persons depends on the respective interpretation of the notion of "usual field of business". If this is limited to elementary core activities, then businesses will frequently profit from consumer protection rules. Conversely, if "usual field of business" comprises all transactions which are not completely atypical, businesses will rarely be considered as consumers.

In the UNITED KINGDOM under section 12(1) of the Unfair Contract Terms Act (UCTA) 1977 businesses engaged in a transaction outside their normal business purposes can claim to be "dealing as a consumer" since the decision in *R & B Customs Brokers Ltd* v *United Dominions Trust Ltd.*[1977] In this case, the plaintiff, a shipping brokerage, purchased a second-hand car for the personal and business use of the company's directors. Several similar purchases had been made before. The contract excluded liability for breach of certain statutory implied terms. According to UCTA sec. 6 (2)(b), where a business sells to a consumer, terms as to quality and fitness for purpose implied by statute (namely sec.13-15 of the Sale of Goods Act 1979) cannot be excluded or restricted by reference to any contract term. Therefore, it was to be decided whether the buyer was "dealing as a consumer". The CA held that no sufficient degree of regularity had been shown by the defendant so as to establish that the activity was an integral part of the plaintiff's business. Rather, the purchase was only incidental to the company's business activity. The plaintiff was therefore dealing as a consumer within the terms of UCTA sec. 12(1). Thus the defendant could not exclude liability for breach of the implied term. Whether this wide definition of consumer can be applied beyond the context of UCTA for other consumer protection legal acts, is questionable however. Firstly it must be noted that UCTA only partly serves the implementation of directive law (namely in relation to the Consumer Sales Directive) and UK otherwise uses a notion of consumer which is closely orientated towards Community law. Secondly, the cited decision has in the meantime been placed in doubt, as in *Stevenson v Rogers* the CA held that for the purposes of the Sale of Goods Act 1979 sec. 14 any sale by a business is "in the course of a business".[1978] Thus a solicitor selling off a computer no longer needed in his office would, for this purpose, be selling the computer in the course of business.

[1975] Cass. Civ. 24 January 1995, Recueil Dalloz Sirey 1995, 327-329.

[1976] Cf. Cass. Civ. 23 November 1999, Jurisclasseur, Contrats-Concurrence-Consommation 2000, commentaires, 25; Cass. Civ. 23 February 1999, D. 1999, informations rapides, 82.

[1977] R & B Customs Brokers Ltd v United Dominions Trust Ltd. [1988] 1 WLR 321.

[1978] *Stevenson v Rogers* [1999] 1 All ER 613.

In ITALY some courts similarly propounded the view for a time, that a person should be protected as a consumer, if the relevant transaction does not belong to his core business activities.[1979] The Cass. on the other hand rejected this view and established a narrow definition of consumer.[1980] This view is consistent with the case-law of the ECJ.

The ECJ has narrowly construed the notion of consumer under Directive 85/577 in C-361/89 - *Di Pinto*.[1981] The ECJ regarded the French notion of consumer as permissible; but at the same time highlighted that Community law does not "*draw a distinction between normal acts and those which are exceptional in nature*".[1982] This view is also confirmed by the preparatory work for Directive 99/44: whereas the original proposal for Directive 99/44 of 18 June 1996[1983] regarded a consumer as a person who "is acting for purposes which are *not directly related to* his trade, business or profession", the amended directive proposal[1984] omitted the words "not directly".

3. Protection of certain legal persons

Under the above-mentioned directives only natural persons are regarded as consumers. In the joined cases C-541/99 and C-542/99 – *Idealservice*[1985] the ECJ expressly stated (concerning the consumer definition of Art. 2 of the Directive 93/13) that Community law in this respect is not to be given a wider interpretation:

> "It is thus clear from the wording of Article 2 of the Directive that a person other than a natural person who concludes a contract with a seller or supplier cannot be regarded as a consumer within the meaning of that provision."

A number of member states follow this concept and expressly limit the scope of consumer protection provisions to natural persons: CYPRUS, GERMANY, ESTONIA, FINLAND, IRELAND, ITALY, LATVIA, LITHUANIA, LUXEMBOURG, MALTA, the NETHERLANDS, POLAND, SLOVENIA and SWEDEN. In ITALY the Italian constitutional court clarified in its judgment of 22 November 2002 that an extension of protection to legal persons is not provided for in Italian constitutional law either.[1986] In LATVIA, there has recently been a reform, so that from now on legal persons are excluded from the notion of consumer.[1987] In the UNITED KINGDOM, by contrast, the law varies: whereas the case-law has declared that a company may "deal as a

[1979] Tribunale Roma, 20 of October 1999, Giustizia civile 2000, I, 2117.

[1980] Cass., 25 July 2001, No. 10127, I Contratti 2002, 338.

[1981] ECJ judgment of 14 March 2003, C-361/89 – *Criminal proceedings v Patrice Di Pinto* [1991] ECR I-01189.

[1982] *Ibid*, para. 15.

[1983] COM 95, 520 final.

[1984] COM 1998, 217 final.

[1985] ECJ judgment of 22 November 2001, joined cases C-541/99 and C-542/99 – *Cape Snc* v *Idealservice Srl and Idealservice MN RE Sas* v *OMAI Srl* [2001], ECR I-9049, para 16.

[1986] *Corte Costituzionale* 22 November 2002, No. 469, Giustizia civile 2003, 290 et seq.

[1987] Amendment of the Consumer Protection Law, which came into force on 11 November 2005.

consumer" within the meaning of UCTA,[1988] in other consumer protection instruments only a natural person can be a consumer.

Through the limitation to natural persons, small and medium sized enterprises and charitable associations e.g. sporting associations or church parishes, are without protection. Thus there are norms in AUSTRIA, BELGIUM,[1989] CZECH REPUBLIC, DENMARK, FRANCE, GREECE, HUNGARY, SLOVAKIA (with some exceptions) and SPAIN,[1990] which treat legal persons as consumers, providing the purchase is for private use (or in Greece, Hungary and Spain the legal person is the final addressee). In FRANCE the Cass. Civ. with judgment of 15 March 2005 has clarified, that the notion of "consumer" (*consommateur*) according to the ECJ decision in *Idealservice* cannot be carried over to legal persons, whereas on the other hand, the notion "*non-professionel*" (used in the context of the articles concerning unfair contract terms; vid. Art. L 132-1 Consumer Code) can also be a legal person under French law.[1991] HUNGARY is currently planning to limit the notion of consumer to natural persons. In PORTUGAL, it is unclear whether legal persons can be protected as "consumers", however, a draft of a new Consumer Code acknowledges that legal persons may, in certain circumstances, benefit from the protection conferred to consumers.

4. Protection of employees

A peculiarity of GERMAN law is that it generally regards an employee, who is also acting within his professional capacity as a "consumer". According to CC § 13 "consumers" are those persons who "enter into a transaction which can be attributed neither to their business nor their *self-employed* capacity". Accordingly, the German Federal Labour Court considered an employee to be a consumer.[1992]

1988 E.g. *R & B Customs*, above.

1989 See Art. 1 No. 7 of the Act of 14 July 1991 on Trade Practices and Consumer Protection (TPA): « Consommateur: toute personne physique ou morale qui acquiert ou utilise à des fins excluant tout caractère professionnel des produits ou des services mis sur le marché « and Art. 2 No 2 of the Act of 2 August 2002 on misleading and comparative advertising, unfair contract terms and distance marketing in respect of liberal professions (LPA): « toute personne physique ou morale qui, dans les contrats visés par la présente loi, agit à des fins qui n'entrent pas dans le cadre de son activité professionnelle « . By contrast, under Art. 2 No. 5 of the Act of 11 April 1999 on the purchase of the right to use immovable properties on a timeshare basis only natural persons are protected: « acquéreur: toute personne physique qui, agissant dans les transactions visées au point 1, à des fins dont on peut considérer qu'elles n'entrent pas dans le cadre de son activité professionnelle, soit se voit transférer le droit objet du contrat, soit voit créé à son bénéfice le droit objet du contrat. »

1990 In SPAIN, however, the "Motives Explanation" of the Law 7/1998 on Standard Terms in Contracts mentions that the consumer is "any natural person". Against this background, it is supposed that the General Law for the Protection of Consumers and Users should be interpreted according to this.

1991 Cass. Civ., 15 March 2005, No. de pourvoi: 02-13285 Syndicat départemental de contrôle laitier de la Mayenne.

1992 BAG, judgment of 25 May 2005, 5 AZR 572/04, NJW 2005, 3305.

This does not however mean that all consumer laws in Germany can automatically be applied to the protection of the employee. Rather, case-law makes the following distinction: whereas standard business terms in contracts of employment are in principle subject to the controls of provisions which serve the transposition of Directive 93/13[1993], an agreement concluded at the place of work to end an employer-employee relationship is not subject to the withdrawal provisions of doorstep sales. In the view of the Federal Labour Court, such an agreement does not represent a doorstep selling situation within the meaning of CC § 312.[1994] The right of withdrawal in doorstep selling situations is – according to the court – a consumer protection right related to the type of contract and encompasses only "particular forms of marketing". Accordingly, the right of withdrawal provided by law does not apply to contracts which are not a form of marketing, such as a contract of employment or contract to terminate employment. Therefore, the employee does not enjoy the right of withdrawal in these situations. Whether the European notion of consumer also includes employed persons is contentious in German literature.[1995]

IV. "Mixed" purpose transactions

1. Community law

For contracts that serve both a private and business purpose (e.g. the acquisition of a motor vehicle for a freelancer), the directives at issue contain no express rule, in contrast to Directive 85/374 (see Art. 9 lit. (b) ii: "used by the injured person *mainly* for his own private use or consumption"). The judgment of the ECJ in C-464/01 – *Gruber*[1996] has brought no clarification in this regard. The Court stressed in this decision that a person can invoke the special rules of jurisdiction of Art. 13-15 of the Brussels I Convention (now Art. 15-17 Brussels I Regulation No. 44/2001) in respect of dual use contracts only if the trade or professional purpose is so limited as to be negligible in the overall context of the transaction (para. 54). However, this decision relates only to European procedural, not substantive law. One might nevertheless wonder whether the procedural notion of consumer can be useful for substantive consumer protection law. Whereas in procedural law terms it can be completely justified on grounds of legal certainty to give standing only in respect of contracts concluded entirely for use for private purposes, in substantive law terms it could be thoroughly justified in the interests of consumer protection to concentrate on the primary use purpose.[1997] Thus for the directives at issue it remains open, as to how dual use cases are to be treated.

[1993] See the judgment of the BAG of 25 May 2005, cited above.

[1994] BAG, judgment of 27 November 2003, 2 AZR 135/03, NJW 2004, 2401.

[1995] In favour thereof: *Faber*, ZEuP 1998, 854 at 873 et seq.; against: *Mohr*, AcP 204 (2004), 660 at 671.

[1996] ECJ judgment of 20 January 2005, C-464/01 – *Johann Gruber v Bay Wa* AG [2005] ECR I-00439.

[1997] See on this *Ebers*, in: Ajani/Ebers (eds), Uniform Terminology for European Contract Law, 115-126 = (2006) Anuario de Derecho Civil (ADC), 229-238.

2. Classification in member states

"Mixed" purpose transactions as consumer contract

Purely private purpose	AT, BE *(2)*
Also "mixed" purpose, preponderant purpose prevails	DE, DK, FI, SE *(4)*
Also "mixed" purpose – unclear whether private purpose must preponderate	IT *(1)*
No clear rule on "mixed" purpose transactions discernible	CY, CZ, EE, EL, ES, FR, HU, IE, LT, LU, LV, MT, NL, PL, PT, SL, SK, UK *(18)*

Member states found different solutions for classifying mixed purpose transactions. The differentiation according to the criteria of the primary use purpose is expressly stated in the DANISH, FINNISH[1998] and SWEDISH[1999] provisions. GERMAN courts also focus on the question of whether the private or business use is predominant.[2000] In ITALY, recent case-law tends towards the same direction, so that a small tobacconist was regarded as a consumer when concluding a contract for the hire of a vehicle which was for both private and business use. However, it is not clear from this judgment whether the private use was predominant.[2001] In AUSTRIA[2002] and BELGIUM[2003], on the other hand, only contracts concluded exclusively for private purposes are considered consumer transactions.

V. Protection of founding activities

1. Community law

Whether a person who makes transactions in the course of preparing professional activity (founding activities) is likewise a "consumer", is not expressly regulated in the directives at issue.

The ECJ decided in C-269/95 – *Benincasa*[2004] that Art. 13 Brussels I Convention (now Art. 15 of the Brussels I Regulation No. 44/2001) is not applicable if a party has concluded a contract for future professional or business activity. In its reasoning the ECJ stated that "[t]he specific protection sought to be afforded by those provisions is unwarranted in the case of contracts for the purpose of trade or professional activity, even if that activity is only planned for the future, since the fact that an activity is in the nature of a future activity does not divest it in any way of its trade or professional character" (para. 17).

1998 Chapter 1 § 4 of the Consumer Protection Act.

1999 Chapter 1 sec. 2 of the Law 2005:59 on Consumer Protection on Distance Contracts and Doorstep Selling Contracts.

2000 OLG Naumburg judgment of 11 December 1997, NJW-RR 1998, 1351, on the applicability of the consumer credit act in relation to motor vehicle leasing.

2001 Giudice di pace Civitanova Marche 4 December 2001, Gius 2002, 1188.

2002 Article 1 (1) of the Consumer Protection Act.

2003 Article 1 (7) of the Trade Practice Act of 14 July 1991.

2004 ECJ judgment of 3 July 1997, C-269/95 – *Francesco Benincasa v Dentalkit Srl* [1997] ECR I-3767.

Thus, for Community law the predominant view is that transactions which serve the founding of a business are also generally not to be regarded as consumer contracts. This view is confirmed by Directive 2002/65. In recital (29) of this Directive it is stated that "[t]his Directive is without prejudice to extension by member states, in accordance with Community law, of the protection provided by this Directive to non-profit organisations and *persons making use of financial services in order to become entrepreneurs*."

2. Member states' law

In most countries the issue of founding activities is not addressed either in legal acts or by case-law. AUSTRIA alone regulates the matter in a legislative act. Art. 1(3) of the Consumer Protection Act provides that transactions by which a natural person, prior to commencing a business, obtains the necessary goods or services do not qualify as business transactions. Founders of new businesses therefore enjoy the protection of consumer laws. In GERMANY, by contrast, courts have regarded founders of businesses not as consumers, but as businesses.[2005]

VI. Final conclusions

1. Issues to be considered for a review of the acquis

The above remarks show that while the member state consumer definitions at times considerably diverge from one another, they are nevertheless by and large in accordance with Community law. Difficulties in application of the consumer protection norms in practice arise above all from the unclear requirements of Community law. In the context of the review therefore the following aspects should be considered:

- Although the consumer definitions in European law exhibit a common core, the wording of the directives uses different definitions, which furthermore diverge in the individual language formulations. Therefore, a harmonised definition for all consumer protecting directives should be found.
- The definition of consumer used in Directive 90/314 is confusing, as according to this definition people who book business trips are also protected. The Community legislator should therefore either avoid the term consumer or restrict the scope of application of the directive to consumer travel services.
- How should mixed contracts be treated? Is a person to be protected as a consumer where the good or service is purchased *predominantly* for private use? Or only if the business use is so limited as to be negligible in the overall context of the transaction?
- Must the consumer prove that he is acting for purposes which are outside of his trade, business or profession? What are the requirements for such proof?

2005 BGH, decision of 24 February 2005, III ZB 36/04, NJW 2005, 1273-1275 on the Directive 93/13. However, according to BGH, judgment of 15 November 2007, III ZR 295/06, NJW 2008, 435 (on the Directive 85/577), transactions with the aim of taking a decision whether to found a business (here: expertises) are not to be regarded as founding activities and therefore very well covered by notion of consumer.

2. Full harmonisation?

If the Community legislator decides to regulate consumer protecting norms wholly or in part according to the concept of full harmonisation, special care with the definition of consumer is necessary. The first experiences with Directive 2002/65 are vivid proof of this. According to recital (13) the Directive aims at maximum harmonisation:

> "Member States should not be able to adopt provisions other than those laid down in this Directive in the fields it harmonises, unless otherwise specifically indicated."

Recital (29) furthermore emphasises that "This Directive is without prejudice to extension by Member States, in accordance with Community law, of the protection provided by this Directive to non-profit organisations and persons making use of financial services in order to become entrepreneurs."

From this, one could draw the conclusion that the directive is conclusive in respect of the question of who comes within its scope of protection. Recital (29) would otherwise be superfluous. If one takes this view, then the member states would be prohibited from using a wide consumer definition and extending the protection to other groups of persons (for example, to businesspersons concluding atypical contracts). Ultimately, the Community legislator probably did not wish such a far reaching specification.[2006] However, this example clearly shows that with a full harmonisation it must be clear whether the member states are allowed to extend the protection to further groups of persons.

B. The notion of "business"

Martin Ebers

I. European Community law

Notion of business in Community Law

Directive	Notion of Business
Directive 85/577, Art. 2	"trader" means a natural or legal person who, for the transaction in question, acts in his commercial or professional capacity, and anyone acting in the name or on behalf of a trader.
Directive 90/314, Art. 2(2) and (3)	"organizer" means the person who, other than occasionally, organizes packages and sells or offers them for sale, whether directly or through a retailer; "retailer" means the person who sells or offers for sale the package put together by the organizer;

2006 This view is also taken by *Schinkels*, GPR 2005, 109 at 110.

Directive	Notion of Business
Directive 93/13, Art. 2 lit. (c)	"seller or supplier" means any natural or legal person who, in contracts covered by this Directive, is acting for purposes relating to his trade, business or profession, whether publicly owned or privately owned
Directive 94/47, Art. 2	"vendor" shall mean any natural or legal person who, acting in transactions covered by this Directive and in his professional capacity, establishes, transfers or undertakes to transfer the right which is the subject of the contract
Directive 97/7, Art. 2(3)	"supplier" means any natural or legal person who, in contracts covered by this Directive, is acting in his commercial or professional capacity
Directive 98/6, Art. 2 lit. (d)	trader shall mean any natural or legal person who sells or offers for sale products which fall within his commercial or professional activity
Directive 99/44, Art. 1(2) lit. (c)	"seller": shall mean any natural or legal person who, under a contract, sells consumer goods in the course of his trade, business or profession

Notion of business in directives not covered by this study

Directive	Notion of business
Directive 87/102, Art. 1(2)(b)	"creditor" means a natural or legal person who grants credit in the course of his trade, business or profession, or a group of such persons
Directive 2000/31, Art. 2(b)	"service provider": any natural or legal person providing an information society service
Directive 2002/65, Art. 2(c)	"supplier" means any natural or legal person, public or private, who, acting in his commercial or professional capacity, is the contractual provider of services subject to distance contracts
Directive 2005/29, Art. 2(b)	"trader" means any natural or legal person who, in commercial practices covered by this Directive, is acting for purposes relating to his trade, business, craft or profession and anyone acting in the name of or on behalf of a trader

1. Common features

Unlike for "consumer", Community law does not use a uniform term for the other party to a consumer contract. That party (hereinafter: business) is variously described as "trader" (Directive 85/577; 98/6; 2005/29), "supplier" (Directive 93/13; 97/7; 2002/65), "seller" (Directive 93/13; 99/44), "vendor" (Directive 94/47), "service provider" (Directive 2000/31) or "creditor" (Directive 87/102). A common feature of these directives, however, is that the business

- can be either a natural or a legal person,
- who is acting for purposes relating to this person's self-employed trade, work or profession.

2. Intention of the business to make a profit (animo lucri)

Whether the Directives at issue additionally require the intention of the business to make a profit is questionable however. Several reasons support the view that a profit motive is irrelevant.[2007] The intention to make a profit relates to an internal business factor, which in some circumstances can be proven only with difficulty and which businesses can manipulate (for

[2007] See also Micklitz, *MüKo*[5], § 14 para 22.

example, by transferring profits within a corporate group). Directive 93/13 also supports the view that a profit motive is immaterial, since this Directive relates to public bodies (see below, 4.). Internal factors of the business should therefore have no bearing on whether consumers are protected. Rather, objective factors should decide whether a person is acting in their commercial or professional capacity. However, legal certainty in this issue can ultimately only be achieved by the ECJ or the acquis review.

3. "Acting in the name or on behalf of a trader"

Community law sometimes contains an extended definition of "business". Thus a "trader" in doorstep sales is also a person who is "acting in the name or on behalf of a trader" (Art. 2 of Directive 85/577). In the same way Art. 2(2) of Directive 2005/29 provides that "trader" is also "anyone acting in the name of or on behalf of a trader". Also the first proposal for Directive 97/7 contained such a definition[2008], however, the amended proposal of 7 October 1993[2009] by contrast refused an express inclusion of auxiliary agents; the reasons for that exclusion being unapparent. Finally, according to Art. 1(2) lit. (b) of Directive 87/102 a "creditor" is not only a person who grants credit in the course of his trade, business or profession, but also "a group of such persons".

When a person is acting "in the name or on behalf of a trader" has not hitherto been clarified by the ECJ. In C-229/04 - *Crailsheimer Volksbank*[2010] the Court of Justice did at least clarify that Directive 85/577 "must be interpreted as meaning that when a third party intervenes in the name of or on behalf of a trader in the negotiation or conclusion of a contract, the application of the Directive cannot be made subject to the condition that the trader was or should have been aware that the contract was concluded in a doorstep selling situation" (para. 45).

4. Inclusion of legal persons/bodies of public law

Some directives (such as Directive 93/13 and Directive 2002/65) make explicitly clear that public bodies can also be "businesses". Directive 93/13 emphasises in recital 14 that the Directive also applies to trades, businesses or professions of a public nature. Additionally, Art. 2 lit. (c) of the Directive makes it clear in the English language version that the nature of ownership of the "trader or supplier" is immaterial (Art. 2 lit. (c): „'seller or supplier' means any natural or legal person who, in contracts covered by this Directive, is acting for purposes relating to his trade, business or profession, whether publicly owned or privately owned."). The German language version, on the other hand, underlines that the Directive is also applicable if the business or professional activity is attributable to the area of public law, ("*dem öffentlich-rechtlichen Bereich zuzurechnen ist*"), whereas the French version speaks of the professional activity, whether public or private ("*activité professionnelle, qu´elle soit publique ou privée*"). In view of these formulations it must be assumed that the Directive in any event

[2008] COM(92) 11 final.

[2009] COM(93) 396 final.

[2010] ECJ judgment of 25 November 2005, C-229/04 - *Crailsheimer Volksbank eG v Klaus Conrads, Frank Schulzke and Petra Schulzke-Lösche, Joachim Nitschke* [2005] ECR I-9273.

extends to private law contracts between consumers and public legal persons/bodies. Whether in addition not only private law, but also public law contracts are encompassed, is by contrast uncertain. In support of this is the fact that the public/private divide is drawn differently in each country and therefore it cannot be at the discretion of the national legislator whether contractual clauses are subject to Directive 93/13 or not. Legal certainty can in turn only be achieved if the ECJ decides the issue, or the Community legislator in the context of the acquis review undertakes a corresponding clarification.

II. Legislative techniques in member states

Most member states have used the terms "trader", "supplier", "seller", "vendor", "service provider" or other terms (like "*Unternehmer*" in AUSTRIA and GERMANY or "*professionista*" in ITALY) in accordance with the Directives at issue; for more detail see Part 2 of this study.

Some member states have introduced a uniform definition for the counterpart of the consumer, in particular AUSTRIA[2011], CZECH REPUBLIC[2012], FINLAND[2013], GERMANY[2014], ITALY[2015] and SLOVENIA.[2016] LATVIA and LITHUANIA define the terms "seller" and "service provider" generally for all kinds of consumer contracts.[2017] SLOVAKIA introduced general definitions for "seller" and "supplier" in its Consumer Protection Act.[2018]

Other member states by contrast (above all FRANCE) abstain from express definitions, relying instead on their case-law.

In MALTA any category or class of persons can be designated as a "trader" by Order of the Minister responsible for consumer affairs after consulting the Consumer Affairs Council, and publication in the Gazette.

III. Content of the definitions in member states

The notion of business is in many member states defined in more concrete terms than in the relevant directives. Many member states have tried to clarify details or give examples.

2011 Article 1(2) of the Consumer Protection Act.

2012 CC Art. 52(2).

2013 Chapter 1 Art. 5 of the Consumer Protection Act.

2014 CC Art. 14.

2015 Article 3(1) lit. (c) of the Consumer Code.

2016 Article 1(3) of the Consumer Protection Act.

2017 Article 1(1) sec. 4-5 of the Latvian Consumer Protection Act; Art. 2(2) and (3) of the Lithuanian Consumer Protection Act.

2018 Article 2(1) lit. (b) and (e).

1. Intention of the business to make a profit (animo lucri)

Some member states have regulated the issue not addressed in the directives, of whether a person who does not intend to make a profit is included in the notion of business. In AUSTRIA business is described in Art. 1(2) of the Consumer Protection Act as "every organisation on a continuing basis of independent economic activity", even if this organisation does not intend to make a profit. In GERMANY, the BGH clarified for consumer goods sales, that the only relevant factors for qualifying as business are whether the seller offers products on the market against payment, normally over a certain period of time. The court stated expressly that it does not matter whether the seller pursues his business activity with the intention of making a profit.[2019] In GREECE, it is likewise recognised that non-profit-making organisations or institutions as well as public corporations and local authorities can act as suppliers. In the NETHERLANDS and SWEDEN the notion business/corporation also includes those enterprises which have no profit motive.

The position is different, however, in FINLAND, SLOVENIA and SPAIN. According to Art. 1:5 of the FINNISH Consumer Protection Act the trader has to act "in order to gain income or with another economic interest." According to Art. 1(3) of the SLOVENIAN Consumer Protection Act, a "trader" is defined as a legal or natural person, who is "engaged in a profitable activity" regardless of its legal form or ownership. SPAIN uses the term "retail trade" in transposition of Directive 97/7, which is defined in Art. 1(2) of the Law 7/1996 on retail trade as "the activity professionally undertaken with the will to earn" (*ánimo de lucro*).

2. "Acting in the name or on behalf of a trader"

The issue addressed in Community law in some directives of whether a person acting in the name or on behalf of a trader is to be regarded as a business, is partly regulated in the member states generally for all or several consumer protecting acts. The BELGIAN Trade Practices Act refers to the term "seller" which is defined in Art. 1.6° as "any other person, whether acting in their own name or on behalf of a third party". The CYPRIOT notion of "supplier" clarifies as well, that the supplier acts "either personally or through his representative". The LATVIAN Consumer Protection Act defines as a "seller" any natural or legal person who offers or sells goods to consumers by means of entrepreneurial activity, as well as a person who acts in the name of the seller or on his or her instruction.

In other legal systems this issue is not expressly regulated, but it does however follow from the general definition of consumer and the rules on agency conducted by a third party is attributed to the business and that a business does not lose its character as such by engaging a representative, who himself would be classed as a consumer (in particular for Austrian law).[2020]

By contrast the legal situation in GREECE and POLAND is unclear. In GREECE - in contrast to Directive 85/577 – no person acting in the name of and on behalf of a trader is viewed as a trader. The same applies for POLISH law. According to CC Art. 43 the nature of the activity

[2019] BGH judgment of 29 March 2006, VIII ZR 173/05, NJW 2006, 2250.

[2020] OGH judgment of 5 August 2003, 7 Ob 155/03z, VersR 2005, 430.

of the trader must be exercised in the person's "own name". This seems to be a narrower definition than the one provided in Art. 2 of Directive 85/577.

Furthermore, the issue of whether consumer protection laws apply if a private person is represented by a business is addressed differently. In AUSTRIA and GERMANY it generally depends on the identity of the contractual partner. A contract between two private persons does not therefore fall within the ambit of consumer protection provisions if it is brokered by a person acting in a business or professional capacity. By contrast in DENMARK, ITALY and PORTUGAL it is clarified that for timeshare contracts, if the vendor is not a professional, but the contract is concluded for the vendor by a professional, then it is regarded as a contract covered by the act as well.[2021]

3. Inclusion of legal persons/bodies of public law

In some member states it is additionally (beyond the scope of application of Directive 93/13) and expressly regulated that "business" includes legal persons under public law. In AUSTRIA legal persons under public law always qualify as businesses.[2022] In BELGIUM, the term "seller" (used in the Trade Practices Act for doorstep and distance selling and price indication) includes governmental institutions that pursue commercial, financial or industrial activity and sell or offer for sale products or services. In CYPRUS, according to Art. 2 of the Consumer Protection Act the word "business" includes "a trade or profession and the activities of any government department or local or public authority", "courts" and "directors". GREEK law also emphasises in Art. 1(3) of the Consumer Protection Act that public sector suppliers qualify as businesses. ITALIAN law includes (for sales contracts) under the definition of "seller" every natural or legal person of private and public law.[2023] In SLOVENIA, a "trader" is defined as a legal or natural person "regardless of their legal form or ownership".[2024] Similarly in the UNITED KINGDOM in the context of transposing the Consumer Sales Directive it is clarified that "business" includes the profession and activity of any government department (including a Northern Ireland department) or local or public authority.[2025] In other member states such as GERMANY it follows from the general definition of legal person that public bodies are also included.

IV. Final conclusions

Most member states do not have a uniform definition for the contractual partner of the consumer (business). It might nevertheless be useful to bear in mind that the main purpose of the notion of business is merely to make clear that the directives apply to B2C transactions, not to C2C relationships. Variations in the notion of business between the member states do not therefore have a great bearing on the correct transposition of the directives, so long as the definition of consumer is precise and the definition of business is not such as to

---

2021 Cf. Part 2 D.II.1.b.

2022 Article 1 (2), sent. 2 of the Consumer Protection Act.

2023 Article 128(2)(b) of the Consumer Code.

2024 Article 1(3) of the Consumer Protection Act.

2025 Section 61(1)(b) of the Sale of Goods Act 1979.

fail to provide protection in transactions where the directives intended the consumer to be protected. This study only shows a deviation from Community law requirements in this respect in GREECE and POLAND with their transpositions of Directive 85/577, as in both countries no person acting in the name of and on behalf of a trader is viewed as a business.[2026]

In the context of the review the following aspects, above all, should be considered:

- Although the definitions of business in European law exhibit a common core, the respective wordings of the directives use different definitions, which furthermore diverge in the individual language versions. Therefore, a uniform definition of business for all consumer protecting definitions should be found.
- In so doing, it should be clarified if the criterion of whether the relevant transaction is made "in the course of a person's profession" should be defined objectively, or more subjectively as being made for purposes relating to the profession.
- Is a person/entity without profit motive included in the notion of business?
- How are cases in which the business is acting for or on behalf of a third person to be treated?
- Besides the Unfair Contract Terms Directive, are legal persons/bodies of public law also covered by the scope of the directives?
- Who has the burden of proving that the contractual partner of the consumer was acting in their commercial or professional capacity? What are the requirements for discharging this burden?

C. Right of withdrawal

Hans Schulte-Nölke

I. Introduction

Another aspect common to some of the Directives within the focus of this study is a right of withdrawal granted to the consumer in certain situations and certain contracts. In this part of the study, we examine the current status of withdrawal rights in the 8 Directives, and consider whether there is room for improvement. In order to establish clear, concise and coherent terminology the term "withdrawal" is used in this study even in those cases where the English version of the Directives uses other terms.

2026 See *ante*, Part 3.B.III.2.

II. Existing withdrawal rights in the acquis

1. Doorstep Selling Directive

On the right of withdrawal, this Directive does not contain much more than what is set out in Art. 4 (duty to inform consumer about this right), Art. 5 (content and basic effect of right to withdraw), Art. 6 (mandatory law clause) and Art. 7 (unravelling of the contract). The terminology used is rather incoherent: "right of cancellation" (recital 5, Art. 4(1); Art. 5(2)), "right to renounce" (Art. 5(1)), "right of renunciation" (Art. 7).

2. Package Travel Directive

Directive 90/314 contains no right of withdrawal. Even when marketed via distance selling, package travel contracts are normally excluded from the withdrawal right granted under Directive 97/7 (Art. 3(2) 2nd indent of this Directive).

3. Unfair Contract Terms Directive

No reference to a right of withdrawal exists within this Directive.

4. Timeshare Directive

Besides an extensive catalogue of information duties, Directive 94/47 contains a right of withdrawal in Art. 5 (partially also called "right to cancel", see also "cancellation and withdrawal" in the 2nd and 13th recital; "right to cancel or withdraw" in Art. 7 and in lit. (l) of the Annex). This right is flanked by a duty to inform the consumer about his right (Art. 3, Art. 4 and lit. (l) of the Annex), a prohibition of advance payments during the withdrawal period (Art. 6), an extension of the withdrawal right to cover credit agreements related to the timeshare contract (Art. 7), some basic provisions on the unravelling of the contract (Art. 5(3) and (4)), a mandatory law clause (Art. 8) and a provision protecting the consumer in case of a choice of law clause (Art. 9).

5. Distance Selling Directive

Directive 97/7 contains a right of withdrawal in Art. 6. There is also a duty to inform the consumer about this right (Art. 4, Art. 5), an extension of the withdrawal right to cover related credit agreements (Art. 6(4)), some basic provisions on the unravelling of the contract (Art. 6(2)), a mandatory law clause (Art. 12(1)) and a provision protecting the consumer in case of a choice of law clause (Art. 12(2)).

6. Price Indications Directive

There is no reference to a right of withdrawal in this Directive.

7. Injunctions Directive

No reference to a right of withdrawal. The Directive is relevant to the extent that it provides a mechanism to deal with a failure to grant the withdrawal rights regulated in other Directives, e.g. Directive 85/577, Directive 94/47 and Directive 97/7.

8. Consumer Sales Directive

This Directive contains no withdrawal right.

9. Other directives outside the scope of this study

Directive 2002/65 contains a right of withdrawal in Art. 6. There is a duty to inform the consumer about this right (Art. 3, also requiring the supplier to inform the consumer about the absence of a withdrawal right), an extension of the withdrawal right to cover related (credit) agreements (Art. 6(7)), some basic provisions on the unravelling of the contract (Art. 7), a mandatory law clause (Art. 12(1)) and a provision protecting the consumer in case of a choice of law clause (Art. 12(2)).

Directive 2002/83 contains in Art. 35(1) a right to cancel an individual life-assurance contract. Directive 2002/65 refers to this cancellation right in Art. 6(1).[2027] The policy holder must be informed about this right according to Art. 36(1) and Annex III (A) of Directive 2002/83. The Directive also provides some very basic rules on the effect of cancellation and on the unravelling of the contract (Art. 35(1)).

Directive 87/102 does not grant right of withdrawal to the consumer, but the annex refers under 1.2. (vii) to a "cooling-off period, if any". By contrast, the proposals for a revision of the Directive contains a right of withdrawal.

2027 Directive 2002/65 refers to Directive 90/619, which has been replaced by Directive 2002/83; the normal withdrawal period of 14 calendar days is extended to 30 calendar days in distance contracts relating to life insurance covered by Directive 90/619 (now Directive 2002/83) and personal pension operations.

10. ECJ case-law with general importance for a right of withdrawal

There are at least three ECJ judgments which may have some importance for a general understanding of a withdrawal right, although they all exclusively apply to Directive 87/577. The C-481/99 – *Heininger*[2028] judgment established that one consequence of non-compliance with the duty to inform the consumer about his right of withdrawal is that the period for withdrawal is extended indefinitely, i.e., the seven-day 'withdrawal period' will not commence until the consumer has been adequately informed. The judgments in C-229/04 – *Crailsheimer Volksbank*[2029] and C-350/03 – *Schulte*[2030] cases also deal, among other issues, with the unravelling of a withdrawn contract.

III. Issues to be considered for a review of the acquis

The withdrawal rights in the Directives have been drafted and enacted one by one. It is nevertheless obvious, that those established earlier have influenced those that followed later. There is a clear tendency in the Directives to follow in the footsteps of the pre-existing withdrawal rights in order to develop the acquis coherently. The main issues regulated in the three withdrawal rights relevant for this study are outlined in the following table.

No	Issue	Directive 85/577	Directive 94/47	Directive 97/7
1	**Length of period**	not less than 7 days	within 10 calendar days	at least 7 working days
2	**Beginning of period** (as to sanctions in case of breach of information obligations see No. 8)	from receipt of notice [unclear: even before conclusion of contract, with the consequence that this period may have expired before the contract is concluded, cf. No. 7 of this table]	both parties signing the contract or both parties signing a binding preliminary contract	in the case of goods, from the day of receipt by the consumer in the case of services, from the day of the conclusion of the contract from the day on which the information obligations were fulfilled, if fulfilled after the conclusion of the contract
3	**Computation of period**		if the 10th day is a public holiday, the period shall be extended to the first working day thereafter	
4	**Dispatch rule:** pure timeliness rule or legal fiction of receipt?	[unclear]: sufficient if the notice is dispatched before the end of period	[unclear, looks more like a legal fiction of receipt]: deadline shall be deemed to have been observed if the notification, if it is in writing, is dispatched	[no provision]

[2028] ECJ judgment of 13 December 2001, C-481/99 – *Georg Heininger and Helga Heininger v Bayerische Hypo- und Vereinsbank AG* [2001] ECR I-09945.

[2029] ECJ judgment of 25 November 2005, C-229/04 – *Crailsheimer Volksbank eG v Klaus Conrads, Frank Schulzke and Petra Schulzke-Lösche, Joachim Nitschke* [2005] ECR I-9273.

[2030] ECJ judgment of 25 October 2005, C-350/03 - Elisabeth Schulte, Wolfgang Schulte v Deutsche Bausparkasse Badenia AG [2005] ECR I-09215.

No	Issue	Directive 85/577	Directive 94/47	Directive 97/7
5	**Rights and obligations during the period for withdrawal**	[no provision]	prohibition of advance payments before the end of the period [unclear whether applicable only with regard to the 10 calendar day period or also to the 3 months plus 10 calendar day period]	[no provision]
6	**Obligation to inform about right of withdrawal** (also formal requirements for this information)	written notice of right of cancellation, together with name and address of a person against whom that right may be exercised, notice must be dated and shall state particulars enabling the contract to be identified	in writing (with regard to the contract, which must contain certain information) in the official language opted for by purchaser	Information about the existence of right of withdrawal and other information (prior to the conclusion of the contract; and, if necessary, later confirmation in writing or on durable medium, cf. No. 7) written information on the conditions and procedures for exercising the right of withdrawal
7	**Point in time when information about right of withdrawal has to be given**	(in the case of Article 1 (1)): at the time of conclusion of the contract; (in the case of Article 1 (2)): not later than the time of conclusion of the contract; (in the case of Article 1 (3) and 1 (4)): when the offer is made by the consumer	provide any person requesting information with a document which shall provide brief and accurate information on lit. (l) of the Annex any advertising shall indicate the possibility of obtaining the document and where it may be obtained contract must include the items referred to in the Annex	in good time prior to the conclusion of any distance contract confirmation (written or on durable medium) in good time during the performance of the contract, and at the latest at the time of delivery, unless the information has already been given in such form in any event (in good time during the performance of the contract etc...): written information on the conditions and procedures for exercising the right of withdrawal,
8	**Sanctions in case of breach of this (and other) information obligation**	MS shall ensure appropriate consumer protection measures ECJ Heininger: period does not begin before information	extension of period: (up to 3 months delay) 10 calendar day period begins with receipt of information, otherwise, 3 months, plus 10 calendar days no defrayal of expenses	extension of period (up to three months delay): 7 working day period begins with receipt of information, otherwise, three months plus 7 working days, beginning in the case of goods, from the day of receipt by the consumer, in the case of services, from the day of conclusion of the contract.

No	Issue	Directive 85/577	Directive 94/47	Directive 97/7
9	**Exercise of right of withdrawal, particularly formal requirements**	in accordance with the procedure laid down by national law.	without giving any reason notify the person whose name and address appear in the contract by means which can be proved in accordance with national law in accordance with the procedures specified in the contract pursuant to point (l) of the Annex.	without giving any reason
10	**Effect of withdrawal for contractual obligations**	renounces the effects of the undertaking releasing the consumer from any obligations under the cancelled contract	[no general provision]	[no general provision]
11	**Effect of withdrawal with regard to credit agreements**	[no provision]	if the price is fully or partly covered by credit granted by the vendor, or if the price is fully or partly covered by credit granted to the purchaser by a third party on the basis of an agreement between the third party and the vendor, the credit agreement shall be cancelled, without any penalty MS shall lay down detailed arrangements to govern the cancellation of credit agreements.	if the price of goods or services is fully or partly covered by credit granted by the supplier, or if the price is fully or partly covered by credit granted to the consumer by a third party on the basis of an agreement between the third party and the supplier, the credit agreement shall be cancelled, without any penalty MS shall determine the detailed rules for cancellation of the credit agreement.
12	**Rules for the unravelling of the contract after withdrawal**	legal effects shall be governed by national laws, particularly regarding the reimbursement of payments for goods or services provided and the return of goods received	purchaser must defray only those expenses which, in accordance with national law, are incurred as a result of the conclusion of and withdrawal from the contract and which correspond to legal formalities which must be completed before the end of the 10 calendar day period; such expenses shall be expressly mentioned in the contract	without penalty supplier shall be obliged to reimburse the sums paid by the consumer free of charge. Such reimbursement must be carried out as soon as possible and in any case within 30 days. only charge: direct cost of returning the goods.
13	**Relation of withdrawal to other remedies**	[no provision, but the ECJ Travel Vac case, C-423/97, illustrates that the Directives may be applicable, in parallel to one another]	In addition to the possibilities available to the purchaser under national laws on the nullity of contracts	The provisions of this Directive shall apply insofar as there are no particular provisions in rules of Community law governing certain types of distance contracts in their entirety.

No	Issue	Directive 85/577	Directive 94/47	Directive 97/7
				Where specific Community rules contain provisions governing only certain aspects of the supply of goods or provision of services, those provisions, rather than the provisions of this Directive, shall apply to these specific aspects of the distance contracts.

The preceding table reveals a number of issues that may require some consideration. The order and numbering of the information laid out below follows the layout of the information presented in the table.

1. Length of period

It is obvious that the different periods cause incoherence within the acquis which may constitute a barrier to trade and an unnecessary burden to businesses. The Commission has already pointed out that it will examine the possibility and desirability of harmonising the existing cooling-off periods.[2031] It also seems that the 14 calendar day period stipulated in Art. 6 of the Directive 2002/65 (apart from life assurance) has been designed as a model for the other rights of withdrawal in the acquis. Therefore, it seems most plausible that the different periods in Directives 85/577, 94/47 and 97/7 should be harmonised in this way. It would have to be considered whether such a harmonised 14 calendar day period should be introduced as a full harmonisation measure. This could help businesses to set up cross-border marketing strategies, particularly in the field of distance selling. As only a few member states have provided longer periods[2032], full harmonisation may seem rather unproblematic from a consumer protection standpoint. However, it would have to be assessed whether in certain cases (in particular with regard to timesharing) a longer period (one to three months) might be desirable in order to improve consumer protection.

2. Beginning of period

A common feature in all the Directives is that the ordinary (short) period, which is applicable when the business fulfils its information obligations, does not begin before the receipt of the information. In this respect, the acquis is coherent.

2031 See Statement by the Council and the Parliament at the end of Directive 97/7.

2032 See the individual reports in Part 2 of this Analysis under A III 2a (Doorstep Selling, e.g. 15 days in MALTA and SLOVENIA); D III 3b aa (Timeshare, e.g. 15 days in CYPRUS, CZECH REPUBLIK, HUNGARY and SLOVENIA; 15 working days in BELGIUM); E III 2c aa (Distance Selling, e.g. 15 days in MALTA and SLOVENIA); perhaps also the one month period in GERMANY in case of delayed information.

Directives 94/47 and 97/7 require, furthermore, the contract to have been concluded, while Directive 85/577 seems to regulate that in certain cases the period may begin (and even end) before a contract has been concluded (Art. 4 lit. (c)). The Directives are therefore incoherent. Moreover, the (non-) requirement of the conclusion of the contract may lead to unwanted results. On the one hand, a consumer may be interested in withdrawing from an offer before it has been accepted (e.g. in timeshare contracts where sometimes a binding offer is pending for months). It would be odd, if a consumer who is already determined to withdraw, were to wait until the acceptance. On the other hand, it may be dangerous for the consumer if the period is allowed to expire before the conclusion of the contract. This would seem strange and could cause unnecessary communication duties for both parties if a consumer, who has made an offer (binding or non-binding), were forced to withdraw from this purely for reasons of precaution in cases where his offer has not been accepted, and he perhaps even suspects that the offer will never be accepted (e.g. an offer made by a consumer who knows that he may not be considered as creditworthy). This issue could be solved easily by a clarification, that the period never begins before the conclusion of the contract, but that the consumer is also entitled to withdraw from an offer or another binding declaration before the period begins, i.e. before a contract is concluded.

A further requirement for the beginning of the period, only regulated in Directive 97/7, is the receipt of goods to be delivered under the contract. This requirement allows the consumer to examine the goods before deciding whether to withdraw. It is a policy question whether a similar requirement also makes sense for doorstep contracts and, in particular, timeshare contracts.

3. Computation of period

The computation of the period is governed by Regulation 1182/71 of 3 June 1971 determining the rules applicable to periods, dates and time limits. Therefore, the express provision in Art. 5(1) 1st indent of the Directive 94/47 is superfluous. It may be useful to refer in future legislation to this regulation, which is perhaps sometimes overlooked.

4. Dispatch rule

Strikingly, Directive 97/7 is (together with Directive 2002/83) the only Directive which does not contain a dispatch rule. Even the later Directive 2002/65 comprises such a rule in Art. 6(6). This seems to be an error which should be removed.

As already indicated in the table, the wording of the existing dispatch rules is non-uniform and also unclear with regard to the effect of a timely dispatch. They allow different interpretation in the case of a letter which was dispatched in time, but got lost and therefore never reached the addressee. If the rule only regulates the calculation of the period, and leaves the consumer to bear the risk of a successful transmission of the declaration, the contract is not withdrawn, if the letter gets lost. The rule that the declaration is deemed to be received could also be construed as being legal fiction. This could be clarified either way.

5. Rights and obligations during the period for withdrawal

Apart from Directive 94/47, which contains a prohibition of advance payments, the acquis does not regulate the rights and obligations of the parties to the contract for which the period for withdrawal is pending. Per argumentum e contrario, one could therefore conclude that in all other cases the Directives allow the business to claim payments during the period. This interpretation is supported by the rules on unravelling the contract (cf. No. 12 of the above table), which regulate the reimbursement of sums paid by the consumer. It goes without saying that the consumer must also be entitled to claim performance during the pending period. The only question to decide for all withdrawal rights could be, whether the member states should be allowed to regulate more restrictive consumer protection rules like a general prohibition to claim payment before the period has expired.

With regard to advance payments under timeshare contracts, it could be clarified whether prohibition is applicable only until the end of the regular (10 calendar days) period or also, in case of breach of information obligations, to the three months plus 10 calendar day period.

6. Obligation to inform about right of withdrawal

The EC legislator should focus attention on this issue, especially due to the fact that this information obligation has enormous importance both for the position of the consumer on the one hand, and the business, which may suffer harsh consequences as a result of a breach of this obligation, on the other. This is also true, because differences of the member states' laws in this field may constitute very effective barriers to trade. The following issues might be considered in this context:

a. Formal requirements

It should be clarified that the information should be in writing (meaning practically on paper) or on a durable medium; the latter only in cases where electronic communication has been established between business and consumer.

b. Language

The language requirement in Directive 94/47 is unique and especially designed for such contracts. As to the other directives, the requirement of information in clear and intelligible language might in some cases amount to an obligation to use a certain (official) language. A general regulation of this issue is hardly imaginable, as the variety of cases and situations is too broad. Therefore, this issue might be left for the courts to decide.

c. Content of the information

The common core of the Directives is the requirement to inform the consumer about the existence of a withdrawal right and the name and address of the person against whom that right may be exercised. It could also be argued that the length of the period must be indicated. Many member states have stated further requirements with regard to the content of the information about the withdrawal right. This difference may constitute a barrier to trade because it might force businesses to draft special information notices for specific member states. Therefore, the acquis should seek to regulate this area in a way which allows for cross-border use of information. Such a regulation could, for example, provide a form which the business can use in order to inform the consumer about his right of withdrawal. EC law could, furthermore, stipulate that a business fulfils its obligation to inform the consumer about the withdrawal right by using this form, notwithstanding any other deviating national law. It is a policy question whether such a full harmonisation measure would displace the national law applicable in all cases or only in cross-border situations.

The content of the information to be provided with the help of such a form should at least encompass

- the existence of a withdrawal right;
- the length of the period; and
- the name and the address of the person against whom that right may be exercised.

Further sought-after information to be included in the form could be the beginning of the period. This issue is connected with the general question of when the period begins. If the acquis contains rules along the lines of the suggestion made under No. 2, it should also be possible to find suitable wording which explains at least the basic rules governing the beginning of the withdrawal period.

An additional element could be to provide the consumer with a form which could be used by him in order to exercise the withdrawal.

7. Point in time when information about the right of withdrawal has to be given

When the acquis offers a form as described under No. 6, the point in time when the consumer has to be provided with such a form (in writing or – if appropriate – on a durable medium) would be, at the latest, at the conclusion of the contract. The actual obligations to inform the consumer about the existence of a right of withdrawal at an earlier point in time could be maintained.

8. Sanctions in case of breach of the information obligation

The acquis is rather incoherent, because it comprises two different approaches. On the one hand, the ECJ decision *Heininger* has clarified that in doorstep selling cases the period does not begin before the consumer has been informed about his right of withdrawal. This may lead to an eternal withdrawal right. Directive 2002/65, which is a full harmonisation measure, seems to follow the same pattern. On the other hand, Directive 94/47 and Directive 97/7 only stipulate a "three months plus" rule, i.e., a prolongation of the withdrawal period up to a maximum of three months. This issue should be solved by choosing either one or the other whereby it may seem more plausible to bring the sanction in line with the ECJ case-law. It is a political question whether the eternal period in such cases is really an appropriate sanction, also bearing in mind that the period might in practice be cut off by national rules on prescription or procedural law. With regard to the laws of the member states, a maximum withdrawal period of one year could be considered as being more reasonable than the eternal period created by the ECJ in the *Heiniger* ruling.

9. Exercise of right of withdrawal, in particular formal requirements

The Directives do not regulate a formal requirement for the withdrawal. However, some member states do. This difference may constitute a barrier to trade, because it might force the business to include any formal requirement for the exercise of the withdrawal right into the information of the consumer about his right to withdraw (cf. e.g. Art. 5(1) 1st indent of Directive 97/7). Therefore, EC law could clarify that the consumer need not fulfil any formal requirement when withdrawing from a contract.

10. Effect of withdrawal for contractual obligations

The Directives contain only rather incomplete provisions on the effects of withdrawal. As the ECJ cases *Crailsheimer Volksbank* and *Schulte* have illustrated, a basic provision along the lines of Art. 5(2) of Directive 85/577 or Art. 35(1) of Directive 2002/83 might be useful for the national legislators to assess the general effect of withdrawal.

11. Effect of withdrawal with regard to credit agreements

Apart from Directive 85/577 (and Directive 2002/83 where it is not appropriate) all the other Directives which contain a withdrawal right, comprise a rather similar provision on credit agreements. Therefore, such a rule could be seen as a general principle and thus be extended to doorstep contracts as well.

12. Rules for the unravelling of contract after withdrawal

While Directive 85/577 expressly leaves the rules on the unravelling of a withdrawn contract to the member states, Directive 94/47 does not comprise a general provision, but regulates some details on the costs of legal formalities. By contrast, Directive 97/7 already contains some basic general rules on reimbursements. The ECJ cases *Crailsheimer Volksbank* and *Schulte* have clarified some further issues. In the course of a review of the acquis these lines could be completed to form a set of basic rules for the unravelling of withdrawn contracts. Such rules would state the general obligation of both parties to return goods and money received and could clarify which defrayals and costs the consumer would have to bear. It would also have to be considered to what extent such a set of rules, which might interfere with national rules on unjustified enrichment, should be enacted in a way of full harmonisation in order to achieve further progress in market integration.

13. Relation of withdrawal to other remedies

Following the model of Art. 5(1) of Directive 94/47, a general rule could be stated that a right of withdrawal does not prejudice other remedies available to the consumer, such as the invalidity of the contract or the right to terminate a contract because of its breach. This may lead to the somewhat surprising result that a consumer could be entitled to withdraw from an invalid contract. Such a remedy can make sense in those cases where the rules applicable for unravelling of the invalid contract would be less favourable than the rules for the unravelling of a withdrawn contract.

D. Information duties

Christian Twigg-Flesner

I. Introduction

One aspect common to several of the Directives within the focus of this study is the requirement to provide information to a consumer, either before a contract is concluded, or immediately afterwards. In some instances, information has to be provided both before *and* after the conclusion of a contract. In this part of the study, we examine the current extent of these information duties, and consider whether there is room for improvement.

The first section of this part will outline the existing information obligations in all the directives under consideration. The second section will then turn to the particular issues that arise from the current state of these duties, and will consider possible suggestions for improvement. This aspect is now firmly tied into the development of the *Common Frame of Reference* on European contract law, and any suggestions we make here need to be set in the context of the CFR.

II. Existing information obligations in the 8 directives

1. Doorstep Selling Directive

This Directive imposes only a very basic information requirement, but the jurisprudence of ECJ has revealed that the consequences of non-compliance can be rather complicated. Under Article 4(1), a consumer must be given information about his right to withdraw from a contract concluded in the circumstances to which the Directive applies within a period of no less than 7 days from concluding the contract, as well as the name and address of the person against who this right may be exercised.

This information must be given in writing. No further requirement, such as the quality of the language used in providing this information, or the clarity of the information, is imposed.

There is no provision in this Directive regarding the sanctions that might be attached to a failure by a trader to give the consumer this information. Case-law before the ECJ has established that one consequence is that the period for extending the right of withdrawal is extended indefinitely, i.e., the seven-day 'withdrawal period' will not commence until the consumer has been informed adequately.

The position regarding sanctions in the member states is therefore rather diffuse. In BELGIUM, failure to provide this information results in the nullity of the contract.[2033] This is also the case e.g., in HUNGARY,[2034] LUXEMBOURG,[2035] MALTA,[2036] the NETHERLANDS, [2037] and SPAIN.[2038] The same may happen in GREECE under generally applicable rules. In the UNITED KINGDOM, it is clarified that the contract remains enforceable by the consumer against the trader, but not by the trader against the consumer,[2039] although the position will be similar in the other countries mentioned.

In IRELAND, a criminal penalty is imposed for failing to comply with this information obligation.[2040] SLOVENIA also imposes criminal liability.[2041] The United Kingdom also provides for a detailed system of criminal penalties in addition to the sanction of non-enforceability against the consumer.[2042]

In ITALY, if this information is not supplied (or supplied incorrectly), the period for exercising the right to withdrawal is extended to 60 days from the conclusion of the contract (for contract of services) or from the delivery of goods,[2043] whereas in LITHUANIA, the period is three months from the date of concluding the contract.[2044]

2033 Article 88, sent. 3 of the Law on Trade Practices and Consumer Information.

2034 Article 3(3) of the Government Decree on Doorstep Selling.

2035 Article 10(1) of the Doorstep Selling Act.

2036 Article 7 of the Doorstep Contracts Act.

2037 Article 24(1) of the Doorstep Selling Act.

2038 Article 4 of the Law 26/1991 of November 21, on consumers' protection in case of contracts executed out of the commercial premises.

2039 Regulation 4 Consumer Protection (Cancellation of Contracts concluded away from business premises) Regulations 1987.

2040 Regulation 4(4)-(6) European Communities (Cancellation of Contracts negotiated away from business premises) Regulations, 1989.

2041 Article 77(1) no. 24, (2) of the Consumer Protection Act.

2042 Regulation 4A-4H Consumer Protection (Cancellation of Contracts concluded away from business premises) Regulations 1987.

2043 Article 65(3) of the Consumer Code.

2044 Article 8, sent. 3 of the Order of the Minister of Economy of the Republic of Lithuania on the Approval of the Rules of Sale of Goods and Provision of Services in Premises not Designated for this Activity.

2. Directive 90/314/EEC (Package Travel)

This Directive requires that information is provided to a consumer at 4 different stages, and the type of information required varies accordingly.

The first stage is where a brochure about a package holiday is given to a consumer. The Directive states that such a brochure must contain information about the following aspects of the holiday:[2045]

(i) the price;
(ii) adequate information concerning:
    (i) destination and means, characteristics and categories of transport used;
    (ii) type of accommodation, its location, category or degree of comfort and its main features; its approval and tourist classification under the rules of the host Member State concerned;
    (iii) the meal plan;
    (iv) the itinerary;
    (v) general information on passport and visa requirements for nationals of the member state or states concerned and health formalities required for the journey and the stay;
    (vi) either the monetary amount or the percentage of the price which is to be paid on account, and the timetable for payment of the balance;
    (vii) whether a minimum number of persons is required for the package to take place and if so, the deadline for informing the consumer in the event of cancellation.

This information has to be included in the brochure. This term is not defined, but it seems likely that the intention was to refer to a written document. Consequently, it is implicit that the information listed above must be provided in writing. In addition, Art.3(1) requires that this information must not be misleading.

It is also not entirely clear if information about package holidays displayed on a website would be a 'brochure'. If this were not so, then these particular information obligations might not apply, although it would then have to be considered to what extent the obligations in the Directive 97/7 might require the provision of the equivalent items of information under its provisions.

The second stage at which information has to be provided is at a point before the contract is concluded. Art. 4(1) lit. (a) states that the consumer has to be provided with information about (i) passport and visa requirements applicable to nationals of the member state(s) concerned, in particular on the periods for obtaining these; and (ii) information on the health formalities required both for the journey and the stay. This information must be provided 'in writing or any other appropriate form'.

The third stage is the period 'in good time before the start of the journey',[2046] which, presumably, means that a contract has already been concluded. Here, the consumer must be given information – again 'in writing or any other appropriate form' about the following:[2047]

2045 Article 3(2).
2046 Article 4(1)(b).
2047 Article 4(1)(b).

(i) Times/places of intermediate stops and transport connections;
(ii) Details of the travel accommodation ('place to be occupied by the traveller'), such as the cabin/berth on a ship or sleeper compartment on a train;
(iii) Name/address/telephone number of organiser's and/or retailer's local representative; alternatively, of local agencies who could assist the consumer in cases of difficulty. If none of these is available, the consumer must be given an emergency contact number for the organiser/retailer.
(iv) Where journeys/stays abroad by minors: information enabling contact with the child/ person responsible for the child;
(v) Optional insurance policy to cover the cost of cancellation by the consumer; or of assistance, including repatriation, in the event of accident/illness.

The fourth, and final, stage at which the Directive mandates the provision of specific information to the consumer is in the contract document itself. Article 4(2) lit. (a) requires that the contract includes at least all the items listed in the Annex to the Directive, which are:
(a) the travel destination(s), and, where periods of stay are involved, the relevant periods with dates;
(b) the means, characteristics and categories of transport to be used, the dates, times and points of departure and return;
(c) where the package includes accommodation, its location, its tourist category or degree of comfort, its main features, its compliance with the rules of the host member state concerned and the meal plan;
(d) whether a minimum number of persons is required for the package to take place and, if so, the deadline for informing the consumer in the event of cancellation;
(e) the itinerary;
(f) visits, excursions or other services which are included in the total price agreed for the package;
(g) the name and address of the organiser, the retailer, and, where appropriate, the insurer;
(h) the price of the package, an indication of the possibility of price revision under Article 4(4) and an indication of any dues, taxes or fees chargeable for certain services (landing, embarkation or disembarkation fees at airports, tourist taxes) where such costs are not included in the package;
(i) the payment schedule and method of payment;
(j) special requirements which the consumer has communicated to the organiser or retailer when making the booking, and which have been accepted;
(k) periods within which the consumer must make any complaint concerning failure to perform or improper performance of the contract.

The terms of the contract must be in writing, or 'in such other form as is comprehensible and accessible to the consumer'. All the information also has to be 'communicated' to the consumer before the conclusion of the contract, which does not seem to require that the consumer is given this information in writing before the contract is concluded. Article 4(2) lit. (b) goes on to say that the consumer must be given a copy of these terms.

The table on the next page seeks to indicate how the various items of information that may have to be provided in the course of concluding a contract for a package holiday are distributed across the 4 stages mentioned above. It will be seen from this that despite the rather extensive list of items, there is only a limited amount of duplication. The only noticeable duplication arises where a consumer is given a brochure and subsequently books a contract based on that brochure. However, in circumstances where a consumer does not rely on a brochure, there will be almost no duplication at all.

Item of information	Brochure[2048]	Before contract[2049]	Before journey[2050]	Contract[2051]
Price	✓			✓(including information about price revision)
Indication of any dues, taxes or fees chargeable for certain services (landing, embarkation or disembarkation fees at airports, tourist taxes) where such costs are not included in the package				✓
Destination and means, characteristics and categories of transport used	✓		✓ (times/places of intermediate stops and transport connections and details of place to be occupied by traveller)	
Type of accommodation, its location, category or degree of comfort and its main features; its approval and tourist classification under the rules of the host member state concerned	✓			✓
Meal plan	✓			✓
Itinerary	✓			✓
General information on passport and visa requirements for nationals of the member state or states concerned	✓	✓		
Health formalities required for the journey and the stay	✓	✓		
Either the monetary amount or the percentage of the price which is to be paid on account, and the timetable for payment of the balance/payment plan	✓			✓(payment schedule and method of payment)
Whether a minimum number of persons is required for the package to take place and if so, the deadline for informing the consumer in the event of cancellation	✓			✓
Name and address of the organiser, the retailer, and, where appropriate, the insurer				✓

2048 It is assumed that the information here must be given in writing.
2049 This information has to be given in writing or any other appropriate form.
2050 In writing or any other appropriate form
2051 In writing or such other form as is comprehensible and accessible to the consumer.

Item of information	Brochure[2048]	Before con-tract[2049]	Before journey[2050]	Contract[2051]
Name/address/telephone number of organiser's and/or retailer's local representative; alternatively, of local agencies who could assist the consumer in cases of difficulty. If none of these is available, the consumer must be given an emergency contact number for the organiser/retailer			✓	
Where journeys/stays abroad by minors: information enabling contact with the child/person responsible for the child			✓	
Optional insurance policy to cover the cost of cancellation by the consumer; or of assistance, including repatriation, in the event of accident/illness			✓	
Visits, excursions or other services which are included in the total price agreed for the package				✓
Special requirements which the consumer has communicated to the organiser or retailer when making the booking, and which have been accepted				✓
Periods within which the consumer must make any complaint concerning failure to perform or improper performance of the contract				✓

3. Unfair Contract Terms Directive

This Directive does not mandate that any particular information is given to a consumer. It may be that the requirement that a term is not contrary to 'good faith'[2052] embodies the obligation to disclose particularly onerous terms to the consumer before a contract is concluded. This is possibly reinforced by one of the indicative terms in the Annex: term (i) states that a term which binds a consumer to all the terms of in the contract without having had an opportunity to become acquainted with them before the conclusion of the contract is potentially unfair. This, in turn, suggests that adequate transparency regarding the terms of a contract before its conclusion would reduce the likelihood of a particular term being found to be unfair subsequently. The Directive also imposes a form requirement in that all written contract terms must be in 'plain and intelligible language'.[2053]

4. Timeshare Directive

The Directive 94/47 contains an extensive catalogue of items of information which must be disclosed to a consumer at two stages in the process of acquiring a property on a timeshare basis: (i) when information about a property is requested; and (ii) when the contract is drawn up. The Annex to the Directive contains a minimum list of information that must be provided to a consumer. The table below illustrates when these items are to be provided.

2052 Article 3(1).

2053 Article 5.

There is no requirement in this Directive that the information must be given in any particular form; crucially, there is no mention of information having to be in plain and intelligible language. A consumer who requests information about a timeshare property under Article 3(1) is entitled to receive 'brief and accurate' information. The contract for the acquisition of a timeshare right has to be in the language of the member state where the purchaser resides or of which he is a national. Also, the relevant information, both at the time of enquiring and in the contract itself, must be written – but there is no mention of alternative forms such as a 'durable medium'.

The Directive 94/47 contains a sanction for circumstances where some of the required information is not given. Thus, Article 5(1) permits an extension of the withdrawal period to up to three months from conclusion of the contract where the items listed in that article are not provided. The final column in the table identifies the items of information which must be provided to avoid triggering the extension of the withdrawal period under Article 5(1). Where there is an omission to provide any other item of information required under Articles 3 and/or 4, no specific sanction is envisaged in the Directive.

As the Comparative Analysis of this Directive reveals, member states have adopted sanctions of varying kinds to deal with a failure to comply with the information duties.

Item of Information	Request	Contract	Withdrawal
(a) The identities and domiciles of the parties, including specific information on the vendor's legal status at the time of the conclusion of the contract and the identity and domicile of the owner.	✓	✓	✓
(b) The exact nature of the right which is the subject of the contract and a clause setting out the conditions governing the exercise of that right within the territory of the member state(s) in which the property or properties concerned relates is or are situated and if those conditions have been fulfilled or, if they have not, what conditions remain to be fulfilled.	✓	✓	✓
(c) When the property has been determined, an accurate description of that property and its location.	✓	✓	✓
(d) Where the immovable property is under construction:			
(1) the state of completion;	✓	✓	✓
(2) a reasonable estimate of the deadline for completion of the immovable property;	✓	✓	✓
(3) where it concerns a specific immovable property, the number of the building permit and the name(s) and full address(es) of the competent authority or authorities;	✓	✓	×
(4) the state of completion of the services rendering the immovable property fully operational (gas, electricity, water and telephone connections);	✓	✓	×
(5) a guarantee regarding completion of the immovable property or a guarantee regarding reimbursement of any payment made if the property is not completed and, where appropriate, the conditions governing the operation of those guarantees.	✓	✓	×
(e) The services (lighting, water, maintenance, refuse collection) to which the purchaser has or will have access and on what conditions.	✓	✓	×
(f) The common facilities, such as swimming pool, sauna, etc., to which the purchaser has or may have access, and, where appropriate, on what conditions.	✓	✓	×

Item of Information	Request	Contract	Withdrawal
(g) The principles on the basis of which the maintenance of and repairs to the immovable property and its administration and management will be arranged.	✓	✓	×
(h) The exact period within which the right which is the subject of the contract may be exercised and, if necessary, its duration; the date on which the purchaser may start to exercise the contractual right.	×	✓	✓
(i) The price to be paid by the purchaser to exercise the contractual right; an estimate of the amount to be paid by the purchaser for the use of common facilities and services; the basis for the calculation of the amount of charges relating to occupation of the property, the mandatory statutory charges (for example, taxes and fees) and the administrative overheads (for example, management, maintenance and repairs).	✓	✓	✓
(j) A clause stating that acquisition will not result in costs, charges or obligations other than those specified in the contract.	×	✓	×
(k) Whether or not it is possible to join a scheme for the exchange or resale of the contractual rights, and any costs involved should an exchange and/or resale scheme be organized by the vendor or by a third party designated by him in the contract.	×	✓	✓
(l) Information on the right to cancel or withdraw from the contract and indication of the person to whom any letter of cancellation or withdrawal should be sent, specifying also the arrangements under which such letters may be sent; precise indication of the nature and amount of the costs which the purchaser will be required to defray pursuant to Article 5(3) if he exercises his right to withdraw; where appropriate, information on the arrangements for the cancellation of the credit agreement linked to the contract in the event of cancellation of the contract or withdrawal from it.	✓	✓	✓
(m) The date and place of each party's signing of the contract.	×	✓	✓

5. Distance Selling Directive

The Directive 97/7 also requires the provision of specific items of information, both before and after a contract is concluded. Unlike the Directives 90/314 and 94/47, the Directive 97/7 specifies broad categories of information, because the Directive applies to the sale of a wide range of goods and services at a distance and can therefore only state generally applicable items of information.

Article 4 specifies a list of items which must be given before a contract is concluded. This information must be provided in a 'clear and comprehensible manner in any way appropriate to the means of distance communication used'. These items are:

(a) the identity of the supplier and, in the case of contracts requiring payment in advance, his address;
(b) the main characteristics of the goods or services;
(c) the price of the goods or services including all taxes;
(d) delivery costs, where appropriate;
(e) the arrangements for payment, delivery or performance;
(f) the existence of a right of withdrawal, except in the cases referred to in Article 6 (3);

(g) the cost of using the means of distance communication, where it is calculated other than at the basic rate;
(h) the period for which the offer or the price remains valid;
(i) where appropriate, the minimum duration of the contract in the case of contracts for the supply of products or services to be performed permanently or recurrently.

Article 5 requires written confirmation of the information listed in paragraphs (a)-(f) above 'in good time during the performance of the contract', and no later than the delivery of goods. Instead of in writing, the information may be provided in a 'durable medium available and accessible' to the consumer. However, it is acknowledged that this provision can result in the duplication of information which has already been given in pursuance of Article 4, and Article 5 therefore provides that where the consumer has already received this information in writing or in another durable medium before the contract was concluded, there is no need to repeat this information. However, there is a requirement to provide information on the following in addition to the items already mentioned:
(i) written information on the conditions and procedures for exercising the right of withdrawal, within the meaning of Article 6, including the cases referred to in the first indent of Article 6(3),
(ii) the geographical address of the place of business of the supplier to which the consumer may address any complaints,
(iii) information on after-sales services and guarantees which exist,
(iv) the [conditions][2054] for cancelling the contract, where it is of unspecified duration or a duration exceeding one year.

The Directive does not provide any specific sanctions for failing to provide the information required by Article 4. A failure to provide written confirmation of the information as required by Article 5 will, however, result in an extension of the period during which the consumer may exercise the right of withdrawal provided by Article 6 from the basic 7-day period to three months.

6. Price Indications Directive

This Directive requires the provision of pricing information in a particular format: the provision of the selling price and the unit price. Thus, in situations within the scope of this Directive, pricing information must comply with the requirements of this Directive. Where the price is given, it must be 'unambiguous, easily identifiable and clearly legible."[2055] Again, no specific sanctions for failing to comply with this Directive are provided, and this matter is left to the member states.[2056]

2054 Note: In the official text of the Directive, the word "conclusions" is used. This seems to be a mistake, albeit one that appears not to have been corrected so far. The German version of the Directive uses the term "Kündigungsbedingungen" (our emphasis), and the French version refers to "les conditions de résiliation", which strongly suggests that the English word here ought to be "conditions", as substituted in the list in the main text.

2055 Article 4(1).

2056 Article 8.

7. Injunctions Directive

This Directive does not contain any information duties. It is relevant to the extent that it provides a mechanism to deal with a failure to comply with the information duties in other Directives, because it enables qualified entities to take action to prevent a continuing failure by a trader to provide information that is required by a particular directive.

8. Consumer Sales Directive

This Directive contains specific information requirements only in respect of 'guarantees'.[2057] This provision requires that a guarantee must contain information about:

(i) the consumer's legal rights under the national legislation on the sale of goods, and make clear that these rights are unaffected by the guarantee;
(ii) the contents of the guarantee, including duration and territorial scope of the guarantee
(iii) the essential particulars for making a claim, including the name and address of the guarantor.

A guarantee must be made available on request in writing or in another durable medium available and accessible to the consumer. It also has to set out the contents and essential particulars in plain and intelligible language. Somewhat strangely, the requirement of plain and intelligible language does not appear to extend to the first item (the reference to the consumer's legal rights). However, if the guarantee is enforceable as a contract, the corresponding requirement in Directive 93/13 may fill this gap in any event.

It may also be noted that it has been suggested by various commentators that Article 2 on 'conformity with the contract' could be read as containing an implied information obligation. This is because a seller who makes a consumer aware of a particular lack of conformity will not be liable for the goods' non-conformity. Commentators have interpreted this in different ways, including as an obligation to disclose information,[2058] an "indirect information requirement",[2059] or a simple "encouragement to disclose information".[2060]

III. Issues common to several directives

The preceding overview of the various information duties in the 8 Directives under review in this study reveals a number of issues that may require consideration. Key matters in respect of which there is divergence between the directives relate to the form in which information is presented, and sanctions for failing to comply with these information obligations. Moreover, there may be circumstances where a transaction comes within the scope of more than one

---

2057 Article 6.

2058 See e.g., *Riesenhuber*, Party Autonomy and Information in the Sales Directive" in: Grundmann/Kerber/Weatherill, Party Autonomy and the Role of Information in the Internal Market.

2059 See *Wilhelmsson*, Remedies against Breach of Information Requirements, in Schulze/Ebers/Grigoleit in: Informationspflichten und Vertragsschluss in Acquis communautaire.

2060 Twigg-Flesner, Information Disclosure about the Quality of Goods – Duty or Encouragement? in: Howells/Janssen/Schulze, Information Rights and Obligations.

directive (e.g., where a package travel holiday is booked via a website), which may result in unnecessary duplication of information. We will consider these issues in turn.

1. Form in which information to be provided

The Directives which impose information duties also specify the form in which this information has to be given. However, as the directives were adopted over a period of 15 years, there is a degree of incoherence/inconsistency in the form requirements. The table below lists the various form requirements found in the directives.

Directive	Form requirement(s)
Doorstep Selling (85/577)	Written Notice (Art. 4)
Package Travel (90/314)	Legible, comprehensible and accurate (Art. 3(2)) [brochure] In writing or other appropriate form (Art. 4(1)) [pre-contract] In writing or such other form as is comprehensible and accessible to the consumer (Art. 4(2)(b)) [contract]
Unfair Terms (93/13)	If contracts in writing, must be in plain and intelligible language (Art.5)
Timeshare (94/47)	Contract in writing and language of member state (Art.4)
Distance Selling (97/7)	Clear and comprehensible manner; appropriate to medium of distance communication used (Art. 4) In writing or in another durable medium available and accessible to the consumer
Price Indications (98/6)	unambiguous, easily identifiable and clearly legible (Art. 4(1))
Consumer Sales (99/44)	in writing or in another durable medium available and accessible to the consumer (Art. 6).

This overview demonstrates that there is a degree of variation in the form requirements for the provision of information. It would be desirable to consider a uniform approach to the question of form of information, to improve overall coherence and to reduce the risk of compliance difficulty for business.

2. Sanctions for failing to provide information

One of the glaring gaps in all the directives imposing information obligations is a consistent scheme of sanctions for a failure to comply with such an obligation. In the directives imposing a right of withdrawal, not providing some of the information, may result in an extension to the period during which the right of withdrawal may be exercised.[2061] However, even in those Directives, this sanction does not extend to all failures to comply with an information duty.[2062]

Beyond these situations, the consumer acquis in its present format does not envisage any particular sanctions, leaving the matter for the member states to resolve. In considering whether to improve the acquis, the question of sanctions for failing to correspond with information duties may be one matter that may need to be given some attention. It was not apparent from the reports by the national correspondents whether the lack of sanctions is an

[2061] See further the section on 'withdrawal' in this study.

[2062] See the table on the Directive 94/47.

obvious barrier to trade. A divergence in the various national laws in this matter does, however, create at least the potential of creating a barrier to trade. Introducing uniform sanctions would, in that case, increase the likelihood of reducing such barriers. A clearer system of sanctions in this regard might also benefit consumer confidence, and therefore the operation of the internal market. However, this study has not discovered sufficiently strong evidence clearly to support the introduction of a coherent system of sanctions from the perspective of benefiting the internal market.

3. Overlapping information obligations

One of the matters which has not been resolved in the directives which impose information obligations is the problem that more than one directive may apply to particular types of contracts, with the consequence that a trader may be subject to more than one set of information rules. Of the Directives under consideration in this study, this problem is most likely to occur in respect of either package holiday contracts or timeshare contracts[2063] concluded at a distance. The Directive 97/7 provides broad pre-contractual information duties, combined with a requirement to confirm information in writing or in another durable medium once a contract has been concluded. The Directives 90/314 and 94/47 contain detailed itemisations of the information to be provided in respect of these particular types of contract. Where both Directives apply at the same time, the two respective sets of information duties overlap and the overall amount of information to be provided is extended. In some instances, information that is required by the Directives 90/314 and 94/47 may correspond to one of the broad headings in the Directive 97/7, which reduces the overall overlap. However, there will be aspects in respect of which there is no such overlap. The following two tables concentrate on the overlap between Distance Selling and Package Travel (grey shaded areas indicate areas where one of the directives adds to the information obligations in the other).

a. Pre-contractual information where package holiday sold by distance selling

Information items in Distance Selling Directive	Corresponding information items in Package Travel Directive
(a) the identity of the supplier and, in the case of contracts requiring payment in advance, his address	No corresponding requirement in this Directive
(b) the main characteristics of the goods or services;	destination and means, characteristics and categories of transport used; type of accommodation, its location, category or degree of comfort and its main features; its approval and tourist classification under the rules of the host member state concerned;

2063 It may be asked whether timeshare contracts come within the scope of the Distance Selling Directive at all. Article 3(1) of the Directive 97/7 excludes "contracts for the construction and sale of immovable property or relating to other immovable property rights, except for rental". Although the provision is not settled, the ECJ judgment in C-423/97 – *Travel-VAC S.L. v Sanchis* [1999] ECR I-2195, which involved an exclusion in very similar terms from the scope of the Directive 85/577, suggests that at least those timeshare contracts which provide more than a basic property right are covered in their entirety by the Directive 97/7 where the transaction falls within the scope of that Directive.

Information items in Distance Selling Directive	Corresponding information items in Package Travel Directive
	the meal plan; the itinerary;
(c) the price of the goods or services including all taxes	Price (Art. 3(2) does not elaborate further on the exact information to be provided)
(d) delivery costs, where appropriate	(not appropriate)
(e) the arrangements for payment, delivery or performance	either the monetary amount or the percentage of the price which is to be paid on account, and the timetable for payment of the balance; whether a minimum number of persons is required for the package to take place and if so, the deadline for informing the consumer in the event of cancellation
(f) the existence of a right of withdrawal, except in the cases referred to in Article 6 (3);	*No corresponding requirement in this Directive* – there is no right of withdrawal from package holidays under the Directive.
(g) the cost of using the means of distance communication, where it is calculated other than at the basic rate	*No corresponding requirement in this Directive* – this provision is specific to the Distance Selling Directive
(h) the period for which the offer or the price remains valid	*No corresponding requirement in this Directive*
(i) where appropriate, the minimum duration of the contract in the case of contracts for the supply of products or services to be performed permanently or recurrently	(not appropriate)
Information not required by the Distance Selling Directive	general information on passport and visa requirements for nationals of the member state or states concerned and health formalities required for the journey and the stay;

b. Confirmation of information where package holiday sold by distance selling

Information items in Distance Selling Directive	Corresponding information items in Package Travel Directive
(a) the identity of the supplier and, in the case of contracts requiring payment in advance, his address	the name and address of the organiser, the retailer, and, where appropriate, the insurer
(b) the main characteristics of the goods or services;	times/places of intermediate stops and transport connections details of the travel accommodation ('place to be occupied by the traveller'), such as the cabin/berth on a ship or sleeper compartment on a train the travel destination(s), and, where periods of stay are involved, the relevant periods with dates the means, characteristics and categories of transport to be used, the dates, times and points of departure and return where the package includes accommodation, its location, its tourist category or degree of comfort, its main features, its compliances with the rules of the host member state concerned and the meal plan the itinerary visits, excursions or other services which are included in the total price agreed for the package

Information items in Distance Selling Directive	Corresponding information items in Package Travel Directive
(c) the price of the goods or services including all taxes	the price of the package, an indication of the possibility of price revision under Article 4(4) and an indication of any dues, taxes or fees chargeable for certain services (landing, embarkation or disembarkation fees at airports, tourist taxes) where such costs are not included in the package
(d) delivery costs, where appropriate	(not appropriate)
(e) the arrangements for payment, delivery or performance	whether a minimum number of persons is required for the package to take place and, if so, the deadline for informing the consumer in the event of cancellation the payment schedule and method of payment
(f) the existence of a right of withdrawal, except in the cases referred to in Article 6(3);	*No corresponding requirement in this Directive* – there is no right of withdrawal from package holidays under the Directive.
written information on the conditions and procedures for exercising the right of withdrawal, within the meaning of Article 6, including the cases referred to in the first indent of Article 6(3),	*No corresponding requirement in this Directive* – there is no right of withdrawal from package holidays under the Directive.
the geographical address of the place of business of the supplier to which the consumer may address any complaints	name/address/telephone number of organiser's and/or retailer's local representative; alternatively, of local agencies who could assist the consumer in cases of difficulty. If none of these is available, the consumer must be given an emergency contact number for the organiser/retailer
information on after-sales services and guarantees which exist	(not applicable)
the conditions[2064] for cancelling the contract, where it is of unspecified duration or a duration exceeding one year	(not applicable)
Information not required by the Distance Selling Directive	Where journeys/stays abroad by minors: information enabling contact with the child/person responsible for the child Optional insurance policy to cover the cost of cancellation by the consumer; or of assistance, including repatriation, in the event of accident/illness special requirements which the consumer has communicated to the organiser or retailer when making the booking, and which have been accepted periods within which the consumer must make any complaint concerning failure to perform or improper performance of the contract

The challenge for the acquis review is to consider whether the lengthy information catalogues in the Directives 94/47 and 90/314, in particular, are still required, or whether they can be shortened. In the Directive 90/314, there appears to be a limited amount of duplication in the way the particular items of information are expressed, but this is only a minor aspect.

2064 See comment made earlier about the use of this word.

IV. Overall recommendations for the acquis review

- There is an obvious need to consider whether the detailed lists of items of information to be provided need to be maintained.
- In particular, it is possible (i) to replace the detailed lists with more general requirements; or (ii) to consider whether particular items are not essential and could be deleted. An analysis of the various items of information found in the directives under review suggests that what is generally needed is information about the main characteristics of the goods or services, the price including delivery charges, taxes and other costs, the address and identity of the business with whom the consumer is transacting, the terms of the contract, the rights and obligations of both contracting parties, and any available redress procedures.
- Regard should also be had to the comparative analysis of the specific Directives, especially Directives 97/7, 90/314 and 94/47, for the national variations regarding the various information duties in these directives. In this regard, the question of overlapping information duties needs to be addressed.
- If it is desirable to retain more precise information catalogues, e.g., for Directive 90/314 or 94/47, it is recommended that consideration is given whether any of the additional items of information required by virtue of the implementing legislation in the member states should be added to the list (even if some existing items are removed).
- At the present time, the form requirements vary between the Directives. It should be made clear that information needs to be clear and precise, and expressed in plain and intelligible language. Moreover, unless a contract is concluded verbally in its entirety, the information should be provided in writing. In this context, it should be clarified that writing may be replaced by another textual form on a durable medium, provided this is reasonably accessible to the recipient.
- Furthermore, there is no coherent system of sanctions for failing to comply with information duties in place. A special position is occupied by information about the right of withdrawal, where a failure to provide this information leads to an extension of the period during which this right may be exercised.[2065] Beyond that, however, the situation is left unclear, and the member states have adopted rather diverse approaches (see the comparative reports on Directives 97/7, 90/314, and 94/47, in particular). A failure to comply with these obligations can be the subject of an action for an injunction (as per Directive 98/27). As far as individual consumers are concerned, a clearer rule regarding sanctions should be adopted; in this regard, it may be considered whether a failure to comply with information duties should result in the non-enforceability of contracts against a consumer (as is the case in many member states), or a claim for damages.

[2065] See further, section on 'right of withdrawal'.

Part 4: Recommendations

Hans Schulte-Nölke, Christian Twigg-Flesner and Martin Ebers

The following conclusions and recommendations are based on the analysis of legal issues carried out in this study. The results of the analysis illustrate and confirm the need for action in the field of EC consumer law for several reasons.

Firstly, the Directives are often incoherent, and contain a significant number of ambiguities, which makes it difficult to transpose them into domestic law, and to ensure correct application by the courts. Consequently, one key recommendation is to remove such incoherencies and ambiguities and at the same time to consolidate and harmonise issues currently distributed across several Directives. This should make EC consumer law easier to access.

Moreover, the comparative analysis has revealed areas where the laws of the member states in the field of the Directives differ considerably. Often, the reason for such variations is that the corresponding provision of the respective Directive contains a gap which the member states have tried to fill with national laws. Many of the recommendations made in this study are based on this observation. Finally, other proposals seek to overcome barriers to trade, which are due to differences between the laws of the member states. Such differences are mainly due to the minimum clauses and options contained in the directives, but sometimes also due to gaps in the Directives, or incorrect transposition. It has been suggested that these differences be removed, in particular, in the field of information duties, withdrawal rights and formal requirements. This should considerably facilitate cross border business, especially for SMEs.

A. Creating common uniform definitions and basic rules for all consumer law directives

Certain definitions and consumer protection devices are to be found in all, or at least several, of the consumer protection directives. In addition to the definition of consumer and the other party to the contract, the business, these are mainly information duties, withdrawal rights and rules making consumer rights mandatory.

The relevant rules in the individual directives show significant differences in wording, style and content. There seem to be practically no differences due to peculiarities of the particular aspect of consumer protection addressed by a directive. The vast majority of these discrepancies are simply inconsistencies resulting from the piecemeal approach in adopting EC legislation over a period of more than 20 years. Such inconsistencies cause difficulties in the transposition and application of EC consumer law, which should be removed. This would identify a 'common core' within the EC consumer acquis. Therefore it has been suggested that the following matters should be treated uniformly in the acquis:

- Definition of consumer;
- Definition of business;
- Some technical definitions like "in writing" or "durable medium";
- Some basic information duties common to the contract law directives;
- General rules on the withdrawal period, the exercise of the withdrawal and its effect;
- A rule making consumer rights generally mandatory;
- Consumer rights in case of choice of law clauses;

B. Re-structuring the consumer acquis through a horizontal consumer protection measure

One possible way forward is to bring together the common EC consumer acquis elements listed above in a horizontal measure (whether that be a new Directive, or a Regulation similar to Regulation 1182/71 of 3 June 1971, determining the rules applicable to periods, dates and time limits, which has horizontal application), which would then contain key general rules applicable also to all relevant consumer protection directives.

Such a horizontal measure should also include those provisions of the existing directives which are applicable to all contracts concluded between a business and a consumer. These provisions, applicable not only to a certain type of contract, but to all contracts for the supply of goods and services, are mainly to be found in the Unfair Contract Terms Directive, the Doorstep Selling and the Distance Selling Directive.
The proposed horizontal measure could have the following basic structure:

Definitions

- Definition of consumer (along the lines sketched out in Part 3.A.; in particular clarification with regard to mixed purpose cases).[2066]
- Definition of business (along the lines sketched out in Part 3.B; in particular clarification with regard to non-profit organisations and clarification that public bodies can also be defined as a *business*).[2067]

[2066] Cf. Art. 1:201 Acquis Principles (ACQP), published under the title 'Principles of the Existing EC Contract Law' (Acquis Principles), Contract I, 2007 (Sellier); cf. also the Definition in the Annex to the Draft Common Frame of Reference (DCFR); *von Bar/Clive/Schulte-Nölke* et.al., Principles, Definitions and Model Rules of European Private Law, 2008 (Sellier).

[2067] Cf. Art. 1:202 Acquis Principles (ACQP), published under the title 'Principles of the Existing EC Contract Law' (Acquis Principles), Contract I, 2007 (Sellier); cf. also the Definition in the Annex to the Draft Common Frame of Reference (DCFR); *von Bar/Clive/Schulte-Nölke* et.al., Principles, Definitions and Model Rules of European Private Law, 2008 (Sellier).

- Definition of "in writing".[2068]
- Definition of "durable medium"(the latter along Art. 2(f) of Directive 2002/65).[2069]

General rules
- Scope of application of the horizontal measure
- Rule spelling out which rules are full harmonisation and which are minimum *(along the lines sketched out below under Point IV).*
- A rule making consumer rights mandatory.[2070]
- Consumer rights in case of choice of law clauses (or – if possible – leaving this to a future Rome I Regulation).

General Information Duties *(along the lines sketched out in Part 3.D.; an indicative draft of the Acquis Group has been published)*[2071]
- Pre-contractual information duties.
- Contractual information duties.
- Formal requirements of information.
- Language in which information to be provided.
- Sanctions for breach of information duties.

Withdrawal *(along the lines sketched out in Part 3.C; an indicative draft of the Acquis Group has been published).*[2072]

Rights to withdraw from a contract
- Contracts concluded outside business premises (Doorstep and Distance Selling).
- Reference to other withdrawal rights granted outside the horizontal measure.
  Exercise and Effects of Withdrawal
- Length of period.
- Start and computation of period.
- Rights and obligations during the period for withdrawal.

2068 Cf. Art. 1:306 Acquis Principles (ACQP), published under the title 'Principles of the Existing EC Contract Law' (Acquis Principles), Contract I, 2007 (Sellier); cf. also Art. I.–1:105 (1) Draft Common Frame of Reference (DCFR); *von Bar/Clive/Schulte-Nölke* et.al., Principles, Definitions and Model Rules of European Private Law, 2008 (Sellier).

2069 Cf. 1:305 Acquis Principles (ACQP), published under the title 'Principles of the Existing EC Contract Law' (Acquis Principles), Contract I, 2007 (Sellier); cf. also Art. I.–1:105 (3) Draft Common Frame of Reference (DCFR); *von Bar/Clive/Schulte-Nölke* et.al., Principles, Definitions and Model Rules of European Private Law, 2008 (Sellier).

2070 Cf. Art. 1:203 Acquis Principles (ACQP), published under the title 'Principles of the Existing EC Contract Law' (Acquis Principles), Contract I, 2007 (Sellier).

2071 Article 2:201-2:207 Acquis Principles (ACQP), published under the title 'Principles of the Existing EC Contract Law' (Acquis Principles), Contract I, 2007 (Sellier); cf. also Art. II.–3:101-3:107 Draft Common Frame of Reference (DCFR); *von Bar/Clive/Schulte-Nölke* et.al., Principles, Definitions and Model Rules of European Private Law, 2008 (Sellier).

2072 Article 5:101-5:202 Acquis Principles (ACQP), published under the title 'Principles of the Existing EC Contract Law' (Acquis Principles), Contract I, 2007 (Sellier); cf. also Art. II.–5:101-5:202 Draft Common Frame of Reference (DCFR); *von Bar/Clive/Schulte-Nölke* et.al., Principles, Definitions and Model Rules of European Private Law, 2008 (Sellier).

- Obligation to inform about right of withdrawal.
- Sanctions in case of breach of this obligation.
- Exercise of right of withdrawal.
- Effects of withdrawal.
- Credit agreements.
- Unravelling of contract after withdrawal.

Unfair Terms *(along the lines sketched out in Part 2.C.; an indicative draft of the Acquis Group has been published)*[2073]

It would then have to be decided whether the remaining contract law consumer acquis, mainly the Consumer Sales, Package Travel, Timeshare, and Consumer Credit Directives (the latter outside the scope of this study), but also, for example, the specific information duties in the field of Distance Selling and Distance Selling of Financial Services, should remain in separate directives or be included in the proposed horizontal measure.

In any case, such a horizontal measure would have to take into account some other fields of EC legislation related to consumer contract law, e.g. the Unfair Commercial Practices Directive, the E-Commerce Directive, the Product Liability Directive, the Insurance Law Directives, Investment Services Directive, the Brussels I Regulation, and the Rome I Regulation.

The Injunctions Directive, the Enforcement Regulation and the Unit Prices Directive mainly deal with matters unrelated to contract law and therefore could remain as stand-alone measures. However, the definition of 'consumer' could be applied uniformly across all these measures.

C. Issues concerning individual directives

The analysis has revealed a number of inconsistencies, as well as gaps and barriers to trade, affecting particular directives, which should be tackled in the course of the consumer acquis review. These proposals are summarised at the end of the Executive Summaries of the report on each of the Directives and therefore do not need to be repeated here in detail. Core proposals are:

I. Doorstep Selling

- Incorporation of the Directive into the horizontal measure.
- Inclusion of contracts concluded in public places outside business premises.

[2073] Article 6:101-6:306 Acquis Principles (ACQP), published under the title 'Principles of the Existing EC Contract Law' (Acquis Principles), Contract I, 2007 (Sellier); cf. also Art. II.–9:103, II.–9:401-9:411 Draft Common Frame of Reference (DCFR); *von Bar/Clive/Schulte-Nölke* et.al., Principles, Definitions and Model Rules of European Private Law, 2008 (Sellier).

- Uniform rules on withdrawal period, exercise of withdrawal, effects of withdrawal (see above).

II. Package Travel

- Definition of 'consumer': adaptation to a coherent definition in EC consumer law by incorporation of the definition into the horizontal measure.
- Definition of 'organiser': adaptation to a coherent definition of the business by incorporation of the Definition into the horizontal measure.
- Inclusion of tailor-made packages offered by travel agencies in accordance with the ECJ ruling *Club-Tour*.
- Clarification that Article 5 also grants a right to compensation for non-material damage, in particular, that such compensation can arise from the loss of enjoyment (ECJ *Simone Leitner*).

III. Unfair Terms

- Incorporation of the Directive into the horizontal measure.
- Definition of 'consumer': adaptation to a coherent definition in EC consumer law.
- Definition of 'seller or supplier': adaptation to a coherent definition of the business.
- Clarifications, e.g., with regard to the scope of application, the unfairness test and the consequences of unfairness and lack of transparency (as sketched out in Part 2 under C).

IV. Timeshare

- Definition of 'consumer': adaptation to a coherent definition in EC consumer law by incorporation of the Definition into the horizontal measure.
- Definition of 'vendor': adaptation to a coherent definition of the business in EC consumer law by incorporation of the Definition into the horizontal measure.
- Extension of the scope of application to contracts where timeshare rights are resold by another consumer through a professional agent.
- Dropping or lowering the requirements of the minimum duration of 3 years and the minimum annual period of 7 days.
- Inclusion of timeshare objects other than buildings, for example, camping grounds, caravans, boats mobile homes and other movables, which can be used for the purpose of accommodation.
- Inclusion of holiday clubs.
- Reducing the detailed lists of information to be provided by using a general clause (to be included in the Horizontal Directive), supplemented by an indicative list of core information; in particular on costs including maintenance costs.
- In principle, uniform rules on withdrawal period, exercise of withdrawal, effects of withdrawal (to be included in the Horizontal Directive), but adaptations due to the peculiarities of timeshare contracts (possibly longer withdrawal period).

V. Distance Selling

- Incorporation of the Directive into the horizontal measure.
- (New) definition of "auction", clarifying that Ebay auctions do not fall under this exception.
- Harmonisation of the pre-contractual information duties with Directive 2002/65 and the law of those member states which made use of the minimum clause.
- Uniform rules on withdrawal period, exercise of withdrawal, effects of withdrawal (to be included in the Horizontal Directive).

VI. Consumer Sales

- Definition of 'consumer': adaptation to a coherent definition in EC consumer law by incorporation of the Definition into the horizontal measure.
- Definition of 'seller': adaptation to a coherent definition of business in EC consumer law by incorporation of the Definition into the horizontal measure.
- Definition of 'goods', in particular with regard to software and other digital products.
- Further consideration of direct producer liability.

VII. Injunctions Directive

- Definition of 'consumer': adaptation to a coherent definition in EC consumer law by incorporation of the Definition into the horizontal measure.
- Clarification of the relationship with Directive-specific enforcement mechanisms, such as Art.11 of Directive 97/7/EC and Art.7 of Directive 93/13/EEC; possibly deletion of the specific provisions.

VIII. Unit Prices

- Definition of 'consumer': adaptation to a coherent definition in EC consumer law by incorporation of the Definition into the Horizontal Directive.
- Establishing a definition of "small retail businesses" with the aim of achieving more coherent national legislation.

D. Full harmonisation and remaining scope for member states

The study, in particular the analysis of the transposition measures enacted by the member states, shows to what extent member states have made use of minimum clauses and options. The results permit an assessment of the possible effects of moving towards full harmonisation in the areas covered by this study. Some aspects, but not as many as may be expected, are likely to be controversial for some Member States, where full harmonisation would force them to reduce their established level of consumer protection. Should the shift to full harmonisation become reality, it would have to be considered whether these areas should not be subject to this approach, and remain subject to minimum harmonisation. Member states might also be keen to have a 'safeguard procedure', allowing them to enact urgent short term consumer protection measures in full harmonisation areas, as long as the EC does not act. The provisions of Article 95 EC would serve as a useful model; indeed, it is unfortunate that those provisions do not currently include consumer protection within its scope.

With regard to the Unit Prices Directive, it must be borne in mind that this Directive has been enacted on the basis (of the predecessor) of Art. 153 of the EC Treaty. Because of Art. 153 para 5 EC Treaty, the Directive would continue to be just a minimum harmonisation measure even if its Art. 10 were deleted.

The analysis reveals also that even a broad shift from minimum to full harmonisation in the field of the EC consumer directives would leave the member states regulatory freedom for all areas outside the scope of the directives or not regulated therein, e.g. with regard to persons other than consumers, other types of contracts or other consumer protection instruments not provided for in the directives.

With regard to all of these considerations, there is no, or at least not a very strong, argument against a selective shift to full harmonisation in those areas where the use of minimum clauses by the member states has clearly caused barriers to trade without substantially increasing consumer protection. Such fields may be, as already said, rules on pre-contractual information duties, in particular on brochures, and the information of the consumer about his right of withdrawal. The latter would consequently also require full harmonisation of certain general elements of the technicalities of the withdrawal rights like the length, the beginning and the calculation of the period, and the formalities for exercising the withdrawal right.

E. Other matters to be considered

I. Translation issues

The analysis of the laws of the member states in the areas covered by the Directive revealed numerous instances of variation, which, as already noted above, tend to be caused by ambiguities or inconsistencies in the relevant directives. On occasion, it seems that these problems might have been caused also by variations in the substantive meaning of particular provisions in the different language versions of the directives. This might be the result of the inherent differences in legal terminology between the various member states, but may also, in part, be the consequence of the challenges posed by the task of having to translate the text of a directive into the many official languages of the EU, where there is a risk that inconsistencies might creep in. The full success of a wholesale reform to the consumer acquis might depend on addressing this risk during the review process.

II. A cross-border measure?

Some consideration could be given to the possibility of adopting a measure dealing specifically with cross-border consumer transactions, to give a boost to consumer utilisation of the internal market, particularly once the Common Frame of Reference project has come to fruition. Such a measure would apply across the EU, and any consumer transaction which is conducted across borders would be covered by this measure. A number of difficult questions would need to be addressed if that option were to be pursued, including (i) would such a measure be mandatory?; (ii) would consumers be permitted to opt-out in favour of a more protective domestic law; (iii) would this measure complement or replace the programme of harmonising domestic consumer law? This possibility would require further careful analysis which exceeds the boundaries of this project.

III. Improving cross-border redress

A gap in the current acquis which is often pointed out is that there continue to be difficulties in enforcing consumer rights across the EU. Although consumers can be confident that they enjoy a minimum level of protection, no matter where they shop, they may be put off doing so by the difficulty of taking action if something they have bought is faulty. The question of cross-border redress in individual consumer cases also falls outside the scope of this study, but it may be desirable to investigate this further as part of the overall improvements to the consumer acquis.

Annex A: Abbreviations

ABGB	Allgemeines Bürgerliches Gesetzbuch, Civil Code (Austria)
AMG	Arzneimittelgesetz, Medicines Act (Germany)
AT	Austria
ATOL	Air Travel Organiser's licence (UK)
B2B	business-to-business
B2C	business-to-consumer
BE	Belgium
BGB	Bürgerliches Gesetzbuch, Civil Code (Germany)
BGB-InfoV	Verordnung über Informations- und Nachweispflichten nach bürgerlichem Recht (BGB-Informationspflichten-Verordnung), Regulation on duties to supply information in civil law (Germany)
BGH	Bundesgerichthof, Federal Court of Justice (Germany)
C2C	consumer-to-consumer
CA	Court of Appeals
CA	Contracts Act (Finland, Sweden)
Cap.	Chapter (Malta)
Cass. civ.	Cour de cassation, Civil chamber (France)
CC	Civil Code
CCA	Civil Aviation Authority (UK)
CCSACCA	Act of 27 July 2002 on specific terms and conditions of consumer sale and amendments to the CC (Poland)
cf.	confer (compare)
CISG	United Nations Convention on Contracts for the International Sale Of Goods (1980)
CO	Consumer Ombudsman (Finland)
CPA	Consumer Protection Act (Estonia, Portugal, Finland)
CTA	Contract Terms Act (Sweden)
CY	Cyprus
CZ	Czech Republic
DE	Germany
DK	Denmark
DKK	Danish Krone
ECJ	European Court of Justice
ECR	European Court Reports
EE	Estonia

EEA	European Economic Area
EL	Greece
ERPL	European Review of Private Law
ES	Spain
ESC	escudo (Portuguese currency before euro)
et seq.	et sequence / et sequentia (and the following one or ones)
F	Franc (Belgian currency before introduction of euro)
FI	Finland
FR	France
HU	Hungary
HWG	Heilmittelwerbegesetz, Medicine Advertisement Act (Germany)
IE	Ireland
InvG	Investmentgesetz, Investment Act (Germany)
IT	Italy
KSchG	Konsumentenschutzgesetz, Consumer Protection Act (Austria)
lit.	litera/letter
Lm	Maltese lira
LOA	Law of Obligations Act (Estonia)
LOCM	Ley del Comercio Minorista, Law of Retail Trade (Spain)
LPA	Liberal Professions Act (Belgium)
LT	Lithuania
LU	Luxembourg
LV	Latvia
MS	Member State
MT	Malta
NB	nota bene
NL	Netherlands
No.	number
OFT	Office of Fair Trading (UK)
OGH	Oberste Gerichtshof, Supreme Court of Justice (Austria)
OWiG	Ordnungswidrigkeitengesetz, Regulatory Offences Act (Germany)
PECL	Principles of European Contract Law
PL	Poland
PLN	złoty (Polish currency)
PrAG	Preisauszeichnungsgesetz (Bundesgesetz über die Auszeichnung von Preisen), Price Indication Act (Austria)
ProdHaftG	Produkthaftungsgesetz, Product Liability Act (Germany)

PT	Portugal
RD	Royal Decree (Belgium)
reg.	regulation
Reisebüroausübungs-VO	Verordnung des Bundesministers für wirtschaftliche Angelegenheiten über Ausübungsvorschriften für das Reisebürogewerbe, Regulation on travel agencies (Austria)
RSV	Reisebürosicherungsverordnung, Regulation on travel agencies implementing Art. 7 of the Package Travel Directive (Austria)
SE	Sweden
sec.	section
sent.	sentence
SI	Slovenia
SIT	currency in Cyprus
SK	Slovakia
SMEs	Small and medium enterprises
sub(s)	subsection(s)
TA	Travel Act (Belgium)
TNG	Teilzeitnutzungsgesetz – Bundesgesetz über den Erwerb von Teilzeitnutzungsrechten an unbeweglichen Sachen, Timeshare Act (Austria)
TPA	Trade Practices Act (Belgium)
UCTA	Unfair Contract Terms Act 1977 (UK)
UK	United Kingdom
UKlaG	Unterlassungsklagengesetz, Injunctions Act (Germany)
UTCC	Unfair Terms in Consumer Contracts (UK)
UTCCR	Unfair Terms in Consumer Contracts Regulations (UK)
UWG	Bundesgesetz gegen den unlauteren Wettbewerb, Act against unfair commercial practices (Austria, Germany)
VVG	Versicherungsvertragsgesetz – Gesetz über den Versicherungsvertrag), Insurance Contract Act (Germany)
ZPO	Zivilprozessordnung, Civil Procedure Code (Germany)
ZVG	Zwangsversteigerungsgesetz, Compulsory Auctions Act (Germany)

Annex B: European Community Sources of Law

A. Treaties and Convention

Chronological order

EC Treaty
(Treaty establishing the European Community, (consolidated text) OJ C 325 of 24 December 2002)

Rome I Convention
(Convention on the law applicable to contractual obligations opened for signature in Rome on 19 June 1980 (80/934/EEC); OJ L 266 of 9 October 1980, 0001-0019)

Treaty of Accession
(Treaty between the Kingdom of Belgium, the Kingdom of Denmark, the Federal Republic of Germany, the Hellenic Republic, the Kingdom of Spain, the French Republic, Ireland, the Italian Republic, the Grand Duchy of Luxembourg, the Kingdom of the Netherlands, the Republic of Austria, the Portuguese Republic, the Republic of Finland, the Kingdom of Sweden, the United Kingdom of Great Britain and Northern Ireland (member states of the European Union) and the Czech Republic, the Republic of Estonia, the Republic of Cyprus, the Republic of Latvia, the Republic of Lithuania, the Republic of Hungary, the Republic of Malta, the Republic of Poland, the Republic of Slovenia, the Slovak Republic, concerning the accession of the Czech Republic, the Republic of Estonia, the Republic of Cyprus, the Republic of Latvia, the Republic of Lithuania, the Republic of Hungary, the Republic of Malta, the Republic of Poland, the Republic of Slovenia and the Slovak Republic to the European Union; OJ L 236 of 23 September 2003, 17-31)

B. Regulations

Chronological order

Regulation 1182/71
(Regulation (EEC, Euratom) No 1182/71 of the Council of 3 June 1971 determining the rules applicable to periods, dates and time limits; OJ L 124 of 8 June 1971, 1-2)

Regulation 2027/97
(Council Regulation (EC) No 2027/97 of 9 October 1997 on air carrier liability in the event of accidents; OJ L 285 of 17 October 1997, 1-3)

Regulation 1980/2000 also referred to as the **Eco-Label Regulation**
(Regulation (EC) No 1980/2000 of the European Parliament and of the Council of 17 July 2000 on a revised Community eco-label award scheme; OJ L 237 of 21 September 2000, 1-12)

Regulation 44/2001 also referred to as the **Brussels I Regulation**
(Council Regulation (EC) No 44/2001 of 22 December 2000 on jurisdiction and the recognition and enforcement of judgments in civil and commercial matters; OJ L 12 of 16 January 2001, 1-23)

Regulation 2006/2004 referred to as the **Enforcement Regulation**
(Regulation (EC) No 2006/2004 of the European Parliament and of the Council of 27 October 2004 on cooperation between national authorities responsible for the enforcement of consumer protection laws (the Regulation on consumer protection cooperation); OJ L 364 of 9 December 2004, 1-11)

C. Directives

Chronological order

Directive 85/374 also referred to as the **Product Liability Directive**
(Council Directive 85/374/EEC of 25 July 1985 on the approximation of the laws, regulations and administrative provisions of the member states concerning liability for defective products; OJ L 210 of 7 August 1985, 29-33)

Directive 85/577 also referred to as the **Doorstep Selling Directive**
(Council Directive 85/577/EEC of 20 December 1985 to protect the consumer in respect of contracts negotiated away from business premises; OJ L 372 of 31 December 1985, 31-33)

Directive 87/102 also referred to as the **Consumer Credit Directive**
(Council Directive 87/102/EEC of 22 December 1986 for the approximation of the laws, regulations and administrative provisions of the member states concerning consumer credit OJ L 42 of 12 February 1987, 48-53)

Directive 90/314 also referred to as the **Package Travel Directive**
(Directive 90/314/EEC on package travel, package holidays and package tours; 1990 OJ L 158/61)

Directive 90/619
(Council Directive 90/619/EEC of 8 November 1990 on the coordination of laws, regulations and administrative provisions relating to direct life assurance, laying down provisions

to facilitate the effective exercise of freedom to provide services and amending Directive 79/267/EEC; OJ L 330 of 29 November 1990, 50-61)

Directive 93/13 also referred to as the **Unfair Contract Terms Directive**
(Council Directive 93/13/EEC of 5 April 1993 on unfair terms in consumer contracts; OJ L 95 of 21 April 1993, 29-34)

Directive 94/47 also referred to as the **Timeshare Directive**
(Directive 94/47/EC of the European Parliament and the Council of 26 October 1994 on the protection of purchasers in respect of certain aspects of contracts relating to the purchase of the right to use immovable properties on a timeshare basis; OJ L 280 of 29 October 1994, 83-87)

Directive 97/7 also referred to as the **Distance Sale Directive**
(Directive 97/7/EC of the European Parliament and of the Council of 20 May 1997 on the protection of consumers in respect of distance contracts; OJ L 144 of 4 June 1997, 19-27)

Directive 98/6 also referred to as the **Unit Prices Directive**
(Directive 98/6/EC of the European Parliament and of the Council of 16 February 1998 on consumer protection in the indication of the prices of products offered to consumers; OJ L 80 of 18 March 1998, 27-31)

Directive 98/27 also referred to as the **Injunctions Directive**
(Directive 98/27/EC of the European Parliament and of the Council of 19 May 1998 on injunctions for the protection of consumers' interests; OJ L 166 of 11 June 1998, 51-55)

Directive 99/44 also referred to as the **Consumer Sales Directive**
(Directive 1999/44/EC of the European Parliament and of the Council of 25 May 1999 on certain aspects of the sale of consumer goods and associated guarantees; OJ L 171 of 7 July 1999, 12-16)

Directive 2000/31 also referred to as the **E-Commerce Directive**
(Directive 2000/31/EC of the European Parliament and of the Council of 8 June 2000 on certain legal aspects of information society services, in particular electronic commerce, in the Internal Market; OJ L 178 of17 July 2000, 1-16)

Directive 2002/65 also referred to as the **Distance Selling of Financial Services Directive**
(Directive 2002/65/EC of the European Parliament and of the Council of 23 September 2002 concerning the distance marketing of consumer financial services and amending Council Directive 90/619/EEC and Directives 97/7/EC and 98/27/EC; OJ L 271 of 9 October 2002, 16-24).

Directive 2002/83
(Directive 2002/83/EC of the European Parliament and of the Council of 5 November 2002 concerning life assurance; OJ L 345 of 19 December 2002, 1-51)

Directive 2005/29 referred to as the **Unfair Commercial Practices Directive**
(Directive 2005/29/EC of the European Parliament and of the Council of 11 May 2005 concerning unfair business-to-consumer commercial practices in the internal market and amending Council Directive 84/450/EEC, Directives 97/7/EC, 98/27/EC and 2002/65/EC of the European Parliament and of the Council and Regulation (EC) No 2006/2004 of the European Parliament and of the Council; OJ L 149 of 11 June 2005, 22-39)

D. European Court of Justice Judgements

Ordered by case numbers

C-361/89 – *Criminal proceedings v Patrice Di Pinto* [1991] ECR I-01189

C-91/92 – *Paola Faccini Dori v Recreb Srl* [1994] ECR I-3325

C-178/94, C-179/94, C-188/94, C-189/94 and **C-190/94** (joined cases)
Dillenkofer v Bundesrepublik Deutschland [1996] ECR I-04845

C-269/95 – *Francesco Benincasa v Dentalkit Srl* [1997] ECR I-3767

C-45/96 – *Bayrische Hypotheken- und Wechselbank AG v Edgar Dietzinger* [1998] ECR I-01119

C-364/96 – *Verein Konsumenteninformation v Österreichische Kreditversicherungs AG*, [1998] ECR I-01949

C-410/96 – *André Ambry* [1998] ECR I-07875

C-140/97 – *Rechberger, Greindel. Hofmeister etc. v Republik Österreich* [1999] ECR I-03499

C-237/97 – *AFS Intercultural Programs Finland ry* [1999] ECR I-00825

C-423/97 – *Travel Vac SL v Manuel José Antelm Sanchi* [1999] ECR I-02195

C-240/98 to **C-244/98** (joined cases) – *Océano Grupo Editorial SA v Murciano Quintero* [2000] ECR I-04941

C-319/98 – *Commission v Belgium* [1999] ECR I-01201

C-381/98 – *Ingmar GB Ltd and Eaton Leonard Technologies Inc.* [2000] ECR I-09305

C-401/98 – *Commission v Hellenic Republic* [1999] ECR I-05543

C-144/99 – *Commission v Kingdom of the Netherlands* [2001] ECR I-03541

C-372/99 – *Commission of the European Communities v Italian Republic* [2002] ECR I-00819

C-478/99 – Commission of the European Communities v Kingdom of Sweden [2002] ECR I-04147

C-481/99 – *Georg Heininger and Helga Heininger v Bayerische Hypo- und Vereinsbank AG* [2001] ECR I-09945

C-541/99 and **C-542/99** (joined cases) – *Cape Snc* v *Idealservice Srl and Idealservice MN RE Sas* v *OMAI Srl* [2001] ECR I-9049

C-96/00 – *Rudolf Gabriel* [2002] ECR I-06367

C-167/00 – *Verein für Konsumenteninformation v Henkel* [2002] ECR I-08111

C-168/00 – *Simone Leitner v TUI Deutschland GmbH & Co KG* [2002] ECR I-02631

C-183/00 – *María Victoria González Sánchez v Medicina Asturiana SA* [2002] ECR I-03901

C-400/00 – *Club-Tour, Viagens e Turismo SA v Alberto Carlos Lobo Gonçalves Garrido* [2002] ECR I-04051

C-473/00 – *Cofidis SA c. Jean-Louis Fredout* [2002] ECR I-10875

C-322/01 – *Deutscher Apothekerverband eV v 0800 DocMorris NV and Jacques Waterval,*

C-414/01 – *Commission v Spain* [2002] ECR I-11121

C-464/01 – *Johann Gruber v Bay Wa AG* [2005] ECR I-00439

C-237/02 – *Freiburger Kommunalbauten GmbH Baugesellschaft & Co. KG v Ludger Hofstetter et Ulrike Hofstetter* [2004] ECR I-3403

C-20/03 – *Burmanjer, Van Der Linden, De Jong* [2005] ECR I-4133

C-70/03 – *Commission v Kingdom of Spain* [2004] ECR I-0799

C-336/03 – *easyCar (UK) Ltd v Office of Fair Trading* [2005] ECR I-01947

C-350/03 – *Eisabeth Schulte, Wolfgang Schulte v Deutsche Bausparkasse Badenia AG* [2005] ECR I-09215

C-229/04 – *Crailsheimer Volksbank eG v Klaus Conrads, Frank Schulzke and Petra Schulzke-Lösche, Joachim Nitschke* [2005] ECR I-9273.

C-302/04 – *Ynos Kft v János Varga* [2006] ECR I-00371

C-441/04 – *A-Punkt-Schmuckhandel* [2006] ECR I-02093

C-168/05 – *Elisa María Mostaza Claro v Centro Móvil Milenium SL* [2006] ECR I-10421

Annex C: National Legislation

AUSTRIA

Act against unfair commercial practices (*Bundesgesetz gegen den unlauteren Wettbewerb (UWG)*)
CC (*Allgemeines Bürgerliches Gesetzbuch (ABGB)*)
Consumer Protection Act *(Konsumentenschutzgesetz)*
Price Indication Act (*Preisauszeichnungsgesetz – PrAG (Bundesgesetz über die Auszeichnung von Preisen)*)
Regulation on travel agencies (*Verordnung des Bundesministers für wirtschaftliche Angelegenheiten über Ausübungsvorschriften für das Reisebürogewerbe (hier abgekürzt mit: Reisebüroausübungs-VO)*).
Regulation on travel agencies implementing Art. 7 Package Travel Directive (*Reisebürosicherungsverordnung (RSV)*)
Timeshare Act (*Teilzeitnutzungsgesetz – TNG (Bundesgesetz über den Erwerb von Teilzeitnutzungsrechten an unbeweglichen Sachen)*)

BELGIUM

Act of 1 September 2004 on the protection of consumers in respect of the sale of consumer goods (amendment of CC) *(Loi du 1/9/2004 relative à la protection des consommateurs en cas de vente de biens de consommation – Wet betreffende de bescherming van de consumenten bij verkoop van consumptiegoederen)*
Act of 11 April 1999 on the injunction for infringements of the Act on the purchase of the right to use immovable properties on a timeshare basis *(Loi du 11/4/1999 relative à l'action en cessation des infractions à la loi relative aux contrats portant sur l'acquisition d'un droit d'utilisation d'immeubles à temps partagé. – Wet aangaande de vordering tot staking van de inbreuken op de wet betreffende de overeenkomsten inzake de verkrijging van een recht van deeltijds gebruik van onroerende goederen.)*
Act of 11 April 1999 on the purchase of the right to use immovable properties on a time-share basis *(Loi du 11/4/1999 relative aux contrats portant sur l'acquisition d'un droit d'utilisation d'immeubles à temps partagé – Wet betreffende de overeenkomsten inzake de verkrijging van een recht van deeltijds gebruik van onroerende goederen)*
Act of 14 July 1991 on trade practices and consumer information and protection (Trade Practices Act) *(Loi du 14/7/1991 sur les pratiques du commerce et sur l'information et la protection du consommateur – Wet betreffende de handelspraktijken en de voorlichting en bescherming van de consument)*
Act of 25 June 1993 on the Practice and the Organisation of Itinerant and Fairground Activities *(Loi sur l'exercice et l'organisation des activités ambulantes et foraines – Wet betreffende de uitoefening en de organisatie van ambulante en kermisactiviteiten)*

Act of 16 February 1994 regulating the package travel contracts and the travel intermediation contracts (*Loi du 16/2/1994 régissant le contrat d'organisation de voyages et le contrat d'intermédiaire de voyages*
– Wet tot regeling van het contract tot reisorganisatie en reisbemiddeling.)
Act of 2 August 2002 on misleading and comparative advertising, unfair contract terms and distance marketing in respect of professional services. (*Loi du 2/8/2002 relative à la publicité trompeuse et à la publicité comparative, aux clauses abusives et aux contrats à distance en ce qui concerne les professions libérales.*
– Wet betreffende de misleidende en vergelijkende reclame, de onrechtmatige bedingen en de op afstand gesloten overeenkomsten inzake de vrije beroepen)
Act of 26 May 2002 concerning intra-Community injunctions in view of protecting consumers (*Loi du 26/5/2002 relative aux actions en cessation intracommunautaires en matière de protection des intérêts des consommateurs*
– Wet betreffende de intracommunautaire vorderingen tot staking op het gebied van de bescherming van de consumentenbelangen)
Royal Decree of 1 February 1995 determining the assurance conditions of the liability of travel organizers and *retailers* (*Arrêté royal du 1/2/1995 déterminant les conditions de l'assurance de la responsabilité professionnelle des organisateurs et intermédiaires de voyages envers les voyageurs*
– Koninklijk besluit tot vaststelling van de voorwaarden van de verzekering van de professionele aansprakelijkheid van de reisorganisatoren en de reisbemiddelaars jegens de reizigers)
Royal Decree of 11 July 2003 containing special rules for price indication in the travel sector (*Arrêté royal du 11/7/2003 portant fixation de règles particulières en matière d'indication du prix dans le secteur du voyage*
– Koninklijk besluit houdende vaststelling van bijzondere regels inzake prijsaanduiding in de reizensector)
Royal Decree of 18 November 2002 excluding certain distance contracts in respect of hotel accommodation, transport, restaurant and leisure services, from the scope of application of the articles 79 and 80 of the Act of 14 July 1991
(*Arrêté royal du 18/11/2002 excluant certains contrats à distance de fourniture de services d'hébergement, de transports, de restauration et de loisirs, du champ d'application des articles 79 et 80 de la loi du 14 juillet 1991*
– Koninklijk besluit houdende uitsluiting van sommige overeenkomsten op afstand betreffende het verrichten van diensten voor logies, vervoer, het restaurantbedrijf en vrijetijdsbesteding, van het toepassingsgebied v. d. artikelen 79 en 80 v.d. wet v.14.7.91)
Royal Decree of 30 June 1996 concerning the indication of the price of products and services and the order form (as amended by R.D. of 7 February 2000) (*Arrêté royal du 30/6/1996 relatif à l'indication du prix des produits et des services et au bon de commande.*
– Koninklijk besluit betreffende de prijsaanduiding van produkten en diensten en de bestelbon.)
Royal Decree of 5 December 2000 declaring certain provisions of the Act of 14 July 1991 on trade practices and consumer information and protection applicable to financial instruments and to transferable securities. (*Arrêté royal du 5/12/2000 rendant applicables aux instruments financiers et aux titres et valeurs certaines dispositions de la loi du 14 juillet 1991 sur les pratiques du commerce et sur l'information et la protection du consommateur.*
– Koninklijk besluit waarbij sommige bepalingen van de wet van 14 juli 1991 betreffende de handelspraktijken en de voorlichting en bescherming van de consument, van toepassing worden verklaard op financiële instrumenten, effecten en waarden.)

Royal Decree putting into effect Article 36 of the Act of 16 February 1994 regulating the package travel contracts and the travel intermediation contracts. *(Arrêté royal du 25/4/1997 portant exécution de l'article 36 de la loi du 16 février 1994 régissant le contrat d'organisation de voyages et le contrat d'intermédiaire de voyages.*
– Koninklijk besluit tot uitvoering van artikel 36 van de wet van 16 februari 1994 tot regeling van het contract tot reisorganisatie en reisbemiddeling)
Royal decree of 6 September 1993 containing special provisions for the distance marketing of certain products or categories of products. *(Arrêté royal du 6/9/1993 portant des modalités particulières pour la vente à distance de certains produits ou catégories de produits*
– Koninklijk besluit houdende bijzondere regelen voor de verkoop op afstand van sommige produkten of categorieën van produkten)
Royal Decree 82 of 28 November 1939 on Itinerant Trade Activities *(Arrêté royal n° 82 du 28 novembre 1939 réglementant le commerce ambulant*
– Koninklijk besluit tot regeling van de uitvoering van het koninklijk besluit nr 82 van 28 November 1939 houdende reglementering van de leurhandel.)
Royal Decree of 25 April 1997 implementing Art. 36 of the Act of 16 February 1994 regulating package travel contracts and travel intermediation contracts *(Arrêté royal du 25 avril 1997 portant exécution de l'article 36 de la loi du 16 février 1994 régissant le contrat d'organisation de voyages et le contrat d'intermédiaire de voyages*
– Koninklijk besluit tot uitvoering van artikel 36 van de wet van 16 februari 1994 tot regeling van het contract tot reisorganisatie en reisbemiddeling)
Royal Decree of 24 September 2006 on the Exercise and the Organisation of Itinerant Activities *(Arrêté royal du 24 Septembre 2006 relatif à l'exercice et à l'organisation des activités ambulantes*
– Koninklijk besluit van 24 September 2006 betreffende de uitoefening en de organisatie van ambulante activiteiten.)

CYPRUS
Misleading Advertising Law *(Ο περί Ελέγχου των Παραπλανητικών και Συγκριτικών Διαφημίσεων Νόμος του 2000 εκδίδεται με δημοσίευση στην Επίσημη Εφημερίδα της Κυπριακής Δημοκρατίας σύμφωνα με το Άρθρο 52 τον Συντάγματος)*
The Certain Aspects of the Sale of Consumer Goods and Associated Guarantees Law of 2000. (L. 7(I)/2000) *(Ο περί Ορισμένων Πτυχών της Πώλησης Καταναλωτικών Αγαθών και των Συναφών Εγγυήσεων Νόμος του 2000. (Ν. 7(I)/2000))*
The Law for the Conclusion of Consumer Distance Contracts of 2000, L.14(I)/2000, as amended by L. 237(I)/04 *(Ο περί της Σύναψης Καταναλωτικών Συμβάσεων Εξ Αποστάσεως Νόμος του 2000, Ν. 14(I)/2000 ως τροποποιήθηκε από τον Νόμο 237(I)/04)*
The Law for the Consumer Contracts Concluded Away from Business Premises of 2000, L.13(I)/2000 *(Ο περί της Σύναψης Καταναλωτικών Συμβάσεων εκτός Εμπορικού Καταστήματος Νόμος του 2000, Ν.13(I)/2000)*
The Package Travel, Holidays and Tours Law of 1998, L.51(I)/98 as amended by the Package Travel, Holidays and Tours (Amendment) Law of 1999, L.72(I)/99 *(Ο περί Οργανωμένων Ταξιδιών, Διακοπών και Περιηγήσεων Νόμος του 1998, Ν.51(I)/98 όπως τροποποιήθηκε από τον περί Οργανωμένων Ταξιδιών, Διακοπών και Περιηγήσεων (Τροποποιητικός) Νόμο του 1999, Ν.72(I)/99)*
The Selling and Unit Price Indication Law of 2000, L.112(I)/2000 as amended by Law 119(I)/2005 and Law136(I)/2005 *(Ο περί της Αναγραφής της Τιμής Πώλησης και της*

Μοναδιαίας Τιμής των Προϊόντων Νόμος του 2000, Ν.112(Ι)/2000 ως έχει τροποποιηθεί από τους Νόμους 119(Ι)/05 και 136(Ι)/05.)

The Timeshare Contract Law of 2001, L.113(I)/2001 as amended by the Timeshare Contracts (Amendment) Law of 2004, L. 127(I)/2004 *(Ο περί Χρονομεριστικής Σύμβασης Νόμος του 2001, Ν.113(Ι)/2001 όπως τροποποιήθηκε από τον περί Χρονομεριστικών Συμβάσεων (Τροποποιητικός) Νόμος του 2004, Ν.127(Ι)/2004)*

The Unfair Terms in Consumer Contracts Law of 1996, N.93(I)/96 as amended by the Unfair Terms in Consumer Contracts (Amendment) Law of 1999, L.69(I)/99 *(Ο περί Καταχρηστικών Ρητρών σε Καταναλωτικές Συμβάσεις Νόμος του 1996, Ν.93(Ι)/96 όπως τροποποιήθηκε από τον περί Καταχρηστικών Ρητρών σε Καταναλωτικές Συμβάσεις (Τροποποιητικός) Νόμος του 1999, Ν.69(Ι)/99.)*

CZECH REPUBLIC

Act No. 159/1999 on conditions of business operation in the tourism industry (*Zákon č. 159/1999 Sb. O některých podmínkách podnikání v oblasti cestovního ruchu*)

Act No. 40/1964, CC as amended by Act 367/2000 (*Zákon č. 40/1964 Sb., občanský zákoník ve znění zákona č. 367/2000 Sb.*)

Act on cross-border payments No. 124/2002 (*Zákon č. 124/2002 Sb. o platebním styku*)

Act on general security of products No. 102/2001 (*Zákon o obecné bezpečnosti výrobků č. 102/2001 Sb.*)

Act on Prices No. 526/1990 as amended by an Act 276/2002 and 124/2003 (*Zákon č. 526/1990 Sb., o cenách v zenění zákona č. 276/2002 Sb. a zákona č. 124/2003 Sb.*)

Act on technical specification of products No. 22/1997, as amended by Act No. 226/2003 (*Zákon č. 22/1997 Sb. o technických požadavcích na výrobky ve znění zákona č. 226/2003 Sb.*)

Consumer Protection Act No. 634/1992 (*Zákon č. 634/1992 Sb. O ochraně spotřebitele*)

DENMARK

Act No. 1257/2000 on the protection of the consumers' interests *(Lov nr. 1257/2000 om forbud til beskyttelse af forbrugernes interesser)*

Act No. 234 of 2 April 1997 on consumer contracts relating to the purchase of the right of use to real estate on timeshare basis *(Lov nr. 234 af 2. april 1997 om forbrugeraftaler, der giver brugsret til fast ejendom på timesharebasis)*

Act No. 315/1997 on the Travel Guarantee Fund as amended by Act No. 164/2000 and Act No. 207/2004 *(Lov nr. 315/1997 om Rejsegarantifonden som ændret ved lov nr. 164/2000 og lov nr. 207/2004)*

Act No. 451 of 9 June 2004 on certain consumer contracts *(Lov nr. 451 af 9. juni 2004 om visse forbrugeraftaler)*

Act No. 472/1993 on Package Travels *(Lov nr.472/1993 om pakkerejser)*

Consolidated Act No. 237/2003 on Sales of Goods *(Lovbekendtgørelse nr. 237/2003 om køb)*

Consolidated Act No. 699/2000 on Marketing Practices *(Lovbekendtgørelse nr. 699/2000 om markedsføring med senere ændringer)*

Consolidated Act No. 781/1996 on Formation of Contract (*Lovbekendtgørelse nr. 781/1996 om aftaler og andre retshandler på formuerettens område*)

Consolidated Act on Means of Payment *(Bekendtgørelse af lov om visse betalingsmidler)*

Executive Order No. 866 of 18 September 2000 on information on sales price and price per unit for consumer goods *(Bekendtgørelse nr. 866 af 18. september 2000 om oplysning om salgspris og enhedspris for forbrugsvarer)*

Regulation No. 503/2004 on registration and security etc.in the Travel Guarantee Fund *(Bekendtgørelse nr. 503/2004 om registrering og sikkerhedsstillelse mv. i Rejsegarantifonden)*
Regulation No. 776/1993 on Package Travels *(Bekendtgørelse nr. 776/1993 om pakkerejser)*

ESTONIA
Consumer Protection Act *(Tarbijakaitseseadus)*
Electronic Communication Act *(Elektroonilise side seadus)*
General Part of the CC Act *(Tsiviilseadustiku üldosa seadus)*
Law of Obligations Act *(Võlaõigusseadus)*
Private International Law Act *(Rahvusvahelise eraõiguse seadus)*
Product Safety Act *(Toote ohutuse seadus)*
Regulation No. 130 of 10 May 2004 *(Majandus- ja kommunikatsiooniministri 10. mai 2004. a määrus nr 130)*
Regulation No. 66/2004 *(Majandus- ja kommunikatsiooniministri 8. aprilli 2004. a määrus nr 66 Koduukselepingu teatise vormi kinnitamine)*
Regulation No. 76 of 14 April 2004 *("Kauba ja teenuse hinna avaldamise nõuded" Vastu võetud majandus- ja kommunikatsiooniministri 14. aprilli 2004.a määrusega nr 76)*
Tourism Act *(Turismiseadus)*
Trading Act *(Kaubandustegevuse seadus)*

FINLAND
Accounting Act *(Kirjanpitolaki 1336/1997)*
Act concerning Transportation in an Aircraft (289/37) *(Laki kuljetuksesta ilma-aluksessa)*
Act of Package Travel Undertakings 28.11.1994/1080 *(Laki valmismatkaliikkeistä 28.11.1994/1080)*
Air Transportation Contracts Act (45/77) *(Ilmakuljetussopimuslaki)*
Air Transportation Act (387/86) *(Ilmakuljetuslaki)*
Act on Cross Border Injunction Procedure *(Laki rajat ylittävästä kieltokannemenettelystä 21.12.2000/1189)*
Com. data protection Act *(Vi 121 Sähköisen viestinnän tietosuojalaki)*
Maritime Act (674/94) *(Merilaki)*
Package Travel Act 28.11.1994/1079 *(Valmismatkalaki 28.11.1994/1079)*
Package Travel Regulation 28.11.1994/1085 *(Valmismatkaasetus 28.11.1994/1085)*
Regulation on Price Indications in Marketing of Consumer Goods *(Asetus kulutushyödykkeen hinnan ilmoittamisesta markkinoinnissa 30.12.1999/1359)*
The Consumer Protection Act 20.1.1978/38 *(Kuluttajansuojalaki 20.1.1978/38)*
The Personal Data Act *(Si 111 Henkilötietolaki)*

FRANCE
Consumer Protection Act *(Code de la Consommation)*
Decree No. 94-490 defining the conditions of exercice of the activites relating to the organisation and the sale of travels or journeys *(Décret no 94-490 du 15/06/1994 pris en application de l'article 31 de la loi Numéro 92-645 du 13/07/1992 fixant les conditions d'exercice des activités relatives à l'organisation et à la vente de voyages ou de séjours)*
Law No. 72-1137 on Canvassing and Door-to-Door Sales *(La loi n° 72-1137 du 22 décembre 1972 relative à la protection des consommateurs en matière de démarchage et de vente à domicile)*

Reguloratory Act No. 2001-741 of 23 August 2001 implementing EC Directives on Consumer Law *(Ordonnance n° 2001-741 du 23 août 2001 portant transposition de directives communautaires et adaptation au droit communautaire en matière de droit de la consommation)*
Reguloratory Act No. 2005-136 of 17 February 2005 on the guarantee of conformity to the contract of the good owed to the consumer by the seller *(Ordonnance n° 2005-136 du 17 février 2005 relative à la garantie de la conformité du bien au contrat due par le vendeur au consommateur)*
Regulatory Act of the 16 November 1999 on consumer protection in the indication of the prices of certain products per unit and prewrapped products offered to consumers *(Arrêté du 16 novembre 1999 relatif à la publicité, à l'égard du consommateur, des prix de vente à l'unité de mesure de certains produits préemballés)*
Tourism Code *(Code du tourisme)*

GERMANY

Act against unfair competition *(Gesetz gegen den unlauteren Wettbewerb (UWG))*
CC *(Bürgerliches Gesetzbuch (BGB))*
Civil Procedure Code *(Zivilprozessordnung (ZPO))*
Commercial Code *(Handelsgesetzbuch)*
Compulsory Auctions Act *(Zwangsversteigerungsgesetz (ZVG))*
Injunctions Act *(Unterlassungsklagengesetz (UKlaG))*
Insurance Contract Act *(Gesetz über den Versicherungsvertrag-Versicherungsvertragsgesetz (VVG))*
Introductory Act on the German CC *(Einführungsgesetz zum Bürgerlichen Gesetzbuch)*
Investment Act *(Investmentgesetz (InvG))*
Medicine Advertisement Act *(Heilmittelwerbegesetz (HWG))*
Medicines Act *(Arzneimittelgesetz (AMG))*
Pharmacies Act *(Apothekengesetz))*
Pharmacy Operating Regulation *(Apothekenbetriebsordung))*
Price indication regulation *(Preisangabenverordnung)*
Product Liability Act *(Produkthaftungsgesetz (ProdHaftG))*
Regulation on duties to supply information in civil law *(Verordnung über Informations- und Nachweispflichten nach bürgerlichem Recht (BGB-Informationspflichten-Verordnung – BGB-InfoV))*
Regulatory Offences Act *(Ordnungswidrigkeitengesetz (OWiG))*

GREECE

Act 393/1976 *(Peri idriseos ke litourgias touristikon grafion)*
Act 2496/1997 *(Asfalistiki simwasi, tropopiisis tis nomothesias gia tin idiotiki asfalisi ke alles diataksis)*
Act 2251/94 on Consumer Protection *(Nomos 2251/94 Prostasia ton katanaloton)*
Act 3927/2004 *(Τραπεζα Νομικων Πληροφοριων: Intracom-Νομοσ)*
Act against unfair competition *(Τραπεζα Νομικων Πληροφοριων: Intracom-Νομοσ)*
CC (Αστικοσ Κωδικασ)
Decree 182/99 on implementing the Directive 94/47 into Greek law *(Proedriko Diatagma 182/1999)*
Decree 301/2002 on implementing the Directive 98/27 into Greek law *(Proedriko Diatagma 301/2002)*
Decree 339/96 on implementing the Directive 90/314 of the Council of 13 June 1990 on package travel, package holidays and package tours *(Proedriko Diatagma 339/96 peri or-*

ganomenon taksidion se simmorfosi pros tin odigia 90/314 (EEL 158/59) gia ta organomena taksidia kai tis organomenes diakopes kai periigiseis)
Ruling of the Ministry for Economy and Development Z1-404 (*Koini Ipourgiki Apofasi ton Ypoyrgeion Ethnikis Oikonomias kai Anaptiksis)*

HUNGARY
Act CLV of 1997 on Consumer Protection *(1997. évi CLV tv. a fogyasztóvédelemről)*
Act CXII of 1996 on Credit Institutions and Financial Enterprises *(1996. évi CXII. tv a hitelintézetekről és a pénzügyi vállalkozásokról)*
Act CXLI of 1997 on Real Estate Registration *(1997. évi CXLI tv. az ingatlannyilvántartásról)*
Act LVIII of 1997 on Business Advertising Activity Act *(1997. évi LVIII tv. A gazdasági reklámról)*
CC *(1959. évi IV. törvény a Polgári Törvénykönyvről)*
Criminal Code (Act IV of 1978) *(1978. évi IV. tv. a Büntetö Törvénykönyvrõl)*
GKM Decree No. 49/2003. (VII.30.) *(49/2003. (VII. 30.) GKM rendeleta fogyasztói szerződés keretében érvényesített szavatossági és jótállási igények intézéséről)*
GM Decree No. 7/2001. (III.29.) on the indication of the prices of products and services offered to consumers *(7/2001. (III. 29.) GM rendeleta fogyasztói forgalomba kerülő áruk és szolgáltatások árának feltüntetéséről)*
Government Decree No. 20/1999. (II. 5.) on contracts for the purchase of the right to use immovable property on a timeshare basis *(20/1999. (II.5.) Korm.rend. Az Ingatlanok időben megosztott használati jogának megszerzésére irányuló szerződésekről*
Government Decree No. 17/1999. (II.5.) on Distance Contracting *(17/1999. (II. 5.) Korm. rendeleta távollevők között kötött szerződésekről)*
Government Decree No. 18/1999. (II.5.) on Unfair Contract Terms *(18/1999. (II.5.) Korm. rend. a fogyasztóval kötött szerződésben tisztességtelennek minősülő feltételekről)*
Government Decree No. 213/1996. (XII.23.) on Travel Organisation and Agency Activities *(213/1996. (XII.23.) Korm.rend. az utazásszervező- és közvetítő tevékenységről)*
Government Decree No. 214/1996. (XII.23.) on Travel Contract and Mediation of Travel *(214/1996. (XII.23.) Korm.rend. az utazási és utazást közvetítő szerződésekről)*
Government Decree No. 249/2004. (VIII. 27.) *(249/2004. (VIII. 27.) Korm. Rendelet az egyes javító-karbantartó szolgáltatásokra vonatkozó kötelező jótállásról)*
Government Decree No. 370/2004 (XII.26.) on Doorstep Selling *(370/2004. (XII.26.) Korm rendelete az üzleten kívül fogyasztóval kötött szerződésekről és az üzleten kívüli kereskedés folytatásának egyes feltételeiről)*
Government Decree No. 89/1998. (V.8.) on Consumer Supervisory Authorithy *(89/1998. (V.8.) Korm. Rend. A fogyasztóvédelmi Főfelügyelőség szervezetéről, feladat- és hatásköréről, valamint a fogyasztóvédelmi bírság felhasználásáról)*
Government Decree No.181/2003. (XI. 5.) *(181/2003. (XI. 5.) Korm. rendelet a lakásépítéssel kapcsolatos kötelező jótállásról)*
Government Decree No. 151/2003. (IX.22.) on guarantees of consumer durables *(151/2003. (IX. 22.) Korm. rendeletaz egyes tartós fogyasztási cikkekre vonatkozó kötelező jótállásról)*
Law-Decree No. 13 of 1979 on the International Private Law *(1979. évi 13. törvényerejű rendelet a nemzetközi magánjogról)*
Ministry of Justice Decree No. 13/2004 (IV.16) IM listing the acts of legislation corresponding to the directives listed in the Annex to Directive 98/27/EC on injunctions for the protection of consumers' interests *(13/2004. (IV. 16.) IM rendeleta fogyasztói érdekek*

védelme érdekében a jogsértés megszüntetésére irányuló eljárásokról szóló 98/27/EK irányelv mellékletében meghatározott irányelvekkel összeegyeztethetőséget teremtő jogszabályok felsorolásáról)
Unfair Contract Terms Decree No. 2/1978 (*1978. évi 2. törvényerejű rendeleta Polgári Törvénykönyv módosításáról és egységes szövegérõl szóló 1977. évi IV. törvény hatálybalépésérõl és végrehajtásáról*)

IRELAND
European Communities (Contracts for Time Sharing of Immovable Property—Protection of Purchasers) Regulations 1997 and 2000
European Communities (Cancellation of Contracts negotiated away from business premises) Regulations, 1989
European Communities (Certain Aspects of the Sale of Consumer Goods and Associated Guarantees) Regulations 2003
European Communities (Unfair Terms in Consumer Contracts) Regulations, 1995 and 2000.
Package Holidays and Travel Trade Act, 1995
Protection of Consumers' Collective Interests Regulations
Protection of Consumers in Respect of Contracts made by Means of Distance Communication Regulation
Requirements to Indicate Product Prices Regulations

ITALY
Legislative Decree of 17 March 1995 No. 111 "Implementation of Directive 90/314/EEC on package travel, package holidays and package tours" (*Decreto Legislativo 17 marzo 1995, N. 111 "Attuazione della direttiva N. 90/314/CEE concernente i viaggi, le vacanze ed I circuiti "tutto compreso")*
Legislative Decree of 2 February 2002 No. 24 "Implementation of Directive 99/44/EC on certain aspects of the sale of consumer goods and associated guarantees" (*Decreto Legislativo 2 febbraio 2002, n. 24 "Attuazione della direttiva 1999/44/CE su taluni aspetti della vendita e delle garanzie di consumo")*
Legislative Decree of 25 February 2000 No. 84 "Implementation of Directive 98/6/EC on consumer protection in the indication of the prices of products offered to consumers" *(Decreto legislativo 25 febbraio 2000, n. 84"Attuazione della direttiva 98/6/CE relativa alla protezione dei consumatori in materia di indicazione dei prezzi offerti ai medesimi")*
Legislative Decree of 6 September 2005, No. 206 "Consumer code" *(Decreto Legislativo 6 settembre 2005, n. 206 "Codice del consumo, a norma dell'articolo 7 della legge 29 luglio 2003, n. 229")*
Legislative Decree of 9 November 1998 No. 427 "Implementation of the Directive 94/47/EC on the protection of purchasers in respect of certain aspects of contracts relating to the purchase of the right to use one or more immovable properties on a timeshare basis" *(Decreto legislativo. 9 novembre 1998, n. 427„Attuazione della direttiva 94/47/CE concernente la tutela dell'acquirente per taluni aspetti dei contrattirelativi all'acquisizione di un diritto di godimento a tempo parziale di beni immobili")*
Law of 6 February 1996 No. 52, art. 25 (amended by Statute 21/12/1999, n. 526, art. 25) "Implementation of the Directive 93/13/EEC relating to unfair terms in contracts concluded between a seller or supplier and a consumer" *(Legge 6 febbraio 1996 n. 52, art. 25 (modificato da (Legge 21 dicembre 1999, n. 526, art. 25) "Attuazione della direttiva 93/13/CEE del consiglio concernente le clausole abusive nei contratti stipulati con iconsumatori")*

Law of 29 March 2001 No. 135 on the reform of national tourist law. *(Legge 29 marzo 2001, n. 135 "Riforma della legislazione nazionale del turismo")*

LATVIA

Cabinet Regulation No. 163 "Regulations regarding Package Tourism Services" *(MK Noteikumi Nr. 163 "Noteikumi par kompleksiem tūrisma pakalpojumiem")*
Cabinet Regulation No. 178 "Procedures for Diplaying Prices of Products and Services" *(LR MK Noteikumi Nr. 178 "Kārtība, kādā norādāmas preču un pakalpojumu cenas")*
Cabinet Regulation No. 207 "Regulations Regarding Distance Contracts *(LR MK Noteikumi Nr. 207 "Noteikumi par distances līgumu")*
Cabinet Regulation No. 325 "Regulations regarding Contracts on Obtaining the Right to Temporary Use of a Residential Building or a Part Thereof" *(LR MK Noteikumi Nr. 325 "Noteikumi par līgumu par dzīvošanai paredzētas ēkas vai ēkas daļas lietošanas tiesību iegūšanu uz laiku")*
Cabinet Regulation No. 1037/2004 *(LR MK Noteikumi Nr. 1037 "Noteikumi par distances līgumu par finanšu pakalpojumu sniegšanu")*
Cabinet Regulation No. 154/2004 *(MK noteikumi Nr.154 (2004.gada 23.marts) "Kārtība, kadā piesakāms patērētāja prasījums par līguma nteikumiem neatbilstošu preci vai pakalpojumu un organizējama preces vai pakalpojuma ekspertīze")*
Law of the Protection of Consumer Rights *(Patērētāju tiesību aizsardzības likums)*
Regulation of 18 June 1994 *(Par likumu un citu Saeimas, Valsts prezidenta un Ministru kabineta pieņemto aktu izsludināšanas, publicēšanas, spēkā stāšanās kārtību un spēkā esamību)*
Republic of Latvia Cabinet Regulation No. 327 "Regulations Regarding Contracts Entered Into Outside the Permanent Location of Sale or Provision of Services of an Undertaking (Company) *(Noteikumi par līgumu, kas noslēgts ārpus uzņēmuma (uzņēmējsabiedrības) pastāvīgās tirdzniecības vai pakalpojumu sniegšanas vietas)*
Tourism Law of 17 September 1998 *(Tūrisma likums)*

LITHUANIA

CC of the Republic of Lithuania *(Lietuvos Respublikos Civilinis Kodeksas)*
Law on Consumer Protection *(Lietuvos Respublikos Vartotojų Teisių Gynimo Įstatymas)*
Law on Tourism of the Republic of Lithuania *(Lietuvos Respublikos Turizmo Įstatymas)*
Order of the Minister of Economy of the Republic of Lithuania on the Approval of the Rules of Sale of Goods and Provision of Services in Premises not Designated for this Activity *(Lietuvos Respublikos Ūkio Ministro Įsakymas dėl prekių pardavimo ir paslaugų teikimo ne šiai veiklai skirtose patalpose taisyklių patvirtinimo)*
Order of the Minister of Economy of the Republic of Lithuania on the Rules of Labeling of Items (Goods) Sold in the Republic of Lithuania and Indication of Prices *(Lietuvos Respublikos Ūkio Ministro Įsakymas dėl Lietuvos Respublikoje parduodamų daiktų (prekių) ženklinimo ir kainų nurodymo taisyklių)*
Order of the Minister of Environment on the Approval of the Minimum List of the Mandatory Data to be Indicated in the Description of the Provided Residential Premises and Agreement when Buying the Right to Use the Residential Premises from Time to Time *(Lietuvos Respublikos Aplinkos Ministro Įsakymas dėl privalomų duomenų, kurie turi būti pateikti suteikiamų gyvenamųjų patalpų aprašyme bei sutartyje, perkant teisę tam tikru laiku naudotis gyvenamosiomis patalpomis, minimalaus sąrašo patvirtinimo)*

LUXEMBURG

Act on injunctions of 19 December 2003 *(Loi du 19 décembre 2003 fixant les conditions d'agrément des organisations habilitées à intenter des actions en cessation)*

Act on Peddling and Itinerant Trade (1970) (Act of 5 March 1970 on Peddling and Itinerant Trade) *(Loi du 5 mars 1970 sur le colportage et les professions ambulantes)*

Act of 26 March 1997 transposing Directive 93/13/EEC and Directive 85/577/EEC *(Loi du 26 mars 1997 portant transposition des directives 93/13/CEE du 5.04 1993 concernant les clauses abusives dans les contrats conclus avec le consommateurs et 85/577/CEE du 20.12.1985 concernant la protection des consommateurs dans le cas de contrats négociés en dehors des établissements commerciaux)*

CC *(Code civil luxembourgeois)*

Competition Act *(Loi du 17 mai 2004 relative à la concurrence)*

Consumer Protection Act of 25 August 1983 *(Loi du 25 août 1983 relative à la protection juridique du consommateur)*

Consumer Sales Act of 21 April 2004 *(Loi du 21 avril 2004 relative à la garantie de conformité due par le vendeur de biens meubles corporels)*

Decree of 4 November 1997 on pre-contractual information and contract conditions of package travel contracts *(Règlement grand-ducal du 4 novembre 1997 déterminant les éléments de l'information préalable et les dispositions du contrat relatifs aux voyages, vacances ou séjours à forfait en exécution des articles 9, 11 et 12 de la loi du 14 juin 1994)*

Decree of 4 November 1997 on the amount, conditions and use of the financial guarantees provided in article 6 of the law of 14 June 1994 *(Règlement grand-ducal du 4 novembre 1997 déterminant le montant, les modalités et l'utilisation de la garantie financière prévue à l'article 6 de la loi du 14 juin 1994)*

Decree of 7 Septembre 2001 on price indication (as amended by the decree of 29 July 2004) *(Règlement grand-ducal du 7 septembre 2001 relatif à l'indication des prix des produits et services)*

Decree of 26 November 2001 amending Decree of 4 November 1997 *(Règlement grand-ducal du 26 novembre 2001 portant modification de l'article 3 point 15 du règlement grand-ducal du 4 novembre 1997 déterminant les éléments de l'information préalable et les dispositions du contrat relatifs aux voyages, vacances ou séjours à forfait, en exécution des articles 9, 11 et 12 de la loi du 14 juin 1994 portant réglementation des conditions d'exercice des activités relatives à l'organisation et à la vente de voyages ou de séjours et portant transposition de la directive du 13 juin 1990 concernant les voyages, vacances et circuits à forfait)*

Distance Contracts Act of 16 April 2003 *(Loi du 16 avril 2003 concernant la protection des consommateurs en matière de contrats à distance)*

Doorstep Selling Act of 16 July 1987 *(Loi du 16 juillet 1987 concernant le colportage, la vente ambulante, l'étalage de marchandises et la sollicitation de commandes (mod. L. 26 mars 1997) et loi du 26 mars 1997 portant transposition des directives 93/13/CEE et 85/577/CEE)*

Package Travel Act of 14 June 1994 *(Loi du 14 juin 1994 portant réglementation des conditions d'exercice des activités relatives à l'organisation et à la vente de voyage ou de séjours)*

Timeshare Act of 18 December 1998 *(Loi du 18 décembre 1998 relative aux contrats portant sur l'acquisition d'un droit d'utilisation à temps partiel de biens immobiliers)*

Act of 27 November 1986 regulating certain trade practices and sanctioning unfair competition (*Loi du 27 novembre 1986 réglementant certaines pratiques commerciales et sanctionnant la concurrence déloyale*).

MALTA

Consumer Affairs Act *(Att dwar l-Affarijiet tal-Konsumatur Kapitlu 378 tal-Ligijiet ta' Malta)*
Consumer Affairs Act (Price Indication) Regulations *(Regolamenti dwar Prezzijiet Indikati skond l-Att dwar l-Affarijiet tal-Konsumaturi)*
Distance Selling Regulations 2001 *(Regolamenti dwar il-Bejgh mill-Boghod)*
Doorstep Contracts Act (formerly: Door-to-Door Salesmen Act) *(Att dwar Kuntratti fuq l-Ghadba tal-Bieb)*
Malta Travel and Tourism Services Act *(Att dwar Servizzi ta' l-Ivvjaggar u tat-Turizmu ghal Malta)*
Package Travel, Package Holidays and Package Tours Regulations, 2000 *(Regolamenti ta' l-2000 dwar Pakkett ta' l-Ivvjaggar, Pakkett ta' Vaganzi u Pakkett ta' Tours)*
Protection of Buyers in Contracts for Time Sharing of Immovable Property Regulations, 2000 (Regolamenti ta' l-2000 dwar il-Protezzjoni ta' Xerrejja f'Kuntratti ta' Time Sharing fi Proprejta' Immobbli)

NETHERLANDS

CC *(Burgerlijk Wetboek)*
Doorstep Selling Law *(Colportagewet)*
Decree of 15 January 1993 containing rules concerning information that organisers of package travel must notify in the interest of travellers *(Besluit van 15 januari 1993, houdende regels inzake de gegevens die de organisatoren van georganiseerde reizen ten behoeve van de reizigers moeten vermelden (Gegevensbesluit georganiseerde reizen))*
Decree of 25 of June 1997 containing rules concerning information that sellers of timeshare rights must mention in the contract in the interest of the buyer *(Gegevensbesluit van 25 juni 1997 rechten van gebruik in deeltijd van onroerende zaken)*
Decree on price-indication of goods 1980 *(Besluit prijsaanduiding producten)*
General act on terms *(Algemene termijnenwet)*
Law of 21 December 2000 on the adaptation of Book 7 of the CC to Directive 97/7/EC regarding the protection of consumers by distance selling *(Wet van 21 december 2000 tot aanpassing van Boek 7 van het Burgerlijk Wetboek aan richtlijn nr. 97/7/EG van het Europees Parlement en de Raad van de Europese Unie van 20 mei 1997)*
Law of 25 April 2000 on the adaptation of Book 3 and 6 of the CC to the Directive 98/27/EC on injunctions for the protection of consumers' interests *(Wet van 25 april 2000 tot aanpassing van de Boeken 3 en 6 van het Burgerlijk Wetboek aan de richtlijn betreffende het doen staken van inbreuken in het raam van de bescherming van de consumentenbelangen)*
Law of 28 October 1999 on the adaptation of Book 6 of the CC to the Directive 93/13/EC on unfair terms in consumer contracts *(Wet van 28 oktober 1999 tot aanpassing van Boek 6 van het Burgerlijk Wetboek aan de richtlijn betreffende oneerlijke bedingen in consumentenovereenkomsten)*
Media Law *(Mediawet)*
Personal Data Protection Act *(Wet bescherming persoonsgegevens)*
Telecommunication Law *(Telecommunicatiewet)*

POLAND

Act of 13 July 2000 on the protection of purchasers in respect of the right to use buildings or dwellings during certain time each year *(Ustawa z 13 lipca 2000 o ochronie nabywców prawa korzystania z budynku lub pomieszczenia mieszkalnego w oznaczonym czasie w każdym roku)*

Act of 15 December 2000 on the protection of consumers and competition. *(Ustawa 15 grudnia 2000 o ochronie konkurencji i konsumentów)*
Act of 2 March 2000 on the protection of certain consumer rights and liability for an unsafe product *(Ustawa z dnia 2 marca 2000 o ochronie niektórych praw konsumentów oraz o odpowiedzialności za szkodę wyrządzoną przez produkt niebezpieczny)*
Act of 27 July 2002 on specific terms and conditions of consumer sale and amendments to the CC *(Ustawa z 27 lipca 2002. o szczegółowych warunkach sprzedaży konsumenckiej oraz o zmianie Kodeksu cywilnego)*
Act of 29 August 1997 on Tourist Services *(Ustawa o usługach turystycznych z 29 sierpnia 1997)*
Act of 5 July 2001 on prices *(Ustawa o cenach z 5 lipca 2001)*
Act on the Freedom of Economic Activity *(Ustawa o swobodzie działalności gospodarczej)*
CC (Kodeks Cywilny)

PORTUGAL
CC *(Código Civil)*
Constitution of the Portuguese Republic *(Constituição da República Portuguesa)*
Consumer Protection Act No. 24/96 of July 31 *(Lei nº 24/96 de 31 de Julho (Regime legal aplicável à defesa dos consumidores)*
Decree-Law No. 138/90 of April 26 as amended by Decree-Law No. 162/99 of May 13 (amended by the declaration No. 10_AF/99) *(Decreto-Lei n.º 138/90, de 26 Abril, na redacção resultante do Decreto-Lei n.º 162/99, de 13 de Maio (rectificado pela Declaração de Rectificação n.º 10-AF/99))*
Decree-Law No. 143/2001 of April 26 *(Decreto-Lei nº 143/2001, de 26 de Abril (rectificado pela Declaração de Rectificação n.º 13-D/2001))*
Decree-Law No. 198/93 of May 27, revoked by Decree-Law 209/97 of August 13, modified by Decree-Law 12/99 of January 11 *(Decreto-Lei n.º 198/93, de 27 de Maio, revogado pelo Decreto-Lei nº 209/97, de 13 de Agosto, alterado pelo Decreto-Lei n.º 12/99, de 11 de Janeiro)*
Decree-Law No. 209/97 of August 13 *(Decreto-Lei nº 209/97, de 13 de Agosto)*
Decree-Law No. 234/99 of June 25 *(Decreto-Lei n.º 234/99 de 25 de Junho)*
Law No. 25/2004 of July 8 *(Lei n.º 25/2004, de 8 de Julho)*
Decree-Law No. 275/93 of August 5 as amended by Decree-Law No. 180/99 of May 22, and Decree-Law No. 22/2002 of January 31 *(Decreto-Lei n.º 275/93, de 5 de Agosto, na redacção resultante do Decreto-Lei n.º 180/99, de 22 de Maio, e do Decreto-Lei n.º 22/2002, de 31 de Janeiro)*
Decree-Law No. 264/86 of September 3 *(Decreto-Lei n.º 264/86, de 03 de Setembro de 1986)*
Decree-Law No. 446/85 of October 25 as amended by Decree-Law 220/95 of August 31, rectified by Declaration 114-B/95 of August 31, and amended also by Decree-Law 249/99 of July 7, and by Decree-Law 323/2001 of December 17 *(Decreto-Lei n.º 446/85, de 25 de Outubro, na redacção resultante do Decreto-Lei n.º 220/95, de 31 de Agosto, tal como rectificado pela Declaração de Rectificação n.º 114-B/95, de 31 de Agosto, do Decreto-Lei n.º 249/99, de 7 de Julho)*
Decree Law No. 67/2003 of April 8 *(Decreto-Lei n.º 67/2003, de 8 de Abril)*
Law No. 83/95 of August 31 (Lei n.º 83/95 de 31 de Agosto)

SLOVAKIA
Act No. 108/2000 on Consumer Protection in Doorstep Selling and in Distance Selling *(Zákon č. 108/2000 Z.z. o ochrane spotrebiteľa pri podomovom predaji a zásielkovom predaji)*
Act No. 258/2001 on Consumer Credit *(Zákon č.258/2001 Z.z. o spotrebiteľských úveroch)*

Act No. 281/2001 on Package Travel *(Zákon č. 281/2001 Z.z. o zájazdoch, podmienkach podnikania cestovných kancelárií a cestovných agentúr a o zmene a doplnení Občianskeho zákonníka v znení neskorších predpisov*
Act No. 634/1992 on Consumer Protection as amended *(Zákon č. 634/1992 Zb. o ochrane spotrebiteľa v znení neskorších predpisov)*
Act No. 99/1963 Code of Civil Procedure as amended *(Zákon č.99/1963 Zb. Občiansky súdny poriadok v znení neskorších predpisov)*
Bond Papers Act *(Zákon č. 566/2001 Z.z. o cenných papieroch a investičných službách v znení neskorších predpisov)*
CC *(Zákon č. 40/1964 Zb. Občiansky zákonník v znení neskorších predpisov)*
Code of international Law *(Zákon č. 97/1963 Zb. o medzinárodnom práve súkromnom a procesnom v znení neskorších predpisov)*
Commercial Code as amended *(Zákon č. 513/1991 Zb. Obchodný zákonník v znení neskorších predpisov)*
Constitution of Slovak Republic as amended *(Zákon č. 460/1992 Zb. Ústava Slovenskej republiky v znení neskorších predpisov)*
Non-Smoker-Protection-Act *(Zákon č. 377/2004 Z.z. o ochrane nefajčiarov v znení neskorších predpisov)*
Price Indication Decree *(Vyhláška č. 545/2002 Z.z. o spôsobe označovania výrobkov cenam)*
Systems of payments Act *(Zákon č. 510/2002 Z.z. o platobnom styku v znení neskorších predpisov)*

SLOVENIA
Code of Obligations (*Obligacijski zakonik)*
Consumer Protection Act (*Zakon o varstvu potrošnikov)*
Medicinal Products Act (*Zakon o zdravilih, ZZdr, Ur.l. RS, št. 31/2006)*
Promotion of Tourism Development Act of 30 January 2004
(*Zakon o spodbujanju razvoja turizma /ZSRT)*
Rules on Price Indication for Goods and Services
(*Pravilnik o načinu označevanja cen blaga in storitev*).

SPAIN
Law 1/2000 of 7 January on Civil Procedure *(Ley 1/2000, de 7 de enero, de enjuiciamiento civil)*
Law 21/1995 of July 6 which regulates the package travels *(Ley 21/1995, de 6 de julio, reguladora de los viajes combinados)*
Law 23/2003 on consumer sales *(Ley 23/2003, de garantías en la venta de bienes de consumo)*
Law 26/1984 of July 19 on Consumer Protection *(Ley 26/1984, de 19 de julio, General para la Defensa de los consumidores y usuarios)*
Law 26/1991 of November 21 on consumer protection in case of contracts executed out of the commercial premises *(Ley 26/1991, de 21 noviembre, de protección de los consumidores en el caso de contratos celebrados fuera de los establecimientos mercantiles)*
Law 34/2002 of July 11 on the services of the Information's Society and on electronic commerce *(Ley 34/2002, de 11 de julio, de los servicios de la sociedad de la información y de comercio electrónico)*
Law 39/2002 of October 28 on the transposition into the Spanish legal system of some Community Directives on protection of the interests of consumers and users *(Ley 39/2002, de 28 de octubre, de transposición al ordenamiento jurídico español de diversas directivas comunitarias en materia de protección de los intereses de los consumidores y usuarios)*

Law 42/1998 of December 15 on timesharing rights on immovable goods for tourist use and taxation norms *(Ley 42/1998, de 15 de diciembre, sobre derechos de aprovechamiento por turno de bienes inmuebles de uso turístico y normas tributarias)*
Law 47/2002 of December 19 on the reform of the Law 7/1996 on retail trade for the transposition into the Spanish legal system of the Directive 97/7/CE *(Ley 47/2002, de 19 de diciembre, de reforma de la Ley 7/1996, de 15-1-1996 de Ordenación del Comercio Minorista, para la transposición al ordenamiento jurídico español de la Directiva 97/7/CE)*
Law 7/1996 of January 15 on retail trade (according to its amendment by Law 47/2002) *(Ley 7/1996, de 15 de enero, de ordenación del comercio minorista)*
Law 7/1998 of April 13 on Standard Terms in Contracts *(Ley 7/1998, de 13 de abril, sobre condiciones generales de la contratación)*
Norms of the Autonomous Communities about Travel:
Aragón:
Act 6/2003 of February 27 on Tourism in Aragón
(Ley 6/2003, de 27 de febrero, de Turismo de Aragón)
Decree 51/1998 of 24 February on Travel Agents in Aragón (Decreto 51/1998, de 24 febrero, del Reglamento de Agencias de Viajes de Aragón)
Andalucía:
Decree 301/2002 of December 17 on Travel Agents in Andalucia *(Decreto 301/2002, de 17 de diciembre, sobre agencies de viajes y centrales de reserva, Andalucía)*
Balearic Islands:
Law 2/1999 of March 24 on Tourism in the Balearic Islands
(Ley 2/1999, de 24 marzo, de las Islas Baleares)
Decree 60/1997 of May 7 on Travel Agens in the Balearic Islands amended by Decree 103/2004 of December 23 *(Decreto 103/2004, de 23 de diciembre, de modificación del Decreto 60/1997, de 7 de mayo, de Reglamento de las Agencies de Viajes de la Comunidad Autónoma de las Illes Balears)*
La Rioja:
Decree 111/2003 of October 10 *(Decreto 111/2003, de 10 de octubre, por el que se aprueba el reglamento de desarrollo de la Ley 2/2001, de 31 de mayo, de Turismo de La Rioja)*

Royal Decree 3423/2000 of December 15 on the regulation of the indication of prices of the products offered to the consumers and users *(Real Decreto 3423/2000, de 15 de diciembre, por el que se regula la indicación de los precios de los productos ofrecidos a los consumidores y usuarios)*

SWEDEN
Air Transport Act *(luftfartslagen (1957:297))*
Act on terms and conditions in consumer relations (1994:1512) *(Lag (1994: 1512) om avtalsvillkor I konsumentförhållanden)*
Consumer Credit Law (1992:830) *(Konsumentkreditlag (1992:830)*
Consumer purchase act (1990:932) as amended by Act 2002:587 *(Konsumentköplag (1990:932) ändrad genom SFS 2002:587)*
International Rail Transport Act *(lagen (1985:193) om internationell järnvägstrafik).*
Law on Group Actions (2002:599) *(Lag (2002:599) om grupprättegång)*
Marketing Act (1995:450) *(Marknadsföringslag (1995:450))*
Maritime Act *(sjölagen (1994:1009))*
Package Tours Act 1992:1672 *(Lag (1992:1672) om paketresor)*

Price Information Act 1991:601, amended by Act 2004:347
(Prisinformationslag (SFS 1991:601))
The Law on Consumer Protection on Distance Contracts and Doorstep Selling Contracts
(Lag (2005:59) om konsumentskydd vid distansavtal och hemförsäljningsavtal)
Timeshare Contracts (Consumer Protection) Act 1997:218
(Lag (1997:218) konsumentskydd vid tidsdelat boende)
Rail Transport Act (*järnvägstrafiklagen (1985:192)*)

UNITED KINGDOM
Consumer Protection (Cancellation of Contracts concluded away from business premises) Regulations 1987
Consumer Protection (Distance Selling) Regulations 2000
Consumer Transactions (Restrictions on statements) Order 1976
Enterprise Act 2002, Part 8 and Schedule 13
Package Travel, Package Holidays and Package Tour Regulations 1992
Prices Act 1974
Privacy and Electronic Communications (EC Directive) Regulations
Sale of Goods Act 1979
Supply of Goods (Implied Terms) Act 1973
Supply of Goods and Services Act 1982
The Civil Aviation Regulations 1995
The Price Marking Order 2004
The Sale and Supply of Goods to Consumers Regulations 2002
Timeshare Act 1992
Unfair Contract Terms Act 1977
Unfair Terms in Consumer Contracts Regulations (UTCCR) 1999